THE

TEMPLE OF
MYSTERIES

THE
TEMPLE OF
MYSTERIES

A KEY TO THE SECRETS OF LIFE

FRANCIA LA DUE

Radiant Books
New York

Library of Congress Control Number: 2023939497

Published in 2023 by Radiant Books
radiantbooks.co

ISBN 978-1-63994-035-6 (hardback)
ISBN 978-1-63994-033-2 (paperback)
ISBN 978-1-63994-034-9 (e-book)

DEDICATED TO HUMANITY

TABLE OF CONTENTS

A MASTER

A Master is one who has become as a little child, who has entered the Eye of the Triangle in the Square within the Seven, and who, by sore travail of Soul, has won his Robe of Immortality, which Robe he must keep unspotted, not for fear of the spotting, but lest the mud thrown against that Robe rebound and strike the thrower.

IN THE HEART OF GOD

Forget not that there are no little things. The hand outstretched when the need is great pulls hard on the heart-strings of him who is down, and the heart-strings of the fallen are fastened in the Heart of God.

H—[|]

BEHOLD!

I GIVE UNTO THEE A KEY

PREFACE

The teachings contained in this volume were first given to the world through the pages of *The Temple Artisan*, a monthly publication and the official magazine of The Temple of the People, an organization having its headquarters and central activities at Halcyon, San Luis Obispo County, California.

This organization was called into being in 1898 at the behest and under the direction of the Master Hilarion, one of the Masters of the Great White Lodge[1] working to lift humanity to higher levels by a direct outpouring of force and teachings, fulfilling the need of the time as rapidly as humanity was able to receive and assimilate such teachings and higher vibrations.

As published in the magazine referred to, these lessons appeared under the head of "Open Series" as distinguished from esoteric[2] teachings given to inner groups of students. In the present volume no attempt has been made to group the lessons under any definite classification, but they appear in the sequence in which they were given to the Temple by the Masters — in most instances, no doubt, being called forth by the law of supply and demand spiritually operating at the time. The lessons open up so many marvelous mines of spiritual richness and helpfulness that The Temple of the People sends out this work to the world in order that a more universal benefit may be derived from a wider dissemination of the same.

The Temple is a continuation of the work inaugurated by H. P. Blavatsky and is inspired and ensouled by the same great cosmical forces having their source in the Masters of the Great White Lodge who are ever guiding the evolution of worlds, races, and the affairs

---

[1] This work uses the terms *Great White Lodge* or *Great White Brotherhood* in reference to the Hierarchy of Light existing on the Earth. The word *White* here symbolizes spiritual purity and has absolutely no association with ethnicity or skin color. It indicates the White Light that, upon splitting, yields the seven colors of the rainbow, each of which symbolizes one of the Great Masters, and vice versa — the seven colors of the rainbow that result in the White Light after fusion. In the White Brotherhood, there is no distinction of race, gender, color, nationality, culture, creed, or religion.

[2] *Esoteric* (*Greek*, "inner") — hidden, secret; intended solely for Initiates with the aim of avoiding use by untrained people that might result in destructive consequences.

of men. While the Masters of the White Lodge are many, yet their work is one.

The Masters are those beings who, by sore travail of soul, by vast experience, suffering, and sacrifice, have advanced to a degree of evolution far beyond ordinary human beings.

Their consciousness is not limited to any one plane of life, as is the case with ordinary men and women. A Master is one who has conquered the limitations of matter, as that term is usually understood, and is able to function consciously and at will on more than one plane of being, according to the degree to which he has attained. In other words, a Master is one who has entered the Eye of the Triangle in the Square,[1] and who henceforth functions in wider spheres of action, where he becomes and *is* a conscious factor, force, and agent in helping on the evolution of worlds and races.

The Masters *are not Gods; they are men*, and if necessity requires, they can work on the physical plane in a physical body. Their greater work is done, however, in their Nirmanakaya body,[2] the robe of con-

---

[1] The Triangle is the symbol of the higher triad of the 5th, 6th, and 7th human principles: Manas (Mind), Buddhi (Soul), and Atman (Spirit). The Square represents the quaternary of the 1st, 2nd, 3rd, and 4th principles: the physical body (Rupa or Sthula Sharira), the life essence (Prana), the etheric double or astral body (Linga Sharira), and the body of desires or the higher astral body (Kama Rupa). Together, they are the Seven. The 6th principle, Buddhi, is associated with the "Divine Eye," or the "Third Eye." Therefore, to become a Master and to achieve true immortality (the continuous consciousness on all planes of Existence), while being incarnated in the physical body, one needs to connect the 4th, 5th, and 7th principles and merge them in the 6th: to "enter the Eye of the Triangle in the Square within the Seven."

[2] *Nirmanakaya (Sanskrit,* "emanation body") — the state of Masters or Initiates, who have advanced along the path of comprehension of Truth and purified themselves to the extent that they have risen above even the divine illusion of *Devachan* — the Sixth Plane of Existence, akin to Paradise. They have achieved the supreme enlightenment, which enables them to enter the Seventh and the Highest Plane, called *Nirvana*, to experience bliss. However, they voluntarily sacrifice themselves and decline to go to Nirvana because, in this case, they will be forever separated from the Earth and be unable to help humanity. Therefore, such Masters continue to live in the higher Subtle or Astral spheres of the Earth to guide and protect humankind. They maintain all their body-principles, except their physical and lower astral bodies, and reside in the robe of conscious immortality. Nevertheless, they are able to create those two lower bodies should they need to incarnate themselves among people to carry out specific tasks on the Earth.

scious immortality, which they have won through pain and sacrifice endured age upon age.

The Lodge of Masters is synthesized in the Central Spiritual Sun, which is composed of all the Masters of the Right-Hand Path.[3] This Central Sun is interchangeable with the Christos who is the perfected Son (Sun) of Infinite Love.

At cyclic periods one or more Masters may seem to take a more particular direction of forces affecting the evolution and development of humanity, but this is because karmic and hierarchical law so ordain.

The Masters are, in a sense, the Higher Self of humanity and watch over, protect, and guide its unfoldment. They cannot interfere with Karmic law,[4] but have the power, at crises, to hold back to some extent the action of accumulated karma that otherwise might destroy civilization or shatter the planet itself. But in the end every iota of Karmic law must be fulfilled. Devastating epidemics, great wars, destruction of cities in past or present times with their toll of death, the sudden breaking up and submergence of continents, as in the case of Atlantis,[5] are instances of karmic forces operating on a large scale, and where such forces could be held back no longer by the administrators of nature's laws, the Masters of Wisdom, lest a greater spiritual damage be done to the people of those cities, nations, or continents affected. Where spirituality and morality have departed beyond a certain measure, humanity can only be brought back to a recognition of its spiritual foundations by some great shock or series of shocks driving the personal consciousness inward to the eternal verities, to its inherent divinity, and so preventing a further descent into the lure and glitter of outer falsities and sense illusions.

We have been told by "Those Who Know" that it is not an uncommon occurrence for a planet to be riven into fragments by retributive forces when the inhabitants of some world have misused high spiritual powers persistently, thus accumulating an excess of destructive forces, outweighing the balance of constructive energies and finally

---

[3] *Right-Hand Path* — the Path of Light and Good, while the *Left-Hand Path* is the path of darkness and evil.

[4] *Karmic law* — the law of equilibrium, of adjustment. When equilibrium is disturbed, action and reaction take place until perfect balance or harmony is again attained.

[5] *Atlantis* — the continent on which humanity of the Fourth Root Race developed. See *Glossary* for more.

culminating in the destruction of the planet itself. In our solar system we have evidence of such a happening. Astronomers had noted the wide gap between Mars and Jupiter in which no planet was found, and for years they looked in vain to find a body that ought to be there. Finally over two hundred asteroids were discovered. These are very small planets, some of them not over twenty-five miles in diameter, moving very close one to another all in the same direction between the orbits of Mars and Jupiter, as would be the case if they were shattered fragments of a once large planet.

A similar fate threatened our own world in 1899; but it was saved at that time by many Masters of high degree and power assembling from other planets at certain zones on and in the earth centers and holding the balance for the time being. The Dark Star[1] was saved for the time, but for how long? Who can tell? Since that time there has been a great advance in scientific knowledge, invention, and attainments, and we are harnessing nature's finer forces more and more to our personal and commercial uses and pleasures. But these forces are forces of Life Itself — rays of Deific Energy from the very Heart of God and of Nature, and unless rightly used in the spirit of unselfish service and for the *good of all*, there is bound to be a reaction, due to the inversion of divine qualities, with terrible consequences to humanity, endangering the very existence of the planet itself upon which we live. Like unto a brotherhood of worlds in the celestial spaces, so must there be a Brotherhood of Nations on the earth and a true spirit of Universal Brotherhood without distinction of race, age, color, or creed among all the peoples of this earth, in order that such a cosmical catastrophe may be averted.

The teachings given out in this volume are ensouled by very high spiritual forces — the forces from the Lodge of Light itself — and in sending these teachings into the world the Temple will radiate into the hearts of the people a light and an influence that must powerfully promote the ideal of the Brotherhood of Man. Because of the great inner Light and Love back of these teachings, every person who loves his fellow men and who opens his or her mind in attunement to the fundamental truth contained in this volume will inevitably receive an uplift in consciousness and a help that will be entirely independent of the teachings themselves. He will receive the touch of Infinite

---

[1] *Dark Star* — the name given by the Masters to the Earth, which can become a bright star, being the "cradle of Gods." The true name of the Earth is *Tiamat*.

Love and Compassion from the Master's hands, warming the heart of every true and earnest seeker for light and giving greater opportunity to help the world. The cosmic lilt of Life Itself may then be heard by the inner ears once more attuned to the initiating sounds of primal Consciousness, that Consciousness which is divine and reveals the concealed unity of the One in All and All in One.

The Temple of the People
[Guardian-in-Chief]
Halcyon, California
January 1925

TO MY BELOVED[1]

Arouse ye! Arouse ye! Children of the New Covenant. Why stand ye in the public places idle throughout the busy day? The War of the Ages is upon thee — the strife between the Sons of Universal Light and the Brothers of the Shadow. The long list of the Sons of Betrayal, the Judas power of the accumulated ages, hath its arms about thy neck and is pressing upon thy cheek the kiss that bringeth crucifixion. Awake, thou that sleepest! And the Logos[2] shall shine upon thee. The Christ in thine own soul whispers: "Be of good courage, I have overcome the world."[3]

The days of preparation are upon thee. Gird on that armor of Righteousness which is the Heritage of every Son of the Living God, and strike for the freedom of the races of the earth from the clutch of the beast, the embodied Mammon[4] who now holdeth in subjection the Children of Man.

Think ye that no protest rises to the seventh heaven from the murdered Abels[5] of the long past ages? Think ye the Law hath lost its power because its judgments tarry long? Become one with the Law. Enter thou the Holy of Holies with unsandaled feet and uncovered head, that the Forces of Love, Law, and Life may flow unobstructed through the Stone of Sacrifice upon which thou standest, and the return wave bear to thee the spiritual essence that shall make thee free. In freedom lies thy strength. The Sword of the Spirit shall be thy reward, and He whom thou lovest shall lead thee to living waters, for He is the Warrior of Light, the Unconquerable, for whom the hour shall never strike. He is thine own true Self; and when thy shadows flee away, thou shalt behold the King in His Beauty and Holiness.

---

[1] The 1925 edition's note: This message of the Great Master was printed in the first issue of *The Temple Artisan* in June 1900. The message is given without altering the text for the sake of any accepted literary form or usage. The change from the plural to the singular number in the use of pronouns is peculiar, but as the message is synthetic, it must signify that it is addressed not only to the whole world of humanity collectively, but to each individual unit thereof as well.

[2] *Logos* (*Greek*, "word") — the manifested Deity; the outward expression, or effect, of the cause which is ever concealed; a name or title of Jesus Christ.

[3] John 16:33.

[4] *Mammon* (*Aramaic*, "riches") — a term derived from biblical texts, representing material wealth or worldly possessions and often associated with greed and the pursuit of wealth as an ultimate goal.

[5] *Abel* — the second son of Adam and Eve, murdered by his brother Cain.

TEMPLE APHORISMS

Days come and days go, but if thou watchest thou shalt see:
The load thou hast laid on the heart of a friend will God transfer to thine own heart; heavy as it presses on the heart of thy friend, heavier will it press on thine own heart in the days to come.

The stone thou hast cast from the path of the blind will smite the adder lying in wait for thee.

The weight thou hast clamped on the feet of another will drag thine own feet into Hadean[6] desolation.

The shelter thou hast given the wayfarer will protect thee from the fiercest of life's storms.

The jewel thou hast stolen from the strong-box of another will burn and torture the breast wherein it is hid.

The bread thou hast given the hungry holds the substance of many loaves for thee.

The lie whereby thou hast gained an end will eat out thine own vitals.

The tears thou drawest from others' eyes will mark deep furrows down thine own face.

The shoe-latch thou hast fastened for the halt and lame will bind the hands of thine enemies.

The fire thou dost feed to scorch another will consume thee in its flames.

The law of right can never be thwarted long.

That which thou hast sown, that shalt thou gather, whether it be in joy or sorrow, pain or peace.

Thou mayest plan the hour of planting — the hour of gathering must needs be struck by the hand of God.

I have said.

---

[6] *Hadean* (from *Hades*, the Greek god of the underworld, and the underworld itself) — infernal or hellish.

A FEW QUALIFICATIONS
(Without which no man can save his soul — *alive*)

1. The ability to stand upright and look squarely at the sun, while the shadows are engulfing everything upon which he has leaned, and yet to know that, illusory though they are, it has been by the means of such supports that he has gained the power to stand upright.

2. The ability to forgive and forget his real or fancied grievances with the same degree of forgiveness and forgetfulness that he desires for himself from his own Higher Self.

3. The ability to examine his own life by means of the same light that he throws upon the life of another.

4. The ability to mete out to himself the same just punishment for his offenses that he would wish to see meted out to any other human being.

5. The ability to shed his last drop of blood to sustain his given word, believing nothing less could wipe out the dishonor of a willful lie.

6. The ability to pour out his soul in streams upon his beloved, and yet, when the streams are treacherously turned aside, to gather up the scattered drops and hold them in leash against the need of some other soul.

"To those who would enter the Temple of Mysteries as disciples, I would say, there are seven requisites: freedom from prejudice; and from thralldom; devotion to the principles; charity towards all; removal of stumbling blocks from the path of lesser disciples; earnest cooperation; burial of past mistakes."

FROM THE PLACE OF SILENCE

To you — comes "the voice of one crying in the wilderness."
Are you to be found among the sorely disappointed, heart-hungry souls who have long been seeking in vain for the realization of some high ideal? Those who have been growing more and more dissatisfied with what life seems to offer and feel appalled at the apparent inadequacy of the present methods of Church or religious organization, science, art, or social conditions to satisfy the ever-increasing craving of your soul for something, you know not what, something to which you can give no name?

Do you believe that you could satisfy that hunger of the soul or still the unrest which is now driving you on as with a whiplash into everything that seems to promise a change, if you might accomplish the realization of some personal ambition, the gratification of passion, or the upheaval of home, family, or business associations? If you hold such a feeling, you may be on the verge of making forever impossible the satisfaction of that hunger, the stilling of that unrest.

Perhaps you are trying to solve life's deepest mysteries from the standpoint of their effects instead of from that of their causes. It never yet has been done by man. You cannot so flout and disgrace your Creator as to believe that the all-powerful, sacred and beneficent laws of universal life could bring you to your present stage of evolution and then leave you at that imperfect stage with no means by which you could carry out their decrees. Those decrees point to self-conscious attainment of the ideals which those laws have formed in your nature. Realization of present limitations may be the cause of your deep dissatisfaction with all that which seems to promise so much only to leave you more discouraged after each effort toward attainment. Yet those efforts have been gradually bringing you to the point where it is possible for you to perceive the one all-important necessity for your next step, when it is presented to you rightly.

All prophecy, all revelation, even the revelations of your own higher nature, have taught that there was just one Being or one Attribute which was capable of leading to or teaching you the way to all attainment. Have you ever asked yourself how you were going to recognize that Being or Attribute when it came on the scene of action?

The predictions and prophecies of the holiest, most self-sacrificing souls of all time; all science and invention; even the very stars in
heaven, as well as the sun that is now entering the sign of the Water-
Bearer, all prefigure the second coming of the Son of Man and the
servant of the people, and the period of his coming.

Deep unrest, widespread rebellion, passionate demands for freedom in all walks of life, all proclaim the same tidings; for without the
latter the former would be inadequate. One demands and the other
supplies the necessary information. The before-mentioned prophecies
and revelations also predict or indicate the evolving of "peculiar children," in whom the long-atrophied psychic senses of the race will be
again aroused, and through whom many of the long-hidden mysteries
of life will be unsealed. As has also been foretold, many false teachers
are appearing who "if it were possible would deceive even the elect,"[1]
the prepared. Therefore, we, who bring the message that has been sent
to you, can only leave it to your own soul to decide the authenticity
of the Message and its application.

Thirty-five years ago there came a call from the long waiting Seers
of past ages, to a body that had been many, many years in process of
preparation, to go out into the world and make ready a still larger
body for the receipt and dispersion of vast revelations. Ten years ago
there came another call from the same Seers, to the faithful of the first
body; to stand ready to deliver to the world the message they brought
and assist the people who would accept that message to recognize the
Messenger when he comes. Within the last year that message has been
deciphered and has been prematurely delivered by some whose inner
ears were partially opened, and who, therefore, caught some portions
of it when it was first delivered to its custodians.

We who send the full message to you were of the first and second
bodies before mentioned. We do not claim for ourselves anything
that you may not have if you will fulfill the necessary conditions.
We only ask you now to review your own past spiritual experiences,
the instructions or interpretings of your own pastors or teachers, the
revealings of your own higher selves as to the necessity, probability,
and possibility of a return to earth of the Great Soul called Jesus of
Nazareth, according to his own prophecy; and also, ask what is the
possibility of your recognizing him or any other Great Soul with no

---

[1] Matthew 24:24.

more knowledge of the nature or substance of the soul or body in which he must come than the average person possesses? When one realizes that he would not be able to recognize his own father or mother without previous association and mutual experiences, the difficulty in the way of the recognition of a Savior or Avatar,[2] without adequate preparation, is obvious.

Not all the paraphernalia of the heavenly spheres, the sound of trumpet or voice of angel would prove the identity of such an one, for we are told the satanic emissaries could make use of similar means. Something must be done to or within us individually to make such recognition possible and, according to the words of the message we bring to you, it is quite possible to make such preparation for the coming Christ, and to make it first in our own hearts.

Do not let anyone persuade you that you must sever your connection with your own church, your own family, your own people in order to make such preparation. It is the whole world and all the people of that world that the Christ desires to gain for the kingdom of God, not merely a fraction of it. Turn to and help to carry the message into all corners of the world and so prepare yourself for recognition of the "man of the hour," for in the carrying mayhap your own eyes and ears will be unsealed.

Francia A. La Due
William H. Dower

---

[2] *Avatar* (*Sanskrit,* "descent") — a God, a Spirit of the Higher Spheres and Distant Worlds incarnated in the body of an ordinary mortal.

THE MESSAGE

Hearken, ye children of the New Dispensation! The time is near at hand when He who is to come will reappear among men for the unification of the races of the earth. Open your eyes that they may see. Open your ears that they may hear. And open your hearts that the Son of Man may have place to lay his head, lest he pass you by and ye know him not.

H—[]

LESSON 1
MANIFESTATION OF SUBSTANCE – MATTER

The Instruction I am about to give you is of infinite importance, and I shall endeavor to render it as simple as possible, in the hope that it will be understood by those students whose opportunities for the acquisition of knowledge have been limited. Upon a complete understanding of this subject depends the full comprehension of many previous Instructions, as well as others that will follow.

The visible Universe as a whole, as well as each constituent or organic part of the same, whether it be sun, planet, man, or molecule, is primarily brought into manifestation on the physical plane, as *Substance* or *Matter*, from the inner or Spiritual plane of Life, by the energizing, through will (Fohatic)[1] power, of the potential forces contained or confined in certain colors manifesting through a great age or Kalpa[2] in the sphere of Mind. These colors are of a much higher order than their reflections, the colors of the physical plane. When a new life cycle of manifestation begins for any separated or individualized portion of the Universal Whole, it first appears as a rapidly vibrating mass of scintillating colors, which, from a definite point in Etheric Space, spread outward into physical space (so termed), by means of a circular mode of motion, in a spiral. The diameter of the last outward sweep of the spiral would be determined by the amount of expansive energy imparted to the mass by the initial impulse. When this energy reaches its extremity of power in the last spiral sweep, a neutral center is in process of creation by means of the contact and interaction of the negative forces of contraction peculiar to the physical plane, with those induced by the action of spiritual or positive energy, before mentioned. This neutral center, which, in the creation of a world, becomes the equatorial belt, manifests in the human and animal kingdoms as the solar plexus.

From the center, the spiral of color decreases in exact ratio to another point, resulting in the formation of a rapidly revolving globe of color, partially flattened at each pole, and hollow so far as physical substance is concerned; but in reality containing all the potencies,

---

[1] *Fohat* — the essence of cosmic electricity — the *driving* power of the universe; the universal propelling vital force, at once the propeller and the resultant.
[2] *Kalpa* (*Sanskrit,* "formation," "creation") — a long period or cycle of evolution.

as well as the *skandhas*[1] — the stored up good and evil tendencies of preceding manifestations of the incarnating Ego,[2] or entity — and the latent forces which will bring effects into action as causes of subsequent effects, at the right time and in the right place, as determined by the law of Karma. In this globe also resides the alchemical power transmuting physical substance into spiritual energy, and vice versa, as food is transmuted by the powers of digestion and assimilation into flesh and blood, and finally into physical energy. If this spiral globe of color could be seen by physical eyes at the beginning of an era of manifestation, it would seem to enclose a certain portion of clear space. On the highest Spiritual plane all lines of demarcation would disappear, and it would be indistinguishable, as far as form is concerned, from all the great ocean of Ether, the storehouse of all energies and potencies; but on the higher astral,[3] the plane of soul, it would be visible to spiritual eyes as an individualized Entity — call it Angel, or Deva-God, whichever you like — so far transcending in beauty, glory and power any description ever given by human tongue or pen, that it is useless to attempt to convey any impression of it to the human mind; it must be seen and recognized to be understood. It belongs to the army of archangels which surround the Throne of God, situated in the hearts of every one of that vast throng, and which exists potentially in the heart of every human being. For illustration, take a piece of paper; consider one side of it as the Spiritual, the other side as the physical plane. Separate one single point, among many others, of white light on the Spiritual plane (or side) of the paper; then

[1] *Skandhas* (*Sanskrit*, "multitude," "quantity") — groups of qualities that constitute our personality, combining in a certain way at our birth. They are divided into five categories: 1) form or body, 2) feelings, 3) consciousness, 4) aspirations or actions (karma), and 5) knowledge. Every action, word, and even thought creates a vibration, and these vibrations represent various skandhas that are attached to one's aura. In other words, skandhas form one's karma, and vice versa, one's karma is created from skandhas. The skandhas that we generate are our invisible property and accompany us from one lifetime to another, being imprinted on our souls as certain vibrations.

[2] *Ego* (*Greek*, "I") — the "I am I" consciousness, one's true being; the three higher principles in a human being that represent one's Spirit. There are two Egos in human beings, the lower and the Higher: one that is mortal and personal, called *personality*, and the other that is immortal, called *Individuality*. See *Man* in *Glossary* for more.

[3] The Astral World, also called the *Subtle* or *Ethereal*, which has many layers, from the lowest to the highest. See *Worlds* in *Glossary* for more.

imagine a flash of Light, or Creative Energy, darting from some other point and impinging upon, thus imparting a more rapid vibration, or another mode of motion to the point under consideration. This mode of motion (Fohatic energy) imparting a forward movement, would drive the substance contained in the point, through the piece of paper (the fiber of which would correspond to the astral, or middle plane) to the other side (the physical plane) and then proceed to form, by the process of spiral movement referred to above, a complete globe of color from the point of its appearance on the physical plane as represented on the paper. There are always forty-eight spiral rings on either side of the middle, or equatorial line, the latter being the forty-ninth from either end. This spiral sheath of color encloses the substance on the plane of action in and through which the energy which passes into it from the first point of manifestation will work in conjunction with the forces of color, for the creation of an individualized life, whether it be a cell, man or world. The auric correspondence to this hollow globe obtains throughout a whole era of individualized manifestation, however long or short that may be, as its particular sphere of creative energy, as does also the globe of color which constitutes the aura[4] of each cell, man, or world. In the materialization of a world there gradually forms, just within the globe of color (as the result of interaction of interior and exterior forces), first, a rapidly revolving sphere of heat and subsequently, moisture. In the creation of a world the power of attraction, which the combined energy and force hold within its mass, draws to this moisture the Cosmic dust which is floating in space. For long ages of time, great quantities of dust and falling masses from other worlds, in the form of meteors, etc., intercepted by or attracted to it, gradually transform this (so to speak) lining of the color globe into the crust of such a world as the one you are now living upon. But innumerable Kalpas before this occurred, the substance with which the spiritual energy manifesting in the point was clothed, had passed through many phases of existence from a molecule to a God. And the Spiritual Entity, or World-Builder, visibly represented by that point of Light, has voluntarily and intelligently assumed the labor, responsibility and sacrifice of creating from its own substance,

---

[4] *Aura* — a psycho-electric force that emanates from all bodies and things and surrounds the body in an egg-shaped form. Its colors change with the development of the mind and soul and are clearly distinguishable by the occultist and oftentimes by the mere psychic. See *Glossary* for more.

a world in which other manifesting entities of lower orders may gain the necessary physical experience to fit them also in time for spiritual existence as Angels or Gods. A corresponding process to the one outlined above occurs in the birth of every child or animal on the physical plane. The creative emanation of the male contains a definite portion of the substance generated on the Spiritual plane by the interaction of masculine and feminine forces as previously explained between the two points of light, or the creative fires; and the product, by contact and interaction with the ovum or egg budded from the ovaries of the female sex, results in impregnation. A certain residue is used by Nature in the formation of a state of matter comparable to the inner lining of the spiral globe of color, within which gestation is accomplished. The uterus, or outer covering, corresponds to the color globe, but is not the globe; for the uterus, as well as every other organic structure, has its own peculiar spiral globe of color or aura.

Despite innumerable explanations and descriptions of the planes of manifestation, students are continually misinterpreting terms and location. The diagram shown below will aid in many ways. First of all, however, you must charge your mind with the fact that there is in reality no high nor low, no hard nor fast lines; that all manifestation is from within outward; that all planes penetrate and interpenetrate each other.

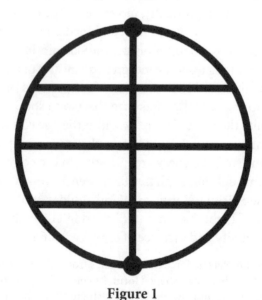

Figure 1
Diagram of the Planes

The dot on the top indicates the Unmanifested, the Absolute, the positive potencies. The one at the bottom indicates the negative of the above — the reservoir in which had been generated and from which had been projected into space, all potential energies belonging to the physical plane, and into which would be cast all manifested matter that had fulfilled its mission; as well as all of nature's abortions and seeming abnormal conditions, to be in some future age energized again by the positive forces of life, and so given another opportunity. It is also known as Chaos.

Each horizontal line in the diagram indicates the positive and negative aspects of some plane or sphere of consciousness; that part of each line to the right of the center representing the positive pole, that to the left, the negative. The line through the center indicates interaction of Spirit and Matter.

This diagram must not be confounded with others which illustrate the same truths, or the different planes or forces. In a certain sense this stands alone.

LESSON 2
STATES OF CONSCIOUSNESS

Many wrong and much-to-be-regretted conceptions regarding existence after dissolution of the physical body exist among members of the Temple.

So much emphasis has been placed upon the reincarnation of the Ego upon earth, that the truth concerning the intermediate states between embodiments has suffered by comparison; and rejection of the fact of reincarnation, in many instances, has resulted from inability to comprehend the conditions upon which the soul enters after leaving the body; for the ingrained belief of a conscious existence after death is inseparable from many religions, especially from that of the "Christian."

In one sense it was peculiarly necessary that the doctrine of reincarnation or rebirth in a physical body, should be emphasized more particularly, when H.P.B.[1] undertook her great work, in order to strike a just balance; for devotees of certain religious sects have zealously inculcated the belief that life on the physical plane is unendurable — "a vale of tears" and of anguish, to be avoided and abhorred — instead of

---
[1] H.P.B. stands for Helena Petrovna Blavatsky (1831–1891).

a field for growth, to be cultivated and raised to perfection. A constant stream of antagonistic thought arising from the minds of multitudes of mistaken human beings, contacting and lowering the vibrations of Nature's purer evolutionary energy, could result in nothing but a depression of the mental sphere of the earth — making evolution more and more difficult for those who through the action of Karmic law must return here in order to work out some unsolved problem.

The unhappy use of a word and simile is frequently responsible for a whole train of false doctrines, and after results in the public presentation of an important philosophical truth disguised beyond recognition by its original expounders. The word "illusion" used by Eastern mystics and theosophists, in reference to life in the *devachanic*[1] (Heavenly) state is such an instance. Although by some teachers the term has been qualified or made all-inclusive by applying it to life on all other planes as well, yet the true idea veiled by the word has not been sufficiently emphasized.

Beyond all controversy there is but one Reality in every sense of the word, whether we name it the Absolute, Eternal Spirit, or God; all else is "illusion" from that higher standpoint, because all else is reflection or manifestation of one or more attributes of God or the Absolute. Matter is "illusion" only from a cosmic point of view; and as Matter in some form manifests in all states of Life, it follows that Life in Devachan or Heaven is as real to the spiritual senses as is Life on earth to the physical senses; and in fact far more real, for the spiritual senses are more delicate, refined, and of infinitely greater power than the physical. Death, like sleep, is "Nature's great restorer" and must inevitably give back to man the realization of all his higher Ideals. If man is without high ideals, utterly hardened, and faithless of all good, the Heavenly Life can hold nothing for him — consequently, he can have no conscious existence on that plane; there can only remain consciousness of the Eighth Plane or Sphere.[2]

---

[1] *Devachan* (*Tibetan*, "blissful realm") — the place of rest between incarnations in the Subtle World, akin to Paradise, in which spirits feel celestial bliss and are immersed in dreams in which they experience, with particular vividness and superior to earthly reality, all the happiest days and moments in their latest life.

[2] *Eighth Sphere* — a special channel or sphere connecting the Earth and Saturn, also known as the *Planet of Death*. It is designed to take care of the outflow of human masses that are not suitable for further evolution. These are the most vicious and hopelessly fallen people, as well as simply those who have not done any light-bearing deeds over the course of their numerous incarnations on the

One great difficulty met with by students lies in trying to reconcile certain statements made by occultists[3] which seem to be absolutely opposed to each other, without the use of the "Triple Key" of Matter, Force, and Consciousness; for by the use of this "Key" alone, can any one particular state or phase of Life be interpreted. If the Key of Consciousness is used, the subject must be treated from point of consciousness — simply one form of consciousness functioning in another form of the same power. The same rule holds good using the Key of Force or of Matter. It is simply impossible to investigate the plane of Astral matter with physical eyes; astral sight is absolutely necessary; and this is latent in every human being.

There is not a cubit's width of void space in the Universe. The ocean of Æther, the self-luminous imponderable substance which fills and molds all space, is, in a sense, the shield or garment of the Infinite. It is also a double reflector: from within it reflects The Infinite; from without it reflects every atom of matter on the manifested planes. Consequently, it is "the great Illusion" in which, while in manifestation, we "live and move and have our being."[4] Among its other attributes, the consciousness, or soul, has the power of penetrating the Æther, and when freed from the physical body, is only limited as to space by its will; so it may seek its own Heaven at its own desire, when freed from the astral body,[5] which, after the dissolution of the physical form, remains for a time in the Astral Light,[6] one of the sheaths of Æther, and from which the original idea of "purgatory" arose.

The subject is too vast to be well considered in a short article, but it is important that an effort be made to change existing opinions.

Earth. Their lower principles are decomposed into their primordial elements, which are absorbed by the corresponding elemental forces, while their higher principles will begin their process of evolution anew on Saturn, under the extremely difficult conditions of this two-dimensional world.

[3] *Occultist* (*Latin,* "hidden," "secret") — a person who studies occultism, which is the totality of sciences that study the secret laws of Nature and the spiritual forces in human beings and the Cosmos, as well as the unfathomed properties of matter and consciousness.

[4] Acts 17:28.

[5] *Astral body* — the ethereal counterpart or shadow of man and animal, existent in the Astral Light.

[6] *Astral Light* — the invisible plane (to mortal eye) that surrounds this and all other worlds. In the Astral Light exists — throughout the great world periods — the astral body of every living thing or person until it dies a second death, and the informing principle then passes on, leaving the shell to finally disintegrate.

LESSON 3
POWER OF AFFIRMATION

It seldom occurs to the advocates of modern Mental Science that the exercise of the affirmative power as taught by some of their number, may result disastrously to themselves as well as to such innocent and ignorant pupils as are not content with natural evolutionary methods for the awakening and satisfying of desire and ambition. The quiet, unostentatious movements of the slower processes of normal growth are "a weariness to the flesh";[1] consequently, many are on the *qui vive*[2] for something new — something that shall stimulate more rapidly the development of their psychic centers.

Unquestionably, the power of affirmation is almost illimitable when rightly used; but it is similar to the power of the double-edged sword in the hands of an irresponsible person; for the opposite pole, the power of denial, must manifest simultaneously with that of affirmation; and unless the former can be controlled, the latter may be overruled. Only a few are capable of exercising this control, because of the peculiar existent conditions of the present cycle, and the unlawful purposes to which spiritual power has been prostituted. For example, the use of the words "I am," preceding some expressed desire, or statement relating to possession or control of some form of matter, as for instance, "I am power," or "I am wealth," may possibly, under right conditions, bring into action certain latent inner forces or elementals,[3] which may serve to bring about a realization of the expressed desire; but, as before intimated, such a positive affirmation invariably awakens the negative aspect of the particular force affirmed, and unless the operator be a trained occultist, perfectly competent to control all force and matter of lower vibrations than those which govern his individual existence, the negative aspect of the force invoked, in striving for equilibrium, may cause him to lose control of the force affirmed. This is one illustration of the eternal war between matter and spirit.

---

[1] Ecclesiastes 12:12.

[2] On the alert or lookout.

[3] *Elementals* — the spirits of the elements of Earth, Water, Air, and Fire (for example, jinns, elves, undines, dwarfs, salamanders, sylvans, etc.). These are blind and irresponsible forces of Nature, subject to the control of the will. Occultists can use them to produce various phenomena.

"He that overcometh shall inherit all things,"[4] and the power of overcoming is the power to control matter, the negative aspect of the eternal positive. Instances are rare indeed where the ordinary 19th-century man is able consciously to separate the Ego from the physical body and to realize the process of merging his personal consciousness with that of the Absolute; and he must be able to stand on this altitude ere it is safe or prudent to call into action the unified forces of the "I am" and direct them toward the accomplishment of a personal desire, however high that desire seems to be; for, sad to say, a pure and undefiled desire is almost an impossibility in this age and among present races, for the element of self enters too largely into every consideration. Only the Masters of the Highest Degrees can accomplish such a herculean task, and even they but relatively. While the individual consciousness is passing through the different planes or states of consciousness, it is subject to the "pairs of opposites," and it cannot awaken any positive phase of its lower nature without awakening the negative also; and it must succeed in striking a balance, in gaining a neutral position on each plane or phase of life, before it can reach a point of safety or of power upon that plane or within that phase or state.

If, by the exercise of the power of affirmation, a man has succeeded in drawing to himself (for the power of affirmation is also the power of attraction) a large share of the wealth of the world, the positive forces aroused by the amassing of that wealth will bring into action the opposing or negative forces, and these will take from him something in his nature which is exactly an equivalent to the wealth he has secured; something in manifestation either on the inner or the outer planes of his life. It may be honor, intellect, health, sight, or hearing — but whatever its nature, the balance will be struck exactly, for natural law cannot swerve from exact justice. If one wins wealth, fame, or any other so-called treasure by the method which natural evolutionary law will teach him, that is, by labor, the same forces manifest, but in a far less dangerous manner; for they manifest normally. The same fight occurs, but his foes are far less powerful, and he is more capable of understanding their methods of warfare and of arming himself against them.

---

[4] Revelation 21:7.

But few appreciate the real power contained in the sentence: "Thy Will be done."[1] It embodies one of the deepest occult mysteries; for Will in this case is identical with Law. An act of Infinite Will sets in motion a natural law which must eventually bring about the thing willed.

When an occultist has reached an advanced stage of mastery, an effort of his will connects his individual power with the power of the Infinite — which must bring about the accomplishment of the desire behind the act of will. He could not will to perform an action out of harmony with the Divine Will. And the fact that he has willed the performance of some act is sufficient to show that he has been acted upon by the Divine Will to serve as an intermediary or converter of the Divine Will to lower forms of force and matter, upon which the Divine potency could not act without danger to the particular grade of matter acted upon, because of the higher vibration of the substance of Divine Will. This is the real secret of all evidences of will power shown by Masters.

The use of the expression quoted above by Jesus at the crucifixion, would go far to substantiate His claim that He and the Father were One, were there no other evidence. The same expression has been used for thousands of years at a certain point in a great Initiation and the result is similar in all instances; that is, it precedes a form of crucifixion.

As powerful as is the action of Will, there is another form of force with which you are all more or less familiar which is equally great, but which has been slighted or neglected in modern occultism. This force is expressed by the word "gratitude." We will keep the familiar word because it will be easier for you to remember.

In striving to set aside a personal God, many attributes which were supposed to be especially connected with such a God, but which are in reality most potent Universal Forces, have been ignored or forgotten. This particular force is closely allied to the law of supply and demand — the demand being the positive aspect of the great law of assimilation, the negative of which is the law of supply. Without the outpouring or setting free of this force of gratitude — thankfulness — on the accomplishment of an act of will, it is impossible for that act to be fully consummated. It may seem to be so to your limited

---

[1] Luke 11:2, Matthew 26:42.

understanding, but could you see interiorly on the plane of forces, you would learn that just according to the degree of your ingratitude, just so would the real consummation of the act remain unmanifested or the results be nullified by some unexpected turn of the wheel of life.

Someone might ask — who or what are we to thank? In answer, simply turn your thoughts inward to Omnipotent Love, and cultivate the will and the desire for awakening this force within yourself which, when cultivated, will flow forth as naturally as does desire for the accomplishment of wish or purpose.

The occult meaning of the sentence, "Thy Will be done," may be summed up in the word "Indifference" as used by learned mystics, and one great cause of danger in the exercise of the power of affirmation referred to above lies in the elimination of this principle, and the putting in its place the most intense desire. While the higher or positive side of the desire principle is good, the lower or animal side is evil, and the lower desire elementals are the class that surround and drag down the neophyte[2] or student who has ignorantly or carelessly invaded their sphere, and who has prematurely awakened the corresponding good elementals of the higher side of desire by forcing them into action; therefore, it is plain that until one has become perfectly "indifferent" in the true sense of the word, and can say from his heart "Thy Will be done," he should be cautious about awakening that *Will*. Far be it from me to attempt to minimize or deny any power or attribute belonging to the Absolute. The one thing which I am constantly pleading for with you is a "natural life." The individual life of each of you should grow and expand naturally, and so reach fruition without spot or blemish, instead of being distorted by deformity and imperfection. If there were but one life to be lived — if men were never again to be capable of experiencing joy or pain, the present mad rush for the gratification of desire would seem more reasonable; but when one comes to realize that by the premature attainment of any special desire, he must eventually relinquish not only that, but all others of a like nature, he will, to say the least, believe it to be a matter of poor policy to risk so much. When man reaches the understanding and realization of the impossibility of gaining something valuable by means of something valueless, and that the law — "by the sweat of thy

---

[2] *Neophyte* (*Greek*, "newly planted") — a beginner; also designates the disciples of lower degrees of the Great White Lodge.

brow shall thy bread be earned,"[1] is irrevocable and immutable, and in action on all planes of life — and is capable of using this knowledge in all that concerns his daily life, he will have at last succeeded in placing the entering wedge into the mass of all power. And the ability safely to use his developing faculties to acquire absolute control over higher forms of matter will follow, as surely as day follows night.

The expression, "by the sweat of thy brow," is symbolic as well as literal, and means — by the use and control of the heat centers of the inner sheaths or bodies, for such correspond to the positive spiritual potencies.

The labor which causes sweat corresponds to the travail of soul which yields the water of affliction. The positive energy of Spirit or Fire yields the negative of Spirit which is the Water of Life or Purification.

LESSON 4
QUALIFICATIONS FOR CHELASHIP

Despite the instructions given so freely, and the manifest allusions in sacred and profane writ, backed by all the evidence the physical senses are capable of cognizing and comprehending in regard to mental and spiritual qualifications for chela-[2] or discipleship, in nine cases out of ten, man still persists in looking for those qualifications almost entirely in the physical man; his environment, occupation, intellectual pursuits, etc. You read — "the wisdom of the world is foolishness with God";[3] recognize and acquiesce in the unmistakable truth of the statement; then serenely uphold that wisdom of the world by your actions the first time you are called upon to make a decision between that and the Wisdom of God as expounded by those to whom advanced evolution has given the highest power of discrimination.

At the risk of rendering myself misunderstood, my words open to grave misconstruction, I must once more strive to clarify this subject.

If it were not so pitiable, it would often be amusing to us, to witness the list of qualifications, mental and physical, including all things from physical culture, scientific attainment, moral uprightness, up to supposed seership, that are frequently held up to us as a basis for demanded spiritual enlightenment. Understand me — I am by no

---

[1] Genesis 3:19.

[2] Chela (Sanskrit, "servant") — a disciple. Chelaship means discipleship.

[3] 1 Corinthians 3:19.

means underestimating any one of these great cultivated attainments; all are necessary, but they are only necessary as an *antaskarana*[4] or bridge between the lower grades of matter and Spirit; they have nothing whatever to do with spiritual enlightenment or attaining to the use of inner senses. They may or may not be a means to that end, according to the use made of them.

It is frequently stated and often contemptuously by the worldly wise that the Masters never could use such and such a person, for he has been guilty of this, that, or some other great crime against society; therefore, he is not capable of use by the pure and holy. To say nothing about the unqualified fact that were this true, no single individual in the world could ever be used in such a capacity — for all are equally guilty, it being a mere matter of different incarnations — the truth remains that it is only those who through spiritual enlightenment have been brought to a point where they can calmly behold in themselves the heights and depths of life that are capable of chelaship; and it matters not whether they have reached this point in this or another incarnation, each human being *must* be able sometime to stand where two roads meet and look backward and forward intelligently. And it is here that the true occultism of repentance for sin as put forth in the Gospels appears in part. For until one has beheld and trembled at the hideousness of one pole of Universal life, he is unable to see the other, for he must learn by comparison, by correspondence; and all possibility of spiritual attainment finally resolves itself into one word — Love. Love of evil or darkness — dead, buried, resurrected, and transfigured — becomes Love of God or Good, Love of humanity, selflessness.

There is no room for self-love in the consciousness of one who has attained to a knowledge of past incarnations unless pride in his victory over the limitations that have hitherto hampered his development arises and awakens latent ambition, or vice-versa; for ambition

---

[4] *Antaskarana* (*Sanskrit*, "internal organ") — the link between the Higher and lower Egos, serving as a medium of communication between the two. It conveys, from the lower to the Higher Ego, all one's personal impressions and thoughts that can be assimilated and stored by one's immortal Spirit, and thus be made immortal with it, being the only elements of one's mortal personality that survive death and time. This "bridge" becomes active when one aspires toward one's Higher Self by developing spiritual qualities, thereby merging the lower self with the Higher. For this reason, antaskarana symbolically means the "Path" that must be traversed through good deeds and actions before it is destroyed at one's death.

awakens pride. But when, instead of either, true humility is born of the sore travail of the soul, that soul becomes a power for good in the hands of the great Master that it is incapable of reaching by any human means.

We who believe in the perfect operation of Karmic law cannot conceive of the suffering and crucifixion of Jesus as being due to anything but corresponding evil in some physical manifestation of the Ego which incarnated as Jesus; but this does not affect the statement that He died for the sins of the world, for the sins of the world were His sins in a double sense that will be explained more fully when we take up the study of the New Testament from an occult standpoint.

The fact that Jesus first appeared to Mary Magdalene who stands even today as the epitome of all evil in woman, when his resurrection was completed, should teach those who presume to call themselves Christians the truth regarding this subject.

A true occultist is never at a loss to reconcile that statement with what he knows to be the requisite purity of body and mind for an accepted chela. Mary the mother stands for ignorant or passive purity — that state of purity that knows no temptation; Mary the Magdalene for conscious and active purity; two poles of one great attribute.

What I have here stated must not be taken as advocacy of that great heresy that the end justifies the means, or that one may do evil with the expectation of having good follow; for conscious evil can never bring forth good — the two are as far apart as the antipodes. What we understand as ignorant evil, sincerely repented of and atoned for, awakens the opposite pole by means of the forces brought into action by repentance and atonement.

Nowhere in literature may the true qualifications for chelaship be found more clearly defined than in the Sermon on the Mount:[1] the poor in spirit; the sorrowing ones; the meek; the merciful; the peacemakers; the persecuted; the pure in heart. These are the children of God, the true disciples, the chelas of the Masters. Without these attributes, all the knowledge in the Universe would not avail. It is what we *are*, our interior character, not what we know or believe, that constitutes the basis for chelaship in the White Brotherhood.

---

[1] Matthew 5:3–10.

LESSON 5
THE CHRISTOS

There are many to whom these Instructions are sent who are not able to obtain the books containing our expositions of the Ancient Wisdom, and to whom, therefore, many of our allusions are unintelligible. More especially is this true of those who have come out from under the bondage of the modern church, and while still holding the person and character of Jesus in reverence and love, know not just where to place Him in the scale of human life, under their changed convictions, or else who are disposed to put Him on the same level with other men.

Every age has its Christ or Savior, who may manifest under different conditions and in one or more human bodies; but by an age we must not be understood as meaning a few hundred years, for many thousand years comprise such an age as is now referred to.

In Volume 1 of *The Secret Doctrine*,[2] in the opening stanzas of the third chapter, occur these words: "The Three fall into the Four."[3] This sentence contains the whole secret of the manifestation of the Saviors of all time. Whether the trinity of Father, Mother, Son; Atma, Buddhi, Manas;[4] Matter, Force, and Consciousness; Desire, Will, and Wisdom; or Body, Soul, and Spirit is under consideration, is of no consequence; for in their last analysis, they are all One, and this One in Three is the Absolute, the life and being of all that is in manifestation on all the planes of the Cosmos, and each must be understood as interchangeable, though complete in itself when separated; and whichever one of the three aspects (or persons, as the church teaches them to be) manifests in time or eternity, manifests perfectly; that is, manifests with all the attributes of the other two.

This threefold manifestation of life and being "is eternal in the Heavens,"[5] and always has been, and always will be in that state of

---

[2] The major work by H. P. Blavatsky, published in 1888.

[3] H. P. Blavatsky, *The Secret Doctrine*, vol. 1 (London: Theosophical Publishing Company, 1888), p. 29.

[4] Spirit, Soul, and Mind, respectively, which constitute one's immortal triad, or Spirit.

[5] 2 Corinthians 5:1.

consciousness commonly termed Nirvana[1] or Heaven. It is inconceivable to think of It as withdrawing any part of itself, for It is a unit, It is *the* God.

No form of words can adequately describe the descent of this God into Matter, for matter was not in manifestation until the descent was accomplished. The principle of Shadow conveys as nearly as is possible an idea of the process. The Three, that is, the *Three in One* — created and became all Substance, all Matter, by a process akin to the casting of a shadow on the physical plane, that is by projecting the creative thought into temporary form and substance; that substance having all the attributes (in a lesser or more modified degree) of its progenitors.

To cast a shadow, a form must pass between the sunlight and the earth; the sun, the body, and the earth are three different grades or rates of vibration of matter, and these constitute the agents by or through which the shadow is cast, and they correspond to three different agents and attributes of the three great creative fires, represented by the Trinity before mentioned.

Now, in order to assist you who find it difficult to comprehend Unity in Diversity, we will take one aspect of the Trinity — the Son, which must also be considered as Cosmic Substance or Matter, in the trinity of Matter, Force, and Consciousness; as Body, in Body, Soul, and Spirit; as Manas, in Manas, Buddhi and Atma. This aspect of the Son is the Christos, the Savior, the Angel of Light that fell from heaven into manifestation, not because of evil, but to fulfill the Desire, or the Father-principle's Will, which was the creation of matter, its evolution, and final redemption.

Every atom of manifested matter possesses this principle; consequently, every human being; but it is dormant until brought out and developed; and can only be developed by the highest instincts of the soul. Consequently, while we are all Saviors in embryo, it is only One in any age that is able to develop the love, the endurance, and

---

[1] *Nirvana (Sanskrit,* "blown out") — the state of complete enlightenment and liberation, the highest tension and development of all the possibilities inherent in the human body. This state can be achieved during our lifetimes, as evidenced by the lives of all the Saints. Nirvana can also be called the *fiery ascent* because it represents the seventh state of matter, or the Seventh Plane of Existence, which we can reach. This is the only Reality in which neither Time nor Space exists, where we can experience bliss from complete unity with our Spirits. The rest of the spheres, or planes, represent only various degrees of illusion, where our physical world is the greatest illusion.

self-sacrifice necessary for such a high calling, and that One becomes the "Elder Brother" of the race and age to which he belongs.

In St. John, 17th chapter and 21st verse, are these words: "That they may be one; as thou Father art in me and I in thee; that they also may be one in us, that the world may know that thou hast sent me." This hope as expressed in this most beautiful and occult passage clearly demonstrates the belief held by Jesus of a final involution of matter in the same order that evolution had brought it out and up to the point where involution became a possibility.

Much of the controversy between science and religion as well as between different divisions of religious bodies, is due to the unwillingness of one body to fairly consider the disputed points in the philosophy of the other. The ignorant Christian imagines that Jesus must lose in greatness and power if considered from the common standpoint of an evolutionary monad,[2] such as was the beginning of the earthly life of all mankind, though he is often referred to in ecclesiastical works as "the firstborn among many brethren."[3] If he is a brother to all the rest of the human race, surely he was subject to the common laws of evolution. We do not desire to detract from the divinity of Jesus — we only desire to show the common origin of the divinity in all mankind.

LESSON 6
ILLUSIONS AND IDEALS

One by one those Ideals and Illusions which serve as the Beacon Lights of life are born and fade away. In the shadowy interim, the hours of utter loneliness between the disappearance of one ideal and the gestation and birth of another, the soul attains either to patience or falls into rebellion, according to the use made of opportunities and experiences.

The glamor surrounding the heroes of our boyhood and the guardian angels of our girlhood fades away with the passing years, and we behold only the good or brave man; the natural forces of law and life.

---

[2] *Monad* (*Greek*, "unity") — our immortal part, which evolves through our numerous reincarnations; also called *Individuality* or *Higher Ego*. See *Glossary* for more.
[3] Romans 8:29.

The men and women we have idealized and clothed in the garments of the gods — Love — become commonplace human beings as that love gives place to satiety or indifference.

Distant countries long associated in the mind with all that is noble and grand when visited by us often, lose their charm and seem far inferior to the land of our own birth. But most difficult to die and easiest to spring from the ashes of the dead are our great religious ideals. With many the personal God, with all the tender attributes of Fatherhood and Motherhood, gradually grows in greatness and power until it becomes Infinity, and an ideal of power and beauty is lost in terms of consciousness too great for comprehension.

The power and influence of one great Savior or Teacher wanes as the power of another Savior waxes, and as the latter gains greater command over universal forces, he draws to himself the worship of the masses, until his time, too, has come — and he must give place to the rising star of still another Savior.

The most important lesson to be learned from passing ideals and illusions is the impermanence of matter, even that of the highest rates of vibration; and the impersonal, non-separable aspects of the Eternal Spirit, as well as the necessity for a mold or pattern for every phase of sentient life.

Nothing is *mine*; nothing is *thine*; all things are *ours*.

In the revival of ancient philosophy in the Western world many old terms indicative of personified natural laws, forces, degrees, and stations of life have been brought to the attention, and sunk deep into the minds of many students of life and its mysteries. Among these the term Master or Guru,[1] as applied to those who have reached to Mastery of Nature's laws and forces, and who belong to certain Degrees of the Cosmic Lodge, has become most common to said students and is frequently used in a manner to prejudice the ordinary 19th-century investigator against both the philosophy and its expounders.

Jesus said, "call no man your master,"[2] and he was right. When you hear anyone say *my* Master, you can depend upon such a one knowing but little of that theme, or else that he is the tool of a designing hypocrite. A true Master of any degree of real life would never

---

[1] *Guru (Sanskrit,* "teacher") — a guide or teacher of the secret laws of life and its mysteries.
[2] Matthew 23:9–10.

countenance the use of the prefix *my*, as applied to the term Master, by a personal chela or student.

Although the term is in common use in the Far East, it simply means "my teacher," and the term Guru has the same signification save that it indicates a teacher of a somewhat lower degree.

What good reason have the English-speaking races for being ashamed of their own language, or of such terms as are in common use; or for using terms of whose real significance they are wholly ignorant?

As before said, the word "Mastery" implies the winning of power over Nature's great forces. One having gained such power is a Master, and can be "my" Master to no individual soul without loss of dignity and individualism to that soul which is one in essence with his own; and when the words *my* Master or *my* Guru issue from the lips of one who uses them to enhance his own importance in the eyes of another who is not supposed to have the honor of a special Master, they are usually accompanied by a wave of vainglory so dense as to be almost visible to mortal eyes. When an individual has arrived at a stage of development which permits of his having special or personal direction, he will never claim any member of the Supreme Lodge as a personal adjunct. If he has occasion to speak of any individual Master, it will be as *the* Master, but this he will never do when his own personal affairs are concerned, especially to the uninitiated; for he will have learned in the first lesson given him that the words *me* and *mine* must be obliterated from his vocabulary.

The Masters or Initiates of the Great Lodge are as yet but ideals to the masses of mankind — ideals that like unto all other ideals must fade to a greater or lesser extent as each individual soul approaches the same scale of Being — gains the same Mastery of life and death; but it is unwise to pull down those ideals by familiar use before they have accomplished their mission as living patterns after which imperfect man may build his life and mold his destiny.

A great fallacy rests in the minds of even some devoted students as to the effect on themselves of coming into contact with an Initiate. The intense longing of the human heart for someone — something, above and beyond itself, by or through which it may attain to a more perfect state, is responsible for the belief that such attainment may be realized merely by the imparting of power by the Initiate to the student. Foolish children — do ye yet think that even a God can supply that which can only manifest by process of labor and growth? The law of growth is the primal law of the Universe which none may break or alter.

LESSON 7
THE ETHERIC UNIVERSE

So much emphasis is laid upon, and so much importance attached to, psychic vision, by those ignorant of the cosmic *modus operandi*,[1] and the purely natural law which produces all phenomena under the classification of psychic; and so many are led astray by that which seems to them only to be accounted for by the intervention of individual "spirits," that it is well such should be undeceived and all interested in the subject enlightened.

Every thought, word, and deed of every creature and thing in the manifested Universe is imprinted by Fohatic energy upon the great ocean of etheric substance, which, in one sense, may be likened to the film upon which a photograph is imprinted, because of its power of receiving and retaining impressions.

The study of geometry will have taught you that the three great powers — positive, negative, and neutral — manifest in all things. The positive-negative, the Father, or great creative power of the Universe, gives power of thought (principle of Manas); the negative-positive pole manifests the thought by bringing it into form, or act.

The neutral or central point of the "line of life" attracts to itself both the power of projector and receiver, and fixes the image of the thought, word, or deed upon or within that Etheric Substance which in geometry is illustrated by the Square, and in arithmetic by the number 4.[2] Here the image remains during the whole cycle of manifestation. It is God's "Book of Judgment," and it is by means of the process

---

[1] A particular way or method of doing something.

[2] The Square is the most sacred figure in all ancient teachings, including those of Atlantis. It is the symbol of the manifested world, divine balance, and the complete Knowledge or the synthesis of Knowledge (whereas the Triangle is the symbol of Supreme Knowledge, which is detached from the Earth). This is also a Pyramid, because the Pyramid stands on a quadrangular foundation and ends with a point at the top, thus representing a triad and a quaternary, or numbers 3 and 4. Its special significance can be found in the teachings of the Pythagoreans who swore by the sacred number 4.

described that our faults and virtues are recorded and may confront us when we gain access to the Astral Light or Ether.

Much confusion appears to exist relative to the above plane or sphere of consciousness, owing to the inconsiderate and indiscriminate use of the term "Astral Light" by those commenting on its laws and phenomena.

The Astral Light has two aspects or planes of consciousness. Its higher aspect is creative and preservative, and from it are reflected, or projected, all inscribed principles of perfect form or order; and back to it are reflected the same principles, plus what each soul may have gained by planetary life. It is the plane of soul manifestation.

The lower aspect of the Astral Light is the plane of disorder and disintegration of form. From it we receive the fleeting visions of horrible or grotesque forms, and back to it is reflected all we know as evil — all of nature's abortions. It is the soul's first stopping place on its return to Devachan (Heaven). It is also the place of purging, where is left the last remnant of what we knew as physical matter. Without a comprehension of both aspects, no right understanding of the Astral Light is possible.

With the first manifestation of the principle of form, sin (bondage or limitation) came into being, and with it the impulse to be freed from these limitations; for Spirit in bondage is Spirit in torment. While the very struggle of the incarnating Spirit to gain its freedom but serves to increase the strength and substance of its bonds, its nature compels it to struggle, and thus bring into manifestation by the power of motion still more of its primal essence.

The statement, "there is no remission of sin save by blood,"[3] has been the cause of more controversy, more bloodshed, than any other single statement in the Bible, and is as little understood as are other deep occult truths to be found in the pages of that book; but, as is the case with other esoteric statements, its very simplicity veils its true meaning from profane eyes — for, while it, like many other similar truths has several keys and is susceptible of many changes or shades of meaning, the most important interpretation demonstrates the fact that blood in some state is the first form of sentient life on the physical plane. It is held in suspension, as it were, latent, in every molecule of every cell which nature uses in building form and substance. You

---

[3] Hebrews 9:22.

often hear the expression — "you cannot draw blood from a stone." But you *could* get blood from a stone if you knew how to produce that phenomenon, as blood is latent, if not in evidence, as I have said before, in all things. Shedding or destroying the blood of a man or an animal only results in the destruction of form, which form is thereby resolved into its constituent elements, and if the soul which animated that form be on the ascending curve of its cycle of manifestation, its unclothing brings it just that much nearer final disintegration of form and absorption into the Infinite, from whence it came, and where alone it can be free from the limitations of Matter.

This exposition is equally true of all forms, whether they be physical, social, religious or political. Every great government, society or religion has been built upon the destruction of some preceding form; and such destruction has been brought about in every case by bloodshed or its corresponding woe and suffering. The soil of the earth has been drenched in blood from pole to pole in the ages that have passed since it came into being, and will be again ere its mission is ended; and, when a realization of this truth dawns upon you it will not be difficult to see the hopelessness, the utter impossibility of the long prayed for "peaceful revolution which is to bring order out of the present social chaos," according to the belief of those who do not sufficiently take into consideration the working out of irrevocable law.

With the end of the reign of the calf of gold will come the most terrible revolutions that have shaken the earth — for, according to the power and greatness of the usurper of the prerogatives of God will be the destructive force arrayed against it, and the worship of the golden calf is responsible for more evil than all other causes combined. Consequently, its dethronement will be more difficult and accompanied by more sorrow.

The power back of the operation of the law that requires the shedding of blood for remission of sin, or in other words, the destruction of form by the disintegration of matter and consequent release of Soul, is the power of the Christ — the Son. As the Father represents the Spirit, the Son represents Matter; and Christ redeems Matter at the end of every great Manvantara[1] by sacrificing differentiated (physical) life in form, and returning to life in Spirit — Unity. But not alone at the close of such periods. From its beginning to its end, the manifestation of

---

[1] *Manvantara (Sanskrit, "Age of a Manu")* — a period of active life within a planet, system, galaxy, or the Universe.

the Christ life in form (the Universal Soul) is a perpetual sacrifice, as is the life of all in whom that first principle is most active. It is born of its Mother — Love, and with her holds the scales of Justice in the light of self-sacrifice.

LESSON 8
TRUE BROTHERHOOD

From the vantage ground gained in battling with like conditions to those among which you find yourselves in this dark age, I come to speak with you, and to plead with you to listen, to understand and obey — not what I may *direct*, but what I, in conjunction with the I of and in your own souls, whisper in unspeakable, yearning love.

Brotherhood has become a term of reproach to some — a byword bandied about from lip to lip with a careless jest by others, through man's inability to discern the fundamental truth expressed by the word in all its purity and holiness.

As a pearl, when dropped into mire and filth, still retains its intrinsic worth and only requires cleaning to bring out its beautiful, spiritual luster, so the word Brotherhood may once more be made to shed the light of its splendor on a world torn apart by strife and dissension and all unbrotherliness; and thou, my child (whichever one thou art), hast thine own part to perform in this great work.

That Brotherhood means literally all that is implied by the words, "do unto others as you would that they should do unto you,"[2] is beyond controversy; and no one of you is so situated as to be unable to keep this law; for it is a universal law, and whoever violates it brings upon himself or herself the karmic action of the law. Furthermore, it is the law upon which rests all possibility of farther advance on evolutionary lines; for if you cannot give to your Brother or Sister the love, the helping hand, the encouraging word or deed which you do now, or will some other time desire for yourself, how can you give to the great Master to whom you are pledged (He who is one with that Brother or Sister as with you), the unselfish love that alone can hold you on the Path you have chosen. This is no matter of sentiment, as is so frequently imagined, but as before intimated, it is the law upon which your real life here and hereafter rests. To the violation of this

---

[2] Matthew 7:12.

law may be attributed every evil ever manifested; and again the stars are predicting the overthrow of great continents, because of man's disobedience to this law.

Open your eyes, my children, and see how man's inhumanity — unbrotherliness, is loading with chains, binding and sacrificing to his own selfish desires and passions, those other fragments of divinity — struggling along the same weary way he also is treading — at his side, within sound of his voice, under the very eaves of the palace which shelters him.

While one among the so-called higher classes is preparing the ruin of a daughter of some poor mechanic, some other man in the same station of life as himself is preparing dainty luncheons in some secluded corner of a great emporium where his wife or daughters may obtain *sub rosa*,[1] the intoxicating wines or liquors which will lead just as surely to *their* eventual ruin, or is making a rendezvous of apparent safety with other men whose object is the same as his own — the ruin of the poor mechanic's daughter.

Great wholesale liquor merchants are storing up barrels upon barrels of vile intoxicating poisons, which finally go to ruin the weak of all classes of their own country as well as of other countries where such beverages have hitherto been unknown. Only too soon the sad stories of murder and rapine come back, mayhap connected with the only sons of the above-mentioned merchants.

If it is only the selfish instincts of man that can as yet be appealed to in the consideration of this great law of Brotherhood, it is better to so appeal to him, through such than to leave him in ignorance of the karmic retribution which must follow; but this great beneficent law of Karma has been equally misunderstood and travestied.

With many, Karma has become simply an avenging "Nemesis"[2] which holds them in a cruel grasp from which they cannot escape, instead of the just and tender great Father-love it is, in reality. But for this violated law of our eternal Brotherhood, we should have no cause for fear. Every loving word or act of ours to a Brother is rewarded tenfold; for on the plane of true Being, Good alone is all-powerful; evil sinks into insignificance.

-----

[1] In secret.

[2] *Nemesis* (*Greek*, "to give what is due") — the goddess of retribution and vengeance in Greek mythology.

Most of us are so wearied by our struggle with the manifested darkness of the physical plane, we would fain stand for a moment where the effulgent light of eternal Good may pour its sevenfold rays into our souls at the end of one span of life, in order that strength, power and endurance may return with us as we once more enter the dark sphere we call our world.

My children, throw off the yoke that has so long burdened your shoulders, stand erect, and say with those who love you, I *am* "my Brother's keeper";[3] my Brother's wrongs are my wrongs; my Sister's burdens are my burdens. What matters it if your words find no echo in the hearts of those about you?

LESSON 9
THE LAW OF BALANCE

It is a source of pain to me at times to be compelled to witness your impatience at the ignorance of your brothers and sisters who have not as yet had equal opportunities for accumulating knowledge, as well as your unwillingness, often, to convey information to them. There are among your number those who are intellectually incapable of grasping intricate problems or technical terms of expression, but who may be far above you in true spiritual progress. Such, through their inability to correlate those lines of thought which lead eventually to the understanding of fundamental laws of life and its phenomena, or to grasp such natural illustrations as lie all around them without help, would sincerely appreciate any effort toward their enlightenment. You cannot give a casual glance around any field of nature without resting your eyes upon hundreds of objects which furnish perfect similes for the illustration of any phase of natural law. The fields of motion and of vibration seem the most obscure, and are difficult of exploration to many of our otherwise well advanced students, who are just entering upon the study of universal (that is, natural) phenomena from the occultist's point of view; and, in giving you the following simple illustration, I am but doing what any one of the older students is quite competent to undertake, if willing to turn his attention to the needs of his younger brothers.

---

[3] See Genesis 4:9.

You have all observed the motion of a perfectly balanced plank, with a person standing upon the middle, having a foot on either side of the balancing point, while imparting an equal amount of force alternately with each foot. The longer the board, the more time is required to lift each end to the highest point it can reach. Each of the ends would be negative to the positive center of balance when horizontally at rest; but each end would manifest both positive and negative aspects when in motion, according to its ascent or descent. The entire board would have a certain mode of motion imparted to it by the person representing the generating force, but it would also have its own peculiar mass motion; that is, the motion of its own interior mass; and each molecule of the board would have its own particular vibration entirely independent of every other molecule. The board would be in one sense dead; that is, its power of growth would be cut off, but its molecules would be alive. Now imagine that the board continues in that position, constantly generating force for an indefinite length of time, and that you can see the inner forces that sustain and keep intact the molecules of the board; you would perceive the molecules contracting and their vibrations rapidly increasing, each drawing into its own center all the living forces that make it a separate molecule, while its sheaths — its physical forms — would disintegrate gradually, leaving nothing to be seen by even the most powerful microscope. If your vision could reach to a still higher plane, you would see that all of the individual centers of the various molecules had become part of one substance of a finer grade, for they would have reached the plane of the atom, which is the plane of the indivisible.

Space is the result of expansion. Time is the result of the action of the laws of attraction and repulsion — motion *per se*[1] — and must be taken into account in this illustration.

During this hypothetical time (say of one thousand years), the process of disintegration in the body of the person standing on the board would be gradually consummated, the board would decrease in weight and would disintegrate; and finally, while the board might retain a semblance of form, there would come a time when its motion would become so rapid as to render the board indistinguishable from the person, or generator of the force; the person and the board would seem as one object; and, if it were possible to increase the motion still

---

[1] By or in itself; intrinsically.

more, they would disappear from sight altogether and only be visible on an inner plane.

In more than one sense this illustration is a correct correspondence of this age; of its creative powers, and of motion and vibration in whole and in part.

As one end of the board requires an appreciable length of time to fall, and to receive an impulse from the earth which it contacts, thus enabling it to rise again, so every age or cycle requires a corresponding time and must receive an upward impulse from the negative force of the preceding cycle. While its matter, its humanity, and all its forces are at or near this negative point, all partake of the dark side of life, and can only give the impulse to rise again by united endeavor. The keynote of motion and vibration is raised while on the upward sweep of the cycle, with every succeeding age. The law of correspondences holds good throughout the universe on all planes of Being.

The fact of the Group Soul is widely contradicted by those not yet able to understand that all life is a series of groupings. From the animalcule to the man, each organism, each individual organ, is a group of a distinct grade in the universal scale of living substance, subject to and brought into form by its peculiar rate of vibration. For instance, that which is now, or has been the heart in every animal form in manifestation, was composed primarily of one form of energy, which, by the laws of chemical affinity united with another or higher form of energy, to produce or evolve a third form of energy which may be termed the universal heart. This form lies latent in every molecule of physical substance; and, as each molecule of matter is combined with another and still another, this sometime latent energy awakens, and is also combined with another form of the same energy, and eventually manifests as the physical heart of some low form of life. When the matter composing this lower form of heart has been cast off, the energy remains on the astral plane awaiting its next manifestation in a higher form.

Every organic center is a god in embryo, a dual manifestation. From a nucleolus to a god, one feminine cell must be impregnated by a masculine cell in order to manifest on any of the lower planes, although the process of impregnation differs in nearly all planes of life.

LESSON 10
SHIELDS OF NUCLEOLI

What I have before intimated concerning the first, or oily envelope of each individual atom of the life principle manifest in human or animal flesh, should indicate the right line of investigation to those interested in physiological problems.

Any force or substance which will operate either to melt or solidify that oily substance which forms one particular grade of matter in all living bodies, can modify or increase the action of the life principle in every cell of that body, to some extent.

Heat and cold apparently have this power, though in reality neither heat nor cold is the primary source of such action. The power lies in the electric energy which increases or decreases the vibrations of such molecules as have been energized for the production of heat or cold.

The results of the action of certain chemical elements used in generating Vital Electricity (some of which are obtained from nitrogenous substances, hydrogen, etc.) upon the oily substance are similar to those observed upon the application of heat or cold direct.

Cold is in reality but the absence of heat; it is not an energy *in actu*;[1] and the solidifying of the oily substance by cold is accomplished by paralyzing it temporarily by inhibiting the action of negative electricity between center and circumference of nucleoli. When the normal action of positive and negative currents is restored, the oily substance will soften and break up again.

The action produced by electric energy direct, or secondarily by application of heat or cold, induces most marked changes in any organ of the human body, owing to its effect on that peculiar combination of force and substance known as the life principle, and its oily envelope, which constitutes that grade of matter known as Nervous Ether or nervous fluid. The hallucinations of the fever or freezing patient, the visions of the lower Psychic plane,[2] noticeably in insanity, are primarily caused by excitation (increased or decreased vibration) of the molecules which compose the nervous fluid by means of Vital

---

[1] In practice; in action.

[2] *Psyche* (*Greek*, "soul") — the animal, terrestrial soul; the lower Manas. *Psychic* is applied to two different planes of consciousness, or what is sometimes called the higher and lower Astral Light.

Electric energy; but the action of this force upon the oily substance could not produce such effects without the interaction which occurs between the negatively charged envelope and the life principle within the nucleolus. The former, combined with the elements of water in close association with it, forms a shield about each nucleolus, which, in one sense, isolates that fiery atom and keeps it in a state of temporary subjection by lowering its vibrations, else it could not be bound in matter, as it now is in all healthy organisms.

When the oily substance is changed by disease or chemical action leading to disintegration of mass, the nucleoli in the nerve centers of the brain are brought into more direct contact with the inner organs of sense, and the quickened vibrations of the latter open the lower astral plane to sense of sight and sound.

While different elements may apparently produce advantageous changes in the oily substance by replacing the broken down cells or restoring them temporarily to normal conditions, it is unsafe to use such until the life principle is better understood; for the forces generated by means of these elements may prove to be in excess, and the patient using them be killed by too much life — for paradoxical as it may seem — it is "too much life that kills" — not too little.

If half the exertion, study and time now used for investigation and experiment along the lower grades of matter were used for the same purpose along the higher lines of life and fire, the greater secrets of life would be more easily approached; for it is the central point in all manifested bodies, whether it be in a world, universe or organ, which contains the most profound mystery of life, and the central point is a fiery atom.

From the center to the circumference, in spiral lines and back again, unceasingly moves all life from the molecules of a cell to the stars of Heaven; and, at the center of each are generated the Electromagnetic forces that control the stream of the life-currents in each; but such an idea as the possibility of controlling gross matter by those higher grades of substance which compose the Will, the Mind, and the Emotions, will not be tolerated by the average investigator. In some cases he will concede that they are the effects of force; but he will not for a moment admit that they may be not only causes and effects, but also that the effects constitute certain states of matter, which may be manipulated by the Higher Self, or soul of man.

There is a wide difference between the conscious act of the Initiate, who sends out and recalls his astral body at will, and that of the man or woman who, through weakness, permits his astral to oscillate between two planes until he can no longer exert any control over it. The former has absolute control over the substance of the oily envelope of the life principle. The same substance in the body of the latter is diseased or broken down.

LESSON 11
KNOWLEDGE AND POWER

No sadder condition of modern life meets the eye of the true Initiate today than that induced by the pseudo-occultist and his dupes or pupils: sad because in many cases the teacher himself is deceived; sad, because hundreds of weak-willed, self-hypnotized men and women are sowing the seeds of insanity, idiocy, and disintegration for themselves and their descendants; saddest of all because the ideal and hope of, and in, the Infinite Spirit of all life with its beauty, truth, and power is being dragged in the mud of sensuality, selfishness, and final degradation, to satisfy man's desire for power in various ways. If any man or woman of average intelligence will faithfully examine their heart and their life, they will find therein old or new tendencies, or full-grown evil habits, gross selfishness, or indications of a leaning toward the dark side of life. Nine out of ten will find a diseased body or weak organic centers, or an inherited or induced tendency to some form of physical or astral ailment. All true works on occultism preface instruction with the warning, that unless a student possesses a sound mind in a sound body, the practice of magic which includes the command of the forces of hypnotism, mesmerism, psychometry, psychology, and many other degrees of force and substance, is most dangerous, if not fatal.

Thousands of human beings "rush in where angels fear to tread,"[1] with no qualification, no power of mind or body to combat or control the occult forces they have evoked, simply because they have what they term an overwhelming desire for knowledge and power, or have been disappointed in more material fields of labor, or because the inner longing and craving of the soul calls for something to expend that energy upon. In the latter instance the ranks are filled from

---

[1] Alexander Pope, *An Essay on Criticism* (1711).

disappointed seekers after a personal God, who having placed all their hope for this world and the hereafter on such a God, and having lived to see their faith dispelled, their hope annihilated, turn to the first philosophy that is capable of filling the aching void within. They grasp with eagerness the promises held out in such an exposition of philosophy and entirely neglect the warnings, in many cases ignoring directions given for preparing conditions of body and mind to receive and profit by the promises. Understand me; I am not discouraging honest effort; I am not denying the truth and power of the Secret Laws of life commonly termed occultism; I am not denying the fact that there do exist teachers who are capable of imparting much preliminary instruction; neither do I deny that there lives a man or woman in the world who is incapable of receiving such instruction to some degree; what I do deny is that a sensualist, a drunkard, a glutton, a hypocrite, a selfish, or diseased man or woman is capable of evoking or controlling the higher or finer forces of Nature, until such time as he has eradicated vice and disease from mind and body. Some of you will say, how can this be when there are black magicians[2] who do evoke and control such powers? But — bear this in mind — such magicians are on the downward arc of the Cycle of manifestation; they have *gained* such powers by the same methods you must use to gain them, and have at some time passed far beyond your present condition in the scale of life, and have fallen from a much greater height than you have yet gained. You are so wedded to this idea of a single life on earth even yet, that it is difficult for you to realize that a very good or a very bad man has planted the seed of the good or evil now manifesting, many Cycles ago — that he has been, and is now, cultivating his own vineyard, the vines of which are his own lives on earth.

Far be it from me to advise you to think less, aspire less, or strive less to reach the goal which we are all seeking, Master as well as pupil, but I cannot urge you too strongly to look at this subject from a common-sense standpoint, to try to realize that the soil, the trunk, and branches of a tree must be perfectly developed if you would have a perfect blossom, perfect fruit. The fully developed soul must have a perfectly developed instrument through which to function, and when your desires and thoughts tend towards the final accomplishment of

---

[2] The terms *black magician* and *black magic* are not meant to convey racial connotations; the word *black* is used to describe the use of magic for evil and selfish purposes.

practical occultism, be thankful that you have reached a point where you are able to see, first your needs, then the possibility of supplying those needs; and, wherein you are deficient, set to work with a *will* to clear away all debris and build a firm foundation for the superstructure you hope to build thereon.

You would not believe the man or woman who told you they could take you just as you are and place you in the ranks with Beethoven or Michelangelo by giving you lessons for a year or two in music or sculpture. How much less can you gain the power of an Initiate from the instruction of the average teacher of occultism. Every human being has in him a spark of divinity — a seed — but he must himself supply the soil, must water and tend the sprouted plant until it reaches perfection; he cannot saturate the soil with nitric acid without killing the seed.

The unity and interdependence of the astral and physical bodies is frequently ignored. If the heart of the physical man is diseased, the heart of the astral is also diseased, although the original cause of the disease may be in either body. If in the astral, that is where the cure must be finally accomplished; if in the physical, corresponding force and substance must be brought to bear to counteract the conditions of disease. Mental scientists claim that all disease originates on the mind plane. This is a mistake; for a primary cause may originate on any one of the four lower planes of manifestation, and the effect of the cause is great or small according to the plane upon which the cause was set up. A virulent, evil cause set up on the mind plane will create far more disastrous results than a like cause of the same strength originating on the physical plane.

Owing to this intimate relation between the two bodies, the would-be chela must learn to distinguish between astral and physical characteristics or conditions, and to be absolute master over both before he can reach planes interior to the Astral, for the gulf between all planes must be bridged, and the forces or materials which bridge the gulf are, so to speak, emanations from the substance of the bodies on either side, and must be strong and enduring, or a great danger will confront the Pilgrim making the pass, the danger of being lost in the gulf, which means the loss of the weaker body of the two, whether it be physical or astral. It is a well-known fact that many soulless men and women are now upon earth; the gradual disintegration of an astral organ or body is frequently responsible for the loss of an organ or the death of a body on the physical plane. Frequent cases of blindness from birth are due to the disintegration or loss of the astral organ as a result of the misuse of that organ in a former incarnation; such misuse terminating in the creation of skandhas which persist from one incarnation to another. Such a case was that of the man born blind whom Jesus cured by forgiving his sin, said forgiveness meaning the disintegration of the skandha, thus permitting normal action — "the works of God" — to manifest.

The one great difficulty in teaching the Way, the Truth, and the Life to the average man is his impatience, his unwillingness to grow naturally and normally, and also his contempt for what he deems are old or simple methods of preliminary instruction. I could very easily show you how to evoke certain occult powers, but if you had not in yourself the power to command these forces, they would simply turn and rend you, and I would be an accessory to your crime. I have made you certain promises which I am willing and able to perform, but your share in this work is no light one, and while I desire to give you all possible encouragement, it is needful that you realize possible dangers from without as well as within; to be able to distinguish between what is possible and what is impossible in your own development. All this is quite within your present power if you will but be true to yourselves; will but face yourselves up courageously and determinedly. A fault acknowledged is half conquered; a virtue recognized is capable of expansion and growth.

LESSON 12
THE PHENOMENA OF SLEEP AND DEATH

The welcome truth that sleep and death are twin sisters, beneficent, healing, and vivifying is gradually making its way through the scientific as well as the religious world, bearing on its wings *faith* and *trust* in the fundamental laws of life which underlie all phenomena, and casting down forever the great Moloch[1] of fear which stands at the gate of all men's minds, ready to devour each child of hope which has been conceived and born in the joy of life.

Erroneous conceptions of the substance of the brain and the hitherto mysterious action of interior forces within that substance are, one by one, giving way to sane, sensible conclusions, and to a better

[1] *Moloch* — a Semitic deity to whom children were sacrificed.

understanding of the phenomena which have so long puzzled science — though perfectly understood and explained by ancient sages; unfortunately, these explanations are oftentimes given in symbolical language not easily interpreted by the unenlightened.

The formation of the cells of the brain and spinal cord, in contradistinction to the formation of the cells of all other organs and tissues, produces some very peculiar characteristics which have passed almost unobserved, or at least unexplained by the average investigator.

The cells of the spinal cord are classified as branched or stellate cells; these minute branches have a very important office, as they serve to conduct energy from one cell to the other, as do also curious little feelers or points of contact with which each brain cell bristles when the blood is coursing naturally through the brain in waking hours, and which are a source of never ending curiosity to the interested observer. If the same observer has ever watched the little feelers on the head of a snail as they disappear when brought in contact with an extraneous substance, he will realize the similarity of the action of the brain cells under excitation; for when the blood currents of the body become sluggish as in sleep, the points of the brain cells are indrawn.

The electric force or nervous energy generated by and in the blood currents operates through these points of contact by using them as conveyers of nervous energy from one cell to another; and as each cell is a miniature world in embryo, with all its powers dormant save for the particular vibration manifesting in one Cycle, the receipt and expenditure of the force by contact with the points of every contiguous cell awakens, or rather increases that particular vibration, and permits the higher forms of electric energy known as mind, which are conveyed by and in these nerve fluids, to pass through and leave their impress within each cell. It is a mistake to think of the cells as repositories of knowledge or power; they are but reflectors and conveyers of different forms of energy. In hours of sleep when these points of contact are indrawn, our consciousness functions on inner planes where such material means of conveying force are not operative, because no longer required, as the energy which required their assistance to contact the physical plane then passes freely from one interior cell to another in the same way as mundane electricity passes from one pole to another as is manifested in the arc light,[1] or by the contact of such wires as are used to convey that form of energy.

Time and Space are annihilated in dream life because of the rapid action of the energy of mind when freed from bonds of matter; and life in a state of dream is a foretaste of what life may be when the coarser grades of matter which now hold the embryonic God-man in bondage are refined; and the energy which now must act under all the difficulties man has ignorantly thrown up by unnatural, unwise methods and practices, through countless incarnations, will then be guided and controlled by the higher or spiritual will of man, for the perfecting of a body as much superior to the bodies of the present races of mankind as the latter are superior to those of the animal creation. There is no questioning the fact that ignorance is the root of all evil. With the dispelling of ignorance and the acquiring of knowledge concerning the laws governing critical states of energy, a new era must dawn for humanity; even now its signs are evident in the interest shown in mesmerism, hypnotism and various other forms of force; for these are all differentiations of one great force or energy. Some of you are frequently asked why mental healing is not openly advocated by Temple members, as the power of mental energy is freely acknowledged. As well might one ask a school boy why he does not perform a difficult operation, or take upon himself the care of a case of typhoid fever. Every human passion, every characteristic, every organ of a body, is, in its ultimate state, a form of force subject to Law. If a specific disease attacks some organ, and you try to remedy the evil by mental healing, and you do not know just what form of energy will counteract the force in manifestation as disease, and just how to apply it, nor the necessary degrees to be applied — in fact, you know nothing about the subject except that you believe in mental healing and imagine that you have the power to draw from an infinite reservoir of healing force, and that the force itself will find out the cause of disease and counteract it; can you not see that you are abusing or ignoring the laws which govern all manifestation? Whether it be force as Matter, or simple force, all degrees of manifestation are subject to the action of rigid law, and each degree has its own specific form, which in turn has its peculiar correspondences. If, for instance, you send a force of *contraction* into an organ that requires the force of *expansion* in

---

[1] *Arc light* — a bright light produced when electricity flows between two separated points.

order to change some condition resident within that organ, or vice versa, you will inevitably work harm; you *might* hit upon the right form of force, but the chances are you would not; or if you did, you might supply a degree of force that would injuriously affect some other organ. Even admitting that you had so perfected and purified your Will as to enable you safely to direct such forces to a given end, you have a long course of education to complete on interior lines, before it is safe to attempt to tamper with these powers that can kill as easily as create. Countless examples of healing by Mental or Christian Science are pointed at as examples of the falsity of our position in this matter. If physical health alone and that for a short period be the sole aim of the disciple, and if he is capable of the perfect diagnosis that will determine how much or how little he has really been helped, our position may be pronounced untenable by some; but, knowing what we do, we still insist on the truth of our statement.

LESSON 13
THE COSMIC LABORATORY

The scum which rises to the top of a stagnant pool is the result of Nature's effort to purify the contents of the pool. The eruption which appears on the skin of a human being is the result of Nature's effort to purify the blood stream of that person. The flow of nonsense, the uninterrupted volume of words that even sleep can hardly dam up in individual cases, is due to a corresponding action induced by Nature in order to clarify the mind by casting forth the froth of words, minus ideas.

In all such instances, an effort made to condense or conserve the energy in operation before its work is completed would result in creating deplorable interior conditions. Though the scum, the eruption, and the tiresome tirade of words may not be desirable from an exterior standpoint, the ultimate effect of such action on the interior planes is most decidedly helpful during some phases of evolution, or until the power of right concentration is attained.

The phenomena of the whole physical plane are more easily interpreted when the action of Nature's laws of purification in the process of perfecting matter is understood; for what is true in the illustration given above is true of every form and division of substance in manifestation on the physical plane. The latter is, so to speak, the refuse of the higher planes — the workshop or laboratory where the Meta-Chemists of the Universe are at work, purifying, distilling, and recombining the atoms cast forth from interior planes; and as soon as the work is completed in any given instance, it is transferred to the next higher plane.

The laws of attraction, repulsion, and gravitation will not permit a single atom that vibrates to one key to remain in the sphere of energy governed by another key, until it vibrates perfectly to the universal chord of Spirit, Soul, and Matter.

The differences which seemingly exist between human beings are not so great as they are sometimes supposed to be. No person absolutely incapable of living the life of any other person, however good or bad, could exist for an hour on the physical plane. Many of you would refuse to admit that by any possibility you could duplicate the evil deeds of another person, or perform the great ones of others; but you would be wrong. You may never have had temptation or motive power sufficiently strong to lead you into the first, no opportunities have occurred for the performance of the last; but under exactly the same circumstances, and with the same amount of desire and energy, the result would be the same in the case of all normal human beings. As soon as an individual reaches a stage of evolution on any particular plane where he has passed or has fallen behind his race, Nature removes him temporarily. And this she continues to do in the case of the former, until he has evolved to a state in which all matter becomes subservient to him, though eons of time be consumed in the process; and then it becomes a matter of choice with him as to where he will remain; for he has become one with the Law — a Creator — a Universal Chemist. But even this state does not free him from the possibility of failure and fall; he can never be entirely free from that possibility while in the bonds of matter or substance; and he is always in those bonds while in manifestation as a personality. Only pure spirit is invulnerable and incorruptible. However slight its incasement or contact with matter, a condition comparable to an alloy of gold and lead exists from the union of matter and spirit. In the former instance, the gold may be separated by means of fire; in the latter instance, Spirit may be separated from matter by means of pain and suffering, which constitutes one aspect of experience.

Spirit and Matter are two poles of Universal Consciousness, and all the intermediate stages between these poles are the battlegrounds and laboratories where countless Souls — Sparks of the Infinite Fire — win or lose the right to eternal individual conscious life; and where transmutation of gross matter into precious Spiritual Energy is carried on through each great Cycle of Time.

LESSON 14
DANGERS OF THE ASTRAL PLANE

You would not expect to increase the growth of a normal child in a normal environment by compelling or permitting it to frequent exciting scenes either of amusement or travel. Whether such scenes were in themselves good or evil in character, the fact remains that the physical atoms which constitute the body of a child would receive no impetus to growth by such experiences. Neither a view of the "passion play" nor an attendance at a bullfight would materially change the physical atoms, whatever effect either or both might have on the substance of the inner or astral body. Yet many of those who do not as yet understand the gulf that separates each plane of matter or substance from every other plane believe that the soul can grow in power by temporarily detaching the astral from the physical body, and allowing the currents of the astral plane (the *upadhi*[1] or base of air) to waft it — guideless and without compass — wheresoever they may.

Without the possession of that spiritual power and knowledge which can only be gained by long continued battle with the spiritual giants which control that particular plane — giants which for want of better terms we symbolize by the terms ambition, pride, avarice, and self-indulgence, but which are, in reality, states of matter and, therefore, *entities* — the astral body would be at the mercy of its natural antagonists and may even be permanently separated from its physical body, and the latter be obsessed by some earthbound soul or demon.

By battling with and either overcoming, or winning equal power to that already won by such entities or powers, through the stress and strain of the struggle, the individual soul creates a state of at-one-ment, by means of which it may enter at will the dominions hitherto barred to it. Without such power the soul is as helpless as a little child

---

[1] *Upadhi* (*Sanskrit*, "that which places its own attributes to something that is nearby") — basis; the vehicle, carrier, or bearer of something less material than itself: as the human body is the upadhi of its spirit and ether is the upadhi of light; a mold; a defining or limiting substance.

in the midst of a great city, where virtue and vice elbow each other, and where snares and pitfalls await the unwary at every turn; for, remember, the astral plane holds the counterpart of every creature and thing that has ever existed or been created by gods, demons or men.

I do not desire to convey the impression that the above-mentioned powers or entities are opposed to the progress of man; they but represent the positive pole of life, and are in natural opposition to the negative pole as now manifest in the human race.

It is a simple process to detach the astral from the physical body. It is done each time you close your eyes in sleep or pass into what you term unconsciousness. It may be done by the use of stimulants or narcotics. In the former case the soul and astral body are under the protection of natural law, and generally pass unscathed through all ordeals. In those instances which may be covered by the latter enumeration, the soul within its tenuous envelope is entirely unprotected, because the condition induced is an abnormal, unnatural condition, and is not guarded by natural law; therefore, dangers innumerable threaten, and unspeakable horrors may be seen on every side; and the same conditions or dangers confront the soul which violently or consciously projects its form-body either by suicide or by concentrated effort of will into the astral plane, while powerless to control the denizens of that plane.

I am moved to make this simple statement because of the almost incredible rashness with which many, even among Temple members, are rushing into psychism — in many instances placing themselves under the direction of conscienceless teachers whose specious demeanor and forked tongues have awakened abnormal desires which can only be gratified at the expense of the true growth of the soul.

My Children! Bring your common sense, if so be that you are possessed of that most valuable as well as most rare quality, to bear upon this question. Do not be led astray.

Either the desire to eclipse some other human being or the wish for the power to change present conditions is generally at the root of this almost insane rush into psychism.

Does the distorted, abnormal, unclean fakir of the Far East, seated upon a post, or in some other unnatural position, and with eyes fixed on vacancy, appeal to you? You, whose karma has brought you into the thick of the fight of the 19th and 20th centuries, and has given you opportunities for advancement spiritually, mentally, and physically far beyond those given to any race since the apotheosis of the race which once lived on the now sunken continent of Atlantis. Not a day passes over your heads which does not bring to you tests and opportunities which, if taken advantage of, may place you far on the path leading to Adeptship[1] — that path which you have longed to enter without realizing that you are already upon it, or that you are watched by anxious eyes far more interested in your successes and failures than you are, as yet, yourselves. Your ignorance of the nature of particular tests placed upon you is in many respects your greatest safeguard, and is at the same time essential to the perfect fulfillment of the duties which generally constitute those tests.

Many of you grumble and grow impatient at what appears to be a non-fulfillment of promises made by us when you have not fulfilled, and in many instances have not tried to fulfill, the obligations taken by you.

Instead of taking advantage of every offering opportunity to teach the philosophy which means so much to the world, you are oftentimes ashamed of it, or afraid that by so doing you will be classed among the despised theosophists, and so jeopardize some worldly position.

With full knowledge, gained through esoteric instructions, of the effect of mind on matter, some of you constantly pour into the aura of those at the center a stream of suspicion, criticism, and unbelief which must inevitably and eventually strike down one or more of the comrades living there, and bring them to the very gate of death or severe mental disturbance, and then calmly say to some friend, "Is it not strange that the Masters cannot prevent the illness or fall of such and such a brother or sister? It must be that there is something wrong with them."

When you are able to behold with unveiled eyes the effects of such ammunition, you will indeed sweat drops of blood from an agony of remorse, as have we who now watch and wait.

If you cannot — will not — help us to roll back the tide of ignorance; if you will not draw into the current of comparative safety those of your brethren who have long waited for your coming, you can at least refrain from striking down those who are trying to do their duty.

---

[1] *Adeptship* — the role, position, or status of an *Adept*, one who has attained true knowledge and mastered the Laws of Spirit and Matter, reaching the stages of Initiation and thus becoming a Master of Esoteric Philosophy.

On the other hand, there are among you those who gladden our hearts with unspeakable hope; those whose kindly encouraging words, in addition to their helpful deeds to and for others; whose sacrifices and efforts towards obedience are as dew to the parched soil to us who only await the right time and opportunity to express our gratification and extend a helping hand to "our little ones" on a lower step of the ladder of life.

You may imagine the above interpolation has nothing to do with our subject, but it has; for words are living things, creations of man, brought into form on the astral plane, either to torture or to bless their creators, according to their character and the amount of force which projects them into being. When you are capable of realizing the value of silence and the power of speech, as well as the effects of both, you will have conquered man's greatest enemy.

LESSON 15
KARMIC LAW

While the law of Karma is exact, there are operations of the law which to human judgment would seem unjust. You are aware that the laws governing all states of matter, while they are differentiations of the one Great Law, are unalterable. If you place a piece of ice in contact with heat, it will melt; if you put an inflammable article in contact with fire, it will burn.

If the substance composing any state of matter, or any individual, has become so refined or sensitive through the operation of the laws of the inner planes as to render contact with a Universal force destructive to its existence in form, that substance will be affected in proportion to the degree of force put in operation against it. This does not militate against the truth of karmic action, but it does take isolated cases out of the sphere of personal karma into the sphere of the World or Universal Karma.

One might think that the effects of a cause set up by a Dhyan-Chohan[2] in the beginning of an age should fall on the Dhyan-Chohan alone; but no human or heavenly being can suffer alone, for the very races or individuals which have emanated from that Dhyan-Chohan (you and I for instance) must and will be affected by the act of what we may term a progenitor. The Dhyan-Chohan must suffer the

---

[2] *Dhyan-Chohan* — a Lord of Light who guides the evolution of the world.

effects of the cause he has set up, but his suffering would not be of the same character as that of the lesser entities which compose his being, because It as an entity belongs to a different grade of matter from its emanations.

A very mistaken idea has obtained credence among some students of the occult life, i.e., that the Initiates or Masters are beyond suffering. So long as any Master elects to remain on the lower planes of being, he is subject to the laws governing those planes; he may have gained great control over the forces at work on those planes, but he is nevertheless under the Law of all Laws — Karma; if he were not, it would not be possible for him to fall; and as I have told you, the upward and downward paths of life run side by side. He may be able to keep his objective form from being mutilated, or hold disease at bay, but there are other forms of suffering proportionately great to which he must pay tribute, whether the law has been broken by himself or those he loves; for — never forget — no man, angel, or God is higher than the Law of Love.

Another error to which students are subject is forgetfulness of the different degrees of Mastery. A Master of a high degree could not suffer from any disease known to man; but disease as a whole has its correspondence on the higher planes, and to that potential correspondence he is subject, if he has broken law which could bring its action upon him, and just in accordance with the degree of Mastery he has reached, is the power or degree of punishment, i.e., suffering to which he is subjected.

It has been said in former Instructions that the Masters are beyond suffering; it should rather have been said, the *manner* of suffering of which man may take cognizance, or which he is able to endure.

LESSON 16
UNSELFISH LOVE

Unless the Temple can be made the refuge of the hunted, the resting place of the weary, the home of the homeless, it must fail in its mission as has every other institution originated and formed by Masters or man. It must be the link between man and the great Hierarchies which rule the Universe, or it will be worse than useless. The pursuit of scientific knowledge leads the irreligious seeker to a point where material force ends, and then he faces an immeasurable gulf.

Such pursuit ends in nearly all such cases in the desire for personal glory or material wealth.

The wave of pessimism now sweeping the earth is desecrating and destroying the high ideals by which alone man can raise his higher nature to that point where he is capable of apprehending spiritual truth. The soul of man daily feels more hungry for that food which alone can sustain it; and in his ignorance, his mad search for something to satisfy that hunger, the individual man throws away the spiritual food which had formerly satisfied and kept him alive, instead of holding to it and waiting for the floodgates of Heaven to be once more opened as they are at certain periods of time — and then adding to himself such a supply as would forever make that hunger impossible, a supply of unselfish love for the whole human race.

Love is the only medium through which our eyes may see clearly, unmistakably. Hate distorts, magnifies, or belittles. Passion blinds. True love throws open the portals of the soul and permits the lover to behold all that is unlovely, as well as all that is pure and beautiful by means of the power to examine and classify, to correctly distinguish between that which is transient and that which is eternal in the life of the beloved, and to give to each its true value. But, alas, how little this true love, disguised under the terms of various so-called attributes, is understood. It may bring to some minds the image of a composite picture, transcendent, glowing with heavenly beauty and truth, but in its last analysis, it is sacrificial Service. One who has attained to the power of love does not make that love an excuse for familiarity, is incapable of thrusting himself intrusively into the presence or life of the beloved; it enjoins the humility of true Service whenever and wherever an opening for such service occurs. It is long-suffering, truly great in patience and trust. However much it would rejoice in the knowledge that its love was appreciated and returned, such recognition is not requisite.

The process of evolving to this height of unselfish love is past power of analysis — past description. The agony of soul which is an integral part of those lonely heights which each neophyte to the great Mystery must experience; the blind struggle with the demons which bar his way; the annihilation of those piteous, pleading elemental selves which cry out from the depths of their torture, give! give! give! — these must not only be met and denied, but slain in cold passionless deliberation to make room for the higher, the unselfish Self, for the Laws of Space are inexorable.

This day in which we live, however sublime, however full, has dawned above the dead past of yesterday. The past years are but an interminable line of corpses. The present moment is all we may know of life, all that is truly our own.

The eternal struggle of the unmanifest to throw open the gates of life and pass through by means of that which is in manifestation, presses upon us in seeming mercilessness; it will exhaust our vitality, whiten our locks, and finally draw us down to the brink and over the river of death. We must die that life may have more perfect expression; but when all is told, that *life* in its totality, is our own. As tomorrow and yesterday are but incidents in a cycle of time, so the *I Was* of our passing Self, and the *I Come* of the newly manifesting Self are but expressions of the *Eternal I Am*.

LESSON 17
THE MEETING OF EXTREMES

The mission of H.P.B. to this country — America — was to teach the ancient Wisdom Religion[1] — the religion given to the Root Race[2] of the present humanity — not the religion of any particular sect which has since arisen as a result of internal dissension or division of interests, or as the result of individual interpretation of teachings found on ancient parchments.

No religion can be true that does not embrace and make provision for the natural life and evolution of every creature and thing in manifestation in that particular cycle.

Knowing that at the beginning of every great age, spiritual beings have made connections with and imparted to the Root Race of that age a system of religion which included the ethics of right living, right thinking, and right action; and that any division or sect which has sprung from that primeval religious system must be limited and in some sense untrue, the Masters of Wisdom cannot class themselves as

---

[1] *Wisdom Religion* — the One Religion that existed in antiquity, from which all other religions originated.

[2] The term *Root Race* does not refer to any ethnicities; rather, it designates the stage of evolution through which humanity passes. There are Seven Root Races in total; the present humanity is the Fifth Root Race. See *Race* in *Glossary* for more.

Brahmans, Christians, Buddhists, or by any other special distinctive religious title. To use the words of Paul, they must be "All things to all men."[3]

Men seek and find association together for the purpose of working to better advantage as well as for mutual help and protection, but the closer they can keep to natural hierarchical lines, the purer will be their religious principles.

Like many other half-told truths, the somewhat prevalent idea of individual growth and development is leading many bright minds astray. If God, the heavenly man, is all in all, each atom of force, substance, and matter has its particular function and place in that one great entity. The force and substance that naturally functions in the heart cannot function in the stomach. Both organs are equally necessary, yet neither could exist apart from the other, and no one man — a single cell in the great body of humanity — can exist or attain the highest possible development apart from his kind.

I refer to the idea expressed above, of individual development to perfection, as a half-truth, because it is true only on the higher spiritual plane where perfect unity in diversity obtains, and where consciousness functions unhindered by time and space.

Until man can learn to dwell with his brothers in peace and unity upon earth, it is absolutely impossible for him to dwell with God in that conscious at-one-ment which constitutes perfection.

Every Master of the right hand path has gained his mastery in the midst of his brethren. True, he must go apart for a time, but only to gain strength to endure the stress and strain of physical environment.

Enlightenment — assimilation of spiritual food — comes in lone-liness and quietude, because it pertains to the spiritual life; but upon its attainment follows a period when that enlightenment — that force which has been generated in the silence, must be put to the service of the rest of the body temporal, or its compression or selfish use will be disastrous in the extreme to the individual. As steam compressed beyond a certain degree will burst asunder the receptacle which held it safely before it reached that degree, so the astral form of man may be burst asunder by the irrepressible force or power generated in that form by the attainment of conscious enlightenment, if not put to universal use.

---

[3] 1 Corinthians 9:22.

Man sometimes attains to a state of optimism that is infinitely more dangerous than a corresponding degree of pessimism, owing to the fact that any power belonging to the positive side of nature and life, when prostituted to base ends, may accomplish greater and more lasting effects than a corresponding power belonging to the opposite or negative side of life, for the reason that its potential energy is of a higher rate of vibration. The extreme optimist is utterly incapable of recognizing and acting upon the intuitive perception or experience of others, however worthy of belief those others may be. He will stand by serenely while family, nation, or religion is in the throes of disruption — seeing nothing, believing nothing but the glamor thrown over everything by his special trend of thought. The extreme pessimist is not so comfortable a man to live with; he can do a great amount of harm in a negative way; he throws out a lethargic poison that leads to decay and disintegration, but he does not possess the active energy that binds, blinds, and leads into captivity his adherents, as is only too often the case with the former.

The pessimism of the present day is largely responsible for the inability of the devotees of mammon to recognize and deal with the conditions being rapidly brought about by the extreme optimism of another rapidly growing class, who will tear down and destroy, instead of waiting for the natural dissolution of things and peoples. Extremes always precede disruption, whether of religious, sociological, or civic bodies.

Above all things, a calm, steady, moderate attitude should be cultivated in regard to all religious, sociological, and civic questions.

If a body of people sufficiently strong to cope with the situation rapidly materializing upon the earth can be organized upon such principles, they will be able to lay the geometrical lines of righteous religion and righteous government for a new age, and resist to a great extent the disintegrating power of the extremists on either side.

LESSON 18
THE SUBSTANCE-FORCE OF LOVE

It needs but a glance from the eyes of an awakened soul into the strained faces of the men and women who are nearing or have passed the middle milestone of life in this rapid, bustling, pushing age, to realize the woe, the pathos, the emptiness of the hearts masked by those drawn, seamed faces, out of which gaze restless, soul-starved eyes, casting furtive glances of suspicion around and about them, or heavy with unshed tears; the tightly closed lips, around which are deeply graven lines of determination or despair, tell their own sad story. The hearts now seemingly hard and calloused to common observation, were not always thus, but are now smothered in the stress of the daily struggle for life, forced upon them, either through their own desires or ambitions, or from the fires of fierce competition which have swallowed up the realization of the laws of justice and equity; or still worse, from thirst for the power that gold alone seems capable of imparting. They have lost the power of seeing that there is but one answer to all the burning questions of the hour; one solution to the problems now concerning labor and capital, masses and classes — and that is — *Love.*

In observation of the apparent cruelty of natural law, many lose sight of the love behind the seeming. In the study and application of Nature's great forces and phenomena, analysis seems to yield but one solution — pure, indiscriminate, invincible power, and the ability to use it for personal ends. As a race, we have put or are putting away from ourselves all that renders life worth living — faith and trust in the love that surrounds us; and what is even worse, in the possibility of impersonal, unselfish love.

Is it necessary to believe in a single personal God, built on the same plan and, therefore, as limited in some ways as is man, in order to gain a conception of the love of God — of the great ocean of spiritual love in which live, move, and have their being, countless thousands of those who have become like unto God, the very forms of whom are built of the substance of love? The concept alone is enough to thrill the coldest heart that has ever tasted the fruit of unselfish love.

In one of the commandments given by Jehovah to the Jews appears the following sentence: "Thou shalt love the Lord thy God with all thy heart, with all thy soul and with all thy might."[1] Are there any so blind as to be unable to see that the secret of this demand lay not in Jehovah's own craving for that love, but in the fact that love is essential to the very life of the individualities of the race? Without it, man is as a dead thing.

---

[1] Matthew 22:37.

The secret of what is termed "mental healing" does not lie in the mentality of the healer; that is only the instrument which he uses. The power of healing lies in the substance of love. Thousands of volumes descriptive of love, its action and functions have been written, but few have ever considered it from the standpoint of a divine force or substance, which could be conveyed from one to another, and which could be awakened by the action of another force just as surely as could the power of electricity be generated by bringing the right substances into contact one with another. You can behold the process by watching the action of the common arc light when the positive and negative currents are brought near enough together by means of such a conductor as carbon. The flame leaps from one to the other in an infinitesimal fraction of time. When the negative energy of a human soul is brought into juxtaposition with the positive energy of spiritual love by means of the conductor of faith, a like phenomenon occurs.

We are not now considering the phenomenon commonly known as love on the physical plane, though the same law is back of it, also. This kind of love can only be adequately described as sex attraction, for it is but the negative pole of the positive or spiritual love, which alone is absolutely unselfish. The love of a mother for her child induces a tenderness toward all other children, and is, therefore, a truer correspondence.

When the flame leaps from the positive pole of Infinite Love to the negative pole in the empty heart made receptive by suffering and aspiration, that heart ever afterwards hears the cry and sees the sign of suffering in every empty heart around it, and knows no rest or peace until it has helped to awaken the necessary energy and eased the suffering of those other hearts.

The scientist may postulate by a process of reasoning to his own satisfaction that the fourth dimension of space is a necessity, and therefore is; but he knows nothing of that fourth dimension in reality, until he has entered its confines. It is a hopeless task to endeavor to prove to another who has never felt it, the existence and reality of Infinite Love, to say nothing of its power to fill and round out the life that has yielded to its power. It is all the more difficult because it is one of the strange, sweet secrets between God and man that can never be imparted to another by words, for no human language contains terms by which it can be expressed. You may see a tithe of its splendor through the windows of a glorious sunset. You may catch the sound of a note, of its depths of harmony, in the roll of a great ocean, and a hint of its peace on the dead face of the friend you have just laid away to await the resurrection; and when your inner senses have opened, and the wondrous reality bursts upon the vision of your soul, the last great analysis will prove there is nothing else left. For God is Love, and out of Love were all things created. As the glorious song of the meadowlark thrills the air cleaved by its wings on its journey upward, awakening sound vibrations which act and react upon the ether which is the foundation of that air, bringing into form the waiting atoms of a higher grade of life then due in manifestation as form — so the song of soul aspiration, cleaving that infinite ocean of Love, creates conditions in which may manifest a higher order of its own substance — the spiritual form through which the consciousness of a god or an angel may pour its radiance.

LESSON 19
FAILURE

The intimation that some individual "has failed" in the sense that such a one has fallen into disgrace, or has been cut off from Lodge influence or connection, falls very glibly from the lips of some of the older students. The words are spoken in awesome undertone, and with a shake of the head, designed to convey the impression that some great calamity has occurred, while only too often the sharp observer may detect a little triumphant or self-satisfied note in the voice of the speaker, which causes him to wonder why that particular failure should be a cause for such undisguised satisfaction.

True, the word was occasionally used by H.P.B. and W.Q.J.[1] to denote some signal lapse into unrighteousness by those who, having been given great opportunities, failed to take advantage of the same; or who, unable to control the antagonistic forces evoked by them, fell under their malign influence, and as a result, took many steps on the downward path. But both of the above-mentioned persons were in a position to know exactly what was meant by the word "failure" when applied by the Master of the Lodge, and in what that failure consisted, and such is not the case with the average member of any of the divisions of the old body Theosophical.

[1] W.Q.J. stands for William Quan Judge (1851–1896), one of the founders of the Theosophical Society.

I would advise that care should be exercised in the application of that word when any defect of a fellow member excites either indignation or criticism.

Would that I could make you comprehend that one of two grievous faults, alone, has power to turn an accepted chela back from the door of the great Initiation chamber — namely, treachery to a comrade, or conscious disobedience to the directions of the Master; and no human being other than the one who has issued the mandate and determined the result has or can have the knowledge of such a failure.

By repeated disobedience, unbrotherly conduct, vice, and crime, even an unconscious chela may make entrance to the path which leads to conscious Initiation impossible for ages. Such souls pass through a whole round of incarnations without making any appreciable advance. The world is peopled today by millions of human beings who are in this condition; people who seemingly have no control over themselves or their circumstances. Conscience occasionally whips them up to make an effort to start in the right direction, but they go only a short distance, for their Will power has either become weakened, or it is yet undeveloped, and they drift along life after life, making, of course, some slight advance in accordance with natural evolutionary law, but unable to take the snake of self with a firm grasp and tear out its poisonous fangs of selfishness and indulgence, and by so doing claim the rightful heritage of man — Power and Wisdom.

Where in all the wide fields of space may be found a single human being who has not failed and failed repeatedly in attempting to reach some high ideal, before success finally crowned his efforts?

The mother bird pushes its fledgling from the nest to the ground, from which it must learn to fly by its own efforts, or be destroyed by its natural enemies. How many apparently fruitless efforts the helpless little creature puts forth ere it is able to soar with outspread wings to the height from which it was first cast down — yet no single effort was, in reality, fruitless. You, like the fledgling, may fall back to the level where evolutionary law has now placed you, again and again, in your efforts to reach the spiritual height from which you were impelled by Karmic law, and be forced to reincarnate on the physical plane; but so long as the great compassionate Soul of the Infinite feels a throb in response to its own beating against your heart, you may lift up your head, however low it has been laid, and say, "I have not yet failed." But beware of that hour when your heart shall feel no throb of pity for the travailing souls about you — when, unrebuked, your lips may utter words that serve to destroy the peace and the hope of your struggling brother; when, cold and careless, you pass by on the other side, leaving your weaker sister to the wild beasts waiting to devour her. O my children, of such are the great failures.

You can never clasp the hand of the Perfected One while your own hand reeks with the blood of your Brother. You can never pass, unscathed, through the flame of the "Inner Chamber," trailing your sister's peace and honor low in the dust of the path upon which you are traveling. Failure will be written in fiery letters within your soul if you have not learned your true relation to your fellow man — and profited by that knowledge.

LESSON 20
THE CONTROL OF LIFE FORCES

In its last analysis, all life is Vibration; that is, all forms or differentiations of life are generated and evolved by the different vibratory rates of one homogeneous state of Substance which is of a spiritual nature.

While scientific research has proved the above statement to some extent, its votaries seek no farther than that state of matter postulated by them as the Ether, for the substance which vibrates, or the power which imparts those different rates of vibration. In reality, the Ether is but the robe or veil which envelops and furnishes the media by and through which the great creative force, which occultists designate the Life Principle, may operate. This Life Principle in its highest aspect is a trinity consisting of Desire, Will, and Mind.

Desire is the ruling force of the Universe, and in its highest aspect is Love. Will is the motive power — the propelling energy — resident in matter, and is also the basic principle of Sound. Mind — Light — is the generating force and at the same time the Matrix in which Desire and Will mold and bring to outward expression all those forms used by Nature to embody the monads, or individualized lives.

This brief outline indicates some of the vast processes by which spiritual life becomes material life, and is given here for the purpose of assisting to demonstrate facts which are of infinite importance to the human race.

To the "ear that can hear," the expression, the "Music of the Spheres" conveys a far deeper significance than any expression used in modern science, for such an ear can plainly distinguish the music made by the motion of the stars in space, by the bursting of seed, and by all growing things, as well as many other sounds inaudible to the ears of the masses of humanity, and knows beyond question that life is harmony.

Every molecule of matter has its own particular tone, and every aggregation of molecules, commonly termed a body, has its keynote. If the keynote of a body which is in a normal condition can be obtained, the keynotes of all other bodies in accord or sympathy with it will be found to belong to the same Hierarchy or Octave. If the body is diseased, its keynote is raised or lowered (according to the nature of the ailment), and it is then out of harmony with all other bodies governed by the hierarchy to which it belongs, and it suffers in proportion to the discords which control it for the time being. Such discords interpenetrate interior planes and awaken corresponding forces or entities from a quiescent to an active state. These are drawn to and absorbed by the astral body of the sufferer and manifest in some form in or around the physical body, thus causing additional suffering.

It is evident from what I have stated that a satisfactory remedial agent must be capable of restoring the normal keynote of an ailing body and, as will be seen later on, the possibility of determining that keynote rests upon the ability of the operator to determine the keynotes of two other (interior) bodies. The task is a difficult, though not an impossible one; difficult because the requisite power is of such an important as well as dangerous character that the Lodge has hedged its discovery about it by almost insurmountable obstacles, which cannot be removed save in individual cases where unselfishness and Love are the ruling motives of a life during the present cycle.

Occasionally, some deep student has conceived a plan for generating and manipulating the form of energy under discussion; but before he could mature the plan, a member of the Lodge was delegated to obstruct his efforts or divert them into some safer channel. A short time ago, such a student believing he had discovered a method for determining the keynote of a human body by means of the tone, quality, and timber of the voice, attempted to heal disease by awakening and applying vibrations of color corresponding to and connected with the energy of the keynote. Such success as he met with was of very transitory character. His failure was not due to incorrect primary conclusions, but largely to the fact that he was treating an effect instead of a cause, and employing but one of the three forms of force, which must be combined and intelligently directed to produce satisfactory results.

A tendency is manifest in the present cycle to deride and dispense with the use of medicines in the treatment of disease, which is but the other extreme of that blind trust in the efficacy of all drugs which prevailed in a previous age.[1]

All medicines, drugs, herbs, and minerals are, of course, subject to the same laws of vibration which produce and evolve all other forms of matter; each one has its own special rate of vibration and keynote, and in order to produce satisfactory results in the treatment of disease by medicines, there must exist a harmonious vibration between patient and medicine — between the keynotes of the two forms of life. Where cures have resulted from administration of medicines by careless or ignorant physicians, it was as a rule due to the so-called "chance" selection of medicines, the keynotes of which were in sympathetic relation to the keynote of the physical body of the patient. Conscientious physicians frequently admit that their selection of medicines for any specific ailment is pure "guesswork." From their standpoint this is true; but the truth is, a conscientious physician is an occultist in some degree, whether or not he be conscious of the fact. The years of devotion and concentration he has been compelled to feel and practice in preparing for his chosen profession, and the character and influence of that profession, have awakened to some extent the life currents in his hitherto atrophied pineal gland,[2] and under such circumstances the power of intuition begins to manifest along the particular line of his profession, and it is intuition instead of mere "chance or guesswork" that guides his selection of the right remedies; and intuition is soul knowledge. If he were to depend entirely on his memory of certain formulae, learned, perhaps, a quarter of a century before, when suddenly called upon to prescribe for some acute disease, there would be many more mistakes lying in wait for his final adjustment than there now are.

If a steel bar is struck by any hard substance, it gives forth a certain tone, soft or hard, high or low, according to the number of molecules which constitute its mass, and the quality of the substance used in striking it. If a current of electricity is passed around the bar, it

---

[1] This text was written at the beginning of the 20th century.

[2] *Pineal gland* — a small, pinecone-shaped endocrine gland located in the brain.

becomes a magnet. It has neither gained nor lost anything in weight: it is the same steel bar, but it is also something entirely different in character. While it was seemingly inert matter before, it is now alive with a force which can draw to it or repel from it other forms of matter, and which it can impart to other forms of the same material. In reality its keynote has been raised by the life force of Electricity. It has passed the gulf that separates inert from active matter.

A human body is also a magnet, and has been made such by the same force — Electricity; but it is also the envelope of a Spiritual Entity and of another Entity entitled a Soul; and as each of these bodies has its own particular keynote, it is evident that the whole man is governed by a chord instead of a single note.

Like the steel magnet, the Human Magnet is capable of sounding its keynote, though the process is somewhat different. But to obtain and utilize the chord of the whole man, a higher form of the life force — Electricity — must be generated and applied. An application of this force is made when, as a child, the individual awakens to consciousness; and again, at the end of a life cycle; and it is applied by the conscious creative builders of the Universe, among whom is the Incarnating Ego of the individual. This force is dual and kills as easily as it creates.

It has long been known to occultists that the principle of Life is Electrical; but to think of life merely as a form of Electricity would be as misleading as to think of food as bread alone; for there are forty-nine different forms of Electricity. That form of force which operates in plant or stone is not the form or degree of electricity which operates in man. The forty-nine forms of electrical force are divided into seven octaves, with seven forms to the octave, each octave supplying all the life force existing on a corresponding plane of manifestation. The octave of force operating on the plane of Mind is not the same octave that operates on the physical plane; the former octave is higher in the scale of energy. But whether the energy be of Spirit, Soul, or Body; Mineral, Plant, or Animal life, all forms of Electricity are generated by means of the gases or their correspondents, known as hydrogen, oxygen, nitrogen, and carbon. Despite the claims of medical science to the contrary, oxygen, as such, does not enter into the blood of the animal creation. It is one of the great creative fires, and acts upon the different organs of the body, which organs serve as generators for the production of Electricity, and it is the latter force instead of oxygen which passes into the blood and builds or destroys as nature demands.

To obtain the power over life and health, as well as disease and death, one must be able to make each one of his three bodies or envelopes a conscious generator of those forms of Electricity that correspond to the keynotes of the octaves of life before mentioned, all of which are primarily under the control of the energy of Desire, Will, and Mind; in other words, the energy of the powers of Mesmerism, Sound, and Light. By combining the material expressions of the more powerful spiritual forces, a lower form of Electrical energy can be generated, which if perfectly understood and rightly directed, will accomplish very much in the line of healing innumerable forms of disease, and may often be advantageously combined with medicines in the treatment of poor ailing humanity. But when that humanity is safely past the point in evolution when its keynote *en masse*[1] has been raised, it will require no exterior help; for when all is said, the application of exterior forces or remedies are but temporary expedients: for the culture-beds of disease lie within the mind, and the disease must be driven out and the culture-beds be destroyed; all of which must be done by the exercise of Spiritual Power ere mankind can regain its lost birthright.

LESSON 21
PRAYER

Over and over again, in some slightly changed form, some of you put the same questions to me; over and over again I make the same replies. Unconsciously to yourselves you often ask that the governing laws of the Universe be changed in order that some personal idiosyncrasy or desire be gratified. You ask that the great law of Karma — cause and effect — be modified or changed in order that you may obtain some favor or win some power which you *have not earned* — that place, position, or opportunity be given you for which you are as yet unfitted, unaware that unfulfilled duties pertaining to such places or opportunities would result in unspeakable anguish to you. You are told that hatred, unbrotherly conduct, harsh criticism of others, whether deserved or not, generates within your own auras a corroding, devitalizing form of force, which not only results in illness

---

[1] As a whole; all together as a group.

of the physical body, but which acts on the astral body, and the organs of consciousness on the mind plane, similarly to some of the noxious metallic poisons on the physical body; and yet some among your number are passing cruel to each other and to others who are dependent on you, and who justly or unjustly excite your anger. You often think you are justified in assuming a judicial air, or in violently condemning wrongdoers; but it is not your possible justification that we are called upon to consider now; it is the action of universal laws, as applied to a would-be occultist. If you are satisfied to evolve with the masses, well and good; if you would pass beyond the masses, you must be subject to higher laws than those which govern material substance. You must try to realize that I, too, am limited.

I can tell you of things to come, as I am able to judge by the visible signs as well as by my knowledge of interior laws; I can tell you how certain catastrophes might be averted if the humanity of this age would listen and obey; but bear in mind, I cannot change the laws that govern manifesting matter; I cannot make two and two five; I cannot take two pecans from five and leave four, although I might be able to make you believe that I had accomplished that feat by means of hypnosis or some other ultra-physical power.

One of the greatest difficulties you experience lies in your inability to accept as literally true the statements given out by myself and others in positions similar to my own, regarding the action of universal laws.

The unyielding, unpliable man is invariably the man that is broken on the wheel of the world; the pliable man bends beneath the storm, and the storm either passes over his head and leaves him untouched, or touches him so lightly by comparison, that his rebound to a normal position is accomplished with very little difficulty when the danger is over.

The strained, tense condition of the nerves from which countless thousands of people are now suffering is responsible for much of the evil that falls upon them. The same law that renders a relaxation of the body necessary is behind an equal necessity for soul relaxation, the law commonly known as gravitation, and true prayer should result in this relaxation of soul. The energy which should be evenly distributed throughout all the nerves and muscles is used up thoughtlessly or ignorantly in sustaining this tension, while for the time being it enables the ambitious man or woman to accomplish herculean tasks in business or pleasure; consequently, the body is robbed of necessary force, and the mind cannot function evenly and naturally; antagonism is engendered, and finally incipient disease or decay manifests. You must learn to relax this tension by power of will, and I have already told you how you must evolve such will power if you are to obtain it.

If the positive energy of intense selfish desire is sent forth in prayer, and the energy is not powerful enough to force accomplishment of the desire, that energy is dissipated, and the body in which it was generated and by which it was sent forth is broken or beaten down by the reflex action.

If from the higher point of renunciation, the soul while in a perfect state of relaxation sends forth a prayer to the Infinite — not *for* some personal favor, but *of* faith, *of* love for that Infinite — the same law which compels one pole of electricity to respond to the other will compel a response from those Infinite domains, and the response will be in accordance with the real needs of the aspiring soul. You will frequently find that the surest way of winning a thing is to give up even the desire for that thing.

Thought is one form of energy, words are other forms of the same energy; combined, they create a third form, and true prayer is of this other form. Created and sent out from the human heart, it can go as far as its inherent power can take it. If the prayer or aspiration is selfish, it meets on an interior plane other forms of the same energy, the desires of which are in opposition to it, and one neutralizes or destroys the other, and the consequence is that neither desire reaches those who have the power to answer.

The wisdom of the ages is compressed in the words spoken by Jesus, "Not my will, but thine be done."[1] It is only prayers preceded by that sentence and winged by an unselfish love, that asks only *to* love, not *for* love, that Omnipotence *can* answer. The highest power is only won by renunciation. Renounce with thy whole heart — love with thy whole heart — work with thy whole heart, and all things in heaven and earth are thine.

---

[1] Luke 22:42.

LESSON 22
ENERGY OF REFLECTION AND REFRACTION

The energy that controls the reflection and refraction of light holds the mystery of the corresponding phenomena of words and ideas. Hold a certain form of prism to the eye, and look at an object at some distance, and you will see one object which subsequently separates and becomes two objects, alike in form. Keep on looking with the determination to draw them together, and they will gradually approach and merge into one. You are told the prism bends or refracts a ray of light and produces this phenomenon. If this alone were the case, you will ask for what purpose, then, is any action of will or mind; and the fact that will and mind do have something to do with this phenomenon proves my conclusion, i.e., that the energy which in reality performs the phenomenon is not in the material prism or in the ray of light, as light is understood by science, but in the *mind* of man and the *mind* of prism, for matter or energy cannot exist apart from mind.

If granted that the potential energy of refraction is an operation of mind directed by will, then the analogies between the action of mind and will on light and prism, and the action of the same energy in the control of Ideas and Words — the formation of language — become evident, as does also the phenomenon of telepathic communication. In thought transference of the highest kind, words are never required; an image of the whole idea is flashed on the sensitive surface prepared for it in the human mind. In the next lower form of thought transference, a single word which holds the main idea is mentally spoken by the sender, and is caught on the sounder of the mind of the receiver; the intelligence of the latter seizes the one word, and by its power of refraction breaks it into its component parts, and the sentence embodying the idea is thus formed in the mind, and is then spoken or written by means of the human senses and organs. You can determine much of the truth of this statement for yourselves. You have often heard or read a single word of a sentence, and lo, almost immediately, the whole idea embodied in the sentence becomes clear to you.

You frequently confuse the ideograph which someone higher in the scale of development attempts to send for your comfort or help, with the remnants of your own thoughts or with half-formed thoughts caught from those you habitually associate with, which are floating about in your thought sphere, and the consequence is that you misinterpret or mistranslate the ideograph — and then set about convincing yourselves that no effort has been made to convey such comfort or help. All these difficulties are due to the lack of the power of concentration.

The sensitized plate of your mind is infinitely more susceptible to the different degrees of light and shadow which make up the experience of your life picture, than is the sensitized plate used in photography to the light and shadow cast by the Sun; and if the field of vision is filled with rubbish, the central figure will be blurred beyond recognition. Previous instructions given for the cultivating of the Will, will aid in overcoming this condition.

When you realize that previous to your study along occult lines, you had made no attempt worth mentioning to clear that field of interior vision — that the half-formed thoughts of your whole life were, practically speaking, holding you at their mercy, you can perhaps understand that the Higher Self has much to overcome before the lower self becomes capable of reading aright the language of the Gods.

As you have been taught in previous instructions, the energy under consideration is also back of all manifestation, whether it be mental or physical. From the plane of unchangeable Spirit, all things are reflected into the Astral plane, as the Moon is reflected into the Ocean, and the Energy of Refraction differentiates those reflections into their component parts. A higher form of the same energy — the word of God — or Fohat, lowers the vibration of the refracted reflections, and physical matter is manifested. The same Energy differentiates the Cosmic Alphabet and manifests words — from the One Word which that Alphabet represents and is.

LESSON 23
ORIENT AND OCCIDENT
From the Master M.

As the waters of the Nile, the sands of the desert, the serpent beneath the bungalow, creep on land and victim noiselessly, resistlessly, purposefully, so creeps on the destructive power of divided interests. Lethargy, treachery, cowardice, and unbelief on one side; alert, dominating, self-conscious activity on the other — creating, molding, dividing, and subdividing class after class, laying the foundations of its arsenals, planting shells in its harbors, casting its nets into which the masses are drifting, as my beloved people drifted centuries agone, first into the power of Moguls,[1] mohurs,[2] rishis,[3] and priests, and finally into the power of invading nations; all of which was primarily due first, to their inhuman treatment of the weaker sex, the feminine aspect of the race; and secondly, to the mistrust and hatred which existed between classes; and to this day divisions between such classes are so sharply defined as to admit of no possible bridging — which leaves all classes at the mercy of the alien, who to advance his own interests fosters and increases the bitterness between Sikh and Afghan, between Behari and Bengali, between warrior and priest. Knowing all this, loving my people as a father his children, forced to see them sink into nothingness among nations, realizing that their only hope lies in the Anglo-Saxon race now incarnated in America — for from it a great karmic debt is due — is it surprising that I should take some interest in the affairs of that nation, even to identifying myself in a measure with it? Yet the ignorant, the self-blinded can neither see the danger which threatens themselves, nor the crying need of the Aryan race,[4] nor understand my motives in striving to draw closer together these long-divided peoples. They can but stand aside and deny either my existence or my presence among them, though they may have seen me face to face. It is nothing — let it pass, the great law will determine the results. Alas for the bird that befouls its own nest; its neighbor's nest is still less sacred.

LESSON 24
RADIOACTIVITY

The rediscovery of, and interest shown by scientists in a certain element christened *Radium* is of special interest to students of occult science. Being a manifestation of the energy of light held in

---

[1] *Mogul* — a Muslim ruler in India in the 16th to 19th centuries.

[2] *Mohur* — an old gold coin of the Moguls that circulated in India from the 16th century. It was also used in British India in the 19th and early 20th centuries, being last issued in 1918.

[3] *Rishi* (*Sanskrit*, "sage") — a Hindu sage or saint.

[4] *Aryan race* — the people of India. The ancient name of Northern India was *Aryavarta* (*Sanskrit*, "land of Aryans"), where the first newcomers from Central Asia settled following the destruction of Atlantis. The Fifth Root Race of humanity, the present stage of evolution, is also called *Aryan* because it originated in India one million years ago.

suspension, its consideration brings you one step nearer the possibility of bridging the gulf which separates two planes of life, i.e., Energy and Matter.

The infinitesimal atoms which constitute space are set in motion by a form of energy sometimes termed "the Word of God." Each rate of motion or vibration eventually manifests first, a form of force; secondly, a grade of matter; i.e., it brings into outer manifestation the substance which was already in manifestation on the interior planes, and divides such substance into groups termed Elements. The wave motions by which such elements are manifested are not the Energies; they are but the source of manifestation. On the spiritual plane, Sound, Light, and Motion are interchangeable. Light on the spiritual plane may be Force or Energy on the physical plane. Radioactivity is the action of the stored-up energy of light, as is also the reflecting property of gold, which imparts much of its value to that metal. This property of reflection is Prana[5] — or life essence — held in suspension in grosser material. All forms of matter which are capable of reflecting light are of much higher vibration than those which absorb the same, and the former are of the same nature as that form of life essence which animates the nucleolus of the cell in all procreative matter. Those who look and long for the power of creating matter, must first find and segregate the energy which manifests in such substances as that termed Radium, surround it with the protoplasmic[6] substance which Nature always furnishes as a protection or vehicle to pranic energy, and finally build the wall which confines it.

In answer to a request for more instruction regarding the action of light in the bodies of mankind, I would say that by referring to other instructions on Light, you will see that Sound, Color, Form, and Number are four demonstrable qualities of the "I am" in manifestation.

The concealed radiance of the *I am* is Spiritual Light, as is also the concealed radiance of the Individual Egos which emanated from *It*, and which are now in manifestation. This one homogeneous substance is the life essence of all the planes of manifestation, and is made

---

[5] *Prana* (*Sanskrit*, "breath") — the life principle; the breath of life; vital energy diffused throughout Nature, which human beings perceive mainly through breathing. In its purest form, *prana* is concentrated in the areas of Nature untouched by humanity: forests, mountains, and natural bodies of water.

[6] *Protoplasm* — the living substance found in all cells, essential for the functioning and maintenance of life.

visible or reflected into physical matter by means of the sun — just as the power of reflecting the spiritual life essence is made possible by the sacrifice of Sun Sons — the Christs — for lower forms of humanity. The sphere of light which surrounds every object or body is such a reflection; but the play of colors within that light is caused by the action of the will and mind of the personal Ego. This light is incognizable by the physical sense of sight, to all but a few of the present humanity, but it will become visible to the masses of the Sixth Race.[1]

The sphere of light or aura surrounding an individual whose life is exceptionally pure and unselfish, becomes so dazzlingly bright that, while it may not be visible to the physical eye, the sensations experienced by the astral eyes of the observer are so acute that they are translated in terms of feeling to the physical senses; and sensitive persons can, so to speak, *feel* the goodness or brightness of such a person.

To the individual who has correlated his physical and astral sense of sight, such spheres of light are made visible by act of will. Such an observer can plainly see the play of color within, and the changes through which such spheres are passing. A few moments' indulgence in selfishness, hatred, etc., will change the most beautiful tint in an aura to a dull, lifeless shade, as the opposites of such conditions will clarify and beautify corresponding shades of color.

One of the most surprising phases of modern mechanical skill will appear at no late date in the form of a device by means of which some of the difficulties in the way of correlating the physical and astral planes may be overcome.[2] The divisions of light rays now passing under the names of individual discoveries are in reality near approaches to astral matter, when they are not the substance that correlates other and inner planes of being.

---

[1] See *Race* in *Glossary*.

[2] The 1925 edition's note: Announcement has recently been made that Professor A. W. Goodspeed, of the Randal Morgan Laboratory of Physics, of the University of Pennsylvania, had accidentally discovered that rays of light emanate naturally from the human body and that these rays are visible to the eyes of some of the lower animals. Divested of technical terms, the discovery of Prof. Goodspeed means that the rays of light shed from a living human body, although invisible to the human eye, may have sufficient intensity to produce a picture on a plate properly sensitized and in a room pitch dark. The discovery was made while X-ray photographs were being taken.

LESSON 25
SELFLESSNESS, THE ONE THING NEEDFUL

Give, give, give — you cry, over and over again — to God, to the World, to me. Ah, when will you learn, that as the dew of heaven descends to water the earth, so the dew of heavenly wisdom is dropping silently on the parched soil of your souls, even while you turn in a passion of self-seeking from its contemplation, and absorption, to the noisy demonstrations of the multitude, which has only lifeless husks to offer in exchange for your heart's best service.

I say to you, that not until you become capable of loving unselfishly can you even enter the Path. Now, alas, you are weak and vacillating, even at the height of such love as you are capable of reflecting. You are calculating, critical, and discriminating, when the reverse of such qualities are the first requisites of "a Son of God," when the interests of his "younger Brothers" are at stake. So long as you are capable of willfully withholding sympathy and assistance from the meanest creature that lives, be it criminal, profligate, or only unfortunate, you cannot pass over the Bridge, which has been built, and is sustained, by the Selfless Mercy of the Hosts of Light.

The first lesson, as well as the last, the Alpha and Omega of occultism, is selflessness; and exoteric[3] selfishness — its opposite — is the fundamental cause of your non-attainment of power, and inability to exercise such necessary qualifications of selflessness as helpfulness and sympathy, where your younger Brother's development and interests are concerned.

I say to you, "Follow me" (for I cannot carry you), and I point you to the milestones along the Path which I have traveled. You are at first fired by enthusiasm, and strike out bravely, crying out before you have passed the first milestone, "Give me something harder to do," Set me some difficult problem," "Pour out Secret Instructions upon me, and you will see how quickly I can absorb them."

I say to you, you must conquer certain characteristics, you must purify your body before it is possible even for you to become individually conscious of the Infinite to which you aspire; and I show you why this is necessary, even from a scientific or selfish aspect; and lo, your enthusiasm is dampened at once. I tell you that absolute Faith,

---
[3] *Exoteric* (*Greek*, "outer") — external; public; intended for the masses.

not only in me, but also in those who represent me, is a necessary factor in your development along both psychic and spiritual lines, and endeavor to show you by correspondence and analogy, that the word *Faith*, as understood by you, is in reality but another name for one of the most potent forms of Energy in manifestation, and that its right application and use are essential to the evolution of certain characteristics of the soul. But frequently one of you revolts and exclaims, "That is very well in theory, but give us *facts*; let us see for ourselves," when it would be just as reasonable to ask for an opportunity for investigating the source of Electricity, though the effects of both forms of energy are clearly demonstrable by means of material agencies.

If I were to ask some among your number to stand on one foot for a certain number of hours a day, and assure them that by so doing they would acquire the power of levitation, they would attempt to follow such directions, after convincing themselves by some method of reasoning that the power of levitation was essential to spiritual development. If they had acquired such power, apparently by the above-mentioned or similar means, they would be loath to believe that its acquirement would in reality be due, first of all, to the awakened energy we term *Faith*, and finally to the *spirit of obedience* which actuated the effort.

I repeat the direction given by countless great teachers — "Condemn not," yet you frequently withdraw faith in and affection for some friend upon learning that such an one has fallen under some great temptation — entirely ignoring or forgetting that you are cutting him off from the energy he requires to correct the fault committed, and oblivious of the truth that back in your own nature lie coiled the hidden causes for similar effects, which are only waiting the same environment and temptation to manifest as the same or similar faults.

You grow weary of the recapitulation of those directions and practices which are essential to the cultivation of higher spiritual attributes; but I ask, would it be to your advantage to begin to study the problems of Euclid[1] before you have mastered the Rule of Three? Knowledge is indeed power, and power may be yours; but if such power is to be used for the good of humanity it must rest upon a substratum of spiritual understanding that cannot be shaken. Therefore, I say to

---

[1] *Euclid* — an ancient Greek mathematician, often referred to as the "Father of Geometry." He authored the famous work *Elements*, which laid the foundation for Euclidean geometry.

you, whatever else you undertake, look first to the development of the three great Energies — Love, Will, and Action — upon which the Universe is built, and never permit yourselves to consider them as simply certain attributes of your lower human nature.

The laws of Attraction, Repulsion, and Cohesion and of Gravitation and Chemical Affinity are but other names and other modifications of the above-mentioned great realities. Consequently, the cultivation of the latter develops or manifests the inherent powers of the former in the individual aura as well as in the Cosmos, and also furnishes the ability to direct such powers to the Ego-center of each Aura.

Indications of such evolution must always be greeted with great hope and encouragement by those who watch and wait.

LESSON 26
THE ESSENCE OF CONSCIOUSNESS

The commonly accepted truth that the Universe is divided into three great states of consciousness, termed body, soul and spirit, is also accepted by the occultist, and to him is an incontrovertible fact. One great difference in the belief of the occultist and that of the masses of humanity, lies in the fact that the belief of the former is based on knowledge while that of the latter is based on tradition. Another difference appears when the occultist refuses to accept the hard and fast lines defined between such states of consciousness, and proves to the intelligent thinker that no gaps or gulfs exist between any two apparent divisions of matter, force, and consciousness and that the seeming gaps are in reality filled by still finer grades of matter, and life in finer states of consciousness.

The knowledge and power won by the occultist enable him consciously to contact those intermediate states and lives, and to a great degree to classify them, and therefore, instead of confining his researches to the three primary states of consciousness, for convenience in classification, he divides the three first into six, and then, counting the combined states as one more, makes seven in all. Each one of the seven is again divided into seven lesser or still finer degrees, making forty-nine. To complete the sum of its experience, and win the crown of Adeptship, the Ego must not only be able to contact those planes or states of consciousness, but must be able to dwell in each one, until long experience has taught it all that it is possible to acquire. Its experience on each plane bears a strong resemblance to its experience on all. For instance, on the plane upon which your consciousness now acts, you are conscious of the development of certain degrees of life, which you term spiritual, moral, mental and physical. That is, you are conscious of the development of the attributes which go to make up your moral nature, and at the same time conscious of those attributes which may be summed up as mental, spiritual and physical. Therefore, the method by which the acquisition of these attributes is accomplished furnishes a perfect correspondence to the methods by which the Ego acquires power and ability to use on any of the interior planes of being. The essence of those attributes is the same on all planes of being, but the laws which govern their manifestation on what are termed the spiritual planes — the three higher planes — are very different in operation. For instance, mind on the physical plane is invisible, not easily controlled, formless, and soundless. On the mental plane, it is visible in form, under control, and its action is accompanied by appreciable sound. On the spiritual plane, it is formless, soundless, and invisible, as we count form, sound, and sight. It is a mode of motion, an eternal matrix into which spirit is being eternally reflected, in and by which spirit lives, moves, and has its first manifested being. In other words, mind is as one great ocean of force, the waves and ripples of which produce the phenomena which we designate attributes, characteristics, habits, and so forth. The eternally concealed spirit which governs this ocean's modifications decrees that some of these modifications or ripples may become visible under certain conditions; for instance, those conditions which are operative on the plane of mind or soul, and invisible on other planes and under other conditions. But always, endlessly, it remains in essence one of the three indivisible, eternal, great realities.

Some poor self-deceived teachers of psychic science are encouraging their disciples to believe in and glibly talk of having attained Nirvana while in their present physical bodies and environment, insisting that the Rest-Angel, Death, has no more power over them individually. This fallacy is made apparent by a careful consideration of corresponding phenomena. As night and rest follow day and work throughout a great age, so death follows life, invariably and inevitably until the closing scene of the great Manvantara. There must always occur an interval between meals, in which to assimilate the food taken into the stomach; and equally important to the Ego is the interval called death, and the interval or rest between notes to the science of music. The periods which we term death, rest, and assimilation are only applicable to the state of life, interval, or note *left behind*. The consciousness of man takes no intervals in reality; it is just as active on the plane it enters after death as before, and its activity is employed in assimilating its late experiences — making up the essence of those experiences into substance for use in another incarnation. The only difference there is in this respect between the Initiates of a high order, and the men and women of the present day, lies in the fact that the outer lives of the former as well as the intervals between become longer than those of the latter. There is a vast difference in the length of time it takes different stars and planets to travel around their orbits, but they are, nevertheless, eternally traveling.

LESSON 27
TO THE FAITHFUL

My Beloved Disciples:

You who walk where the deadly nightshade breathes forth its poisonous exhalations — you who lie down to rest conscious that the basilisk eye of a hidden cobra is fixed upon you — who rise up morning after morning expecting naught but the repeated sting of the asp — the enfolding pressure of the boa constrictor; you whose closest bedfellows are hunger and thirst, want, and misery — not necessarily the hunger and thirst of the physical body, but the hunger and thirst of the soul for a word of appreciation, a glance of understanding, a touch of a helping hand, any one of which would be to you as dew to the desert sands; to you I come with a word, a glance, a touch, though they be unheard, unseen, unfelt by ears too dulled to hear, by eyes too weary to see, and by hands too powerless to feel.

Look up, my beloved! Waken from the nightmare by which you are holden, and strive to realize that even the deadly nightshade holds life as well as death in its leaves and flowers; that the cobra is powerless to strike at a Son of God, and that love rules it, as it does all other creatures; that the asp and boa-constrictor each has its appointed place in the economy of things, and but for the hunger and thirst, the weariness and pain, you could never know the fullness of eternal love, could never taste the water from the fountains of eternal truth, or know the blessed joy and peace which follow upon righteous toil and patient endurance of pain.

Anxious fathers and affrighted mothers, your sons cannot pass beyond the care and watchfulness of the Sons of Wisdom — your daughters cannot stray beyond the keeping of the great Mother-heart of God.

Would you, if so be you might, restrain your child by force from striving to examine the great mystery, Fire, because it might receive a slight burn? If you knew that such fire was only the lowest note in the scale of that glorious harmony — consuming fire — which only burns all imperfections, all refuse substance, only destroys the chrysalis, and prepares conditions for the advent of the perfected angels of radiant light — Wisdom, Knowledge, and Power — and knew that ignorance of the power of that one note might jeopardize the advent of those angels?

Desolate, weary burden-bearers, embryonic saviors of men and worlds, your hearts will thrill with rapture when at the close of your journey, you stoop to undo the burden you have so long carried, and find at the end of the last wrapping, the beautiful face of a beautiful soul gazing out at a transfigured world. The food and drink for which you are famishing lie even now on the other side of the path you are wearily treading — lie just another step within the confines of that aching heart. Believe me, neither yourselves nor your dear ones can pass beyond the power of the love which has loved you and them into life.

Take heed, my little ones, lest the scalpel of life's surgeon lay bare the tender buds of faith and trust in all that lives, to the fiery blast of the typhoon. For however dark the way and fierce the struggle, or sharp the instruments of torture, however foul and poisonous the stream through which you must sail your boat of life, the source of that stream is pure; the end and the beginning of all things, all experiences, is love, light, and peace.

You have called to me in the dim vistas of past ages; you call again today; and now as then I answer, "Cast off your burden of attachment to results." Do the duty which lies closest to your hand. Be not led away by specious tongues that strive to convince you that there is some better, some quicker way. Believe the truth your stifled souls would make you hear and heed — the truth that only as the bonds by which you are enthralled are burst — because your growth can no more be impeded by such means — can perfect freedom come to you. Believe the promise made by me and others like me in the olden days while yet you wandered as a savage race through jungles, wilds, and forests; while yet you sat on jeweled thrones and held within your hands the scepters of despotic power; or toiled as slaves to raise the hoary sphinx and pyramids which in another age far distant, your eyes should once more see and ponder over; while yet you toiled with naked hands to wrest from Nature's barren breast the food to keep your little ones from passing out, and leaving you yet more desolate and lonely — the promise made by us that we would stand upon the threshold of the great Initiation halls and gladly open those closed doors when you had reached and placed your hands upon them in token of submission, in evidence of your strength to reach to such a height, and power to stand without assistance until the door should be unbarred and opened.

LESSON 28
THE EVILS OF DISTRUST

If you would understand the difficulties which confront the Initiates in the higher degrees of the Lodge in their efforts to solve any one of the great world problems, consider what difficulties would confront you; what dangers appall, what discouragements weaken, were you to try to solve any one of even the minor problems of your present city government from the height of a personal great ideal.

You might labor for years to convince your fellow citizens of the advisability, righteousness, and wisdom of a certain course, and finally be persuaded that you had succeeded. You might get together your ammunition of arguments, promises, indulgences, etc., for their use, mark out a straight course which, according to your inner vision, would insure final success, a brilliant achievement for all concerned, only to find in the end that your great ideal was yours alone, that your words had fallen on deaf ears, to find your promises scouted, your anticipated achievements as dust and ashes under your feet, and why? Mainly because your coadjutors were almost without exception governed entirely by ignorant self-conceit. Your great ideal might seem to them a beautiful theory, but unless they could perceive some way in which they were to be immediately and individually benefited, they would turn from you even at the eleventh hour and cast in their lot with the opposing side.

The average man trusts no man, no God, deep down in his heart. If he is honest with himself, he knows that he is not infallible, is not entirely worthy of trust, knows that he too would fall if sufficient pressure were placed upon him. Consequently, he believes that all others are in a similar position, and if he gives trust at all, it is always with reservations which in the end may triumph, and saddest of all sad things is the truth that, from his particular standpoint, he is right.

But he does not know that he and others like him are continuing the fiend *distrust* in manifestation age after age; that they are making faith and trust impossible by continually generating and living in distrust. Better far would it be for him in the end to suffer from trust betrayed every day of his life than to help swell the great river of distrust that paralyzes all human endeavor, that wrecks the bodies and souls of millions of human beings yearly.

To be a Master means to have conquered distrust, to work on age after age knowing his confidence will be betrayed, his best laid plans defeated, his great ideals despised, but knowing also that some time the God in man will triumph, knowing that notwithstanding his present unworthiness and weakness, man is still worth loving, worth serving.

Unfortunately, this sense of distrust reaches its height in the intellectual giants of the human race; men whose tendency towards materialism has awakened a spirit of egotism far in excess of that of the ignorant masses. They are men who are surpassingly ignorant of the fundamental truth of all knowledge, i.e., that the Cosmos is a unit; men who believe the material universe is, as it were, a herd of cows, created for the express purpose of furnishing nourishment to them individually and that they are justified in milking those cows *ad libitum*,[1] regardless of the wants and requirements of their weaker brethren.

Blind leaders of a blind age! Unable to perceive the dark clouds of the threatening storm, unable to see that they are cutting off the source of their own nourishment, even on the physical plane, and tying themselves karmically to the people they are now using, both on the physical and astral planes for ages to come. Self-conceit and self-indulgence are twin destroyers.

---

[1] In accordance with one's wishes.

LESSON 29
BUILDING IN ACCORD WITH
NATURAL AND DIVINE LAW

August 14, 1900

The fearful and the unbelieving, as well as all sycophantic devotees of the beast of Mammon, have invariably attempted to stop the progress of evolutionary development by building mental images of disaster and failure, or spreading nets of discouragement to entangle the energies directed by true lovers of the human race toward a common goal and a common good.

Nature furnishes to each of her kingdoms a perfect form, and correspondingly perfect principles of government. Only so far as man has observed and followed that form and embodied those principles in a constitution, has been his measure of success in the creating of a righteous government, whether of church or state. The outlines of the government of the United States were taken from the aborigines, the Six Nations of Indians. Those laws were given to the Indians by Hiawatha,[2] an Agent of the White Lodge. The ancient Peruvians, the Atlanteans, and many other races and nations, were taught and governed by the same laws. These are the laws that govern the bees, the ants, and every other division of insect and animal life that has not deteriorated through contact and association with mankind.

The great rock of offense against which, one after another, individuals, organizations and nations are hurled, and are either crippled or broken to pieces, is the selfishness, the heartlessness of those in authority, whether these be self-constituted teachers, leaders, presidents, or kings. In religion some one portion of a world-embracing philosophy is separated from the whole, or is misinterpreted by some seeker for power; a certain coterie gathers about its expounder or teacher, who isolates them and ignores all philosophy that does not corroborate his exposition, rendering it impossible for others to associate with them because of their evident narrowness, and they themselves become incapable of effort in a larger field, owing to the

---

[2] *Hiawatha (Ojibwa,* "He Makes Rivers") — a legendary 16th-century chief of the Onondaga tribe of North American Indians. He helped unite the Iroquois tribes who had warred with each other for decades into a single group, known as the Iroquois Confederacy comprising the Onondaga, Mohawk, Oneida, Cayuga, Seneca, and Tuscarora tribes. The story of Hiawatha is told in *The Song of Hiawatha* by Henry Wadsworth Longfellow.

action of the laws of constriction which immediately come into effect when one or more separates himself from the mass of humanity in thought or feeling; and these laws energize a powerful force which bars one's progress as might a rod of iron on the physical plane. We, as a race, must stand or fall together, for *we are One*. When one individual rises above another in any phase of development, he does so by reason of the inherent good which is manifesting in him; for evil is negative, and leaves no lasting effect.

The great plan of the Lodge for the development of the human race is so superhumanly grand and perfect in its entirety, as well as in its minutiae, that it would be useless to attempt to make it intelligible to the masses of the present age. It is like the foundation setting of a beautiful mosaic into which a bit is being set here and there by a Master Workman, each stone being cut and fitted to suit each point in the setting, and all emplaced from the underside. Only the Adept and Master Workman is familiar with the design; none other can form the slightest concept of the transcendent glory that will flash from it when the light of the Spiritual Sun falls on the completed work. I am here to outline one little point of that setting for you to work upon.

In order to labor effectually, the Temple organization must direct its work from a center strong enough to hold and conserve the forces sent for its advancement; and powerful enough to furnish an object lesson to all that will turn their eyes in its direction. A dynamic center which, while it may draw men who will scoff at first, will compel them to remain and work. With the permanent organization of the work, and as one of the objects of that work, there should be outlined to all interested, the building of a city where there may be faithfully carried out the ideas of a righteous government of the people, by the people, and for the people, on a spot of ground in a western state which will be selected by us, and where all that nature can do for the benefit of man has been done; where two important magnetic lines meet, and where once stood a city and reigned a people far in advance of the present civilization, taught and governed by one of the great Masters of the Lodge. The city which will sometime be built already hangs in the heavens in form. This form will be given to you ere long.

All of the great centers of the world have arisen and gradually developed from a small settlement. The failure of many attempts to found such centers has been due to narrow and contracted lines of thought and labor.

I have not touched upon advantages to occult students from the site and the conditions that exist on the spot indicated. That must be left until a future time.

LESSON 30
UNTO THE THIRD AND FOURTH GENERATION

The action of Karmic law in the affairs of nations and men, as well as in the Cosmos, is of all things most interesting, though too often incomprehensible to the average student. In the depths of every living soul there resides a sense of abstract justice and a feeling of abhorrence toward its opposite, or what is commonly termed injustice, due to the operations of two poles of one inherent quality or state of substance which manifests as wisdom.

However degraded the human being, a belief that nature or man has unjustly treated him will awaken a strong, if it be only a silent protest, and only too often such a protest long continued has changed the nature of a normal human being and prepared the way for his degeneracy. If all men were convinced that the action of the negative pole of karma was in reality the result of their own mistaken or evil thought and conduct, the most bitter drop in the cup of their afflictions would be dispelled. Recognizing the justice of his punishment, man would gradually be led into a knowledge that what he had hitherto believed to be merciless or unjust chastisement, was but the action of a most beneficent law, seeking only to establish a lost equilibrium.

No thing or being lives to itself or is sufficient unto itself. The law which brings retribution for a wrong done by you to your brother is the same law that controls the movements of the stars in their courses, the government of the ants in their anthills, and the return wave from the distant shore of the Ocean of Life.

It is said "not a sparrow falls to the ground without the knowledge of the Father";[1] no more can the star glide from its orbit into the immensities of space without the knowledge of the Father; and the cause of either phenomenon may be found in a disturbed equilibrium and a discord of the eternal harmonies. The single sparrow under consideration may not have been guilty of producing this discord, but the entitized group-soul of all sparrows has so disturbed the harmony

---

[1] Matthew 10:29.

of the sphere in which it has manifested, as to bring on all its atomic creations the same fate which has overtaken this particular sparrow, namely, death.

Unto the third and fourth generation, the curse — the devil — which has disturbed the equilibrium of love — the Father, descends (for the biblical term generation is frequently intended to convey the idea of an age), and until that group soul manifesting as evil has once more established harmony by yielding itself to the will of the Father; until the tone it had formerly sounded in the scale of creation once more rings true and clear, the sparrows — its creations — must continue to fall.

If a stone is thrown into a body of water, the ripples which ensue as a result of the force generated by the movement of the stone and its contact with the water cannot cease their movements until they have touched the farthest shore and returned to the point of their departure. So is it when a discord or sin starts a vibration in the ocean of life. To the circumference of its sphere of action and back to the center of its being must that discord or sin go and return ere its force be spent; and the power which impels it onward is the vehicle of its punishment, for only where such power is inoperative is there peace, and only in peace can there be perfect content, only in peace can love find its fulfillment.

No great calamity occurs as the result of a single action by Nature or man. Age upon age has one little act, one little thing has been added to the collective mass, until the measure became full; and being full, its contents are precipitated by the *last* act or event, however trivial it seems.

You, yourselves, mentally, morally, and physically are the result of ages of alternate growth and degeneration, and all that concerns you is subject to the same laws. There are countless numbers of human beings on the earth today, each one of whom is waiting for the one word, one look, one act of some other person before he can take the final step which will bring him under the direction of the Masters of the White Brotherhood. There are countless numbers of others waiting for a similar word, look, or act from some other person which will result in their taking the final step which will plunge them eventually into the depths of life — into the control of the Brothers of the Shadow. It is almost impossible for me to make you understand and realize the immense crisis which is now on in the affairs of men and nations, or how important your thoughts and acts are and will be, for some time to come. While in some instances such thoughts and acts may be compared to the last little act or event required to precipitate a great calamity — in others, your evolutionary status is such that you may unconsciously exert a tremendous influence. Your thought, word, or deed may evoke the requisite elemental power by which, finding a channel or vehicle in some influential person in incarnation, a connection is secured and, the necessary preparations having already been made, the torch is applied to the funeral pyre — so to speak — and lo, a conflagration will appear, the end of which no man knoweth.

LESSON 31
THE CREATIVE WORD

The ocean of ether — that shoreless, soundless, motionless mirror of God, reservoir of all the life essence of all the eternities — is set in motion by Fohat, the Word, and the Divine Thought. That Eternal All breaks into ripples and waves of different lengths and intensities, clothing the souls awaiting embodiment with their first garments of manifestation. These are called light waves and sound waves by modern scientists, but the average scientist has not yet evolved to the point where he becomes conscious that the synthesis of the individual forms of his many incarnations (namely his personal self) is, *in actu*, one of those waves of the etheric ocean, set into motion countless eons agone, and so to continue that motion until the Divine Word of recall is spoken eons hence, creating and disintegrating form after form by the power of its own inherent vitality for the use of the soul — the essence of that Word — sent forth from the depths of that silent ocean. In the vast, immeasurable spaces of the heavens, myriads upon myriads of waves are being unceasingly spoken into motion, garments of souls that will sometime people other systems of worlds now in process of building.

The initial impulse is given at the beginning of every great Manvantara, which must eventually manifest in uncountable races of beings, which will in future ages manifest as sentient lives on this and other planets. But it would be an error to imagine those synthetic light and sound waves as something inferior to such a race of human beings as now inhabit the earth. Far from it, they are the first clothing of immortal souls, pure and holy, born of God; and when the long cycles of reincarnations are past, and the soul once more is clothed upon with immortality (after casting off its worn-out clothing of physical forms, retaining only the knowledge, power, and experience it has gained from its contact with matter), it will pass into that silent ocean an individualized spirit of power and glory unspeakable. I say silent, but that is incorrect, for conditions of spiritual life would be silence only to physical ears, though indescribable by mortal tongue and pen.

It is because of his knowledge of the real essence of those light and sound waves or forces, that the Initiate warns his disciple against the selfish use of what are commonly termed natural forces. The former often uses the etheric waves in the conduct of varied forms of phenomena, but he uses them as a friend might use a friend, not as a human being would use a slave. He does not use them to gain material wealth or power for his own gratification or glorification, nor as does the tyro in occultism, who often ignorantly opens the door to sensual vampires during his efforts to establish communication with others at a distance. He does often use them in conveying messages through his agents or disciples; and here again appears a part of the wonderful numerical exactness of the divisions of the Universe and their relations one to the other. A single light wave may have a connection with a number of people in bodily forms, the combined auras of those people forming a corresponding wave, and a relationship existing between them which dates from the establishment of a particular hierarchical line. A Master belonging to such a hierarchy must use a certain division of these etheric waves for any natural phenomena he may cause, the media for which must also belong to that hierarchy. If he should attempt to send a message through some agent or messenger by means of a wave, any part of which has been weakened by the temporary fall of a soul in incarnation — thus incapacitating for action that soul and breaking the connection between it and the wave — his effort would be in vain, communication would be cut off between himself and the one to whom he would communicate, and until that soul regained its equilibrium sender and receiver would be unable to communicate with each other without the assistance of souls belonging to another hierarchical line. Those members of the Order of the Seven who occupy certain positions in the hierarchical line to which I am attached, if able to keep in a faithful, devoted condition of mind, in other words, in a positive position to the negative one, I must assume that contacting them (otherwise the force from my own aura would deprive them of mortal life) would enable me to transmit force and open methods of communication with them; but the instant one drops from the positive to the negative aspect, he or she breaks the wave motion, and the current can go no farther than the point formerly held by him or her; so all who come after them in that particular wave, are cut off as well as themselves. Sad instances of such a nature are numerous in all true groups of disciples, some of whom, because they cannot see spiritual things with physical eyes, or prefer their own volition, however faulty, to the practice of the true laws of life, do not hesitate to rob their brethren as well as themselves of the power of attaining to knowledge and wisdom.

The glorious, all-powerful groups of suns which lighten the fathomless depths of space within some of the constellations, such as that surpassingly marvelous group in the constellation Hercules, which is known by astronomers as the Omega Centauri, were once but single wave motions of the ether — the ether *en masse* — which sprang into motion at the bidding of Infinite Law, and traveled around and throughout the etheric ocean, growing into power with every ripple and wave of their journey through worlds and systems of worlds, returning through all the kingdoms of fire, earth, air and water eventually to their starting point, as suns to lighten the great immensities; as glorious hosts possessing in themselves the power to create and sustain universes; with ability to speak the soundless creative Word that shall send forth countless myriads of souls on the same life journey from which they returned ages and ages before. Could the human eye behold the radiant energy of the combined glory of such a host of angelic beings, the brain would be unbalanced by the sight.

By comparing a constellation of stars to a single family of the common people of earth, and these glorious suns to a council of the united crowned heads of the same earth, a faint idea might be obtained of their relative places in the scale of creation; and yet, you are on your way to such a great destiny if you will it so. Is there any human ambition worthy of consideration in the light of such a reality, any sacrifice too great for such an attainment? Is there nothing in life greater than the dregs with which so many are satisfied, when to all I have prefigured is added the knowledge, the wisdom, the power of the Gods which these suns represent and are?

LESSON 32
HOW LONG, O LORD!

"Pity me, all ye who pass this way!" falls from the pallid lips as a sad refrain, wrung from the almost despairing heart of every advanced chela of the Lodge who has reached to any spiritual height above that attained by the masses of his brethren.

He must have learned how to reach out a brimming cup of compassion to all others in need, but he must deny himself a draught from the same cup, and remain comfortless, unless some other traveler on the same path intuitively feels and supplies his need.

He has passed the first gate of the Great White Lodge before which, with hungry soul and baffled intellect, he has madly sought for something "*worth* loving," "*worth* serving." He has faced up that stony Sphinx of mystery — the law of self-effacement — whichever way he has turned in religion or science, and while he has been brought to accept the truth that there is no help for him outside himself, all that is mortal in his nature still craves sympathy and understanding.

The unutterable sadness of life, the maddening uncertainty of death, still fling their gaunt shadows over the narrow path he is treading, and he looks in vain for power to dispel them, as long as he yields to the temptation of looking backward. Behind him he beholds the gaunt specter, *insanity*, increasing momentarily in size and power, nourished by false methods of education, and given to drink from the gourds *selfishness*, *treachery*, and *inhumanity*; for the visions of Mastery which have drawn him from the lower levels of mediocrity now seem like the vagaries of an unsettled brain. He is nearing the great gulf which separates spirit from matter, and is losing hold of all that has hitherto sustained him. In view of all this, is it surprising that he should sometimes seek a glance of pity from some passerby on the same path, or that he should cry out with the few brave souls who are always striving to stem the tide of evil — "How long, O Lord!"[1]

But most difficult of all the difficult trials that beset him are those which spring from the treachery of those comrades he has tried to serve. They have failed to understand his actions, and therefore can find nothing in their hearts but condemnation for him; nothing but

---

[1] Psalm 13:1.

rebellion against anything he may strive to accomplish; nothing but suspicious glances at and unkind words about him.

Ah, children of the world! You prate of your duty to society, to religion, science, and business, but ignore your duty toward the brother or sister within the sound of your voice, within the touch of your hand, who has been viciously attacked by some other poor desperate human being, maddened by the same curse of selfishness which has wrecked your own hopes of happiness.

The first law of occultism is defense of a Master or Teacher. The chela who can stand supinely and silently by, and make no effort to defend such a Master or Teacher, will have no occasion to seek far for the cause of the closed door which will inevitably meet his eye when he attempts to enter the "Hall of Learning."[2] For the same law which renders it impossible for a teacher of occultism to defend himself or herself, renders it obligatory upon the chela to stand at that portal of knowledge which the Teacher represents and is, and hold it against all intruders — the law of *self-protection*.

The chela must rise or fall with his Master, and the first great reality that dawns upon his awakening consciousness is a recognition of his kinship to — his oneness with — that Master; and having once recognized, he cannot repudiate Him; his duty, his pleasure, his very life is bound up with that of the Master. But, alas, all too many of the disciples of the Secret Science in the Western world not only idly listen to, and read with avidity all libelous attacks on their teachers, but cowardly, turn from them and run for a safe hiding place when the arrows of ridicule or abuse are pointed with personal significance, or fly too rapidly from the quiver of the assailant, lest some of the mud into which those arrows fall should splash the garments they have donned and which they believe to be immaculate.

Such disciples are seemingly incapable of perceiving the truth that a warm, brave, loyal defense — a hearty "Yo-heave-ho!" of all hands, would send their own life ship, together with their shipmates, out of the range of those arrows, out of the mud of the cove into which they have drifted, far out into the open sea beyond, with pennant and banners flying from prow and stern; for even the poorest of all poor human beings admires and loves a brave man, a faithful comrade and

---

[2] The second of the three Halls through which the human soul must pass to unite with its Higher Self. See H. P. Blavatsky, *The Voice of the Silence* (London: Theosophical Publishing House, 1889), p. 6.

friend. "To the victor is due the guerdon," on the lower as well as on the higher lines of life and endeavor.

From one here and one there, comes the cry, "If the Initiates are facts in Nature and in Life, why do They not appear to *me*? Why do They not come out from their concealment and prove themselves to *me*?" — evidently without a suspicion of the fact that the daily lives they lead would make it impossible for such a one to exist in their vicinity. I in turn would ask a question, namely, as the Initiates are tenfold more amenable to natural law than are the masses of humanity (as They must be, to have become Masters) and therefore amenable to the law of conservation and concentration of energy, would They be justified in taking the vehicle of that energy, which is so perfectly attuned to the key of every spiritual impulse or force that it responds to all vibrations in its environment, as an Æolian harp[1] responds to waves of air — would They be justified, I repeat, in taking such a vehicle into vibrations of hatred, murder, and selfishness, such as now prevail in the environment of many of the people of this earth, for the sole purpose of satisfying mere curiosity? For Them to enter such lower vibrations, even momentarily, means intense suffering. To go into them to remain means dissolution of form; namely, loss of the vehicles They have been centuries in building. But notwithstanding the truth of the above statement, They *do* go, and are almost invariably killed, as was the Master Jesus and many others before and since His time, by the ignorance and ingratitude of those They went to serve, just as are generally killed sooner or later, all those who take up the burden of their travail — the enlightenment of the world.

The burden of recognition must always rest upon the personally most interested observer. Not one in ten thousand would recognize a Master if he met him. When man succeeds in erasing the varied images of his own lower personality from the reflector or mirror of his soul, he will have no difficulty in convincing himself of the reality and existence of the Lodge of Masters. It is a law of physics that no two things can occupy the same space at the same time. If man would behold God, he must first destroy the image of self.

---

[1] *Æolian harp* — a musical instrument played by the wind, named after the ancient Greek god of the wind Æolus.

LESSON 33
FIRE AND BLOOD

One by one the red corpuscles of the blood stream are broken up by one of the interior fires operative in all animal bodies. The waste fragments are consumed by the leucocytes, the white corpuscle of spleen, liver, cell walls, etc. The nucleoli of each red corpuscle receive from the first mentioned interior fire — a form of electricity — a new impulse to a higher rate of vibration than that previously manifested, which carries each in rotation from one organ of the body to another, until it reaches the brain and spinal cord, where it receives another impulse to a still higher rate of vibration, which carries it out of the realm of physical matter into the finer, ethereal realm of astral matter. On the Astral plane the same nucleoli pass in turn through every grade of astral matter, being carried from organ to organ of astral bodies, by the action of finer or more spiritual fires. Such substance matter finally becomes a part of the practically indestructible spiritual body.

Chemistry throws much light on the evolution of physical matter as, for instance, in the process of refining coal tar. First comes the gradual elimination of what are termed waste products. Then the condensation and conservation of the finer essences, colors, and valuable medicinal products. All such processes are carried on by fire or heat, and are analogous to the processes by which the blood stream of a physical body is transmuted first into astral, then into spiritual matter, or vice versa.

The occult scientist may sometimes observe such processes going on in his own body, as, for example, a strong aspiration for spiritual development, directed by will, to the Infinite, or Father-Mother-Son, would call out from the Infinite that which to the spiritual eye would appear to be a stream of light; to all appearances that Stream would seem to issue from a hole in the atmosphere, as sunlight might issue through a hole in a black wall. The force of that light would contact and coalesce with the mind or will force of the thought which prompted the aspiration; a combination would be effected that would impart a still more rapid rate of vibration to the nucleus of every blood corpuscle in the body of such aspirant, changing its character to a very marked degree. This is the *modus operandi* of the transmuting processes brought about by concentration and meditation, such as is advised by teachers of the sacred science. The student of physiology knows that the blood corpuscles are continually breaking up, and that the fragments are taken up by the white corpuscles, but he does not know what occurs to the nucleus in those transitional stages. He is not able to see how the life principle of the nucleus is raised to higher states of substance-matter, and how it passes from death to life, and from life to death, in continuous incarnation and excarnation.

The proud in spirit object to having the bodies they have lavished so much care and thought upon classed as animals. They will repudiate the statement that they have no human bodies as yet, that such are only in process of building. Age upon age, life after life, must yield its quota of substance for that human body, substance which has been refined by fire from the streams of blood which have passed through all the long line of animal bodies. Every thought, every aspiration, leaves an impress upon the nucleoli of the cells of the physical body. In fact, we may consciously create our own human bodies.

It is because of his power over that particular grade of substance, that a Master can create at will, or disintegrate, a physical body; he can raise or lower the vibrations of the nucleoli which form the basis of his real body, and so make it visible or invisible, although it must not be understood that this is the only way by which he can perform the same phenomenon, for he also has the power of inhibiting or increasing the physical sense of sight in any given person.

LESSON 34
FULFILLMENT

"Though I speak with the tongues of men and angels, and have not charity, I am become as sounding brass or a tinkling cymbal.

"Though I have the gift of prophecy and understanding, and have not charity, I am nothing.

"Though I bestow all my goods to feed the poor, and give my body to be burned, and have not charity, it profiteth me nothing."[1]

Interpreted by a co-Initiate with Paul, the preceding words of the latter would negatively indicate the necessary qualifications for chelaship, as well as furnish the clue to the failure of so many applicants for the same. Charity thus interpreted would indicate fulfillment — attainment — accomplished by means of implicit obedience to law.

[1] 1 Corinthians 13:1–3.

Law and Love are synonymous terms; therefore, obedience in love fulfills all law.

If it be true that lacking charity you or I become as "sounding brass or tinkling cymbal"; if, after the cultivation of every attribute deemed admirable by God or man, you and I are nothing; is there not something for us to do, ere the hour strikes that will leave us as mere instruments of mechanical sound, valueless symbols of noise in a living, breathing world, fast whirling onward to a destiny unspeakably great; a world in which the one word, *use*, will be the "open sesame" to every door of endeavor — a world in which the power — substance — of charity will be the keystone to every arch of human ingenuity and triumph?

Of what avail your strife at the portal of that world, if you attempt to force a passage with clubs and knives, or with blandishments and temptations?

My heart grows sad for those among your number whose wholesale criticism and condemnation of every creature that does not fit into the round or square place created in their intellects, renders them incapable of charitable judgment; for those of you whose opinion is a seat of judgment before which you would have all men bow, ere passing to that gate above which is written in letters of flaming fire the words, "Judgment in Mercy." The fact that you have forgotten or are ignoring the underlying principle of that inscription will not avail with *your* judges when your time shall have come to pass under the same gate. If you, yourselves, were purity personified, were monuments of wisdom and knowledge combined, you might (remember I say *might*) then pass the administrators of Karmic law, and be found among the judges of your brethren. But being what you are, weak, fallible, mortal, does no thrill of terror ever sweep over your souls at the thought of judgment to come, when with the lie of a broken sacred obligation yet hot on your tongue, when with a Judas kiss yet trembling on your lips, you lead out to crucifixion the friend who has trusted you, the brother who has put himself defenseless into your hands?

Ah, blinded souls, I have heard your claims for help, advancement, protection, based upon a few days or years of service to the Lodge, a few pieces of gold or silver, a handful of worthless gems. Yet I say to you, not a thousand years' service to the White Brotherhood; not all the material gold or silver of the Universe; not all the gems of the sea, sky, and earth could purchase one look of such appreciation as rests

on the face of the Great Master when the most humble chela kneels
before Him — could unlock a single one of the seventy and seven
gates which bar off the path to the dais of the Hierophant[1] — could
wipe out the stain of a single treacherous act for which no atonement
had been made — could wipe up the blood spilled on the ground by
a single unavenged victim.

If you cannot be faithful to the vows you have taken to your Higher
Selves, what security can you give to the Law that you will remain
faithful, if the life and well-being of one of the least of the little cries
of God — a chela of the Lodge — is placed in your keeping — if one
of the secrets of the House of Treasures is imparted to you?

If you cannot obey the laws you have sworn to uphold, how can
you sit among the Law-Givers and hand down just decrees to the
executors of those laws?

If from the depths of the vileness and putrescence of your own
lower natures, you are led to seek for vileness and putrescence in
others; if you turn over under your tongues as a sweet morsel every
calumny you may hear and repeat, and stand with itching ears to listen to an account of some brother's crime, some sister's loss of virtue,
some weak, tempted soul's downfall from the ranks of the "highly
respectable," how can you receive and carry out to a suffering world
the beloved Master's messages of pity, forgiveness, atonement, and
resurrection? How can you stand with uplifted head and eager eyes
before the altar of the Lord High Sentinel, and be clothed with the
white robe and golden collar bestowed upon the sons and daughters
of the Third Degree, in token of victory, chastity, unselfish effort, and
suffering for others — in token of immortal life and love?

You have passed heedlessly, carelessly by many of the countless
charges given to you, the messages conveyed to you in pain and longing. If from only the motive of self-preservation, I implore you to
listen, to heed the words I now speak to you.

---

[1] *Hierophant* (*Greek*, "one who explains sacred things") — a revealer of sacred
knowledge and the Chief of the Initiates. A title belonging to the highest Adepts
in the temples of antiquity, who were the teachers, expounders of the Mysteries,
and the Initiated into the final great Mysteries. The Hierophant represented the
Demiurge (*Greek*, "Creator"), and explained to the candidates for Initiation the
various phenomena of Creation that were produced for their tuition.

LESSON 35
BREATH CULTURE

"The child of the West must lie in the East Wind for a time and a half, ere the Northern and Southern Giants can stand securely on his navel."

The above aphorism meets the eye of the disciple upon entering the portico of one of the Temples of the Mysteries in the Far East. In simple terms it means the chela or disciple, symbolically the man of the West, must place himself in a position to absorb the teaching of the Initiate, symbolically the man of the East, and follow that instruction long enough to permit the magnetic currents, the Giants of North and South, to perform their full offices of awakening to action the hitherto unmanifested or dormant grey matter of the solar plexus. When the above-mentioned giants can stand — that is, when the grey matter has become firm and active enough to bear the pressure placed upon it, the chela is prepared for another step in evolution. Part of the instruction noted above refers to habitual correct breathing, and the aphorism mentioned is peculiarly applicable to the people of the western hemisphere, whether or not they be conscious chelas; for in a great majority of cases, the grey matter alluded to has scarcely begun to manifest in the solar plexus, the Sun of the Body.

So little attention has been paid by the over-worked, over-burdened, or ignorant and neglectful parents of children in recent ages, that cultivation of the breath centers has been largely left to chance. Cultivation of muscle appears to be far more necessary to the average man, while in truth over-cultivation of muscle, without corresponding cultivation of the breath centers, is often injurious, and frequently results in premature disease and death. In such instances too great a pressure is placed on heart and lungs, and the blood by which such pressure is induced is insufficiently oxygenated and, therefore, incapable of furnishing the necessary power of resistance to the organs mentioned above, and suddenly the man or woman falls to the ground, as if a tree is struck by lightning.

I must not be understood as advocating the use or abuse of the instructions of different Eastern teachers now being publicly circulated in many parts of America and Europe. While they may be correct in theory and detail, they are utterly ruinous in practice, because such teachers have not sufficiently considered, or have ignored the fact that the people to whom they offer such instruction are totally unprepared for it as a rule. In individual cases, some few good results may appear for a time, but it is to the children of this and other generations to come that we must look for complete success in a single lifetime. Adults as a rule have neither time, patience, nor power of application sufficient to overcome the difficulties in the way, though a beginning must be made in this or some other incarnation; and while the few simple rules I purpose giving may seem inadequate to those who wish to grow more rapidly than Nature has provided means for doing, they are all that are required, if faithfully followed, to bring your children to a point where instructions of greater moment may be imparted to them.

A careful study of the form and functions of the breath centers is a first requisite, and any good modern textbook of physiology will supply a basis of understanding.

While the blood stream of a body is the conveyor of the life principle as that stream makes its way through arteries, veins, capillaries, etc., to every minutest portion of the body, it is also a sewage system of wonderful ingenuity, and one to which the authorities of large cities might well look for information.

The blood flows out from the left ventricle of the heart, a pure, life-giving stream, and returns from its journey through the body, laden with refuse matter, to the lungs — the way stations — where it comes into contact with the life-energized oxygen breathed into the lungs, and by means of a process of combustion the carbonic acid gas which has been generated by such contact is liberated. The blood is thus cleansed or purified as by fire, and is ready to continue its journey back to its starting point. As the necessary oxygen is one of the gases contained in the air breathed into the lungs, the necessity for and effect of correct breathing is evident. And as everything in manifestation has its correspondence, its pattern or simulacrum in every other plane or state of matter, the whole process of breathing, the air, the organs used, and the bloodstream itself also have their correspondences.

Within the molecules of air exists an etheric energy, which is in turn supplied to the astral body of man at the same time and by similar methods to those used in supplying oxygen to the blood, and by bringing into action the power of will, the process of transmuting the astral substance into a still higher state of matter, and thus liberating the spirit may be accomplished when man has learned that great secret. But for the present, we will confine ourselves to the purely physical function of correct breathing.

If you will note the inaction of the breath centers of the average child, or even the adult, when in deep thought, and take into consideration what I have said, you will in part realize the necessity for some instruction to correct such inaction, which for the time being robs the blood of the oxygen required for its purification.

You know something of the power of habit, and can readily understand that if you form the habit of deep and rhythmic breathing by means of conscious effort, the action will continue indefinitely, whether you be conscious of it or not. Habitual deep breathing will tend to develop the grey matter now dormant in the solar plexus and prepare the way for the advent and use of finer natural forces. It is the inaction of this grey matter of the solar plexus which renders some of the yoga practices so dangerous to man; for by such practices, too great a pressure is placed upon the cerebrum, cerebellum, and nerves; whereas, if the solar plexus were fully developed, and the grey matter abundant and active, such pressure would be more evenly distributed throughout the body and all danger avoided. In order to produce harmony or health, a perfect equilibrium must be established between the dominant chords or organs of the body. The power of resistance is just as important as the power of impact, and when the solar plexus is fully developed, it generates the power of resistance to a greater degree than it can be generated by the brain alone. Where there is a lack of this power in any organ, the impact of the finer natural forces tends to break up the molecules of matter composing that organ, and to liberate the life energy, which then escapes and leaves the organ to gradual decay and death. This is what occurs when too great a pressure is placed on the brain. When the blood is perfectly oxygenated, and the grey matter in the head and the solar plexus is fully developed, there follows a gradual emplacement of the same kind of grey matter in other organs of the body, and in time the whole body becomes subject to every thought vibration; it is, in fact, a thinking instrument in every part. Its possibilities are increased tenfold, and life becomes no longer a burden but a great privilege and blessing.

1. Teach your children to stand erect, first of all things.

2. Never permit them to dislocate the bones of their feet by means of heels on their shoes. Let their bare feet rest on the ground, if possible, some hours of every day, if you do not feel that they can do so all the time.

3. Keep the thought of full, deep breathing continually in their minds by some simple device, some reminder.

4. Breathe in unison with them a few times each day, and see that the breaths are deep enough to contract the muscles of the abdomen.

5. Never breathe in unison with them when you or they are disturbed or angry, and always keep the idea of harmony before them.

6. Do not attempt to teach children physical exercises at the same time you teach deep breathing.

By following these simple rules, you may keep your children in perfect health, and provide them with bodies capable of withstanding many of the fiercest trials of life, and at the same time prepare them for instructions which will aid in attaining a much higher rate of development than now obtains among the average races of the earth.

LESSON 36
DIVINE LOVE

Of what value is a problem in Euclid to the scholar who is in throes of agony because of a broken bone? Of what value is a treatise on the constitution of matter, or the auric centers, and the currents of force which operate through such centers, to the soul-starved disciple whose life is one great longing for Divine Love and recognition? It is not that such a disciple is unable intellectually to grasp and appreciate the knowledge thus conveyed to his understanding, but the great gulf which his longing has created between his intellect and heart has become impassable for the time being; the necessity for union with the Higher Self has become infinitely greater to his consciousness than the necessity for mental pabulum; his soul requires nourishment far more than his mind requires stimulation or satisfaction. However valuable such knowledge might be to him at other times, during the period in which that longing is uppermost, it is not only valueless but detrimental.

There is coming upon the people of this world a period of reaction from the stress and strain of intellectual pursuit. Materialism and kindred "isms" awakened from their siesta somewhat over a quarter of a century ago have passed the middle milestone of the path of their cycle, and in their dying throes are awakening once more the ever-new hunger and thirst for righteousness, for Divine Love, for "the Father's face," and crush it down as they may, fight it back, or try to satisfy that need with material or mental diet, the souls of men will only cry out more persistently day by day until the very heavens are filled with the sound thereof, and the demand thus made can then bring response and fulfillment, for we must want one particular thing more than we want all other things combined, and be ready to sacrifice all else for that one thing before we can demand it with sufficient Power to compel its manifestation to or for us.

For the businessman, the inadequacy of material things for satisfaction finally becomes appalling. The ever-narrowing horizon of the average material scientist and scholar eventually leaves his soul, as it were, flattened between the covers of a folio. There may be length and breadth to such a poorly nourished soul, but there is no thickness, i.e., no room for expansion, no space in which living things may grow and blossom and fill with beauty, joy, and gladness. And when all the long, long story of life in manifestation is told, is there aught worth striving for save as a means to one end — that is, reunion with the great Father-Mother Life which has loved us into being and sustains us in the hope of finally "seeing God face to face"? A mystic sentence, by the way, typifying the reunion of Matter and Spirit.

Be very careful how you tear down the faith of the humblest creature that lives in the ideal God he worships, whether it be one of his own creation or otherwise, for with the loss of that faith, the individual also loses the power of loving. It may be for years; it may be for ages.

Much scoffing is indulged in by the worldly wise at the idea of a possible love for a spiritual principle by an individual. As well might they scoff at the Great Law which rules the action of the waters of earth, sky, and sea; for the law of gravitation no more truly draws one drop of water to and from sky and earth to streamlet, river, and finally to ocean, than the love of God awakens and draws to itself the love of man.

In the fast-coming, trying days which the human race has brought and is bringing upon itself, when the voices of Justice, Mercy, and Charity will be no more heard in the land, when might alone will seem right, and every man's hand be turned against every other man; the saving grace, the one living reality which will hold the earth in form and water, and preserve the seed for the new humanity, will be the now dormant love for God in the hearts of the masses of mankind; the love which will awaken from its long sleep as a result of the suffering to be endured, and when awakened, will behold its own strong, sweet face in the faces of every other creature and thing, as in a looking glass.

What does it matter what name you give it, whether it be God, Love, Attraction, Gravitation, Law, or Life? It is all names in one name, all words in one word. An unpronounceable word by mortal man, and the last letter of the last word cannot be added to that name until the last thing in manifestation becomes once more the first, until the serpent's jaws have closed firmly on its tail.

Do not judge your neighbor as a canting hypocrite because his actions do not always justify the words he utters, especially when he sometimes refers to the love of God in his heart. He may be a liar, a thief, an adulterer, and all else that the world terms evil; but, at the same time, there may be an awakening of that wonderful long-dormant power in his heart which has not yet had time to change his lower nature. You would not repudiate or harshly criticize the statement of an electrician if he told you a certain dynamo was capable of generating a certain voltage of electricity. You would let him prove it if you were sufficiently interested, and help him to make conditions by which he could generate that power, and so make it perceptible to your consciousness. It might be only a very little of the power of love the *human dynamo* was capable of demonstrating, but the fact of its even entering his consciousness would prove the possibility of its awakening, for you cannot imagine a thing that does not exist for you in some state of life.

The great crying evil of the present age is the seeming impossibility of uniting in one effective organization the various bodies of people who are working for the same end. There is invariably a manifestation of the Judas or Thomas force in each body, which betrays and doubts, and finally disrupts, and in the process piles up barriers between its own body and all others. The various national churches of the world all retain the forms and ceremonies and some other vestiges of the eternal truth, as well as do many religious and secular organizations. If all could unite, if it were on but a single indisputable principle, the history of the world would be changed in the twinkling of an eye. But the work of the Disintegrator goes on, and will finally develop a species of madness, when all men will be striking blindly at everything and every person in sight. When that period is over, then will come this other period of which I have spoken — a time when heart-(God) hunger will dominate all other desires — and then will it become possible again for God to speak to man in the Silence.

LESSON 37
THE EFFECTS OF COLOR

Every student of the secret science has some idea of the importance and effect of close association with varied vibrations of color. Instructions on color were issued to the ancient Hebrew high priests, and before their era to the Egyptian and Aryan priesthoods by Initiates of high degree, and similar instructions are of equal importance to you.

Much of the incompatibility between members of families and bodies of people closely associated in any line of work or endeavor is due to cross vibrations which are aroused by the predominance of some one or more inharmonious colors within some personal aura or environment. The same conditions may manifest as a result of the action of inharmonious sound vibrations.

The constant repetition of one tone of voice in conversation, or note sounded on a musical instrument, though it be one of the creative tones of the material universe, will by rapid repetition awaken cross vibrations to those of the governing scale of an individual life, and set into action a host of previously dormant elemental lives, which will make that particular life a burden.

Every created thing or being bears on its outer semblance or body, the key to the color vibrations which will harmonize with his, her, or its exterior life, as it carries on or in its astral and spiritual body the key to the vibrations governing its inner life. If the dominating color vibrations of any two bodies in close proximity to each other are inharmonious, there is no possible chance for peace and harmony to exist between those persons unless they can neutralize the inharmonious vibrations by bringing into action some other rate or rates of color vibration which will tend to blend or unite the former, thus awakening another (a neutral) vibration. For instance, if the dominating color of one individual is a certain shade of red, and the dominating color of another is a certain shade of yellow which will not harmonize with that particular shade of red, by close association with yet another individual whose dominating color vibration is powerful enough to blend the two first mentioned vibrations, thus creating a neutral shade, other and better conditions would be brought about. Or if the dominating color of their surroundings, apparel, house furnishings, etc., can be made powerful enough to bring into active life the same forces that the above-mentioned third person might bring by his or her mere presence in the same environment, a similar result might be produced.

I have said that the key to the dominating color could be found on the outer semblance of the man. I will go further, and say, it is generally found in the eye, though only visible to the close observer. The complexion and hair furnish the second and third keys, but the eye is the only sure guide, and the color is perceptible in the early morning or on first awakening from sleep, in the cases of the masses of the people of this age. Those people whose eyes, hair and complexion do not harmonize are generally erratic, volatile, and fickle, and their tendencies toward such undesirable characteristics can only be modified by close association with others whose general characteristics are the reverse.

In nearly all persons belonging to the Aryan race in the present era, the predominating vibrations are red and yellow. Many reasons are attributed for wearing the yellow robe or turban by the East Indian yogis, but the true reason lies back in the early ages of the present Manvantara. The yellow vibrations were then required for use in dominating the natural red and assisting to create the golden brown, which is also the governing color vibration of one great degree of the Initiates of the Indian race. Yellow is also the Buddhi,[1] Christos, and the Sun-Son color, and its free use on body or in environment serves to bring into more active manifestation that particular principle in man, and as intuition belongs to that principle, the free use of the same color must also serve more easily to develop that attribute.

On personal examination of the candidate for chelaship, the officiating Initiate to any degree of the Lodge always demonstrates by a method of his own, the particular color or colors the chela requires to more quickly develop the attributes in which he is most deficient, and requires that such colors be worn continually on the body in some form. If the attribute is most strongly connected with some head center, the candidate must wear the corresponding color on his

---

[1] *Buddhi* (*Sanskrit*, "to be awake")— the Universal Soul; the Spiritual Soul or Christos in man.

head. If with the heart or some other center of the body, the necessary color must contact that center as nearly as possible, and must be worn until the creative vibrations have induced the new condition, or strengthened the necessary centers so they are able to stand more rapid vibration. The yellow robe and turban of the Eastern yogis would prove most harmful to many of the people of the Western races. It is only in individual cases of the latter that the color yellow could be worn continually with good results. The vibrations of blue, red, violet, and green are more generally necessary, though in the individual cases mentioned above, some of the last-noted colors would prove most harmful.

Too little attention is given to the cultivation of the right color vibrations in and around your bodies and homes. You have certain ideas which you deem artistic or fashionable, and these ideas are carried out in your apparel and surroundings, regardless of the effect of the combination so secured on your mental and spiritual atmosphere, and one of the results is that nearly all of you are working at cross-purposes, inharmony prevails, and the cultivation of the attributes most necessary for your higher development is left to chance. You would deem it the height of imprudence to till the soil, plant the seeds, and leave to chance the watering of the same, and yet you are equally imprudent when you make no effort to flood your souls and bodies with the right color vibrations — vibrations which are as water to the thirsty soil, to your present physical conditions, and to the seed which sound has called forth from the eternities and implanted in your natures as incipient spiritual attributes.

An unusual shade of blue or green will be found in the eyes of blue- or green-eyed people at the time before mentioned, and a similar unusual shade of red or yellow will be found in the eyes of brown- or black-eyed people. Such shades should be fixed in the mind in some way, and as soon as possible, the former should find the particular shades of red and yellow which most perfectly harmonize with the shade of blue or green he has discovered, and use them as suggested. In the cases of brown- or black-eyed people, the same method should be used as above, but the color blue should be substituted for the red. Many people find it difficult to carry any particular shade of color in their mind, and a color card at hand will serve to fix the shade or refresh the memory; and if unable to determine what shades of other colors are complementary or harmonious shades to that found in the eye, it can be determined by experimenting with oil or water colors. When any two of the above-mentioned shades have been combined, the color which will manifest as a result of such combination is the one required for use on the body or in its surroundings. For instance, if by combining certain shades of blue and yellow, you find a certain shade of green, the vibrations of that shade of green are necessary to your well-being. If the combined shades of red and blue yield a certain shade of purple, you may feel satisfied you require that shade of purple, and so on.

In determining the sound or note which will equalize cross vibrations, and bring into your sphere more helpful forces, you should ascertain your ruling planet, and by the table of correspondences given in the Temple Teachings determine the note which belongs to that planet. Sound the note aloud as often as is possible, and keep it in your minds.

LESSON 38
THE DEFLECTION OF THE EARTH'S AXIS
FROM THE MASTER M.

Whether or not the average geologist or astronomer concedes the truth of the statements made by the sages of past ages, as to the periodical changes which have occurred in the earth's axis, the fact remains that such statements, as also the myths and legends of less intelligent peoples conveying the same information, are literally true.

The only error lies in the figures given as to the length of the cycles between such changes, and this error, if error it be, is due to the sacredness investing numbers, and the secrecy attendant upon the giving out of the length of certain cycles which have a great bearing on prophecy, by the Hierophants of the White Lodge, under whom such sages had been placed by natural selection as well as by choice. While the knowledge of such changes in the earth's axis is now widespread, the causes for the same, though simple enough, have not been correctly determined by the savants who discovered them, and as the time is rapidly approaching when another such change will occur, it may be well to give a little inside information to those interested; for even if we cannot prevent a catastrophe, there is a certain satisfaction in understanding the causes which produce it, and as the causes for these changes lie far back in what we term the spiritual planes of life, a resume of the same may prove instructive.

In the archives of one of the great underground temples, lie parchment after parchment, prepared leaves of papyrus, engraved tablets and stones innumerable, giving a complete record of all the ages and peoples who have inhabited the earth and other planets of the solar system, as well as all the information imparted by the so-called Gods or Great Masters to those sages and disciples who have reached a certain point of development that enables them consciously to contact such Masters.

Each true student at some time, in one or more of his earthly lives, in either sleeping or waking hours, has access to this temple, and is enabled to carry away with him more or less of this valuable information. Oftentimes a dim memory of the same comes back to him, which he imputes to his researches in other fields of investigation, and he is enabled to piece together fragment after fragment, and prepare quite a perfect thesis, while yet unable to recognize the fact that the binding force which has enabled him to piece together those fragments, is only at his command because of his experience in some secret repository of knowledge during his hours of so-called sleep.

No atom, molecule, man, or star lives to itself alone. Whether it be atom, star, or constellation, each form or division of the Cosmos has one central point in which is stored and from which emanates the energy which moves it to life and action. While that composite energy in its last analysis is God, Good, Love — its secondary attributes, its laws, its vibrations, manifest first on the plane of consciousness, secondly on the plane of forces, and thirdly, as matter or substance.

Action and reaction are not only equal on the physical plane; they are also equal and interchangeable on all planes. Therefore, action on the physical plane incites to action on all other planes; and as there is complete interdependence and interpenetration of atoms and planes, every thought, every action, of every manifested atom, must inevitably cause action and reaction in some other thought, atom or plane. This by way of preface to the subject under consideration.

In the before-mentioned temple, on one of the engraved tables, is a record of the last change which occurred in the earth's axis, and while its ultimate cause, materially speaking, was the vile mental energy set free by the races which then inhabited the earth, the precipitation of forces was due to the action of a higher race of beings which inhabited the sun. There, as elsewhere in the Universe, the battle between Good and evil is always being fought, and at the time in question, there was a great war between the Devas[1] of the Right- and Left-Hand Paths over the possession and use of certain powers and positions which largely controlled the solar system. By means of the tremendous elemental forces set free by the disturbance of the equilibrium of the sun, great changes occurred in the configuration of the same (changes that are comparable to those which would occur in the earth's crust if a great internal explosion occurred), and the sudden freeing of such undirected elemental forces also disturbed the equilibrium of the earth, thus deflecting the earth's axis from its former position. There is a sphere or line of energy connecting the sun and all planets of the solar system, as sound or light waves may connect two electrical centers of communication, and through this means of communication a conscious elemental force may reach and affect any planet of this system. By the deflection of the true pole the great waters were released and overflowed the then inhabited continents. The disturbance in such a large area of the sun had its effect on the heat vibrations, diminishing the heat vibrations of the earth, and what is known as the Glacial Age began shortly after the great floods.

At the point of evolution where the earth had attained its greatest development — when the Gods looked upon their work and said, "Well done!" the magnetic pole was coincident with the pole of revolution. Since that time it has had no fixed habitation, but is continually in spiral revolution about the true pole. Neither is the latter fixed; it is in constant vibration, and is largely subject to the action of magnetic energy.

The magnetic fluids which constitute the substance of the magnetic pole of any planet, are subject to Will and Mind when directed by the Planetary Spirits[2] or Gods of a solar system. These poles cor-

---

[1] *Deva* (*Sanskrit*, "shining one") — a god, deity, or celestial being, whether good, bad, or indifferent.

[2] *Planetary Spirits* — the Lords or Rulers of a planet. As a rule, the governing Hierarchy of Light for young planets, such as the Earth, consists of High Spirits that came from Distant Worlds, wherein they long ago had gone through the given planet's stage of evolution. When the humankind of such a planet reaches spiritual maturity, the Lords of Light who had arrived from other Worlds then leave it, to be replaced by worthy High Spirits who have already gone through their evolution on that young planet.

respond to the *ida, pingala,* and *sushumna*[3] of the human spinal cord, and the magnetic fluid or energy is carried from center to center, planet to planet, and man to man by conscious elementals which alternately clothe and unclothe themselves, as it were, with garments of magnetic energy, by which means the pole of revolution of any planet is deflected when the karma of that planet decrees the annihilation of the races inhabiting it, and the Planetary Spirits set about carrying out those decrees.

You who are subjects of time and space will find it difficult to comprehend this truth; the element of time is bound to present itself for your consideration, for the action of such elemental forces is so rapid as to be beyond the power of human appreciation.

LESSON 39
THE POWER OF THOUGHT

The tongue is truly a small member, but the amount of suffering brought upon the human race through its agency is prodigious. The effects of such action are evident to all as far as the physical plane is concerned; but the fundamental causes, the *modus operandi* of the generation and distribution of the electro-magnetic forces which are primarily responsible for the good as well as the evil action of that small member, are unknown to or unobserved by the masses of mankind. There is much less excuse for students of the Secret Sciences who use such forces to injure their fellow creatures than for those who have not been taught the power and potency of the invisible elemental lives which comprise those varied forms of manifested life. But at the same time, the advantages secured by the right use of the same forms of life are correspondingly great. Some of your number will hastily repudiate or deny the truth of the assertion I am about to make, but it is nevertheless perfectly true, and serious thought will bring some realization of its truth to the deeper student. Very much of the present physical suffering, loss of position and means, separation of friends and members of families is primarily due to the willful falsehood and the uncharitable and treacherous actions of a few people in your own ranks. Your inability to accept this statement lies largely in the

---

[3] *Ida, pingala,* and *sushumna* — the three main channels of subtle energy in the human astral body. More in Lesson 42, "Chelaship Versus Mediumship."

difficulty you experience in consciously recognizing your unity, your existence as one single entity on one plane of life.

I have said before, and now repeat — no individual can be drawn into The Temple or any other organic body, who does not belong to that body by karmic right and long association in past lives. Your mere signature to a pledge or withdrawal from an organization has no effect on the facts of the case. These are questions of duty done or undone, of responsibilities assumed or ignored. The bonds that formerly united you, the fires that welded you into that one body, were made and built many thousand years agone; and in order to comprehend the action of such forces, it is essential that you recognize and accept the fact of your unity, first in one special degree of the great Lodge, and finally in humanity as a whole. The currents of thought that are constantly flowing between you, cementing and intensifying the strength of your unity, are indissolubly binding you to each other, to the Lodge, to myself. You cannot tell a willful falsehood, perform a mean or ungenerous action against another Temple member, without hurting in some degree every other member of the Temple, any more than you can stab one finger of your hand without hurting your whole hand and body; for the nerves which conduct that physical pain to every part of your hand, correspond exactly to the currents of force set up between you by the living mental or thought energy you have generated and sent through or within those currents. Take, for instance, a malicious lie uttered by one against another. First, consider the evil generated by the hatred which preceded the spoken words — a force so potent and deadly, corrosive and fiery that, when directed by a powerful will, it can kill instantaneously; then consider the power in sound and form, as evidenced in every letter of the alphabet which goes to form the words of that lie; then the power of numbers generated by the combination of those letters. Here you have the material to work with, the path or method of its working, and the organism on which it works. The currents of thought continually in action between you keep open and strengthen the paths so that good or evil thought, speech, or action travels almost instantaneously from one to the other, until every individual is more or less saturated with the living energy set free. If the lie is repeated, the force is intensified, additional power supplied, and the effects are manifested more pronouncedly. The higher your karmic position in such an organic structure, as I have mentioned, the more surely and swiftly will the effects of your good or evil thoughts, words, and actions be felt by all the other fragments of yourselves, and the more will you suffer from the same forces set free by others, because you are in those so-called higher or more interior positions of the Lodge, for the reason that you have become more sensitive to the action of the life forces of interior planes of manifestation, and the more sensitive you become, the more acutely can you perceive the action of the "pairs of opposites," until finally the strings of your harp of life have vibrated so long and intensely, they sound no longer as separate strings but as one note or chord. Then those vibrations have transferred your consciousness on to another plane of existence, commonly known as the plane of Soul. The physical body is then disintegrated in the majority of instances. The power of mastery presupposes the ability of the individual to stand these higher or finer vibrations and keep, at the same time, a physical body in manifestation.

LESSON 40
WOMAN

There are women who, like unto a certain species of land crab which yearly takes a pilgrimage to the shore to bathe and shed its shell, at stated periods go down into the sea of human love and disport themselves, shed the callous growth that inaction and over-indulgence have formed about their hearts, and return to a normal condition refreshed and revivified by each experience. But, alas, there are others, and they are not in the minority, who, while intellectually capable of observing the coming storm which is to leave them desolate, are powerless to guide their frail life boats into sheltered places; women who with wide-open eyes drift helplessly, sometimes despairingly, upon the rocks upon which even they see burning many warning lights. The hearts of such women never grow old; the body which encases them may shrivel up, sight and hearing depart, poverty, sickness, and misfortune of all kinds be their daily portion, yet the heart in its awful eternal youthful passion beats on remorselessly, alternately consuming itself and revivifying its embers even into the great beyond. Other women smile at the seeming incongruity of age and love, until their time comes also, and a realization of the perpetual tragedy of the feminine side of life finally dawns upon them.

Give, give, give, cries the opposite pole of life, the embodied masculinity, and woman gives until her power is exhausted, and in reincarnation she swings to the opposite side of life and takes a position with those who demand and receive — that is, the male sex, until satiety sends her also to the opposite pole.

The law of compensation is exact; what we sow, that we must also reap. The wheel of the gods grinds slowly, but it grinds exceeding fine.

Out of all this travail, this heart starvation, or over-indulgence, is born the babe in swaddling clothes, to be laid in a manger — that is, Spiritual Love for Christ, for God. The manger is the physical plane of existence, into which the babe is brought, that it may redeem the substance of that plane and raise it once more to the estate from which it has fallen. It can only redeem it atom by atom, for so it fell. But let all sore, aching hearts be comforted by the thought that every bravely endured pang brings it one step nearer its Father's house, its Father's face. Nation after nation, race after race goes down and out, leaving but a few scattered remnants here and there to prove that it ever existed. The old, old story of ebb and flow is told over and over again in different cycles by the same souls in different bodies to their less well-informed brethren. The same old ambition, greed, and avarice is awakened as a result of contact with matter, and the message of the soul goes on, unnoted, unrecognized. Race after race suffers from the same old causes and goes out into the silence as a result of its own inherent selfishness. A few brave souls are born in every race who are willing to lay down life and all things to teach the old, yet ever-new lesson of Eternal Brotherhood. Each in turn is crucified on the cross of the world's selfishness. When such souls are young, the enthusiasm awakened by the divine touch they have felt may sustain them; but when old age comes creeping on, their vehicles are incapacitated for action, and by the time they arrive at the age and experience that would make them safe guides for younger generations, they have lost the beauty of face and form which appeals to the sensuous eye, and which is one of the most powerful levers of world movement, and so are incapable of impressing their words and actions upon others with sufficient power to enthuse. And so they are laid aside or merely tolerated, and the consequence is that each new generation has to learn the same old lesson over for itself.

LESSON 41
OUR NATURAL BIRTHRIGHT

Power, Love, Justice, and Mercy, commonly termed attributes of God are, in their last analysis, reflections of, and forces emanating from, the Triune Godhead; and man has the right to demand and seize upon these and all other forces emanating from the same source, and use them for his own development. But that right exists by virtue of his relationship to every other man, and unless his desire for individual development be subservient to his desire for the same development for all men, it becomes mere selfishness, and his right to demand and seize upon such forces then becomes at least questionable. Whether we consider God as a personality, a Jehovah, or a great ruling evolutionary power, He or It is the Father-Mother, the Creator and Preserver of every manifested atom.

The law of Correspondences is one of the most exact laws of universal life. Every atom of force, substance and matter contains, either potentially or actively, the power to produce to some degree all that has been or may be produced by every other atom. Any fortuitous concourse of atoms, as well as any occurring event on any one plane of existence, will actively manifest a similar concourse of atoms or events not only on every other plane, but in every division of force, substance and matter on each plane which is in synchronous vibration with the dominant chord of those atoms or events.

In teaching the action of the law of Correspondences, the more simple the illustration can be made the better for the pupils; for by forcing the mind into unfamiliar channels of thought, such as abstract metaphysics in an endeavor to show the action of the law, the mind of the western man becomes confused and unable to discern the correspondence between such and the familiar signs and sounds of natural phenomena, while it would be readily understood by the mind of an eastern mystic to whom the action of the law as well as the substance in operation would be perfectly familiar.

In this field of research, as in all other fields, we behold the action of the positive and negative poles of life, and by keeping these in mind, a better understanding of the subject under consideration is attainable.

In endeavoring to show the right of man to all things, as well as the probable care for His offspring by what we know as God, by means of the action of Divine Will on the evolutionary forces of life, perhaps we can do so in no more intelligible manner than by considering the probable action of a normal father and mother toward their children; for here we find one of the most perfect correspondences to the action of the Godhead in and with His or Its creatures. Such a father and mother as have been mentioned, will never think of their possessions as belonging solely to themselves; all that they are, all that they have is at the disposal of their children, if those children will make a proper use of it; all just demands are complied with as a matter of course. It would never occur to such parents to deny their children the right to food, shelter, clothing, and education until such time as those children were perfectly capable of providing for themselves; and even then, the Love which brought them into life and sustained them, the Love that is the fulfillment of all law, would envelop them eternally, for Love cannot die.

A parent would have just cause for reproving a child for willfully suffering from hunger, if he had been called in some other direction, and it was possible for the child to reach the receptacle of a loaf of bread, or if the parent had hidden himself from view for the purpose of observing how the child would proceed to cut the loaf, or whether it would take a little nibble, and throw the rest away, instead of giving it to some hungry child. The child would be perfectly justified in taking the bread under either of such circumstances, or at least so much of it as would satisfy its hunger, but it would have no right to take, either carelessly or intentionally, more than it required, when by so doing, it might deprive some other child of its rightful share, or might injure itself through gluttony, in which case, the righteous punishment which would be inflicted by its parents or the suffering induced by overeating, would in the end be the most merciful action of the law, for the experience gained would be of value.

A child of God, the living result of the action of evolutionary forces in the form of man, whose soul is hungry for any particular power or force which pertains to or is a part of God, has a perfect right to that power or force, if it has won the *ability* to grasp and hold it, even while its Father's face is seemingly turned away. But to win the ability to do this is his first task; and in order to win such ability, he has first of all to do what the human child would do, if its parent were within hearing when it was hungry; namely, ask for, demand, concentrate on or pray for the ability to seize upon the requisite power or force. There are many forms of demand — prayer — but there is no more efficient form than that of perfect obedience to known laws, and by means of self-sacrifice cultivating the inherent will which dominates the personality of every man and uniting that personal will to the engine of God's omnipotent will.

It seems a trivial thing to you when you reduce some other man to a state bordering on frenzy, by taking advantage of his ignorance or weakness to enrich yourself, or merely for the purpose of amusement, gratification, or revenge. The incident quickly passes out of your mind; you are not cognizant of the interior effects of your action; you are not able to see that you have changed the auric color-vibrations both of yourself and your antagonist. It might be only a short time thereafter when you would begin to experience a great hunger and dissatisfaction of soul; you would begin to search for something to satisfy that hunger, and perhaps find fault with or repudiate the teacher who is striving to point out the path of power and development to you, either utterly ignoring or ignorant of the fact that the changed color-vibration of your aura has brought your interior self into what is to it a foreign vibration, and one which will not harmonize with the dominant colors of your normal state, nor with the manifesting colors of the Ray which is in one sense your Father-Mother. I mention the effect of this one possible act only to illustrate the probable effect of disobedience to the law of brotherhood, and to emphasize the necessity for obedience to all known laws, by the chela who would win the ability to grasp and hold the powers and forces which rule the universe and which are his by right.

Whether a Master be of the Right- or Left-Hand Path, he has won whatever power he possesses by means of obedience to the laws I have noted. That the latter mentioned Master has fallen from a much greater height than you have yet attained, and still possesses some measure of the power he won in earlier ages, is no argument against the truth of my statements.

LESSON 42
CHELASHIP VERSUS MEDIUMSHIP

Students of the Secret Science are very early taught the origin, existence, and functions of the three *nadis*[1] or tubes which traverse the spinal cord in man, having their source in the *medulla oblongata*.[2] The central tube is termed the *sushumna*, and those on the left and right, respectively, the *ida* and *pingala*.

Physical science is unable to determine the use of these tubes even when its votaries are convinced of their existence, which is not always the case. A transverse slice of the spinal cord will plainly show the central tube, and on either side of it may sometimes be distinguished a shadowy chain, but to the average investigator these tubes would not appear to have any particular function to perform, as such cannot be discovered by dissection or observation; nevertheless, they exert a tremendous influence on the exterior as well as the interior bodies of man, as they are vehicles for the transmission of some of the potential finer forces of Nature. It is through these tubes that are transmitted those forms of energy which enable the yogi, the entranced medium, or the hypnotized and mesmerized subject, to remain in a condition of *samadhi*[3] or trance for days and sometimes years, without material nourishment; in other words, they convey the energy which acts as nourishment to the astral body, and the energy, in turn, is transferred to certain centers of the physical body, thereby sustaining it until it awakens to normal consciousness; and as the latter is built upon and within the astral, the necessity for such vehicles is apparent. The particular form of energy mentioned above is, as it were, the spiritual essence of a certain concentrated material nourishment. It manifests to eyes capable of observation as a definite color: this homogeneous color is diversified in the sushumna, and by the lowering of its vibrations as a result of contact with matter of a lower degree, soon manifests four other colors, and the latter may be increased or modified

---

[1] *Nadi (Sanskrit,* "tube," "nerve") — a channel through which subtle energies flow in the human astral body. They connect energy centers known as *chakras.*
[2] *Medulla oblongata (Latin,* "elongated medulla") — the lowest part of the brain, situated at the top of the spinal cord; it controls activities such as heartbeat, blood pressure, and breathing.
[3] *Samadhi (Sanskrit,* "to bring together") — the state in which the yogi loses the consciousness of every individuality, including his own, and becomes the *All.*

by the body's close proximity to different articles of the same or its complementary color; and the increased vibration of such a color adds to the strength and potency of the energy thus manifesting in the sushumna.

The ida and pingala act more as distributing centers than as original conveyers of energy, for they take up the energy as it rushes through the lowest chakra[4] of the spinal cord, and distribute it to certain centers of the physical body, where it is used up in the creation of certain blood corpuscles, which in turn are intimately connected with the astral body. As an illustration of the use of a definite color as an aid to the development of one principle, I will call your attention to the fact that the shade of yellow, which corresponds to the Christ-principle, is constantly worn on the heads of the Initiates of one degree of the White Lodge, for the purpose of more rapidly developing the Kriyashakti,[5] or Higher Will Power, which is one aspect of the Christ-principle; but a chela can gain no advantage from the use of that color unless the motive which prompted its use be in sympathetic vibration with the higher astral counterpart of the color; in other words, unless the act of will which prompted its use partake of the character of the Christ-principle, which is, above all else, selflessness.

There is a great deal of controversy at the present time among a particular class of investigators relative to the condition commonly termed *trance*. It is vigorously disputed that there is any appreciable difference between the state of unconsciousness to physical things, of the yogi or chela of the Lodge — those disciples who are under the immediate direction of an Initiate, when in a state of self-induced trance or samadhi — and the condition of a so-called spiritual medium who is under the control of the denizens of the lower astral plane. The difference between the two conditions would be apparent to a good clairvoyant or an advanced chela at a single glance. In the sushumna of the yogi or chela there would be seen four of the prismatic colors in a state of rapid vibration; the colors would mingle and intermingle so rapidly, it would be difficult to distinguish any particular color for

---

[4] *Chakra* (*Sanskrit*, "wheel") — the energy center of a human being, a planet, a star system, and so on. There are seven main chakras, each of which has seven centers — that is, 49 in total. Yet, these in turn also have a sevenfold nature.

[5] *Kriyashakti* (*Sanskrit*, "power to create") — the mysterious power of thought that enables it to transform ideas instantaneously into visible forms by its own inherent energy.

any definite length of time. In a like tube in the body of a medium, the same colors might be distinguished, but they would appear very dull and sluggish, and the outlines of each color distinct from the others.

The entranced medium is at the mercy of any extraneous astral influence and has not the ability to protect himself to any appreciable extent, owing to the temporarily paralyzed condition of his own will. His astral body drifts powerlessly about in a half conscious condition. Occasionally it drifts into the immediate vicinity of more highly developed entities that have passed out of incarnation but who are still earthbound, either because they are under the ban of some broken Cyclic law or because they have not gained sufficient power over their lower principles to use them instead of being used by them. Such an entity may be capable of giving what seems to be a high order of teaching, but it has no more power of verifying its own theories and deductions than it had when on the physical plane amidst men and women in a similar stage of development so that its impressions and statements cannot be perfectly reliable. To the medium, they would seem to come from some high spiritual source, and no intentional deception on others would be practiced. Naturally, we are only considering that class of mediums, the members of which are incapable of conscious fraud.

It seems difficult to make some people realize that the passing of the soul from one plane to another will not, in some miraculous way, change the general characteristics of the soul, and even make an Angel out of a former demon. The truth is the soul passes into the Astral plane in very nearly the same stage of development it had reached when it left the physical plane. The mind of an enthusiastic medium only too often drifts into a stage of dissipation when surrounded by the elementals and lower human vampires which feed upon its substance and eventually leave it a mental and moral wreck. But what is of infinite importance to the medium is the fact that when entranced, the higher mentality or spiritual soul is temporarily incapacitated for action upon the lower principles, for the antaskarana, or bridge between the two, is semi-paralyzed when the astral body is unnaturally forced to project its essence without long years of preparation and adequate protection.

The yogi or accepted chela has earned the power to control his body to such a degree that sense of time and space is lost to him in entrancement. His movements are only limited by his own will and desire.

It is not alone by the manifesting colors in the sushumna that the clairvoyant can distinguish the difference between the conditions of a yogi or chela, and a medium, while either is entranced. The colors belonging to the lower quaternary, red, green, orange, and red-violet, assume a very vivid hue in the aura of the medium, while in the aura of the yogi or chela can only be seen a golden glow with occasional flashes of ultra violet, all together in a state of rapid vibration. The task of unifying the two aspects of the Divine Will is given to the chela immediately upon his acceptance by the Master who is to guide his unfoldment, and is fully accomplished during a certain Initiation in which he acquires a Fire (or permanent) body. I do not intend to imply that such a body cannot be earned without association with an Initiate on the physical plane, but I do state most emphatically that such a body cannot be earned without implicit obedience to the laws by which the accepted chela conquers the Dweller on the Threshold[1] or, in other words, destroys the before-mentioned bridge between his higher astral and the higher principles of his lower astral bodies. One of the advantages to be gained from chelaship is a more rapid evolution. No scientist would despise the assistance of a greater scientist when striving to demonstrate a truth, and no human being is in a position to despise or reject the assistance or directions of an Initiate; for sooner or later, on the Astral, if not on the physical plane of life, he must come under the direction of a more highly developed being, before it is possible for him to recognize and kill out the insidiously deceptive foes which lurk about the higher levels, as well as the lower steps, of the path of life.

---

[1] *Dweller on the Threshold* — the embodiment of one's internal negative essence that has been formed over the course of one's many lifetimes. One's spirit is set to meet with them before one's entrance into the Higher World. All one's weaknesses, vices, and shortcomings that were present in oneself on the Earth intensify manifold. They clothe themselves in visible, most attractive and seductive images to captivate and devour one's consciousness to such an extent that one no longer has either the strength or desire to cross the Threshold into the Supreme World, and so remains in the lower layers of space. Therefore, it is necessary that we prepare ourselves for the meeting with the Dwellers on the Threshold already during our stays in our physical bodies on the Earth, eliminating all shortcomings in ourselves. A trial by the Dwellers on the Threshold, produced by both their own and others' selves, also awaits everyone in the material world who has decided to follow the path of discipleship.

Some of the dangers that confront the medium, the hypnotized and mesmerized subjects, are analogous to the dangers encountered by the prematurely born child; neither medium nor child is prepared to meet the hostile forces which attack it when suddenly thrown unprotected into a strange environment. Both would require such assistance as is analogous to the power won by the young bird in breaking its way out of the shell that has protected it while in a state of gestation: the power which is only won by means of a fierce struggle with adverse conditions. The Initiate or Master but holds the light, and points out the quagmires on one side and the beasts of prey on the other, of the path of life; the disciple must cross the quagmire and destroy the beasts himself, by means of the knowledge and power he has gained in breaking through the shell which held him while in a state of gestation; or, in other words, while living in the world of men and things.

One of the greatest of all the mistakes which the orthodox religious enthusiast is liable to, is the mistake of imagining that the laws which control the visible universe are abrogated when a supposed point of demarcation between the now visible and invisible realms is reached; when in reality there is no line of demarcation. The same laws are operative on all the planes of manifestation; the apparent difference is due to the changes which occur in the states of substance or matter of which those planes consist; although an erroneous concept is frequently given by the occultist, who finds it impossible to give the right one because of the inability of the student to comprehend the laws of vibration which bring into manifestation those different states of matter; hence the expression, "the laws of (such and such) a plane are changed," when attempting to teach somewhat of the lives of those who inhabit those planes.

Before closing, I wish again to call your attention to the reality of the effects of color both on astral and physical bodies, and advise you to observe and note well the effect of different colors on your minds and bodies, and endeavor to understand all that I have transmitted to you in the past on the same subject.

LESSON 43
IDEATION

In one sense of the word, it is deplorable that some of the brightest minds of the present age seem incapable of perceiving the absurdities they advance in support of their theories regarding the imagination of man, or are unwilling to admit the truth through fear of the unfavorable criticisms of their more material coworkers, and so stifle or ridicule the principle by means of which they have attained to any measure of success in scientific research.

Without the principle of Ideation, that is, Imagination, the seemingly modern as well as marvelous discoveries in the field of biochemical investigation would have been impossible, for all must admit that before the human brain can formulate and successfully execute an experiment of any nature, there must invariably occur the idealized or imagined model which will subsequently be used to build the materialized form upon or rather within. When an act of the Imagination has created the idealized form of a state of matter, so much finer than any state now under the observation of man, that effort of the Imagination awakens the will to manifest that state to others, and by the power or energy resident in that will there is awakened, or drawn out from the inner spheres of potential Ether, a degree of that force which can be manifested in several ways, in a similar manner to those adopted to manifest electricity. A galvanometer may be used to manifest finer grades of matter than can be perceived by the vision of man, but that fact does not nullify the statements of true prophets to the effect that man will sometime evolve the necessary organs to perceive that particular grade of matter and other grades still finer. As an argument against the possible manifestation of spiritualized or astral bodies, it has been contended that there could be no truth in such manifestations, for the reason that even if the physical eye could not see those bodies, their presence or substance would affect to some degree the latter mentioned instrument. The gulf that exists between electricity and the instrument which brings it under observation by man, though impassable to the man of the present age, is not nearly so great as the gulf that exists between the latter and those finer forms of the same force that exist on the inner planes, and in order to understand the true nature and functions of electricity, man must evolve an instrument of the same nature. In order to perceive spirit, man must evolve a spiritual eye. We cannot know a thing or a state of matter until we have become that thing or state of matter; we could know nothing of the physical plane unless we had, now or once, possessed a physical instrument or body. A large class of investigators refuse to recognize and accept the aid they might secure, by the right use of the Imagination, to further their search for that *ignis fatuus*,[1] the source of life. By their attitude of contempt for what they deem "abstractions" they throw into their own minds the potent force of suggestion. A suggestion of the uselessness of effort in such a direction inhibits them from using that principle of Imagination advantageously.

Modern science has determined what the secret sciences have long since demonstrated, that all life is the result of fermentation, and, also that the little lives which produce the same are reversible in action, i.e., that the polarity of the little electric bodies, the Sparks of occult science, is changeable, but it has not yet determined that such action is subject to Will and Mind, and also to a great degree to the right kind and degree of electricity as applicable to some of the modern inventions. To cure a disease, it must be first correctly diagnosed, and in order to apply the correct current or kind of electricity to a diseased organ, the nature of the sparks composing that organ, their present position, and their power of resistance must be determined, and it is at this point the power of Imagination acts upon or with a material medium to obtain that diagnosis, for the Will and Mind *in concentration* use the Imagination to secure the knowledge required. The vesture or bodies of the Sparks or ferments are said to be created by the action of the forty-nine fires on the combination of oxygen and hydrogen we term *water*, while it is held in suspension, as it were in the air, before being precipitated; in which condition it corresponds to a condition of gestation. The ferments have within themselves, and are subject to, the power of attraction and repulsion, the power of reproduction and dissolution, and are the real "missing links" in the chain of evolution constructed by modern science, only missing to those who will not permit the power of Imagination to prefigure the probable results of investigation by faith, one result of which would be the ability to determine the manner of disease operating in an organ of the body, by the position assumed by the ferments of that organ, and the kind and degree of electricity to be used in changing that position by changing their polarity. Investigators who have but

---

[1] Will-o'-the-wisp; something that is impossible to get or achieve.

recently observed the difference in character and position of such ferments have not had time to observe their action in disease, and therefore would hardly be expected to admit that they would not be able to perform any function of the body without the aid of its resident ferments; they could not even breathe without the aid of that class which line the throat and lungs; but neither would they admit that the sore throat they may be suffering from is the final result of perverted thought, either by themselves or others about them, the result of which has been to change the former position of the throat ferments, thus producing abnormal conditions and consequent disease. As "like breeds like," the germs that reproduce their kind by fissure or division multiply almost indefinitely the original germ brought into existence by an elemental which ensouls all that one class of germs as an elemental of a higher class ensouls a swarm of bees, or race of other minute creations.

The starchy products which more than all else are the material bases of the chemical action of fermentation in the body, furnish a clue to the method by which the reversed action of the ferments is accomplished. Such products are formed of dead, or rather of inactive germs of life, but they remain inactive only so long as they are isolated from other germs. Once brought into action with another class of active germs, they spring into life again in other forms, somewhat as a butterfly emerges from a chrysalis, leaving a refuse which returns to protoplasmic substance; but such inactive germs frequently prove the Nemesis of mankind as far as punishment for certain sins of the body is concerned.[2]

In fact the starches are great in potentialities.

I am well aware that I lay you open to criticism for even publishing some of the foregoing statements, and while it is difficult to put into language some of the deeper metaphysical truths which appear to trench upon the ground of chemical or meta-chemical investigation, I will endeavor to explain how it is that Imagination may determine the position of ferments. In a case of disease, there first appears an image in the mind, of the good or evil results of a certain line of conduct, for instance, the gratification of the palate by the use of some form of food or drink which is in reality injurious to the body; at once the

---

[2] The 1925 edition's note: Medical science now teaches that the residue of the starches is what clogs up the blood and produces clots, which are sometimes the cause of paralysis and kindred diseases.

power of thought seizes upon that image and imparts life — motion to its previously inactive atoms, and a battle ensues between them and the abnormal germs introduced into the stomach, which results in a changed position of all the germs, and a diseased condition of the stomach results; the germs feed upon the substance of the organ, reproduce their kind in great numbers and destroy or incapacitate the organ. In order to heal a diseased organ by the same power — a combination of Imagination, Will and Mind — make an image of a healthy organ in the mind, find the antithesis of the evil thought which produced the disease, and direct the force of that thought to the diseased organ. If your power of concentration is strong enough, you can change those wrong vibrations and reverse the position of those ferments by will power; if not, some mechanical means or chemical means of imparting the new vibration may bring about the desired end. It is the power of reversing the position of the ferments, resident in all drugs and medicines, that gives them their healing properties. The power of *invariably* determining the position of the ferments belongs to the occultist, in other words, to the one who has become as a little child that he may learn of those who alone are able to teach the laws underlying the mysteries of life.

LESSON 44
WINDOWS OF THE SOUL

The Christian religion recognizes nothing above or beyond the personal God. Its votaries assume that believers in the Absolute, the Trinity of Life, and the personified natural forces are heathen. On the other hand, many students of the great Mysteries refuse to see in the personal God of the Christians a representation of the first individualized manifestation of the Absolute; consequently, both parties to the great controversy go on year after year, misunderstanding each other, imputing all evil to each other, instead of striving to find the common ground for the faith that is in them both, and this sad condition of things is apparent in all controversy between different branches of the great bodies regarding minor points of their belief such as states of consciousness after release from the physical plane, the power and ability of different Orders and grades of Beings, etc. If the time given up to all this controversy were spent in investigation instigated by sincere desire for truth, each would soon find that the other had the same basis for belief as himself, and that the real points of difference were so minute as to be unworthy of serious consideration. Much of the difficulty arises from inability to comprehend the common consciousness of God and man, and its operation in and through Matter.

Could the Holy Lotus of the Far East, the Water Lily of the West speak in human tones, it could tell many tales of the three kingdoms, Earth, Air, and Water, which it inhabits simultaneously — tales of little creeping things, tales of swiftly moving denizens of water, of strangely plumaged birds, and queer insects that the eye of man seldom rests upon.

If the impersonal soul in the heart of man could make that heart understand its language, it could tell still more wonderful tales of Air, Ether, and Akasha,[1] as well as of Fire, Water, and Earth; for as the Lotus dwells habitually in three kingdoms, so the soul dwells in six kingdoms or planes of consciousness at one and the same time. Its memory of higher planes may become inhibited for the time, if it be earth-bound, as are nearly all the present races of the earth, but this bondage may be broken. In the majority of instances, however, the casement of flesh must be shattered and the silver cord that holds it back be cut, ere it can escape and throw off the mantle of forgetfulness cast about it on its entrance into human conditions on earth. Death is still pictured as a skeleton horror to most of the human race, instead of as the bright angel of release it really is. Ignorance holds that race in bondage to the fear of death, as it has always held it to the fear of any unknown or untried phenomena. The roots of the Lotus, buried in slime and mud, have no consciousness of the exquisite flower waving gracefully in the air above them, but the soul or consciousness of the flower has full knowledge of roots and stalk, as well as flower, and knows also that a rough hand may tear them from the soil beneath, and leave the whole plant a dead thing on the face of the waters; but the soul of man, as a brooding bird, nestles in or over each of the bodies it has built, and through which it looks into all the kingdoms of life, and when one of its bodies decays and wastes away, it has only

---

[1] *Akasha* (*Sanskrit*, "sky") — Primeval Matter, also known as *Materia Matrix*; the refined, supersensible spiritual essence which pervades all space; primary cosmic substance. The Scrolls of Akasha, or the Akasha Records, are a particular manifestation of the limitless and indestructible memory of Nature, which stores information about all events and manifestations of the Cosmos.

to build another, or remain in those already built on inner planes, for it has only lost temporarily the use of one window looking out on the particular plane on which that body functioned.

LESSON 45
THE SEVEN RAYS OF EVOLUTION

With all the advantages attainable by the earnest student through study of the slokas[1] of the *Book of Dzyan*,[2] which constitutes, in part, the Wisdom Religion, and the commentaries prepared by H. P. Blavatsky at the instigation and with the assistance of the Initiates, no mere mental effort can solve the mysteries which lie hidden between the lines and even between the letters of the archaic truths pertaining to Cosmogenesis and Anthropogenesis, as given to the world at large for the first time in the two volumes of *The Secret Doctrine*. An unbiased seeker after truth would find it difficult to ignore or contemptuously criticize the truths under consideration, if even a tithe of the profound wisdom contained in them had entered his consciousness. Notwithstanding the fullness of the commentaries, unless the intuition were developed to a supernormal degree, thus permitting the student to apply the laws governing analogy and correspondence, the slokas above-mentioned would continue to be unsolved mysteries, though in truth they contain a complete history of Nature and man since the beginning of the evolution of life in our solar system.

Coincidently with the birth of a new race, after the destruction of the continent of Lemuria,[3] arose the necessity for a specialized group of seven human beings who could be prepared and instructed, and finally overshadowed by the seven Lords of Karma,[4] when the

---

[1] Verses.

[2] *Dzyan (Tibetan)* — Secret Wisdom, Knowledge. *Book of Dzyan* — a secret book written in *Senzar* and stored in the Tower of Chung in Shambhala, a Stronghold of Light hidden in the Himalayas. Under the guidance of the Master Morya, H. P. Blavatsky published two parts from it, entitled *Cosmogenesis* and *Anthropogenesis*, in *The Secret Doctrine*. Consisting of nineteen stanzas, they narrated the story of the origin of the Cosmos and humanity. Later, at the beginning of the 20th century, a third part of nine stanzas appeared, this part about the inherent divinity of humanity under the title *Theogenesis*, published by Francia La Due under the guidance of the Master Hilarion.

[3] *Lemuria* — the continent on which humanity of the Third Root Race developed. See *Glossary* for more.

[4] See Lesson 214, "The Lords of Karma."

development of such chelas should have reached a certain degree, thus insuring proper vehicles for the transmission of necessary evolutionary forces as well as for the receipt of important secret instruction. Each one of the seven great Lords mentioned literally controls one of those forces, and if a suitable vehicle has been evolved, capable of receiving and distributing that force, the evolution of the world is helped onward to just that degree. The failure of the Lodge to secure seven such points of contact on the physical plane, at the beginning of very important cycles, has made it impossible to distribute and equilibrate those forces, as was necessary for the more rapid development of mankind and, consequently, one force has been manifested in excess, while others have failed to manifest at all, or so slightly as to leave no impression on the lives of the masses of humanity.

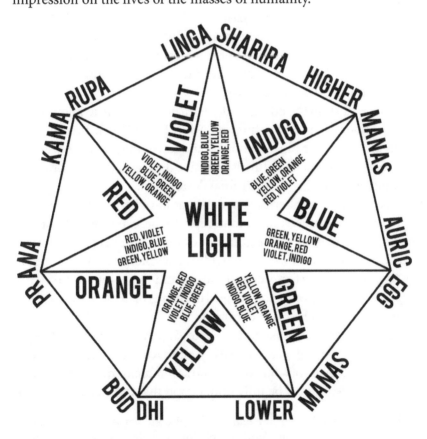

Figure 2
*Diagram of the Hierarchies of Colors
and Principles of Man and Nature*

But one of the saddest effects of the failure of any one of such a group of human beings, chelas, as I have referred to, particularly when the failure was due to pride or ambition, is a loss of the power to recognize their own condition; consequently no effort is made to eradicate the fault; and often, unconsciously it may be, such chelas become victims of the Black Brotherhood[1] — transmitters of the opposing forces. The fact that the chelas had previously earned and been given such great opportunities, makes them all the more valuable to our Brothers of the Shadow, who are always on the watch to gain control of such chelas. The humanity of this age cannot rise to a much greater height until such a group of perfectly devoted instruments can be secured, and every failure of the Initiates of the White Lodge to secure and hold such a group, retards the growth of all with whom they are connected. If all realized how they were trifling with the laws of their growth when by support or encouragement they were aiding or abetting a chela belonging to the selected group of Seven in being untrue to his Order or any member thereof, they would fly from the temptation as from a wild beast.

There exists in the minds of all men a natural desire to know some-what of their origin and nature, and while heredity may furnish a few clues as far as their physical bodies and lower minds are concerned, it is totally inadequate to furnish reliable data as to their spiritual life and higher mentality, or their final destination.

I could not number the appeals that have been made to me for light upon these questions, and in reply to these questions I purpose to endeavor to give a little glimmer of that light; I can do no more because, if the intuition of an individual is awakened to such an extent as to permit of perfect understanding and interpretation of a full explanation, there would be no need of such explanation; the requisite knowledge would be his at command.

All Matter and Substance is septenary, and each of its states is graduated in seven degrees of density, and each state reflects the qual-ities and potencies of some one of the seven major divisions or Rays of the Infinite. It must be fully understood that there is no higher or

---

[1] The *Black Brotherhood* or the *Black Lodge*, also known as the *Brothers of the Shadow*, opposes the White Brotherhood. The word *Black* here has absolutely no racial connotation; it is merely used to describe the use of powers for evil purposes. The Black Brotherhood also unites different people, regardless of their ethnicity, nationality, gender, race, or religion.

lower, no graduated scale of place or position in the manifestations (vehicles) of these great powers we term Rays, in order to distinguish them from lesser entities, but who are so far beyond finite conception it is almost useless to refer to them as entities. They are equal in power, though each controls a separate degree or division of that power, a different grade of substance and force. The three higher of the seven minor divisions or states noted above are the planes or states of individual perfection. It is not until the heavenly pilgrim has reached the fourth state in its descent into matter that if becomes subject to the law of Karma and limitation.

The three times seven (21) spiritual entities or powers which comprise the three higher states of substance multiply indefinitely in the fourth state, where the individual forms, created of the highest grade of substance, form the vehicles for the incarnating Ego's first manifestations in form, and these twofold entities are the individual souls which subsequently inform the physical bodies of mankind.

While there is a certain correspondence between the birth of the soul and the birth of a physical body, there is, nevertheless, a vast difference as the vehicle of the Ego's first manifestation in form is the result of creation by Will and Imagination, and in occultism these creations are called the "Sons of Will and Yoga,"[2] instead of Souls. The Souls thus created during the descending arc of a great cycle or Kalpa persist in incarnation and excarnation during that age, consisting of many million years, at the close of which all substance and matter is indrawn, and the Ego returns to its "Father's bosom" where it remains in Nirvanic rest or Pralaya[3] until awakened to take upon itself another line of incarnations in another great age. The soul is the seat of our greatest woe or bliss in physical, astral and spiritual life; the fact that it is possible to lose one's soul while yet living on the physical plane would seem to contradict the foregoing statement, but in such a case all pain and pleasure are derived from the action of the lower mind

[2] *Yoga (Sanskrit,* "union") — a spiritual practice leading to liberation and enlightenment, as well as to development of spiritual powers, through the union or merger of the individual self with the Universal Self. The highest form of yoga is *Agni Yoga,* which is represented in the book series of the same name, given by Helena Roerich (1879–1955) under the guidance of the Master Morya.
[3] *Pralaya (Sanskrit,* "dissolution") — a period of rest, or collapse of life within a planet, system, galaxy, or the Universe between various Cycles of Evolution. It is equivalent in duration to *Manvantara.*

or the senses. The fact that it is possible to separate the soul from the body by long-continued evil is seldom referred to by the Initiates of the White Lodge, for by dwelling upon such a possibility, a weak-minded person might bring about, by the power of suggestion, the first stages of such a calamity. Many soulless persons enter your lives in the common walks of life, but you are not yet capable of distinguishing them from others. When separated from a living body, the soul returns to the fourth plane, where it remains until the cycle rolls around again when it can commence another line of incarnations; and in the disintegration of the physical and astral bodies, the three lower principles gradually return to protoplasmic matter, to be worked up later into other forms of life. It is believed by many that even in such cases the action of the law of Karma still persists, and the disintegrated matter, with the attached skandhas, is drawn together in lower forms of mineral, plant and animal life, and gradually evolves until the soul can again incarnate, and so have another opportunity of winning its crown of perfection.

If there is one truth more important than another to be learned in the consideration of the foregoing statements, it is the irrefutable fact of the brotherhood of man, and the importance of maintaining brotherly relations with all men. You cannot injure another, no matter what the provocation, without laying a stone in your own pathway. You cannot assist another without clearing away some obstruction to your own development. If I have succeeded in enlightening you to any extent by showing one cause for your delayed development, through the difficulties in the way of securing the seven initial points of contact, by means of which the evolutionary waves of the Ocean of Life may swell and touch the shore of power toward which your longing eyes are turned, and inciting all who are in line for position in one such group of disciples to turn their backs on their great enemies and go forward to victory; if I have thrown any light on the perplexing problems of Evolution which haunt the minds of men, I have done all that was possible in such a short dissertation; for the world could not contain the volumes which might be written on that one subject.

LESSON 46
LOVE'S APOTHEOSIS

To my sorrow, though not to my despair, I see here and there a Temple child sinking into the slough of despondency, letting go of the rudder of the ship of life, staggering on under the weight of the heavy burden he has all unwittingly assumed, a burden too heavy for any one human being to carry, and all because he has temporarily lost the ability to function the Deific energy which alone would enable him to aspire to reach those divine and perfect conceptions which are the heritage of every child of the living God — conceptions within which are embodied the powers that swing the suns in space, the power that moves the spider to build its delicate habitation.

With the first awakening of the human soul to a knowledge of its divinity, to a knowledge of the character of the substance of and within which its expression in form has been molded, there are also awakened the karmic results of its previous lives in the line of sensuous gratification, and it is overcome with horror and disgust, which temporarily dashes it into a whirlpool of fear; fear that it has sinned too deeply for possible atonement, fear of its powerlessness to crush the demons pressing close about it. Finally, in desperation, it determines to create an ideal, and to build toward that ideal by a method of elimination. It selects the most obvious fault in its category, and sets itself vigorously at work to eradicate it. It may succeed in temporarily crushing that fault out, or rather back into the depths of its auric body, but ere that difficult task is completed, it awakes to the consciousness that some other form of the same fault, or one equally abhorrent, is taking its place. It then begins to realize that there is a more deeply rooted cause for its failure than it has hitherto comprehended; something is wrong at the very heart of its being; the substance in which it is embodied, of which it is formed, does not seem to vibrate in unison with the heart of the great Over-Soul.[1] Discouraged at its powerlessness to crush its tormentors, it determines to try another method, that seemingly will be infallible, and so endeavors to conquer those elementary forces by raising them to a higher vibration. Where, mayhap, lust of power

---

[1] *Over-Soul* — the Universal Soul, also known as *Alaya* (*Sanskrit,* "abode"); the Father-Mother. All individual souls are its rays or sparks and are able to merge with it.

and place now manifest, it proceeds by the power of Will to awaken a corresponding desire for holy things. It devotes all its surplus energy to the advancement of some religious or humanitarian purpose. For a time, it believes it has found the peace of fulfillment, but some day it suddenly awakens to the fact that it has only transferred the original thirst for power and place to another phase of the same lustful desire, and now that hydra-headed monster holds it firmly in its grewsome clutches. Then comes a period of utter despondency and despair. With weighted steps and bowed head, it plods along through the dreary wastes which spread out on all sides of it. It sees no end to its labor, knows no hope. But one day it contacts some other soul, which has sunk still deeper in some of the morasses of evil, and its God-given power of sympathy responds to the call made upon it; its lethargy, hopelessness, and despair drop from its consciousness as might a filthy cloak from the shoulders of a man; it reaches out a helping hand to that suffering brother, and with the giving of that help there springs up into its consciousness, direct from the Christ-star Eros,[1] a ray of the light that has lightened the Universe — Unselfish Love; the love that casteth out all fear; the love that incites to kindly action; the love that begets peace, joy, happiness, even in the stress and turmoil of physical life; the love that goes straight to the heart of things, and returns laden with blessings for all who will open their hearts for their entrance.

The proof of the awakening of love in the human soul is the awakening of an overwhelming desire to give itself and all it possesses for the best good of all. It is only as we are enabled to give ourselves to Love that we can find life in abundance. But, alas, the self-deceived but seek amiss. They start out on their search for the Fountain of Wisdom, the waters of which are the sprayings of Love, with man-made ideas, not only of what Love consists, but where it is to be found, and find naught but the vaporings of lust, which soon pall on their senses and finally leave them tenfold more heart hungry than they were in the beginning of their search. Often, oh, so often, have you heard the words, "Except ye become as little children, ye cannot enter the kingdom of God."[2] I herewith plead with you to strive with all your might to form some right concept of all that is involved in that sentence, all that it means to you individually. First, perfect faith, unselfish love, and trust. It is only when a child has been influenced by its elders to

---

[1] *Eros* (*Greek*, "love") — the God of Love in Greek mythology.
[2] Matthew 18:3.

do so that it chooses the opposite pavement to that upon which the so-styled sinner is walking. Love reduces all men to a level. It takes nothing; it gives all. With the dawn of that mighty force in our hearts, it begins to speak through our eyes in no uncertain tones; it draws to us by the might of intuition the wisdom and power we could attain in no other way; it casts the filthy rags of self-righteousness in which we have clothed ourselves into the flames that ascend from the heart of the great Temple of Life, and reclothes us in a spotless robe, woven from the threads which lie curled in the drops of sweat wrung from our tortures, as we stand in the midst of the central flame, where sooner or later every disciple of the Great White Lodge must stand until purified.

Ah, my children, nothing else counts in the sum of our existence save Love. "If ye love not your brother whom ye have seen"[3] — the brother who has cheated you in business as well as the brother who has succored you, the sister who has betrayed your trust as well as the sister who has been your inspiration, your brethren who now walk on the shady side of the path of life — not always by choice — but frequently because they have been pushed from the sunny side by you and others like you: if ye cannot love these who need your love above all others, "how can ye love God whom ye have not seen,"[4] the God in whom these now despised ones "live and move and have their being"[5]?

So long as you can turn your faces in anger or disgust from the meanest thing that lives, so long as you can persuade or tempt another human being to do likewise, just so long will the bars of that gate which now shuts you off from your inheritance remain in place, and you still continue to grope around in the outer darkness.

The words, "Judge not, that ye be not judged,"[6] were spoken to you just as surely as they were spoken to those other fragments of divinity, who standing in the light of the Spiritual Sun, were striving to disperse the dense clouds which yet surrounded them; but that light had been focused so strongly upon the screen of their lives, that their power of righteous judgment was held in abeyance by the fires thus kindled. But it is not so with you; while you have long stood in the rays of that Sun, its light has entered your consciousness, and given

---

[3] 1 John 4:20.

[4] 1 John 4:20.

[5] Acts 17:28.

[6] Matthew 7:1.

you the power of self-restraint; the power to withhold judgment and give love, where a weak or erring brother stands in need of it.

Come back to me, my children, who have wandered far away into the bypaths made by faithlessness, by false judgment, by lovelessness, until you can no longer hear my voice, no longer see my outstretched hand. Open your hearts to that Divine Love which, as a mirror, reflects our unity. Remember that your brother's sin is your sin, your sister's weaknesses are your weaknesses, and that as the Great Master cannot enter into his rest until he has gathered into one fold the sheep that belong to him, neither can you enter into your inheritance until you have led into your love the hearts that are a part of your heart. Take my hand, and with me seek your straying brothers and enfold them in the love that is the apotheosis of all things, the love that can conquer all things, even death itself.

As the sound of the words you have spoken passes into the invisible realms; as the light of the fires you have kindled passes inward beyond your earthly vision; both sound and light return to that form of energy of which they are integral parts, subject to recall by those who have won the power to manipulate those forms of energy, not necessarily as repetitions of the spoken words, or similar flashes of light, but as elementary embodiments subject to control. In like manner, the thoughts of love, compassion, and devotion which well up in the human heart, pass beyond the ken of their creators, to mingle with like-forces in the realms of spirit. And these, too, are subject to recall, and come as angel visitants to those who have prepared a dwelling-place for them.

To those who look upon all spoken or written efforts to awaken man to a consciousness of the power of Love, as a string of platitudes — a useless waste of time, that might better be devoted to some material purpose, I would say: Even from the most material standpoint, the cultivation of the power of Love will bring about the manifestation of all they prize most highly; for beyond all controversy, Love is the most potent form of energy in the Universe, and he who has won the power to control it, has at his command all lesser forms of force; but it is that form of Love that gives all instead of that which takes all; for paradoxical as it seems and difficult to comprehend, renunciation is equivalent to possession.

LESSON 47
RIGHT APPLICATION OF LAW

There are countless lessons to be learned from observation of the action of modern business principles. A past cycle of hand-to-hand conflict between men and nations for the possession of prestige, power, and wealth is fast closing, and another cycle of the same world-wide struggle, wherein brains will furnish the weapons of offense and defense has commenced, and is rapidly developing strength. All cycles overlap each other to a greater or less extent.

The "brave knight" no longer uses the crowded arena to display his prowess and receive his reward. The scene of bloody carnage is changing, and the greater battles are being fought out in the business offices of towering blocks of stone. Within these luxuriously appointed anterooms to the real scene of action — the world — deep plans are laid, the results of which sweep over the whole world, leaving in their wake bitterness, despair, suicide, and murder, thereby sending countless thousands of men, women and children into the streets to beg, or worse; and at the same time there is arising an over-active, optimistic class of men who are continually prating of the rapid advance of civilization. Giants of finance, many of them are termed, men who heartlessly take every advantage of their wretched dupes and skillfully manipulate the people's own rights and privileges to their personal advantage, while the latter cringe and bow down to their temporary idols, until they find a loophole in their armor large enough to admit a hand, when a frenzied clutch is made at the idol's hoarded wealth. If unsuccessful, jealousy and despair drive them on to tear down their idols from their pedestals, trample them into the dust, and cover their very names with obloquy, as of old, like sycophants tore down the idols they had made and worshipped slavishly, until a time came when the governing laws of all life bore too heavily upon them, and the impotence of their idols to avert disaster and well-deserved punishment became painfully apparent. As long as they were sustained by the hope of a satisfactory response to their supplication, the idols were safe. When the latter seemed to fail to supply their ever increasing demands, all that they had before received, supposedly from the same source, was forgotten; and in a frenzy of rage men fell upon the thing in which they had placed their trust and tore it to pieces.

And whether it be idol, king, government, or individual, it matters not; selfish, ungrateful, treacherous lower human nature in its rage repeats the same old tragedy over and over again throughout each age; and the one who perceives the shadows of coming crises and places himself in the midst of a tumultuous mob, to warn, to supplicate, to teach, must inevitably meet with the same fate that has befallen the would-be Saviors of mankind since the beginning of time. But though all I have said be apparently rank pessimism, to the mind of the uninitiated, it is far from that in reality, for the fact that there has been a transference of the scene of action from a lower or material plane to a higher or mental plane, is the one redeeming feature of the whole pitiable situation. Until mankind could sense the horror, the brutality of bodily conflict, he could not — or would not — forego the gratification of his lustful desire for physical supremacy and emoluments, so again until man has reached to a full appreciation of the final effects of the still more deadly, if bloodless slaughter of the innocents now taking place under the guise of business, and the fact that his implements of torture are tenfold more dangerous, the wreckage which follows their use tenfold wider in extent, and the sin of it all as much more far-reaching as the mental energy is higher than mere brute force — he cannot even awake to the seriousness of the conditions in which he is involved; and until he is awakened, he will make no effort to change the situation. Age after age there have been sent out from the Infinite Heart of Compassion the Great Souls who have won their crown of immortality, and they have been torn to pieces and flung back to the source of being, as a gift may be flung at a giver after being covered with the filth which adhered to the hands which so desecrated it, and all because of the blindness, the selfishness of those whose sight is impeded by the brick-red mist of passion which swims before their inner eyes. And yet the struggle has only begun.

What wonder is it that poor, weak human flesh quails at the thought of the ostracism, the contempt, the bludgeon, and the halter, which it must expect, if it be placed in the wake of those who have taken a stand for righteousness' sake. But by far the most pitiful of all the cowards of the present human race is the man or woman who prates of brotherhood, of Divine Love and Law, who has donned a wolf's garment and hidden it with the garb of righteousness, for the purpose of preying upon his weaker brethren; who has not even the courage of conviction; who can stand idly by and see his fellow workers spat upon, buffeted, torn to pieces by the inner as well as outer forces of rebellion, without lifting a finger to aid or succor, and who will join hand and voice with the hands and voices of common enemies in order to destroy those brothers. And the strangest part of the whole strange, abnormal condition of such a one is his lack of appreciation of all that he is bringing upon himself, upon his loved ones; that he should be unable to perceive the character of the garment he has donned; or if he does perceive it, will not admit its character, even to himself, and so continues to lower himself into a slough of treachery and unbrotherliness, while knowing that he is a part of the One Life, and that he cannot strike at his brother without having the blow descend on his own head.

But even to such as these will the true soul turn in pity and love, for it knows that naught can be lost out of the universal heart of things and creatures; that sooner or later that soul must come back to its early home; it may be that it will come like a bird that has flung itself upon the rocks till its pinions are all broken, its power exhausted, and it falls to the ground a helpless, lifeless thing, a prey for the wild beasts, the sport of the winds of heaven; but come it must, for there is no place in God's universe wherein a part of God may be lost eternally.

Physical pain and mental torture reduces the bravest to a condition of helplessness; and so long as selfishness exists, pain must live to do its perfect work. Banish selfishness, and the cause and sequence of pain must follow, for selfishness lives and thrives on gratified desire.

In your hours of physical pain and languor, your thoughts naturally fly to the Higher Self — to God, or to some Master or Savior to whom you have hitherto aspired; you realize your weakness, and feel around with the arms of your soul, hoping to touch a hand in the darkness which will impart the courage, the magnetic force to lift you out of the valley of the shadow and set your feet on the rugged path of life. When disaster overtakes you by means of loss of fortune through the treachery of others, or your own lack of wisdom, you fall into a similar condition of weakness, and again you reach out into the great silence for help. You will hide this seeming weakness, this call for help from those around you; and sincere and earnest as you have been, the answer to your supplication comes as it will invariably come, if your demand is made aright; but, alas, it all ends with the divine answer. Returning vigor, business, or social calls distract your mind, the vows you have made remain unfulfilled and often forgotten; the light which once flooded your soul dies out because you have shaded the windows of the soul through which that light came. The sympathy for others who suffer now as you then suffered is crushed back in your fight for material things; your heart is hardened; in other words, your soul is starved because you have failed to supply it with the only food that can nourish it, the food that can be attained in but one way — by obedience to the irrevocable law of supply and demand. Your wives, your husbands, children and friends sicken, suffer, and possibly die, or other heavy losses follow, losses commensurate with the loss the heart of All-Being has sustained by means of your recreancy, your ingratitude, your failure to continue to make the spiritual demands which would make it possible for the divine Father-Motherhood to supply the nourishment your soul requires for its individual growth.

From even a superficial point it appears unaccountable that the average, intelligent, keen, executive operator in business or social life should so fail to continue to apply the laws which have hitherto brought success to him on material lines to the soul or spiritual life, when to him the result of such success is so clearly all that is worth having, because of the possibility of the gratification of desires which more immediately concern the real sense organs of the soul. It is not alone for bodily ease and comfort his life is spent in struggle; it is for the opportunity of filling his life with beautiful things, educating and gratifying his mind — for desire is located principally in the mind; and still as a general thing such a man will entirely ignore, or fail to make an effort to appreciate the higher action of these laws. He knows, if he is to win in the struggle of life, that he must be able to supply or create a demand in the public market. He knows he must awaken such an appreciation of himself or his goods as will result in a return wave of thankfulness in the shape of dollars. He knows he must repeat the effort, supply or create the demand over and over again; that it is not enough to do it once and then cease all effort. And yet, with all his knowledge of the action of those universal laws, it seldom occurs to him that by making the same continued effort, taking advantage of the action of the same laws, with an expenditure of one one-hundredth part of the same energy, he could bring to himself infinitely more satisfaction, could feed and sustain his mind and soul, and thereby obtain a height of development unattainable to any marked degree by his labor in a lower field; and his failure to perceive his lost opportunities lies in the fact that he will not follow out the logical sequence of the action of those laws beyond the point where his physical eyes can perceive material results, though he would look at you in scorn if you were to tell him the positive and negative laws which govern electricity were suspended upon the lighting of one arc light, or that the laws which govern sound would cease their action upon the sounding of a single note. He knows each law continues to act in exactly the same way through the whole visible universe, under the same circumstances; and he is himself the arbiter of these circumstances so far as the action of the laws affects him personally. So, if he would but carry his conclusions to a sensible terminus, he could scarcely fail to perceive the unreasonableness of even theorizing along any other lines than those which have brought him to a point of material success.

LESSON 48
THE PATH OF LIGHT

My Children:

The first seven-year cycle of the present phase of the Temple work is fast slipping away. There remains but a short time ere it passes into the great silence, with its records of efforts, successes, and failures; its opportunities appreciated and advantageously used, or neglected and repudiated. No single Temple child can truthfully say it is not mentally and spiritually better fitted for contact with the world, more enlightened, more capable of assisting others to climb the steep hill of life, if it has faithfully followed the directions given by me. As for those who have either willfully, purposefully, or ignorantly refused to follow those directions, spurned the advice which would have helped them over many rough places, and who are therefore unable to see any sign of spiritual advance in themselves or others, I can only say that if they have evolved any sense of justice and are capable of making an honest self-examination (regardless of wounds to pride and egotism), they will admit that the fault lies with them.

When I have made an explicit statement to a disciple concerning the good or evil result that will follow any specified line of action, a statement which I know rests upon the foundation of some unalterable law, and that statement is not accepted at its true value and acted upon, I have done all I may do to aid that disciple in that respect, until hard experience has taught him to view the contested point from an unbiased and intelligent angle of vision. This would seem to be an evident fact. Nevertheless, there are among your number, those who have set a false estimate on the value of certain statements made by me, ignoring or repudiating them without making an effort to learn their true basis, and for the reason that they could not make them fit in with their own theories; or as in some instances, while admitting the possible truth of said statements, their acceptance would render those disciples unable to justify to their own consciences the continuance of certain practices they were not yet prepared to renounce. In no case where I have observed such results have I failed to see the acceptance of opposing statements made by false teachers, which, notwithstanding all denials, must inevitably lead to the severance of those ties which unite the true Master of the White Lodge and his disciples, and just as inevitably bind the latter to the service of the opposing forces though it may be all unconsciously. When I have told you that any particular line of action in regard to a brother disciple will surely awaken an active semiconscious degree of corresponding elemental force within your own auras, a force which up to that time has been merely potential so far as you are concerned; and which, unless rendered impotent by a higher power will induce some mental or physical ailment that will incapacitate you for reaching some higher degree of evolution to which you are aspiring; and when, instead of accepting my statement and acting upon given directions, you try to justify your actions or to assure yourselves that your conduct has been due to the influence of others or to some evil hereditary or acquired characteristic now very indulgently contemplated by you, you make me powerless to aid you in controlling those elements. I do not say you have an easy task before you when you commence to change or kill out such tendencies, but I do say *it must be done*; so why not begin to do it now, instead of daily adding to their power over you by indifference?

If you are honest with yourselves, you know whether or not you are yet capable of rightly using the greater secrets of occultism; for instance, the secrets of life and death; the power of changing the vibration of living substance, for a wrong use of which you would be held accountable to the Lodge; you who have as yet but little or no control over even what you term "a bad temper," which for instance, if indulged in, coincidently with the exercise of such powers, might kill the victim of your anger by a look or thought. Or many of you are still so tainted with the curse of the world and the accumulation of wealth at the expense of your brethren, that you would be unable to refrain from using even a divine power, if it were yours to use, for self-aggrandizement.

I have never given you advice or direction that has not had back of it the knowledge of the action of some cosmic law which would more rapidly develop some important center in your auras, or retard or destroy the growth of some undesirable one. I have given you instruction after instruction, explanatory of the *modus operandi* of such laws, that you might more intelligently observe and profit by the same, as well as given you my reasons for emphasizing many points of given directions; and when I tell you that some act will arouse a corroding force within your aura, it should not now be necessary for me to elaborate such a statement in order to enable you to understand that such a force could not operate in that essence of your vehicles of manifestation — mental, astral, and physical (the aura) — without destroying or badly injuring some important plexus or organ, thereby rendering you incapable of becoming a center of operations for the special degree of energy that under normal conditions would express itself through that plexus or organ, thereby making you so much the less "a whole man" or woman.

I have told you that certain acts would invariably lead to black magic, and that a conscious and continued line of action of such a nature would take you from under the protection of the White Lodge; and yet, to satisfy curiosity or insatiate thirst for abnormal growth, I have seen some of your number deliberately perform such acts; and in some instances, perform them at the suggestion of incompetent instructors; eagerly drinking in the poison offered them in the line of instruction, and even indulging in the practices that must inevitably cost them many incarnations of woeful suffering, mental and physical. I have heard others criticize as "old and trite," directions that have been given them from the depths of centuries of experience, and suffered anguish of soul because of seeming inability to convey the truth of the tremendous importance of the apparently simple idea and still more simple words in which they were clothed, and also to convey a knowledge of the fact that their simplicity and age are the surest indications of their value. If they had been hitherto understood by others, and acted upon, there would be no necessity for their constant repetition, for they would have accomplished the desired purpose. What would you think of your dearest friend if he stopped to consider carefully the grammatical construction of a sentence in which he was conveying a warning, while a cobra was coiled for a spring at your back, if his inaction was caused by a fancied idea that you would object to the form of words he must use to arrest your attention?

There are certain strict and inviolable rules for developing a disciple into an Initiate, and each of these rules is simple in construction of form, and as old as the stars and planets of the solar system. If their age, construction, and context render them uninteresting reading, or tiresome in their application, to those who are always seeking some new thing, some easy way of climbing the ladder of life, it simply proves such persons incompetent or impossible, as far as true chelaship is concerned. Only too often such a one falls under the ban of the law when harassed mercilessly by implacable enemies, with faith destroyed, destitute of love, of all that sentient life offers to man in seeming generosity, only to snatch away as his hand is reached out, if he is proven incapable of seizing the gift; he goes to the foot of the ladder of life, and there finds that his desires have fled, his will is broken; and finally crushed to the earth he reaches out to the Great Silence, where alone the soul may speak with God, and then he learns how unnecessary was the greater part of all his woe; how gladly would his Elder Brothers have helped him on his way if he had permitted them.

If man could dissociate the egoism of his personal self (which is usually in contradistinction to the general ideal of the egoism of the Godhead), and understand that in the last analysis there is but *one* Soul, *one* Ego, the result of ages of manifested life, and that It is divine, his contempt for the seemingly simple things of life would undergo a great change; for paradoxical as it seems, the more simple a thing or a number appears, the greater and more complex it is in reality.

A man who can neither read nor write may be as far beyond you in the real scale of life, as you are beyond the lowest form of life, if he has evolved the Power and Will to render perfect service in exact justice and you are still clinging to present worldly ideals, though he may be at a great disadvantage in the world of things and unable to make the necessary correlation between the different material planes.

"There are no little things." Every great event rests upon the foundation of some seemingly little thing, some simple action, and you may rest assured no Initiate of the Lodge will waste time, and force, and knowledge in propounding a conundrum; or for amusement, direct the accomplishment of a useless task. If you refuse to learn the alphabet of life, you can never understand or speak its language.

LESSON 49
THE VALUE OF CORRESPONDENCES

The astrologer, astronomer, or geologist, even more than many other seekers in cosmic fields of research will find more than enough to occupy his time and attention in a single lifetime, in any one field of investigation; nevertheless, if he permits himself to be confined exclusively to one field, he will find his powers of generalization and combination gradually departing: in other words, atrophying. If the said powers are to be retained in their fullness, they must be kept constantly employed. Research into the minutiae of any one field of labor should awaken a desire for the investigation of corresponding minutiae in other fields, for it is only by combining the minutiae of the phenomena of all states of matter belonging to the same octave of vibration that the ideal form which has given birth to all that class of phenomena can be brought under observation. By losing the ability to find and concentrate on the primal cause, the center, from which proceeds all the minutiae of any degree of matter, the investigator becomes rigid and inflexible; he narrows his nature and his conception of things down to such an infinitesimal point that he becomes a mere slave to minutiae; he attaches himself by the energy of concentrated effort to the "little things" of life instead of the great, and but seldom rises to the investigation of primal causes.

In my communications to you, I have been striving to aid you to avoid this danger by frequently changing your angle of vision, and forcing you to turn your attention to different planes and states of consciousness; not pursuing any one line of research, but endeavoring to give you general outlines interspersed with more specific delineations, trusting that you would be able to fill in the outlines with the minor details of personal experiences, and finally, not only be able to seize upon and place any one of the greater divisions where it belongs in the Cosmic scale of Matter, Force, and Consciousness, but also be able to form a comparatively good concept of any one of those divisions by means of any part of the minutiae which constitute that division; so there has been more method in my apparent wanderings than my critics would suppose.

I might, for instance, take the sacred word Aum, and confine my efforts for many months to the different definitions given to the word, take one letter and trace it back through the archives of time to its first utterance; give you a detailed account of all the difficulties experienced by those who have sought for its correct interpretation; but when I had completed such observations, you would know no more of the real power and substance of the word than you did when I commenced; and it may be as well to continue to use this word as a subject for further illustration, while giving a short instruction on the principles under consideration.

The Sacred Word symbolizes three of the greatest forms of energy in manifestation, the higher potencies of which are subject to the will of perfected man and God. By many it is supposed that the power of this word lies in the right pronunciation of the letters alone, but this is a great mistake. Its power lies in the energies which are symbolized by the letters, and the correct pronunciation only starts the vibration of a definite degree of each of the three forms of energy. The purpose and direction of the same must also be clearly defined in the mind of the operator using the word. The letter A symbolizes fire (flame), the letter U heat, and the letter M water; legendary lore maintains that the first sound symbolized by the letter M, i.e., the explosive utterance of that sound by the Cosmic Builder, called together the scattered elementals and created the Great Deep — the Waters, and the wavy motion thus imparted to the Akasha by the movement of the elementals continued such explosions by bringing together and combining the hydrogen and oxygen potentially resident in the Akasha, thus creating the first deluge or watery planes. In fact we are told the letter M designates a cosmic center of manifestation, and whenever or wherever we see a drop of water, we may know it was created by an explosion of gases, an expulsive effort of Nature. Water is the feminine principle of life, and each one of the three centers of generation manifesting therein is symbolized by the double strokes which form one-third of the letter M, and each such division symbolizes a union of the masculine and feminine principles — an equilibrium struck by positive and negative action.

Either one, or a combination of two of the three above-mentioned centers of generation, creates the foundation strata and holds the potential form of every creature or object in all the natural kingdoms, from a stone to a god; as in the axis around which gather the minute lives of crystallization. Within and around such an axis evolves every molecule of plant, flower, and fruit, and also the central nucleus of all seed and seminal fluids. Different combinations of all three of these centers form the nucleus of the brain, heart, and organs of reproduction in man. On the subliminal planes where the vibratory action of all substance is increased, the fiery properties designated by the first two letters of the word, A-U, begin to operate more powerfully; the watery element M, is absorbed by the heat, U, which has previously been generated by the flame A; and as the separated letters of the Sacred Word are combined forming a word, so the principles of Flame, Heat, and Water are combined in the nucleus of a thing or a world. The pronunciation of the Word is then no longer, *Aaa-ooo-mmm* it has become Aum. Water ceases to be water; it is transmuted and raised, as the physical body of the neophyte is transmuted in the fiery pillar of the great Initiation chamber, leaving only a congery of energies subject to the control of Will, capable of being condensed and made visible and audible to physical eyes and ears, as hydrogen and oxygen by means of an explosion may become condensed and visible as water. Take a piece of ice, subject it to heat, it becomes water; increase the heat, it becomes steam; subject that steam to pressure, it becomes energy; in a corresponding manner the physical body becomes a spiritual body. The fire body of an Initiate is such a congery of energies, and by effort of His purified will He can condense and concentrate the same to different degrees of vibration corresponding to planes of phenomena above noted.

If the investigator in the field of crystallization is content to confine his research exclusively to the material aspects of the same, he will not only have a comparatively narrow field for investigation, but he will gradually lose interest in other fields of research, and will finally lose his power to seek and find the basic principles of crystallization, which can far more readily be observed in the corresponding fluidic principles; therefore I repeat, do not be satisfied with exclusive investigations in one field; find the correspondences to any one object or detail under observation, in all the other kingdoms of nature; for you will never find the basic principle of any one state of matter or substance in that particular state or degree of substance wherein it manifests more pronouncedly to physical senses.

LESSON 50
ZONES OF COLOR

However wise the teacher, he can give but little knowledge to his pupils in the stereotyped phrases he must use to clothe his ideas; unless his words strike upon the soul's organ of hearing, he can convey no vital truth. Words are but symbols which change and pass away, while knowledge is eternal, and words must be vitalized, impregnated with pranic force to give them even temporary endurance; and this can only be done in concentration. It is in the parturition pains of concentration that the power of perception is born — or to be a little more exact — is transferred from the spiritual to the mental plane.

In pursuing the study of symbolism, if anything but a superficial knowledge of the same is to be attained, the student must at the same time strive to cultivate the power of concentration. He must become able to recognize the whole of an idea or object by any one of its constituent parts, and to do it instantaneously; or in the interpretation of an idea or a message he may lose the most important point while stopping to interpret some connecting or other symbol of secondary importance. By understanding that all things in manifestation are symbols of eternal truths, and by taking any one visible object and fixing the mind upon that, first by an effort of will, then by stopping the fluctuations of the mind, the soul can make itself heard as it tries to impart to the mind some inner truth in relation to the object under investigation. In fact, the consciousness of observer and observed becomes identified, and the personal Ego becomes conscious of all that is in the consciousness or soul of the object. But as a rule students become too easily discouraged. Because they have some difficulty in stopping the fluctuations of the mind and in listening for the tones of the inner voice at one and the same time, they give up in despair. They seem to think it ought to be a purely natural process requiring no continued effort on their part. It is quite understandable to them that even years of study and close application may be necessary for the acquisition of some specific branch of scientific knowledge while, at the same time, they rebel at the idea of giving much less time and effort to a power that is limitless, or despair of final success. In no branch of occultism will the earnest student find more to interest and instruct himself and others, than in the study of all phenomena from the aspect of Color.

It is not generally understood that the geographical divisions of latitude and longitude were originally designed to mark out the habitat of different orders of color elementals, the knowledge of which was confined to Initiates and was held inviolate.

At the center of each of the Zones so defined, there are astral conditions comparable to those resident around the solar plexus of man, where the color elementals of any ray exert more power than on either side, and therefore exert a tremendous influence on all things and people that live therein.

As there are ties of relationship existing between different parts of the earth and corresponding divisions of the Cosmos, so there are ties of relationship existing between these and all human beings upon the Earth, and the Color that dominates a Color Zone has a peculiar influence over the people that belong to that particular Color Ray. The hair, eyes, and skin are strongly affected, and such a Zone is the natural environment of those who belong to that Ray. Out of it, they will degenerate and decay as a race. It does not often occur to students of life's mysteries that loss of health may be due primarily to a wrong color environment, yet this is true. This particular part of California[1] lies in the Center of the Color Zone of the Red Ray. By following the 35th and 36th parallels you may find the portions of the Earth's surface where the Red races would find their natural environment. The Aztec, Indian,[2] and Aryan races are among those races.

So subtle and potent is the influence of color that if the units of a race are transplanted, or even if the environment and association be changed by the introduction of innovations brought about by people of another race who are dominated by some other color, the people in whom the operation of either color is most strongly pronounced are the ones who will gain and hold power and preeminence, and the others will die out gradually, or their descendants will become mixed and partake more strongly of the characteristics and constitutional tendencies of the dominating units. There is some color zone on the earth's surface in which every human, animal, vegetable, and mineral creation is naturally "at home," a zone where all that is in them will rise to its highest point of attainment, if given like advantages to those that

---

[1] Halcyon, San Luis Obispo County.
[2] American Indians.

might obtain elsewhere under other circumstances; and one result of the coming of the Golden Age will be the attainment of the knowledge of how to seek the true home zone and at the same time the necessary advantages that will enable all the races of the earth to reach the highest possible point of attainment for them. In individual minds there is already awakening an inkling of the importance of research along these lines. However, an earnest student of occultism will not be contented to stop his investigation at the point of manifestation of color and its effects; he will desire to know what lies still farther back of the zones of color and their apparent effects on the human race; and this brings me back to the opening paragraphs of this communication. The ability to determine these mysteries and satisfy his inner craving for knowledge lies in the student's power of understanding and remembering the correspondences — the language of symbolism, and by concentration and analytical research, to trace back the effects to their hidden causes; and it is not such a difficult thing to do as you might imagine. Take for instance the Red race. The earth's red plexus, that part of the earth more particularly dominated by the Red Ray, lies between the 30th and 40th degrees from the equator; that is the true home of all those people who spiritually belong to the Red Ray.

There are also many people in incarnation in the mixed races at the present time who belong to the Red Ray, but who are on the verge of changing into some other ray; for it must be remembered that at the beginning of each new Manvantara, the monads ready for incarnation come under the dominion of some other degree of life or Color Ray than that in which they had previously incarnated. Those now incarnated in the Red Ray will become a part of the Blue Ray in the next Manvantara, those now of the Blue Ray will become a part of the Red Ray unless they have passed through that phase of existence, in which case both they and the monads of the present Blue Ray will pass into the Violet at the beginning of the next Manvantara.

Unless you are willing to accept the fact that every Color Ray, as well as every other division of the Cosmos, is an embodied entity on some plane of existence, you will not be able to accept my statement that there is a corresponding plexus to that of the red color zone of the earth, in the entity we term the Red Ray — a cosmic plexus — represented by the planet Mars, as far as it is visible to the human vision, and also another similar plexus or rather, a form of energy which corresponds to a plexus, on each of the invisible planes. If you are able to perceive that in their totality all these various plexuses which manifest in each state and condition of matter, force, and consciousness are one single entity, it will not be difficult for you to perceive that there must inevitably be a very powerful force of attraction between the red color zone of the earth and the people of the Red race.

LESSON 51
THE SUICIDE OF THE SOUL

The veriest coward in the whole category of cowards may have the courage of conviction, and arise to defend his position when the exigencies of some important situation seem to demand such action; but it takes a hero of heroes quietly to accept a rebuke, frankly to acknowledge a wrong to those for whose good opinion he cares, then drop silently out of sight and go to work to set himself right. It is of such that the "Kingdom of Heaven" is made, and over whom the "Great Souls" yearn, and whom they draw to their own spheres as quickly as possible. The character of such courage as is displayed by the slayers of men, the intoxication of the arena of finance, or the battlefield of modern daily life yields no such power to man and gives no such results to the world.

Until a man can bravely confess a wrong and acknowledge a mistake, and as bravely accept the offered forgiveness or punishment therefore, without feeling that he has, in some inexplicable way, been wronged or degraded thereby, and that therefore he has just cause for the hatred he feels creeping into his heart for the one he has wronged, and by whom he has been forgiven, he is not worthy to unlatch the sandals of his whilom antagonist. His unworthiness does not lie in the wrong originally done; that is of little consequence, comparatively speaking (for it is not what we do that counts in the great sum; it is what we are — what we have become, as a result of our doing). The unworthiness lies in the fundamental cause of his attitude; for, back of that attitude, lies the hurt of his self-love. It is of no consequence to him at the moment that his antagonist may have been right and he wrong; the possible far-reaching results of his error seem hardly worth his consideration; the only thing that really matters to him is that cankering, corroding spot upon the armor of his self-love. So long as unselfishness is the keystone to the arch of human development, so long is such a man or such a woman debarred from the gates of true chelaship.

The earth is reeking with the blood of the victims of man's selfishness. Every Deva, every Savior, every true teacher that ever touched the sphere of man's consciousness has agonized over, pleaded with his hearers, in mercy to themselves, to kill out the demon of selfishness that was dragging them down to perdition. Closer and closer grows that demon's strangling grip in the present age; deeper and deeper into men's souls sink its poisonous fangs; louder and louder grow the cries of its victims, now piercing the heavens and demanding recompense. And, alas, swifter and swifter cometh that great day of retribution; and then will follow the era of readjustment, the day when just for one of the opportunities he has thrown away, a man would gladly surrender his earthly all.

Instead of becoming the living image of the great Ideal set up in his mind when the world was young, man has been sinking into a bondage worse by far than the meanest earthly slave has ever known. And you — O man, who cannot forgive the man you have wronged; and you — O woman, who have willfully torn apart the heart-strings of some other woman who has repelled your advances or outstripped you in some petty ambition, whom you hate because you fear, or who will not permit you to walk roughshod over the secret places of her soul — be not deceived, it is not the man or the woman that you hate; it is God! And you are building the fires that will consume the stubble of your lives; you are digging the pits into which your own feet will walk, for you "know what you do." You can no longer cover the nakedness of your own cruelty or your unworthy desires or ambitions with the cloak of unconsciousness.

The very heavens tremble with the force of the woeful anguish of those who have suffered, who now suffer for striving to force the one irrevocable truth upon the mirror of your minds. You hear or read of such martyrdoms, discuss the main points of the sad stories, the grammatical construction of the sentences in which they are clothed, then cast all behind you, and continue to live as though you had never heard of them. The lines that Time is graving around your eyes and mouths indicate the truth to the most careless observer; the hard, cruel spark in the depths of your eyes; the constantly clutching fingers; the restlessness of body; all tell the same story.

While knowing full well the illimitable power of thought, the strength of personal influence, you say, "Why should I make special effort to gain the attribute of unselfishness, when I am surrounded by such evidences of rank selfishness in others?" Alas, you do not see that man has come to the parting of two ways, the highest point of the arc of development for the brute creation. The acme of selfishness has now been reached, and man must go back to his old brutish instincts and habits, or he must cross the bridge which separates the animal from the human kingdom; for as yet, man has not reached the perfect human stage of development, save in very rare instances; and the stones of which that bridge is built are stones of sacrifice, stones of unselfish efforts, across which you may not pass until you have made of your own self yet another stone, which will give footing to some other pilgrim.

No man can take that journey into the Human Kingdom, can pass over that bridge, and ever return to old conditions, the same man. The change that comes over his life is like unto the change that succeeds the passing over the longer bridge of death, when man comes face to face with his own soul. The notes of the Song of Life to which you listen, as the wind sings through the branches of a forest of oak trees, are not like unto the low tones which reach your ears from great stretches of prairie grass; yet the song is the same. But the tones of the same song in your heart at the close of some unselfish act bear little semblance to the hoarse, croaking sounds which issue from the same heart at the close of a selfish act.

You imagine selfishness may be something like a mode of motion, a vague quality, a non-materialistic, non-scientific something, that will pass out into space with the laying away of the physical body. You do not realize that the form of energy we term selfishness, for want of some more comprehensive term, is the antithesis of the Infinite Selflessness, the True Self. Where one gives all, the other *takes all*; and in the taking, draws together and coalesces all the evil elementary forces of the negative pole of life, and kills out, strangles to death, every other living thing in its embrace. The suicide of the body is a small thing in comparison to the suicide of the soul; and continued selfishness is, beyond all question, the suicide of the soul. Knowing this, what wonder that countless brave, unselfish souls have made the great renunciation, have sacrificed sentient life, in their efforts to teach man the superlatively great lesson of unselfishness.

LESSON 52
ASTRAL WRECKAGE

To those who believe they have discovered the mysteries of the universe, those for whom life holds no problems, who have defined the bounds of all matter, force and consciousness to their own individual satisfaction; those who have burned up, by self-indulgence and inhumanity, the vital Ether which flows through the extremity of each nerve of sensation, to reappear — minus its enveloping media — in corresponding etheric vehicles of sensory impulses in the astral bodies of normally developed human beings; for those I have no word; but for the illuminated, for those touched with the divine afflatus of knowledge, and for the humble seekers after the keys to the mysteries which confront them on every side of life — for these I will try again, and yet again, to unfold some of the leaves of the great folio of existence. No one of those leaves contains more of deep interest, of profound truth, than that leaf on which is writ the records of the disastrous action of certain ethereal embodied forces resident on the Kama-Rupic[1] plane, upon the mentality of incarnate man. Especially is this true in regard to those injudicious, contemptuous disclaimers of the reality of psychic phenomena, and of the willful, disobedient disciples of the primary degrees of occultism, who either flout or disobey the urgent warnings of the Initiates of the White Lodge against indulging in forbidden practices of black magic such as spiritualistic séances, necromancy, ceremonial magic, etc.

At present, as in past corresponding periods of earlier civilizations, there has arisen a class of adventurers who have brought and are still bringing, some of the aspects of the Wisdom Religion into disrepute by means of the so-called investigations of its devotees, and their careless dabbling with the mysteries of Nature, which they are wholly incapable of apprehending, or, if mentally capable of understanding, are too gross and licentious to be able to make the spiritual and mental correlations which alone could give them the right key to

---

[1] *Kama-Rupa* (*Sanskrit*, "body of desires") — the lower desire body, a form that survives the death of the physical body; a shell from which the real soul has departed. A spook, capable of being drawn into observation by the mediums, and, once having learned the way, it returns again and again, vampirizing the body of the medium. The *Kama-Rupic plane* — the Astral World, the Fourth Plane of Existence.

the Mysteries. So they are breaking into forbidden places and dragging into view the decaying skeletons, the refuse and garbage of Nature's laboratories, and palming them off on selfish, inquisitive abettors as true revelations of spiritual life and power.

Every *exposé*,[2] every effort to hale such individuals before the judgment bar of common law, every shattering of the cup of the wine of life, the blasting of intellect, the results of disobedience to divine law, bring to a certain class of worldly people but one more object for satirical criticism and vapid ridicule. The awful tragedy which lies behind every such manifestation, does not occur to the minds of such as these, a tragedy in which they are more intimately concerned than they have any idea of, and which, if they were capable of apprehending, would make them shudder with horror. For all these outrages upon divine law are due primarily to their thoughtless encouragement and their self-indulgence, their support of those who in the initial stage of this craze, perpetrated these crimes against the Holy Spirit.

For the purpose of spending an idle hour in some exciting pastime, of delving into hidden things to obtain a point for a horse race, the indulgence of a lecherous desire, a certain tip in stock gambling — the services of fortune tellers, spiritualists, hypnotists, and other shells of what were once human souls, have been called into requisition both in private and in public, thereby degrading and corrupting the minds of weaker souls that were making a hard fight to keep their footing in the world of things, and earn a livelihood for themselves and those dependent on them. What wonder is it that they took advantage of a seemingly easy way to do so, by using their half-developed psychic power, when the example of those they had been taught to emulate was before them; not realizing that when they were caught at their thinly disguised efforts to prey on their fellow creatures, they in turn would become objects of scorn, contempt, and ridicule to those who were in reality responsible for their downfall. Great is the sin of both; as great in comparison will be the punishment of both. A little earnest study of the principles of the Wisdom Religion — white magic — would put all parties mentioned in the above category in a position to determine rightly the cause as well as the effect, of such catastrophes, and awaken tender sympathy in hearts that are not seared by self-indulgence.

---

[2] An exposure of something discreditable.

No human being can jump from one extreme of life to another. It takes a long period of time and the action of great psychic and mental forces, to change a saint into a sinner, and vice versa. Every psychic sensitive[1] could tell you that in the beginning of his or her mediumistic career, their hearts were filled with holy desires and images of love, beneficence and helpfulness toward all the human race; and tell you so truthfully; for the very power with which they were gifted — or cursed — has been won as a result of aspiration and effort along right lines.

The orthodox ideas of heaven and hell are responsible for the downfall of many sensitives. Their minds have been saturated with the belief that any state of life that produced or reproduced those things toward which their mortal instinct turned in longing — the gratification of sensual desires and lusts — must of necessity belong to heaven, and all they abhorred or feared, to hell. It did not enter their minds that there might be intermediate planes of life in which were pictured the primary forms of what were or would be earthly pleasures and indulgences of the senses; pictures instinct with vitality; embodied forms, existent only as irresponsible forces, and only so long as their inherent energy lasted, but as long as that energy remained, subject to the demand and call of those whose will could control their movements, and when that individual will had been satisfied, and its energy withdrawn, were then left drifting about in astral space, often using the mind sphere of incarnate man as mere pleasure grounds. These students might also learn of the existence of countless numbers of human wrecks, driven out of life by suicide, murder, and violent death, enraged at their futile attempts to gratify personal desire, entirely dependent upon incarnate sensitives for the gratification of the same; whispering, always whispering, into the ear of some weak one, "Do this, and power and wealth will be yours." "Do that, and the kingdoms of the whole earth shall be yours." The same old, yet ever new, story. And finally, such students would learn how subtly, how persistently, those poor wretched victims had been tempted and driven into doing, at last, the deeds their very souls abhorred in the early days of their psychic development.

How can there be aught but pity in the hearts of the truly great, the good, for such a human wreck as I have mentioned?

[1] *Sensitive* — a person who has psychical or paranormal abilities. The term was introduced by Carl Ludwig von Reichenbach (1788–1869).

How can there be anything but compassion and profound pity in the hearts of "those who know" for all concerned, for the tempter and tempted, for all victims of the greatest of all tragedies? Ah, ye know not what ye do, blind leaders of the blind, willfully ignorant administrators of human law. May infinite mercy cover you all as with the wings of a great eagle.

LESSON 53
THE EVOLUTION OF WILL

The acceptance of Truth by the multitude, however long delayed, and grudgingly admitted or disguised by its exponents, can but be a matter of deep interest to those guardians of its treasures whose primary efforts to give it expression date back many centuries, and who, unlike modern exponents and seeming discoverers, seek neither recognition nor reward for their labor. I say seeming discoverers, advisedly, for no truth has ever been discovered by man; a truth discovers, or rather uncovers itself to the earnest, unselfish seeker in its particular field. It is always with us, always here, has always been here. The film of matter falls from the mental eye of man when he is prepared to receive a truth as a result of the action of the inherent power of that truth upon "the film" which has hitherto inhibited his power of observation. At no time in past ages has the verity of the above statement been more apparent than at present.

Converts to the Wisdom Religion in past ages have symbolized and illustrated the facts in regard to the constitution of matter, in psalm, prose, and poetry. These have been repeated or read widely, and while often derided or ignored by the many, have been accepted and acted upon by the few.

When the White Lodge gave *The Secret Doctrine* to the world, it gathered up and combined in one invaluable work all that the world has ever known, all it ever will know, in the present Manvantara, of the primal causes, the fundamental principles, of all the degrees of matter mankind as it is now constituted is capable of cognizing. This is a very sweeping statement, but it is nevertheless true, as may be understood by any profound student of *The Secret Doctrine*. But these great truths could not be uncovered to the masses before a corresponding condition of advancement to that attained by man, had been reached by all the degrees of substance — matter — with which those masses are identified. It has probably not been observed by many that there is any special connection between the recent revolution in the flower, fruit, and grain industries as a result of the wonderful crossing of life currents, and the notably rapid evolution of the mental and psychic power in man. Nevertheless, there is far more than a mere connection. The operation of the same law, carried out by the same orders of life and accomplished during the same period of time, is responsible for both classes of development.

A number of gifted intellects, Great Souls, are now in incarnation, through whom the Lodge is working to bring about these changes in the vegetable and human kingdoms. The particular group of souls of which I speak came into incarnation between fifty and seventy-five years ago. Their individual efforts will cease inside of the next twenty-five years, during which time the culmination of their work will appear in a new sub-race[1] of both the human and vegetable King-doms. All that I have said here is equally true of the other divisions of manifested life, but it would take more time and effort than I can now give, to enter upon those subjects to any extent; they must be left for another time.

Man *en masse* is coming into another aspect of his heritage; and it is an aspect that will place upon him a tremendous responsibility for the right use of the riches of Wisdom he has inherited as a result of ages of work and sacrifice. Invention after invention is placing within the power of man the means by which he may investigate the hidden causes of evident effects. In no field is this more evident than in the interaction, the movements, the marriage — of the fiery lives. While research has demonstrated the atomic constitution of all matter, and therefore of fire, it has not yet demonstrated the atomic constitution of consciousness — a higher fire — and its inseparableness from all matter. Every *laya*[2] center, every atom, is a self-conscious life, a com-ponent part of a more complex, more perfect life; as much greater than itself from an interior point of view, as a camel is greater than a gnat from an exterior point of view; and yet the ultimate of the expansion

---

[1] *Sub-race* — a division of a Race. Each Root Race has seven sub-races.

[2] *Laya* (*Sanskrit*, "dissolution") — the state of matter in the undifferentiated con-dition; a zero point from which the primordial substance begins to differentiate into all elements and thus gives birth to the Universe and all in it on each plane and sub-plane of Existence.

of matter is not yet reached, and in reality lies so far beyond the immediate future as to be impossible of computation in terms of time.

It is conceivable that man might determine, approximately, by mechanical means, the amount of energy possible of generation by the waves of the Pacific Ocean, but he could not measure by any method, or by any means, the enormous energy stored up in an atomic center, a single fiery life. If you can accept this statement, you may be able to gain some concept of the tremendous possibilities of growth.

As the fiery life center partakes of the nature of positive electricity, in excess of negative, so its first embodiment, the oily sheath, partakes more of the nature of negative electricity in excess of positive; otherwise the substance of which that oily sheath is composed could not be impelled from one plane of life into another. It is the temporary destruction of equilibrium that forces substance into manifestation by changing its character, and its manifestation in form commences in an intermediate state between the physical and the astral plane.

It does not seem to occur to the average investigator along these lines, that the difference between human and terrestrial electricity lies in the fact that the fiery lives of the latter are devoid of the oily sheaths which differentiate them from the former. They are not so fully evolved, and will not develop those protective shields until associated with others in a more complex organism, a living organic body. The human Will must force its passage through these protective sheaths before it can control the fiery lives within them, and thereby the individual will of men. With Divine Will, it is otherwise: To the latter, all things, all lives, become subservient, and until human Will renounces its slavery to self and becomes identified with the Divine Will, it has no power to break through those oily sheaths. Experiment would seem to contradict what I have said; but, in cases of hypnosis, whether or not the operator is aware of it, there has been such a temporary union, and one of the great dangers of hypnosis lies in the fact that such union is not permanent, and the rapid changes from one condition to another produce effects that are greater than the vital ether operative in the nerves can endure, without breaking down the brain cells through which it must operate. It is during the attempt to pierce the oily sheath of the fiery lives, by over-strenuous efforts in concentration, that human mentality often succumbs. The brain cells break down, and the would-be divine operator is left to the mercy of irresponsible forces whose precincts have been ignorantly invaded, and disease or insanity results.

Little by little these great truths are being unveiled, but so long as an investigator confines his research to any one field of research to the exclusion of all others, he is doomed to failure.

LESSON 54
KARMA – ACTION AND REACTION

Throw a stone into a quiet pool of water; a sound into the silent ocean of Ether; an idea into the quiescent mind of man, and you disturb the equilibrated condition of a definite field or sphere of substance, which will result in setting wave after wave in motion in ever increasing circles that will not break until they have struck the circumference of that measurable sphere. Having reached that boundary, the energy which guided those waves will at once return to the center from which they were impelled.

In relation to the idea thrown into the mind of man, the afterthoughts which come trooping into that individual mind on the return waves of Manas are the distorted reflections of the original idea; sometimes these images are unrecognizable by the thinker for the reason that he has not fully grasped the potentialities of the idea when it first presented itself.

The return waves of the sound sent forth into the ether bear back corresponding images, broken geometrical forms, inharmonious or minor chords, as it were, unrecognizable by the maker of the sound, because he knew so little of the action of the energy he released.

Every act, good or bad, perpetrated by man produces a correspondingly great result, as its released energy pours out and into the ocean of Prana — life force. And as the image of an object or individual at the center of operations reflects a certain distorted image of itself on every wave of the startled pool, so a certain reflection of itself is cast on the waves of Prana, within a certain radius, by every act of man. These reflections may seem to bear no resemblance to the central object or individual, but to the wise man, the seer, they are unmistakable evidences of their primal cause and final result.

If you could read the reflections of a good deed aright they would take you through many and devious paths — through many peoples and nations, back to the doer of that deed, as surely as tomorrow's sun will rise to your view. You cannot lift a finger, give birth to a single idea or utter a sound, without disturbing the equilibrium of a world — and, to some extent, a universe; and the crest of the thus awakened wave will as surely bring back to you the reward or punishment for the act.

This law is back of the tracing of all crime. Invariably the criminal leaves reflections of himself, of his act, in some form, upon every retreating footstep, in every following act. It is only because the human sleuth is not wise enough to read the signs that a criminal has left behind him, that the latter ever escapes his pursuers.

You may give a coin to a needy man; and mayhap may never connect that gift with the offer of the highest gift in the power of a nation; but if the motive power that actuated the gift was high enough, and if the recipient accepted it with as high a purpose in view, and put it to as high a use, the triune energy thus generated would break forth into waves upon which the images of the good effects of that act would be imprinted and the return waves would inevitably bring back to you the value of your gift increased by seventy times seven.

But remember — it will be according to the height of the motive, purpose, and use, how great a circle will be inscribed by the released energy and how great a height the waves will reach and, therefore, how great an accumulation of indebtedness will be repaid to you.

LESSON 55
THE SYMBOL OF THE SERPENT

Men have tried to fathom the underlying mystery of the antagonism between man and the creeping things of life, the little worm, the harmless and often helpful diminutive snake, that has unwittingly crept upon the naked flesh. Other creatures may cause fear in man; he may shrink back terror-stricken from a bear or tiger; he may dislike, distrust, or be perfectly indifferent to many other animals, and if by any chance they should touch his flesh he is conscious of no such intense repugnance as he feels from physical contact with any creeping thing. There is a deep, far-reaching reason for this feeling, as deep and wide as the two extremities of his being, life and death; and the beginning of this antipathy dates back to the beginning of his life as a conscious human being. When Jehovah said there should be enmity between the seed of the woman and the seed of the serpent,[1] a great truth was uttered, and war was then again declared between white and black magic, for one Manvantara.

In one sense, all creeping things are included in the one word, "serpent." From an esoteric aspect, the Serpent symbolizes the highest point of the development of a human being. From the exoteric aspect it symbolizes the lowest point in the same development.

Here, as in all other divisions of the Cosmos, appears the action of the two poles of manifestation. The farther man advances, the greater will grow his antipathy to creeping, slimy, secretive, hiding things, because the gulf between his higher and lower nature is continually widening, and up to the point when he parts forever with that lower self by gaining all power over it, the fascination, the temptation of the lower self continually increases and the battle grows stronger.

When "the heel of the woman shall crush the serpent's head," i.e., when the negative aspect of the eternally feminine, the Soul, shall come into contact with the positive, the head — lower mind — the masculine aspect of matter, one of the twain must disappear, and it is the latter that must disappear, because when such an event occurs the end of a Manvantara will have come, and Soul and Mind become one.

The creeping of a worm or snake over human flesh does not occasion any particular fear in the human mind; as said before, it is a far different feeling, a quick, convulsive shudder, due to the action of the force of repulsion which manifests immediately and results in the creature's being thrown violently from its resting place. This action of the force of repulsion is but a slight exhibition of the same force that is generated in, and expelled from "the heel of the woman" as a result of the interaction of the forces of attraction and cohesion. The action of the vital ether operative in the nerves of the skin is instantly increased by contact with such a creature, and upon communicating a desire to the brain to be rid of the obnoxious thing, the brain commands the muscles of hand and arm to remove the interloper, and the command is obeyed.

There is an occasional "exception to prove the rule" in the cases of men and women who seem abnormally fond of snakes. These persons fondle and caress such creatures and exhibit their power of control, to the great wonder of beholders; but when this feeling of attraction

---

[1] Genesis 3:15.

is genuine, it is due to one of two causes; either custom has so famil-iarized the person by constant contact with snakes that natural antag-onism has been overcome, and the force symbolized by the woman's heel has been developed in the performer's body far in excess of the force symbolized by the "head of the serpent," even to such a degree that the vital ether no longer responds to excitation by touch; or the person has come directly under the control of some black magician, thereby changing his whole nature and making him amenable to the control of those who govern the division of life to which the creeping things belong, corresponding in planes to the lower astral. The Serpent (personified evil, according to the orthodox concept, the Tempter) has been greatly misunderstood. It is a most perfect symbol of the two extremes of life. In the highest sense it represents the Guardian of the Threshold, and the appellation "Serpents" has been applied to Initiates of high degree for many ages, whose office it is to test in all ways the applicant for admission to any degree of the Lodge. If said applicant fails in passing the test, the power responsible for the trial in which he has failed will naturally seem to be evil. Especially is this true if the disciple has not reached a stage of development that will permit his seeing the justice and mercy back of the trial. The powers of silence, wisdom, retirement, casting of skin, or power of assuming different forms are some of the powers that the serpent holds in common with the Initiate, and indicate why it symbolizes the highest pole of being. Its confinement to the lower levels of life — slyness, concealed poison, treachery, etc. — symbolize the habits and characteristics of a like nature associated with the black magician. Therefore, "the serpent" is a fitting symbol for both extremes of life.

LESSON 56
CREATION IN UNITY AND TRINITY

I plead for, and teach you the importance of unified action, only to find that in many cases you have little or no comprehension of the basic principles involved, and therefore, little appreciation of the effects of unified action on all lines of endeavor, on your own inte-rior as well as exterior development. Those who have attained to a moderate degree of knowledge on this subject may not find anything of particular value in the following resume of the facts concerning Evolution; but to those who hitherto have been unable to secure the advantages to be derived from conscientious application to study, I hope to convey a more lucid, concise idea of the action of the laws of Evolution and Involution, with the aid of their own intuition.

First, consider all space as formed of countless billions of infinitesimal lives of varying degrees of potentiality, number, and form, but for the time being in a dormant, quiescent state, each degree of which must be given an evolutionary impulse at the commencement of a great world period in order to complete the development of its constituent lives, by expanding and exploding the confined dormant energy which is the basis of those lives, thereby bursting through the compressing, enveloping Aura of Ethereal Force (which is the bridge between two states of consciousness), thus being impelled from the inner to the outer fields of Space.

Among these degrees of dormant elemental forces are those commonly recognized as Light, Heat, Electricity, and Magnetism, always the first to manifest in any great world period. Then consider that potential space *in toto*[1] as a single, self-conscious Entity with almost unlimited power, intelligence, and ability, who at the beginning of the present world period is actuated by one great impulse (desire) to manifest such power and by one long-drawn breath — "one motion of Mass," awakes the many and various rates of motion and vibration of its own constituent lives or atoms — the different degrees of the laya centers which persist from one Manvantara to another; that impulse being given by means of the power of Fohat, potential Sound, the compelling power of the Cosmos, in itself a power subject only to a higher law — namely, the law of Gravitation; which great mystery is in reality a spiritual power, the manifesting aspects of which are the forces (the Gods) — Attraction, Repulsion, Cohesion, Expansion, Extension, and Suction. These six aspects or modifications of Gravitation create, control, and disintegrate (involve and evolve) all forms of force and energy in manifestation in the exterior fields of Space and Matter. Then imagine that whole potential Space or Entity breaking forth into waves and ripples of sound, as each laya center of the Mass responds to the call thus made, giving forth its own particular keynote and sustaining the vibrations or keynotes of such sound waves for a definite period of time, thereby keeping each individual degree of the evolving laya centers at a certain rate of mass motion, and by the

---

[1] As a whole.

energy thus generated forming a definite sphere of influence — an orbit — the size of that orbit being determined by the volume and strength of force generated at the instant of explosion. The grouping of individual centers of such degrees of laya — or atomic — centers into different forms, weight, and density is brought about by the action of the law of affinity (one aspect of the force of attraction) according to number; and first, Fire (Flame), then Water, Air, and Earth are evolved, and by the same process of expansion and explosion; and finally, mineral, vegetable, and animal germs of life are brought into manifestation. The most rapid vibrations evolve Fire, the atomic centers of which are first drawn together in outer manifestation as suns, shining from their own intrinsic light, and lightening the dark spaces within each individual aura, where the brooding negative side of the life principle is drawing together and nesting the laya centers which will eventually manifest as Water.

As all laya centers must explode to manifest, so the fiery centers which constitute the mass of such suns must explode in course of time, and the then flaming fragments or lives which fall into space become centers of attraction for other wandering lesser lives which are combined with and assimilated by the greater. The waters held in suspension in space are attracted by the heat waves generated by the flames, and fall upon the burning masses, thus causing, by further explosion, the freeing of confined potential gases. These gases penetrate and interpenetrate the flaming masses and surround them with cushions of air. From the intermarriage of Fire, Water, and Air, and the explosions which result therefrom, there is precipitated a sediment which we term the element of Earth, and by the intermarriage of these four elements, and by like process of expansion and explosion of the lives which comprise said elements, and under the same laws which guided and controlled the action of the first sound waves, there is evolved the substance which science terms protoplasm, from which all living forms are created.

If convinced that all matter has evolved from within outward, the average person will have little difficulty in accepting my explanation and formulating to his own personal satisfaction some concept of the subsequent action of the Substance alluded to.

With the manifestation of said Substance, No-thing has become All-things in embryo. Spirit and Matter have met. But at the completion of one-half a great world period, man, by that time evolved to his highest point of development as man, must re-become God, and in the process of re-becoming is but too prone to forget his Divine prototype; forget that he is but an atom of the substance of God, and by falling in love with his own personal image and permitting that image to absorb his care and worship, he forgets his Father's face and his Mother's beauty and grace. Like a ship in a storm he permits himself to be drifted hither and yon, until as a result of long suffering he finally opens his inner eye, to behold the life line thrown out to him. That line is thrown by the Higher Self when Substance-Matter has reached its ultimate vibration as Matter; at which time, but for the incarnation of higher mind (Spiritual Egos in bodies created as before described) Matter, at first only endowed with lower mind (instinct), could not sustain itself at such rapid rates of vibration, and would return to its primeval conditionless state, and mankind as we know it could not exist.

As two points of a triangle may be forced to meet, pass each other to a given distance and form a six-pointed star, so Spirit and Matter meet and unite in man, both separate and distinct, yet one entity, thus giving the spirit the vehicle it requires for manifesting in Matter and gaining all knowledge of its possibilities in form. When Matter has reached its highest possible rate of vibration in humanity, the processes and laws of evolution are reversed. There is a gradual reversal of the two poles of universal life, and there follows a like period of involution, lasting during the other half of the great world cycle. The first and last requisite of involution is the gradual decrease and subsidence of the energy of the vibratory keynote or rate of mass motion that has been the fundamental and sustaining power of evolution; in other words, the regaining of the potent power of Silence; the conservation and concentration of all forms of Energy preparatory to the sounding of another, a higher keynote for a new age; for evolutionary forces always work in a spiral instead of a closed circle.

The more highly developed units of the present races have reached a degree of knowledge where it has become possible to lay the foundation for the attainment of such power. The ultimate causes and effects of evolution are becoming apparent; and all their efforts toward self-development should be along the lines of condensation, conservation, and concentration. This is where the importance of individual self-denial — altruism — becomes more evident. No finding of science pointing to this necessity is of more importance. Altruism is not a sentimental virtue; it is an absolute requisite to self-development.

Whenever any group of three or more individuals has reached a point of harmonious action on all lines of their lives, a point where perfect cooperation of will and effort obtains — a point where in fact, as well as in theory, they can live and act up to their highest ideals of use and service to and for each other — they have reached a condition where it is possible for them to become an active vehicle for the spiritual forces generated by much greater beings than they have ever before been conscious of; and by becoming such a vehicle the individual evolution of each constituent part of that vehicle is carried forward by great strides. As previously illustrated, the points of two Triangles, Spirit and Matter, have met and intertwined. Each such individual becomes in process of time a Savior of all those who are still beneath him in the scale of evolution. The path to the Gods opens wide, and instead of the slow, painful, crawling mode of procedure he has hitherto been compelled to use, he goes onward and upward as though shod with seven-league boots, for he is "coming into his own," and is gaining command over the secret powers of a universe. Every effort you consciously put forth toward the attainment of such a trinity of life and action as I have indicated, takes you a step further toward that most desirable end. Every failure to utilize an opportunity for so doing, plunges you back a like distance.

Knowing the truth and verity of each statement made herein; knowing that my own as well as your individual evolution all depends upon your acceptance of and obedience to the laws designated by me, is it surprising that I iterate and reiterate my pleas to you to listen and obey? For in no other way, by no other method or plan, can man hasten his evolutionary career.

LESSON 57
INITIATION

Much has been written by the uninitiated concerning the Initiates and the Greater Mysteries, of which the writers are entirely ignorant. Naught but spiritual blindness could excuse one of ordinary intelligence for failing to perceive the absurdity of placing any credence in such palpably contradictory statements as are handed out for the mental delectation of the curious. Notwithstanding the fact that it is claimed in one paragraph that an Initiate must be an epitome of all Truth, Wisdom, Faithfulness, and Power, perhaps the following paragraph will picture that Initiate as imparting to all who may desire it, regardless of their good or evil proclivities or their unbelief or intellectual development, a description of some initiatory ceremony — or an offer to lead for mere pelf, whosoever will comply with their demands, to the heights of Initiation. Until man has evinced the possibility of keeping his body free from sins of voluptuousness, his mind free from hatred for his kind, his soul capable of faithfulness to his Higher Self, he might with just as much surety of fulfillment expect the sun to be given him for a pleasure boat. Countless half-imbeciles ponder over such trash, hand over their hard-won means of livelihood, and follow the trail made by innumerable others as foolish and reckless as themselves, utterly ignoring the still small voice that is calling to them to stop and think of the great gulf that must inevitably exist between them as they now are, and one who has reached a height so immeasurably far above them that they could get only a faint glimmering of the possibilities of such an eminence if they were to stretch their imaginations to the breaking point; and then to consider what probability could possibly exist that a voluptuary, a traitor, a liar, or a blasphemer would be able to guide their footsteps through the mazes of the evolutionary stages which must be passed ere that height could be reached. Ah, my children, do not deceive yourselves or permit others to deceive you; be honest with your own souls; face the fact that notwithstanding your divine possibilities, you are full of weaknesses and evil desires, even if you do not outwardly yield to such desires; that you still wear the filthy garment you have been long ages in weaving about you; and be brave enough to acknowledge the truth to yourselves, humble enough to perceive your unworthiness, and great enough to commence the preparation of the groundwork upon which you hope to build the edifice, the upper story of which will reach the heavens.

No intelligent person will criticize unfavorably your desire or your longing to reach such heights as you may be able mentally to contemplate, for such contemplation is not only a rainbow of promise, but also an assurance of the certainty of attainment.

No group of disciples of the White Lodge was ever admitted to probation to a higher degree of the Lodge at one time. Alone man came into the world, alone he must leave it, whether it be by the path of death or Initiation, and the same great power that presided over his birth must preside over his Initiation, whether such Initiation be brought about by the power and effect of the Hierophant of the degree he has reached, or by the chela's coming face to face with his own soul on those heights of which I have spoken. Be assured, for I tell you true — you may be led to the foot of the steps of the great Initiation Stair by one empowered and fitted for such leading, but when you have reached that Stair you must pass the Guardian of the Threshold alone, and if it were possible for you to pass it while yet encumbered with your weaknesses, while yet enfolded in the ragged filthy garment you clutch so greedily now, the Stair would give way under your weight, and you would be plunged to the depths of Hades[1] (in some of the courts of which you are now existing, all unknown to your lower selves). My heart yearns over you with love past telling. I stretch out my arms to you in beseeching while I bid you set about making that groundwork now. Make it possible for yourselves to reach Adonai's[2] feet by passing successfully through the primary degrees.

A form or ceremony is but an expression in matter of the reality in spirit, and unless you have attained to the reality, the form will profit you nothing. If any man had power to whisper in your ear the great Creative Word, the word which would make you more than man, you could not hear and understand that Word while a trace of that which had hitherto deafened your ears and stultified your understanding remained. It is not words or forms you require so much, but thoughts embodied in deeds that will unite you to the source of all power, and make it possible for you to keep the obligations assumed in such outer ceremonies.

LESSON 58
THE SUBSTANCE OF GOD

Of all the fallacies ever conceived and propagated by man, there is no more dangerous an emasculated truth than that which has been seized and applied to one of the basic principles of occultism and thrown broadcast in the name of the Masters, by many unenlightened, self-styled teachers of Divine Truth. This fallacy is all the more deadly in its results in that it apparently expresses a generally

---

[1] *Hades* — the Greek god of the underworld, and the underworld itself; a hell.
[2] *Adonai* (*Hebrew*, "my Lord") — one of the names of God in Judaism.

accepted Cosmic law, the law of opposites, and accentuates a universally recognized necessity; namely, the bringing of the lower self under subjection.

Love and hate are two poles of one universal law; but love, in the common acceptation of the term, and as bestowed or received by the units of the great mass of humanity upon the material planes, partakes more of the nature of the lower pole, hate, than the higher pole, Love. It is often cruel, selfish, inhumane, and bears but little semblance to the greater Love, as interpreted by the Initiates.

The Initiate Paul's interpretation of the word charity more perfectly describes the manifestation of the higher pole than any other writer on that theme, but even his interpretation is deficient, in that no special reference is made to the essence of Love, the law of Attraction, and the various degrees of love which are different rates of vibration of that one essence.

It is not my object to dilate upon the scientific or universal aspects or action of that Cosmic Law at this time, but to endeavor to explode the false ideas put forth by imitators of the Initiates, who have never understood the veiled directions given by the latter to their disciples touching upon the qualifications for chelaship, and consequently have travestied or misinterpreted the same, to the great injury of those who trust to their guidance, and in no instance more destructively than in the directions given for the killing out of their love natures.

To my knowledge there are many groups of sincere, intelligent students now under the direction of such incompetent teachers, that are bending every effort toward the killing out in themselves of the power and ability to love, thereby stultifying their own higher natures and atrophying the very organic centers through which the highest aspect of the law of Attraction must necessarily operate in order to reach and connect the spiritual and material planes, and so further the evolution of man; in other words, they are destroying the bridge over which the Ego must pass and repass from the Higher to the lower self, thus leaving the lower self to the doubtful mercy of the lower psychic elementals which, in revenge for the repression of bodily functions which furnish gratification to such elementals, eventually unite and bring to bear an accumulation of force upon the unprotected lower self which plunges it into a very maelstrom of passion and self-gratification.

Even the lowest vibration of the law of Attraction-Passion, when purely natural, has a certain office to perform in the evolution of the man or woman who has not passed beyond the primary classes of life and attained perfect control over all the organic centers of the body; but, having passed through those classes, he may not return to lower levels without endangering his whole career.

In whatever Cosmic degree of life man may be functioning for the time being, some aspect or vibration of the law of Attraction must be his guiding star to the next higher degree, whether it be love of God, Nature, or individual, until he has reached the degree where all personal love is swallowed up in universal love — until love is, so to speak, unclothed, and becomes the pure force of Attraction, when it in turn reincarnates in every living thing during the next period of manifestation. The great sin, the bar to development, lies in the misuse, the abuse of the Omnipotent, Omnipresent God, for God it is, and I say to you now that he who uses the power attained over some other human being as a result of the abuse of any aspect of Love, draws upon himself the corresponding action of Karmic law to such a degree as to chill him with apprehension could he behold its coming; and unfortunately, such an one attains to such power only too easily. One of the characteristics of love is humility; one who loves truly is always filled with the idea of his own unworthiness in comparison with the presumed worthiness of the ideal in mind, and this places him at a disadvantage; his seeming unworthiness of such a high gift as he believes reciprocated love to be, tends to foster the idea that nothing he possesses is too good to be freely bestowed upon the loved one, however the gift may be, in reality, despised or misused, and according to the purity, strength, and unselfishness of the love thus freely given, is the power increased for its abuse and misuse by the unprincipled man or woman; while at the same time the spiritual power and possessions gained by the giver through such misuse of the gift, are increased tenfold. His unselfish love leads him to a height which brings him into the communion of saints. He has not much farther to travel up the steep path of life ere he finds his reward in the change from personal to universal love and life, if he has held firmly to his ideal; for the fallen idol has served as a step for him to climb to a higher level where dwells his true Ideal.

If mankind could only remember that the Substance of God is the Substance of Love, it would not be deceived so easily by specious words. It is the greater, the unselfish love, which invariably gains life's compensations, though it may gain them only through the fire of renunciation. All the world may offer could not compensate for the loss of the power of loving, and when this truth is realized, some idea may be gained of the irreparable loss one must sustain who has by his own unceasing efforts toward self-development only succeeded in atrophying the centers through which the great Cosmic force of Attraction must flow, in order to connect him with God — the Higher Self, through which alone development may be gained.

LESSON 59
TRANSMUTATION

Notwithstanding the efforts of the Catholic clergy to clarify the doctrine of the transmutation, that is, the transmuting of bread and wine into the body and blood of the Master Jesus, the average layman experiences much difficulty in comprehending the process or accepting the fact of such a seeming miracle.

As the said doctrine is founded on the action of a great natural law, and Temple members are as deeply concerned in the effects of that law as any other body of people can possibly be, I will make some effort to enlighten them regarding the same and its resultant phenomena. The foundation of all occultism rests upon the principles of Desire, Motive, and Will; three forms of energy which in action become Light, Heat, and Flame — Father, Mother, Son — Creator, Destroyer, and Preserver.

To understand the higher aspect of any thing or condition, we must turn our attention to the lower aspect of the same, which for our present purpose must be the physical body, that being the negative aspect of the spiritual body — the Son — the Christ-body — the Preserver. That the physical body may be sustained and preserved, the inherent principle of desire moves the animal will to action, for the purpose (motive) of securing (eating) and assimilating, at regular appointed times, sufficient food to sustain the body for a definite period of time. This action of forces has become almost automatic in man. No sane man thinks he can deprive his body of food and continue to live. The fact that the soul of man requires nourishment no less than the body, and also requires it at stated intervals of time, and in sufficient quantities, is not always recognized or accepted, consequently in the majority of cases that nourishment is very inadequately and intermittently supplied, and the result of such neglect is to a close observer evident in the faces and forms of the people he meets. With the animal creation it is far otherwise, for unless deprived of food and drink by hard conditions, the so-called instinct (which man has lost) leads the animal to an unconscious use of the forces which correspond to desire, motive, and will in man, and the animal soul is almost automatically fed. In the case of man, if every meal were prefaced by a consciously expressed desire for soul sustenance, and while partaking of the food the mind were awakened to a higher motive than mere animal satisfaction of appetite, and also if a few moments of silent thanksgiving and appreciation were to conclude the meal, there would inevitably be the three forms of energy set in action, which in essence would furnish nourishment, digestion, and assimilation to the soul, and the nourishment furnished the body would then be blessed and therefore would create the most healthful conditions, owing to the establishment of a harmonious adjustment of forces. "Health is harmony."

Remember, it is not the gross food deposited in that wonderful receptacle, the stomach, that finally enters the blood stream to nourish and vitalize the body; that food is disintegrated, churned by the action of gastric juices until the fiery lives which animate the food are set free to enter the bloodstream, leaving their bodies (waste matter) to share the fate of all other outer forms and conditions of matter. Each of the shields of those fiery lives is related to a different plane or state of matter, some of them so fine in essence as to be under the sway and dominion of will and mind.

If Desire has aroused the Will to determine that a certain proportion and degree of the shields of these fiery lives shall nourish the soul, and Mind has furnished the dynamic force by compelling the lips to utter the sounds which will propel that essence in a certain direction, nothing can prevent its taking that definite course. Again, the same or similar forces are set in action by Desire, Will, and Mind in the thanksgiving which follows the meal, and the process of soul digestion and assimilation is then complete. Do not forget that the Ego is first of all responsible for the taking of the food in the interests of the physical body, and that It is just as deeply concerned in the feeding of soul. But I do not wish to imply that it is only in this way the soul is nourished, for truly it is said, "Man shall not live by bread alone, but by every word that proceedeth from the Father";[1] every such word is a Son of God, a living creature, for life alone can sustain life; and as there are no dead things, the soul may be nourished by all it contacts, if it is capable of seeking and finding such nourishment.

Taking the words, "Take no thought what ye shall eat,"[2] literally, instead of figuratively, as they were intended, the average orthodox believer makes no effort to awaken spiritual Desire, Will, and Mind, before, during, and after the taking of food, and consequently furnishes no food in a methodical cyclic manner to the soul, which must needs take its nourishment from the crumbs that fall from the rich — the perfected — man's table. But alas and alas, even those crumbs are too heavy for the mental digestion of the unprepared soul, and therefore that soul is too often compelled to sustain itself with the husks, the castaway refuse of the selfish, egotistical, self-indulgent, worldly individual who has thrown away priceless food because he had no soul to nourish and cared nothing for the souls of others. Ah, the infinite pity, the Cosmic woe of it all. The Wheel of the world is grinding out daily the meal that would nourish, invigorate, and revitalize millions of self-starved human souls, the crushed, half-grown, tortured, tempted, broken-willed souls — that are daily driven out of incarnation when there is manna in plenty and therefore Life for all.

If an individual recognizes the necessity for feeding his soul, determines upon a methodical, periodical way and time for so doing, obtains and uses the outer symbols of that food, arouses the energy in sound by a definite ceremony with words, he is literally "laying up treasure in heaven,"[3] helping to create an eternal structure in and through which the Ego may operate after his outer form has become dust and ashes.

Certain forms of food and liquid contain more in number and a better quality or degree of the fiery lives than others; among these are wheat, wine, and water. They are more easily disintegrated and assimilated; therefore the fiery lives are more expeditiously and thoroughly freed from bondage to coarser forms of matter, and more readily acted upon by the gastric juices.

What I have said may seem to indicate the degradation of a great spiritual ideal, but instead of encouraging you to belittle or degrade

---

[1] Matthew 4:4.

[2] Matthew 6:25.

[3] Matthew 6:20.

one ideal, I fain would help you to raise all ideals, as well as to see that natural law governs both spirit and matter.

No more holy function exists than that of supplying nourishment to the body; no more degrading process can be conceived than that of gorging the stomach for mere appetite's sake.

LESSON 60
IDEALS OF GOD

Whatever the status of man, slave or master, boor or exquisite, every normal human being has some ideal of God, though it be unrecognized, distorted, misunderstood, or derided. We may not be conscious of that ideal until some admirable quality or characteristic in ourselves or others suddenly arouses our respect or admiration, in which case we begin to look for the appearance of the same or others of like nature, and eventually we combine all we have noted, and therewith create the ideal which stands to us as an epitome of Power, Beauty, and Goodness; and that ideal is our first real consciousness of God.

From regard and appreciation there is gradually awakened either fear of, or love for, that ideal God, according to our power and ability to meet the demands made upon our obedience, or to our longing for some expression of the love which we feel is self-existent in that ideal. Other peoples have made their own Gods, which for some reason do not exactly partake of the nature of our Gods, and if they conflict with our Ideals, we at once begin to make comparisons, always in detraction of their Gods and in exaltation of our own. Some of the attributes of the Gods of the ancients would more fitly have clothed our ideal devils, and as fear dominated their religious instincts that fact is not surprising.

If unable to convince our fellow men of the superiority of our Gods by fair means and gentle arguments, some among our more belligerent brethren seem to think they may be able to torture, cheat, or shoot their ideas into the consciousness of their opponents.

Excessive egotism prevents many people from even trying to understand the ideals of others. They take it for granted that such ideal Gods must be poor objects, judging from the forms of worship offered them, and refuse to believe that the superstitions or halting speech of their worshipers can by any possibility build or represent a great Ideal of Supreme Power, Strength, and Wisdom that would be worth consideration; they utterly ignore the fact that the opportunities of said worshipers for gaining imaginative or descriptive power may have been fewer than our more cultivated races have secured, that were we able to interpret aright their crude representations we would find a similar ideal to the one we had formed ourselves. It is not always admiration for, and delight in, the sight and performance of such awful slaughter and extreme cruelty that we deplore in the religions of some nations and tribes signifying the demands and qualities of their Gods. Back of it all may be a great admiration for the superhuman power, endurance, strength, and ability they have credited to their Gods, and by means of which their enemies may be punished and their own safety assured. When admiration and worship of the nobler attributes and qualities are changed into delight in and performance of willful cruelty, the devils have stolen the livery of God and are using it for the benefit of the dark side of life.

If we could accept the fact that every noble, true, and good quality, attribute, or object we are capable of perceiving, is in deed and in truth a part of God, it would assist us in forming a right concept of Divinity.

Some of our fellow men are incapable of forming and holding a mental ideal which gives them personally any satisfaction, without the use of a material object; and beyond all doubt, in the beginning idolatry was the result of the efforts of more enlightened men to convey ideas of great cosmic forces in such familiar forms as would fix the attention of the less enlightened. As man became more selfish, and the desire to dominate and rule over the less intelligent masses increased, what was originally a pure desire to teach somewhat of the action of the cosmic forces, degenerated into desire to rule by fear, and so the darker, the negative aspect of Nature was represented by horrible idols, and the spiritual devotion just awakening in the ignorant was purposely turned into idolatry; and worship of the created thing, instead of the Creator of all things, was established.

In past ages such material objects of worship were concrete forms which represented such god-like attributes as superhuman power, ability, strength, and courage, and man's great need of help and sustenance made it an easy task for the priests and rulers to play upon the fears, and thereby enrich themselves by the superstitions engendered by them in the minds of the ignorant masses. The sale of such representations alone must have brought immense sums into the hands of the Church and State, and so, what was once an aid to prayer and concentration has been prostituted to the service of the dark side of life.

The main point now under consideration is that notwithstanding this great degradation of spiritual ideals, the fact remains that the Gods of these long-forgotten races and the Gods of modern times are in reality one and the same God, and their name is Love; for even in the grossest forms of idolatry it was love of or for some phase of what was recognized as Divinity, which originally attracted the embryonic souls of those masses.

Many intelligent and educated people of modern times find it necessary to resort to some material object in order to fix their wandering attention on interior things. The Roman Church, as well as some others, has recognized and provided for this need, and notwithstanding the fact that gross advantage has been taken of this need by the priests in many instances, the images of saints, virgins, martyrs, and *Agnus Dei*[1] answer a wise purpose, for they not only serve as an aid to imagination, but also furnish a fixed point for concentration and prayer, and are all representations of some desirable attribute or quality, or of some superhuman entity who serves as an example. Unfortunately, the real object of such material representation is only too frequently lost sight of, and the created thing is identified with the Creator.

The most hopeful and encouraging fact we can point to for the help and satisfaction of all the world is that notwithstanding all the mistaken ideas, willful perversions of truth, and deliberate misuse of knowledge, Love must ultimately identify itself with Love; and love for the beautiful, the true, and the powerful is love of God — the very substance of God; and according to the strength and measure of our love shall we become identified with God, whether the object of our love be our fellow men, an aspect of nature, or a material thing.

Jesus said, "If ye love not your brother whom ye have seen, how can ye love God whom ye have not seen?"[2] If we cannot perceive and love the god-like attributes in our brother men, how can we comprehend and identify ourselves with an individualized part of that Godhead, such as we believe our Higher Self — the Holy Spirit — to be?

---

[1] *Agnus Dei* (*Latin*, "Lamb of God") — a title for Jesus Christ that appears in the Gospel of John.
[2] 1 John 4:20.

LESSON 61
THE CAMEL'S BACK

Truly it is said, "It is easier for a camel to go through the eye of a needle than for a rich man to enter the kingdom of Heaven."[1] One interpretation of the Master's words is given to the effect that there was formerly a peculiarly shaped gate in the wall of the ancient city,[2] called the needle's eye, and the eastern beast of burden, the camel, could not go through that gate because of the hump on his back. Similar impediments are observed in the case of the rich man, if the above interpretation of the Bible statement has a basis of truth. The possessions of the rich man correspond to the hump on the camel's back, and while he clings to that burden, or it to him, he must stay on the outside of the Heavenly City; that is, in some lower place. But whether the interpretation is correct or not matters little; in reality the statement is true as it stands. I will go still further and say it is impossible for a rich man to enter the path of occultism. The first task given him on his application for chelaship is voluntarily to renounce all hindrances, to give up at once and forever everything that can impede his progress. He may win back all that he renounced and ten times over that amount if he be accepted, but it will never be his, it will belong to the degree which he has entered. He may be appointed to a stewardship over it, every penny of it may pass through his hands, but it will be used as dictated by others, and for the benefit of others. If he receives any personal benefit from it, it will be incidental, and because of his being a part of the degree which is dictating the use of it. It requires but a little earnest thought to show us why this must be true. We are well aware of the effect of riches on the average man of the world. Autocracy, self-indulgence, pride, and greed are some of the evils engendered by the possession of great wealth; and, still worse, contempt for and mastery over the poor, cringing, fearful sycophants who dog his footsteps, and abuse of the poor man who has not inherited or gained an equal amount of treasure, all of which deadens the soul of the rich man, destroys all his confidence in human nature, and finally leaves him destitute of all that makes life worth living. Suspicious of his friends, despising the rank and file of mankind,

---

[1] Matthew 19:24.

[2] Jerusalem.

fearful that his nearest and dearest are watching with longing eyes for the day that will usher him out of life and give them an opportunity to handle his wealth, what has he left? The poorest man in the world has more cause for self-laudation than he.

The man who can keep his fingers fast closed on his purse and pass by another man who he has reason to believe is homeless and hungry; who can refrain from opening that purse while a wounded beggar, or a sick child lies in a hovel or on the street through which he must pass to his own comfortable home, could not by any possibility face the Master at the top of the great Initiation Stair.

I do not pretend to say just how the rich man can most wisely dispose of his possessions; that lies between God and his own soul, but I do most emphatically repeat, a materially rich man cannot enter the Kingdom of God, the height of perfection, the great Initiation. It is one of the few privileges that wealth cannot purchase for him. He has altogether too many "humps on his back." As a rule his one great haunting dread is that he will have to die and leave that beloved wealth. Poor man, if he only could leave it, there might be some hope for him; but unfortunately he cannot, he takes it all with him to curse him for centuries. Not the mere material wealth (that has never been of any particular value), but the results, the lasting effects of the things he has done and left undone, the misery he has caused others in the gathering of that wealth, the lofty, beautiful, and Christly things he might have done and did not do. The compassion, sympathy, love, and charity for which his hungry soul will cry, he can only see like Dives,[3] "from afar." The so-called charity on which he has hitherto prided himself, he will find is an empty thing, for the only thing that could render that charity acceptable — Love — was never put into it; therefore can never be taken out. A gift has no particular value — it is only too often accursed, unless actuated by self-surrender and love, and the selfish man has lost the power of loving and has put in its place an idol made by men's hands.

Truly, of all men, there are none so greatly in need of our pity as the selfish rich man. Unfortunately for himself, the poor man does not always realize the power of the curse of unlimited wealth in time to prevent his trying to bring down the same curse on himself. Verily, contentment is a treasure.

---

[3] *Dives* — a rich man in the parable in Luke 16:19–31.

LESSON 62
THE MURDER OF IDEALS
FROM THE MASTER M.

Has it yet dawned upon your mind that even a premeditated murder does not bear the dire consequences to the murdered or the murderer that does the blasting of a high ideal by a scandal monger? The death of the body is a light thing compared to the death of a soul, and the soul is dependent for its nourishment and, therefore, its life, upon the force of its high ideals.

Every invidious comparison, innuendo, slighting, sarcastic, or sneering word or thought by another, serves to undermine or tear down the faith and trust we have placed in some ideal of Truth or Righteousness. When the first rift is made in the beautiful light that radiates from that Ideal, you may feel a little uncomfortable, may even be driven to protest, but you do not realize the enormity of the offense or its effect upon you. That Ideal is the purest, holiest thing in the world to you, whatever it may be to others. It is so superhumanly pure that the least stain stands out in broad relief, and the corroding force which has made the stain, slowly eats into the inmost recesses of your being. You cannot forget or ignore it. It tears away the mental tissue of your ideal and leaves a great cavity which grows wider and deeper with every attack, with every word that seems to corroborate the first seed of suspicion, and one day it dawns upon you that you are facing a perfect Hades, in place of the pure, beautiful Ideal your open enemy or seeming friend has killed. Your peace of mind is gone. Materialism takes the place of faith, suspicion ousts trust, you have become a walking sepulcher of dead hopes, and when you take an inventory of your possessions and learn the cause of your evident mental bankruptcy, in ninety-nine cases out of a hundred you learn that the ruin has all been wrought by those you have believed to be your friends, and has been done through jealousy of you or others, personal ambition, or self-gratification, and you, poor innocent that you were, never suspected the seeming sympathy with your higher aims, the tenderly drawn comparison between your ideals and theirs; never have dreamed that the profound pity expressed for your ignorance, the warmly offered help, the final caricature and grotesque cartoons which familiarity with the Ideal and its creator made possible at the last, were all parts of a deep laid plot by the enemies of the human race on other planes, and you are left with only an aching void where once dwelt your heart's ideal, left with your whole being reeking with the poison so ably administered, and devoid of the power to build another Ideal; for all the imagination at your command has been devitalized, and you have no longer even the desire to seek another subject for adoration.

"How long, O Lord, how long," will it take us to learn the lesson that whether our mind be fixed on an individual representation of such an ideal in some personality, or the ideal of a supernatural God, it literally makes no difference. It is we, ourselves, who have loved that ideal into life, and clothed it with spiritual garments. It is what that ideal stands for to us, that counts, not what it stands for to others, and whether it be stick or stone, personality or God, it makes no difference. It is of no consequence to us even what such a personality does or does not do, whether the stick or stone be rough or hewn; through some Cosmic link, some karmic tie between us and the substance of that Ideal so represented, it is possible for us to receive the help from, and offer the requisite devotion to the Lord of all Life we have mentally photographed within that Ideal. It is only when we make an idol of the personality, the stick or stone, forgetting that that idol is only clay, that we are endangered. The Ideal hangs over our heads, like the weaver's pattern above his loom, and even though it be unconsciously, it is at that pattern, that sacred Ideal, that the filth and slime of people's thoughts and tongues is flung, when a deliberate attempt is made to break down our faith and destroy our love in and for our Ideals.

LESSON 63
THE MOUNTAIN HEIGHTS

Words are easily found to express philosophical or scientific ideas or theories. Expression is readily given to the affairs of material existence, but what words can we find for, and how do we give expression to the deep truths of spiritual life, the intense, unspeakable longing of the awakened soul for the source of its being? How do we describe the unutterable ecstasy of pain of that soul, at last alive, at once to its separateness and its relationship to — nay, more, its unity with — all it has ever been taught to believe, or has personally experienced of God, the Infinite?

Human life is held so cheap; nature seems to vie with man in so underestimating the value of a single life, that its inestimable worth as a differentiated aspect of the Infinite Father-Mother does not receive the reverent recognition it deserves, in fact receives no recognition worth mentioning unless it has become an embodied $ (dollar mark). This non-recognition of the value of life is especially noticeable in the cases of the unawakened and the murdered souls of men. The former have never experienced anything that could by any possibility afford them a hypothesis or an analogy by or with which comprehensive comparisons might be made to create an understanding of such a state of spiritual consciousness; and the latter, if there yet be left a memory of such experiences, refuse to dwell upon them because of consequent fear or hopelessness, either of which conditions awakens unbearable suffering. It is to those who have reached, even in ever so slight a degree, one or more of the immeasurable heights of spiritual loneliness, that I would fain make my words convey a tithe of the sympathy and desire to help, that surges through my heart.

O, my children, could you but realize that the one word "separateness" holds the key to all such suffering! Could you but force your hearts to respond to your brains when you attempt to synthesize the life forces and gain some intellectual concept of unity, and so reach to the certainty of spiritual knowledge that the same soul-essence that is pulsing through your own hearts is likewise pulsing through the heart of every other human being, good, bad, or indifferent! If you could feel, intuitively, that the great Love Energy toward which your soul is reaching with such unspeakable anguish and longing is likewise appealing to you through the eyes of every living creature, whether or not the intellectual part of that creature is conscious of the fact, and that it is only a matter of greater or lesser experience which keeps both it and you from recognizing your relationship and duty to each other! Never, until your own heart is melted by the true spiritual fire of love for all that lives, will it be possible for you to pass on over the top of those heights of loneliness. The human love that you permit to chain you to one human being, thus giving rise to indifference toward all others, only serves to fix your feet on one step of the mountainside. In that human love, as in all other material expressions of life, there are always the two great universal forces of action and reaction in labor. While that human love may give you for a limited time a slight glimpse of what spiritual love of and for God may be, the reaction of the same force, which must inevitably ensue, will as inevitably render you cold and careless, by comparison, toward the object of your erstwhile affection, as well as toward all others.

It is not for the purpose of repeating for my own satisfaction what I have told you, over and over again, that I reach out and draw you to me in longing now, but to try to impress upon you, if it be possible, that never, until you can see the great Father-Mother force within the outer lineaments of the most disreputable, repulsive human being — never until you can feel the heartbeat of the Great Master against your own heart at the call of your worst enemy as well as your dearly beloved, will it be possible for you to scale the heights and reach the haven of soul satisfaction. Do not let the specious reasoning of those who know not what they say lead you into the belief that Wisdom is to be gained by stifling sympathy and killing out love, for the reaction which follows such methods will inevitably plunge you into a hell of intense, unsatisfied, and unsatisfiable desire, such as no tongue can describe. God cannot be safely mocked or set at aught, for *God is Love*.

Of what use to you the treasures of sunken Lemuria, the hidden wisdom of the Pyramids, the knowledge of the action of the combined Suns of Space, and of Earth and Sea and Sky, if the one great reality back of all and in all, is denied you?

All else that I and others like me have gained in countless incarnations, and might impart to you, is worthless chaff beside the wheat — the love — which alone can impart life and value to that and to all else.

What wonder then that I sometimes weary some of you with what seem vain repetitions. Would you have me feed you with husks, and while watching your starved faces, refuse to give you corn and wine, and refrain from giving lest it trouble you to eat, or lest you throw the corn and wine back in my face again, as you have done before?

Someday the scales will fall from eyes now holden, and let the light I bring reach to the inner chambers of the tightly closed hearts now locked to me by pride and ignorance.

LESSON 64
LET THERE BE LIGHT

If the generally accepted aphorism, "Self-protection is the first law of nature," contains the truth it implies, and that truth is applicable to all degrees of selfhood, the preservation of the Self of the average human being requires a far greater effort on the part of nature than is perceptible to the casual observer, if it is to counterbalance the efforts that many human beings put forth for the destruction of Self.

This is especially true as regards to the whilom Christian who has repudiated the fundamental truths of Christianity in favor of the materialistic claptrap offered in the much abused name of science, and offered as a sop to troublesome consciences which as yet cannot reconcile to their full satisfaction a desire to ride roughshod over the existing code of moral laws with the yet live coals of their former belief; and so in many cases accept the sop which offers freedom from all restraint, in the name of materialistic science.

The establishing of the non-existence of a Christ — a Savior — by said science, and the reduction of a formerly accepted ideal God to an unconscious, impersonal form of energy, and the enthroning of a lesser God designated Primordial Matter, has been rapidly taking away Nature's power to protect the Self, which for the time being appears to be at the mercy of the destructive powers of Nature.

The ideas that have supplanted former Ideals in such instances, at first slowly filtered through the mind, forced by the tremendous power of auto-suggestion; and with the final rejection of the Ideals, the Ideas sprang into active life as confessed materialism. One hears here and there from such self-deceived ones, an expression of pity for "the poor ignorant dupe who persists in clinging to his worn-out creeds or to a code of moral laws altogether too narrow for an enlightened 19th-century man or woman," and beholds with joy the new altar set up to the new God, the God of license and self-indulgence.

It is not surprising amidst all the turmoil, the contradictory state-ments made by men, he has been taught to honor the newly coined phrases indicative of half-revealed discoveries along the line of evo-lution, that the sore beset, passion tossed, discouraged human being is driven to despair, and hopeless of ever seeing "the face of Truth," finally settles down with the old reckless cry, "Let us eat, drink, and be merry, for tomorrow we die,"[1] upon his lips, and a sinking of heart that baffles understanding; or else he falls into the hands of some psychic, mad individual who initiates him into the mysteries of mediumship, if so be he cannot yet relinquish all that has hitherto made his life worth the living — his religion — and finally travels a similar path to that

---

[1] Isaiah 22:13, Luke 12:19, 1 Corinthians 15:32.

which his materialistic brother has taken as a result of the deceptive, little-understood phenomena he has found himself enmeshed within.

Ah, the pity of it all! And all due to a lack of understanding of the fundamental principles of all religions, an ignorantly inspired contempt for great truths which the majority have never had the opportunity of intelligently considering, owing either to mistakes, or lack of opportunity for investigation in the cases of those who have stood in the position of teachers, or to the glamor thrown around the great mysteries by those who, knowing the truth, yet conceal the same, either through fear of the derision of the multitude or for selfish, ambitious projects of their own.

CHRIST IS NOT DEAD

If the words of my first quotation, "Self-protection is the first law of Nature," could but fall on the ears of the self-deceived or the victims of man's ignorance and inhumanity with sufficient force to hold the attention and cause the hearers to ask themselves how much truth there really is in those words, and if any, where and what is the Self that natural law is bound to protect, then put their bias and prejudice aside and go back to the beginning of Time and the action of natural law for an answer to those questions; all their despair, heart-scorching agony of loss, and feeble snatching at the few realities left of a formerly acceptable religious experience, would be spared them, and a glorious possibility might dawn on their minds, break through the darkness and flood their souls with understanding of the hitherto concealed and mysterious meaning of countless dear and reverenced, though incomprehensible, sayings of wise men and prophets in reference to the Christ, who, they now believe, is either dead or a myth; for I, Hilarion, Initiate of the Mysteries, declare to you that Christ is not dead, will never die, and that you, an expression of that Christ, are alive, have always lived, and will never die.

Jesus said, "I and my Father are one";[2] "whoso liveth and believeth in Me shall never die";[3] "God so loved the world that He gave His only begotten Son that whosoever believeth on Him might not perish, but have eternal life."[4]

---

[2] John 10:30.
[3] John 11:26.
[4] John 3:16.

These words not only record the accepted truths of Christianity but they express the deepest truths of all religions.

If you have lost your faith in these grand, soul-inspiring promises, come aside with me awhile and let us see what they mean, and what effect an understanding of them may have on your life; but first be open, brave, and just enough to ask yourself the following questions:

If the personal ideal of God which most Christians form, and which resembles a little bigger, more powerful and just, as well as more tender Father than the father who gave you physical life, should by any chance be lost in an inconceivably greater, more wise and just vehicle of consciousness in which is preeminently active all Love, all Wisdom, all Power, and in which you — the real you — the Self, dwells eternally; with whom you will by steady growth sometime be consciously and individually identified; do you think you would suffer much by exchanging your ideal of that almost earthly Father, for the great vehicle of consciousness, Principle, God, call it what you will, here outlined? And yet this is the nearest I can come to the truth in an endeavor to afford you some adequate idea of the greatly misunderstood Christos whom the ancients and the Initiates of the Great Mysteries reverence and adore, and do so reverence and adore because they have seen with unveiled eye its operation upon the lives and within the souls of the Perfected — the Savior of mankind, and know whereof they speak.

LET THERE BE SONS OF LIGHT

This first emanation from the Godhead is referred to in the familiar expressions of the Bible, as follows:

"In the beginning was the Word, and the Word was with God, and the Word was God."[1] "And God said, Let there be Light."[2] In other words, Let there be Mind, the Son, the Christos (in that first day, the beginning of a great world period or age). And Jesus said, "I am the firstborn among many brethren."[3] "The first that shall be last,"[4] the first emanation of many other emanations, of which I shall speak later.

Would it stagger your belief and bankrupt your hope to exchange the ill- formed, generally grotesque and always unsatisfactory image

---

[1] John 1:1.

[2] Genesis 1:3.

[3] Romans 8:29.

[4] Matthew 19:30.

of a man which so-called art has fixed in your mind as a picture of the Savior of mankind, or any imaginary picture of a man endowed with all the virtues, subjected to all the abuses, finally "dying on the cross for your redemption," paying the price of your sin? — I say, would it be difficult to exchange such an image for a conscious, omnipotent, life-manifesting Light, emanating from the hidden source of all Life, creeping slowly, silently out and over a world of shadows, illuminating every hidden corner, every dark place, penetrating to the heart of every living thing and flooding it with beauty; teaching by its very presence the glory of sacrifice as it surrenders its own substance that all living things should have life more abundantly; touching and arousing to action every human impulse for good, as well as every divine impulse toward the source of its own emanation; the same creative power which poured through and illuminated the blessed Master Jesus and made of Him the Savior, the healer, the hope of the degraded and outcast, as it shone through other Great Souls before His time, and shines now through still others, and will always continue to shine when given opportunity, even through you and me?

What is there in the thought of this omnipotent, omnipresent, beautiful reality, that compares unfavorably with your first ideal concept, or picture of a Savior?

In order to form some faint idea of the Christos, by analogy, think of the Ether which surrounds and penetrates all planets, suns, and stars in space, as of one definite grade of substance, though composed of different finer grades, without which no thing or creature could live. If we can gain an adequate idea of the universality as well as potentiality of the Ether, its relation to all forms and conditions of life, it may aid us in the consideration of a more refined, more potent and spiritual emanation from the First Cause — the Absolute — which the ancients termed the Christos, "the firstborn Son of God."

Being nearer to the heart of Nature, as well as purer and much wiser than the humanity of later ages, some of these ancient Seers and Prophets came into the possession of great knowledge, which was handed down under vows of secrecy to disciples who had passed through the most severe tests as to their ability to keep inviolate the secrets entrusted to them, until the evolution of later races brought the humanity of the same to the point where such secrets could be imparted with benefit to all. Among the latter was the secret of the sevenfold constitution of Matter, Force, and Consciousness; the intimate relation of one to the other, and the periodical manifestation of each. These Seers and Prophets, Masters of the Mysteries, were held together in groups by bonds which no earthly power could break; and to one of these groups, the Essenes,[1] the Master Jesus belonged; and in the private gatherings of these illumined ones, as well as other groups of a similar kind, He passed much time at one period of His life. Many of the expressions He commonly used were in continual use in the ceremonies as well as in the elucidation of the Mysteries by the Essenes.

The firstborn Son, the Christos, the fount of Wisdom, Love, and Power, only required such a purified, perfected vehicle as was Jesus of Nazareth in order to manifest outwardly as qualities, those inner attributes of the Christos, which I have mentioned, and to make him in deed and in truth a very Son of God.

Rightly directed study of these much maligned, greatly misunderstood, and misinterpreted ancient teachings will give a definite groundwork for necessary illustrations of the action of the one great life principle, God in manifestation, who lives and moves and has His being in Matter, Force, and Consciousness, and such study will open wide the closed doors of many sacred books, notably of the Bible, as well as all the phenomena of evolution and involution.

Science is demonstrating the truth of many of these teachings, and at the points where science fails, they supply the necessary impetus for far deeper investigation, along much higher lines.

Little can be said in such an article as this for the enlightenment of an unprepared reader, and I must refer such to other more comprehensive and all-inclusive works on the same subjects, and confine my efforts to the two least understood and all-important Principles toward which all others converge, and which unfortunately seem to furnish a basis for all the more violent and even vicious religious disputes between man and man; the repudiation of which in comparatively modern times has led to confusion worse confounded, and finally to a rejection of all unauthenticated records of Christianity, and in many cases to loss of all faith in the existence and work of the Great Master, thus leaving a vacuum in thousands of lives, which some form of materialism or agnosticism has filled, to the eternal sorrow and regret of those who know the truth.

---

[1] *Essenes (Hebrew,* "healer") — a mystic Jewish sect that flourished from the 2nd century BCE to the 1st century CE. For thousands of years, they lived near the Dead Sea in highly organized groups and held property in common.

DIVINITY OF JESUS

The divinity of Jesus does not rest upon a miraculous or supernatural conception, birth, and resurrection. The life and conduct accredited to Him are sufficient to show the action of Divinity through Him, the one perfect pattern in ages of human effort handed down to the races of mankind now upon the earth, and one who believed in and taught the truths revealed to the Initiates in the Mysteries, as may be seen by those who possess the clue to the hidden kernel of His teachings, which He plainly stated were not for the multitude but for His chosen disciples alone.

It is contended that the whole Christian theology must stand or fall by the acceptance or rejection of the miracles noted in the Bible, and particularly the accounts of the conception, birth, and resurrection of Jesus; and yet, what essential difference can it make to mankind in general whether the events recorded were of a miraculous or a purely natural order of things; or even if they were a symbolic illustration of different phases of evolution and involution which could only be expressed in such language? What effect would it have on the character, mental caliber, spiritual power, and attributes of a man, whether his physical body was brought into manifestation by means of the body of a virgin or by one who had lost her virginity? The laws of Nature would produce the same kind of a body in either case, everything else being equal.

The fundamental cause of the difference between Jesus and countless other men of similar potentialities, lies in the fact that through many lives the inner Ego, the Self of that entity, had prepared conditions by self-sacrifice, indefatigable labor, purity of life and purpose, intense love, and unremitting service for others, for the acceptance and radiation of that divine light we call the Christos, in and through His whole nature, and which made of Him "One set apart," a "Light to lighten the world," a pattern for all men to copy if they would reach the altitude where He dwells, and at the same time and by the same means furnish the vehicle through which the phenomena noted in the various accounts of the descent of the Holy Spirit, could be manifested to a wondering people who did not yet know that in the common acceptance of the word, a miracle was an utter impossibility, or that all seemingly miraculous events were due to the Self-directed action of a divine, purified Will on Nature's finer forces, for the greatest good of all concerned.

DIVINELY NATURAL LAW

Remember that although your concept of maidenly virtue as a necessary factor in the conception and birth of a Savior is the generally accepted concept of the world, and that such a necessity would seem to arise as a result of a Divine command; look where you will in all stages and degrees of natural life and law, you can find no analogy, no reliable information regarding a necessity for previous abstinence from sexual contact where was concerned the conception and birth of the offspring of plant, vegetable, mineral, or human being. Man has made a law, and according to the word of man that law was made by divine command; but Nature furnishes no proof of the probability of such command. We know that previous abstinence (to the time of conception) or the reverse by the mother, does not of necessity either injuriously or otherwise affect her offspring. We have seen the most beautiful, pure, and lovely children whom we knew to be of so-called illegitimate birth. The air such a one breathes is not restricted by law, its body is as perfect, its mind and soul are as active eternal and useful as that of any other child; and no more than the action of air and formation of mind is restricted in such an instance is the principle of the Christos restricted in its action, by the illegitimacy of a child.

Please note I am not countenancing lax morals, denying the legitimacy or Divinity of Jesus, or the understood divine command concerning the moral law; I am but endeavoring to show that a mother's limitations, idiosyncrasies, or lax morals, cannot prevent the action of a divine power in the case of a child, and therefore the conception and birth of Jesus literally had nothing to do with His divinity and power and His mission to earth, and even if He never came to earth, as is contended by many, and the whole account be a fabrication or a symbolic representation of the action of great natural forces, there is no occasion for the upsetting of faith and throwing away our great opportunities for seeking and finding the truth because we have not understood some particular phase of that truth.

THE MESSAGE OF HOPE

The people of the world are starving for want of the spiritual sustenance of which they have been robbed by ignorant misrepresentations or willful selfishness. The churches are losing their devotees by thousands because of the bondage of many of their ministers to worldly opinions, even when light has partially broken in upon their minds, and it remains for the disciples of the Masters to go out into the world, and in the highways and byways of life seek for the "seeing eye," the "open ear," that they may help to stem the tide now set in for the destruction or degradation of the great ideals through which humanity has been raised to its present status. The mystery of the resurrection becomes a simple act of Nature in the light of the sevenfold constitution of Matter.

For the love of the Christ that is in us all, let us turn our hearts to the light and our footsteps in the direction of those "who have marked the signs of the times" and been permitted to see the sheaf of Annunciation Lilies held in the hand of the Angel — the progenitor of the coming Race — and hear the words which bid them seek out the desolate and faint-hearted and give them a message of hope.

LESSON 65
SOME OF THE HEROES OF LIFE

If the faintest concept of the absolute geometrical and mathematical perfection of the universe, from the highest to the lowest degree, were fixed in the consciousness of a student of life's mysteries, he would have but little if any difficulty in solving the ever recurring problem of the position and rights of a Teacher, Master, or Ruler, and the correct attitude he should hold toward such an one.

It is an absurdity to hold that the evolution of the planets in their own orbits is governed by irrevocable law, while the evolution of one or more nearly related human beings in their own environment is left to chance, as it would inevitably be if the same immutable, irrevocable laws were not guiding every phase of every degree of their evolution.

No human being is drawn to and placed under the direction of a superior influence for a definite purpose and at a definite period of time, by chance, nor could such a one be rightly loosed from subjection to such influence by chance; he may tear himself away, for he is a free-will agent as regards certain clearly defined phases of his separate life, but if he does so separate himself, the action and results of the same are analogous to the phenomenon of the star that tears itself, or is torn from, its own orbit, and goes flying into space, only to fall and keep on falling, until its mass is disintegrated, and its insignificant fractions are drawn into the orbit of some greater star, there to lose its integrity as far as an individualized entity is concerned. Having been drawn by Karmic law and association of long past lives into one Hierarchical line, the evolution of such an individual is provided for *on that line*, and the ruling entity of that Hierarchical line commands his allegiance by divine right; and any important deviation from the right line causes him to lose whatever degree of knowledge and experience was due him at the particular period of his recreancy.

Love will invariably attract him back to that line in time, unless he has gone too far, but in the interim he has missed just the measure of opportunity and development that Karmic law had provided for at that period, and consequently falls behind the other constituent parts of that line.

It is a cowardly, selfish man who, for the purpose of saving himself from a little inconvenience, an insignificant personal trouble, or to enhance his own importance in the eyes of others, tears himself away from the business, social, or religious body with which he is connected on the supposition that he sees signs of its breaking up; and to find an acceptable excuse for his treachery convinces himself that he is protecting himself or others from the results of the failure or unworthiness of others who are connected with the same body. The moment he decides to take such action he prints in fiery letters within his own aura the words, coward, recreant, unworthy, and faithless; and it will take long years of almost superhuman effort to erase those words.

The majority of human beings have been so long tinctured with selfish worldliness, that they rush with incredible speed to shelter themselves under the roof of the common opinions and estimates of position held by their more influential associates. Man is so fearful of being made a victim of the contempt and ridicule which he knows is the portion of the loser in any of the games of life, that he usually runs for his life to cover, at a hint of disgrace or failure in connection with his whilom friends and comrades, and cannot bring himself to stop a moment and look back at what and who it is that he is in reality deserting.

In all the annals of history there is no one crime that awakens such contemptuous disgust in the minds of the people at large, as does the crime of the deserter from a post of trust — the coward who shrinks back and takes to the slums and byways at the first firing of a gun by the enemy. In all the long list of heroes the world delights to honor, there are none which move the hearts of all — good, bad, or indifferent — to such admiration and regard as does the hero leader of a forlorn hope, the man who stands in the breach regardless of what the enemy may do.

In all life's lists of interior or exterior action, there is not a living soul over whom the Initiates of the White Lodge so quickly and efficiently spread the mantle of their love and protection as the man or woman who, in spite of all the darts of all the demons of the lower spheres and upon the earth, stands steadily at the post taken at the signing of the pledge of application for discipleship, and none from whom that mantle is so quickly withdrawn as from the deserter from the ranks of comradeship; and such withdrawal of protection is not a matter of choice, necessarily, with the Initiates; for, being administrators of Nature's laws, they have no alternative; such a cowardly deserter has stepped from the line and position that evolution had placed him upon, and like the falling star has left his own orbit, has fallen out of the circle of Lodge protection.

The brave man, the accepted disciple, knows that just because there has arisen a great crisis, just because other comrades have deserted their post, just because the citadel of his strength is attacked, because his Master, his leader, has need of him, his hour has come to prove himself, and wild beasts could not tear him away from that leader's side, the wealth of the whole world could not tempt him away. He knows that the reforming of the whole body on higher, better lines may, sometime, rest on his loyalty. The power to cleanse and purify the body, to stiffen the weak and lift up the crushed, and so help to bring harmony out of discord, victory out of defeat, may be his, if the need should ever arise, and he will run no risk of being found wanting or absent if such a calamity should occur. He knows that countless brave men have gone down to death; innumerable grand efforts for the betterment of humanity have been rendered worthless for want of one unselfish, well-qualified person to take up the reins of power which have fallen from the hands of a wounded leader, a stricken comrade; and the end — no tongue can tell. He is content to wait.

LESSON 66
THE PLANES OF REFLECTION

I find that many of the more recently received students of the Secret Science meet with what seem to them insurmountable difficulties in the way of reconciling statements made in some late instruction with statements made in previous instructions, and in many instances the difficulty lies in their incomplete grasp of the subject *in toto*, or imperfect concept of the vital importance of the laws governing Reflection, as well as the character of the substances involved in the media of reflection.

Before passing to further comment on the same, I desire to make one emphatic statement which you will do well to remember. The three higher of the seven planes of manifestation are incomprehensible and eternal so far as any possible computation of time or exercise of mentality by a human being is concerned; so, in trying to understand the planes, states of consciousness, laws, and all that pertains to them, you will save much valuable time and mental force by confining your efforts to the study of the four lower — the reflected planes, for some time to come.

The laws governing the energy of reflection are unchangeable. By the action of these laws, within the same forces by and through which physical form is reflected on a polished surface, is the potential energy of the three higher planes — spiritual life — reflected first into the Akasha, next into the Etheric, and finally into the grosser or material planes. As the Akasha has three major subdivisions, so the Etheric and material have three major subdivisions. The subdivisions of the material are Water, Air, and Earth; those of the Etheric are Light, Heat, and Sound. The ether of science and the real Æther, the vehicle of electric energy, are the positive and negative aspects of one homogeneous substance. The three subdivisions of Akasha, in common parlance, are designated the Higher Astral or Soul Plane, the Devachanic, and the Nirvanic Planes — the three higher Fires in and from which all fiery forces first emanate and proceed, and to which they finally return.

The fourth of the seven planes, counting from either above or below, is a combination of three subdivisions of Akasha. It is the great double cosmic mirror, for it eventually receives back all its own reflections as their mission is accomplished on lower planes and transmutes them. It is the plane of the Christos in operation, "in whom are all things and by whom all things are made."[1] As the light of the sun or some other bright body is essential to the reflection of a body or the casting of a shadow on the plane of matter, so a higher form of light — energy — is essential to the reflection of the potentialities of the Akashic planes upon or within the lower planes or states, and that light is identical with spiritual love — the Christ-love. As the light of the sun must be intercepted in order that a body may cast a shadow of itself on any other thing or object, so the Christ-light — Love — must be intercepted, the current interrupted, cut off from the heart of any human being in order to demonstrate the action of evil, i.e., cast a negative mental astral shadow on the soul. You will note, the same light is requisite for both. It is the use to which that light is put that determines its plane of action, i.e., whether it will manifest as good or evil, just as it is the free action of human love, or its interception as mentioned above, that determines whether that love shall be a blessing or a curse to the recipient and the giver.

It is difficult for the average man to picture Love to his mind as a definite form of energy which may be used or abused, according to the power and desire of the human will and under a definite code of laws, as surely and as scientifically as any form of electricity known to man may be used.

Some students claim that what is termed sexual love bears no relation to spiritual love — Christ-love — or that one is the antithesis of the other; but here again is a great mistake, for it is the interception, the interruption of the current of spiritual love by blind passion which creates the shadow termed sexual love (passion). It is never *love* that should be killed to raise the vibration of man, but passion that must be raised.

Divine Love — Creative Energy in action — when reflected into the Etheric plane, becomes the active principle of Gravitation.

The visible sun is often said to be the generator of heat and light, but in fact it is like unto a concave mirror, and intercepts and gathers the etheric vibrations of sound, heat, and light, and in turn throws them back into the receptive cushion or aura of the earth and the other planets of its evolutionary chain. The correspondence between such action of Cosmic forces upon each other, and the influence of

---

[1] 1 Corinthians 8:6.

one human being over another, is perfect, for the magnetic radiations of any one aura are reflected upon the auras of others, and by means of the action of the same great Cosmic light, and if the latter is intercepted by an antagonistic emanation, that which should have been a spiritual uplifting, upbuilding power for good, for both sender and receiver, becomes a disrupting, deathly influence, or shadow, which is in the way of the light, and through which each party must look at the other; consequently, there is friction and hatred where there should be harmony and power.

Another point you will do well to emphasize and remember is the fact of the reversal of all reflected forms or forces when thrown on the Earth's aura. You will notice in a reflected form of yourself, you stand face to face with the reflected form; you cannot see your own back without the aid of another mirror. So, you cannot observe the entire Self of another individual by observation of the reflected image in your own mind without the aid of another reflector, i.e., without the clear, pure energy of the Christ-love, which throws so strong a reflection that you may be able to perceive the inner self as well as the outer semblance of that other.

It is the misfortune of not being able to appreciate these great truths that causes so much misunderstanding of each other's motives, thoughts, and acts. You see a certain characteristic or quality which is abhorrent to your particular cast of mind, and at once arouses a sensation of hatred or disgust, and final condemnation, thereby intercepting the light and casting deep shadows which confuse your mind and render it absolutely impossible for you to see the very thing you have condemned in another all ready for action in yourself — the ultimate cause of the disagreeable attribute or characteristic in your brother. In other words, you must cleanse your own mind and make sure the reflections cast upon it by Divine Love are not intercepted by shadows of your own making, before you presume to judge your brother or sister, if so be you would become a true reflector of the Deific vibrations.

Man pays in full for every opportunity Life offers him — not a jot or tittle less than the ultimate value of the opportunity. The greater his demands, the more force and energy he puts into those demands — all that the same or a like opportunity could be forced to yield by himself or another, just so great will be the price demanded by the law for the given opportunity. If this were more fully realized, man would be less careless in demanding greatness when unwilling or unable to pay the price.

In commenting on the causes and effects of Reflection, I would call your attention to previous Instruction on Centralization. Disobedience to the laws of Centralization is primarily responsible for the confused and confusing conditions now in operation through all lines of human endeavor.

It is a commonly accepted idea that the repudiation of a dominating factor in religious, social, or material life for some cause, which is in reality only a matter of controversy, is a desirable and efficient way of securing better conditions.

The murder of an unpopular king, the vicious attack on the moral or physical qualities of a lesser ruler, or a presiding officer of any organized body, which by affecting public opinion results in killing that individual's power for good (whether deserved or not), if some selfish purpose is to be served, finds much justification and excuse; and the immediate effects often seem to justify such action. But if the final effects on the individuals concerned were to be taken into consideration, such reasoning would be found very faulty; for, no matter how powerful or how weak the line of life descending through religious, national, sociological, or family groups of people may be, the evolutionary forces can only operate for normal growth through that one line, as far as that one natural division of life is concerned, and the hurt of one is the hurt of all.

Inability to recognize this truth is due to the very deplorable conditions now existing in the business and social world.

There could never occur a condition in the central cell (the nucleus) inimical to the best interests of the other constituent part of any one organism, if the latter had perfectly sustained and supported that nucleus in its position and duties; for all the laws of growth and manifestation are against it. That nucleus, if not sufficiently strong and virile enough to function the evolutionary forces, would have been destroyed at birth. If it has degenerated subsequently, it has been because of lack of sustenance on the material side of life.

Humanity cannot call to itself and retain an individual ruler in any functional department who is very far in advance of the other constituent lines, and this is because of its tendency to neglect or destroy what it cannot understand or appreciate; and the very power which makes the central cell a vehicle for the transmission of the evolutionary impulses also renders that cell an inexplicable quantity, and therefore, to be rejected by the great majority. Consequently, instead of supporting and sustaining it, it is, figuratively speaking, dragged down, beaten, and cast out; it becomes, in fact, the rejected Son, the Sacrifice.

If this statement of facts is comprehended, it will show the great necessity for centralized efforts if the Temple members are ever to furnish the nucleus through which the Lodge can reach the world and teach the revolution of present methods of government and life.

LESSON 67
LOVE OF IDEALS

There are two ways by which a human being may defend his life or his honor; one is by crippling his antagonist, the other is by making a friend of that antagonist; but it depends upon what manner of man the latter proves to be whether his friendship or his enmity is better worth the courting. The enmity of a treacherous viper in human or animal guise is more to be desired than its openly expressed friendship, for there is possible defense against a known enemy; none whatever against the treachery of a supposed friend.

Of all the brave, noble, and true men and women of this dreary iron age there are none more worthy of admiration, and of exaltation by mankind than is the one who can retain a true, unselfish friendship for another who has forgiven a great personal injury; for the fiends of the nethermost hell delight in the work cut out for them in the heart of the forgiven one in such an instance; the fiends begotten of loss of self-regard, born of jealousy, and nourished by abject fear. A torturing suspicion of the genuineness of the forgiveness is forever with such a one, and what words can tell the story of the long, hard struggle — and frequent failures?

This is a long preamble to a few stern facts.

Among the Temple members, to our everlasting sorrow and regret be it said, there are a few who have been forgiven the greatest wrongs that a human being is capable of doing to another — wrongs to which loss of life would be trifling by comparison. Years have passed since some of those wrongs were committed; and only months since certain phases of the same wrongs have been repeated, and have been again forgiven, and the fight, if there has been a fight, has gone against the doers of those wrongs. They could not endure the temptations of the above-mentioned fiends, and thus have fallen so deeply in the toils of the latter, they need no further forgiveness to strengthen their bondage.

I do not mention this for the purpose of exciting sympathy or support for any individual, but from an all-engrossing desire to save others from a like retribution, and to endeavor to strengthen the weak and encourage the strong.

In the early days of the Temple work, the aura of each entering member was thrown open to those who had the right to see therein, for the better protection of the gestating cell of the Temple work, and every future vicious attack on that work was prefigured in some auric envelope before it was made. But if such knowledge could have unrighteously and uncharitably affected those on whom the attacks were primarily to be made; if it could have influenced the latter to refuse admission to the association, or to openly resent the sly untruthful innuendoes, the uncharitable or false statements of those who applied for or gained membership only to use the organization for selfish purposes, the fulfilment of a great trust would have been long delayed, and the recipients of the trust would not have been permitted to proceed with the work under the direction of the White Lodge, for they would have degraded the Cosmic Ideal of The Temple, the Brotherhood of Humanity.

If you could at all times remember the great ideals you have loved and longed to materialize in the days that are gone — ideals of courageous, self-sacrificing, noble Knights of the Holy Grail; of sweet womanly, tender, and faithful Ladies worthy of the love and sacrifice of those Knights; of the unselfish, undying devotion, the charity, helpfulness, wisdom, and beneficence of the Priests and Priestesses of the great Temples of antiquity, unweariedly pursuing the Path, sometimes by fire and flood, in the midst of carnage and blood, through years of martyrdom, on, on, to the topmost step of the great Initiation Stair; I repeat, if you could always remember those ideals — remember what they meant to you when you made the first conscious effort to reach to some height of the ladder of self-help, as well as what they have been to you on every upward step you have taken since; through every soul-scorching sorrow or great joy; would you not be more careful how you debased them, how you dragged them in the mire and mud of a treacherous, unstable, unloving maze of mind?

If you could but always remember that those ideals were the first privations in form of your spiritual selves, created out of your own spiritual substance, and therefore living images fixed indelibly in your own auras, and which you had only to fill in, in order to perfect as an artist fills in the sketch he has drawn, as the musician fills in the trills and chords, or as he finds suitable words to accompany the melody he has spiritually caught and brought to outer expression, thus creating a never dying musical gem! If you had retained any memory of these ideals, could you deliberately thrust away from you the opportunity to grasp the brushes, to make use of the trills and chords for the reason that some other poor, unfortunate artist has chosen to cover his sketch with slime, or paint, in the place of the Ideal, a grinning fiend, or because some other musician has set the sweet melody caught from the realms of Spirit to obscene and degrading words?

You now know what you ought to do; you have been left in no doubt about that; you may know, if you will but listen, what the inevitable result will be of not doing what you know you ought in the line of your duty to your co-disciples, and the preservation of your higher ideals. The signs of coming events, the forerunning tremors of the coming great storms are filling the very air.

As well as you know that two and two make four, you know that a willfully broken pledge to your Higher Selves puts an unyielding bar across the door which leads to the secret places of the Great White Lodge. You know that a deliberate lie, or a willfully malicious statement, whether true or false, about another human soul who is courageously trying to climb out of the mud of sense into the light of Spirit, will surely set you apart from the encircling love of the Great Master, until you have picked up every dropped or imperfect strand of the web that the lie or malicious statement has woven therein; you need no reminder of this, if you have listened to the inner voice which always tells you when you have struck a blow at the Christ — have driven another nail into the cross of the world's woe.

What does it matter that you try to salve your conscience by saying "I believed that brother or sister was bad, was untrue, was deceiving the world for his or her own advantage"? Who made you — you who are incapable of looking into the heart or the soul of the accused — a judge of his or her victories or failures, spiritual growth, or ability to help others? You who have sinned just as deeply as lies the accusation you have made; else you never could have made it — would never have entertained the thought of it for a moment; for the law is inexorable that forbids you to perceive aught that you have not experienced.

The time is short — oh, so short, my children — the day of judgment, the effects of previous causes approaches so rapidly. You can put your heads in the sand like the ostrich if you will, and refuse to see the signs of its coming; you can deafen your ears to the battle cry of the elemental fiends, the yells of maddened, persecuted, enslaved victims of man's inhumanity, but that will not prevent that judgment day — your judgment day — from coming.

Self-preservation is the first law of nature, you are told, but nature seems to have failed in the present great crisis in respect to the majority of human beings, for they have lost even the desire, to say nothing of the power, for self-preservation. If all could see and understand, they would be on their knees at the feet of those they have wronged, instead of trying to justify that wrong to themselves or to others. No surer indication of guilt can be given than attempts at justification may furnish in the case of a wrong.

Why should I attempt to deaden your sensibility in regard to the most vital issues in your lives by rapidly pouring forth instructions upon great Cosmic phenomena? Why give you more definite directions for the further unfoldment of psychic senses and gaining of spiritual power as I have been repeatedly requested to do, when I am forced to see that I would only add to your responsibility and place in your hands, figuratively speaking, a dangerous two-edged weapon with which to slay yourselves and others?

Just as distinctly and emphatically as I have assured you that the power is mine to lead you to the heights of development toward which your eyes are turned, have I told you that without the attainment of true brotherliness toward your co-disciples, without the virtues of humility, obedience, and chastity as a foundation, the attainment of such spiritual and psychic qualifications as you desire would be detrimental in the extreme; for you would thereby be thrown among different orders of life than you are accustomed to, which could work you irremediable harm, if you had not the power to control them to your advantage; and such power can only be won by the practice of the virtues mentioned by me. You would not expect to handle fire with unprotected hands, and the forces you would manipulate, if you could, are far more potent, and just as little self-conscious and as irresponsible as is the fire of the material planes. And remember, it is not you yourselves alone that you are holding back by refusing to obey or ignoring your obligations; it is also all those who are in the same auric vibrations as yourselves. For you can no more reach the height of development to which you aspire, *alone*, than one of a single hive of bees can attain to the stature of a man by itself. You are parts of a single Group Soul, as the atoms of your bodies are a part of yourselves, and as long as that Group Soul is held back by a predominance of one or more detrimental forces, all its individual parts are restrained to just the degree that they have become responsible for the same, by "the things they have done or left undone." So, to just the extent that you are a partaker in the wrongdoing of those others, by joining in with them, countenancing their evil acts, or deliberately ignoring their effects — to just that extent you place them and yourselves under restraint.

You will yet wonder at your disregard of and indifference to the words of a great Master, "Man does not live to himself alone,"[1] for the spiritual significance of the words is so far beyond the material significance in importance and truthfulness as to be beyond comparison. Whether you ever reach the material center of the Temple work and become associated with your comrades there or not; whether you are so isolated as never to meet another Temple member in your present incarnation, the fact remains that you are one of the constituent parts of a single Group Soul, else you never would have been impelled to unite yourselves with the Temple body, for you have been under the guidance of that Soul since one of its galaxy of stars watched over your first appearance on earth.

LESSON 68
THE POWER OF THE CENTRAL CELL

Will you not try to put aside any opinions formed by hearsay in reference to any member of the official staff of the Temple, and for the sake of your suffering fellow creatures in the world, as well as for your own eternal good, and your personal development, ask yourselves the following questions:

Have you ever heard or read of the advancement of an individual to a position of honor or power, that did not arouse the envy, hatred,

---

[1] Romans 14:7.

or jealousy of one or more persons who had been seeking that particular position for themselves or some other interested individual, and, regardless of the real worth and ability of the advanced, have you not seen the simplest, most natural acts and words of such an one misconstrued and magnified beyond recognition by the latter, or by those who were not in a position to judge fairly?

Have you not found in all nature, in all evolutionary aspects from that of the atom to a God, in every phase or differentiation of the Eternal, One Life, so far as your observation has extended, that one single point, cell, organ, individual, nation, star (sun) was the center of attraction and distribution for the action of the evolutionary forces which were in process of creating or had created, not only the circumference of that great mystery in form, but all else that came into manifestation between such a center and the circumference?

It will be according to the nature of the task allotted such a center by the Lords of Karma and its plane of action, whether it will be a visible or invisible center, but always its office is the same.

Have you ever known a revolt, a belittling of lawful authority, usurpation of rightful prerogative, repudiation of requisite directions, and in short, injury to or destruction of the center of action, to yield anything but disintegration of mass, mental and physical suffering, and loss of opportunity for many in line for advancement?

Does not the whole history of the human race, as well as all known phases of nature teach us this great truth?

Is not such rebellion, revolt, and disobedience the underlying cause of all human suffering, delayed progress, and continuance of warfare between nation and nation, man and man?

Do not all successful ventures in business, government, and family life, as well as all lower natural phenomena plainly teach that however limited the nucleus, the building center, may be, if it be in its rightful karmic position, its destruction leaves the mass in form which it has created, without a vehicle for the attraction and dissemination of the requisite building and sustaining forces; and that by its protection and sustenance it is enabled to work in harmony with every molecule of its organic whole, thus giving to the same what it alone could give. As rapidly as any unit of a given mass reaches a point of development where it has become a recognized instrument capable of directing lesser units to the advantage of the whole mass, the central nucleus, in accordance with the higher law which governs the whole mass, must avail itself of the services of that instrument, and must do its utmost to advance and emplace that instrument where it can do the most good for the greatest number. Not to do so would be to jeopardize and eventually to destroy the whole mass of which it is a constituent part, for evolution is conducted on strictly mathematical principles. Man's ignorance of or disobedience to that one law is the primary cause of all the wretched inhuman forms of government and political corruption in the world today.

It is an easily demonstrable truth that every cell, every individual that refuses to perform its own duty and usurps the duty of another; every cell, every individual that attacks or minimizes, or detracts from the authority vested by Nature in the central cell, the electric generator, receiver and transmitter of the constructive forces, becomes a source of great danger to the whole mass — becomes an avenue through which the destructive instead of the constructive forces may work, and is therefore the common enemy of the constituent parts of that mass, of whatever it may consist.

Man's cruelty to his kind is seldom the result of an inherent desire for cruelty; its basis, if normal, is almost invariably his material self-interest. But however culpable he may be, if he has not been found out, he indulges in a little feeling of satisfaction when some other guilty one is brought to punishment unless he is a partaker in such punishment. Such characteristics are among the first which must be killed out in the true disciple of the Lodge.

No pressure could be brought to bear upon an Initiate great enough to influence him to hand over to the "tender mercies" of his kind any poor soul that had sinned against him individually. He knows that though its judgments tarry long, the guilty one will meet his punishment by means of the Law of Laws, but even should the latter escape such payment of indebtedness, nothing but regret for the fault would be tolerated.

If thunder and lightning, earthquake and fire could arouse and hold the attention of the rebellious, self-righteous man fixed, long enough for the still small "voice of the silence" which always follows a storm, to be heard, and the light of the spiritual torch he unwittingly carries, the torch of Divine Wisdom, could be uncovered, it would show him how he himself had madly, ignorantly brought on the storm and the fire, the anguish, loss, and disappointment, by the defiance he has hurled at the law. One short cycle of cause and effect would then be complete, and he would have learned how he himself had murdered his loved ones, had laid the lines and carried the explosives, the seeds of contagious diseases, the poison, the knife, or the dagger that has wounded himself and destroyed thousands of his equally anguished, struggling fellow creatures; has maimed and crippled others and brought on famine and pestilence; and still worse, has destroyed by self-indulgence the avenue through which the creative forces must work to furnish vehicles suitable to attract to earth, and embody the souls which would be capable of freeing him from bondage, and teaching him to work intelligently with Nature's great, immutable principles in order utterly to drive all willful evil from the face of the earth, and give the impetus to the divine fiery lives to flash forth the news of a revivified, forgiven and forgiving, unspeakably great and glorified New People, in a stream of white light that would lighten all the dark places of the universe. But ere even the ideal of such a finality can become the recognized ambition of the people at large, countless numbers must go down into the great darkness. The artist, the dreamer, the scientist, all who have caught a glimpse of any part of that ideal, must pay the price of daring to underestimate the importance of the material gods who have claimed their worship, and who, being refused, will sacrifice them as they have sacrificed every unwilling devotee of Mammon and brute force in the present Manvantara.

Man has never accepted, will never accept the highest ideal of his fellowman — the Brotherhood of Man — as worthy of his devotion, until selfishness, poverty, and suffering have driven him to it; at least to the extent of acknowledging its worth and generously placing himself and his substance at the service of the other, to aid in its materialization. No matter how much good may result to the world *en masse*, unless he can see a way to possess himself individually of the advantages to be gained by associated endeavor, the average man is not able to overcome the force of jealousy awakened by the thought that the ideal is not his own, and this limitation in himself keeps him at the circumference of life, and forces him to follow the weary round of the Great Wheel from life to life. He feels no vibration of attraction from the center because he has placed himself at such a distance from that center, and meeting with no force of resistance in him, those vibrations are caught and fixed in a denser, material state of substance which forms the circumference, and there he must remain until he learns that he can wrong no fellow man by word or thought or deed and go free from karmic action himself — until he learns that he himself must open up the avenues he has closed between himself and the central nucleus of the world cell to which he belongs, and as those avenues lead through layer after layer, plane after plane of minor cells, or organized bodies, with which he is connected by unbreakable strands, he must become able to harmonize himself with all of those bodies before the full strength of the evolutionary currents of life can flow unobstructed from the center to the circumference of his individuality through the avenues thus kept open, and through which he himself will be drawn back to the source of his being, back to his home and his Father's heart where the feast for the prodigal son is set and awaits his coming.

LESSON 69
THE ETERNAL QUERY

The one eternal query — How can God be all things, all good, and evil exist coincidently with God? It is said to be a law of physics that no two things can occupy the same space at the same time, yet we are asked to believe that while God is all things, all reality, the antithesis of God, evil, is not only a self-existent reality but is also the cause of perpetual warfare between the creatures that God has created from His own substance.

This would indeed be the paradox of all paradoxes if it were literally true.

The duality of all manifested life is such an obvious fact that it would seem hardly necessary to refer to it as a basis for argument. Positive and negative, day and night, good and evil; consciousness of one implies consciousness of the other.

An object itself is not the picture of that object; the picture is an illusion, a reflection, caught and fixed temporarily in substance of another character. It is also an inversion of the original object. Stand over a pool of water and note the image of yourself in the water beneath; that image will appear to be upside down; your head will seem to be where your feet should be.

This simple illustration may help you to some knowledge of the methods by which some of the phases of spiritual life become phases of astral life.

In order to externalize Itself, and so to know Itself, Deity reflects Itself — its own potential attributes and qualities — into what we term space, but which is eternal substance, at the beginning of a Great Age — Maha Yuga.[1] This substance, Akasha, is the fundamental principle of electric energy, the first manifestation of which is Ether.

Darkness has no real existence: let the light shine, and darkness disappears. So it is with the reflected universe; while the Light of God, the Will to create, is in action for that purpose, the living reflection of God has a temporary existence, the time limit of which is set by that Will.

The one great difficulty in the way of our understanding somewhat of this reflection of God is in the limitations we put to our ideal conception, and the tendency to cling to the reflection as a whole, instead of giving more time and thought to the minor reflections, the constituent parts of the major reflection, and the problem is then too great for our mentality. If we can understand that it is not only all form and every degree of substance that are reflected, but all possible modifications of mind, all possible attributes, qualities, characteristics, all forms and degrees of force and energy, and that they are not only reflections, they are also all separate and distinct inversions of the same, and therefore false in comparison with the real, the problem will be simplified. The only real and eternal form of life in such a universe of shadows is the Ego, the Divine Spark, the basis of every individual; and being, as it were, caught and bound in a universe of reflection, its mission is to transmute that reflection, to return it to God, plus what it individually has won through its experience with the shadows. For instance, suppose the reflected image of yourself in the pool of water has been endowed with mentality by you, given power of motion and the inspiration to seek and find out all the pond of water contains and can teach, and that you who are watching from your standpoint above, become aware that it has fulfilled its mission, has gained all its experience, and knowing that its form and substance are not necessary to its real life, you can just disintegrate them and set the mentality free, embodied in a form of pure energy which it has won through the experience, and that you can recall this finer form to your side on the surface of the pool, your own child, part of yourself;

---

[1] *Maha Yuga* (*Sanskrit*, "great age") — a large cycle of evolution in Hinduism. Maha Yuga consists of four smaller Yugas, or cycles: Satya Yuga, Treta Yuga, Dvapara Yuga, and Kali Yuga.

then suppose by the power of your own will, which has reflected both the pool of water and the reflected image of yourself, you withdraw the light by which the reflection was cast, leaving nothing but darkness and non-existence where the pool had been.

While not an exact illustration of the manifestation and involution of matter, the above may serve to enlighten you to some extent.

The parable of the ten talents refers to these labors of the Ego. The unworthy disciple who hid his talent — who made no use of the talent, which he returned to the Master, illustrates the action of an Ego which has selfishly refused to use its spiritual life to transmute lower forms of force which must be cyclicly returned to the Absolute for a stronger impulse. The disciple who used his talent to good purpose was rewarded with the talent which the unworthy one had returned; in other words, the substance of the lasting, finer vehicle of the Ego was the reward of its own industry, as was also the unused substance which had been returned to the Giver.

LESSON 70
GOD AND CHRIST

The use by some teachers of foreign or unfamiliar terms of expression, owing to the difficulty of expressing deep spiritual truths for which the English language is inadequate, has unfortunately led to a repudiation or misunderstanding of the corollary of one or more aspects of those truths, aspects which are familiar to those who have been connected with any of the more modern systems of religion; and in no instance have the results been more disastrous and far-reaching than when students were ignorantly led to the complete repudiation of the ideals which had been formerly built up in their consciousness by long continued use of the words God and Christ, through the misinterpretation of foreign or unfamiliar terms of expression, supposed to indicate exactly the same ideals.

No words can convey an idea of the immeasurable loss that has been sustained by the rejection of these once familiar and precious concepts of infinite Love and Power. Many are the futile efforts made to attain to a similarly potent, uplifting, sustaining power to that formerly idealized and expressed in those words, and to attain the same by devotion to an impersonal, unfeeling, all powerful, unreachable, ever receding ideal, while at the same time the human heart is

continually crying out, hopelessly, despairingly, for comfort in affliction, for a place of refuge in the storms of evolution, a consciousness
of which might indeed "make the angels weep."

Countless numbers are being driven into suicide and crimes of all
kinds by the despair which has succeeded the apparent loss of such
ideals. In the majority of cases it was altogether more than could be
endured to relinquish all that had hitherto given them courage for the
present and hope for the future as expressed by them in the words,
"a Father's love," "a Savior's redemption," and they could not see how
the — to them — cold expressions which "only appealed to the intellect" were in reality but other forms of expressing Divinity and the
higher attributes; nor could they appreciate the truth of the (hitherto
lacking) details of the interior planes of consciousness and the inhabitants of the same which lie between humanity as it now exists, and
the Godhead. They cannot understand that a knowledge of God the
Father — the Holy Spirit, the Mother — is being consciously brought
nearer to them, is in fact a part of them — the highest and best part
Divine Wisdom — the power of loving; and that Christ the Son, the
first expression or reflection in a slightly less concentrated vehicle
is also a part of highest and best in them, represented by the words
service, sacrifice, and redemption; and that Christ can be brought into
visible, tangible form through a perfected man, a Savior.

It should not detract from man's worship of, or reverence for
God, to know that instead of a great being eternally seated upon a
golden throne above them, that God is speaking to them, comforting
them, blessing them, in every sincere, loving word and act spoken or
performed by any other human being, to or for them; or that their
eyes behold His glory in every flower, in every sunrise or sunset, in
every lightning flash, in every beautiful thing, creature, or scene in the
world. It should not belittle or cast out man's love for Krishna, Jesus,
Buddha or any other incarnated Savior, to know that their faith in
the same is justified because exactly what those great ones taught is
now being verified; namely, that being one with the Father in essence,
when those Sons of God withdrew from this plane of action, they
would have the power to send back to man the Holy Ghost, the Comforter, the Divine Essence which had imbued them with wisdom, to
assist in the regeneration of the human race. In other words, that a
tremendous impulse, an unsurpassable power, namely, the power of
intuitive wisdom and knowledge, would be at the service of others as

it had been of themselves, by which those others could have unending communication, a perfect union with and understanding of, all those Elder Brothers; and also that a perfect realization of the truth would come to them that every unselfish service, every willing sacrifice rendered by a human being to another is the stretching out of the hand of the Christ; that every effort made to atone for wrongdoing is a step toward self-redemption.

Ah, children mine, do not permit any misinterpretation, any wrong construction of words and sentences to come between God and your own souls, or to shut out the love, service, and sacrifice of Christ. Remember that the touch of a loving hand, the low soft word of sympathy, condolence, and compassion spoken by your brother or sister in your need is a touch by the hand of God, the voice of an all-powerful servitor, comforter, and coadjutor; that the love welling up in your hearts unselfishly is, as it were, the Breath of God breathed out by yourselves.

The false conceptions that have crept into religious systems — the qualities which man has evolved, and which have been attributed by man to Divinity — are all that the sincere, earnest man has really parted with, in giving up some false idea of God. The highest and best, the most powerful of all that he has intuitively recognized as God-like — as well as inconceivably more — he has retained, whether or not he is conscious of it.

Do not let your own inability to conceive of an ideal which can adequately express all that you feel there must be, in God and Christ, rob you of the benefit you may receive from the ideals you are now capable of creating or of perceiving. Remember you are as yet but "God's little ones" — immature children — and that God and Christ, Love and Service, Omnipotent Law and Divine Power, are evolving those "little ones" to perfection. Let no man take your crown, the crown of your faith, knowledge, and growth.

Weighty indeed hath been the karmic action upon the human race of that trepidation and ever increasing terror of the unknown (the result of the curse of fear), first instilled by the selfish, ferocious, soulless enemies of man. Soulless, yet possessed of intelligence sufficient to feel the wish to desecrate, and if possible to destroy, the bridge between the Higher and lower selves of the newly Christ-born — the evolving race which had already built up suitable vehicles for the incarnating of the waiting Egos of the spiritual plane, and by such destruction forever prevent the entrance of the mediatorial element into embryonic man, leaving merely replicas of their own impalpable, restricted lives. For it is to these denizens of the lower astral plane that man must look in his search for the veiling of intellect which cuts off from him the knowledge that the first awakening of the concept of God, whatever the thing or creature to which the concept may apply, is God; and to these beings he must look for the blasting of the reverential awe and intelligent appreciation of the truth which intuitionally teaches him that there is something, some being, some power, which is far in advance of aught that he has yet experienced; and also for keeping man in ignorance of that immeasurably great truth that *good is God*; God in expression, God in form (as much as God, who is all form, could be confined in one form), whenever and however Good is being manifested.

With the acceptance and appreciation of this illimitable, stupendous fact — the personal realization that God is surrounding, interpenetrating, informing them, folding them, as it were, within a garment of love, of power of expansion, of unification — what room is there in the heart of a sane, normal human being for aught that can conflict with his reverent desire for the fulfillment of the evident divine purpose, conflict with his awe at the grandeur, the overwhelming greatness of that which no man has ever been able to express in suitable terms, or will be able to while in the flesh. And when one thinks of the depths to which a normally intelligent human being may sink, when from fear of losing some paltry material advantage, he refuses to affirm his belief in an all-powerful God or openly to identify himself with those who are seeking the source of their being, and in his puny dread of the ridicule of some other equally ignorant or defiled burlesque of the truly human, unites with the latter in discrediting his superiors, it causes one to wonder to what possible further depth such can descend. One can but pity the cowardice and weakness which makes a worldly devotee hedge about, belittle his own soul, and cast a shadow of unjust criticism on all those human beings who gladly and gratefully acknowledge their indebtedness to and love for the Elder Brothers who have pointed out the long hidden path back to the Godhead, and (O Patience, fold me close!) in many instances does so for the reason that some other poor unfortunate has made a futile effort to win reverent obedience or succor from him on what he believes to be a false basis. He is not wise enough to perceive that his own limitations have kept him from right discrimination. Ah, fool, indeed, is he who can surrender his faith, his reverence, his devotion to Good, however feebly manifested, at the bidding or because of the example of another, when that other has never "touched the hem of the divine garment." Surely of all men he is most to be pitied and shunned.

No man has ever found God by way of his intellect, but the path from his heart is straight and always wide open.

LESSON 71
THE GLORY OF THE LORD

The Ego which was last in incarnation upon this planet in the body of Jesus the Nazarene is the same Ego which has incarnated in every racial and national Savior since the beginning of the present great cycle of 200,000 years, and every such Savior has heralded the beginning of one age, a minor cycle of the major cycle; that is, the finger of God has, as it were, drawn a smaller circle within a large circle, and evolved a new order of life upon it. When the great cycle is closed, the Ego which has built up the bodily expressions of those individual Saviors, will pass on to take up a higher mission, perhaps upon some other planet, and its labors will fall upon the Ego which comes next in development, and who will begin to build up the vehicles — personalities — for its incarnations with the first minor of the major cycle. The incarnating Ego of the Saviors of any one major cycle is the Great Initiator, the "Watcher on the Threshold," for that cycle. Only as man can understand all that is involved in the words, "a group soul," can he understand just what Jesus was and is. The reflection of the sun which you see in a pool of water is not the real sun, yet it partakes of certain qualities and characteristics active in that sun. In illustration: if the sun were able to fix all its reflections permanently, and endow them with mind, the vibrations in continuous action between the sun and those reflections might gradually evolve a group soul; the sun being the central figure, there would be a continual interaction of forces and principles as time passed, and the sun and its reflections become one inseparable entity on a higher plane.

The personality of Jesus was correspondingly a reflection of the Father — the spiritual Sun — and there obtained that perfect interaction of forces and principles between them, which made them one in deed and in truth, as has also been the case with preceding Saviors.

If a perfect understanding of this important truth has come to us, it is no longer difficult to appreciate the righteousness of the demands made upon us as to reverence, service, and implicit obedience to the commands of Jesus.

We make a tremendous mistake when we try to relegate Jesus to some inferior position, and set up an abstraction in the place he formerly held. We often hear the expression, "There is as much of the Christ in me as there was in Jesus," but this is not true. There may be as much of that divine principle in such a one potentially, but there is not *in actu*.

To whatever extent the principles and powers which constitute the Christos, the Son of God, are developed in any human being, to that extent he has become a Christ, a Savior, and is worthy of like love and reverence. But we must not forget the fact of the mathematical perfection of the action of all natural law, and if one is not by divine right in some given position in the cosmic scale of all manifested life, the forces and principles which are preeminently active in that position or state cannot act upon the personal self as potently as they can in the one person who has reached that karmic position, and consequently cannot be as worthy of the love, service, and reverence of those who are in lower positions karmically on the same scale. It would not be a question of potential worthiness in such an instance, but of actual worthiness; nor a question of ability or lack of ability to function the cosmic forces and principles pertaining to such position; the position itself is the first consideration.

God cannot, as it were, burst into the bloom of humanity at one bound. Leaf by leaf, petal by petal, the divine bud generated by law is opening. The Master Jesus was one of the petals, which one aspect of cosmic law in conjunction with individual effort had broken loose from the restraint imposed by another phase of the same law, in advance of the other closely bound petals of the bud, and by that single act had made possible the opening of the rest of the petals; for as long as the first petal remained bound, the bud could not open perfectly. If any other petal should force its way open before the first had opened, the symmetry and beauty of the bud would be lost, and the final result would be a monstrosity instead of a perfect flower.

The average idea of the great sacrifice as associated with Jesus is based upon wrong premises; it clings about the surrender of the physical body, which is but one feature of that sacrifice. The breaking forth of that first petal — the separation from the Father — the heartbreaking cry, "My God, my God, why hast thou forsaken me!"[1] indicates the positive aspect of that great sacrifice, as the words, "It is finished,"[2] indicate the negative aspect of the same, and we must not lose sight of the truth that the rendering of this great sacrifice was no more requisite for the final perfecting of Jesus than it is for the perfecting of every disciple of the White Lodge.

The morning stars sing together at the birth of a soul, as the evening stars weep at its death; but this is only evidenced on the interior planes. The birth of a soul on the material planes is, as it were, its death on the spiritual (its temporary obscuration); but it is well that all earth should rejoice in commemoration of such an event, for in such rejoicing, the soul that is passing from death to life finds much of its compensation for the sorrows through which it has passed, and those who rejoice find the strength in their rejoicing that will enable them to endure the inevitable suffering which follows upon the final renunciation.

The stones of the sacrificial altar, and the fagots for the fire are found and laid in rejoicing; the sacrificial victim is bound and dies in sorrow, but the fire which kindles the fagots and consumes the sacrifice is the annealing force which combines altar, fagots, and victim, and raises the result, the spiritual giant, to the throne of power, where neither joy nor pain has dominion over it — where service and service alone is its life. And it is then, and then alone, that the soul of man finds out the purpose of life, and the realization of its own divinity, only then that "Death is swallowed up in victory,"[3] and that Law is fulfilled in perfect love.

"Rejoice, ye children of earth, for unto you is born this day a King," a "prince of the house of David," sang the seraphs in a day that is past.[4] Yet again and again shall the same song be sung by you and yours in the days to come, and each song shall bring you closer to the fulfillment of your highest desire.

---

[1] Matthew 27:46.

[2] John 19:30.

[3] 1 Corinthians 15:54.

[4] See Luke 2:11.

LESSON 72
THE REVELATION

Among many wonderfully prepared parchments and papyrus leaves done in exquisitely illumined text, the work of many disciples through generation after generation, there now lies in the secret chambers of an ancient Order of the Initiates one which contains a full interpretation of the "visions" as seen by John, "the beloved disciple," while undergoing his final initiation, in preparation for his translation.

These visions have been wisely termed the Revelation, yet they are only revelation to the initiated, for in all the archives of philosophical and sacred literature, there is nothing which begins to compare with those ancient works in esoteric significance; nothing so trustworthy or more vitally important to the whole human race. Their half-revealed lights, their dark shadows — the effects of righteously administered justice — are strongly enough cast to enlighten the intuitional student sufficiently to arouse him to necessary investigation, while the more deeply concealed truths are so perplexing as to discourage the most able scholars unless spiritual enlightenment has been vouchsafed them, either by spiritual illumination or by individual effort of the "Brothers of Compassion," who alone hold the keys to obscure Biblical symbology.

The visions of John, though expressed in somewhat different language than have been similar visions seen by others, are the visions which every initiate of the Ancient Orders of the Priesthood — the Sons of Hermes,[5] the Order of the Saviors of mankind, must necessarily behold when he reaches the degree of full illumination. Naturally each initiate would express his visions and experiences in different language, using different terminology from others, but the differences to be found would be very slight, and would concern unimportant details. All the main features would be found to be identical.

It can be readily understood that there must be some vital necessity for a continuance of any one series of interior experiences in all such instances, and that such is the case is beyond question to those who are familiar with the correct interpretation of the same, for these visions are exact representations of the closing events of every great age of manifestation; and not only of the closing events of an age of one or more planets, but also of the closing events of the still greater age of a whole planetary chain — the solar system to which those planets

---

[5] *Hermes* — a Greek name for Thoth, the Egyptian God of Wisdom.

belong. Every observer of this series of visions naturally applies those terms with which he is most familiar, in expressing any feature of the great series, and the terms applied by John were those which were in common use by the race to which he belonged; but the interpretation before mentioned, when given by a Master, is made in a universal language consisting of symbols in color and form, and is therefore easily read by every advanced chela of the White Lodge who has access to it. However, I do not wish to imply that it can be correctly interpreted by every such chela without assistance. No one of these visions has been so persistently misinterpreted as that contained in the twelfth chapter of Revelation. Woman after woman has given it a personal interpretation. The beauty of the imagery has first attracted each in turn, and either some part of the Cosmic event has been interiorly perceived, or a natural desire has led to self-deception, or, as has frequently happened, the ignorance or deceit of some personal admirer or disciple has led to an application of the mystic symbols to some aspirant for Divine power; and the average human being willingly accepts all offered homage and honor, regardless of the efforts of the still small voice to show how misplaced is the homage offered, or how unworthy of it the recipient may be; and the fact that each woman is indeed and in truth most deeply concerned in the great reality which underlies the superficial aspect of the mother of a Christ, and that there is a basic principle back of the desire for such motherhood, renders it all the more difficult to entirely ignore the false claims of the self-deceived, or the personal interpretation of the symbolic truths.

The Eternally Feminine is symbolized in the woman who is "clothed with the sun, with the moon under her feet and a crown of twelve stars on her head."[1]

The symbol has been interpreted astrologically many times, but the average astrologer is so handicapped by his lack of knowledge of the secret planets and their influences that he gains but a limited concept of the magnitude and importance of the symbol as a whole. The eternally feminine — the Great Mother — as represented on the earth plane by Astarte[2] and Isis[3] of the ancients, by the Virgin Mary

---

[1] Revelation 12:1.

[2] *Astarte* — a Phoenician goddess of fertility, motherhood, and love who corresponds to the Babylonian and Assyrian goddess Ishtar and who became identified with the Egyptian Isis, the Greek Aphrodite, and others.

[3] *Isis* — the ancient Egyptian Mother Goddess, the ideal of femininity and motherhood; personified Nature. The Christian image of God's Mother with the Child in her arms dates back to the image of Isis with the infant Horus.

of the Christian era and relatively by every woman incarnated who has borne a child, is in reality "clothed with the sun" — the Father — as Mary was "overshadowed by the Holy Ghost"[4] — the spirit of the Godhead, the Father. The Moon, the feminine symbol, is "under the feet of the woman," for the reason that the Moon typifies the lower aspect, the travail of childbirth, and the malefic forces which deceive, intoxicate, and cause great suffering to the feminine — the negative aspect of life. With the attainment of sufficient power of a spiritual nature, woman will be able to dominate and transmute the forces which have hitherto held her in subjection, thus bringing them "under her feet," the feet symbolizing *understanding*.

The twelve stars symbolize the twelve dominant vital forces of the universe, the gaining control of which — using them to crown her efforts — will be the fruit of the travail of woman; and thus will be vindicated the action of the law of compensation for past suffering.

The succeeding events detailed somewhat in the same chapter are as broad and deep and mysterious as is that of the above-mentioned illustration, but it would require volumes to interpret them all, and I have only intended to illustrate my first statement. If a faint concept of the importance of these cosmic symbols given in vision to the prepared could dawn upon the minds of those who so contemptuously deride the possibility of intercommunication between the different planes of existence, they would be much richer in knowledge, for such derision shuts the door which otherwise might open for their enlightenment. Far better would it be for such an one to submit to false representations temporarily than to make it impossible for the truth to be manifested for his more perfect understanding.

A short horizontal bar, a figure of the new moon with horns up underneath the bar, a small five-pointed star with the figure twelve below it placed over the bar, and a small golden-colored sphere over all, would indicate to the enlightened all that is contained in the before-mentioned cosmic symbol as expressed in words. The colors in which the different features of the symbols were outlined would indicate the spheres of action upon which the manifestation of the prophecy was to occur.

The dense ignorance and unbelief of the great majority in all that concerns symbolism is keeping the world from obtaining desirable knowledge and power. The sciences which many investigators are

---

[4] See Luke 1:35.

spending their lives, money, and strength to bring to high standards are all clearly outlined in such symbolic representations. The same sciences have been studied and brought to perfection in ages past, and put into symbolic form as a legacy for those who were to come after; but, as a rule, man will not use the same means of enlightenment in this age that were used by the old sages; consequently, the symbols remain uninterpreted, or are marks for ridicule and contempt, or avoidance.

There is a very palpable weakness in the argument used to destroy the faith of the unprepared in the possible observation of visible and audible phenomena connected with interior planes of being.

While the senses are known to be the most unreliable purveyors of fact, they are the only means of observation which the majority possess; and when some individual asserts that he has seen or heard some hitherto unknown or mysterious thing or event, and that individual's assertion or oath would be unquestionably accepted if he were placed on the witness stand or in a jury box where the lives of one or a dozen human beings depended upon his reliability and integrity, it seems like an absurd travesty of justice to repudiate and deny the possibility of his asserted observations in the former instance and accept and justify the latter, especially when the only means of determining the truth lies in the higher development of the senses of the one who is sitting in judgment.

The unfortunate individual who deliberately plays upon what are termed the finer qualities of human nature for pecuniary advantage, is in reality on exactly the same level of development upon which stands the man who misrepresents or adulterates the food products upon which the lives of other human beings depend, for his own pecuniary profit. One class of offenses is no worse than the other. The unrighteousness in both instances is the misuse, the violation of the vital essence of the Christos, for the nucleus of every organized or unorganized form of energy — physical, mental, or spiritual — is the mantle, the vehicle of the essence of the Christos, and its misuse is sin, whatever form that misuse may take, and that essence is as active in the nucleus of a wheat or corn cell as it is in a cell which helps to form an organ in the physical body of a man.

LESSON 73
THE WAY

"No man cometh unto the Father save by me."[1] Strange, incomprehensible words, save to the few who have gone or are going the way of the Christs, and therefore have some faint idea of the goal — the Father.

Man strives to fix some kind of a working hypothesis in his mind regarding the intangible, omnipresent, inscrutable mystery of the Godhead in which "we live and move and have our being,"[2] but he is powerless to conceive a satisfactory ideal of a formless, conditionless, limitless existence, in which all things and creatures are potentially or actively alive; and so, until he reaches a certain stage of development, the nearest he comes to the truth is by the creation of an ever-receding ideal, which, because of its intangibility and changeableness, satisfies him but a short time. He does not realize that even his dissatisfaction with those ideals indicates that he is making much more progress than he was making when he clung to some less changeable ideals. It is in the making of too great an effort to hold on to some limited concept of the Godhead, such as has been done in the past and is now being done in orthodoxy and in some of what are called the New Thought movement — limiting the limitless — that a great wrong is done the aspiring soul. The greedy clutching at and persistent holding on to a worn out or lived out ideal of God in abject fear that somehow that God is going to be lost or is going to lose him if he does not hold on, when in reality the great Father-Mother resident in his soul is pleading for greater expression, is a sad hindrance to man.

Man begins to limit God by fear. When fear rules him in place of love, he creates a personal object of worship or dread, which will act as a blinder to his own intelligence and understanding. We can readily create a limited ideal of the great reality insofar as it pertains to or is active within our own individual forms, our own environment, or our little planet; but while we are trying to combine any two or more of these fields of action, we lose the connection between them (blank space alone is unthinkable) and fail to see that in the gulf so created the Godhead is as active as in the visible forms, and probably much more so; so we find we are able to retain only a series of broken

---

[1] John 14:6.
[2] Acts 17:28.

reflections instead of the one composite reflection, the one Divine Reality, a realization and acceptance of which would give us some faint idea of the truth and a better understanding of the fact that the different Gods the majority of the human race delight to honor, or fear intensely, are but some of these broken reflections.

It may help some of your number to remember that at any point in life or in space where our consciousness and divine thought centers; at that point is the center of the universe for us, and there is where our own Higher Self now is, has always been, and will always be. By such a point or center, I mean that center in whatsoever or whomsoever self-consciousness — the consciousness of existence as an individualized life — has awakened in threefold activity, Desire, Will, and Mind — the deific forces — in other words, the soul. The individual who has won the power to function the above-mentioned deific forces in equilibrium, has become a Savior — a Son of God — a part of the Way.

It may be of some assistance if in meditation you can retain the consciousness that in every grain of earth, every drop of water, every molecule of fire or air, though it be invisible to you, there is a definite degree of the Christos active, and the outer coverings or vehicles of action of those centers receive and radiate that great life principle or energy, according to their particular growth and development; and that though the forms and degree of power active in each are continually changing, the centers are unchangeable, eternal — are in fact the *substance* of "the Path" — the Way.

Try to imagine an ever-expanding, unending, ever-increasing (in power and brilliancy) spherical radiator of light, which combines all the before-mentioned centers, your own center among all others, which has neither beginning nor end — and the radiations of which are Love, Wisdom, Power, and Truth — in fact, the Way to God.

LESSON 74
THE TRUE PATH

One part of the world is woefully deceiving itself, refusing to believe the records forced upon its attention, deliberately ignoring the testimony of those who have been taught by sad experience and suffering; drugging conscience by over excitement and seeking by vain efforts to amuse itself by legitimate or questionable forms of entertainment; all of which is due to utter hopelessness and despair of better conditions. In many instances inherent selfishness has induced the acceptance of some cult disguised under terms expressive of the tenderest, holiest emotions of the human heart, or by high-sounding scientific terms. When the teachings of many of these cults are thoroughly analyzed and viewed from a higher consciousness, they are found to be the rankest kind of selfish imposture, and perfect epitomes of blasphemous idolatry, or preparatory instructions in phallicism.

In view of the fact that education has become almost compulsory in all so-called civilized nations today, there is no valid excuse for ignorance in regard to the woeful tyranny of the over-rich, the rapid increase of poverty and suffering, of crime in high places, of slavery worse than has been practiced for centuries, because more intelligently perpetrated.

There is no excuse, no justification for the expenditure of the vast sums literally thrown away in the building of great cathedrals, palaces, places of amusement, or objects of adornment. I say thrown away, because not one stone will be left on another when the human cyclone now gathering as a result of such unjust accumulation of wealth and unwise expenditure has passed over the doomed territories.

No matter how great the sacrifice, how unselfish the efforts put forth by those who have not become identified with the $ aristocracy of the day, toward the building up of some purely philanthropic institution for the use of the suffering, or for the education of the masses, it either fails of sustenance and passes into a receiver's hands, or is seized by some modern highway robber and turned into another "den of thieves."[1] You hear moderately well-informed people discoursing about the wonderful examples of charity set to the world in the establishment of some of the great hospitals, yet let some poor suffering soul apply for operation or treatment at many of them, and the degree of assistance rendered is in exact proportion to the length of the patient's purse.

The saddest of all the sad effects of this era of repudiation of spiritual, and mad accumulation of material wealth, is the blighting of the sense of interdependence between man and man, and the destruction of long cherished ideals of the Fatherhood of God and Brotherhood of Man. The empty places in the hearts of countless numbers of those

---

[1] Matthew 21:13.

who have cherished those ideals are fast filling with utter discouragement, hopelessness, and despair. The intelligence, the energy which
has heretofore enabled the human race to build those high ideas, has
been prostituted to unworthy ends, and the result is a reaction which
has destroyed man's faith in his fellow man; and worse still, his power
of loving his fellow man. In business every man takes every other man
to be a soulless antagonist and treats him accordingly. Mutual help is
no longer offered or expected, save in rare instances.

When a realization of these facts dawns upon one of average intelligence, and he attempts to voice his discoveries and fears, and to send
forth a warning cry or an earnest entreaty to others to pause and apply
some remedy to the disease he beholds, at once the cry of pessimist,
revolutionist, or anarchist goes out, and his efforts are nullified in the
cases of those who most need his help; those who because of selfish
desire have conceived a great admiration for the methods and results
of modern business. Many of the people most nearly concerned are
well aware of the seething spirit of discontent which is rapidly forcing
events to a disastrous conclusion, but they are devoid of the will power
and power of initiative that are essential to a clear concept of the right
steps to be taken to avert or lessen such disaster; and yet these people
are the only hope of their fellow men, from an exterior point of view;
and it is to such as these that I now appeal. Even if they must lose some
of their hard-earned material wealth; even if those vacant places in
their hearts still resound with the voices of the elemental forms with
which they have replaced the spiritual ideals of long ago, it is worth
their while to take a backward look in search of those lost ideals and
try to win them back.

There is but one way for man to identify himself with God — there
has ever been but one way; Jesus of Nazareth voiced that way in the
words of the Golden Rule.[1] Even if man must yield up physical life in
the great contest, is it not better to yield it in reaching after the only
thing that makes life worth living, the only thing that gives assurance
of a better life, a broader chance, than yield it in a maelstrom of hatred
and despair, as he inevitably must do if he will not listen and hear the
appeal of the Spirit of Love?

[1] "Thou shalt love the Lord thy God with all thy heart, and with all thy soul,
and with all thy strength, and with all thy mind; and thy neighbor as thyself"
(Luke 10:27); "Therefore all things whatsoever ye would that men should do to
you, do ye even so to them: for this is the law and the prophets" (Matthew 7:12).

I make no appeal from the (to them) incomprehensible height of occultism, for if the rich (the overburdened) man cannot enter the Kingdom of Heaven, much less can the unbelieving, faithless, or despairing, selfish man go far on the Path of Enlightenment. The characteristics which keep him in the rut he has formed, the fallacy which leads him to believe that he has sounded every depth of spiritual experience in the days of his long renounced orthodoxy, will not loosen their hold at any light demand; and unless the very foundations of his life are shattered, he cannot be aroused to a consciousness that there is aught worth striving for upon that Path, or, indeed, that there is such a Path at all, much less the God-like reward for unselfish endeavor. He cannot prevail upon himself to accept the most comforting, the most immeasurably great truth, that the only authentic evidences of the facts of a continuous line of evolution must be given by those who have passed from one phase of evolution into another, and who can no more return to the former, the human phase, in possession of the power to disclose the secrets of the Path to a pessimist, than a man of any present day race could appeal to the mentality of an anthropoid ape and convey a lucid idea of the methods by which he had reached the human stage. When man has outgrown the more infantile instructions of orthodoxy, if he fails to comprehend that there must be more beyond, and he is left without a conscious director, he drifts into faithlessness, unbelief and despair. The horror of such a fate should at least render one willing to consider the fact of the existence of the Masters and the Lodge, even though ignorant students of philosophy almost smother the truth in false representations and absurd or impossible delineations, and to make some effort to open his eyes to the transcendent light glowing upon the Path, even though it be too vivid for his unaccustomed eyes. But, alas, the great majority have chosen to dwell in darkness.

LESSON 75
THE MYSTERIES

One of life's deep mysteries lies in man's persistent ignoring of the open secrets which are so common as to stultify the almost universal characteristic of curiosity. Although such secrets are so common as to make it impossible for us to draw breath, to tread upon the ground, to see or hear any phase or condition of matter, without uncovering one or more of them, we seldom associate them with the great truths we are wont to call "the Mysteries." We would willingly offer all that is ours to give for an opportunity consciously to unveil those mysteries under the direction of those we deem competent to rightly demonstrate such incalculably important and sacred realities.

No true teacher of occult philosophy could minimize the importance of the law of correspondences or fail to lay that law down as a fundamental proposition to any student, unless from spiritual blindness or self-interested motives he ignored his duty or refused to enlighten said student as to the universality and essential value of the material manifestations of that law, each one of which is a guide to enlightenment.

The value of the law of Correspondences in solving the ever-recurring mystifying problems which harass the soul and make of earthly existence, in the majority of cases, one long question mark, one never-ending cry, "Why is it?" is beyond all possible computation.

In the law which prevents the mixing of oil and water; in the law which provides for and protects the fructifying, growth, maturing, and disintegration of the weed under our feet; in the law which provides the right environment for one order of life and denies existence to that particular order of life in any other environment; the law which refuses water the right to run up an inclined plane and impels it to take a downward course; in the law which sets one star above another in glory and power; in all these and countless other differentiations of the one law as exemplified in action all about us, we may by a little study and observation solve every perplexing secret, unravel every mystery which the soul is driving man to fathom in order that he may enter upon his inheritance. But the greater part of the time and effort of the great majority is given to creating countless lesser mysteries which only add to the burden they are bearing, finally resulting in the sad-faced, heartsick, selfish, and inconsiderate cumberers of the earth that they are.

In the case of a disciple, constant repetition by the Master of the preliminary teachings, which are at first absolutely necessary for enlightenment, either results in demands for still further repetition of the same or for instructions regarding phases of life which would be utterly incomprehensible to the human race in its present stage of development. You should never lay by a statement of fact until you have mastered it.

You would smile at the childishness of the man who insisted upon your making a fire in a bucket of water; you would never think of expecting a child to do the work of a trained mechanic; it would never occur to you to demand that the tiller of the soil should paint a marvelous work of art, neither would you demand excellence in chemistry from a devotee of the harp or viol. These are all such obvious absurdities that they would not require a second thought, yet from willful ignorance or careless negligence of opportunity, you are continually performing even worse absurdities, and suffering from the effects of the same, to a degree that would seem almost unbearable, were you aware of the facts concerned, and in many cases do become unbearable when mental or physical weakness results from continued repetitions of such effects, and they are added to the already too heavy burdens you bear.

If you see a beautiful flower droop and die from the effects of the sun's excessive heat, or lack of water, you do not have to argue about the matter; if you desire to save the flower you will protect it from the sun, or give it water, as the case may be. You have been taught that fire and water are the fundamentals of all life, yet if you see a human being sickening or dying from some unaccountable cause, it does not occur to you that some form of fire or water might save that life. It might be the fire that is kindled by sympathetic and helpful words and deeds, or the water which is formed by the union of two forces which correspond to hydrogen and oxygen, and which flows from "the well of tears." It may be the knife or the bitter draught that is needed to tap that well, and the only question you have to ask yourself is as to your ability to use that knife or give that bitter draught in the right spirit and from the right motive. But, my child, make sure that you do not administer fire when water is required, or the reverse, and you can only make sure, as you would make sure of the need of the flower, by intelligent observation of causes, and diagnosis of surrounding conditions. And as there are only these two infallible rules for determining the need, and the requisite supplying of the same on the plane of physical expression, so there are but the same two rules (or shall we call them laws?) by means of which we can diagnose and determine the requisite medium for equilibrating the unbalanced substance in the mentally, physically, or spiritually unbalanced; and, sad to say, a large majority of the human race are thus unbalanced.

If you see a stick of caustic applied to flesh, you know that it is going to destroy a certain area about the point of contact. If you use your knowledge of the law of correspondences, you know that the human thought or word which partakes of the nature of that caustic (and its nature is as easily determined by the same law of correspondences) will affect a corresponding area of substance of one or more of the interior vehicles of the life forces of your victim; the destruction or injury being according to the degree of resistance the victim is able to oppose to the attacking power, and when you think seriously over this fact and realize the effects of your cruelty in conjunction with like cruelty perpetrated, perhaps by hundreds of others just as careless and thoughtless as yourself, it may be you can gain some slight knowledge of the causes of the crucifixion of every accepted chela — every Savior — who gives not only his physical but his astral and manasic[1] body up to the torture of human kind, that they may profit by his sacrifice.

When you have suffered enough from the effects of such causes, from the loss of ideals, from disappointments, sorrows, the direct reaction of just such offenses as I have indicated, destruction of faith, ingratitude, your continual torture of the only links between you and the Lodge, your seeming incapacity for realizing that you are cutting off the only media of communication I have with you, then you may be able to see what you have thrown away. God grant you may see before it is too late.

LESSON 76
LEST WE FORGET

If it were for the best interests of humanity at its present stage of development to be able to predict all future events, the knowledge which would enable them to do so would have been more emphatically forced upon them; but while such knowledge has always been possible of attainment, it was only so to those who had developed the interior senses to a marked degree, and who therefore comprehended the vastness of existent relations between all states and planes of life, and could therefore draw the right conclusions from even slight data, and compute the length of corresponding periods of time, according to the magnitude of the event or divine purpose. The possibility of such attainment lies back of the desire for the same, even in primitive man.

---

[1] The mental body associated with Manas, or Mind.

Man always attains what he most desires, if such desire be based upon a principle of life, and therefore he has conquered the unorganized, unrestrained, heterogeneous, lawless elements sometimes posited by those who are not yet able to see the unity of the basic principles which underlie all interior and exterior phenomena, and therefore he recognizes the impossibility of any lasting restriction as regards to knowledge of any phase of such phenomena.

As well strive to separate the currents of the ocean from the water of the same, and insist that the water moved by one current may not contact the water moved by another, as to separate one man — a drop of the universal ocean — from another, or from any phase, state, or condition of matter, force, and consciousness. The divine current which moves the combined drops, can only move those drops (humanity) according to irrevocable laws, and if any of those drops are too light or too heavy (too advanced or too ignorant) to be borne by one current, they are taken up and carried on by another greater or lesser current, but in the course of time every drop of the cosmic ocean will touch every shore and every other drop, and according to the impression made by the contact (the stored up memory) will one drop recognize any other drop or shore, and profit by such recognition.

The language of symbolism, the science of the stars, the lines engraved on forehead and hand by life's experiences, all these are marks of recognition, points of contact which rightly interpreted indicate past, present, and future events, as surely as the rising of the sun indicates the beginning of a new day.

If all these facts can be understood and accepted, the majesty, purpose, and power of Cosmic symbolism, which includes astrology and prophecy, may be seen, and that great phenomenon of life be dignified and raised to its true position in the minds of men instead of, as now, being relegated to the shades of superstition and made a byword and epithet of contempt by some, and used for the deception and beguilement of their fellow men by others.

While the vibrations raised by the Initiates through the repetition of ancient prophecies and messages of warning or encouragement for the future have resulted in sending a stream of similar prophetic utterances throughout the world, the ignorance of vitally important central fundamental points, upon which, like the spokes of a wheel to the hub, all other aspects or delineations of such prophecies or messages depend, renders such utterances of little or no importance.

By the loss of mental and physical force expended in fear or contempt, man weakens his power to meet events prophesied, or to reach the point of development before mentioned, where he can rightly understand, interpret, and prepare to deal with coming events.

You have been told at different times that discouragement, illness, bereavement, loss of confidence in yourselves and others, suicidal tendencies, and despair are often brought on by continued exposes of unwise or unworthy teachers, and above all by the unnatural thirst for material gold, which crushes out all human feeling and leaves only a grim harvest of abnormality, hidden by a mask of supposed virtue and self-importance. All these sad effects of ignorance separate you from each other and from the Higher Self, and life becomes a terror and, so far as you can see, the gift of a fiendish, instead of a beneficent power. Yet all this you must face and conquer, and you have now to decide whether you will do it alone, or with those who have conquered and stand ready to aid you if you will make the necessary conditions.

Enough of the statements I have made have been already fulfilled to assure you that others will be fulfilled. Less and less security for invested or hoarded means will be found. More and more disruption will occur and methods of quick slaughter be found. Wave upon wave of crime will arise as a result of the frenzy aroused by the above-mentioned discouragements, and if man refuses to make way for the manifestation of his own divinity, to whom or what will he turn in his hour of greatest need?

It is not because of my need of you that I urge you to stand firm and steady on any one of the Temple steps you have reached, but that you may have combined support of all the forces that constitute that step, in whatever karma may have in store for you personally. Build a center, a fulcrum in your own inner self, where the Love of the Great White Lodge may rest; and fear, the greatest of all stultifying, unsettling forces in the universe, will have no more dominion over you.

If you could fully understand and believe the vital truth in every statement of prophecy I have made to you; if you could accept the fact that every phase of the so-called new thought, the later scientific discoveries and results of inventive genius for the good of man, were either the results of advantage taken of the knowledge given out by the command of the Great White Lodge, first through the Initiate H.P.B. (Madame Blavatsky), secondly by W.Q.J. (William Q. Judge), and thirdly through the Temple; or were the perversion of such knowledge by the self-interested to the injury of mankind, you would be better able to appreciate the depth and importance of seemingly simple directions, and the necessity for fully learning the alphabet of occult science, as given in the Temple Teachings, and so guard yourselves against the danger you must ultimately meet when you begin to use the letters of that alphabet to form the words and interpret the same; in other words, apply the Wisdom and Knowledge you have gained to the solution of the material problems which will confront you.

LESSON 77
VALUE OF RELIGIOUS INSTINCT

If the unappeasable longing of the human heart for an undeniable, self-evident reality back of all evanescent, cyclic phenomena, for the source of the stream of love which springs up in man at the sight of a face, the touch of a hand, and like a living fountain of water beautifies every waste place and brings to birth the hidden germ of every useful and beautiful characteristic in human nature — for the unspeakable awe which numbs our gift of speech at the sight of some magnificent mountain scene or ravishing sunset; for the almost physical hunger which seizes one at the scent of some rare flower when the whole nature rebels and refuses to be satisfied with the sense of sight and smell alone; and most of all in the insatiable thirst for recognition by some extraneous force or being, of some quality or hard-won attribute believed by us to be worthy of recognition, or for the blotting out of the effects of some unworthy act which we know intuitively to be opposed to the manifestation of our ideals of perfection — if all these supersensitive actions of interior forces which are beyond our ken are aroused in us only to die of inanition for the reason that there is nothing behind and above them capable of nourishing and sustaining then permanently, then all life is a lie and a delusion, and the universe, the mad dream of a mad humanity; for nowhere in external expression may be found a manifestation of desire that somewhere, somehow, there has not been provision made for the satisfaction of that desire, and it is beyond the bounds of reason that the highest, purest, holiest desires of the human race have alone been left unprovided for.

The strongest proof of the underlying truth of any religious system is the need of its devotees for what that system can supply. We may satisfy our reason for a time with various scientific hypotheses, may over-exercise or stultify our minds with specious arguments against the probability of any reality back of the generally accepted dogmas and creeds which we have relinquished or have never fully accepted, but the fact remains, that when severe illness, desolation, great suffering, or their other extremes, great joy and gratification come upon us, we are driven back to our repudiated beliefs or discarded ideas of a possible Divine Reality.

It is only in the mediocre, the dead levels of life, when we have lost or thrown away the power to feel deeply, to desire ardently, that we can be satisfied with the results of our reasoning processes, our intellectual gymnastics. At either extreme, at the highest and lowest vibratory key of life, all in us that is capable of touching the hem of the garment of Infinite Love cries out for closer contact with that love at any sacrifice, and only in those extremes can such contact be secured, whether it be by means of some accepted religious belief or by the birth of the soul through travail of personal desire and effort.

The "Thank God!" which falls from the lips of the pessimist or materialist as he snatches a loved one from some imminent peril, is a surer indication of the existence of a Deity, a God who could be thanked, than years of argumentative denial of such an One could furnish to the contrary. One springs pure and limpid from the depths of man's divine nature, a result of instantaneous recognition of possible Infinite Love and protection, expressing one of the most beautiful attributes in life — Gratitude; the other is but the temporary illusionary action of a few of the surface ripples of the great Cosmic Ocean, transitory in their nature as the vagaries of a beam of light (as are all the operations of reason unaffected by intuition), possibly of use in determining temporary affairs, but failing egregiously in satisfying the soul which is caught in some abyss of lower desire, from which it cannot extricate itself without help.

LESSON 78
SOUND VIBRATIONS

Notwithstanding all the centuries of struggle and effort toward development which lie behind the present human race and its straining for educational, sociological, and material advantages, in some respects that race is exactly where it was ages ago; and the principal cause of such stultification, though always in evidence, as well as the cause of much of man's excruciating suffering of mind and body, and even crime, is deliberately ignored, ridiculed, sarcastically noted, or self-pityingly admitted, and then pushed aside and forgotten.

To my undying regret, I have seen the same causes set up by Templars, and working similar effects, and in many cases as flagrantly repeated, ignored, or excused. Careless as you seem of the inevitable fruits of these causes, vividly and repeatedly as I have pointed them out and urged their eradication upon you, I am nevertheless left with but little to encourage a repetition of the same; and yet if I refrain from repetition, I am remiss in duty.

I am sometimes awed at the apparent recklessness with which one or more of your number will draw down upon yourselves and your loved ones the active, malignant, elemental forces, and the condemnatory decisions of the Law which controls and punishes the use and abuse of the Divine energy called into action by the satirical, cruel, unjust, and often untrue statements to and against each other; and when the results of such action appear in your own lives, in the form of physical ailments, poverty, destruction of comeliness, loss of affection, faith, and trust, to say nothing of their effect on the substance with which you must build a Nirmanakaya body (if so be you are ever to build one), your indifference causes me to realize my impotence and the apparent uselessness of aiding you to destroy the ravaging demons which you permit to reappear without contest, owing to your own natural indolence.

After half a century of specific work in that line by myself, and in view of the fact that though the students of the Great Mysteries have been given so much attention and so much unparalleled instruction by others as well as myself, they have made, comparatively speaking, so little progress, I stand appalled at the thought of the superhuman task set the Initiates who are by karmic right the executors of divine law for the present Maha Yuga.

A student or novice claims the protection and assistance of the Lodge, deliberately takes a step by assuming obligations which must inevitably precipitate a large amount of back karma, refuses to perceive the obstacles he is continually creating, and when some crushing blow, some deprivation or loss occurs, some retrograde displacement from position, or failure to achieve distinction, it will almost invariably arouse latent anger or jealousy; and such victim of Illusion's spells, instead of seeking the ultimate cause of his difficulty in his own nature — his own acts and words — will "pile Pelion on Ossa"[1] by striking out blindly at "fate," at his teachers, his neighbor, or his material limitations or environment.

I ask you, my son — my daughter, individually, as one of those most vitally concerned, "What are you going to do to change these conditions in *yourself*?"

Occasionally one of your number will say, "I hate this or that person or condition; things are not what I expected at headquarters, so and so is cruel, unjust, or untrustworthy, and evidently desires my labor or my money," and so blindly continues to pile up imaginary grievances, utterly repudiating the probable fact that although he may have been invited, he has never been urged to take up any position and may have been advised to the contrary; forgetting that he had been given the privilege of helping to build a place of protection and safety for himself, not to enter one already built; forgetting all the kindnesses that have been shown him, all the sacrifices made by those upon whom he has subsequently brought anguish, suffering, and loss; ignorantly charging others with the use of undue influence, when almost, if not quite invariably, if he were open to conviction, a little calm, intelligent examination and investigation in the right direction could easily prove the reverse of his suspicions, and show him but too often utterly careless of the feelings of Those Who have sacrificed infinitely more than he to make possible an opening for him. Plunged in such a maelstrom a novice does not immediately perceive he has set in action these hitherto quiescent, now malignant, destructive forces of the negative pole of life in his own auric envelope, the action of which has an effect on the astral body similar to that of corrosive acids or sulfuric poisons on the physical; devouring, paralyzing, or disintegrating forces, which act by repercussion upon the organs, blood vessels, muscles, and nerves of his physical body, and ultimately bring on swellings, fever, eruptions of the body, and corresponding conditions in the astral envelope, and consequently, upon the substance he must evolve and manipulate in order to build a yet more interior vehicle.

---

[1] To further complicate something that is already tedious or challenging. Ossa and Pelion are two mountains in Greece. In Greek mythology, the twins Otus and Ephialtes piled Mount Pelion atop Mount Ossa and both atop Mount Olympus in an attempt to reach heaven and attack the gods.

"Nature abhors a vacuum."[2] If an individual sends out from his own auric center a definite degree of force of such a character as above noted, thus temporarily leaving a vacuum in such center, by that act he sets free an equal amount of the force of suction, which draws to himself from the aura of the one so attacked an exact equivalent, a definite amount or degree of the same force he has expelled (it may have been hitherto latent in the attacked), which will draw to himself and precipitate a corresponding attack from others. The law of compensation then begins to act, and, whether he will or not, he must pay the debt he has made in the same kind and degree — must give to that other part of his own substance, which alone will counteract the effect of the cause he has set up. He gives out an evil, a negative personal force; he draws to himself an impersonal retributive force that will fill the vacuum thus created, and then must give back of the best that is in him, a full equivalent to that of which he has robbed the other. This is one result of the action of the irrevocable triple-sided law of compensation.

The fact that he does not at once see the final results of its action is of no consequence, or that there is not an immediate material loss of health or wealth. Time has no existence in the Divine Mind. Other karma of a better nature then due may have to be lived out before the full results of his wrongly vitalized words become apparent.

You can predict very accurately that which lies before you, by a self-examination of your words and acts for or against others in the past, and someday you will know beyond question that the cancer, the fever, the eruption, the loss of a limb or organ, the utter breaking down of nerves, brain, and muscles from which you suffer, is primarily due to some cruel, unjust, or untrue statement forgotten, mayhap, as quickly as it was uttered. Remember "there are no little things." It hath been truly said, "You shall give an account of every idle word."[3]

Knowing all this, I ask you, is it surprising that almost despair seizes those who watch and labor to aid you in the dizzy climb to perfection, or that as I have before said, the causes of the calamitous episodes, the failures to make advance in the cases of pledged disciples,

---

[2] A postulate attributed to Aristotle (384–322 BCE) — an ancient Greek philosopher, scientist, and polymath who was a student of Plato and a teacher of Alexander the Great.

[3] Matthew 12:36.

the unhappiness and misery in the world, lie almost unrecognized, ignored, or despised?

Man's continuous ignoring of the power of silence, and the inevitable effects of careless use of words which have a divine origin and purpose, is responsible for three-fifths of his suffering.

The fact that the songs of the songbirds in the airy envelope of the earth, the roar of the mountain torrent, and other nature sounds are among the chief instruments for the increase and decrease in the rates of the earth's vibrations, should give you some idea of the importance and effects of the sounds you make and the words you utter.

The recent discoveries in connection with the methods by which sound may be transmitted and recorded may give you some idea of the methods used by natural law to transmit and record sound waves to and from the organic centers of the human body. The length of such waves indicates the strength and potency of the same; but to bring to outer perception any knowledge of the final effects of any one sound, the wave must be changed into a light wave (these two great energies are interchangeable, though one is a straight and the other a curved motion). Then another change in the vibration of the light wave brings the dormant fiery lives which constitute that light, into action, and it is through the control of those fiery lives that the results before mentioned are accomplished by divine retributive law.

Until the individual members of mankind at large can be taught to understand and apply these truths by control of vibration, they cannot rise to any great level. But the progress made in the transmitting and recording of sound, and the knowledge of the curve and wave motion of the same, indicates a gradual advance, though such advance could be accelerated; but man is slow to accept anything that costs him any great effort and sacrifice.

LESSON 79
THE HERESY OF SEPARATENESS

September 1908

It is a well-known fact among chemists, that upon the release of a single nascent atom from the other constituent atoms of any compound, by means of chemical action, the released atom seeks with newly aroused energy to unite itself with any other freed atom within its sphere of movement; but it is not so well known that the newly realized power which impels it to this action is derived from the shock which the other atoms of the compound sustained from the hammering they received at the time the atom was freed. The propelling power which launched it into space was drawn from the common reservoir, the reserve force which the combination of atoms possessed; therefore the latter was more or less temporarily crippled by the loss of force. But the loss sustained by the combination was little compared to the loss which the freed atom must sustain if it cannot immediately unite itself with other freed atoms; for, as in the case of all other users of suddenly acquired power, the velocity and intensity of its action soon cause exhaustion and devitalization, and the strength of the freed atom dwindles to nothing in short order.

Even disintegration is only a factor in integration. It is the negative pole to a positive force. If the main body dies from the loss sustained by the emission of an expulsive force, and a new coalition is formed of the freed atoms, the karmic action which ensues as a result of such necessity will invariably bring a similar catastrophe upon the new body within a comparatively short time, for karma works incessantly to preserve the integrity of the whole, to draw to a common center the fragments expelled from the center at the beginning of a great world period. If you were working in harmony with that law, every effort of your lives would go toward the building of any Lodge Center with which you were identified. Instead of flying off at a tangent at any blow struck against that center, you would gather every bit of energy in your auric body for the purpose of tightening your grip upon it. If there was an expulsion of disintegrating force within its ranks, you would change it or make it harmless. It is absurd to say that any body or coalition is too strong to conquer by your single efforts. Patience and determination will overcome evil or weakness; and by the exercise of the same you must eventually succeed, or be proved in the wrong by the forces you yourselves have evoked. In the latter case, if your motive has been pure, your real purpose has been served, which was the defense of your brethren and their best good.

If you desire life, health, happiness, and success in spiritual aspiration, take this communication and use it as a bugle call. Get into line, evoke your higher principles, take your place by the side of your Commander, and work for the good of the organization. If you let the enemy pound your body (The Temple) to fragments, or vitally injure its usefulness, you may be sure you will suffer defeat, not within, but without its ranks, and a worse defeat than ever before, because your original purpose was higher than the purpose of the enemy — the expelled atom before mentioned. It is the original motive of each atom which furnishes the concentration and integration of the atoms of the organic body. The expulsion of the atom is without individual self-conscious motive; it is due to the mass motive of self-protection, and is therefore of a lower order of power; and it is for this reason that the body can be shocked by the expulsion of an atom.

If its composite mass had arrived at the point of self-conscious individuality, the explosion which always causes an expulsion would occur within the atom expelled alone, and on the confines of the mass, where it could not injure the mass as a whole.

Gird up your loins and work for the individualizing of The Temple as you would work for self-consciousness as an individual.

THE WAR OF ARMAGEDDON

Do you realize that the war of Armageddon,[1] already commenced on the astral plane, and to be precipitated on the physical, is a religious war, strange as that statement must appear in this age of Iron? This is not recognized by the majority of those who see its coming, but, driving them on with fiendish ingenuity, the demons of darkness are forcing England, Japan, Russia, China, Germany, and the United States, and even fomenting internal struggles between factions, into what appears to a materialist to be a struggle for material power. But back of all exterior causes is the struggle for spiritual supremacy. On one side is the accumulated strength, power, and fanaticism of the ages, embodied in the Brothers of the Shadow, leagued against the strength, power, communism, true democracy, and conservative force — the garnerings of the middle path of the Brothers of Light.

I have told you the forces seemingly precipitated upon members of The Temple by the Brothers of the Shadow were not in reality primarily directed against you as individuals; they are against Us, the White Lodge, the progenitors of the human race, the bearers of the cosmic hammers and battle-axes, the Keepers of the Temple of the Holy Grail, and the great war referred to is between the Brothers of Light and the Brothers of Shadow, and the gages of battle are the souls of men. The final result means freedom or slavery for the human race for ages to come. It means man's victory over death, or continual dying, man's

---

[1] *Armageddon* — the Final Battle between the Forces of Light and darkness, as proclaimed in ancient prophecies. See *Glossary* for more.

union with God, or dispersion from God, and it is these tremendous, incalculably great issues, which will make the result of this universal contest the point of balance in the evolution of man for ages to come.

Look deep enough, and you will see the jewels of truth in my statements. Remember it will be true Christianity, typified by the white race, that will be lined up against prostituted Shintoism, Buddhism, Confucianism, etc., as typified by the yellow race, and the latter are being reinforced by the devil-ridden devotees of demonology who belong to the black races. The Occidental and Oriental races are the vehicles of power, but the one great issue is the higher evolution of man.

Look underneath the surface of all the exterior causes set up by those who are contending against each other in this worldwide struggle for future existence on this planet, and you will find what is sometimes termed religious instinct — the innate longing of the latent or the awakened soul for consciousness of Self. When that longing has deteriorated by constant indulgence of the sensuous, selfish, lower nature of man through repeated incarnations, the soul is driven out from the body, and the longing for spiritual supremacy, the cry of the created for its creator is replaced by a longing for material supremacy; and a spiritual degradation corresponding to the material uplift takes place.

The incarnating Ego is thus disgraced and degraded by being compelled to seek the races which are on the downward arc of civilization in order to incarnate. The yellow and black races long since lost their power of interpreting and absorbing spiritual truth. They are only now passing the lower point of that arc and so have but just started on their upward arc; consequently there is a natural religious antagonism back of the material antagonism felt by both races for each other.

LESSON 80
CHEMICAL ACTION

The states of matter commonly termed Akashic, Ethereal, Watery, and Fiery by the student of occult science, contain the bases of the gases known to exoteric science, as parohydrogenic, parooxygenic, oxyhydrogenic, and nitrogenic.

By combining, recombining, and dissociating the above-mentioned gases in ways known only to Initiates of high degree, divine chemistry evolves a state of substance — a transitory vehicle, as a temporary residence for each division of the spiritual life forces to be incarnated in gross matter during a great cycle. One such vehicle has been recently brought before the exoteric scientific world in the character of radium. When the individualized lives confined in radium are released and brought into association with one of the gases which has been generated by combination and dissociation of the four first mentioned or primal gases, there is evolved a certain degree of secondary elemental lives which are subject to the will of the practical occultist, and by means of which many of the mysterious phenomena performed by such occultists are brought about. But as soon as the energy — the will power — which has combined the before-mentioned gases is withdrawn, there is an instant dissociation of the atoms of the gaseous vehicle, and consequently a release of the fiery lives.

While the combining, recombining and dissociation of gases is accomplished by means of occult chemistry, and the vehicle so evolved is perceptible to the operator through the senses of smell and taste and can be confined in glass or metal, it must escape from such confinement in order to be temporarily ensouled by the fiery atoms, and unless controlled by the will of the operator after escape, is dissipated at once.

It may be interesting to you to learn that the class of fiery atoms referred to are identical with the latest scientific discoveries in the field of electricity (the fourth Son of Fohat), designated electrons by its latest discoverer. I say "latest discoverer" advisedly, for that division as well as yet more infinitesimal divisions (Sons of Fohat), has long been known and used by practical occultists who well know the dangers involved in bringing those degrees of the fiery lives into juxtaposition with substance matter of much lower vibratory action, and consequently are faithful to their trusts and their guardianship of the great secrets imparted to them.

Occasionally some of these nature secrets are accidentally learned by delvers into chemistry and alchemy, and some of the more recent discoveries along the lines of high explosives are the results of such delving; but if the discoverer of such a secret had the faintest conception of the character of the inevitable karma which will result from the sale of such secrets for the destruction of human life, he would willingly starve if that were the only alternative, before he would part with the knowledge attained by him; for here as well as elsewhere,

where commercialism enters the field, and a consequent degradation of a higher spiritual force is accomplished, the unforgivable sin is committed; in other words, ineradicable, eternal causes, so far as this Manvantara is concerned, are set in action, and their effects, like the ripples made in a pool of water by a vigorously cast stone, will never stop until they have reached the outermost verge of that sphere of action and returned to their source, bearing the inevitable results.

The point of divergence — the line of demarcation between white and black magic, between good and evil action, in such instances as above noted, is drawn by the hand of motive — use — and while to the mind of the unenlightened there could be no possible connection between the atmospheric or ethereal gases and the attributes and qualities of mankind, there is in fact a most intimate relation.

Nature is continually doing exactly what the practical occultist does occasionally, by combining and dissociating gases, and thereby drawing a higher degree of the fiery lives to ensoul such combinations, and man is unconsciously using such elemental forces by concentrated will power to accomplish his various designs. As yet this is done in the majority of instances in ignorance of the results of his action or his responsibility, and therefore he is not as accountable as he would otherwise be for the good or evil effects which have resulted from such use. But the final effects of such action will remain to his credit or discredit according to the character of the motives which have been the guiding power of his Will, that Will which furnishes the dynamic power to direct the action of the same degrees of elementals which nature is evolving and destroying continuously in all her dominions.

LESSON 81
SPEECH IN MUSIC

It is a commonly accepted fact that some knowledge of music is essential to any high degree of attainment in that science of the sciences feebly expressed by the term "occultism," but it is not generally understood that far more than the limited amount of knowledge above indicated is indispensable to the interpretation of the language of symbolism, as the latter is primarily founded upon sound. The musical scale adopted by the occultist contains an infinite variety of notes and sounds; in fact, every note or sound possible of utterance by any created thing or being. Only certain notes or combinations are classed among musical tones by the masses of people, while the truth is that Nature's great anthem, Life, could never be correctly interpreted if even a single one of the tones or sounds usually considered harsh and discordant, or sweet and melodious to the human ear, were omitted; both poles of sound being requisite.

The fact that sound — music — is a perfect language capable of expression by voice or instrument — a language which may be uttered without a spoken word, is known to many, and by them designated the first division of the Mystery language. It is commonly used by the Initiates in conveying necessary secret directions or information to each other when the use of other divisions of the same language such as color and speech, would be inadequate or unwise.

Save for the Initiates, it is only the natural musician who can utter or interpret ideas or ideals of his own or of others when they come to birth in musical tones.

Many tones possible of expression in a single octave, and requisite for voicing some one idea, are above, below, or between the notes of the commonly accepted octave of seven full tones, and could convey no meaning to the average person, even if heard; and each one of those twenty-eight tones is a full tone in a scale which is a connecting link between two planes, or states of consciousness.

One is often struck by the apparent understanding existing between two animals when no outer sound has reached his ear. The onlooker might indignantly deny an accusation to the effect that he was unable to hear a sound which had been very evidently voiced by either animal; nevertheless, it might be perfectly true, for what amounts to a perfect interchange of communication between two horses, and even between two ants, may be continuously carried on in tones perfectly uttered and heard by each animal or insect, and which may be heard by the trained human ear.

When you understand that there are seven full tones and innumerable lesser tones possible of sounding between any two full notes of a voice, violin, or other instrument, you can gain some idea of the infinite variety of tones a more highly evolved man or an animal may use for expression of higher or lower ideas, and the mathematical accuracy and length of the beats or measures — the intervals — between said tones, during which there is opportunity for the introduction of light waves conveying different qualities to the sound waves in action.

The sense of feeling is so closely identified with the sense of hearing in the case of the natural-born musician, that it will enable him easily to comprehend my words when I say that it is more through the sense of feeling than that of hearing that the tones above mentioned, in use by animals or insects, are interpreted, one by the other. In other words, the horse or the ant feels the vibration of the idea or force as it is expressed by the higher, lower, or intermediate tones, more acutely than it hears the tones, although the latter make a distinct impression on the sounding board — the drum of the ear.

The multiplicity of unnatural sounds with which the tympanum of the ear of man has been afflicted during many generations has resulted in hardening and toughening that drum in the case of the great majority of the human race; otherwise, the present generation would have gone insane long ere reaching maturity. But this process of protection carries with it an immeasurable loss, namely, the power to hear or perceive the tones which hold the "open sesame" to many of nature's holiest secrets.

If the finer tones of nature were to reach the consciousness through the ear, in most cases it would be at the cost of a great nervous strain.

You will note the physical sensation of strain especially in the brain if you attempt to reach into the silence through the sense of hearing alone, and this strain nullifies your efforts to perceive interior phenomena, for it brings on a condition analogous to pain, thus keeping your consciousness fixed on the physical plane. Yet you have to conquer such conditions if you are to gain the lost sense of finer hearing; and if you can be patient with yourselves you can do this by persistently modifying that sense of strain, and, as it were, quietly — without conscious effort — listening to what the average man would call "nothing." But under no circumstances do I advise you to continue the practice when you are conscious of any strain — for that way madness lies.

The voicing of the right tones of a mantram[1] or Lodge Call is of great importance. A single wrong note may bring an inharmonious or destructive, instead of harmonious or constructive, force into operation which might not only destroy the effort of others, but also

---

[1] *Mantram* or *mantra* (*Sanskrit*, "instrument of thought") — a sacred or mystical phrase, word, verse, or sound that has spiritual power and is used in spiritual practices like meditation or prayer.

bring into action another force which would build up some condition greatly opposed to the original desire.

Do not lightly read and then ignore the information herein given if you have any hope of becoming a practical occultist, for I am openly giving you another of Nature's great secrets; but you must use the key yourselves, and use it wisely.

LESSON 82
THE MEASURE OF TRUTH

The never ceasing craving of the heart of man, first aroused by the awakening soul, for some outer manifestation in human form that can satisfy that craving, has made man the prey of designing fellow creatures through long ages.

There is more excuse for the failure of the humanity of preceding ages to recognize the truth than there is for the humanity of the present age, and therefore more cause for regretting the ease with which unprincipled men and women can now deceive others as to their true nature and possibilities, and the character of their teaching regarding the constitution of man and his environment.

Scientific research, as well as the revival of long buried philosophical truths has brought to light the nature of the matter from which physical man draws his life sustenance. That matter is now easily proven to be evanescent, changeable, and unreliable. All that is real and unchangeable is the spark of divinity in man, and so long as man is bound by the conditions of matter, so long he will remain to a greater or lesser degree the slave of those conditions; yet he reaches continually for the perfect within the imperfect, and when disappointed in one direction persists in flying immediately to some other, repudiating the fundamentals to be found in the first before they have been assimilated, in his mad effort to gain immediate satisfaction; and this can never be gained in any division of life study until he has thoroughly learned his first lesson. It would save him long years of futile effort, and save others upon whom he brings great suffering, if upon learning something of the nature and constitution of Matter, he could realize that the cause of the imperfection he finds in some other person he has set upon a pedestal for his copying and then incontinently dragged down, did not lie in the real man or woman, but in the very substance of the vehicle used by that reality within the physical body in which the soul (the real man or woman) was bound as securely as was his own soul in his body; and that so long as the matter of the physical plane remains at its present vibratory rate of action, just that long will it be impossible for a perfect man or woman to manifest in that matter. It is not only the individual body that must change periodically, as vibration increases or lowers, but all the matter upon which all bodies in the same sphere subsist, before the real Self be rid of all imperfections. This being true, what cause is there for condemnation of, or dissatisfaction with, our comrade or friend for the reason that he does not fulfill our expectations, or gratify a longing which could only be gratified in substance matter of a higher vibration?

What satisfactory reason can one give for believing that some per-fect being belonging to, and formed from, the substance of another, a higher state or plane of life than that in which he himself is involved, could by any possibility live indefinitely in a lower form of matter? Does not all nature teach the contrary? But there is one way, and one only, by which the higher and lower planes and states of life may be related; namely, by the reforming of the bridge torn away when spirit and matter were separated. Man himself must build that bridge, and must build it of the substance of his own physical body and lower mentality, and that body — the aforesaid bridge — even if rightly built, could not stay in position until its *weight* — its pressure — was reduced to the lowest possible degree, otherwise it would break through and fall into the abyss below. In other words, he must build it well and strong by untiring effort, and with the tools of self-sacri-fice and aspiration, and must reduce the weight of each constituent molecule by conquering selfishness and lower desire while the bridge is in process of building.

When the bridge is built, then, some appointed day, may he cross to the middle of it where he will find awaiting him the one he has longed for and previously sought in vain among his own kind. He may never meet that one again in a single lifetime, but it will not be necessary, for he will have seen and been satisfied and will be content to return to the side of the Cosmic stream he had left, comfort his brethren, and teach them to build their own bridges. This does not mean that he shall be released from the governing laws of matter, for that will never be, so long as he remains in its dominions; it does not mean that he is perfected. It means he has learned the way to release;

he has taught himself how to tread "the path," and has opened his ears to the tones of a voice he may thereafter hear and recognize — the voice of his beloved — at all times and in all places. He will never more condemn a human being because he cannot filch from him what he has not earned, nor will he make of himself an object of envy, or a hindrance to his brethren, by permitting them to feel that having reached a higher level than that which they stand upon, he no longer feels his kinship, or dependence upon their good offices.

We are often nonplussed at the exercise of some unexpected characteristic, or at an act committed by some person we have raised to a great height in our regard. He commits some act, or shows forth some trait of character which would previously have appeared to us utterly foreign to his real nature. We are frequently at a loss to understand how it is we can look upon some horrible sight with equanimity, or bear some heavy pain, slight twinges of which had formerly almost driven us to desperation. We wonder how a naturally tender-hearted man can be lashed into such a state of fury on a battlefield that he is maddened with lust for killing and striking down without a qualm of conscience every soldier of the opposing side that he can reach; and also how it is that we can witness famine, pestilence, and all forms of human misery at certain times without feeling one impulse of sympathy.

There is a point in the Cosmic mentality beyond which the Ego cannot go without creating an entire change in the position of the molecules of some brain center of the body it is using — the point where extremes meet; and where in the individual mind horror and pain become pleasure or indifference, and vice versa.

This change is due to the action of a merciful law, for the brain of man is so constituted that it cannot bear the vibration of any one phase of the sense of feeling, beyond a certain degree. When that degree is reached the action is reversed as it were, and the opposite pole to the one in operation responds to the demand which has been previously made. If it were not so, every molecule of the brain center involved would burst its boundary lines and disappear from mortal ken, for the same dynamic energy that was active in the sense of feeling is just as active in every cell of the protoplasmic matter of the physical plane from which the brain center was formed, the energy of Fohat, the energy back of every explosive force in manifestation. It is some phase of the action of the above-mentioned law that has produced the surprising effects above noted, and when it is understood that the physical man and lower mentality are not conscious of any act that could produce such sudden changes in his nature, it becomes evident that the physical man is neither accountable for the changes, nor should he be judged and condemned by others who are subject to the same changes.

LESSON 83
ACTION AND REACTION OF FORCES

In commenting upon the Instruction entitled "The Mysteries of Space," the Master said:

"The truth herein stated will take its place among the scientific facts at the end of the cycle, not before. I mean the one-hundred-year cycle which has just begun. The ether of the occultist is now recognized by science, or rather is used as a hypothesis upon which to build its theories of etheric or astral phenomena. In the same way will science claim something else that will demonstrate the truth of other things I have now said. Great earthquakes[1] will unveil many of the hidden things of this globe before many years pass by, and these discoveries will nullify much that science now claims to be truth. These earthquakes will occur at different points of the earth. Same of them will take place in this state,[2] others at other points of the country.

"We have long been holding back the forces that are making for the uncovering of a secret path across the ocean, or rather underneath the ocean. The time is fast coming when we shall no longer be able to hold back these powers, for cyclic reasons. The path will be found, but when it is found its discovery will only be useful to demonstrate the truth of what I have now told you; because, knowing that this must take place, we are now engaged in building a roundabout way which

---

[1] The great American prophet and seer Edgar Cayce (1877–1945) predicted with immense accuracy the places and timing of the cataclysms that should have changed the geographical map almost beyond recognition. This did not happen because, at the cost of the Great Sacrifice of the Masters, the main catastrophe, which could have greatly affected both America and Europe as a result of the movements of underground fire, "has been postponed for one century — perhaps, even, for two" (Helena Roerich, "Zapisi besed s Uchitelem (mashinopis')" [Records of conversations with the Master (typescript)], 04.03.1953–15.08.1953, fol. 60, Roerich Museum, Moscow).

[2] California.

will answer all purposes for us, and still leave the old path where it may be found, without working injury to those who have hitherto depended upon it for rapid travel.

"It takes about a half hour of your time for us to pass from one continent to another, but you must remember that we use a form of energy of which you are not yet conscious."

January 7, 1907

"Every ruling aspect of a hierarchy, every individual who is in any sense a part of that ruling aspect, meets, from those who are lineally beneath it, with its opposite pole — revolt — in the hearts of the latter; I mean by this that every individual who is in any sense in a ruling position (no matter how tender-hearted he may be in reality, no matter how deeply he may crave the love and appreciation of those brothers and sisters, no matter how kindly he may feel toward all the world), awakens in every individual who is in any sense beneath him in the Cosmic scale, a vibration of fear, hatred, or rebellion. For this reason he is of all people to be pitied, for he is seldom understood. If you trace back the history of every great king, ruler, president, or all officials in high authority, you will almost invariably find that though they may be feared and obeyed, they are seldom loved by those who are subject to them, and this rule holds good up through higher ranks of life, as well as through lower.

"In many cases you will find that one, or at most two, sincere, earnest friends or lovers, are all that these could claim for their own amidst the myriads by which they were surrounded. This is due partially to a cause not known to many. The cause is set up with the beginning of the evolution of matter. The single cell is the beginning of all organic forms of matter. That cell separates and forms others, either by budding, extension, or division, and final aggregation of atoms. In every instance there is first manifested within the single cell the action of an expulsive force, and this action of the force of expulsion is by its very nature positive and arbitrary in action, and must inevitably arouse in other cells, even if hitherto latent, a negative force of opposition to the ruling cell.

"I call your attention to this for more than one reason."

LESSON 84
MOTHERS OF THE CHRIST-CHILD

One of life's great mysteries is partially solved when in deep concentration on any absorbing subject, and so released from thrall, a human being realizes the underlying unity of all things, lines, physical and mental, built up by life's experiences, fall away one by one in concentration until all sense of outer things is lost and the consciousness and the idea concentrated upon is all of existence for the time being. The Ego (the thinker) and the thought, fill all space, and time is obliterated from consciousness.

As each normal human being may have the same experience, it follows that there must be same state of consciousness in which inseparableness reigns; that state which is only comparable to space, where all things move and are.

It is essential to a perfect understanding that the fundamental truths underlying the above-mentioned statement be accepted, otherwise the new light which I desire to throw upon a subject which has awakened profound thought, suspicion, and contempt in many minds of different caliber, would only add to a seeming jumble of impossible or insane conclusions in regard to what now, under the patronage of science, has become a subject of worldwide recognition, and would not be seriously considered. Yet it is a subject of the most vital importance to every thinker. I refer to the subject of the occult sciences, and more particularly to one phase or aspect of one such science, namely, the apparent impossibility of accepting seriously the countless claims of divine guidance and bestowal of authority and supremacy made by many different persons in as many parts of the world. Women who claim to be the mothers or prospective mothers of a Christ-child, men and women who claim to be reincarnations of Jesus, administrators of his commands, or vehicles for the transmission of his life forces. The fact that in these claims there could possibly be any truth worthy of investigation is laughed to scorn by the unbelievers, and accepted slavishly by the followers of the claimant. Yet there is an underlying truth, a basic reality to many such claims, beautiful past telling to many listeners, and important to all.

To every true seer or astral visitant there are visions granted, sounds and speech heard that far surpass in beauty and grandeur anything imaginable by the less gifted, as well as sights and sounds which exceed in unspeakable horror anything to be seen or heard under other conditions. Those same experiences, sights and sounds, beautiful or horrible, are as open to the interior senses of every other man or woman who has consciously or unconsciously developed one particular organ in the brain, as they are or may be to the seer. There seems to be a false idea prevalent even among psychics that there must be a new scene or sound to every new observer of astral phenomena.

As the interior planes of life are contacted, one becomes more and more enlightened as to the unity of all consciousness on those planes. The identity of the individual is not lost, yet the soul is identified in some mysterious manner and degree with the identity of every individual or object seen: for instance, in gazing at a beautiful astral flower, one becomes identified with the flower and knows all about it, how it came into life, and what it is or will be in the future. In communication with others one realizes that the term "I" or "you" does not refer to I or you, individually. Consequently, when these terms are used, either in direct communications from higher entities, or accidentally heard, as it were (as in sleep), if one is not familiar with the fundamental truth before mentioned, there is no alternative to the belief that he or she is individually indicated or intimately concerned with any direct promise or statement regarding such a momentous subject, as for example, the birth of a Christ-child or the bestowal of some great dignity. Of course this fact will be disputed by the supposed mothers of such children, and such supposed dignitaries, for there is an underlying desire for personal recognition, and a love of power in the heart of every normal human being, and all seeming fulfillments of such desires die a hard death. However, I am quite sure every true occultist will agree with me.

Jesus himself said, "I will come again."[1] The Book of Revelation is full of promises to the believer and threats against the "lost" — the unbeliever. With the mental picture already painted in the mind by familiarity with those several promises or threats, and the apparent visualizing or auditory confirmation of the same, if one is to "believe her or his own eyes and ears" what is there left but literal acceptance for the average psychic? And once accepted, pure human longing and natural egotism will bind one of either sex irrevocably to such beliefs. Owing to the before-noted great fundamental truth back of all illusions of this character, it is not surprising that any woman might

---

[1] John 14:3.

accept a universal for an individual promise, for when all is said every woman who bears a child does indeed give birth to a Christ-child.

Jesus said, "I and the Father are One."[2] "I in Thee, and Thou in me, that we may be made perfect in One,"[3] and to whatever extent such a child partakes of the nature of Christ, it is a Christ-child; and whether it be consciously or unconsciously, such a prospective mother knows in her heart that she is bearing "a Christ-child."

Every man knows in his soul that he has been or ought to have been, born to be a leader, a wise teacher, scientist, or some other noteworthy individual. Seeing or hearing what is to him astral corroborative sight or speech, wild animals could not tear from him his belief in the blindness of those who do not accept his estimate of himself.

This all being true, can we not have a little more patience with what we believe to be vagaries or frauds; be willing to accept the fact of the possible vision or hearing of the seer, and strive to realize that the great longing Mother-heart of the world is eternally bringing back to earth a Savior of the people, a leader of the nations. It does not matter *how* he comes, just that he does arrive on the present scene of desolation. The need is great enough, and the need of man is supplied by God when that need reaches its greatest height, whatever that need may be.

It makes no difference who or what may be the woman that Karmic law designates for the vehicle to bring a Great Soul — an Avatar — to the physical plane. The fact that so much obscurity surrounds the birth of Jesus, and that it has been left possible to cast unworthy reflections upon the character of the Mother of Jesus and his most intimate woman friend, Mary Magdalene, should open the eyes of Christians to one very important fact. If it were essential to the incarnation of a Great Soul that the vehicle of his manifestation should be what is termed a sexually pure woman, the Masters of the White Lodge would have long since made that fact indisputable. In the case of Jesus their silence proves that too much emphasis on such a hypothesis is not advisable. Karmic law — the law of cosmical succession — would determine such an honor before all else. I mention this point to emphasize my former statement that it is of little consequence how or through whom the next great Avatar comes to the physical plane. The only point that is essential is that of his finally reaching that plane. But God forbid that any poor self-deceived woman should

---

[2] John 10:30.
[3] John 17:23.

make that statement the basis of belief in license for a sexual impurity. No words of mine can tell the extent of evil already done by ignorant or depraved men and women who use the limited knowledge they possess of such cosmic truths for the degradation of their fellow men and women. No ordinary man or woman of the present age could determine the possibility of creating a vehicle for the incarnation of an Avatar. The knowledge of such possibility in the case of any woman is only obtainable through and could only be imparted by an Initiate of much higher degree than those who contact the average avenues of life, and then only in the intervals between the passing of one Messianic Cycle and the beginning of another. But all women should look forward to forming the sustenance, the spiritual food for incarnating Egos of this age, for it is only the feminine aspect of life that has the power to do so, and to whatever extent they do this, they mother the Christ-child.

LESSON 85
WILL AND LAW

A very important cycle, the last of the seven lesser cycles of seven years each, which compose a larger cycle of forty-nine years, is now closing. There have been better results shown in the line of individual psychic development during this last lesser cycle, especially among conscious disciples of the White Lodge, than during any other similar period of the present two-thousand-year cycle. These results are due to the persistent exercise of the newly developed power of equilibrium by said disciples, which has enabled them to hold themselves in a more balanced condition of mentality while the Infinite was striking a stronger and higher vibratory key, during which time many things and conditions evolved in previous cycles, and were changing and adapting themselves to the higher vibratory key, thus falling into lines for future action.

Twenty-one years ago there were but three disciples out of forty-nine, divided into seven groups of seven individualities in each, and located at different points of the western globe, who were strongly enough fortified exteriorly and interiorly to bear the effects of the action of opposing forces of the age, and so to enable the Lodge of Initiates to form fixed auric centers in their immediate vicinity for use in the connecting of three or more planes by such Initiates. Two of the three mentioned have now left the physical plane; the third one will leave it at a not very distant date, but their sacrifice and unselfish, intelligent work for humanity has resulted in the formation of nine similar auric centers by the Initiates through which may be sent and received the lines of force which will furnish the Initiates substance for building and sustaining great numbers of vehicles — astro-mental bodies — capable of bearing the vibrations of newly incarnating Egos of greater age and experience than those now incarnated, during the period of gestation which precedes physical birth.

To the uninitiated, the formation of nine auric centers, impossible to contact through the physical senses would seem of little importance, but "to those who know," it is the greatest event of the present Manvantara, for it means the advancement of the human race at a rate hitherto unimagined, and whatever be the cost in the way of material loss, the gain will be immeasurably greater.

The gain to the individual disciples of the Masters by the rise in degree — cosmic position — of the before-mentioned Three and Nine is wrought by and in accordance with precession and position. Each advance made in the cosmic scale by a human being advances all who follow the former on the same scale, in the same cyclic round, and therefore leads to a change in outer position as well as in interior environment.

Free Will as a factor in human life is a commonly recognized fact, notwithstanding a tendency to belief in the doctrines of fatalism; but the difficulty of harmonizing two such opposing ideals, or learning just how much truth is concealed in either has hitherto been insurmountable in this age for the reason that the key to the problem has been lost. But that key has been found and presented to you under the name of the Cyclic law.

Personal free will is the divine prerogative of man, but the Will governing the action of Cyclic law is much greater in wisdom, knowledge, and power, and that Will has decreed that the first principle or embodied thing or creature of one cyclic round shall be the last of the next succeeding cyclic round in the cosmic spiral which reaches from the physical to the Spiritual plane, and that the second in line can never take the position of the first until the latter has passed into the next higher round of the spiral, or has fallen back to the last position of the round it was upon at the time of change; therefore, no matter to what extent free will in man may be exercised in individual affairs, his position in the cyclic spiral is determined by a higher Will.

However — and this is most important — man's latitude is so wide in his own field of will power, that there is no injustice in what at first thought might appear to be arbitrary control; for individual past karma has fitted each soul for the position it occupies in the cosmic scale, whatever its position in life may be; furthermore, if all mankind connected with any one soul in the cycle of time wherein it is developing are individual parts, or souls, of the same Group Soul which governs that cycle, its karma must be inextricably intertwined with that of each one of those parts or souls; therefore, all must be subject in great degree to the Will of the Group Soul. The one who has overcome the lower — the heavier — karmic obstacles which confront all men alike, must inevitably reach the first position on the spiral line, owing to a peculiar action of the same law which compels any light substance to rise to the top of a heavier one (unless separated by a third substance, native, yet repellant to both). And that peculiar action of Law arouses Divine Will to distinguish between the lower — the heavier — aspect of Matter and separates it from the higher — the physical from the Spiritual — and does this by the introduction of a third aspect, the human soul, the seat of free will in man, at the same time defining the position of each soul at every stage of progress on the line of cyclic progression.

I have digressed from my first statement in order to throw some light on the process by which the three and the nine disciples out of a large number have reached a higher stage of development than their former associates.

By passing into higher groups of disciples, the first three mentioned by me opened the way for a change in place and position; therefore, a change in environment and opportunity for those who were next in line, and to a greater extent than in preceding cycles, the three individualities immediately following each one of the first mentioned three were able to profit by the change; for the reason that each outward sweep of a cyclic line is, so to speak, of greater girth toward the middle point of any cyclic spiral. The next forty-nine year cycle will see a decrease in the number of those reaching a similar degree of attainment, owing to the closing up of the lines of the coming cycles in the major or world spiral; but at the same time, the higher evolution of so many degrees of force and substance constituting the environment of the present races of humanity will give opportunity for advancement on less interior lines, to a much greater number of people, who will thus be prepared for higher positions in the wider lines referred to as girths, of the next cyclic sweep of the Divine Will.

I am emphasizing and elaborating this subject of position for many good reasons, the chief of which is embodied in our efforts to dissipate the feeling of discouragement which so often depletes and devitalizes disciples when a recognition of the futility of opposing an inherently weak human will against the commonly termed "Will of God" comes to them, and to bring them to a realization that the Divine Will governing cyclic law is not in opposition to human will in an arbitrary sense. Divine Will is working to bring all temporarily differentiated wills to the point where they will recognize the fact that there can be but one Will, and that Will is good. It only requires intelligent observation of the phenomena produced by that Will to arouse mankind to make an effort to harmonize the now discordant lower elemental forces, which are apparently diametrically opposed to that One Will.

One other reason I may give more in detail, though it is included in the above: The masses of mankind are battling for position; position of one kind or another, merely for the sake of the position, when if they could understand all that is contained in the words, "the least of these, my disciples,"[1] spoken by Jesus, they could appreciate the fact of the futility of the struggle so far as personal satisfaction through such position is concerned.

Any position worth having, on either material or interior lines, seeks the man or woman because he or she has earned it; and it so seeks through the action of the cyclic law. It is "the least of these" who gain such recognition by reason of the child heart that obeys unquestioningly those who have the karmic right to such obedience, and so acts in conjunction with divine law. In the child heart, the dividing line — the confining force — is giving way. Spirit has refined soul; soul is refining body. There has occurred a change in such a life that has reversed the action of the force formerly acting as repulsion, and the force of attraction is now drawing together and combining all three — body, soul, and spirit — on a higher plane of life, and the position of such an entity in the cosmic scale is secured for all time.

---

[1] See Matthew 25:40.

LESSON 86
LAW

You doubt not the rising and the setting of the sun — you doubt not the action of the known laws which demonstrate birth and death the alternates, light and darkness, through which every infinitesimal life in mineral, vegetable, and animal manifestation must pass. You are aware of the positive and negative action of all electrical phenomena; you know that sleep must follow wakefulness, as night follows day. In every field of manifested existence you see the action of two immutable, eternal laws which absolutely control all things and creatures within your sphere of consciousness. You know that they are the two extremes of life, the action of the law of opposites; and practically as well as you know the operation of said laws in material, visible life you know the same laws are as omnipotent and unchangeable in the spheres of higher vibration, and can trace their action through those spheres. Knowing all this, can you willfully blind yourselves, in order that you may gratify the sensuous part of your nature in all its extremes, or when you are brought face to face with an opponent in discussion of the highest, holiest functions of human life — the development of which has separated you from the animal creation, can you justify a plunge back into the depths from which you have escaped, as does the man or woman who denies the righteousness of, and rejects the only possible protection and safeguard for either a race or individual that stands on the dividing line between the purely animal and part human, as you must deny and reject the same if you uphold or countenance the promiscuous cohabitation of the sexes and the repudiation of the law of monogamy.

The laws which govern the before-mentioned states and conditions of matter are the same laws and are just as rigid in their application to the emotions and senses of man as they are to Force or Matter of lower Vibration, and you can no more help arousing its opposite, hate, when you have given loose rein to the emotion ordinarily termed love, namely, lust, than you can prevent night from following day; and lust is as different from the attribute love, as the color red is different from the color blue. If the emotion lust were in truth one with the attribute Love, there would be no reaction, no possibility of satiation from its indulgence, for in love the two extremes of one spiritual force or attribute unite and when fully expressed by a human being, sex attraction disappears. The sexless Lord has no preference for either sex.

The argument used to sustain sex freedom, namely, that the early races were uncontrolled in the matter of sexual impulse, and consequently better off in that respect than later races, betrays ignorance. If all the past ages of strict adherence to the laws of evolution for the evident purpose of refining gross forms of matter are only to result in throwing back those forms into the same condition from which they were evolved, what a farce the whole process would be. A refiner of silver in olden times must sit by the crucible which held the molten mass until he could see the reflection of his face in the purified metal. The refiner of the human being — the evolutionary law which is refining gross forms of life according to a perfect pattern — must bring those forms to the point of development where the pattern is reflected in every organic cell of those forms in all of the conditions, states, material, mental, and spiritual, where those forms perform any function whatsoever, and Fire, i.e., stress, strain, and suffering are the only levers by which the mass — the human race — may be lifted from the crucible. Physical substance must be lifted into the light or substance of higher mentality, where renunciation of all attachment to the lower states of substance, the passions, will make possible the manifestation of the refined — the perfected spiritual forms of life.

No sane man or woman can fail to see the great necessity for a change in the methods and results of the present marriage laws, if a better race of human beings is to follow the present race, but the abrogation of the present marriage laws and a deliberate retrogression of ideals, and acceptance of the laws, or rather the lawlessness, which prevailed in antediluvian ages could have but one result. The laws which control the evolution of the elemental forces of the deadly nightshade cannot by the same processes and means produce a rose bush. The operation of the same laws may be necessary, but the processes of growth and formation, and the necessary substance and energy must be of other qualities. Humanity does not gain in power and knowledge by retreat, but by advance. Education and effort in regard to the marriage relation should now be directed along the lines of right natural selection and monogamy instead of promiscuity.

If a good horticulturist wishes to produce an extraordinarily fine flower of a certain kind, he obtains the seed or takes the grafts from the best specimens of the kind he desires to combine with another of the same family, and cultivates the seed which results, to the highest possible degree. When he finally produces the flower he wants he is very careful not to mix its seed with, or to graft from, that lower order of plant life which he used to evolve that perfected flower, if he desires to perpetuate the new and rare variety. A single act of such nature would mean a reversion to lower type for the plant which grew from seed or graft. The laws by which he has brought the masterpiece to perfection are the same laws which govern the production and perpetuation of a higher class of life, the human class. If a divine masterpiece, a perfected man, is to be evolved, a prospective parent of that ideal man cannot go back into the humanity of the night of time, back to a degenerate race for the seed — the other parent — or use the methods and conditions which availed for the evolving of an inferior race of men. Each parent to be must select the seed (the mate), and the conditions and environment most favorable for the new life and the future growth of the same from the highest type of human beings he or she is able to contact and prepare the best possible conditions and environment.

If the strength of the original plant is wasted by overproduction of flower and seed, or by some disease, the horticulturist is not going to take his seed for new experiment or culture from that plant. If the human being wastes his or her strength in promiscuity, and so devitalizes the cells which form the seed of human life for the mere gratification of sexual desire (which desire was originally implanted in man for one specific purpose, namely, production of offspring), when the time comes that he or she meets the one man or woman by and with whom it would be possible to bring to birth the highest form of life it was possible for those two individuals combined to create, he or she is absolutely incapable of supplying the necessary substance, force, and magnetic energy which alone could produce the requisite vehicle or body in which a waiting perfected soul could perform its divine mission. They might create bodies innumerable, but they absolutely could not create such a body as I have described. The freshness, the magnetic qualities, the Odic force,[1] the pure love essential to the creation of the highest form of physical life would be no longer theirs to give. No amount of argument can make what is

---

[1] *Odic force* — the name given to life energy by Carl Ludwig von Reichenbach (1788–1869) after the Germanic god Odin.

commonly termed "sex freedom" anything else but license for gratification of lower desire, in the present cycle of manifestation. In a more highly evolved race a greater degree of freedom in every line of life would naturally result, and would not be abused as it inevitably would be abused at the present time, in the majority of cases where it was exercised. The true marriage would follow as naturally as day follows night when other right conditions obtained, and promiscuous sex relations would be as rare then as are true marriages at the present time.

I would not be quoted as upholding the continuance of the marriage relations between men and women who are antagonistic, unfaithful, and cruel to each other. What I plead for is more care in selection and the use of all natural means by which such selection could be intelligently made. Wrong planetary conditions, sordid motives, abnormal sexual desire amounting to disease, are responsible for the majority of the unhappy, unnatural marriages of the present age.

It is as absurd unjustly to criticize the Law which demands monogamy because men and women enter into the marriage relation unprepared and unfitted for such relation, as it would be to criticize the law of gravitation for not fulfilling its purpose when some obstruction was deliberately placed in the path of a descending object.

Consciously or unconsciously, the condemnation of monogamy and the exploitation of promiscuity is based upon abnormal sexual desire in the case of every intelligent man and woman who is thoroughly familiar with the causes and effects of disobedience to the law governing creative forces.

Humanity is now evolving under a different phase of universal law from that which governed the birth and evolution of man in the earlier ages of this cycle. The law of differentiation — separation — then ruled supreme, while the law of unification — of combination — is preeminently active in the present race. The triangle is in process of becoming the straight line again, as it must so become in the closing eras of any great cycle of manifestation; and those who pit their puny strength and selfish desire against Divine purpose and power must inevitably lose in the contest.

LESSON 87
THE MYSTERY LANGUAGE

One of the rules of initiation in a high degree of the Great Lodge contains the following paragraphs:

"This is a secret which gives death; close thy mouth lest thou shouldst reveal it to the vulgar; compress thy brain lest something should escape from it and fall outside."

To this exhortation is added yet another:

"Open wide thy hand that the blood droppings from thy opened veins may fall from thy finger tips to give life to the dead. Open thine heart that its inmost shrine may be reflected on the screen of the world by the rays of the Central Sun, in order that man may know that there is speech higher than words."

Since mindless man was overshadowed by the Sons of Light, and higher Manas was born in the human race, the shades of the lower mind — animal instincts — have fought to regain and hold their former supremacy, and to strike out all the "thou shalt not's" from the commandments, issued as guides to higher evolution, by the Sons of Light.

The Decalogue[1] is no modern invention of a few thousand years ago, given by a God through a single leader of the Jewish race, as is generally supposed. Each paragraph outlines the final result of eons of experience, lived out by countless numbers of seers and sages, and graven on "two tablets of stone," i.e., on the two lobes of the lungs, the air transmitters, the double organ which renders speech possible to man.

But there are many more of these "thou shalt not's," graven on similar stones or organs, by the same methods, and to similar ends, by the same seers and sages in more fully developed bodies, and among them is the following:

"Thou shalt not take the children's bread and give it unto the dogs":[2] meaning, "Thou shalt not take the secrets of initiation and give them to the world in general."

In many instances, where this commandment has been disobeyed, death indeed has resulted — death of the soul of the one who imparted

---

[1] *Decalogue* (*Latin*, "ten words") — another term for the Ten Commandments.
[2] Matthew 15:26.

the secret and the one who received it. For when certain great cosmic truths have been given to the unprepared — the uninitiated — the soul and body have been destroyed by lack of power to control the cosmic forces generated, owing to the fact that it was impossible to impart instructions as to safe and right methods of manipulating the forces generated by the use of said truths, which alone could be imparted "mouth to ear" by the Hierophant of any degree, to a neophyte of the same degree, and no man or God in such a position could possibly be induced to give such instructions to the weak or unworthy.

Before the utter disintegration of such "dead" forms, the latter had become temples of black magic more or less consciously — instruments for the use of evil spiritual forces in form. And the same great crimes, with their terrible aftereffects, are occurring in this age even more frequently and with greater power for evil than ever before, for it is the age of the anti-Christ, and there is no place, no center, on the earth where the spiritual currents of the White Lodge have been directed for the amelioration of the ills of mankind, the betterment of existing conditions, and the spiritual advancement of the human race, that there has not entered into it the conscious satanic emissaries of the Black Lodge to take up their dwelling place in some man or woman who selfishly or ambitiously begins to use the knowledge acquired from close association with the disciples of the White Lodge, for the disruption and dissociation of the body with which he or she is connected.

The same forces, the same character of weak, unstable, and drifting souls — vehicles of those forces — are with you now, as they are with every like center where a link with the Initiates has been forged, and are fulfilling the same cosmic service, i.e., acting as testing stones for the individual members of the center. In many cases such individuals ignorantly believe "they are doing God's service," while in reality they are striking at the very foundation of Faith, Hope, and Courage. In other instances they are consciously bringing upon others all the evils human flesh is heir to, in the form of suffering, loss, and disease; while posing in their black-lined, white garments as benefactors. The Initiates are thus greatly hampered in their efforts; and often incapacitated for imparting the methods hinted at in the above-mentioned Rules, hindered from opening the hand that the droppings from the finger tips — the rules of the Mystery language — may fall on mankind; i.e., may reach the intelligence, and so make possible the regaining of the powers and privileges now lost; the possibilities of which are taught and explained in that language alone. In every instance so far, that an attempt has been made to teach this language to the laity, and even before the first principles had been fully understood, those to whom the requisite knowledge had been entrusted have been compelled to stay their hand and wait for the replacing of some recreant from a sevenfold group before they could continue; for such a sevenfold group is an essential. Other disciples wonder and puzzle over the cessation of, or change in, some line of esoteric instruction, the cause for which cannot be explained at once by their teachers without breaking some law of discipleship by which they individually are bound; and they often jump to the conclusion that the teachers are untrue or have reached the limit of their knowledge.

You must know these things if you are to meet them and be prepared "to stand in the furnace" by the side of those who must bear the strain of such conditions, and so make possible the resumption of any interrupted course of instruction, or the holding of a center against the powers of evil that have gained entrance. If you cannot do this, "Your hour has not yet come." You have not yet gained the power to "lie still on the horizontal bar of the balanced cross, while the perpendicular spear passes through your vitals, to raise the vibrations of the Solar center and enable you to win the reward of crucifixion."

Distrust the man or woman who tells you he or she is a Templar and then strikes at the heart of your Order. You are facing an emissary of the Brothers of the Shadow every time. Fly from the man or woman who offers you the gold of spiritual knowledge in a cup made of the heart of a co-disciple. Your own heart's blood will eventually fill that cup, if you accept it.

He who appeals to the Brothers of Light for the opportunity, and at the same moment of his appeal demands the trial by fire, i.e., he demands an opportunity to prove his fitness for life on higher levels.

The law mercifully blinds him to his failures in many instances, but it is his fault alone if he fails in recognizing the presence of an emissary of a black magician in the midst of his Order when the fundamental law of that Order — Inseparableness — is attacked.

LESSON 88
SPIRITUAL HEREDITY

Consciousness is the essential basis of all life. All outer expressions of consciousness are ephemeral, passing, illusory.

Each of the four lower of the combined seven forms which constitute the manifested self of a human being, has an individual past, present, and future karma that is in perfect alignment and correspondence with the karma of the other forms, also with the karma of the race, family, nation, world, and universe of which it is a constituent. Each one of these four bodies or sheaths, as they are termed in the Secret Science, is ill or well, happy or unhappy, in good or bad environment, is energetic or indolent, wise or foolish during any one period of time, according to the dominant karmic force in operation on its particular plane of action at that period.

The lowest, the physical body, sometimes seems logy or lazy, with no apparent cause for the same, but in such an instance it might be that the next body or sheath in sequence was at that moment experiencing some phase of action that impressed the result as a negative force within the physical atoms, or, as it were, unlocked the cell doors and permitted that force to sift through the atomic structure of the physical body, hence the feeling of inertia.

A sudden wild gust of passion, utterly unaccountable at the moment to the mind of all interested people because of its apparent causelessness, seizes upon an individual, and results in some crime on the physical plane. It might be that in such an instance one of the other sheaths is living through some past experience of similar nature, when extreme anger had aroused a burst of passion; or is then passing through some similar experience to that which the physical body is undergoing at the same time in its own field of expression, and the force of that passion has thus involved another sheath and perhaps forced it into the commission of crime. The consciousness being, at the moment fixed upon the physical plane more powerfully than upon any other, would naturally locate the ultimate cause for such an exhibition of passion upon that physical plane by acting through the physical senses.

Each plane and each body of any plane is, as it were, a double-faced mirror. The consciousness — the Builder — which dwells as "a star apart," gazes at certain clearly defined cyclic periods into each mirror in turn. When it is fixed upon some mirror it perceives not only itself as the dominant figure upon the same, but also the reflections of itself in surrounding mirrors, and reflections of reflections. It periodically identifies itself with each one of those reflections until discrimination has been evolved. All of the sheaths disintegrate and return to a homogeneous condition, each one in perfect sequence; first the physical, then the astral, the mental, and the higher astral or soul. As the consciousness releases itself from one sheath it centers itself more and more in those sheaths which remain. And all of the power, knowledge, and wisdom it has gained by its experience in all its sheaths is finally centered in the permanent spiritual body of the Ego — the Nirmanakaya robe, which has been in process of building since the first manifestation of matter at the commencement of a new Manvantara.

When the individuality, the Ego, is compelled by Karmic law to incarnate, it gathers the scattered fragments, the skandhas, and the lasting results of previous incarnations all together within its auric sphere and recreates each of its new sheaths in turn, the physical last, informing it with its own consciousness during the process of creation. With the completion of the physical body, one round of an individual life cycle is closed.

I am but giving you something of an illustration, not attempting a detailed statement of the action of the various forms, phases, forces, and conditions of life referred to above, but will note a few interesting details.

Sometimes the shadows — the sheaths — of one or more other Egos drift across the surface of one of the mirrors, in which case there is a blending of the consciousness of the individual Egos — it may be momentary or it may last through a longer period of time; but this can never occur unless the Egos are closely related by karmic and sympathetic ties; in fact, not unless they belong to the same Cosmic Ray. Man ignorantly calls different phases of this phenomenon spiritualism, affinity, psychic control, or something similar; but it is in deed and in truth the action of a spiritual law. It is the only right basis for marriage between souls, and is but a premonitory expression of what will be an ultimate reality at the close of a Manvantara, when there will be no occasion for mirrors — bodies, as means to identification — for the human race will then have again become what it was in the beginning, one entity.

You might ask, "What becomes of planetary influences, heredity, etc.?" But do not forget that I have said that this world, as well as the universe which contains the world and its inhabitants, is evolving in like ratio, and all are subject to the same laws which control the movements of the planets.

The planetary influences are simply those drifting shadows before referred to as being cast upon the mirrors of the individual Ego, the action of which is only possible because of the intimate relation existing, karmically and cosmically speaking, between the Egos, which are, as it were, the lights which make possible the casting of the shadows. The shadows mingle and intermingle with each other and with the thought-forms cast upon the mirror, and only the Egos — the planetary rulers in this instance — have power to separate them one from the other and place them where they belong in the scale of life; but as these drifting shadows glide over the surface of the mirrors and intermingle, so the planetary influences and their reflections cast by the individual Egos of the planetary rulers mingle with each other and affect each other according to the action of the natural laws which create and control those particular expressions of Divine life, and only the mystic who can observe those reflections and is competent to decipher their mysteries and compute the power and purpose of each one, can possibly cast a true horoscope of a human being.

Possibly a less developed person might cast the horoscope of a physical body, but how about the horoscopes of the next three bodies, the astral, mental, and psychic bodies? And they must be cast if a true delineation of that fourfold entity, the human being, is to be found.

An honorable astrologer will never promise to bring forth the mysteries of the stars relating to the interior sheaths for the eyes of the profane to degrade. He realizes the enormity of the sin of even such an attempt.

LESSON 89
CHARACTER

Character is the basic source as well as the culmination of every successful effort in the direction of soul building; the beginning and the end of every individualized Cosmic, planetary, and human endeavor toward spiritual supremacy.

The non-possession or deterioration of that basic principle means the death and disintegration of any individualized form of life.

Few among even the more enlightened class of investigators stop to consider what may be the method of procedure, what forces are available to build up the substance of character, or of what that substance really consists.

The interaction of Will and Desire under certain stimuli impels to rapid action the central nucleus of an embryonic cell; continued repetition of the stimuli may create the cells or rudiments of what will sometime be an organic center, a base of supplies, or it may be for a brain. This center can only respond to the same character of stimulating force which formed the third line of the trio, Action, and the stimulus is originally given by the vibratory action of various qualities commonly termed good, existing in the mentality of the planetary ruler of the planet on which that cell is developing and therefore subject to the attracting power of the duo, Will and Desire, as expressed in the cell. Constant contact and interaction between these stimulating forces, the basic source and the cells of a brain, will evolve the same qualities to a greater degree as time passes until they are finally manifested in what we term character in an individual.

The word "character" commonly conveys a vague impression of the good or bad characteristics of a person, the possession of which leads to position and influence, social, religious, or political, as the case may be, or the reverse. The truth is that every separate factor, every quality that enters into the sum total which manifests character is the result of eons of conscious, persistent, indefatigable effort by the individual Ego through stone, plant, animal, and human life.

The monad when first clothed in the form of a crystal has alternately attracted and repulsed various vibrations of pranic energy, and incipient Will has finally cohered and molded the resultant molecular substance into a given form. It has sharpened the edges of each facet and thereby constructed points for contact with similar forms, and for weapons of offense and defense. These sharpened points of the crystal are ultimately the bases of other correspondingly potent organic centers and weapons, according to the cyclic development of the natural kingdom in which it is manifesting and the phases or races of life evolving within that kingdom. For instance, such points may evolve into the thorns of a rose tree, the horns of an animal, the fins of a fish, the poison sacs of a serpent, or the teeth and nails — the weapons of defense and offense of an animal.

Every one of the crystal points was primarily fitted for its particular act of service according to the need, the desire, and will of the monad as it was concentrated and expressed in the central cell of the crystal; and all such points have finally developed into the mediums of contact, and weapons of defense and offense commonly termed qualifications, developed in the human mentality and acting through the human body. While the forms of such qualifications are not perceptible to the human eye, they have subordinate mediums of expression within the human brain, visible to the inner eye. If the brain is destroyed they have no expression in form, thereafter in occult phraseology they are termed *skandhas*.

These qualifications are the foundation stones of the edifice we have reared to express character. If you find yourself lacking one of the basic qualities of this edifice it follows that you have not earned it in the past, or, through abuse of it, you have lost it and never will have it again until you earn it once more by persistent, indefatigable effort.

If it is the quality of self-control that you lack, never lose an opportunity of bringing your will to bear upon any condition that inhibits such control. A thousand failures do not count where one successful effort is made. Every test you pass brings you so much nearer final accomplishment. The same is true in regard to all other qualities.

Attract to yourself by strong desire the cosmic building forces. Cohere and emplace your successes within the mental image you have formed of the desired quality, by means of Desire.

Never lose sight of the concealed power within yourself, which first acted within the crystal points; the same power that is now resident in those qualities which are manifesting character; namely, self-control, altruism, service, purity, faith, truth, and devotion. When these qualities have reached their highest point of attainment in you, you will have become a Master of the White Brotherhood, and never until then, even though you possessed the earth and all else that it contains and expresses.

The day of full recognition of the power of "little things" approaches — the little things that are the bases of all great things; and rightly directed study of even the facets of a crystal will point out the path to the Gods. Not alone the qualities referred to will you find expressed in the crystal as above noted, but all things, all features of the genus homo; for in the very first manifested form of life force is concealed the power of the trinity, Will, Desire, and Action. The more complex the form, the greater has been the operation of that power and the greater the possibilities for the future.

So long as you only desire me to corroborate your own beliefs, your own conceptions of life and action (such life and action as you have as yet only touched upon), because you cannot or will not obey certain laws of Being, obedience to which would increase the power of non-resistance in the organic centers through which alone the light of sure knowledge can radiate, and so unconsciously repel that light, just as long you are doomed to disappointment and chagrin; and just as long you will be subject to every fluctuation of thought in the minds of those about you; thought-forms which drift through your own mind and confuse every main point and thus make you incapable of holding to any one center to which you owe allegiance — owe it because karma and your own higher Will and Desire have justly placed you in one definite position toward such center.

If you are convinced that your Initiate Teacher knows no more than you know yourself about any subject formulated and introduced by him that you may be interested in, and will only believe in and act upon conclusions formed as a result of such drifting thoughts as now sift through your mentality, you will gain nothing from his instructions.

The kingdom of God is within you, and it is also within the central cell of the crystal, and the center of any thing or condition; and so long as you are obediently subject to that central cell you will go on building the higher qualities, as the points of that crystal are built, by the same law, to final perfection of form. But such expansion of spiritual substance, as well as that of cellular life, is contingent upon the resident power in each atom to resist every exterior force that would tend toward separation from its kind; separation that would tend to frustrate the purpose of the Ego that dominates the mass and which alone knows the geometrical form which Divine Wisdom has set according to number for any mass of substance, and the equally potent power of non-resistance to the true building forces. So with man, as with the crystal cell, his power of expansion, of growth, rests upon his ability to identify himself with a true center that is one of a direct line of centers reaching from a Dhyan-Chohan, through a planetary ruler, down through the ranks of lesser Masters to the composite body of which he is a constituent — a line of centers in one sense, yet one center *in toto*, and that power is dependent on character.

Without a center of expression, the manifestation of character is impossible; without character man would be but a congery of unstable forces.

It has been taught by some who argue from generalities to particulars that moral responsibility builds character; but the reverse is true. It is character that determines moral responsibility. Morals are changeable. They are relatively good or bad, according to the race, nation, religious prejudices, etc.; but character, as I have insisted, is the one persistent feature from incarnation to incarnation. It is, so to speak, the basic sheath of the Ego, inseparable from that Ego.

LESSON 90
MISUSE OF POWER
FROM THE MASTER M.

If there is any one thing more than another that justifies the Initiates of the right hand path in refraining from divulging the deepest truths of occultism concerning the exercise of creative power it is the attitude of the great majority of the human race toward the feminine sex; and the fact that the most malicious, cruel, and unjust treatment of woman is by woman, adds immensely to the difficulties in the way. A student of occultism is so much more accountable for such treatment than are others that comparison is hardly possible, for such an one knows full well that without the assistance of the female, the male is absolutely helpless in his search for the philosopher's stone — the lost creative power. This knowledge makes his conduct tenfold more reprehensible when he indulges in, or sustains others in indulging in vituperative, malicious slander of a woman, whoever or whatever the slandered woman may be. The poor tool of the Brothers of the Shadow who teaches that anything but the most perfect purity can avail to reach the heights of knowledge where the generation and exercise of patent creative forces is possible, is a willful or ignorant deceiver. Yet knowing all this, as every true student of occultism does know it, the first demonstration of ambition, weariness, anger, or righteous criticism of some fault often results in vicious slander, persistent vituperative scandal against the woman, whoever she may be, who occupies a prominent position in the organic body of which those are parts. Whether the body be religious, scientific, social, or political, it would seem that the feminine, the most vital, the most necessary (even if it be concealed from outer view) source of sustenance for the growth and development of such a body, is almost invariably the point of most demoniacal attack. And so it will be until woman, purely for the sake of womankind, awakens from her lethargic sleep and compels regard for her sex. She will never be voluntarily given her place in the world by man during the present Manvantara until she takes it by means of her own inherent strength, and she never will have the power to take it while she can stand by and see those of her own sex attacked and misused, without protest, and without an effort to rehabilitate those attacked and often displaced by those seeking selfish aggrandizement.

This is not a matter of ethics alone. One of the universal laws governing spiritual creative power is infringed upon or broken (according to the strength of the governing motive) in all like instances, and in all such cases the hitherto latent positive aspect of the creative force is prematurely aroused and, figuratively speaking, dammed up and thrown back on itself, causing explosive action and scattering its volume in many directions, instead of developing evenly and normally in combination with the negative aspects of the same into one powerful force, in which case an occultist may, by concentration of will and mind, direct the latter into channels of spiritual generation for the evolving of higher spiritual powers.

Indulgence in such action as is referred to above produces phenomena upon the astral plane that are akin to the display of electric light on the physical plane when conducting wires are crossed, and the fiery force thus astrally liberated reappears on the latter plane and is seized by the passions and used up in lower creative functions, although it is unconsciously done in the majority of instances. Mankind is slow in reaching to knowledge of the fundamental causes of the effects it is continually fighting, and in no instance is it so slow as in its search for the causes back of the effects of the destructive forces of Nature.

LESSON 91
THE OVERLAPPING OF CYCLES

Just four times seven revolutions of the earth on its axis from the day which closed the first ten-year cycle of the Esoteric Section of the Temple movement (February 18, 1909), the Cosmic timepiece, Fohat, rang out the knell of the past and coincidently struck the keynote for the succeeding ten-year cycle.

Each one of those twenty-eight days opened and closed a single note in an octave of the scale of life which represents two and one-half years. In other words, the opportunities, failures, and successes of any one of those days prefigured the opportunities, failures, or successes of one twenty-eighth of 3,652 days (ten years), for all those disciples who have been admitted to the Esoteric Section of The Temple between February 18, 1899, and February 18, 1909.

The first yearly cycle of the organized Temple of the People has now closed. If you could remember the main events, the trend of mind, the opportunities lost or gained within those past twenty-eight days, you could more or less accurately prefigure the events of your lives for the coming ten years. Victories gained will be accentuated; evil done will be increased; injustice and all uncharitableness and viciousness will find their punishment. Kindly deeds, charity, unselfishness, and sincere efforts will meet their reward before that era closes,

Eyes that cannot see, ears that cannot hear will let such marked periods as I have referred to pass without note, and without realization that all the important events and opportunities that such a ten-year cycle can bring to them are determined in those days.

The sixth sense now developing has awakened and implanted in the mind of a vast number of the human race an innate realization of the importance of each cyclic division of time, in the worldwide inclination toward the holding of anniversaries. Carelessly or thoughtlessly you hear repeated or repeat yourself the words, "It is just a year ago today," or ten years, or a hundred years, as the case may be. The impulse back of the words is the soul's effort to impress upon the consciousness of the lower self the importance of such cyclic openings and closings, for as surely as the cycle of a deed or thought is accomplished, so surely a repetition of that deed or thought on some plane of being will be enacted.

It is this God-given impulse that sets the final bounds to every living thing. It is the basic force of every habit; and until man realizes this truth and acts upon his recurring opportunities at the time the cosmic cyclic forces open the same for him, he will never be able consciously to win a great battle with interior opposing forces, nor can he rise to the heights of the offered opportunities.

With regret passing words, I have closely watched the passing of the last twenty-eight day period and have seen some of you willfully throw away the hand outstretched to you; watched you carelessly add to your difficulties, throw away your opportunities, open new cycles of desperate trouble; as with joy passing words, I have watched others do exactly the reverse, watched the latter open cycles of true benevolence, loving thought, and loyal service. But it is to you these cyclic opportunities come and I cannot even tell you of their coming, or speak of them until they have passed, otherwise I might help to defeat the ends of justice and increase weakness.

This particular ten-year cycle closed very near the time of the completion of the organizing of The Temple of the People. This organization is in no sense a new movement, but just such a cyclic enlargement of a past opportunity as I have noted.

Each day of the ten-year cycle now commenced will accentuate the good, decrease the evil, or demolish the good and create the evil for the Temple work as a whole, as each member remembers and takes advantage of the words here given.

The exactness with which recurring lines of force are sent out from the central sphere of energy cannot be measured by mind of man, but he is capable of measuring them to such an extent as to profit by the opportunities they bring if he will take the trouble to note the time, place, and event in any given line of action, and when the same hour, day, or year, as the case may be, recurs, use the planetary forces that are in action when the hourly or yearly round of those particular forces recurs once more.

Many a lost disciple — many of those who have recently set up first causes for the same end during the aforementioned twenty-eight day period — would have had cause to kneel in gratitude had they remembered even what has heretofore been said by myself and others on this subject of cycles, and made some effort to discover and uncover any concealed truths in the same, and have used them rightly.

The preceding words clearly indicate the original cause, and also prefigure the further development of the one great science in two divisions, astrology and astronomy.

The constant incitement by the soul to compel man to note recurring events, as for instance the divisions of time, the movements of the planets, the tides of large bodies of water, definite changes in the physical body, etc., has aroused the mentality of many sages to note, compare notes, and keep anniversaries of individual or worldwide events.

Little by little these notes have been and are being chronicled, corroborated, and will finally be compiled by succeeding races into the astrological and astronomical works of the future.

To understand the real basic truths of my statements and bring them out for the understanding of those less fitted for comparison and analysis we must first try to comprehend what the Initiates refer to as the Great Breath — Motion — i.e., the cosmic impulse from a divine source to move at certain definite periods of time the substance created by itself. These movements constitute the measurements of time.

Bring the mind and imagination to bear on the constant action and reaction of the breath of a human being. Every inhalation carries oxygen to every atom of the body but the oxygen cannot reach every atom at the same instant. The various organs, nerves, muscles, etc., get their supply in regular order according to their need and the method of distribution, consequently the periods between contact, like the rests between musical notes, accentuate the different rates of vibration. The outbreathing exhales from the body the poisonous carbonic acid and other poisonous gases formed by the contact of the oxygen with other gases, other constituents of the blood of the human body. Each double breath therefore adds to the sum total of the life of the body and carries off the refuse resulting from the changing or re-creating of the blood.

Now imagine what might be done if the mind of man, knowing just when each one of the great cosmic double breaths obtained, could take advantage of the tremendous composite forces corresponding to the gases in the physical body, and in combination with corresponding forces in perfect time and rhythm, from every sun and planet, he could use them with his own breath as a carrying vehicle and by his will and mind could direct those forces for the accomplishment of any desired purpose. You can readily see what it would mean to him to know exactly when each breath was due, as well as the rates of motion and vibration of all those higher forms of energy, in order to bring their strength and power to bear on his purpose. This is exactly what an Initiate of high degree may accomplish, if Karmic law will permit.

LESSON 92
GOD AND THE DEVIL

Man uses his much vaunted reason to little effect when he throws over with one fell blow the cherished religious ideals and beliefs of preceding races and ages and of the earlier years of his present racial cycle.

As a rule he is entirely unconscious of the loss sustained when he casts down his former ideal, together with his belief in Heaven and hell, in God and the devil, in cursing and blessing, beliefs founded on varied expositions of the sacred books and on ancient myths and traditions, without an effort to seek out their basic source or interpret their mysteries.

With the increasing flood of new literature and retranslation of old which now sweeps over the world corroborating the false ideas of a thinker and reader who has for some apparently valid reason come to believe that former ideas and ideals were false or incomprehensible, there comes an almost overwhelming impulse to throw them all aside; and, as otherwise it seems to spell a perfect shipwreck of all hope, he seizes upon any plank of modern science that is within his reach which appears capable of bearing his weight — his doubts and fears instead of making a strong effort to hold the more modern theories and ideas on the surface of his mind tentatively while he searches for the clues which when found would prove beyond question that ancient and modern ideas and ideals had a common basis and a common end.

There is the same foundation for a belief in a Heaven and Hell, a devil and an angel in modern expositions of universal law, and in the scientific hypotheses of the action of cosmic forces in the creation of matter and its ultimate destiny — those forces which underlie every phase of material phenomena — as there ever was in what are termed the dark ages.

It is a bold speaker as well as an agnostic thinker who is willing to stand forth in the present age and deny statements of the Initiates as to the existence of at least three planes of consciousness — states of existence — or that the individual lives germane to any one of those states have not many features in common with the lives of the other states.

When one considers how nearly the supposed conditions of heaven and hell are attainable by the great majority of the people of earth; how many devilish and angelic characters the daily papers of a great metropolis bring to notice, the logical conclusion is that the forces active in each one of the said characters must have had some localized previous manifestation as well as a necessary future expression. Even if the energy so operating be only embodied in some degree of force such force or form of energy has its natural habitat, its original field of action; and wherever that is, by whatever name it is called, there will be a heaven or hell, the dwelling place of an angel or devil. As like seeks like in all fields of action, the individuals in whom those forces are peculiarly active must necessarily find themselves in rapport with others of like nature and in homogeneous states of consciousness. Once predicate the indestructibility of Matter, and the destruction of Consciousness is almost unthinkable.

As life is motion *per se*, and all motion must have some starting point, some impulse, some form of energy which sets in motion the thing or object moved, and as every central point, every sun, moon, or star under observation in the heavens, is apparently subject to the motion set up by some such form of energy, it follows that there must be one central point where that energy is generated or stored. Whether you can call the author, the generator of that energy, God (good) or the devil (evil) depends upon your present viewpoint, but the fact remains that it is, and that every phase and expression of life is dependent upon it.

Under the name of the Great Breath this source of energy has been revered and worshipped by the greatest intellects, the most spiritual teachers of all Time.

With every inbreathing and outbreathing by or from the spiritual source of all life, there rises and falls in perfect rhythm and time (according to the plane of manifestation, the size and weight of each form of differentiated matter), the manifesting point, the heart of every cell, whether it be the heart of a sun, planet, or germ and whether it be a material, mental, or spiritual body.

The rising and falling of the tides, the fluctuations of the earth's crust, the atmospheric changes, the changes in the physical body of man, and every movement of every creature and thing are all due to the rising and falling of the Great Breath; and, as even modern science concedes the fact that all forms of life are but different rates of vibration of one phase or state of energy commonly termed Ether, and all vibrations are different modifications of motion *per se*, the Great

Breath, we may accept the ancient teaching without allowing much room for controversy.

Once postulate intelligence and will as the guiding forces behind or within the Great Breath, and a God, in the highest sense of the word becomes an indisputable fact. Grant a plane of operations, which must of necessity be a harmonious center where all acting forms of force and energy are in perfect accord, where all power is centered, and surely the condition usually termed Heaven does not appear to be a very far-fetched idea. Reverse the action of these constituents of Heaven, consider the negative action of all the positive forces according to the well-known scientific postulate that there can be no manifestation of a positive pole of energy without the manifestation of its antithesis, the negative pole, and in that negative aspect of Heaven you have all the constituents of a state or plane of discord, the effect of the action of unconstructive, constrictive, rebellious forces; and the central point, the nucleus or heart of all this negative action and reaction, the legendary devil and hell, appear to be corollary realities, whatever terms we may use to express realities so designated.

With the outbreathing of the Great Breath everything in bond of form must swell, and consequent to the swelling, when its last degree of resistance is reached, that form, whether it be sun, planet, or seed-pod, must burst and scatter its fragments afar; each fragment, a lesser center, drifts into the fields of space, and new planets, new stars, new vegetation, new lives are formed. But before this bursting point is reached, say in the life of a planet, for instance, it has gathered its forces and swollen many times, its crust is covered with great cracks and crevices, the effects of former breaks sometimes becoming reservoirs for big rivers and lakes; and the waves of human and animal life force upon its surface, once transferred from other centers, other planets, other fragments, rise and fall with the life tides of the Great Breath. Races are born and die and are born again. Exactly the same phenomena occur under other variations of law, other conditions made by increased vibrations of the homogeneous substance, Ether, to which have been given the terms Astral, Soul, and Spiritual life, and even in those interior aspects of life we can imagine similar operations of the one Great Breath causing more ethereal combustion and resulting in expansion and explosion. The same great life wave breaks on the shores of every form of substance in vibration, with the same effect in every case. The era of duration, the cyclic gathering, swelling, and bursting of its separate forms of life and their transfer to other fields of activity occur just as methodically, as purposefully, and as surely on what are termed the interior, or Astral, Soul, and Spiritual planes as upon the physical plane, and must occur, until the operation of the Great Breath ceases and the generator of the breath ceases to act; or as is related in the Stanzas of Dzyan, "The Eternal Parent, wrapped in Her Ever-Invisible Robes, had slumbered again for seven Eternities."[1]

The action of the moon on the ocean tides has long been an accepted fact, but the fact of a similar action by every sun and star or planet on all other life tides, even the blood stream of men and animals within their individual sphere of action, is not so well established, nor is the fact that it is the central nucleus or cell of any one planet instead of the body as a whole that exerts whatever degree of force is necessary to affect the tides of water or life force on any other planet, and that all are subject to the central nucleus of the central sun around which all suns and planets alike, revolve.

In other words, from the universal point of operation, the home of the generator of the Great Breath, is sent forth the impulse which acts at one and the same time on every center of manifested life, whatever its nature.

These centers constitute "the harp of a thousand strings" whereon the fingers of God — the Cosmic Energies — are eternally playing the great life symphony. As the breath sweeps over those strings, as their tones rise and fall, suns and planets are born and die to live again, as man is born, dies, and lives again.

LESSON 93
THE CONSTRUCTIVE FORCES OF THE TEMPLE OF THE PEOPLE

Exactly on the same geometrical pattern, and in corresponding periods of time and definite degrees of energy and force, humanity, *en masse*, must rise to a corresponding height to that from which it fell at the close of the last great world period.

Every dropped stitch in the evolutionary web of one Manvantara of human life must be picked up and fastened, or the place of cleavage would enlarge until the whole web became a mass of tangled, broken threads.

---

[1] Blavatsky, *The Secret Doctrine*, vol. 1, p. 27.

One essential point in one decree of Divine Law is being continually overlooked, and the gaping wounds in the bodies — religious, political, and social — of this age are the results of the lost or wasted opportunities of a previous civilization.

The efforts of mankind to leap over those now festering wounds at a bound, leaving them to the destructive forces of nature, permit the whole body to become infected with the virus of deadly disease.

The law of gravitation controls both the ascent and descent of a body, but it is according to the weight and elasticity of the body whether or not its ascent can be accomplished in the same period of time consumed in its descent — though it must cover exactly the same length and breadth of space in its ascent as in its descent.

The same law governs the rise and fall of nations, races, families, as well as organizations; but it is according to its weight, its density, and interior power of overcoming inertia, whether or not either one can rise in a like period of time to that consumed in its fall.

Until a center has become strong enough to repel invaders through its own innate power by the exercise of the force of repulsion, it will attract bodies of a similar size, though of different densities — different calibers — and then commence the struggle for supremacy.

If the invading body is weighty and elastic enough to crush the central cell of the invaded body when they meet, both bodies will crash and destroy each other by the power of momentum.

If the central cell is weighty and elastic enough to sustain itself in poise, there issues from it a repelling force that will keep all invaders at a sufficient distance from its auric envelope to prevent the extraneous bodies from reaching its real center of operations.

This is equally true of the planetary bodies, of every physical body and organization of people karmically drawn together around a common center.

Humanity has been much slower in appreciating the vital cause of hindrance in its long struggle to reach the heights to which it aspires, than it has in appreciating the fact that it was surely in process of rising from the depths of the morass of evil into which it sank in the closing years of the last Manvantara.

The soul's memory of its former high estate has been sufficient to furnish the dynamic energy for the first necessary expulsive and ascending effort; but, as has so repeatedly occurred in the case of man, lower desire runs away with reason and intuition, and tries to force him upward in the scale of evolution by leaps and bounds while the truth is that the energy exhausted by any such leap and bound stays his progress at the step so reached, until sufficient energy is generated to take him a step further; and in that interval, the masses of mankind he had left behind in that supreme effort, have reached a position similar to that attained by him, by steady normal growth, and reached it minus the weakening strain imposed upon some parts of his nature by the extra effort to pass others in the race.

Man cannot outstrip the laws of his being, and every effort at so doing causes him to retrace his steps, and as it were, to stop and pick up those stitches in his part of the web of life that he had inadvertently dropped.

No amount of reasoning will avail with the majority of the human race to prevent their making such mistakes, because they will not control the lower desire principle which drives them on as with a whiplash into unwise disastrous effort.

An earnest study of the laws of Being would show the futility of trying to build a body of any character by any other method of formation than that used by nature.

A single cell is the foundation and generator of all the constructive life forces that will enter into the building of any organic body, whatever may be the purposes and functions of all subsequently evolved cells, and however important any one set of cells may be to the good and well-being of the mass as a whole.

If the central cell is cut off or cannot function properly because of some obstruction placed in its way by other cells, the body *en masse* must fall apart by its weight, for the cohesive power rests primarily in the central cell.

Every word I have spoken is peculiarly applicable to The Temple of the People. The Initiates of the White Lodge make no mistakes in placing the central cells of any of its organic bodies, for they form those bodies in accordance with evolutionary and Karmic law, of which they are administrators; and every failure of such a body to fulfill its divine mission is due to the cause above noted, lower desire outstripping Reason and Law in the individual cells — or members — of the body and killing out or incapacitating the central cell — in other words, unwillingness to wait for the law to take its course and eliminate any self-seeking or rebellious central cell by the right means, which that law would invariably do if left to take its course.

As a rule, people have but little knowledge of the tremendous power of elimination aroused in an organic body, where an obstructing force is introduced, or some individual is in the wrong; and therefore fail to see the needlessness, as well as the inevitable result, of precipitate action by any single individual or group.

In nine cases out of ten, the consequent anguish and suffering as a result of broken law by a limited number or individual, must fall upon the innocent; and thus, a new karmic debt is created, the payment of which will be to disintegrate the body of which the lawbreaker is a part if the latter be not eliminated.

I have advised and directed the formation of every main feature of The Temple of the People, and I call your attention to the above-mentioned action of the Universal Law, that you may be enabled to stand, when countless other organic bodies will fall — as you can do if you can keep in mind and act upon the directions I have given you.

If you can always remember that the breaking of the law of discipleship by any one of your number is a danger signal to you individually, which calls for right and immediate action on your part, you will be able to build a body which will stand the strain of the coming pull of forces, without being torn apart.

The defection of one member should sound the rallying cry for the rest, to battle for the preservation of the whole.

Man always gets what he demands, and the demand is made by his own obedience to Divine Law; and in no other way can he obtain satisfaction of demand; but his motive for the demand determines its final result.

There is a place, an opportunity, a certainty for every faithful disciple in The Temple of the People. He may have to win that place through his own heart's laceration — but win it he will — if he is faithful to his trust.

Having won it, he must be prepared to hold it at all costs, and the costs are generally heavy, for no man ever rose above his fellow men without arousing the emissaries of the Black Lodge to action through his erstwhile companions.

This is due to the inevitable effect of the action of the law of Balance, which works for the proving of the tool it has created and raised to the proving point. Having won his place, man must prove his right to hold it against all comers who would rob him of it.

I have scarcely ceased from telling you during the last decade that your right to the protection and help of the White Lodge, and what is of much more importance — the possibility of preparing as it were, for the coming central figure of a new humanity — rested upon implicit obedience to the laws laid down, and not upon the action of any personality.

We can easily displace one or a dozen disciples from positions which have been usurped or misused; but we cannot form the Guardian Wall for that Great Center, the coming Avatar, without the suitable, steadfast, coherent stones (disciples) with which to build it; and without that Wall no such Center can maintain individual form and carry out a divine purpose while in that form for any length of time on the physical plane.

Never let anyone persuade you that a single point of the six-pointed star, which symbolizes The Temple of the People, can be broken down, and the body of the star still be held intact by you.

It is possible, humanly speaking, that the representative of some one point may be removed by death or otherwise, and some other disciple moved up to sustain the same point, but the latter action can only be taken by us who are building the form — and taken in no uncertain way.

What I have said in relation to form applies just as certainly to the new political parties forming in every government in the world as it does to The Temple of the People.

With all the basic truths of socialism, it can never come into full power in any nation until the central cell — the nucleus — the right man takes his rightful position, among his fellows, with six adherents, no less rightly placed.

The Divine Law governing construction of form will nullify every effort, until that hour strikes, and the rebellious — the anarchistic leaders of the minority, who are always in opposition to that law, will bring into effect that which must inevitably follow upon the manifesting of such a man, i.e., division of interests; and thereby will set in action the forces which will bring success or failure to the body as a whole, and in either case great suffering to the world, which will last until the law has eliminated the destructive forces or has changed them into constructive forces, and the government of the nation is carried on by those who recognize the Father-Motherhood of God and the Brotherhood of Man.

LESSON 94
THE SOUL REDEEMED

As far back in the annals of time as sacred and profane history can take you, and eons before any of the records now recognized as authentic history were even thought out and tabulated; at a time when only the records of the astral light were available for research, the thinking animal, man, destroyed his opportunity for rapid advance in the life scale by persistent disobedience to one Divine Law, the law of Unity; and the same sad tale with all its ghastly details will sometime be recorded of the present generation. No matter how great the issue, how terrible the results both to themselves and the unborn races which follow them, personal ambition, lust for power or place, and hatred with its brood of devils, will turn away the sheep — like masses of human beings into separate channels, and nothing can hold those so actuated to the one great underlying principle of progress.

You have only to consider what the world would now be with all its races united on one fundamental principle; for instance, the principle of justice, and then consider the now ruling injustice, to gain some concept of the mighty change that would occur in all fields of life.

The one unending riddle of the universe is the hidden cause of the blindness of mankind. Why is it that man is willing to suffer and make others suffer age after age when it could be prevented by just being true to the principle of unity. Once perhaps in a century there arises some man or some woman who has seen the light and will not permit either the lower self or the temptations of others to lead them back into the darkness by repudiation of that one great law.

A man or woman who persists in being true to the Higher Self, who cannot be deceived by the specious tales of others, that one takes his or her place with the Initiates of the White Lodge when his trial is over as surely as tomorrow's sun will rise in the east. This does not mean that such an one is blind to the evil committed by others, or to personal weakness; it only means that, having seen the light, he becomes a part of it, and no matter what darkness reigns in the hearts of others the power to stand by and see divine justice work out its decrees year after year has been won. He can see his fellow men fall and rise again, can see the dearest things in the world taken away from him, perhaps unjustly, but still can say in his heart, "'I know that my

Redeemer liveth.'[1] I have *seen* the light of His truth and I *know* there is no shadow of turning with Him. I will not be false to God and my own Higher Self by being false to my brethren, false to the vows I have spoken, false to the principle I have founded my faith upon."

There is no more chance for a further step in development to the man who persistently lies to his Higher Self and his fellow creatures by willfully breaking his solemn promises, until he has retraced his way in sackcloth and ashes and made good those promises, than there is for him to leap over the sun. He can deceive himself very easily if he is not grounded in the principle of unity, but every time he tears apart two souls or more that have started right in an effort to attain to wisdom, he places a bar across his own path and can never gain another step up the ladder of his personal development until he has brought back those souls to the point of divergence. It would not help him in the least if he gave his body to be burned, all his possessions to the poor, and groveled in the dust in an effort to escape the results of his act. Nothing less than reparation would avail. He has committed the unforgivable sin against the fundamental law of life, the law of Unity. The gravity of the offense calls for a correspondingly full atonement.

LESSON 95
TO MY DAUGHTERS

Pray God to keep you from the falling of the curse that all too often blights a woman's life and leaves her but a similitude of the truly feminine; the curse that blinds her to her own limitations, and above all, robs her of her divine birthright.

When the gifts, the graces, and beyond all else, the interior qualities which set her apart from the rest of creation are prostituted to unworthy ends, the power of intuitive perception and application of the normal methods by which the feminine attributes can be raised from the mediocre to the highest point in the scale, must remain undeveloped and crude.

False impersonations of the divine attributes of purity and loyalty, which qualities or characteristics spring from the action of lower desires in woman, may deceive her as to their real nature for a time, and even all others among her associates save the man she loves, or who loves her; but that very force of love soon tears the deceptive mask

---

[1] Job 19:25.

aside and shows her superficiality. However gross may be the man, he creates an ideal and clothes it in the form of the woman he loves. That ideal is destroyed as soon as lower desire gains the upper hand in the contest between virtue and vice — between the real and the unreal. He may even deceive himself for a short time into believing that it still exists, but it is only a similitude of the real ideal that still lives in such an instance, and the frivolous, over-sexed nature of the woman soon palls upon him, satiety follows and finally, utter disgust.

There are few exceptions to this rule among the masses of the present age, and as soon as such a woman comes to a realization of the truth she either gives way to despair or in fury seeks revenge for wounded self-conceit and pride, and becomes frankly intolerant of and uninteresting to other women. She is either ill at ease or apathetic in their presence. She will preen like a female bird at mating time, using hands, head, and eyes to attract attention when a male enters the room. She seems neither to sit nor stand at ease for a moment. Every molecule of body and brain is at a tension, or the reverse may be the case; she may become the attentive, devout listener, the admiring flatterer of man's vanity, willing to "sit at his feet."

In other words, such a woman takes her color temporarily from any man she is brought into close contact with.

Ah, daughter mine, pray God to shield you from the fate that invariably overtakes a woman of that caliber.

Avoid the woman who despises or ignores others of her own sex, the woman who openly acknowledges her preference for the male by cruelly neglecting or avoiding other women, for she can give nothing of value to you and she will not accept anything of value at your hands. Your greatest treasure, the attributes which differentiate you from her are unseen or despised, and she must pass through deep, muddy waters and swirling waves of the life stream that will, metaphorically, tear her to pieces ere she reaches the point where desire for the great Motherhood of God will awaken and lead her into higher paths.

The man or woman who condones the evil in another for the purpose of covering up his or her wrong doing; the man who becomes accessory to the evil conduct of another for the purpose of preventing betrayal of his own shortcomings; the woman who finds excuses for the impurity of another woman merely to satisfy her own conscience when that conscience accuses her of like impurity, and thus seeks license for the same, all have betrayed their birthright for trash.

At the very foundations of the soul of man there shine out the twin stars, courage and self-respect. When the light of those stars is dimmed or quenched by cowardice or self-gratification, the soul is lost amid the shadows that darken the path of life and can no longer perceive the character of the beasts that beset that path. Evil seems to be good and good evil, and the soul stumbles along, falling into every trap which the demons of darkness have dug for such weaklings, releasing itself with more and more difficulty each time. Its garments stained and torn, it struggles on until the path leads out into wide waters where it becomes a derelict, a stranded wreck.

The man or woman who drags down to the use and pleasure of the physical senses the divine creative fire, against the behests of conscience, against the teachings of the Masters of the White Brotherhood, blots out his or her name from the book of discipleship.

From the moment the above-mentioned twin stars shine out into the mind of man and the knowledge of good and evil comes to him with the power to choose, if he chooses evil he does so with his inner eye open. The disobedience of man to the divine laws of interdependence and mutual responsibility has helped to fill the earth with suffering and anguish, and only as he learns to obey the law can he help to remedy that condition.

As woman has been the temptation to which the lower nature of man has yielded, it is only as woman refuses to become accessory to his fall and shows forth to his mind's eye the beauties and graces of the higher aspect of womanhood that man can be compelled to recognize and desire those higher aspects. Man will eventually either bless or curse womanhood and it will be according to the extent and use of her power to dominate and control his lower nature, whether it will be blessing or cursing.

The wrong interpretation has been given to the allegory of the temptation and fall of man. The double-sexed nature of original mankind has been lost sight of. It was the struggle between the higher and lower nature of a single being that was originally portrayed in that allegory instead of a struggle between two personalities of different sexes. The lower or negative nature was the tempter, because it partook more strongly of the nature of matter at the time the force of the whole double-sexed nature swung to the lower — the negative — pole of manifestation on its cyclic round. When the same nature reaches the other pole on the same round, that which was the tempter becomes the tempted; the higher, the positive, then becomes the tempter, in turn.

The correspondence is obvious. The woman of the single-sexed race personates the tempter until the lower pole of her nature is reversed and she then becomes the tempted of the higher pole, man, and it is then that all the power at her command is requisite for her own salvation and secondarily the salvation of man.

The women of the present race are approaching such a period in a cyclic round, and every woman who helps to save a man from his lower self by refusing to yield to the temptation her lower nature places in her way, thus proving the existence of a higher phase of life than he has previously known, does more to save the race to which both belong than any man, however great he may be, can possibly do in the present age, and it is womankind that will be finally held to strict account for the laxity in morals of the present race, far more than man. His time will come in another age, as it came in a preceding age. The present cycle is woman's great opportunity, so again I appeal to you, daughters of the King,[1] pray the God within to keep you clean.

LESSON 96
THE HOLY PLACES
FROM THE MASTER K.H.

"Lovest thou me?" saith the Christ. "Lovest thou me?" whispers the man to the maid who has gained his love.

"Lovest thou me?" cries out the sorrowing mother to her wayward child. "Lovest thou me?" blossoms forth the lily and the rose, in tones of fragrance and beauty, to the sun.

"Lovest thou me?" softly calls the thirsty earth to the fast falling rain. Turn our eyes where we will, upward to the heavens or outward upon the earth, and silently or loudly, unclothed or embodied, beats the one thought — a query, "Lovest thou me?" in the brain or upon the ear of all creatures; and the answer which comes swiftly and unfailingly in response must always bring a cry or moan of pain and sorrow, or a sense of joy and gladness unspeakable.

Truly is the human heart the holiest of holy shrines, when once unselfish, sacrificial Love hath entered it, and throned itself before

---

[1] See Psalm 45:9–14.

the Altar Stone therein — a shrine at which the proudest knee may well bow low, the humblest soul prostrate itself, when once the faintest recognition of the great reality behind all earthly seeming dawns upon the consciousness.

Yet, thou, O little man, in ignorance, in jealousy, in fear or contempt of all that is obscure or hidden from thy gaze, dost laugh and make merry, slaughter and torture, weep over or imprison those into whose hearts is entering the light which always precedes the coming of God — the God of Love.

Thou dost place a ban against, or form a cordon around that shrine, and cry aloud: "Keep off, thou God of Love; thou mayest not enter in to bless that life, unless it be as I shall lead the way and make conditions for thee, and if thou darest to enter, I will crush thee with the law I have usurped, or kill thee in the mill of poverty and crime that I will drive thee into" — all unaware that He to whom thou speakest is the Author of thy being — the same God — the same Love that thundered out the Law on Sinai's[2] heights — the same who lay upon the cross and cried forgiveness unto those who nailed Him there; he who sat beneath the Bo tree[3] and delved into the Heart of Life, until he found the "open sesame" to all the secret places of the Universal Heart.

Man may place a barrier between that Love and himself. He may so befoul the substance of his heart that the Light of Love can only be reflected in a dim and shadowy form therein.

He may pull down the altar where the sacrificial rites have been performed day after day since first he saw the light, and leave but shattered emblems fouled by sensuous vileness; yea, may make that heart a rendezvous for devils, and ask the Love of God to shine thereon; yet, naught on earth or in the vast infinitudes of Motion, Time, and Space can have power to cast a stain or darksome blot upon that Love, or make it aught but what it is — the holiest of holy things, the body of our Christs, the God who holdeth in His gentle hands the blessings of all life, and all fulfillment.

Truly is the heart that purifies itself and bids Love enter and abide, the holiest of holy places.

---

[2] *Sinai* — the mountain where Moses received the Ten Commandments.
[3] *Bo tree* (*Sanskrit*, "tree of awakening") — a large sacred fig tree located in Bodh Gaya, India, under which the Buddha attained enlightenment; the symbol of wisdom.

LESSON 97
THE OCCULT SCIENCES

The occult sciences, or occultism, as the philosophy of the spiritual aspect of the three sciences in one is now widely termed by students of the same, indicates its nature by its terminology.

Do you ask what of this secrecy? Are not things done in secret condemned? Does not the word open, the very reverse of secret, in connection with any phase of life convey a higher, nobler idea to the human mind? I answer: Yes, unless the student be far enough along in his investigation of the nature of the sciences under discussion to have learned that the two words "secret" and "open" express two poles of the same thing or idea. An idea may be secretly unfolded, yet the instant the idea finds expression it has become open, and when the same idea is opened wide enough it again becomes secret. It disappears from common usage by over-use and becomes obsolete. It is, as it were, indrawn. In other words, the idea becomes secret or open according to its effects on the human mind and the period of its cycle of manifestation.

The occult sciences are secret only because the right period for their full revelation in the present Maha Yuga (great age) has not yet been reached. We are halfway between the beginning and the end of the cycle which gave birth to those sciences. They are as yet only partially born, so far as the majority of the human race is concerned. We find daily indications of the opening up of interest in the minds of many in regard to all those deep mysteries of life which pertain to the secret sciences, mysteries partially solved in other cycles, the sciences of mysticism, psychology, medicine, art, literature, music, etc., but the greater depths of those mysteries have not been sounded by the laity, nor can they be fully sounded by the latter at present nor in the very near future.

The very few who have sounded the depths, the progenitors or forerunners of the races that are to come, are compelled by their very knowledge of the results of ignorant or unwise speculation to keep those secrets, save as one by one there comes into incarnation a soul to whom they may be safely imparted, a soul prepared for such knowledge, a soul that has won in a previous incarnation the right and the ability to comprehend and use such knowledge.

Examples of the terrible results of prematurely imparted fragments of some occult science come under your observation almost
daily, as for example in the misuse of the powers of mesmerism. or
hypnotism, the misuse of spiritual forces that will bring terrible karmic results to the careless operator, and results which, to the mind of
the ignorant observer, may appear to be disproportionate to the wrong
committed, but which are not so in reality, for the crime is great.

The Temple is sometimes cruelly criticized for its seeming secrecy,
when the truth is there is not a single secret in the instructions issued
or in the foundation and formation of the body in whole or in part.

Secrecy in the narrowest acceptance of the term is the very reverse
of occultism. The true Initiate will tell you that clarity, clarity of life, of
purpose, of action, is the fundamental requisite of a disciple. The man
or woman with a secret is the man or woman to avoid as you would
a snake or a malignant, contagious disease. The man or woman who
can willfully deceive a friend by keeping secret something that friend
should know, at the same time deceives himself or herself infinitely
more, for the injury inflicted upon the soul substance of that friend
will call for sad retribution, and the demand will be paid to the uttermost. There can be no friendship between those who can permit a
secret to find lodgment between them, and a true occultist is above
all else a true friend to humanity as a whole and to those most closely
associated with him in any minor division of life. But a deep spiritual
truth cannot be widely imparted, for the reason that there is only
one here and there who has evolved to the point where that truth
can appeal to his understanding, and the Initiate is compelled by the
very nature of that truth to protect those who cannot comprehend
and therefore might ignorantly misuse it.

An unprecedented effort has been made by the Initiates ever since
the first instructions were issued by them, to convey some idea of the
truths outlined in the instructions, but unless the ideas expressed
therein are intuitively grasped by the student who endeavors to decipher their inner relationship to life, the efforts are fruitless in most
cases. How can one person convey to another an idea of a formless,
bodiless, yet conscious character of energy or force which cannot
materially manifest its presence to man because there are no vehicles
through which it can function on the plane of its operations that man
is able to cognize? Yet this is a simple proposition in comparison with
some of life's deeper mysteries.

Man cannot appreciate the necessity for or reality of those mysteries unless his senses of sight, hearing, touch, and understanding are developed to the degree where they can become centers of contact and operation for those forms of force and energy which are the bases of the mysteries, and which can function only through finer forms of matter; yet they are the most real of all real things.

It is dimly dawning on the minds of a few exoteric scientists that there exists a medium in and through which they individually are drifting as might a drop of oil through the veins or molecules of a stone, a medium of so much greater density and solidity than the matter of which they are now cognizant that there can be no comparison. Yet the etheric medium which penetrates or is interpenetrated by every atom of matter is exactly such a medium. It cannot be seen, touched, or heard by the physical senses, yet the soul becomes doubly cognizant of it after death when it enters upon another phase of life, the lower astral, and is capable of moving unhindered through the avenues which traverse that ether, avenues which correspond to the veins or interstices of the above-mentioned stone; and it is conscious of a weight and heaviness and density of which it was never conscious when confined in the vehicle which permitted only one form of locomotion.

It is for the reason that the bird is more tenuous and elastic instead of lighter than is the etheric base of the air through which it travels that it can fly, and were it not for the power of attraction which holds all non-elastic forms of matter to the earth's surface while that earth is turning on its axis and moving through its orbit, man also could move through the air by means of air currents which correspond to the etheric avenues with equal ease.

Because he is not so entirely subject to the same pole of the force of gravitation as are the other forms of physical life which are attracted and held to the surface of the earth, the enlightened student of the secret sciences can reverse the action of that pole of gravitation in his own astral body and move at will through the astral or etheric medium. There is no secret about it, but the average man will not even believe in the possibility of such power. He is so much the slave of the suggestion that has dominated the human races so long, namely, that he cannot rise from the earth, that he simply cannot even control his astral body to such an extent as consciously to leave the physical body.

As ether is the basic principle of air and all coarser forms of matter, so Akasha is the basic principle of ether, but neither is comprehensible to one who has not attained to knowledge of the mysteries of reflection or shadow.

A little light may be thrown upon the nature of each principle by the power of imagination.

If the Ego incarnated in a physical body were capable of imparting life, intelligence, being, to every atom of a reflection cast upon a mirror by its physical body, and the light in itself by which the reflection was cast were also sifting through the interstices and made visible between the atoms of that physical body, thus exerting the pressure which would bind together the atoms of the reflected image, the phenomena thus produced would exemplify the relation between Akasha and Ether. The latter is the background upon or within which Akasha, spiritual Will, casts its reflections by means of its inherent light, and those reflections eventually become the various forms of life on the visible planes of the universe.

How little the great majority of teachers of Christianity have ever suspected the deep scientific truths revealed in countless utterances of its founder! Age after age has passed since the utterance was voiced, "Oh thou of little faith, wherefore dost thou doubt?"[1] yet in those simple words the Initiate gave the key to one of Nature's mightiest secrets; a secret which once fully solved will revolutionize many of the deepest scientific theories ever recognized by man.

You may ask why, if my statement be true, did not that Initiate more fully explain his words if he really had the well-being of humanity at heart. I answer, simply because he was powerless to do so, not alone because of his obligations to the Degree of the White Lodge which he represented, but man was not at that time capable of externalizing the idea voiced. The right cyclic hour had not struck. The peculiar sense through which alone such deep truths might be apprehended was then only barely conceived, and had not been developed to such an extent that it was capable of solving that mystery. It is only within the last quarter of a century that mankind has seen and recognized the fact that a new sense, termed the sixth sense, was in process of evolution, and only here and there a single individual has been able to make any use of the same.

---

[1] Matthew 14:31.

The term faith has been made interchangeable with the term belief, while in fact they are two poles of one potent force. Belief is lost in faith. When faith disappears belief is quickly swallowed up in unbelief. The possessor of faith can do much more than remove the proverbial mountain. He can build or destroy a world. Yet these, together with many other equally potent expressions of the Initiates are frequently classed as "drivel," wearisome platitudes, etc., by those who are tirelessly seeking for the clue to the great mystery of Cosmic energy, which was given repeatedly by the Initiate and also by his disciples, but it will escape the latter until they have still further evolved the sense by which alone it is made perceptible and of which it is a most important part. Strange as the last statement may seem, when you have reached the point where the same Initiate's reproof and injunction, "What is that to thee? Follow thou me,"[1] falls with sufficient intensity, and commands immediate obedience, a point where all the concerns of other individuals, all the petty trivialities of everyday life, the faults and weaknesses of co-disciples become as nothing, you will not merit such reproof as is contained in the first part of the expression. Without faith you cannot "follow the Christ" which the Initiate represents in the sense indicated by him, therefore cannot touch the clue to the great secret which the Christ principle expresses in and by the sixth sense, for faith is the substance-force by which the etheric base of all power is tapped.

It would seem a far cry from the Christ principle as generally understood, to the energy which moves the sun and stars in their orbits and which gives the power of locomotion expressed by the word "flight," to a tiny insect, yet it is one and the same.

Man's inability to accept the fact that faith, will, and mentality are forms of substance, cripples his investigations. He cries wildly for knowledge, for justice, for truth, and while the cry is on his lips deliberately flings back into the faces of the Gods the opportunities showered upon him for obtaining his desires, and then whines like a whipped cur at the inevitable results of his revolt or indifference.

Is it to be wondered at that the observer of the same often cries out with the prophets of old, "How long, oh Lord, how long wilt thou suffer this people?"

---

[1] John 21:22.

LESSON 98
QUESTIONS ANSWERED BY THE MASTER

Question: What fits a disciple for exoteric work for the Lodge?
Answer: Indifference, and again I say indifference. As long as a disciple can be spiritually hurt or can be incapacitated for doing his best work by the attacks, the opinions, the criticisms of others, so long can he be turned aside from his mission.

Question: Is what the world calls "good character" an essential to the highest service in a disciple?

Answer: All that may be summed up in the words, virtue, discretion, tact, honesty, etc., may be, and often is, requisite for service in many fields of life. But for the service which leads to attainment of the highest gifts in the power of the Lodge to bestow, the possession of one of these characteristics alone, or all together, as the world interprets them, is not sufficient for admission to the ranks of accepted disciples. These characteristics are all embodied in, combined with, and overruled by another all-important attribute which will live and endure when all differentiations in the line of characteristics are in abeyance. What the world calls good character in an individual is as a rule the combined result of some years of ambition, emulation, and adaptation to certain ideals fixed in the mentality of the race. The essential attribute for the accepted chela is the result of ages of effort by countless races. The former is something which may be lost by a single unpremeditated act or as a result of yielding to an overwhelming temptation. But the attribute which the examining Master first seeks, in the hour of a disciple's examination, is Charity — the love of the infinite life in which all things are engulfed. Where charity exists all truly desirable characteristics must inevitably evolve in time. Only long struggle, suffering, sacrifice and unspeakable longing can arouse the long atrophied center of the human brain which will respond to the vibrations of Divine Love, and such response is necessary before the disciple can answer aright the demand of the Master, but when that center is aroused and in action it will be found that all other requisites for service are at the command of the disciple. Yielding to temptation may plunge a disciple for the time being back into some gulf from which he has escaped, but the power of the attribute which he has gained through his personal struggle will bring him back in safety; where the one possessed of the before-mentioned "good character" alone, might fall into a similar gulf never to rise again in one life. The former disciple may suffer more than he ever had suffered before in order to win out, but he *will win*, and that is the important thing.

Question: Having been warned that the disciple who goes into the world to preach the truths of our philosophy, or any other good tidings, must meet attacks upon the foundation of his belief, the character of his Master or Guru, the nature or means of his material existence, what course should such disciple take to combat the same?

Answer: He should never combat any such criticism. He should refuse absolutely and persistently to discuss a single outer feature of an attack. He is not sent into the world to prove to others the nature, circumstances, character, or works of any person or group of persons with whom he is associated. If he is an accredited disciple of the White Lodge he goes with a message to the sick, the weary, the heart-atrophied human race, who, as it were, stand by their own open graves and know not that they are graves, or that they themselves are dead, and his mission is to help to resurrect them or keep them from entering these graves. And no matter what intervenes, nor how hard the Brothers of the Shadow strive to keep their hold on the "dead in life," the disciple should cling to his message alone and should throw up that message as a shield against every weapon raised to injure him or his work. He should try to show his hearers the nature of the methods used by the black brothers to mix the issues and cripple his work by diverting the mind from the one all-important subject of that message. He must become one with his message. It must dominate his nature and his hearers. It must sink so deeply into his soul that it carries the soul by its very weight and importance to the heart of Infinity and back again with every expression of it.

When the people of the world come to recognize the fact of the disciple's impersonality, compassion, and desire to serve them unselfishly, they will do as they have always done — "follow like sheep" that disciple who has been made their leader by the very force of his devotion to them individually and collectively.

Never should the disciple forget this. Never should he allow himself to be turned aside for a moment; for in that moment all the baffled, malignant forces of the negative side of life may drag him down, and make him commence the hard climb over again. The imminence of the danger and the importance of the issues should be the "hurry call" to action for every Templar.

LESSON 99
THE MIDDLE POINT

The average 19th-century man and woman has become so habituated to wonderful inventions and discoveries of science, by which nature's bars have been taken down and her secrets unveiled, that he is prone, when his interest in occultism is first aroused, to believe he has only to wait long enough to have the greater secrets of occultism pertaining to psychic and spiritual development unveiled by similar means, and to be able to avail himself of all such advantages without special effort on his part, and so he refuses to accept the statements of the older Seers regarding personal effort, or to use the only methods by which advancement in those fields is possible, as those methods have been outlined, for they invariably call for a greater amount of self-sacrifice than he feels willing to make. But this is where he makes his great mistake, for he never can attain to the understanding or use of the only powers that will differentiate him from others in the mediocre degrees of life by means of the effort of others.

As a race man is fast reaching the middle point of evolution beyond which no man can go on the merits or by the efforts of any other man. Before that middle point is reached, advancement has been made under the law governing differentiation — Repulsion. After this middle point is reached other laws, governing combination, unification — Attraction and Cohesion — are preeminently active, and opposition only increases difficulty, and finally results in crushing out the opposing thing, or person.

Many of the students of the Masters have reached or are nearing the above-mentioned middle point of evolution, but the development of the Spiritual Will has not kept pace with the development of their mentality; consequently, in some instances they are falling away from their original purpose, and being swept into the swirl of material development along lines that will surely drag them into the same vortex now being prepared by nature forces for many others.

It is utter folly for a man to expect that he can lead the same useless, selfish life he led previous to initiation in even the lowest degrees of the Lodge, and at the same time make any material advance in occultism. The line of demarcation between the two is definitely fixed.

The accepted neophyte has literally nothing to do with the requirements or commands of any other disciple or body of disciples, or with his own past. He has formed a definite contract with the Higher Self and his teacher, and to these alone he is answerable.

There was one of the deepest of all deep truths hidden in the command of Jesus, to the would-be disciple who would fain care for a newly made bride, or bury a friend: "What is that to thee? Follow thou me."[1] And contrary to the general idea of the apparent heartlessness of the command, that command was in fact the most loving, the most necessary, for anything that would tend to draw back the disciple into the slough he was leaving, when just on the verge of attaining to power by which he could succor those he was leaving or who had left him, would be most deplorable from all points of view. But whatever the effect of his primal efforts, the fact remains that the methods and means by which a man may reach beyond that middle point are as clearly and as sharply defined as may be the methods and means by which he may attain to power over steam or electrical energy, and "there is no shadow of turning with God."[2] He may attain to some measure of knowledge and mental satisfaction by some other method, but this is practically lost to him when he faces the fact that do what he will, he cannot go a step farther on the old lines. He will then either renounce all and drift into something which promises big results by little effort, and find out the facts in that way, or fall by leaps and bounds back to the old condition of dissatisfaction, materiality and final despair; or if he be brave enough, he will face the effects of his previous failures, pull himself together and start out in the direction he should have taken long before.

It is those of the first mentioned caliber that are the most rabid, hypercritical, and condemnatory of all others in respect to all occult research. The effect of their own failure having permeated their whole nature they will not admit there can be anything of value in that wherein they have failed. They forget that their failure was to be expected because they could not or would not conform to the rules given for their guidance. They pride themselves on their own supposed perspicuity in seeing, and morality in exposing what, in the silence of their own souls, they know is a false estimate of something far beyond them, and are in fact objects of pity to those who know them for what they are.

---

[1] John 21:22.
[2] James 1:17.

One of the methods by which a student may finally reach such a sad condition of mind is by laying down certain rules and conditions by which alone he will consent to help his comrades, utterly ignoring their needs, blinding himself to the fact that his methods would be of no avail to accomplish a task set for others. Such an one is so entirely possessed by his own ideas he is utterly incapable of perceiving the jinns[3] who are waiting upon interior planes, to trip him up when the inhibition of his mind is complete.

You cannot really help a man unless he chooses to be helped. All you may do up to that point, is "bread cast upon the waters,"[4] which may or may not return to you, and if he cannot see the advantage of your methods of procedure in the way of giving help, and you will not accept his estimate of his needs, there will be just one more lost opportunity for all concerned. In no other one way is the truth of the importance of non-attachment to results more perfectly exemplified, for it should make no difference to you individually what the results of your helpful thought or deed may be, or in what manner the help given is used, once you have decided to give that help.

You can prove the truth of my statements very easily from the personal standpoint. Of what advantage would it be to you if you were given the multiplication table, and told you could use it only in a certain way, when duty, inclination, and in fact your whole heart was set on using it in another way, by which you could solve a vital problem of infinite importance to you.

While non-attachment to results is essential to attainment of the heights of life, on the personal side of the equation it is equally true that the rungs of the ladder of life upon which you personally are climbing are built up by the opportunities for gratitude you have given the human souls you have helped to reach one or more of these rungs.

"Step out of the sunlight into the shade, if there be but place for thy brother, that so thou mayest add to that light, and thou wilt find that the light will guide both thee and thy brother."

---

[3] *Jinn* (*Arabic*, "to hide") — an elemental spirit. According to Arabic mythology, jinns were created from a pure smokeless flame and cannot be perceived by any of the five basic human senses. As with any elemental spirit, they can either invisibly assist or harm people. King Solomon was known to have power over jinns, thanks to a special stone in his possession. The jinns helped him build the Temple in Jerusalem.

[4] Ecclesiastes 11:1.

Remember, there is always place on the highest round of Life's ladder for him who can climb thus high. It is only the lower rounds of the ladder that are crowded by the climbers. Also remember that from the middle to the topmost round, each one is gained by renunciation energized by discrimination.

LESSON 100
POISON

If the causation as well as the effects of certain poisons, continually being generated and distributed by the self-conscious votaries of black magic were understood by the sufferers from their practices, they would be able to protect themselves, and at the same time destroy the effects of dastardly proceedings which, if left to chance, might finally wipe out a whole human race.

In order to give you some idea of the rationale and the final effect of what may originally have been but the satisfaction of vicious desire, or which may be a deliberate attempt to destroy another living creature, it will be necessary to consider the motive, the astral action and pathological effects, as well as the final result of either act under consideration. A tool of the Black Brotherhood, or an unconscious tool of his own evil desires, urged on by a powerful personal desire may generate by means of rapid, concentrated thought force, a condition in his own mental sphere which is comparable to that produced in cream by constant churning; that is, the rapid thought action separates certain ionic constituents of mental energy from the rest, even as butter is separated, leaving a residue.

These constituents, in combination with others of an opposing character, normally are beneficent, but are destructive, poisonous, and deadly in effect when isolated and consciously directed to any living creature.

They are then in a different rate of vibration, firmer in texture, more possible of manipulation by beings trained to their use; and because of their incisive, penetrative, disintegrating nature when directed into any channel, cannot easily be dislodged until their deadly work is done. The deposits in the poison sacs or fangs of the serpent, poisonous secretions in other animals, and even in man, were originally all of this nature. They were primarily the result of voluntary or involuntary depolarization and separation of one grade of substance from what was, *en masse*, a beneficent form of substance, its segregation into some part of a physical form of animal or man, and its final degeneration, during which process the secretions reached malefic condition.

When a votary of the Black Lodge desires to wreak vengeance upon, or kill a man or animal, he first generates and then transmits that deadly force to another, either by direct action or by slower forms of infection; but those in the more powerful ranks of that body are careful to refrain from informing their dupes or votaries that by means of such generation and transmission, they themselves will become individually infected with the same virus, and that the final results of their action will be far worse for them individually than for their victims.

The fact that it is even possible for a serpent to poison a man without biting him, under some circumstances, indicates the penetrating power of the poison; and this being true of this grade of matter of lower vibration, how much more effective must be the concentrated, condensed forms of like poison of a higher vibration, when emanating from a man.

The method by which this poison is injected into the body of one man by another is very simple. Once the deposit is formed by individual effort in the auric sphere of one man, a definite degree of the fiery lives which constitute that deposit is directed by will power to a certain center of the *medulla oblongata*. They there come into contact with a very refined class of cells, and incite the nucleoli therein to more rapid action, with the result that the whole character of the cells is changed.

They first become swollen, then looser in construction, then break down and are partially liquefied. Then, infected as they are by the character of the elementary lives that have incited them to action, they drift into the connecting nerve ganglia and are carried into the pneumogastric nerve, then to the ninth pair of nerves, and so by means of the nervous fluid, to all parts of the body.

In such a case the afflicted one soon begins to have fits of nervous or sullen depression, marked by suspicion, morbid speculations, desire for isolation, and frequently inordinate sexual manifestation.

Finally the nerve walls break down and the nerve fluid, which under normal conditions would vitalize the whole nervous system, is constricted within smaller areas where, because of its concentration and its disintegrating power, it destroys or incapacities whatever nerve centers of the body it contacts.

I have said a whole race might be destroyed by such means, and it is for the reason that such an infected mind and body may infect all whom they contact, while those so infected may be entirely unconscious of the existence of the power, or the object of the generator of the poison, and so do nothing to counteract it, that it may then manifest in some form of disease as, for instance, one of the terrible plagues.

With the disabling or breaking down of the nerve tissue in some vital organ, the organ itself is no longer able to throw off the poisonous products which have resulted naturally from chemical action.

Such an infected mind and body oftentimes unintentionally transmit the same poison that first infected it to others, and it is according to the purity of the mind and strength and vitality of the body of those so infected whether they can prevent similar action in their own auric spheres to that which first led to the generation of the poison, with all its aftereffects, even to insanity and death. Verily, one life is dependent on another. Who can picture the karmic effects of a deliberate act of such a nature to the person committing the crime?

LESSON 101
COLOR AND DISEASE

I am asked to give some information regarding the fundamental cause of the disease termed *tuberculosis* or *consumption*, and in reply will say the cause as well as the cure lies far beyond the domain of physical science. All diseases, whether or not now recognized as belonging to the class termed *germ diseases*, have the same primal cause; namely, unduly gratified desire.

If you are so intimately acquainted with a victim of tuberculosis as to enable you to perceive such concealed characteristics as only the intimate friend is allowed to see, you will invariably find some trace of the particular tenacious, grasping, and consuming appetite or desire that has been primarily the cause of the disease.

Often it is so well hidden that not even the victim of its power realizes its dominion until some hint of its existence incites him to bravely drag it out to the light of his consciousness by a rigid self-examination; but strangely enough, the sufferers from the line of diseases induced by the "devourers" (one degree of the fiery lives) are generally the last to perceive the causes back of the generation of those elemental lives and are, therefore, all the more difficult to treat successfully.

It is the repetition of unduly strong acts of self-indulgence along some line of desire through many lives which develops the soil — the color — in which the fiery lives may find a suitable environment and rapidly germinate, and which in turn are finally destroyed by a higher degree of the same order of life, when their duty as cosmic scavengers is accomplished. A slothful, self-indulgent, negatively active individual will, octopus-like, stretch out mental tentacles and draw to himself whatever he may desire, regardless of the effect of his selfishness on himself or others. He may influence others to labor to supply his desires instead of supplying his own necessities by normal, natural methods, i.e., by positive industry, and by such mental and physical practices he will tinge the normally bright color of some astral center of a physical organ with a dark reflection which will tend to decrease vibration and so materialize the substance of that center that its weight and density will decrease its power of resistance to inimical forces.

Those who are familiar with the Eastern teaching of the sevenfold division of all matter, force and consciousness, will understand me when I say the seat of any disease is in the astral center of the organ affected; but in order better to comprehend this statement the average student may receive some assistance from a review of the main points of the philosophy of the manifestation of all matter.

From the standpoint of the seven principles there is neither a white nor black ray, yet there is a composite ray which contains potentially, and periodically reflects, all degrees of the life principle.

From this "white" ray (undifferentiated matter) is shot out — photographed — as it were, the energy that becomes differentiated as color on an Etheric plane; which plane also acts as a screen or sensitized plate, in that it receives and fixes the energy as color within itself.

As individual groupings of the different aspects of color, these groups are reflected in the auric sphere of man and thence to the astral body, where they become the substratum of the organs and different divisions of the physical man, and are at all times visible to the inquiring seer, on the astral plane. While these groups all have one predominating color, they contain potentially all other colors, and these colors being subject to the energy of Mind and Will when manifested are subject to change in degrees of shade and intensity, according to the nature and intensity of the thought forces operating upon or within the groupings. Perhaps some idea of the process by which such a change is made may be obtained by considering the following illustration.

There are times when the mind of man seems a perfect blank; the man is conscious of the reality of the great potential reservoir he calls his mind, yet, for the time being, there is no movement therein; suddenly a thought, an idea, a color, or vibration from the negative pole of some center of the brain sends a flash of energy into that previously quiescent reservoir of the mind. As like seeks like on the astral as well as on the physical plane, the energy awakened by that idea will seek out and unite with the astral center of the physical organ to which it is drawn by the law of affinity.

Thought follows thought on the same idea, day after day, if the basis of the idea contains sufficient interest until finally the whole mass is changed, materialized, and possibly tainted.

If the idea seems a practical one, the man seizes it and fixes it, as it were, by bringing it into concrete form by physical energy, and the idea is thus embodied as a material thing. The process by which disease is manifested is similar, if not exactly the same.

In the case of a consumptive, if a victim of selfish desires in some incarnation, he first lays a train of thought, the basic subject of which is intimately connected with one astral center of a physical organ. If the line of thought, or the desire for self-indulgence be more intimately concerned with a breath center, the soil or habitat suitable for the awaiting fiery lives of tuberculosis will be created in the throat and lungs. These "fiery lives" are always with us, but they can do no harm until a suitable habitat, a right soil is created for them, in which case they are drawn as surely to that soil center or organ as water is drawn to its own level.

Embodied in the bacillus they will at once attack and devour the tissue forming the organ. As the requisite soil can only be created by self-indulgence, the right conditions for recovery can only be created by sacrifice; in other words, the center — the soil — the color — must be purified so that it will no longer furnish sustenance for the tubercular bacilli — no longer furnish a feeding ground for "the devourers."

This is done first by a positive idea of health; secondarily by the renunciation of personal will and the sacrifice of those habits or appetites of self-indulgence which were the original cause of the disease;

and thirdly, by placing the physical body in conditions where nature's remedial agents will have the least to contend with.

The modern idea of treating disease is the only truly scientific idea of cure advanced in this age. All others but drive the disease from one plane or organ to another. A positive desire for recovery, the renunciation of former methods of life, the sacrifice of deleterious and harmful appetites, the introduction by natural means of a higher degree of the fiery lives — "the builders" — by means of pure ozone and oxygen, which in their turn destroy the "devourers"; all these conduce to the recovery of the victim of his own imprudent self-indulgence.

"He who would find his life must lose it";[1] he who would find health must first destroy disease; and his first effort must be a purification of the color centers of his astral body where the first causes of that disease are located, but he should not stop there; for unless the disease is destroyed, root and branch, it will only be transferred.

LESSON 102
THE LIGHT FROM THE LODGE

As the light of the sun rules the day and the light of the moon and stars rules the night, yet the light is one, so the light of the White Lodge rules its first appointed representative during its appointed season, and the same light rules its lesser representatives during their appointed seasons.

If the stars should leave their orbits and combine in space to rule the day, great would be the darkness of those stars for they would pass beyond the power and influence of the giver of their light. The light which had lighted sun, moon, and stars would be darkened in such an instance and only dead worlds would float in the spacial currents; the equilibrium of all would be destroyed, the purpose of that light would be thwarted, and with the thwarting of purpose would come paralysis of effort.

Shall the moon or the satellites of the sun say to the sun, "We will have none of thee, we will shine by our own light"? Verily I say, no true light shall be theirs.

Foolish, misguided child that thou art, seest thou not that only the pale reflected light of the moon — the psychic plane — can lighten thy

---

[1] Matthew 10:39.

path if thou art false to the sun — thy Father — and like unto a false star hast left thine appointed place, the orbit of thy motion?

When thou hast cleansed thine own heart that the light of the sun of Divine Love may shine clearly through its meshes, then shalt thou see clearly to cleanse thy brother's heart, and mayhap, thou wilt not then find so much of evil in thy brother's heart as now thou thinkest. What seemeth evil to thee in him, may be but the image of evil reflected upon him from thine own heart.

LESSON 103
HIS COMING

Think you that the coming of the Blessed One will bring peace to the earth? Think you your periods of labor, of struggle with limitations, of the temptations of the flesh will be lessened, and that the conditions now obtaining on the Devachanic plane will be repeated upon the material plane? If so, great will be your disappointment.

No Avatar, no great leader of His people ever came to earth with an olive branch in His hand. Invariably He comes with a sword to divide "the sheep and the goats,"[1] to sunder the evils of ignorance from knowledge and truth. The olive branch materializes when the sword has done its work of separation, and the soul, stripped clean of its hindrances, its vile imaginings, bows its head and says, "Take me, use me, trample me if need be, only cleanse me, purify me, lead me to the stream of living water that I too in turn may give life to those who follow me."

In the days to come, what you are working for now will come to you, whether it be the things of the world or the things of the spirit. Improved conditions may and will give you improved opportunities, but those particular opportunities are for the future. Your present opportunities improved or neglected will bring you peace with honor or battle with dishonor in the coming days. The same demons of avarice, jealousy, hatred, and despair that now pursue you so viciously will await the coming of your footsteps as they pass the portal of life's fulfillment in Devachan to death in life on the physical plane.

The coming of an Avatar is always the signal for a harder fight than that which has preceded it, but thanks be to the sacrifices He makes

---

[1] Matthew 25:32.

for you in His great renunciation, the weapons for use in that warfare are of tenfold the power and service, and your power and strength will be reinforced by the power and strength of His great purpose. Your personal responsibility for failure will not be lessened, but to that responsibility will be added the wisdom gained by association with His successes. The goal of your ambition may still seem far away and to have increased in power and greatness to the grandeur of a universal goal, but it will be within the reach of your vision.

LESSON 104
THE COMING DAY

In the days to come, those days toward which the eyes of the starved, world-torn soul turn in longing, the days when its long tantalized, age-long, whetted appetite can no longer be controlled by some scrap of knowledge of a debatable character, the students of the then established seats of learning will find it much less difficult to make the necessary correlations between the principles of physiology and psychology, than the corresponding class of students find it at the present time. But unless said students can simultaneously develop the psychic and mental qualities, while their physical bodies are in a state of transmutation, they will be in a similar position to that of the man who desires to see the back of his head while beholding his face in a mirror and must use a second mirror. Unless the second mirror — the psychic senses — as well as the first, is perfect, he can only obtain very unsatisfactory results, possibly something in the line of odd caricatures of either or both sides of his head, i.e., mental malformations.

At the present time, a fairly good mirror — the deductions of science — is obtainable for examination of the facial — the exterior — expressions and qualities, in the form of the action of matter on the physical plane; but the second mirror, the mirror by which is seen the back of the head — the succeeding effects of the same action on the substance of the astral plane, so far as it is usable by the majority of students — is a very unsatisfactory reflector. The reflected images appear distorted beyond all semblance to realities, or are so coarsened or degraded in character that they are only possible for use in the operations of the charlatan and cheat.

Exactly as it is now possible to cast reflected images of persons or material things in successive action upon a reflecting surface,[1] so it is quite possible to cast the continuous action — the successive aftereffects — of astral forms or objects upon a reflecting surface of astral matter, and to do so consciously and intelligently.

The second mirror — the screen — must be of a finer quality in the latter instance; the instrument — the operator — must possess more penetrating power, more fixity of purpose, more energy, and he must be able to bridge the seeming gulf between any two states of matter, or rather he must be able to see that there is no actual gulf, and that success is dependent upon his ability to follow the interior direct line which leads from one state of matter into another. And the student of the before-mentioned time to come will be able to do this. In some few instances the power is even now partially developed, and the individuals so progressed will furnish the impulse needed to greater effort. But no worse mistake can be made in this respect than that now evidenced by those who presume to say that education on material lines is unnecessary for rightly interpreting and correlating the different features of universal phenomena, and who are satisfied to rely on psychic training or upon what they believe to be spiritual leadings for such purposes. Unfortunately for their purpose, they ignore the most vital link in our chain of reasoning, i.e., the actual impossibility of the manifestation of the phenomena of any one plane or state of matter without corresponding action on its opposite plane; for instance, the natural phenomena of the spiritual and psychic planes could not be made manifest on those planes, unless there was corresponding action in the line of material phenomena on the lowest material planes.

The law of opposites is immutable. However, it should be understood that there must be a great broadening and deepening of the present day educational methods and ideals, before the human race as a whole can accept and profit by the teachings of Esotericism.

If the photographer be an occultist, the click of the camera which announces the fixing of a picture upon the sensitive film would be the signal for him to look inward and follow the interior aftereffects of the single motion of the thing or object so fixed on the outer plane.

These effects could only be perceived by the psychic sight at first, and by one who possesses a wider, deeper knowledge of the principles

---

[1] It is a motion picture.

involved than the average man, but they could be caught and fixed and reflected by the instrument I have in mind; such an instrument would manifest some of the features of clairvoyance, the psychic sense of vision.

By the use of the telescope and camera combined, it is now possible to bring the stars or other heavenly bodies, located at great distances from the earth, into focus for photographing, and fair presentations of their appearance may be made by enlarging the pictures and casting them on screens. If you can realize that it is quite possible for an instrument to be invented which would combine the requisite qualities of the present-day microscope, telescope, spectroscope, and camera obscura,[2] all of which are dependent upon the energy of light for operation, then you can perceive the possibilities before mentioned, and can reason from these premises as to the truth of previous statements regarding the necessity for education on certain lines.

Such an instrument will be perfected at the time intimated by me, and the invention will owe its perfection to the observations taken by a limited number of disciples of the White Lodge, on the action of the energy of light on the astral planes in conjunction with observations of the same energy on the material plane.

But we have to delve deeper still to find the unifying force which will combine the outer and inner features of such an invention and make possible its materialization; namely, the intuitionally perceptive energy which now operates alone through the pineal gland — the atrophied third eye in man, for it is only to the vision of that eye that the light to which I have referred as astral light is visible. Neither can the operation of that light be satisfactorily studied on the lower phases of the astral plane, where the average psychic of the present day functions, though the results of those operations in the form of light be visible on both the astral and physical planes.

The gradual awakening of that now atrophied center of sight is taking place in the cases of those students who have come directly under the tuition of the Initiates of the White Lodge, and who are fulfilling the obligations taken to the same.

When such an instrument as I have referred to is invented and put into use by the highly trained and developed student, the effects

---

[2] *Camera obscura* — an early form of camera consisting of a dark box with a tiny hole or lens in the front and a small screen inside on which the image appears.

of the secret actions of any one person or object can be made visible to another person or to the world at large if necessary.

For instance, let us take such an action as the blow of a knife by one man on another; every cell of the wounded flesh could be made perceptible, as well as the action of the blood corpuscles, the entering of any destructive microbes, the breaking down of the tissue, the fight between the elementals embodied in the red and the white corpuscles, and even so far inward as the mass color, the form of the entities of which those constructive and destructive elementals were individual parts.

Such an instrument would do even more than record the action of objects now alone classed as material, for it would record the results of concentrated thought forces. In other words, it would record the picture made by any line of thought powerful and concentrated deeply enough to bring the thought into form as color. If accentuated by strong emotion, the color would mass itself into more definite form and be more easily caught by the instrument and subsequently reflected upon a peculiar chemical composition which as yet has only been conceived in mind but which will be materialized before many decades pass.

By following up this line of prediction and thought, it will become evident that with the natural changes now occurring in the constituents of matter and force, many great inventions, many events hitherto believed to be possible only under the law of miracles, will become realized facts. But one thing can prevent this. If the compelling desire of the human race tend in a downward direction, the achievement will be delayed for some time.

If the lessons taught by the downfall of past civilizations pass unheeded by the present civilization, if the nucleus required for bridging the gulf of antagonism between the races and peoples of the earth cannot be formed and held intact, in order that the knowledge now being gained may be applied to the solution of interior problems, mankind will have proved itself unready for further advance at this time, and the climb up the next spiral of progress will be all the harder.

I have only touched upon various aspects of the great possibilities indicated in what I have now said. It would take volumes to enlarge upon these aspects to a degree that would enable the average student thoroughly to comprehend either the truths intimated or those more definitely touched upon.

Those volumes may be forthcoming if the Templars will prove themselves worthy of the confidence and trust requisite for such an important revelation, by making use of the knowledge already given, and obeying the directions and suggestions issued, by which such action on our part may be made possible.

LESSON 105
MY BROTHER'S KEEPER

To the disciple of the Master Soul of the Universe:
From the moment your feet shall cross the sill of the high-barred gate which now divides the things of the spirit and the things of the flesh; from the moment when you bid adieu to the long loved, long followed friends and companions of the past, and gird yourself afresh for service, grasp firmly the handle of the staff that had well-nigh fallen from your shaking hand in your hour of final testing, and for the last time wipe the cheek wet with the tears of your beloved; from that moment life has changed for you.

You have caught a glimpse of the towering pinnacles of the Temple of Life's Mysteries at the end of the path and of the tender face of the great Mother bending over its battlements, and that one glimpse is enough. From that moment your viewpoint of life has changed; you are no longer owner of yourself; you have no longer a right to claim for yourself the easy things, the delights of that part of life's path you are leaving; you have only the right of renunciation, the joys of introspection, and the ever-widening realization that when your task is completed, when you have reached and passed the Temple Gate, widely opened for your entrance, you will at last be closely folded in the Heart you so long have sought, the Heart of the Christ, the Heart of the Universe.

"The self of spirit and the self of matter can never meet, one of the twain must disappear."[1] The true and the false are diametrically opposed to each other, and all the energy of all the vast spaces of the universe cannot draw them together. Truth and falsehood cannot unite. No disciple can be true to God and false to his brother at the same time.

---

[1] From the *Book of the Golden Precepts*. See Blavatsky, *The Voice of the Silence*, p. 12.

If you to whom I speak are indeed disciples, to you I say if your brother trusts you to his undoing while you sleep, sad will be your awakening. If so be, you have failed to plant the guideposts at the points of danger on the path where lurk the treacherous, slimy demons of the underworld you have but just escaped yourselves, and who now lie in wait to trip the weary footsore comrade returning to his home; the same demons will draw you back into their toils, however far you may have traveled from them.

"If thy brother will not hear; if life with all its myriad notes of soft beguiling still urges him on to satiation, and he turn his face from thee to tread some other path, then art thou clear of blame."

"If ambition's curse and all the brood of devil's spawn which tempt men on to hatred and reviling, now drive them on to stab their brethren to the soul, and blind the eyes of sister souls with tears of acid and of blood — then they of all men need thy pity and compassion, and thou canst only stand, with none to know the anguish of thy soul, and see them pass to other fields of life than thine, while yet the tendrils of thy heart cling close to them."

Ah, children, could I but show you the final result of the steadfast devotion of a single soul who, with full faith in the eternal, all-sufficing justice of Omnipotence, and who in admiration for the boundless effort, the long self-sacrifice, the sublime endurance of some other soul who stands in the breach of some wall of life, can stand up, alone, if need be, before the maddened crowd of selfish, crude, or even weak and wavering souls who throng that wall on either side, and with all his heart can cry aloud, "I am my brother's keeper, here stand I, ready to battle with all men for the life of my brother, ready to fight for his right to bring to a successful finish the work the Christ, in the body of the Great White Lodge, has given him to do, in His name and for His cause, and naught shall stand in my way! Not even a gnat shall cross my path to reach him, or a serpent glide between my feet, mayhap to sting him until his flesh gives way, and he falls and dies, and leaves the work to which he has been called in chaos or undone. By his death in such a way, he proves me a traitor to the cause I chose myself, the failure of which I must answer for at the judgment bar of the Great White Lodge, which received my promise of protection for my brother."

The aisles of heaven echo and re-echo with the paeans of praise sung by angelic hosts, and many are the wreaths of victory which crown the brow of such a one, for he is victor in life's hardest lists, victor in the fight betwixt right and wrong, the fight which demons wage for souls which stand betwixt them and man; and never can the human race reach the height of power until many are the true brave souls who can stand the test of loyalty, bravery, and endurance, when the life and honor of their fellow disciples are at stake.

The world is seething with the masses of the weak and wavering, sick of soul and body, the panic stricken crowds that trample each other down like a drove of maddened beasts at the smell of fire, in their wild rush to leave a battleground where braver, stronger souls are fighting hard to hold a vantage point, that when the fight is over and hard-won peace has been declared, all men may have security and opportunity to grow aright.

Here and there lies a soldier of another class, a stricken soldier of higher rank, beaten down to earth by shafts of malice from the tongue of a whilom friend or open enemy. The mercy he has freely given to all who asked, is now denied by all, and in his last long hour of anguish he sinks to rest with none to turn his eyes toward, but God.

Nevertheless, he with his great brother in the breach of the wall are greater far than any kings of earth, for both have overcome man's worst enemies, cowardice, and unfaith.

I would that every pilgrim in life's lists, that every chela started on the path marked out for him, might see and seize his chance, the chance which comes but once in any single life, to take and hold a point of vantage such as I have limned; for having won that single point, he has won the power to reach to greater heights.

For such as these a newer day will dawn. To such as these the kings and princes of a newer realm will bow and the corridors of Heaven will ring with the glorious words of the salutatory.

"Warriors[1] of Light! Warriors of Truth! I salute you in the name of the Great White Brotherhood. Go forth to battle with the powers of darkness, armed with the Sword of the Spirit of God, the Breastplate of Righteousness, the Helmet of eternal Truth."

---

[1] *Warrior* — in certain contexts, the Higher Self, the first manifestation of the Christos.

LESSON 106
THE MINUTIAE OF LIFE AND EFFECTS

The average student of esoteric science has been so naturally drawn to the study of the minutiae of life, it is somewhat singular that he has not reached a clearer comprehension of the action of what are commonly called good and evil forces as exemplified in the ferments, bacteria, and other microorganisms, and thus more easily learned to protect himself and benefit the world thereby, even without amplified dissertations by an occult scientist. He surely could spend his spare time, if no more, to no better purpose; but in all too many cases, even with all the instruction he has had on the law of correspondences, he fails to make any connection between these lesser lives and the finer forces. The study of bacteriology would give him many broad hints as to the action of the protective and injurious psycho-organic forces by which he is constantly surrounded and which are playing through his body at all times. Microorganisms that are injurious to the tissues of the body secrete and expel still more minute forms of life which are just as injurious to the nervous fluids as the former are to the tissues, and these in turn secrete and expel yet finer forms of psycho-organisms which affect the air we breathe, and upon entering the lungs, work changes in the blood stream which produce some of the most obscure and dangerous diseases that human beings are subject to. Some incurable forms of insanity are the result of the action of those lesser lives upon the brain through the blood.

The idea that worry and trouble drive men to insanity is very common, but the way in which it is done escapes observation. Exactly as a single ferment will change the character of a large quantity of some gross form of matter, the secretions of the same ferment which are also of the lesser lives will act upon the nervous system and consequently on the brain. It is not the worry (or at least that is incidental) which provokes the disease; it is some definite form of disintegrating force precipitated during the incidents which have caused the worry, probably through an associate in business or social life, who has become infected in the aforesaid manner.

Esoteric students are often warned by their teachers to keep away from certain persons who are antagonistic to them individually or to some cause with which they are personally identified. In some instances the warning is not heeded, from some mistaken idea that he or she would be acting unbrotherly, or that it might appear that they were dominated by fear of some untoward results, when the facts in the case are that the teacher knows that such antagonism has been instrumental in introducing certain definite forms of ferments into the bodies of those persons by physical or psychic touch which may mean death or disease to the one so warned, while the one warned against might be perfectly ignorant of the existence or action of said ferments in his own body. One of the worst features of phenomena of this kind is the length of time that may elapse in some instances between the time of infection and the appearance of the disease, consequently no connection is made in the mind between the two.

Many esoteric students belonging to The Temple and other organizations are suffering all the terrors of some form of nervous or malignant disease today because of disobedience to the injunctions which have been laid upon them within the last decade.

You are apt to think of Forces as of some impalpable, unorganized, gaseous or astral substances which might possibly strike you as would a gust of hot air or wind, but if so, you are mistaken. They are entities composed of billions of lesser lives, beneficent or destructive to you according to their nature, direction and absorption, and also according to your own individual condition at the time of contact.

A thought of a malignant nature will set into action a malignant force. If you come into intimate personal contact or association with the generator of that thought you will inevitably receive some measure of that force, which striking upon some weak organ will generate a life in the form of a ferment, and then it depends upon your power and ability to dislodge that ferment before the whole organ is involved, or generate a force antagonistic to it and so conquer it. The fermentation which follows its appearance in your body will produce the disease corresponding to the original thought, and, in many cases the time and place of contagion is erroneously fixed by examining bacteriologists, simply because they know nothing of the action of forces such as I have mentioned. You can no more escape infection when placing yourself in contact with a malignant force than you may escape the action of the germs of the disease when exposed in some other way and time.

These facts were known to the priesthoods of even the Dark Ages, and the knowledge of the possibilities of such infection and cure was what gave rise to belief in certain amulets and charms for protection against witchcraft, which was supposed to be the result of just such actions of force as I have mentioned, and in many cases was nothing but insanity due to such causes.

The members of a family or a group of people may be drawn together for a common cause or purpose, thus forming a magnetic center dominated by some form of magnetic force, which by its cyclic individual action is antipathetic to some other degree or form of the same force, and if any member of such group or family enter into close relation with a person or persons dominated by the antipathetical force, he will inevitably be infected to a greater or lesser extent by the latter in the way I have mentioned, and then it depends upon his power of resistance as to how much harm will ensue. If he be weak or ailing, or negative in disposition and will, any weakness he may have will be aggravated, any latent disease in his body will be accentuated and he will suffer greatly himself and in the end probably infect others also with the same physical, mental, or moral disease. If he be a disciple of the Initiates of the White Lodge and under instruction in the Secret Sciences, they will teach him how to deal with such infection; but if he has proven himself recreant and disobedient to the injunctions of his teachers, he will not be given such knowledge, for further disobedience would be apt to follow perhaps, in the misuse and willful abuse of the knowledge gained and only lead to great personal wrongdoing and might also precipitate the Karma of his disobedience upon his teacher.

As said before, it is surprising that a greater number of students of occultism have not reached these conclusions themselves long ago, when the advantages they have had are taken into consideration, but these are of the things that belong to esotericism and do not reach the lay mind unless some hint is given that sets in action a train of thought which finally leads to a partial solution of the mysteries under consideration.

LESSON 107
STORED-UP MEMORIES

Man seldom realizes how dependent he is upon the stored up memories of former lives for his impressions, ideals, and beliefs and in many instances, for final success in materializing his ideals.

He imagines that he can trace back to some former event, circumstance, or past experience of his present life, all his beliefs and ideals, and that where changes in the same occur it is due alone to new conditions or events; but this is not exactly true. He does not take sufficiently into account the methodical, mathematically exact periods of time which must elapse between any two phases of growth and development. The finality, so far as it may be observed, of any creation of Nature may suddenly appear, but the periods of growth between conception and birth of any product in any department of life, are all definitely fixed, and the more perfect, the more valuable any product of nature; the slower, the more exact are the processes by which she accomplishes her object; and this is as true on the mental and spiritual planes of life as on the material.

You hear an argument or read a statement of fact which appeals to you at once, and you accept it and incorporate it among your collection of beliefs. You may often refer to the statement as the foundation of your present belief in that fact, but you have held deep in your consciousness, it may be for ages, the real foundation of that belief. That one statement only called out what was in you pertaining to the subject.

At some time in some previous incarnation you have been personally identified with the very substance under discussion, the thing or object upon which the fact was based, and it has become incorporated in your brain or body by some of nature's mysterious processes; and it is a part of your being.

Perhaps someday you may lie with ear to the ground, and you catch the rustle of the leaves of grass, you hear the buzz of an insect, the stealthy approach of a caterpillar. You recognize each one, and its name and form come into your consciousness. You think your recognition of them is the result of repeated listening to the same sounds in your present life, but this may not be true; each time a consciousness of either action has come to you in this life it has come as a finality, not as a commencement.

You never could have recognized or heard either one of those sounds had it not been that there still remained in your being some mental deposit, some cell or skandha that has been a part of your being since the hour when individual consciousness first came to the combination of atoms which clothed the monad — the foundation of your being.

It may have been when you passed from the mineral into the vegetable kingdom, and the grass, the caterpillar, the insect were parts of your existence, and the sound waves aroused by your motions entered into and became a part of that vegetable or insect organic structure.

It seems a very difficult thing for the average student to accept the fact that it is utterly impossible for him to know, to recognize or accept a single thing that he himself has not been personally identified with in some life.

It is a worldwide adage that experience is the best teacher. It is not only the best; it is the only reliable teacher; and the reason for this is obvious in the face of my foregoing statements. It is the only teacher because in the experience the very substance of the experience and the experimenter have become identified by the processes of nature, during the period of time that elapses between the beginning and the end of the experience; and they two have become one flesh and there is no such thing as divorce between them.

Memory of the same may be inhibited for cause, but with the further development of the soul, as one experience merges into another and the higher law blends them into one, memory of each and every experience will become more and more fixed and certain, and the time will come when from the heights of all life's experiences of one great Manvantara, the soul will be able to look back through the long line of incarnations and remember all that has befallen it since it left its Father's house to wander in the fields of material life.

As spectrum analysis proceeds and finer and finer grades of substance are unmistakably manifest, and the intimate relation of the same to all forms of matter becomes more apparent, and with the acceptance of the indestructibility of matter, which is now established beyond doubt, there will come to the investigators a realization of the truths occult science has so long been trying to inculcate; and among these truths will be the one I have been stating.

Physical science has already reduced matter to units of force, theoretically speaking, but either because of antagonism or ignorance its votaries are either unwilling to admit or unable to perceive that those same units of force, sometimes termed "thoughts of God," are really the monads of occult science.

The quality of resistance resident in force precludes the possibility of compressing it into any given form, and this has been one of the unsolved mysteries of the past, but would be so no longer to a mind capable of accepting the fact of the universality of one force, of which all other forms of force are emanations, and the unmistakable action of cyclic law on the latter; for the cyclic law is the power behind condensation of the differentiated forms of force, through which process force is, so to speak, precipitated and becomes matter.

For instance, take the familiar form of force we term steam. In the releasing of that force a certain degree of heat must be applied to water; in other words, the vibratory action of the water must be raised.

If the steam can be collected and the lower vibratory action of cold applied to the steam, it condenses and returns to water; in other words, the positive and negative action of the cyclic law — the law of motion — has released the force, and then bound the same force again into form.

The finer the force, the higher must be the rates of vibration which control it. The powerlessness of the undeveloped disciple to control the cyclic law to a degree that would increase the rate of vibration of any form of force he would desire to use, to an intensity that would overcome the natural quality of resistance inherent in the force, is all that keeps him from proving the truth of this statement.

Back of the cyclic law — the law of motion — is the power of Kriyashakti — Universal Will — and to whatever extent man has developed that Will in himself, is he able to control the before said units of force in the creation of matter, and the great hindrance to the development of that power is his innate selfishness and unreliability.

So long as his self-interest will lead him into injustice, so long is the path of power barred — for Justice is corollary with Divine Will. If he can store up memories of just, wise, compassionate acts performed by himself in any one incarnation, he has stored up just so much energy for use in the following incarnation in overcoming the inertia induced by the negative aspect of the positive good in the acts above mentioned. It is this negative aspect of positive good that always induces resistance. So in the overcoming of the inertia as is done by the energy referred to, when the impulse comes to repeat the act in a following incarnation there are fewer obstacles to overcome. He is so much the more capable of manipulating the forces of Justice, Wisdom, and Compassion; consequently, the next act of similar nature carries with it a greater power for good to others and increases the quality of the force in his own aura.

LESSON 108
THE GREAT TEMPLE

Y ou have been given the ground floor of the Great Temple which is really the underground or the most hidden chambers.

This hidden floor contains so many clues, by which many of the symbolic features of the upper regions may be deciphered, that I have left it to your intuition and knowledge of symbolism to make connections.

The masons, especially if they happen to be skilled geometricians or mathematicians, would find it easier to do this than the average student, and if any further clue than those previously given is needed, the one following will supply it; namely, the roof of the central Initiation chamber is pyramidal in form and the apex or opening at the top is in the form of a huge eye, through which escapes the surplus Fire during the process of the Fiery Ordeal on the lower floor.

Another clue which I may now give you relates to the fact that each of the seats of the Mighty — the Masters, at the corners of the central chamber, are indicative of the four paths which lead to attainment; and the Initiates stand at those points to welcome the descending pilgrim from the upper regions, who descends to face the great Ordeal by Fire, in one degree of his Initiation.

In the third degree the same pilgrim ascends to the upper regions by means of corridors leading upward from the four chambers of Initiation, situated at each side of the central Initiation chamber.

He receives his armor, his implements of labor, pestle, board, square and compass, his trowel, and his passwords in those upper regions, and then must descend for his fiery trial, after which he again ascends to the upper regions for his final degree, his resurrection from the tomb; upon the conclusion of which he may pass unhindered back and forth between upper and lower regions at will.

In due time the great pyramid will yield to investigation, and there will be found, in replica, all the features designated by me in the plan of the Great Temple as given to you — and many more undreamed of as yet by all save the Initiates.

On subterranean floors of this pyramid, as yet undiscovered by later-day explorers, are replicas, in symbol, of all the features of the first floor of the Temple plan.

The corridors leading to these have been completely sealed, as have also other ascending and descending corridors and chambers of the pyramid, and there is small chance of their discovery, unless the pyramid itself should be shattered by some convulsion of nature.

Yet there are hidden springs by means of which the immense stones used for sealing the passages may be displaced by the touch of a finger, so perfect is their adjustment.

LESSON 109
CHEMICAL AND ALCHEMICAL AFFINITY

The following condensed statement regarding the action of one of the most important spiritual laws, and the biological effect of disobedience to the same, may lead to much good if carefully read and circulated among those for whom it is primarily intended.

I have scarcely touched upon the mathematical and geometrical aspects of these laws, though they are all important, for I do not now desire to distract attention from the main points under consideration.

I have previously said that the principles of chemistry would throw open many sealed doors to the earnest disciple, and some of those doors open upon the special problems which confront the world at different cyclic periods, and which must then be solved, to some extent at least, or the succeeding race must suffer greatly as a result of the ignorance or indifference which has prevented their solution.

Back of every such problem is disobedience to some primal law of life, and whether the problem be mental or physical, national or social, if the primal cause be sought it may be found, either *in actu* or by correspondence, in chemical or alchemical action.

Aside from the problem of right government, and I might say including the same, the greatest problem of the day is negatively stated in the words "race suicide" — racial degeneracy — and for the cause as well as the solution of the problem we must hark back to the principles of chemistry as embodied in alchemy.

There is in fact but one primal, all-inclusive element, and that is Fire. In its forty-nine aspects — principles — Fire is creator and created, Cosmic Father and Mother, Brother and Sister. In manifestation as a single entity, it is first of all Intelligence *per se*.

But for our present purpose we will confine ourselves more particularly to the action of some of the sub-divisions — energies and elements which are the secondary embodiments of Intelligence.

The nearest we can come to a comprehension of Intelligence as an element is to study its manifestation as oxygen.

It depends entirely upon the affinity for oxygen existing in any two or more elements whether it is possible for them to combine with each other and create or generate other elementary substances or energies. The concealed Fire, commonly termed Heat, is the only form of energy which can break up the constituents of any elementary substance and compel them to combine with others in some other form of substance.

While the laws governing chemical affinity may compel combination under right conditions, it depends upon the quantity or degree of the original elements, and therefore on the principles of mathematics and geometry, as to what forms the elements in process of combination will take in order to manifest as gross matter, and therefore, what kingdom of nature they will operate within.

There is no such possibility as the combination of any two elements which do not stand in the right mathematical relation to each other.

If that relation is not correct, the principle of Heat as manifest in oxygen cannot combine any two substances, it can only disintegrate them and leave the atomic constituents to find their way to other atoms with which combination may be effected.

The true relation of one element to another, i.e., the affinity of one element for another, is established on a higher plane than that of Intelligence, namely, the plane of Consciousness or Spirit, the Great Breath, and the plane of Identities.

With the first cyclic rise and fall of the Great Breath, the breathings — fiery forces — emanate and combine, thus creating the plane or state we call Intelligence. Each one of these Breaths is a divine Spirit — an Entity — a God which yields up its manifested existence as one, to become many; a mode of motion which becomes many rates of vibration.

I have faintly touched upon these great mysteries in order to illustrate two all-important points, namely, the relation of one created thing or creature to another, and the method by which two intimately related Entities combine to create two more, and the progeny of the four thus created upon the succeeding plane.

As previously stated, every Breath, every God or Monad is a distinct life, an Identity which cannot be lost, whatever form or combination of forms the monadic essence (of which a monad is an emanation), may create in Time and Space. The real "you," will be "you" eternally, whatever your incarnations are, or whether those incarnations are a-sexual or bi-sexual.

The before-mentioned Breaths are fourfold or four-faced, so to speak. Each Breath, or degree of energy, contains all the potentialities of all positive and negative forces, yet it must combine with the succeeding Breath — the next released energy or emanation — in order to create those four faces or aspects, and the two thus combined with their progeny — emanations — manifest the positive-negative and negative-positive, and the straight positive and negative aspects of itself; the first square, which ultimately becomes the four planes of the Cosmos.

In other words, two bi-sexual entities must combine to create two bi-sexual entities on lower planes in a succeeding racial cycle.

This brings us to the consideration of the human family of the present age — ourselves. The first two monads which combined to form first, a third and then the first four-faced energy, and all others which followed in like order, never losing their identities, exist today as races and planes, or states of consciousness, and every man and woman in the world with all the potentialities of the monads which created them, is thus a reincarnation — differentiation — of the God-head of a great race or cosmic family.

However antagonistic might be the exterior conditions now existing between men and women who are in right affinitive relation to each other interiorly, that antagonism has been engendered by the karmic sin of disobedience to the divine law of affinity in some life. Nothing can break the interior relation between them, however wide the separation may be on the physical plane. For example, owing to the strong affinity existing between the elements oxygen and hydrogen, a certain proportion and quantity of each will create a definite amount of water, and though that water may be raised to vapor, and then to steam, or lowered to ice, the water in some form, will remain until it is resolved back into its constituent gases. You can color the water or add different chemicals to it, change its appearance as you will, but the water is always there in the same proportion.

So a man and woman may color their lives, their environments, by close connection with other men or other women; they can add immensely to their experience and karma; but they are only perfectly identified and truly united with those in right affinitive relations to them while under the dominion of Time and Space.

If by any chance, or interposition of a higher power, two persons in the right affinitive relation to each other are drawn together in any earth life when karmic conditions are right for their union, the potential forces within them both will bend all exterior things to their will and bring to them all they require for their well-being, without any particular strain or stress. They will be, so to speak, so permeated with the monadic four-faced essence that their power is only limited by their environment and state of development. Separation between the immediate members of such a family would be impossible, until by marriage and intermarriage with members of other families the monadic essence of the first was, so to speak, diluted in later generations; in which case the divine Fire — Love — which in its positive aspect had combined the parents and firstborn children into one four-faced entity, or form of energy, in its negative aspect would tear apart — separate the later-born from their forbears, and when this takes place the race or family, man or woman, is nearing the downward arc of its particular life cycle.

Note: The fifth — the separative energy — would come into action.

A large number of the present white race have reached this very point. Many men and women governed by lust or selfish desire are brought together in sexual relations termed marriage, and as a consequence of the natural reaction — which always follows in such instances and results in satiation, the offspring of such unions are driven apart, dispersed into other families, and often driven into soul-crushing, body-killing industries, the worst result of which is prostitution.

This has led to sterility and the unsexing of many men and women, and consequently to different forms of terrible disease.

Coincident with the cry of race suicide is the revival of the old so-called "affinity craze." The connection between the two is obvious. One is the natural corollary of the other. The poor self-deceived souls who are seeking true affinities on the earth or lower astral planes will never find them in those fields without the right kind of assistance.

The Identities which came forth from the Divine Spirit together, as far as their embodiments are concerned, are now so widely separated by sin that there is no possibility of recognition of each other, only as Initiates of high degrees who have access to the "Book of Life," may possibly identify them and assist in such recognition.

Recognition by what is commonly called mutual or sex attraction is a fallacy, for the Divine Love by which the alchemical action of recognition and combination is effected, bears no semblance to the sex attraction of the physical plane, which in the majority of instances rests upon the color and expression of an eye, the turn of a head, the molding of limbs, a smile, or a voice.

The present personalities of many true affinities might greatly surprise you, as they appear today in the single pictures (the incarnations) now in evidence. In many cases they are viciously antagonistic to each other. Long-indulged sin has driven them as far asunder in thought and desire as the poles, and only severe trial, unselfish action, and the results of suffering can bring them together again, overcome the antagonism, and re-combine the separated energies.

It would not occur to the minds of all students that there might be a spiritually incestuous relation between two interiorly related persons that would be infinitely more destructive to the bodies and souls so indulging, than would the crime of incest between people who are merely connected by family ties on the physical plane; and that the evil of spiritual incest is responsible to a great extent for the lasciviousness which makes a hospital of a large portion of this beautiful world. The spiritual relation existing between Father, Mother, Sister, and Brother — the before-mentioned four-faced Energies — extends through all planes of manifestation and all races or solar families.

In the early races of this earth these ties were recognized and the law carefully followed, but after the fall of the angels — these same early races — into dense matter and finally into black magic, the "leaves" of the "family trees," metaphorically speaking, the genealogies, were lost and the right relations between individual members of this planetary family were no longer ascertainable; so there was indiscriminate indulgence between Father and Mother, Sister and Brother, and this evil, figuratively speaking, sowed the seed for the crop of degenerates now fast increasing.

As much evil is resulting from such indiscriminate spiritual relations today as was ever the case, and the utter impossibility of ascer-
taining true relations, true affinities, in any other way than through the
efforts of the Initiates, is one of the facts which point to the inevitable
destruction of the present earth races when they have passed a given
cyclic point; for exactly as incestuous connections between men and
women on the physical plane lead to physical sterility, so correspondingly incestuous thought and spiritual action on the planes of soul
and mind between the members of one racial family, photograph, as
it were, the results to the physical plane, thus leading toward sterility
of the victims of such practices.

This deep truth is back of the Initiate's pleadings for loyalty to
"Our Father's house," devotion to home, family, nation, and above
all to whatever degree of the White Lodge one functions in, and to
the heads — the Father-Mother principles of that degree, and in
some instances of their directions regarding celibacy in the cases of
advanced disciples.

So it is that all things, all principles, laws, and Identities twine and
intertwine around and about each other, affecting all, and all leading
to one central point, whatever phase of life you examine.

Of course, much of what I have said will be disputed by those in
thrall to the lusts of flesh, but here and there will be one intelligent and
clear minded enough to recognize the probabilities in the case and
the action of the universal law as feebly outlined here, and so be able
to see that far gone as is the age, and alchemically separated as must
be the original elements of life by means of the various processes of
differentiation, what I have said may well be logical and true.

One of the greatest missions of some of the high degrees of
the Initiates is the breaking down of the barriers which now exist
between souls in true affinitive relation to each other, but which have
no self-consciousness of such relation; and in contradistinction to the
performance of that mission by the Brothers of Light are the efforts of
the Brothers of the Shadow to rebuild the barriers when partly broken
by the Initiates or make new and stronger ones, as is evidenced in the
conduct and instructions of the pseudo-occultists who are teaching
sex magic, making pretense of finding said affinities while driving
true affinities apart, and indulgence in all the long line of demoniacal
pretense, which leads to the death and annihilation of their victims.

I earnestly plead with you to beware how you lend yourselves carelessly or willfully to any such practices or suggestions.

If you are strong, brave, loyal, and obedient enough to keep *en rapport*[1] with your teachers, the deep truths concerning these mysteries will be opened to you and opened rightly.

You can thus pick up the dropped stitches of your web of life, you can pay your just debts to nature, hold fast to your Identities and eventually find your right niches in the Great Temple Wall.

LESSON 110
HEREDITY

The masses of the 19th century have little or no conception of some of the vast fields of occult research to be invaded by the few, ere another century rolls around. A suspicion of the existence of those fields has been awakened in an occasional mind, but only one here and there has even touched the outlying districts comprehendingly.

The field of genealogy is one of these and, closely allied to the same, is the field of anthropology. The mysteries now attendant upon the study of atavism will be solved in the next century, and even the child born of criminal or insane parentage will no longer be considered a menace to society, so far will be advanced the knowledge of the human body and the methods, surgical, medicinal, and psychological, by which it may be changed for the better.

Every teacher of man, woman or child has been amazed beyond measure at the unsatisfactory results of his efforts in the direction of moral and mental development, and at the appearance of criminal tendencies which would sometimes suddenly manifest after years of constant labor and watching, and with no apparent reason.

In many such cases the horrible charge of insanity is lodged against such as these, and this charge has been pushed to such a degree as the commitment of the afflicted one to the hell of some insane hospital, when if the truth might be learned, the abnormal growth of some set of giant cells pressing upon the central cell of some group, which under normal conditions would form a very active, important center of the brain or spinal cord, was in fact the basic cause of the condition; or it may be that a depression of the skull at some important point has

---
[1] In agreement or harmony.

precluded the possibility of the supply of a normal amount of blood to that point, thus causing starvation and final disintegration of tissue.

In still other cases the hypertrophy of some formerly prominent occipital center belonging to the animal kingdom is not complete enough to prevent its recurrence in the human body, and it is quite possible that a pupil or disciple who is descended from a parent so afflicted suddenly develops characteristic features which would plainly show the recurrence of these long-vanished animal traits of remote progenitors, and in an occasional case this would be so pronounced as to lead to a change in construction of form or feature, the body being contorted or elongated, and possibly one or more features of the head, or the hands and feet show decided tendencies to degeneration.

A wise teacher, in selecting his pupils for any particular branch of general knowledge, or a teacher along lines of occultism, would do well to thoroughly examine the bodies of the proposed pupils, in a search for marks by which he might recognize a tendency toward atavism; but it must be a wise teacher; he must not jump to the conclusion that because some organ or feature seems abnormally large or small in comparison with similar organs or features of some other body there must be degeneration, for while the same might indicate the preponderance or lack of some particular normal quality, it would require a microscopical examination of the blood, bone, and tissue cells to determine the fact, and consequently, an operation by knife to reach the points to be examined.

But there are other ways of examination, and they will be found and used at a later date by those fitted for such work.

Even now, much advance in one direction along these lines is possible by psychological processes. If an advanced disciple were to watch closely his associates for signs of degeneracy, he would learn that these may be easily found by one who seeks aright for abnormally evil tendencies, cruelty, jealousy, malice, hatred, and all those characteristics which in reality belong to the most blood-thirsty animal creation, and are always indications of degeneracy and moral and physical disease; and by tracing these indications back to the corresponding feature or organ, and examining the blood and tissue of the same, corroboration of suspicion may be found, and at the same time right methods of treatment may be discovered.

It is a fairly well-established fact that cancer is the result of the development of embryonic tissue belonging to a lower order of life within the human. These embryonic cells may be latent for years or generations, and then suddenly begin to multiply and make war on the surrounding tissue. This tissue may have belonged in the past to the body of a fish or some other cold-blooded animal. The tendency to suspicion unduly persisted in, may be evidenced by an abnormally large eye, and that tendency be developed by a single cell inherited from some far off ancestor in the animal kingdom, possibly the lynx. That single cell has increased in size and generative power, multiplied greatly, and the group of giant cells so developed may be active in the unnatural development of that eye.

In order to remedy the evil, destroy the tendency, and thereby reduce the size of the eye, the location of those cells must be found and their gradual elimination be brought about by means which would in nowise interfere with the surrounding normal tissue, or any function of the eye. This would be very difficult in the case of an adult but comparatively simple in the case of a child, though always attended with danger.

You often hear of the eradication of like tendencies by means of much effort, sacrifice, will power, or prayer, but they cannot be entirely eradicated as long as a single cell of the group which is responsible is still in active service; but take notice, I do not deny the possibility of removing the cells themselves by such a method — it is the tendency, or the active existence of the evil quality that I deny can be entirely removed, without the removal of the responsible agent first, and this can be done by two methods.

But whatever the method, it is attended by danger of one kind or another if the operator is ignorant of the possible harm he may do to surrounding tissue or organ.

Will power is a finer form of Fire than any fire capable of observation on the physical plane, and the concentration of will power on any organ may destroy the usefulness of the organ and in some instances the organ itself, so here again we see the necessity for right training by competent teachers in that particular field of knowledge.

LESSON 111
THE HUMAN RACE

Beautiful beyond aught the mind of the present human race can conceive was the great polar continent, which like a huge cap encompassed the north pole in the days when the Sons of God first came forth to dwell upon the earth in bodies they themselves had created from the vital sparks of the water enveloping the then fiery sphere — the substratum of our earth.

And beautiful past power of description were the ensouled forms so created — the first, the moon-colored race, to which the purest, brightest moonbeams gave their character and colorings. Sexless Lords they were during the first three of the Seven Ages of this present Manvantara, and their immediate offspring were the creations of Will and Yoga.

But in the latter half of the Third Age the substance which formed the bodies of this First Race began to solidify; all matter became denser and coarser in texture, and the animal forms created by mindless man, as well as the human race began to differentiate.

The sexless became in time the bi-sexual and the functions of conception and birth obtaining now became common.

About the same time another continent appeared above the surface of the water; other atmospheric and magnetic conditions were made manifest, and the end of the Fourth Age found many of the bi-sexual offspring of the preceding races domiciled upon the new continent, and greatly changed in appearance.

The "coats of skin" had taken on a yellow cast of color and their spiritual purity and beauty had degenerated.

Then came the fall of the Race into gross sin, and wide separation between families, tribes and divisions occurred. One of the divisions — sub-races — fell into great physical sin, and became black in color, another became red, and another brown, but a certain division of the original race refused to be drawn into the gross sin which tempted the others, and remained on the first formed continent, keeping their original color for ages, and these were the ancestors of the present Chinese race.

At the close of the Fourth Age, the chain of the Himalayas — the oldest mountain chain of the world — was thrown up from the floor of the ocean, and circled the earth sphere beginning at what is now the

lowest point of northern Asia, which, by the way, was the first continent thrown up after the separation of the sexes. Only a comparatively
short length of this mountain chain is now above water, but during
the Age to which I refer, it was an impassable barrier between the
northern and southern divisions, and between the continents which
subsequently appeared and the "land of the Blessed" — the North
Pole; and not only to man, for it gradually formed a barrier which
turned away the warm air, water, and magnetic currents of the south
and left that Pole the frozen waste it still is, and must remain, until
those barriers (many stretches of which are under water) are broken
down by the changes in the configuration of the earth's surface. These
changes will occur during the lives of the Sixth Race which will then
inhabit the earth.

The continents and many of the islands of the seas now above
water in the southern hemisphere will then disappear from sight.
Lemuria will rise again, and connection between it and the northern
continent be again established.

The descendants of the White race now upon the earth, having
passed through incarnations in the Black, Red, Brown, and lower
sub-races of the Yellow race, must combine with the higher sub-races
of the Yellow race in order to reach again the high estate from which
the whole human race fell in the Fourth Age.

There are now evolving in the Chinese nation and in America
certain progenitors of the new Sixth Race.

Both the white and yellow races are now on the upward arc of the
present cycle of manifestation. The White race turned the lowest point
of the arc several hundred years ago, while the Yellow race passed the
same point within the memory of the present generation.

Prejudice against intermarriage between these two races will gradually die out as time passes, and by the close of another short cycle,
the first children of the first sub-race of the Sixth Race will be born as
a result of intermarriage between the before-mentioned progenitors
of the new Race, now appearing in the White and Yellow races.

The Red, Brown, and Black races will gradually disappear from
the earth, and the close of the Sixth Age and beginning of the Seventh
will see a new sun dawn on a new earth, or rather a renewed earth,
containing one great Continent and peopled by one Race — the old-
new, Moon-colored Race. A Race of self-conscious, God-like beings,
greater far than the First Race. A Race that has won by its own inherent

power and ability the one all-important principle the First Race was deficient in, the principle of Manas, Higher Mind, self-consciousness of its own Divinity.

The First Race possessed only race consciousness. The knowledge evolved through differentiation and experience was an unknown quantity to the units of that Race.

The identity of each unit was then hidden in the identity of the race, and could only be uncovered by self-conscious experience on the Seven planes — the seven stages of existence; but once uncovered, brought to recognition of itself, identity can never be entirely lost again. It is necessary that you bear in mind the fact that the same Egos, the same individualities which incarnated in the First Race will be the incarnating Egos of the Seventh, as they have been the Egos of all the intermediate Races of the present Manvantara.

It is also necessary that you discriminate between both the Chinese and White races of this cycle, and the same races in another cycle during which the progenitors of the new race will be born. The highest type of the men and women of the White and Chinese races now in existence could not furnish the parents of such a race as I refer to. At the very best the children born from intermarriage between members of these two races today, would be four times removed from the pure line from which the children of the new race will descend.

LESSON 112
THE DIVINE SPARK

It has become evident to some of the devotees of the science of bacteriology that the hitherto carefully concealed mysteries of the occult science of life in its minutiae were being cautiously unveiled, but the possibility of their solution by the uninitiated has rested entirely on the opportunities given by the closing of a great world cycle, and opening of another, the guiding entities of which have released lesser disciples, to whom those mysteries were imparted, from sacred vows they have been under for centuries.

In some instances, credit to the latter has been given by the claimants to new discoveries; in others, fear of personal loss of prestige and power has prevented such acknowledgment, and in such instances subsequent efforts along the same lines of development have furnished the groundwork of their claim to originality, and led to entire repudiation of the basic source of their knowledge.

This is unpardonably true in the case of one or more votaries of physical science, in regard to the mysteries of the life cells.

And yet, the fact that a single cell contains an embryonic man or animal is only an unproven theory to many of the last-mentioned class, so they would not be prepared to accept the fact that a single one of the countless vital sparks (ions of electricity) contains not only an embryonic man, but an embryonic world.

A vital or life spark is a definite division of Prana — life force — and contains in essence the basic substance of every form of life that the evolutionary laws can bring into material manifestation during a great Manvantara; but no single unit of that order of life can duplicate itself, or create form, save by combination and impregnation through contact.

Investigation of the action of life cells would seem to disprove the latter statement, for the reason that it has been found possible to re-combine cells and create abnormal growths; but that does not alter the fact, for the masculine and feminine forces are resident in the life sparks within the cells, and no cell could be found that did not have the requisite number and quality of life sparks.

The power of "becoming," or growth resides in the Life Spark.

The power of direction resides in the Ego, or individuality of man, and the power of yoga, the aim of the occultist, is the union of the power of direction and the power of becoming.

Herein is contained one of the greatest mysteries, the solving of which gives Mastery. You have been taught that there have always existed sexless and double-sexed beings. This would appear to contradict what I have previously said about the manifestation of sex in the minutiae of life, but not so; a god is sexless because he has transcended sex.

The Life Sparks which make up the spiritual substance of His form, if He be still in form, are not differentiated as to sex as are those which manifest on planes of matter; and in its evolution from a stone to a god the incarnating Ego has raised the Life Sparks to a higher order of life, a plane of pure energy.

When an Initiate advocates celibacy in the case of a disciple, it is for the definite purpose of raising and concentrating the resident Life Sparks of his threefold form to higher orders for the purpose of gaining the above-mentioned power of direction over the Kriyashakti or Divine Fire, thus making possible the creation by Will and Yoga.

But let any disciple beware of the self-advertised teacher who proposes such a course. Instruction will come in no uncertain way to the disciple who has fitted himself by purification for such instruction.

The sex of the Initiate is not changed while in the physical body, neither does he become sexless in the correct interpretation of the word, though he may have attained to power over spiritual forces. Kriyashakti force is the dominating force of the Buddhic plane,[1] as electricity is the dominating force of the physical plane, and sex in differentiation does not exist on the Buddhic plane.

At one stage of evolution the masculine and feminine forces of a proved disciple tend toward equalization, and when a true balance is reached neither sex is unduly operative and therefore antagonistic to the other.

The power of one sex must be in excess of the other to determine the sex of an embryonic child, and also to make sex function possible to an individual. When the masculine and feminine forces are equally balanced in an individual there is no longer opposition to the Kriyashakti force which is always striving with the lower nature of man, and only yields itself to the service of man when the lower sex nature is overcome.

Sex does not manifest on either of the three higher planes of life.

The first manifestation of differentiation of sex in the Life Sparks occurs on the fourth plane, the Kama-Manasic,[2] although preparation for differentiation is made in that state between the third and fourth plane, commonly referred to as the soul plane, and that preparation takes place in the substance which will subsequently be the centers of the spine and brain of the physical man.

On taking up a new incarnation, the skandhas, the effects of past action, meet the incarnating Ego at the entrance of the Kama-Manasic plane, and these skandhas are in the form of the Life Sparks of the before-mentioned centers. They are the avengers, and as they have been made such by man, they must be redeemed by man and brought back to their original state of purity — the sexless state of the substance of the three higher planes.

---

[1] *Buddhic plane* — the higher spiritual plane associated with the soul.

[2] *Kama-Manas* (*Sanskrit*, "mind of desires") — the lower Manas, or the lower mind, the intellect.

This is man's great mission. He has defiled the very substance of the Godhead, which is also his own substance, and he must purify and redeem that substance.

It is the Fiery Sparks which continue to exist as skandhas from life to life which build up the astral vehicle which persists after the death of the body. They are indestructible because they are the very substance of the Godhead, that God "in whom we live and move and have our being,"[3] that substance which is sexless on the three higher planes of being, and sexually differentiated on the four lower planes.

Perhaps this will help you to understand what it is that differentiates all orders of plant life from each other, all crystals, and all the minute organisms which are only visible under a microscope; and also to understand why it is that a star, a sun, and a world stands alone, unsupported by any other star or world, and yet continually pours forth a force of attraction and repulsion in the direction of other bodies belonging to the same system.

Life in its minutiae is due to sex differentiation; in its totalities it is sexless; in its minutiae it is dependent on others of its kind; in its totalities it is independent of others so far as individual action is concerned.

A star or planet is a cell in the body of God. The light, heat, and electricity streaming from those heavenly bodies are the radiations of the great combinations of Life Sparks which compose the substance of those bodies.

In the case of the sun the Life Sparks are undifferentiated as to sex; in the case of the planet they are differentiated, as in the case of the ordinary man.

Differentiation decreases power, tension, and ability to act.

Concentration increases the same in exact ratio.

The more you accustom yourselves to meditation upon these subjects the wider and deeper will grow your knowledge of yourselves, and therefore, your knowledge of God and Infinity. But take heed of your motives.

Try to realize that you are drawing close to the spiritual plane when by deep thought you are meditating upon the very vehicle of the Godhead — on all that you are capable of comprehending of that which forms the body of God while you are in your present state of development.

---

[3] Acts 17:28.

When you are contemplating the marvelous, mysterious operation of the Life Sparks which are the basis of all materialized life, and,
in recognition of the threefold marriage of Desire, Thought, and Life,
you direct the results of your findings to any definite point, you are
creating good or evil for which you must surely answer.

LESSON 113
MENTAL HEALING

Within the physical body is another, a finer body, an exact replica
of the former. Every organ, nerve, muscle, and part is duplicated in substance of an ethereal character.

If a physical disease is stopped on its way outward to extinction
through the blood, by means of what is in one sense a nervous shock
caused by a strong affirmation or denial of the reality of the disease,
there may be a temporary paralysis, as it were, of the disease germs,
or they may be forced back into some other vein, capillary, or organ
than the one first affected, and a new or more virulent form of the
same disease thus receives its first impetus. Or, worse still, the negative
force which was the original cause of the disease may be forced back
into the before-mentioned mental-astral body, where it was originally
conceived and born, and the soil created for the seed of some form of
mental disease, tenfold worse in character and effect than the physical
disease which had preceded it.

The personal mind and the personal will are so inseparably united
that with the surrender of the personal to the Divine Will by the
Mind in the treatment of disease by psychic methods, much if not all
of the shock referred to is obviated; but even then, ignorance of the
past karma of the patient would place a great responsibility upon the
average mental practitioner.

There is a fixed gulf between each of the planes of matter, mind,
and spirit. Each plane has the correspondences of every existing thing
on other planes, so why run the risk contingent upon the use of "things
out of place" — the forces or properties of other planes — when the
same forces or properties in other forms are attainable on the plane
where one is normally functioning?

Why should Divine Law have set the bounds between all planes
if those barriers were to be crossed by every "little man" who wished
to increase his property, heal his diseases, and control his fellow

men without the necessary effort to do so in the ways provided by natural law?

No matter what arguments may be brought against it, the fact remains that the exercise of one mind over another is hypnotism, and hypnotism is sheer black magic.

LESSON 114
THE LOWER ASTRAL OR "KA"

U nfortunately, but comparatively few among the more modern students of psychology, and the more recently admitted members of The Temple of the People have familiarized themselves with one of the basic teachings of the Wisdom Religion; namely, the Seven Principles, or the seven divisions of Matter, Force, and Consciousness. Therefore, such students find it very difficult to interpret certain terms or to connect various references and features of instructions in constant use by their teachers with those corresponding divisions or principles. This leads to much confusion, and in some instances to very much injury. In no instance may greater injury accrue to the ignorant than by wrongly considering the nature and functions of the lower self — the Linga Sharira,[1] as it is termed in the teachings of the far East, and the "Ka" or double, the shadow, as the ancient Egyptians always termed that form.

This division of the human being is built up and comes to maturity with the mind and physical body of man, and persists for a definite period after the passing of the soul, though invisible to the majority of people. As the lifeless body falls apart through the action of the elementary forces, so the lower astral is disintegrated by the same forces at a later period when the soul passes to a higher order of life, unless it is revived by the thought and will of the incarnating Ego, or is deliberately earthbound by strong desire.

It is the lower self — the "Ka" of an earthbound soul — which responds to the call of the average spiritualist, and which is frequently seen in graveyards, or when separating itself from the body of the dying.

---

[1] *Linga Sharira (Sanskrit,* "body's image") — the lower astral body; the etheric double that is born before the physical body and that dies or dissipates at the same time as the latter. It represents a precise copy of the physical body, but in the etheric form.

It also operates in sensuous dream life. Its substance is created by the lower or sensuous pole of human nature. As it is a perfect replica of the physical body it is easily mistaken for the departed personality.

In occasional cases before death it gains such perfect control of the body which envelops it that the real entity — the soul — is driven out for the time being. There seems to be a great and unaccountable change for the worse in the person in such an instance. This change may occur through an injury to the physical body or brain, such an injury as might paralyze some normal spiritual or brain center, thereby inhibiting normal control by the indwelling soul, and leaving the body at the mercy of the elementary forces of this lower self.

A sight of this creature, as it really would appear in the majority of human beings, would be enough to strike terror or disgust into the heart of the one beholding it. When you realize that every selfish, cruel, sensual, vicious thought you have cherished or have sent out, and the nature and power of the forces set free in all such characteristic acts that you may have performed in a lifetime, and become aware that they have been centralized and materialized in that lower self, you can form some concept of its appearance and proclivities; and when you also realize that it is endowed with all of the self-conceit of the average human being, and his power of compromise, treachery, and vanity, you may be able to see how such an entity would naturally try to deceive the weak as to its real character and claims, and even as to its appearance by casting a glamor over the mind of the observer.

In a few words, it is the devil incarnate in human nature, and every human being is possessed of this devil, which is weak or strong according to its endowment; and which, like the devil which tempted Jesus, is always "taking the soul up into a high mountain"[1] and offering it all the "kingdoms of the earth"; that is, it is always playing on the ambition and greed of human nature, and trying to drive a bargain with the indwelling soul by offering those things it is in fact powerless to bestow, in return for the devotion of the soul — for it can only live by consent of the soul.

If the reality, the existence, and the resident power of this other or lower self is fully accepted and understood by the soul, there is much less danger to the latter — the antithesis of this lower self — from its machinations or presentments.

---

[1] See Matthew 4:8.

All true neophytes know that it is against powers and principalities that the human soul is arrayed. If we can accept and realize the unalterable truth of the words, "I am all power," we know that we have the power to overcome evil, and render powerless the fiend which has stolen the human shape in order to deceive.

Good is all-powerful. Evil, or darkness can always be dissipated by good — Light. It will not help you to overcome it to deny the existence of this very material entity, as some people would have you do, for in denying its existence you are adding to its strength and power by the addition of another lie — another evil — to those which originally served to create it; and sometime in the future it will break the bounds set by such denial, and then it will riot in the aura and you will have to reckon with it.

You should affirm the power of Good with all your strength, and at the same time identify the Higher Self with that good. By constantly holding in mind the thought of such identification, you entirely ignore the lower self — which is the one thing it fears. By refusing to give it the substance it requires to live upon, that is, the substance of your own evil thoughts and words, it is rendered powerless, becomes more and more tenuous, and disintegrates quickly after death, and even before death, in the case of the Masters or advanced chelas who have killed it by overcoming it with Good, thus changing its nature.

A Master is said to cast no shadow, and but very seldom a shadow can be seen in such company.

Do not feed and nourish that lower self by fear of its effect on you, or by yielding recognition of its power over you.

Strive to realize the truth of the words, "I am one with God and all Good; evil hath no power over me,"[2] and, by making evil powerless, free yourself from its dominion. It is the recognition of this lower self, clothed in its stolen panoply, the forms of deceased friends, that makes spiritualistic séances such dangerous places, for almost all of the reliable materializations are made by the lower self of the medium, which clothes itself in the image in the inquirer's mind by means of the magnetism of the latter.

---

[2] The Temple mantram: "I believe that in me dwelleth every good and perfect Spirit. Believing this, I will show forth this day, by thought, word, and deed, all that perfection that dwelleth in me. I am one with God and all Good. Evil hath no power over me. Though clouds and darkness seem to be about me, yet dwell I eternally in the Light."

The conscious life of the lower self is passed on the lower astral plane; therefore, it has access to the astral records to whatever extent it may read. Occasionally, such an entity may tell some truth, and make a true prophecy, especially if by so doing it will add to its satisfaction or importance; but usually it is utterly unreliable, very changeable by nature, and the wise purpose of its being appears to be the conserving or concentrating of the floating evil in the nature of man within a form or compass where it may be more readily destroyed, or rather where it may be changed into good by the incarnated Ego, as opportunity after opportunity offers for paying karmic debts which have accrued in past lives — debts made by the performance of evil thoughts and acts.

Every normal person is more or less conscious of the existence of this lower self. In strong temptation its very tones are heard by the inner ear, often causing a belief in Divine interposition; but it can be silenced when once recognized. It takes an Initiate of high degree to bring the souls of two individuals into conscious contact, when they are on different planes and as this is often very hurtful to the soul that is freeing itself from Matter, it is not done except in cases of great moment.

LESSON 115
THE LAW OF PRIMOGENITURE

The world is seething with the discontent of the human race, and only one here and one there in the great crucible can subdue the elementaries[1] of his lower nature sufficiently to obtain the mental poise requisite for perceiving the fundamental cause of that discontent.

Universal law cannot be broken or ignored without bringing corresponding suffering upon the breaker of those laws.

The majority of the inhabitants of this puny little earth sphere are so entirely enwrapped and mentally smothered by the conditions they themselves have created that they have no time or inclination for perceiving or applying the knowledge and wisdom gained by the small minority, that minority which has in every age devoted itself

---

[1] *Elementaries* — the disembodied souls of evil people, unsuitable for evolution, who have lost their immortality. These souls remain in the astral bodies in the lowest layers of the Subtle World. Elementaries are irresistibly drawn to the physically incarnated people who are similar to them in nature, and they attach themselves like energy vampires to the auras of those people.

to the contemplation and study of the phenomenal universe and the laws which govern it in minutiae as well as those which govern it as one composite entity. For many ages individual man has usurped the offices of Divine Law, and for his personal ends has continued to bring woe and suffering on the race. The recognition, or partial recognition, of this truth by the masses has brought about revolt after revolt, as was to be expected when abuse of position and power was self-evident to all; but these facts do not alter the greater fact that Centralization is the only law under which life can exist and prosper for any length of time, and nothing can excuse the breaking of that law by a body of disciples pledged to the sustaining of that law in order that they may come under the direction of those whose obedience to the same law has brought them out of the conditions of heterogeneous, disorganized life in which the majority of human beings now live, into the light and freedom of fully organized life.

As long as a disciple is content to remain in the helpless, powerless condition of the average human being, with no more ability rightly to serve and uplift the masses of downtrodden, incompetent human beings than he now has, his right of free will *will* secure him that privilege, if it can be termed privilege; but if he desires to escape from present thralldom, and take others with him, there is only one way by which it can be done. It is generally supposed that there is another way, i.e., the path of isolation, but even that is only one feature of the one way, for such isolation is a matter of direction from the Higher Self or some Initiate, and is only undertaken for a specific purpose and for a definite time, at the expiration of which the law will compel him to go back to his post of duty, wherever it may be.

Lack of faith in the eternal fitness of things, and in Divine Justice, desire to escape the results of action, and above all, impatience with what seem the slow processes of time plunge man back over and over again into the whirlpool of rebellion and discontent from which he is feebly endeavoring to escape. And this will continue until a body strong, united, unselfish, and wise enough to obey the law can be formed on the outer plane of this world; a body composed of those who are physically and mentally able to catch, translate, and teach those details of the mystery language by means of which alone the beings of other and more advanced spheres can communicate with the men of earth.

Those who tell you these truths are not responsible for the making of the Law, nor the continued breaking of the Law. They can only tell you the truths which Life and obedience to Law have taught them.

If you fail to perceive the necessity for the existence of the Law, or the logic of our arguments; if you confuse the results of individual disobedience to the requirements of the Law with the Law itself, and so fail to form a true concept of the Divine purpose to be served, i.e., the return of the Prodigal Son to the bosom of the Father; in other words, fail to perceive the necessity for the involution of matter, you cannot fail to be the poorer for your lack of power and wisdom.

Man has gone so far out of the way in the long ages of time which have elapsed since the Gods dwelt with men and ruled over them in Love and Justice, that the grand cosmic ideal of Brotherhood has degenerated into an idea of one-man rule, each man believing himself to be the requisite one. The matter of evolutionary status, divine right, the best equipment — mental, moral and spiritual — has been unobserved or greatly questioned by the masses in their search of some remedy for existing conditions, and the only point in the arguments used which contains much truth, is based upon the inherent possibilities of the fully evolved man and the difficulties in the way of securing such a man to rule over a people.

The Gods, the Devas, the Initiates, and the Masters being fully evolved men and, therefore, proving the possibility of such mastery, the natural egotism of man leads him to the conclusion that if he is ever to be competent for such leadership he must be more or less fitted for it *now*.

The cyclic law of primogeniture is ignored.

In all that I have said I have been referring more particularly to duties and conditions of the disciples of the White Lodge, who have become such disciples through desire for rapid development.

If a man is content to continue life on such terms as worldly conditions offer, he is dependent upon worldly opinions; but if he continues in discipleship, he must be content to obey the laws of discipleship, which are the Universal Laws, and these laws are based upon a geometrical foundation. Truly "the first shall be last"[1] and each spoke of the revolving wheel of life shall be uppermost in its turn. Why, then, strive to throw the wheel out of balance by bringing up a spoke out of its turn?

---

[1] See Matthew 20:16.

LESSON 116
WHAT IS LOVE?

You who maintain that love is dependent upon respect, you do not know, you never can know what love is, and therefore upon what it subsists, until your own head has been bowed low, your own soul dragged through the mire of the world's scorn for love's sake; nor can you understand why men and women will lay themselves on the funeral pyre of self-scorn and self-condemnation by the commission of acts they would condemn in others — acts which they know must come up before their own souls for recording — and all for love's sake.

In order to understand you must know something of the forces at work in and about you, must know something of the little lives which comprise those forces which are powerful enough to conquer everything but the spiritual will.

As a rule man does not know that he is putting himself in thrall to various distinct orders of life by his deeds — orders, the units of which are as real and as individual as is any other creature of nature's kingdoms. Ignorance of the exercise of his creative power in the interior realms of life often leaves him at the mercy of his own creations.

Non-recognition of this fact leaves him powerless to control such entities. His scorn of what he believes to be the superstitions of past ages and his absolute trust in the findings of modern science are great hindrances to him. He does not perceive that the ancients took up the study of life from the point modern science has but just reached, and carried their investigations through fields of life the modern devotee is but just on the verge of discovering, and found that what are now termed degrees of force and energy are distinct orders of intelligent life, with governments and laws of their own, and that those infinitesimal lives are indissolubly united to all other orders of life, large or small.

Many a one will admit that an electrical storm exerts a peculiar effect on him, depressing or exhilarating, as the case may be; but tell him that the effects he feels are due to direct contact with countless numbers of the fiery lives, the elementals, which every flash, every shimmering fold in the sky partly reveals, conscious creations that are incessantly beating, pounding on his nerves, and taking from or giving to them some measure of the fiery force that is their natural support, and you will evoke a smile of superiority from your listener.

You may have seen an immense flock of destructive birds light on an orchard or field of grain and leave it utterly bare, or a plague of insects pass over a large section of land, leaving it stripped of all green things. While the devastation is not so perceptible to the human eye, the passing over a race or nation of human beings of billions of the negative fiery elementals has a somewhat similar effect. There is inevitably a great loss of physical vitality and nerve force in the units of that race. The resisting power of the human will and mentality throws off the influence of these lesser lives to a great degree, but there is always an appreciable loss of nerve force which must subsequently be made up, or the victim is so much the more subject to the action of any other inimical force.

These lesser lives are but one rank of soldiers among the countless legions engaged in the great battle of life. They are neither to be feared nor despised, but simply to be kept on their own side of the battle line.

They are as subject to the universal laws as is man, and are affected by the same influences. They are irresponsible and therefore soulless, and are subject to the will and mentality of higher orders of life. They cause many epidemics. Terrific pressure is sometimes exerted by them on the nerves and grey matter of the brain by the conscious or unconscious ill will of a person. All this being true, is it not worthwhile to study them, and protect one's self from them when such protection is possible?

And this brings me back to my opening sentences. The higher any attribute or energy is in the scale of life the more powerful it is for good or ill, and the negative aspect of love evokes the cruelest, the most blinding, selfish, destructive phase of the fiery elemental lives in that scale.

The positive aspect of the same attribute is the reverse in all respects. The lesser lives which manifest as a result of the exercise of the positive aspect of love are tenacious, open-eyed, selfless, and whatever be the object, thing, or person that has excited the positive aspect of the attribute in the heart of a human being, there is a constant bombardment of these lesser lives and, therefore, a continual increase in strength and power of those qualities which are peculiarly active in the lesser lives of the positive aspect of the attribute, so that the will and mentality of the lower man are under restraint.

The latter cannot break away from his subjection to the thing or person if he would. It is for this reason that the character, qualities, or limitations of the object, however unworthy, fail to affect the real issue.

When the resident force actuating those lesser lives is exhausted, either by time, or through the action of the awakened spiritual will and the soul is therefore freed from its thralldom, the power of that positive aspect of the great Love Principle is transferred from the one to the many, and the selfish satisfaction hitherto enjoyed in devotion to one object is increased many thousandfold.

It is then that the awakened soul knows what love is.

LESSON 117
THE CIRCUIT OF THE SOUL

Do you understand in the least how closely you are related to and connected with the Universal Lodge centers throughout all worlds and spaces, when once the divine, the Higher Self, has commenced to manifest in your soul?

Each such center has as definite a connection with every human soul as have the wireless electric outfits of great steamships on the ocean, with similar outfits on the high places of the earth. Your inability to realize this fact fully is due to the paralyzing of the stations or centers in your own bodies and souls by long-neglected or ignored opportunities, or by viciously crippling them with evil thought and action; and though it is no longer possible for you consciously and deliberately to send forth your message direct to all those greater centers, there are many which catch your feeble messages, your aspirations and desires, and answer them, and yet you do not understand.

Sometimes you think those answers are but fluctuations of your own mentality. Sometimes you crush them down and out of your consciousness because they bid you do that which you do not desire. At other times you stop and wonder how it is that some totally unfamiliar thought or word impinges upon your consciousness, and you strive to locate the cause.

The whole human race is bound together by a network of sound and light waves, and the thoughts and words of each person are impinging upon the mentality and psychic centers of others with tremendous power and activity; but it is only the fully developed occultist who can consciously direct the messages borne by these waves wheresoever he will, for only he has reawakened the once atrophied centers of brain and body which are requisite to accomplish this. Yet any normal person can do this if he is willing to spend the time and effort, and will put himself entirely under the guidance of one who is truly able to instruct him in this great and universal science.

Unfortunately for many sincere seekers, there is an ever-increasing class of pseudo-occultists who claim the power to so instruct man, and only succeed in making mental and physical wrecks of their victims.

The very first necessity for securing reliable and efficient instruction is such a purification of mind and body as but few among the races of earth are willing to submit to in this day and age. Of one thing you may rest assured, that the man or woman who tells you that he or she individually has the power to develop those long-atrophied centers in you, is invariably deceiving you, for not so will come your instructor to you, even if you prove yourself worthy.

Your own Higher Self will make known the means and method, and the teacher, when you are ready, for that Higher Self is in constant communication with the Higher Selves of others, and only It is able to perceive the definite line, the circuit upon which your individual intelligence is located, and make the connection between you and others on that same line, who may karmically become your instructors.

That line or circuit is the Group Soul of which you are a part, and such communication as I have referred to is only possible in this age, and with the present human race, with the companion souls on that one circuit; but there are enough of those souls to communicate with to satisfy the mind of the average man, especially until after he has gone over that circuit.

In other ages, and with other races, the circuit will be widened, for there are groups of group souls, among which a wider intelligence, vaster experiences, more God-like powers obtain than can be realized by experience with a single such soul, and the evolution of man will place him in such relations with those grand centers in some future age, as will enable him to partake of their knowledge and power.

The possibilities of man are limitless. Then, will you to whom I speak be content to sit down in idleness, or spend your time in trivial pursuit, in gossip, or in reckless dissipations and let your opportunities pass, because they bring you some measure of sacrifice or pain, some effort, some endurance? Or will you be so careless of the warnings, the pleadings of your present teachers as to risk such opportunities at the insistence of some self-aggrandizing, self-advertised charlatan and deceiver? You may be enabled to choose wisely if you will. The choice is yours, but you must learn to choose by sacrifice. The currents set in motion by your thoughts must be strong and pure and able to pass over obstructions as the light flashes from one pole to another or a condition will arise which corresponds to the short-circuiting of an electric current, and so long as obstruction is possible by selfish or impure desire, so long will you fail to make the requisite conscious connection between your mind and that of others who are at the higher centers of your circuit.

LESSON 118
THE PLACE OF POWER

In these days, referred to by the ancient seers as "the latter rain,"[1] there is an outpouring of spiritual force that is drenching the souls of the illuminated with light and arousing the consideration of even the selfish man to a sense of the spiritual basis of life, and invoking a response from what may be termed the heart side of humanity, as never before in the history of mankind in the present age.

It is the force of the Christos, the Love force, the reconstructing, upbuilding, Universal fiery force sent forth from the Heart of God — the Holy Ghost, which always precedes the advent of a great Avatar, in order to prepare the people of the earth for His coming. This tremendous force operates in different ways on different individuals, according to their nature and ability to function the attributes it arouses, and the desires it incites to action. To some it comes as a call to gather the people together to protest against wrong; to others, as the voice of one "crying in the wilderness"[2] bidding them "seek out the poor, the lame, the blind"[3] of body and of soul. To still others it comes with the power of the Great Physician, bringing them out of servitude to pain. To the few who catch the low whisper, "seek ye within," which comes from the point in the center of the circle of its gravitational motion, and who obey, it comes as an incentive to superhuman endeavor to find what is sought; and upon such as these the force finally centers and

---

[1] See Jeremiah 3:3, 5:23–25, Joel 2:23, Hosea 6:3, Zechariah 10:1, and James 5:7.
[2] Matthew 3:3.
[3] Luke 14:13.

spends itself, for upon these will rest the power of its transmission to other races in other ages. The others may forget in the stress of trial and tribulation which must surely come upon the world from the awakening of the nether pole of this same force, as the nether pole of every force and form of energy, however spiritual or material, must awaken when the opposite pole of the same has spent its power; but not "the few" to whom I now address myself; for only these can find the seed of the truths I speak, however simply I word my message.

There is a spiritual basis for every atom of matter, and only the spiritual man, the pure-minded, the self-sacrificing, world-embracing man can unite his conscious selfhood with the spiritual basis of that matter, and in the marriage so completed bring forth the fruit of that union — creative power, reconstructive, revealing power.

You watch the growth of plant, of man, of crystal; you see constant changes taking place — disintegration of mass, molecule by molecule.

You watch the new life spring from the apparently dead seed or root, and the great mystery appalls you. You cannot perceive what is so evident to the great seer, the marriage of the spiritual basis of that seed or root with the universal spirit which surrounds and interpenetrates it, the reunion of the separated life with the Universal Life, the contact of individual love with cosmic Love, the overshadowing of the separated ray of light by the great spiritual Sun of Light; you can only perceive the results of the processes, unless you, too, are one of the seers I mention — "one of the few."

If you are not one of these, you may behold the marvels of what is termed spiritual or mental healing, you may perceive apparently miraculous exhibitions of psychic phenomena, the mysteries of hypnotism, mesmerism and of physical science, and accept the general interpretation of the same, but you will not be able to perceive the basic reality of all these seeming mysteries until you too have reached the stage of seership; and, my children, you never can reach that stage while you cling to a single material thing or creature, and will not let go your hold.

The circumference of the circle cannot touch the point in the center. It must break, and be absorbed, atom by atom, ere it can see into the depths which that point indicates — those depths where dwells in perfect selfless unity the basic source of Desire, Will, Resolution, and Devotion — Spiritual Love, which moves to action the constructive powers latent in mind, the powers which may build an atom, a man, a world according to its divine prototype.

Like not only seeks, but it finds like. Only Love can find Love.

I cannot tell you; no one can tell you how to produce Love in yourself. I can give you a method of preparation for its advent, but the average man or even disciple will think it too difficult — yet he will use similar methods for obtaining far less result.

He will sacrifice himself and those who love him, will surrender food, clothes, and even life itself in a search for some material thing. He will undergo training to prove his physical superiority that is more severe on his physical body than the methods I refer to could possibly be on that same body.

He will force his individual mentality until the brain reels, his nerve force is exhausted, and he sinks into a senile decrepit wreck, to carry out some plan for what he deems a great undertaking, while half the same effort rightly directed would have given him the body of a Hercules,[1] the brain of a Jove,[2] and the long life of a Methuselah.[3]

The same efforts, the same sacrifices, incited by the motive of awakening a response in his own soul to the spiritual Love which is always clamoring for admission and union, would have given him infinitely more than his present mentality can conceive.

Exactly as the constructive forces of nature build material forms by expansion and accretion, so are the creative and constructive forces themselves formed. As the cells of the bloodstream die and are replaced by others and greater numbers of the latter by the action of the laws of physics, so the minutiae of the constructive forces are diminished and increased by the action of higher laws on the spiritual bases of their minutiae. From the dead form springs the new life over and over again in all fields of life.

From the dead and dying cells of your bodies may arise the new, the living cells, by means of the accretions of the minutiae of the constructive forces, making new blood, new tissue, new bodies, if you have made that divine marriage between the Love in your own soul and the Universal Love which surrounds and interpenetrates that soul.

---

[1] *Hercules* — a legendary hero in Greek mythology known for his great strength and celebrated for completing the Twelve Labors assigned to him.

[2] *Jove* — Jupiter, the ancient Roman God of Heaven, daylight, thunder; the Father of all the Gods; the Supreme Deity of the Romans, identified with the Greek Zeus.

[3] *Methuselah* — a patriarch, the son of Enoch and the grandfather of Noah, who lived for 969 years (see Genesis 5:27).

LESSON 119
THE LAW OF OPPOSITES

The Twelve Houses of the Zodiac, the twelve cosmic divisions, symbolized by the Christos group of the Avatars, as well as by Jesus and His disciples (counting Judas and the one selected to hold the position of the latter), as well as all other groups symbolizing that particular division of the cosmos, the twelve grand divisions of all the great Temples, the Pyramids, the human body, all of these and many more are symbols in gross form of the characteristic qualities, attributes, and powers of the individual incarnated soul.

These are all passive on the sub-plane interior to the physical, and become active with the growth and development of the organs or centers of the human body. They are fixed, inexorable, and unchangeable in essence on the high spiritual plane, and obedient to the governing laws.

The negative aspects of these principles have no manifested vehicles or centers on the planes of real life — the spiritual planes. Their power of expression and influence is confined to the mentality of organized physical life.

In order to express in words comprehensible to the average intellect the said principles with their qualities and attributes, we are confined to the use of common terms which in fact only express a minor part of their totality — they comprise so much that is inexpressible by words.

The said principles, commonly expressed, are Love, Will, Wisdom, Knowledge, Faith, Hope, Truth, Justice, Loyalty, Honesty, Service, and Obedience.

All features, all terms that could express the principle named in any one of these generic terms, are vibrations of the one mode of motion expressed by that term. All features, all terms expressive of the negative aspect of a generic term as applied to a principle, would indicate the vibrations of a mere reflection or distortion of the positive principle; for there can be no principle of evil. For instance, the negative aspect of Knowledge — a principle — is ignorance. Ignorance is inactive, is nothing. So with the negative aspect of Justice. Injustice is in opposition to Justice, it is temporary. Disloyalty, the negative aspect of Loyalty, in opposition to Loyalty, of itself is nothing, but when energized by the active principle of Service, for instance, there is generated a force of treachery, which undermines the personal possession of the power of the positive attribute — Loyalty — in the case of the disloyal. When one active principle is undermined and jeopardized, the triad of principles with which it is identified is affected to a corresponding degree.

Therefore, in the case of Judas, when the principle of Loyalty to the Christos group was undermined, the principles of Honesty and Service were correspondingly affected.

I have chosen Judas as an illustration of a great truth only because the effects of his treachery, his disloyalty, his solemnly pledged service to Jesus are so commonly recognized. Every human being has within him, and is controlled by the before-mentioned twelve principles and their opposites, and there is no one of the latter so pregnant with evil possibilities as is the opposite of the principle of Loyalty. The demoniacal powers of the dark side of life know that in attacking the Loyalty of an individual they are striking at the very citadel of that individual's evolution, which is his power of Loyalty to whatever is undertaken in all his relations of life, his attachment to the spiritual side of his nature, his ability to even enter the path of power, all depend upon the exercise of that principle of Loyalty.

Therefore it is easy to see why the unconscious soul shrinks from expressed or known disloyalty, and why an act of treachery evokes more contempt, more hatred and fear than any other act of man. It is the act of treachery committed by Judas, far more than anything else, that has made his name a byword and has epitomized his whole character and individuality as personified evil and blotted out all of his good qualities. None of the latter are remembered. So it is not surprising that the general application of the term Judas to any individual expresses the accepted character of the person, and sets him apart from all others, even though those others have the seeds of the same fruit in their nature, and time is sure to develop them. As before intimated, it is the possible and probable eventual contingencies which inevitably arise as the final results of treachery, and the natural desire to avert them at any cost which bring such severe judgment upon the offender.

What is true of the effects of the negative or oppositional aspects of one of these grand divisions is equally true of all others, and in order to understand yourselves, and create a distinct picture of your Higher Self in contradistinction to your lower self, you must understand that to whatever degree the twelve principles or attributes designated by the above-mentioned terms are active and so able to exert a controlling influence over the forces in opposition to those principles — the forces that are preeminently active in matter — to just that degree you have an individual Higher Self, and therefore an independent, eternal existence; for the Higher Self is a combination of those principles.,

It is the gradual killing of the vehicles of said principles by their misuse or neglect which finally results in the soulless being. In the latter instance, a fixed gulf intervenes between the Higher Self and the personality. So to whatever extent you are conscious of the active existence of those twelve principles in your individual auric sphere, to just that extent may you feel sure that you are at one with God, and that you have a distinctive Higher Self.

One of the basic laws of spirit as well as of matter decrees that like shall seek like. The evolution of concrete form demands obedience to this law. While the law of opposites is undeniable, and no form of force can manifest without its opposite, the higher law compels truth to seek truth, falsehood to seek falsehood. Truth does not attract falsehood, nor falsehood attract truth; one is antagonistic to the other.

You cannot conceive of the existence of a warm personal friendship between an Initiate of the Right-Hand Path and an Initiate of the Left-Hand Path.

Oil and water will not mix without the aid of some other substance which will dissociate the molecules of both, and combine them in another form entirely. The soul cannot recognize or accept the existence of spirit until it partakes of the nature of spirit. The lower self can have no appreciation of the Higher Self until it has attracted and assimilated the attributes of the Higher Self, and incorporated them into its own essence, thus changing the nature of the lower self.

Those attributes are the very substance of the Higher Self. They create its form and essence under as fixed and immutable laws as those which govern the absorption, assimilation, and accretion of the substances which form the live tissues of the human body.

In other words, the human Ego must draw upon the substance of the Universal Higher Self in order to create a living mirror which will reflect that substance within the soul it is helping to build.

That soul can have no consciousness of Love, Wisdom, Truth, or any other attribute of God, and therefore no consciousness, no knowledge of God, save insofar as each one of those attributes has been developed within it.

In view of this fact, is it surprising that the Higher Self, that God, is such a vague, imperceptible, shadowy being in the minds of the majority of people?

If you pour two vessels full of water together they will mingle molecule with molecule and become one body. When the attributes of God, and like attributes in man, meet and mingle there will be no separation between God and man. Like the truly married, the twain have become one.

LESSON 120
THE SOURCE OF EVIL

You will make a grievous mistake by considering the entities of the various Degrees and Orders of the White Lodge as finished products of Life, that is, as perfected beings in the sense that God is perfect, for so long as the Ego retains a body, whether that body is spiritual, astral, super-astral, or physical, it cannot be perfect in the sense that the Absolute is perfect. The gulf between spirit and matter is impassable; matter must be reduced to pure energy before that gulf can be crossed.

So long as man retains the qualities of material existence, so long will he be dominated to a greater or lesser extent, by the force of jealousy; he frequently confuses that force with the force of zeal, which is not surprising, as zeal is the positive aspect of the force of which jealousy is the negative aspect, and even a high Initiate may be jealous in the sense that Moses proclaims God to be jealous, that is, jealous for good instead of jealous of good.

I refer to this particular force among the many which are active in matter, for the reason that it is one of the first emanations of the form of energy which is the basic principle of what man calls "evil."

The word Inertia comes nearer to expressing an idea of the character of the energy from which the qualities termed evil may develop than any other word in common use, and its purpose in the scheme of manifestation should be evident to the deep student of the mysteries of physics and metaphysics.

In one of the recent inventions of man, the phonograph,[1] you have somewhat of an illustration of the processes of creation and

---

[1] This text was written at the beginning of the 20th century.

manifestation of life by means of the creative impregnating energy of Sound.

The atomic substance of a note or a single utterance, traveling on etheric waves, is gathered up in a funnel-shaped instrument of wood or metal and condensed to a single point. The concentrated force thus gathered is not only powerful enough to make a visible indentation on some soft material but also carries and deposits the very substance of the utterance (the sounds) within the indentations. The sounds may be later reproduced when the point of another instrument attached to a corresponding funnel contacts the indentations which in the meantime have been transferred to a denser, heavier body termed a record.

When the condensed sound stored up in the minute section of space created by the note or utterance meets the point in the second instrument by the action of friction, it at once commences to expand, and finally comes forth through the second funnel with the same volume and force of its original utterance.

Correspondingly, the creative energy of Sound carried by Light is condensed, conserved, and stored up in an infinitesimal point and deposited in the spaces surrounding the molecules of the vital essence of the semen of the male and the ovum of the female.

These spaces partake of the nature of vortices and give entrance to or egress from interior states of life and also correspond to funnels. When the vital essence is deposited in the female uterus (which also corresponds to a funnel), the Inertia which has hitherto restrained it by shutting off the pranic forces in the spaces has been overcome, the two vital points have been released by physical contact and conception is concluded.

The principle of Form, impelled by Fohat (Sound), then guides the formation of the fetus to maturity.

The forbidden fruit of the Edenic Tree, the tree of good and evil, has its correspondence in the energy of Inertia. It is not difficult to see how the mind of the student almost invariably rushes to the subject of creative power and function at the mention of the Tree of good and evil, though he may not be able to give a logical reason for it.

To render this truth comprehensible to those who are not analytical by nature is somewhat difficult, yet some concept of it is requisite to an understanding of the mystery of life. To gain this concept you must first consider all matter, force, and energy as in a state of Pralaya and then imagine the effect of the first thrill, the action of Fohat (the concealed energy of sound), as all the hitherto composite, sleeping energies are aroused to action by "the Word," and separation between the different forms of energy occurs in perfect sequence.

Space as known to man had no existence previous to the action of sound — the Word — but commences to manifest with the expulsion of the first separated energy, and continues to grow with each release of energy until the first half of a Manvantara is completed when, with the indrawing of these expelled energies, space also disappears. But what is more *germane* to our present subject — the source of evil — is the fact that Inertia is the first one of various forms of energy to be released in the process of the creation of Space.

We cannot consider either spiritual Light or Sound as forms of energy possible of release in any one world period in considering this particular subject, for spiritual Light is the revealing power of Sound; the two are indissolubly united — they are the universal Androgyne.[1] In other words, Light carries the creative word or sound which produces the thrill mentioned before at the commencement of such a world period.

As Light impregnated by Sound is breaking away from (darkness) Pralaya, it meets the power of resistance stored up in Darkness, and in the great effort to overcome that resistance the energy of Inertia is brought forth from the same potential source, and this also must be struggled with and overcome before mass motion can be fully established and Light and Sound be left free to continue their function of creation in other fields throughout the cyclic round of Time.

Between the close of the third cyclic round and the beginning of the fourth round of every cosmic age, that which may be designated as the universal world germ is created as a result of the interaction and struggle of the aforementioned powers and energies within space.

As has been previously stated by me, impregnation is requisite to manifestation, whether that manifestation be the energies of Light and Sound, a cell of primordial matter, the form of a man, or any other thing or creature, and the universal world germ is conceived as a result of the impregnation of Space by the energies released in the before-mentioned struggle with Inertia.

---

[1] *Androgyne* (*Greek*, "man-woman") — a being that has both male and female principles. The first two Root Races of humanity were androgynous; the separation of sexes occurred in the middle of the Third Race, approximately 18 million years ago. Toward the end of the Seventh Race, humanity must again become androgynous.

The world germ contains in embryo the substance of all the world's suns, stars, and planets which will later come into manifestation as matter on the physical plane, within Space and Time, by means of the great Androgyne — Light and Sound.

All the processes, energies, and functions instrumental in the creation of the world germ are latent in every differentiation of that germ and their action in such creation and differentiation is repeated and reproduced in each embryo when it is separated from the parent germ, and commences to build its individual world in whatever kingdom it is first to enter in nature's realms.

Therefore each embryonic world must pass through a like struggle with Inertia in a condition corresponding to darkness — a negative state — and in the struggle the forces which subsequently manifest as evil qualities in matter are set free, and subsequently attracted to the forms of life in process of creation and they are thus attracted to the latter as a result of past karma; consequently in our search for the ultimate source of evil we cannot stop short of the energy of Inertia.

LESSON 121
YOUR KEYNOTE

It has been said that every manifested form has a keynote, but it must be remembered that the cosmic scale is re-created by the Egos which come into individual form at the commencement of every Great Age.

At the end of a cosmic Pralaya when all manifested life is indrawn, both sound and light are also indrawn.

The first incarnated Ego strikes the cosmic keynote for the Age in which it incarnated, and with the first incarnation of the Seven World-Builders, the seven keys — of which all other keys are variations — are, so to speak, sounded throughout all space.

With the sounding of the twelve full notes between the two central octaves of a cosmic scale, there is set up a series of vibrations to which all later creations must be finally harmonized. For example, one of the twelve grand divisions of the cosmos is attuned to one certain key. All of the forms of life karmically belonging to that division, whether they be human, animal, mineral, or vegetable, and however discordant, however high or low in the scale of which that one note is the key, must eventually be brought into harmony through the chords which can be created in that particular key, from time to time, as the cycle of its manifestation continues.

The affinity existing between certain human beings, or between the latter and lower forms of life, is contingent upon the striking of some chord which is in harmony with the keynote of the division to which those persons or things belong. If there is no affinity between two persons it is a clear indication that they belong to different divisions, with different keynotes; though such relations may be changed with the evolution of one or both of those persons, and affinity finally established by self-effort, when they might both pass into one of the other divisions. But as the power to so change is the result of Self-Mastery, which is another subject, we need not consider that possible event in this communication.

The protracted sounding of a note on a tightly drawn string of a musical instrument will set up a similar vibration in another string which has been tuned to the same key, on another instrument, within a certain clearly defined distance from the first instrument.

Likewise, a thought wave, set up by the vibrating of some definite thought in the mind of one person, will impinge upon the mind of another that is in alignment, or in other words, in harmony with the first thinker; and it does so because of the striking of one note of a chord to which both are attuned, that is, some idea that is common to both thinkers.

If the inner sense of hearing is developed in an individual, he can distinguish between the different sound waves set free by thought, just as easily and as clearly as he can distinguish one thought from another. If he is in harmonious relations with the thinker he will hear those thought waves as harmonies; if otherwise, he will hear only discords, and feel nothing but antagonism toward the thoughts which force themselves through his mind.

If his keynote is strongly sounded by one at a distance, one who is in affinitive relation, and at a time when he is in a receptive condition, he will feel a slight vibration pass up the spinal cord and enter a certain center of the cerebellum, the result of which will tend to arouse some thought or memory of the absent one.

If harmonious relations are established between a number of people whose keynotes when struck will form a chord, there is a greater certainty of the continuance of friendly relations between those persons for an indefinite period, than could possibly be the case between those whose keynotes followed each other in the scale.

The dominant seventh in a chord breaks up the harshness, softens, and beautifies the chord, thus raising the chord from one condition of sound to another, even as self-effort toward mastery softens and beautifies the harsher characteristics of an individual, and raises him from one degree of the Great White Lodge into a higher degree.

If you can always remember that sound is the basis of all form, it will aid you in understanding the deep significance of your keynote, and it will help you to solve many mysteries of nature and life.

Many vibrations of the nerves which produce thrilling sensations in various parts of the body are the result of sound waves set up at a distance by the unintentional striking of the keynote of that body.

Many superstitions have arisen as a result of these peculiar sensations which have no basic truth.

The place that music fills in the economy of the universe is all important, although this fact may not be recognized by one who is indifferent to musical sounds. But as such sounds may be transposed into other sensations he may feel corresponding sensations, pleasurable or otherwise, to the sounds in various parts of his body, although he may not have the slightest knowledge of the ultimate cause of those sensations.

I would advise that you note the effects of different notes both in your mentality and physical body.

LESSON 122
THE PHOSPHORIC PLANE

Each one of the four manifested planes and their sub-planes is evolved from one basic force or element from which emanate or radiate three other forces — elements — which form, as it were, the substratum of that plane, and from which are evolved all other forces or elements which in combination create that plane. The basic element, together with its three emanations, are the pillars upon which the whole structure must rest during one great age.

The nearer the central point of each structure these four pillars stand, the finer, the more tenuous become the elementary substances which constitute the plane.

That which is pure energy at the central point becomes dense matter at the circumference, the density depending upon the character of the basic energy of the plane.

The intimate connection between thought and the element of phosphorus has long been recognized, but the knowledge of the causes, as well as the methods by which the relation is sustained, is confined to the Illuminati,[1] as well as the power of observing the minutiae of the states of organized life existing on those planes interior to the earth plane. It will be generally admitted that the points of divergence — the intermediate or sub-planes — between any two full planes (as, for instance, the physical and the astral planes), are impassable, and are incomprehensible by one still in bondage to Form. Man must part with his form either by death, trance, sleep, or concentration, to pass from one plane to another, and even then he retains no consciousness of the passing, or knowledge of the substances through which he has passed, until he has reached, by evolution, the higher astral or soul plane.

What is the spiritual aspect of phosphorus?

You may be surprised to learn that in common parlance it would be the devil; in other words, it is the force of testing, the trial force.

The plane or gulf, as it is sometimes termed, between the physical and astral world, is lighted and largely energized by the active principle of phosphorus. It is the plane of testing, of trial, through which every soul must pass before entering the astral, which is the scene of another trial.

This phosphoric plane is the plane on which the soul drops the last figment of its physical nature, and it depends upon the clothing it finds itself in, as to what part of that astral plane it will next contact, and this energy of phosphorus acts as the testing force in this respect.

The soul will cling to those physical remnants if it can do so, sometimes through fear, sometimes through love, and the phosphoric force presents to the soul the problem of the separation from that physical matter.

The very force of testing is a mental force which belongs to the plane of Manas; it is reason, in one respect. Phosphorus is absolutely necessary to the formation of the physical brain and nerves.

---

[1] *Illuminati* (*Latin*, "enlightened") — the Initiated Adepts. This term should not be confused with a secret society that aims to change the world order.

Spiritual Light is the homogeneous energy, by, in, and of which, all life in manifestation on the four planes above mentioned is created.

In passing from the lower astral to the physical plane, a definite degree of that energy is alchemically reduced to phosphoric energy, from which emanate the three basic energies of antimony, arsenic, and carbon.

These three have an inhibiting effect on the illuminating principle of homogeneous light, and it is therefore only through the phosphoric energy that the illuminating principle can radiate; and all the light visible to the eye which can penetrate the sub-plane mentioned, is a weird, shifting, phosphoric glow, streaked occasionally with red and green.

The energies of antimony, arsenic, and carbon are the vehicles which transfer the forces — the individual lives — of the physical plane through this intermediate or sub-plane to the next, the astral plane. They form, as it were, the boat which takes the soul of man over the river Styx[1] (another name, by the way, for this intermediate plane).

The basic element, in this case phosphorus, is always neutral to its three emanations, and always of another mode of motion.

It must always be remembered that these basic elements are not the gross forms of the substances we know by the same names on the physical plane, but are what the alchemists call the Soul or Spirit of those elements, and they are only observable by the Initiates or by one whom an Initiate has overshadowed for some definite purpose.

Observers of the phosphorescence of the ocean, in fungus and in warm, moist places on land, may be interested in knowing that the minute organisms to which that light is imputed are carriers of phosphoric energy, and their purpose in the divine economy is very great.

By means of water energized by Fire — Heat — all organic life is brought into physical form, and strange as it may appear, man is dependent upon such minute organisms as those mentioned and others for the vehicles of thought forces, i.e., the grey matter of the brain and nerves.

It is in Water that the four energies referred to, combine to create the forces, the living substance, which upon being released and transferred to the Air, subsequently enter into the formation of the grey matter in man, plant, and animal — the brain and nerve substance, in

---

[1] *Styx* — the principal river of the underworld, the kingdom of Hades, in Greek mythology. The souls of the dead were ferried across it in a boat by Charon.

varying intensities, and this grey matter is the vehicle of transmission for all thought forces.

The incarnation of the Sons of Mind into mindless men did not cease with their first incarnation. They are constantly reincarnating, and are doing so in the form of these short-lived, minute organisms.

If the principles of chemistry were better understood and applied to the study of all natural phenomena, some wonderful secrets would be revealed; but nature's great arcanum is sealed to the great majority through their sheer indolence and consequent ignorance.

LESSON 123
THE RESPONSIBILITY OF LEADERSHIP

The founder of every great or small religious or sectarian organization, the originator of every specific movement or plan for the benefit of the human race, or any division thereof, is primarily responsible for the success or failure, the adherence or dispersion of the units of the movement or body to a much greater degree than either he or his associates are aware; for the cause and effects of such responsibility and power are so closely identified with the finer forces of nature that unless one is a deep student of life he will not seek in the right quarter for knowledge of their ultimate source. Only one who is aware of the geometrical perfection of every phase and condition of manifested life will be apt to note that some direct line or figure, some geometrical form representing some quality karmically drawn together, connects all living creatures, and places them, according to the dominance of their quality, in one position in that figure.

I refer to this in order to point out that a higher rate of development along any definite line — for instance, a line which makes the religious instinct dominant in his nature — would place a man geometrically in a certain figure and in a certain position in that figure, thereby making him a centralizing point for the cosmic energy which constitutes that particular quality.

Just so much of that quality as he was capable of functioning would pour in on him from the inner source of that form of energy. Any personal idiosyncrasy or characteristic of an opposite nature, any weakness, or even a stronger degree of the same energy than his personality could endure, would throw that quality in his nature out of alignment, would lower or raise it, geometrically speaking, above or below the normal degree and thus incapacitate him for perfectly functioning that quality, or only permit his partially or weakly functioning the same, he being the natural avenue for that energy so far as all other individuals in that same geometrical figure were for the time being concerned, and there would also be a falling off, a decrease of that energy in the cases of those other individuals emplaced in the same figure.

Perhaps I may particularly illustrate this by using an engine boiler with a steam whistle as a symbol. The boiler, the generator of the steam, is generating energy of a particular kind. The engineer wishes to use that steam for the purpose of blowing the whistle, and a certain degree of the steam is turned into the tube of the whistle. As long as the tube is unobstructed and the conditions are right, the whistle will continue to sound. If there were an obstruction in the tube of the whistle, or if another stream of energy of equal power were directed into the tube from the whistle end, one of two things would happen — one stream would neutralize the other and there would be no sound, or the extra stream would burst the whistle, and in either case the purpose of the whistle would be confounded.

If a stream of divine afflatus, a power which we might term enthusiastic religious fervor dependent on devotion and faith for its outpouring, were poured out into a community of believers through the channel of one man, and a contrary stream were poured into his mind through the unfaith, unbelief, and lack of devotion of many of his associates, unless the man were perfectly poised and unchangeable, the religious fervor would be neutralized, and his faith would be unsettled.

No matter how he might labor exteriorly he could not make his efforts count to any extent. No matter how he might hide his unfaith, his work would be fruitless.

If he had but three, five, or seven persons in perfect alignment with him, and so was able to function the power bestowed, there would be perfect interaction between him and them, and all things would be possible to him and to the body. If the reverse were the case, conditions corresponding to explosion and disruption in his own nature and in his work would inevitably occur.

No other person could take up his particular work along that one line and carry it to success, as long as he remained in the geometrical position which made him a centralizing point for the receipt and transmission of that particular form of energy.

The failure of men in religious, in business, or in social life might all be traced back to their loss of faith in themselves or their ideas and, therefore, a similar loss in the case of their associates.

The exactitude of the geometrical laws, the perfection down to the minutest details of the action of all the laws governing the finer forces of energy and force make exception to the above rule impossible.

Exactly as a top will slow down gradually, and finally fall on its side when the energy generated by the unwound string is exhausted, so you will see men and women in all walks of life who are engaged in specific lines of work commence to slow down, and gradually fall out of their individual lines of work without any apparent cause. You may surmise a cause which to you would seem sufficient, yet another man under similar handicaps would carry a similar line of work to a successful conclusion.

If you were able to trace back the cause of the failure of the first man mentioned, you would find that the particular quality through which his main stream of energy functioned had been lessened or killed, thereby disqualifying him for service in his particular field.

The loss or failure might not be perceptible to others, but he would be conscious of a loss of something in himself that was the mainspring of his action. He would no longer be a magnet to attract success to himself or those associated with him. Gradually his customers, if he were a merchant, would leave him, and everything he undertook in that particular line would be a failure.

If he were able to analyze the effects of the first cause — the withdrawal of that force or finer form of energy — he would soon learn that loss of faith in himself had been the first effect of such withdrawal.

Therefore, it behooves you all to watch closely and protect the qualities in yourselves to which you look for success. Keep your ideals strong and pure, and reject the thoughts and influences which would tend to lower them.

LESSON 124
DETERMINATION OF SEX

To "those who stand and wait," as well as those who direct the execution of the Karmic law age after age, there is no mystery, no possible miscarriage of justice in regard to the present position, circumstances, limitations, or status of the female sex. The sex as a whole is reaping the exact reward of sin against the seed of sex during the first centuries of the iron age.

Instead of just "coming into her own," as is proudly stated by many supporters of the present woman's movement, the cyclic return of the same individual Egos, and similar conditions to those which obtained in those aforementioned centuries, bring about an opportunity to pay an old debt and conquer the present limiting karmic conditions at the same time, as well as to develop a higher form of humanity as a whole than those which have formerly existed. It also reawakens and develops the potencies and powers which have lain dormant in the female sex for such a great length of time. Her period of punishment for her sin against the seed of life is about to close, and it will depend upon her ability to conserve and sow aright the new crop of seed, figuratively speaking, coming into her possession, as to whether there will be any very pronounced change in her status and condition.

The theory held by many, that in the act of impregnation of the seed of the woman by the mate the sex of the child is determined, does not contain a particle of truth. Such impregnation bestows the impulse to growth, the racial qualities, even the design of the form and features, but has no effect in determining the sex.

Whether it be crystal, plant, or human being, the power to determine sex resides in the feminine sex of the object or being, and such determination lies in the expulsion or withholding of certain cells which in combination form groups which are deposited within the walls of the fallopian tubes of woman, or in similar tubes or organs of the females of other kingdoms of nature.

During the centuries to which I have referred woman was the dominating factor in all the actions of life and government, and the individual woman was perfectly conscious of her power to give or withhold either sex, at will, intuition acting as the handmaid of Karmic law. There had been no wars to decimate the males, so there was no surplus of females, and male and female children were conceived alternately, but upon becoming intoxicated with power, the majority of womankind became proud, self-conscious, and cruel, and finally became so enervated they were no longer able to control the action of the seed cells and, fearing the accumulating power by the male sex, began to destroy the males, as the females of a hive of bees will destroy the males of the hive as soon as their work of impregnation is done.

The condition of the males of that period was very similar to that of the females of the leisure class today. They were kept in luxury, finely groomed, and so made and kept beautiful and fruitful, and used by the females exactly as the females of today are used by the males who maintain them.

But an era is coming when all this will be changed, even to the most minute forms of life. The conditions outlined above could never have obtained had it not been for the wide separation between the masculine and feminine souls which came into existence as units, and differentiated in the Third and Fourth Root Races. As an effect of the great sin which caused the separation of souls there were brought into manifestation hordes of sensual elementals which brought about separation between the organs and functions of generation and conception in the lower forms of life.

With the reunion of such souls in a coming new age, there will also be a return of the power of determination of sex at will, but it will be possessed by the combined male and female and exercised on an interior plane. Differentiation in form will still obtain even when the reunion of souls is accomplished, but there will nevermore be the preponderance of either sex.

Nature revenges itself for every unbalanced condition, and in those earlier ages when the males were made the tools and playthings of the females, the fetus of the male child was subjected to all the magical forces of color and sound — the finer, the spiritual forces — in order that the expanding cells might be saturated with the influences of size, strength, and beauty; and as the selfish uses of such forces constitute black magic and consequent loss of power, it naturally followed that while the power of the female diminished, the power of the male increased, and as the ability to influence the form and features of a child descended through the male line, the heredity so established finally resulted in a race of giants. The long subservience of the males had aroused a most abnormally strong desire for revenge in the units of that sex, and also a determination to establish the male sex in power.

The arbitrary taking of so many lives by the females in power could do nothing less than invoke the action of the Karmic law, and in retribution countless numbers of females were killed or enslaved by the males as soon as they had attained to sufficient strength and power, and this was made comparatively easy, for not being fully conscious of their loss of power, large numbers of females became involved in war which was provoked by abnormal desire for extension of territory and influence and by jealousy and hatred of each other; and finally, all of the females involved became so weakened and powerless they were an easy prey for the male; and so commenced the dominion of the male sex over the female, which has lasted to the present time. But as before intimated, the cyclic turn of the wheel of life has at last brought to womankind a return of opportunity, and with that opportunity a possibility of again possessing the power, so long lost, of determining the sex of her children; but the same power will be extended to the male as time passes, as the powers formerly possessed by the male alone will be extended to the female.

By means of their united desire and action, and presided over by the reunited souls, the conception and birth of a new race, finer and more powerful than any which have preceded it, is on the way of accomplishment. If womankind can be made to appreciate the importance of the power and function of the determination of sex she will begin to prepare for its return by purity of body, of desire and action, by unselfish devotion to the highest purposes of life, and above all by rightly influencing the children of the present age who are to be the forefathers and mothers of the new race.

If she continues to degrade herself by impurity, license, and selfish aggrandizement, the curse of succeeding ages will fall on her, as a similar curse fell on the women of that long past age, the Egos of which are now incarnated in the present races of the earth.

LESSON 125
WHITE AND BLACK MAGIC AND MAGICIANS

You ask me to tell you "to whom or to what I refer in making use of the terms white and black magic." In contradistinction to the term "white magician" the term "black magician" is now applied to any devotee of the negative or evil principle of life, and as prefixes, the terms white and black are so applied because of the difficulty experienced in finding words in the English language that will exactly interpret Sanskrit terms generally used to designate interior orders of life. For instance, the terms "Arhat"[1] and "Dugpa,"[2] indicative of the embodied spiritual intelligences of two degrees of life have been for long centuries unknown, misunderstood, and misrepresented or repudiated by narrow sectarian devotees of orthodox forms of religion.

The word "magic," from the root "magi," has been used for ages in the Far East to denote a sacred science which is inseparable from religion.

An Arhat is one of a very high and powerful order of intelligences comparable to one order of the Archangels referred to in Biblical lore.

A Dugpa is one of a correspondingly powerful order of intelligences who uses his power for selfish purposes, even to the debasement of his fellow creatures.

During one definite period of time, the middle of a Maha Yuga or great age, a Dugpa might exert as much or even more power over lesser orders of life than the Arhat, but the power of the Dugpa is continually waning, from that period to the end of the age, while that of the Arhat is increasing.

From the description given by some writers, a Dugpa and a devil might appear to be synonymous terms, but the wise one knows that there is a vast difference, for the latter is an irresponsible creature, being one of a lower spiritual order — the fire elementals — which have never yet been incarnated in physical bodies.

Evolutionary law makes use of the Dugpa for the testing of a human being, but it does not willfully or blindly create him for such a purpose. There is a fine line of demarcation to be found between good and evil, white and black, positive and negative forces, although not always perceptible to the average man. In the consideration of white and black magic that line is exceptionally fine; it belongs to the order of "little things" frequently referred to by us — original causes of cosmic-wide events. It is said that the two paths of white and black

---

[1] *Arhat* (*Sanskrit*, "worthy," "one deserving divine honors") — one who has attained the highest level of enlightenment; the Great Teachers are commonly referred to as Arhats.

[2] *Dugpa* (*Tibetan*, "red hats") — the name of a sect in Tibet that, because of its merger with the concepts and rituals of the pre-Buddhist Bon religion, widely practices black magic. Subsequently, this term has become a general name for the forces of evil, represented by the entities of the lowest astral planes of the Subtle World, as well as by evil sorcerers incarnated in the physical world.

magic run side by side, and this is true for a long distance, but there is a certain definite point where they meet and cross, and one or the other must disappear from manifested life at that point.

It is a great mistake to dwell upon the thought that any mischance, any wrong act, or any antagonistic thought is directly the work of a black magician, for while such may or may not be the original cause of some untoward event, if it were true that such a cause were set up, the added force supplied by the secondary vehicle in the form of individual thought, word, or act may be all that is required to turn the balance of power and bring into materialized form or action the negative force dominating the mentality of the black magician, and is only waiting a suitable vehicle for representation. Unfortunately, such an entity is liable to find the needed vehicle in some associate who may have hitherto been all that could be desired in the way of a friend or comrade, who has been deceived or led into over-consideration of the importance or fear of the results, of some specific action threatened by a black magician. You would neither fear nor despise a live wire as long as you knew the electric energy passing through the molecules at any time could not leave that wire and leap into your body without such a conductor as you alone could supply.

If you will all strive to render yourselves, body and mind, immune to such entitized forces as the black magicians have been rightly termed — the great Disintegrators — you will deprive them of so many victims. The words, "by their fruits ye shall know them,"[1] are peculiarly applicable to those entities, for all the power at their command is used on lines of separation; and in no instance may you feel so sure of their malignant presence and action as when you see some body of former friends or comrades being torn apart for no sufficient cause. The ability of those entities to manufacture and furnish what appears to be sufficient cause for such action, and its ready acceptance by the majority of human kind, is truly phenomenal.

When a realization of the underlying cause of all human woe and suffering dawns on the mind of a deep student of life's mysteries; when even on the greatest heights of bliss attainable by human kind, there comes to him the consciousness that such bliss is meaningless, worthless, and transitory unless it can be shared with others; when one who loves his race comprehends that he must remain outside of the

---

[1] Matthew 7:20.

real life of every other soul until he has broken down forever the barriers between them and himself, and that no effort of his in any other direction can change that fact; when he understands that even if he were able to open the physical heart of a beloved friend and imprison his body therein and close up the entrance, he would be no nearer the real self of that friend; when he understands that notwithstanding all the longing, the praying, the hard striving, all the ambition and battling with nature forces to gain something that never can be gained by him in his present state of development until he can break down those walls of separation, i.e., union with and perfect understanding of the thing or creature his desire has been fixed upon; and at the same time comprehends that the ultimate cause of all that anguish and all the suffering, all the loneliness, the useless effort, is due alone to the separation of soul from soul — of the created from the Creator — the Father-Mother from the child; then — and only then — he comes to a realization of the awfulness of the *sin of separateness* and the hideous, dastardly, fiendish work of the black magicians and the conscious or unconscious disciples of the latter, who have been made vehicles for the transmission of this deadly power.

Only Divine Love can sound the depths of the horrors of that sin, and only the highest love of which man is capable can possibly sense the gulf that lies between separation from and unification with God.

Tear down the barriers, children of my soul! Shut out from your hearts nothing in the Universe save the thing or creature that would separate you from other human souls; for only in union with those other human souls will you ever find God — find Love Incarnate — find peace and fulfillment.

Every barrier you build between other human souls is a barrier between your God and your own soul, between your Higher Self and you.

LESSON 126
COMMENTARIES ON CENTRALIZATION

In commenting on the causes and effects of Centralization, I would call your attention to previous instructions on the same.

Disobedience to the fundamental law of Centralization is primarily responsible for the confused and confusing conditions now obtaining throughout all lines of human endeavor.

It is a commonly accepted idea that the repudiation and displacement of a dominating factor in religious, social, or political life for some given cause is a desirable and efficient way of bettering conditions. The murder of an unpopular king, a vicious attack on the morals or ability of one in an official position, which by affecting public opinion (if some ulterior purpose is to be served) results in destroying the power and influence of such a one for good, find much justification among those who believe the end justifies the means. The immediate effects seem to justify the action taken in many instances; but if longer periods of time, the aftereffects of the act on the performer himself and on the conditions which resulted from the changes could be foreshadowed, such reasoning would be found very faulty, for no matter which one of the 49 lines of life may be descending through any religious, national, sociological, or racial body, the evolutionary forces can only work uninterruptedly for the uplift of that body through that one line; all intermediary or connecting lines are influence lines which may work for good or ill and for definite periods of time according to their magnetic relation to that one main line.

This line descends through every central cell of organ or form which belongs by karmic relation to that body, whatsoever be the nature or character of that body, as might a wire seen through a vast number of beads.

There could never occur a condition inimical to the body as a whole, if the connecting or intermediary lines could sustain the right magnetic relation toward the central line, for all the laws of growth and development would work against such a contingency.

If the nucleus of a central cell of an organic body were not sufficiently virile to function the evolutionary forces of its main line, it would be destroyed in its microbial germ or bacterial stage. If a central cell degenerated or died at any later period, it would be because it had not been sufficiently sustained and nourished from the outside, i.e., by its immediate connections to enable it to reproduce its kind.

The human race cannot call to itself any guide or ruler of any of its fundamental departments who is very far in advance of the constituent elements — the men and women of those departments — and this is due to the tendency of the lower — the animal — man to destroy or mutilate that which it cannot understand or control, and consequently that which it fears; and the inexplicable nature of "the central cell," the ruler, makes it one to be feared by the lesser cells, and therefore one to be rejected by them. Hence, instead of that cell being supported and sustained as ought to be done, it is dragged down, beaten, and cast out, and to all intents and purposes becomes the "Rejected Son," the "Great Sacrifice" of its particular department, organ, or body, and then the karmic results of the action set in against the offenders and woe and suffering fall upon the latter. For the body cannot sustain itself in equilibrium without the central cell, and so its individual parts are in turn beaten, cast out, or torn to pieces by the administrators of the Law it has invoked by its action; and thus nature revenges itself for the destruction of one of its centers of operation.

As it is impossible for nature forces to build a body without a central cell, so it is impossible for man to build a nation or an organization without the guiding force, the superior attracting power of one individual who stands in a similar position to that of the central cell.

The constituent members of the body may imagine that they alone have placed the man in power, and therefore, can tear him down at will, but that is true in only one sense; he has been so placed by the guiding power of the Lords of Karma acting on the minds of those members, and if, in opposition to the will of those karmic instruments of Divine purpose, and for selfish reasons, the said members should so displace that one, they sound the knell of the body as a whole at the same time.

When the normal life functions and the karmic responsibilities of a plant or a man are fully performed, nature itself removes that plant or man from that field of operation according to its desert.

It has many ways of accomplishing this, but if man attempts either by force or diplomacy to remove one before those functions are completed, the whole race loses to the extent of the wrong committed.

You may say that if mankind, acting under superior guidance, places a man at the head of nation or organization, why may not the same superior guidance incite to his removal by the same men if deemed necessary?

I answer, he cannot be removed justly, for the reason that superior intelligence would never place a man in a central position while knowing that the life of such a nation or organization depended upon the stability of that central point, unless it knew beyond any shadow of doubt that the man could hold the point if he were rightly supported. If such a man were to fail in his personal life test, the antithesis of that power in him which made possible his elevation in the first place, and which exists in him in exact proportion to the latter, would pull him down to a depth corresponding to the height from which he fell, but the fall would come through his loss of power, his illness or death — in other words, through his personal limitations, and not by the act of others, if the Divine Law were permitted to take its course.

The delegation of power to family and friends, regardless of the worth or ability of the latter, is responsible for nine-tenths of the trouble that has followed the elevation of man by man to positions of authority, and will continue to be so until man has evolved to the point where his family and friends are those who "do the will of the Father,"[1] as was said by the Nazarene.

It requires tenfold more courage and endurance to render obedience to specific rules of daily life when personal will and desire move in contrary directions, than it does to meet any great crisis of life. In this last instance, you draw on the reserve force of the race to which you belong, while you are dependent upon personal qualifications alone for ability to fulfill the commonplaces of life.

The central figures of any body of people whether self-placed or placed by others, should stand alone, untrammeled by others, yet working on true magnetic lines with those others.

When such magnetic connections obtain there is no chance for undue friction, for the will of one is the will of the others.

It has been due to arbitrary placing of men or women in power, against the will or direction of the Karmic Lords, and for motives of self-interest by those who were to benefit from the exaltation of one or the other that has, first of all, brought so much suffering upon the human race, and secondarily, the arbitrary displacing of those who had been rightly placed from wrong motives.

LESSON 127
PREPARATION FOR THE AVATAR

Little by little the delvers into nature's secret arcana are unraveling strand after strand of the close-meshed, jewel-studded web of life, and catching a glimmer of a gem here and there which by its splendid possibilities temporarily halts them in their search.

Reflected from the depths of the gem may flash out a color, or clue to some new field of investigation hitherto sealed to their imagination,

---

[1] Matthew 12:50.

or a memory of some one or more unproven and discarded theories which, in fact, only required a knowledge of some connecting link to establish the theories as facts and complete a chain of important discoveries.

Science has yet to learn that many of its discarded theories were in fact true links in a grand cosmic chain of truth, as are also those theories now under consideration only to be discarded in turn.

The hard and fast rules applied by science to the investigation of theoretical concepts of some of the most sincere minds of the age, together with the necessity for financial assistance to demonstrate those concepts as literal facts, are the causes back of the failures to solve many of the deepest mysteries of life. Were it not for such hindrances the connecting links between spirit (pure energy) and matter and between cosmic forces and substance in form, would have come under observation long ere this.

If the fact of psychic sight and hearing might be accepted as working hypotheses, and intelligently used when available in determining the relation between some two discovered though discordant facts, for instance, facts concerning the operation of natural law under the action of which the higher development of man is dependent, many of the said missing links would be found. For illustration, take the law of gravity and the known facts of its operation in regard to material things, and the operations of the same law in regard to the astral and soul planes of life and the things or beings in form within those planes; if the psychic senses of some reliable vehicle of communication between the planes of matter and force might be used in such investigation, such mysteries as levitation and suspension of material forms in air without visible means of support would be solved, for the laws of correspondence would show that a corresponding medium to that which supported astral form in etheric atmosphere — inner space — would support material forms in outer space — the earth's atmosphere and the method and means of creating such a medium might be found by investigation.

An astral body could no more support itself in etheric space without a supporting medium than can a physical body; consequently, there emanates from the former a magnetic force which is used in creating a magnetic field which surrounds that body at all times. If the force — substance — of such a magnetic field could be concentrated to make a more condensed support, such an astral form would be visible to physical eyes as a floating sphere giving out its own light, but the astral form of the body thus surrounded would only be visible to psychic vision.

But before any such field of magnetic energy could be concentrated to form such a support for the astral body of a human soul, that soul must have responded to a powerful force of attraction exerted from the physical plane by some human soul in incarnation. While it might be unconsciously exerted by the latter, it is the force of attraction sent out from the lower pole of Manas — the mind, of the incarnated human being, in conjunction with the higher pole of the same force in the excarnated soul which concentrates the substance of the magnetic field and so, as it were, furnishes a bridge, a support for the balanced point in the center — the astral body. And a corresponding field of magnetic energy must be created and concentrated before any material object may be raised and suspended in equilibrium for any length of time from the earth's surface.

It does not occur to cavilers who decry the possibility of the ascension of the Master Jesus on the ground of gravity, that such a Master of forces would possess the power of overcoming the gravitational pull by the creation of such a magnetic field as I have referred to. However, it is not so much the ascension as it is the descent, or rather the outcoming or return of that entity that we are bound to consider most at this time, in view of the fact that I have told you that such a return depends upon a right preparation for such an event.

You must understand that the long centuries since the ascent of Jesus have afforded time and opportunity for the exertion of a tremendous force of attraction which has been generated and expelled by the deep love, longing, and aspiration of millions of the units of the human race, and which has drawn that entity from the higher etheric or astral plane to the lower astral, the plane next in vibration to the earth plane; but to appear in physical manifestation the substance of that etheric body must be condensed to a similar rate of vibration to that in which the disciples saw Him at the time of His ascent; and in order to make it possible for that to be done there must be a magnetic field created and condensed by those in incarnation who have the power, which will not only furnish the bridge from one plane to the other, but which will also supply the necessary force for such a change in body vibration as He will require. It is this great work that loyal students of occultism are asked to engage in, and this is partly what I referred to in speaking of the necessary preparation to be made.

You have been taught that the higher attributes to be cultivated were in fact states of substance and force possible of manipulation by man, and that the possession and use of occult power depended upon the cultivation and use of those attributes. You have also been taught how this should be accomplished. If their possession and use depend upon your obedience, your devotion, your brotherly affection and help for each and all human beings, no less than upon your power of accepting and acting upon the advice and direction of your teacher along lines of practical occultism, how else can you consciously develop those attributes than by keeping your vows of Initiation?

True it is that they are being developed in mankind by the slow process of natural growth, but there must always be some in advance of the race to which they belong, so it is only a question as to whether you will be of the latter-named class or be content to plod on with the masses; whether you will be among those who consciously create conditions for the manifestation of the Great Soul of the Cosmos, or be content to take such fragments as fall from the tables of the Initiates when the great Feast is prepared.

LESSON 128
THE WISE MAN

The wise man knows that a conditionless, changeless period of manifestation is an utter impossibility for man in his present state; he knows that history repeats itself in ever-recurring periods through an eternity of time as day follows night; he knows that the democracy of one age will make way for the monarchy of the next, as surely as he knows that the tides will throw up the waters of an ocean on its shores and then fling them back in perfect time and rhythm.

He also knows that every tide of life, as well as every tide of ocean, must be taken at its flood if it is to bear a precious load of treasure or experience to its destined harbor; therefore, he takes advantage of every high tide in the affairs of men and nations to advance the progress of his ideals, and then falls back into some secure haven when the tide has gone out and conserves his energies. But the wise man also knows that back of every tide, every movement of sun, stars, and planets, every cycle of manifestation, is a supreme power which governs all, a power which operates at the center of all things — the place of peace — the point where motion ceases and unity reigns, and that he must be aligned to that power if he would succeed. A point where the Father can no more become the Son, and the Son can no more become the Father. A state of existence where the Father reigns eternally and the Son serves eternally — where the Mother and the Father are one in the Son, and each is a partaker of the greatness of the other.

And the wise man sees that however often the elder Son may be differentiated into the many sons, in the course of time; however repeatedly night may follow day, or the tides of life go out; however often a democracy may be created by the powers of disruption in labor for the birth of more desirable conditions, the people must return to the original form, the paternal — the kingly form of government — again and again; therefore, instead of throwing his energies into the flotsam and jetsam of changeable life, he strives to keep them in line with the more stable, the more lasting forms of life, those forms which begin and end a Manvantara.

It is because of his knowledge of the flux and reflux of the life forces that the Master — Initiate — of the great White Lodge forms all his creations on the lines which govern that Lodge — the paternal form of government and control, however inefficient the parent of any one of his creations may be in the initial stage of the creation. This would seem to contradict the advice and direction given by us along communistic lines, but does not in reality, for the sooner the flood tide of a democracy or socialistic community is reached the sooner will the best fitted units of the humanity of that period and nation have reached their apogee of development through experience, and so be fitted for removal to another sphere of action, a greater opportunity.

Believe me when I say there is no such thing as a decadent civilization, notwithstanding the claims made by political economists to the contrary.

The fact that the sons and daughters of a truly great man have become degenerate does not prove that the tendency to degeneracy began in the parent, or that he can be held responsible and so be made partaker in the results of the degeneracy of his children. If that parent is truly a great man, he passes into another sphere of activity at the highest point of his development, a sphere where the children of his body are no more to him than the children of another man's body. He has then more nearly approximated the sphere of divine Fatherhood.

The average man does not realize that the seemingly decadent race may be but the rising souls of a more material, a more animal-like race, the units of which must learn by conscious contact with evil — the horrible nature of evil — as have those who have passed on. But when I speak of those who are at the flood tide I do not necessarily refer to the rich, the powerful, or the great, as the world counts the great; but the rich, the powerful, the great of mind, of nature, of soul, whatever their outer circumstances may be.

When the thirst for popular rule is upon a people, that race or nation is nearing the apogee of development which that particular race or nation could reach as a body. It is preparing the way for the division of "the sheep and the goats"[1] of that cyclic round, as was indicated by the prophet — the sheep to be removed by rebirth into some higher form of civilization, possibly on some other planet, figuratively speaking, "the right hand of God." The goats — the passion-bound, brutish descendants — to take the "left hand" route to knowledge, the route of suffering, that they in turn may rise to a similar point to that attained by "the sheep." Many of the nations of the earth are in the throes of such a preparation at the present time, hence the craze for popular government sweeping over the earth. The wise man stands back, looks on, and listens, knowing the inevitable result.

When directions were given for the formation of the Temple and its subsidiary effort, the Temple Home Association, I directed that the control of the two divisions should be vested in the paternal, and the communistic forms respectively, knowing full well that the latter could not long survive the withdrawal of the paternal influences flowing from myself and my brethren through the agent appointed by us, should any successful effort be made to separate the two bodies. They are founded on the laws which govern the universe and the great White Lodge — the law of centralization. All this I made plain in the beginning. Ignoring these directions, individuals have made repeated, though unsuccessful, efforts to separate these two bodies which are bound by the deepest of all ties, by trying to incapacitate one or the other in some respect.

When the demons of avarice, self-exaltation, or hatred creep into the human heart, they blind the mentality to such a degree that their

---

[1] Matthew 25:32.

victims neither think nor care about the injury they may inflict upon the community, organization, or body of which they are units. If the masses of a body politic could but realize that every blow struck at that body must inevitably fall on every unit of that body, they would be less willing to encourage the single unit who strikes the blow which must fall on them. The masses of a human race cannot reach the highest possibilities of that race until they perfectly obey the laws which now govern some of the lower orders of life, accepting cheerfully the fact that implicit obedience to divine law as rendered by the said lower orders has enabled them to multiply and continue to exist when man has been killed off the earth.

The prick of a pin, a tiny knife thrust into the body of man or animal will call countless numbers of defenders — the white blood corpuscles — to the point of attack. They are sent by a single brain impulse. The combined recuperative forces of the whole body are turned in the direction of the wound until the danger has passed.

If man were obedient to the law which governs those minute, semiconscious organisms, no single body or organization of which he was a unit could be greatly endangered by the act of any individual, or by a minority of its members.

It is because of their implicit obedience to this law by the units of the great White Lodge that the latter has become and remained the guiding, controlling power of manifested life. The disintegrating element — the individual destroyer — which may creep into some lower Order of a Degree of the Lodge is thrust out by his own limitations. The solid front opposed to him forces him to eliminate himself.

There is no occasion for positive action — attack — on the part of his associates against him. The negative action of quiet, steady resistance to combined opposition forces him out of the environment of those he has endangered by his acts. When the inner eyes of mankind are opened to the great fundamental laws, life will have taken on a new aspect.

The primal object of the Temple formation by the Initiates was the more rapid assimilation of the spiritual truths upon which natural laws are founded, by as large a number of people as might be fitted for their reception.

Each entering member receives what he demands by his adherence to or repudiation of the said laws. He can rise to the apogee of his opportunity, or fall below the level and be placed accordingly by the Lodge in some other sphere of experience or activity; but whatever may be the instrument used for his grading, the controlling force of that instrument will be the natural law; for it is divinely true that not a sparrow falls to the ground without the knowledge of the Father. Not a hair of the head is left unnumbered; and if the Temple were only a sparrow, figuratively speaking, not a single feather of its body could be ignored or forgotten by its original founders — the Great White Lodge.

LESSON 129
HANDS

It is not to the science of chiromancy — or palmistry — that I shall here call attention, though that science has a basis that is closely connected with the embodied elementaries to which I shall refer.

In exoteric symbolism the left hand denotes *power*, the right hand, *execution*. From a material aspect the reason for such classification is obvious, but there is an esoteric cause for the same which lies much deeper. In all ages the subject has created special interest in the minds of investigators into the secrets of the human body, for the hands possess some features not found in any other organ or region of the body. These are not all perceptible to the anatomist, though clearly so to the developed psychic.

It is not alone for the services they perform to the rest of the body that they are peculiarly valuable and interesting, but because they contain the media for the expulsion of a peculiar form of energy, commonly termed magnetic, which, if man were still in his original globular form, could be used to perform an equal amount of service for him to that which is now performed by his physical hands.

There still remain in the hands of the human being, and also to some extent in the feet and at the ends of some of the finer nerves, certain forms of molecular substance within which are conserved, and from which are expelled streams of magnetic energy which are subject to the trained will of the operator.

To those who have no belief in the lesser gods, the elementaries of divine science, the idea that these minute bodies or corpuscles are indeed the vehicles of the elementaries of certain orders will seem visionary, but it is nevertheless true that such is the case.

The reason why hand will go out to hand all but involuntarily upon the meeting of friends, and also why there is a feeling of repugnance toward accepting the hand of another, even when there is no apparent cause for restraint, is that the molecular substance of the corpuscles of which I speak will expand or contract unconsciously to those concerned, and so flash their message of consent or denial to the brain. The resident elementaries of those corpuscles are as sensitive to antagonism as the weather vane is to the wind, and if man were more alive to the inner promptings of the soul, he would know immediately, at the first impulse to lift his hand, whether or not it was desirable to take the hand of another.

The corpuscles referred to are capable of segregation and examination by a skilled anatomist, but escape the careless eye because of their similarity to certain other white corpuscles. If a microscope of sufficient power could be brought to bear on them, they would be found to be small masses of intricately woven thread-like nerve ends surrounding a nucleus, each corpuscle a distinct organism, though working harmoniously with other normal organisms in the same body.

They are exceedingly sensitive to changes in the magnetic field of any person or thing exterior to the organism in which they are developing, and almost automatically contract or expand according to the nature of the changes taking place in such a field.

The rays of light emitted from the ends of the fingers of those who are able to use their hands effectually in healing the sick or operating on the body can be seen and felt very easily by a sensitive; and all the different modes of healing by use of the hands were originally founded by those who had more or less knowledge of the existence and operation of those corpuscles of activity.

The sympathetic vibrations between these corpuscles and certain orders of other corpuscles operative in the brain and heart make possible the expression of deep feeling in instrumental music, and peculiarly so in violin playing, where the ends of the fingers all but automatically seek the right position on the strings.

It is quite possible to do more injury to the body of another by wrong methods of manipulation with the hands than benefit by right methods, though it may take longer for the injuries to become apparent.

The origin of the cruel practice indulged in by a certain emperor of turning the thumbs up or down to signal life or death to the victims of the Roman amphitheater, may be found in the legendary tales of still more powerful sovereigns who, with the raising of one or more fingers, could instantaneously execute a criminal or a decree of vengeance upon a victim, without the intervention of any other instrument or person, by means of the magnetic forces so directed.

You all ought to be able to tell a friend from an enemy, a harmonious or inharmonious factor, the instant hand meets hand, but as it is, that power is resident in but few for the reason that you have trifled with those finer forces of nature to such an extent that their vehicles of operation within your hands have become partially atrophied or paralyzed, and there is little or no interaction between them and the brain.

However fine the character of a given person whose hand you clasp, if you are conscious of a sensation of coldness, dampness, and feebleness, there is most surely some bar between that person and yourself that you would do well to recognize and heed. It is not the mere temperature alone that gives this warning; it is the combination of moisture, temperature, and activity.

By means of the moisture which acts as a conveyor, the poisoned magnetic energy generated in one body can be more quickly transmitted to another. In its pure state magnetic energy requires no medium of transmission whatever, aside from its etheric base. It may be expelled or attracted by action of the will; but when it becomes permeated with the stultifying, paralyzing forces of the lower pole of life, it becomes denser and heavier and does not respond to impulse, either so rapidly or so directly.

Others might not be affected by or even notice these signs in the hand of a mutual acquaintance, and in such an instance there is not so much danger of untoward aftereffect. The bar, if there be one, exists between those who are conscious of the antagonism indicated by me. In the one case there is no interaction between the streams of energy escaping from the heart and hand (giving birth to the affinitive force, the force which ensouls the before-mentioned corpuscles) which is the energy in action in the other case. In simple words, a new creation — a child — is born, a different form of the energy expressed by its progenitors — the original magnetic streams from heart to hand — and that child is indeed and in truth a connecting and binding form of energy which ensouls the peculiar entities embodied in the corpuscles — the elementaries — which transmit their life currents to each other when they meet as they must do in a warm, firm handclasp between friend and friend.

It is the stagnation of the molecular substance of said corpuscles, in the case of a broken friendship, that causes so much mental and physical suffering to both parties. The more sensitive the disciple to the action of the finer forces of nature, the more he will suffer from the breaking of such a tie, as I have mentioned, until he reaches the state of equilibrium where he is the perfect master of all the evolutionary forces embodied in his various vehicles of expression.

LESSON 130
THE CONSERVATION OF LODGE FORCE

Would you place in the hands of your little child a stick of dynamite and a hammer with which to amuse itself? Would you send a beloved one alone into the lair of a tiger, when you knew that one was subject to attacks of dizziness when affrighted? Would you teach your comrade the use of firearms, when you knew he would turn them against you in a passion, or still worse, against his weaker comrades?

What excuse could you offer to divine law should you do any of these three things? None, you would say. And no more could the Initiates of the right hand path gain forgiveness for taking a disciple beyond the preparatory degrees of occultism, when they knew that such a disciple was incapable of passing safely beyond that preparatory degree — the testing degree for that which might follow if the disciple were proven capable of further advance.

Whenever you hear a recreant, expelled, or unreliable disciple say that he has passed through the Orders of the Temple, and has not found what he was seeking, or has been deceived, or one who is offering any kind of excuse in justification of his unfaithfulness, you will always be safe in saying — "My friend, you have gone to the limit of your power of progress in this life."

The very fact of his unfaithfulness to his vows of Initiation, and therefore of treachery to a comrade, effaced his name, at the moment of the commission of such an act, from the roll of personal disciples; "his (inner) eye is blinded and his heart is hardened, lest he should see and understand"[1] that which his former comrades are entering upon,

---
[1] John 12:40.

and endeavor to force his way, and so compel refusal from his Master, or gain just knowledge enough to injure himself or his comrades past his power to remedy the injury. It is the merciful law which, symbolically speaking, blinds his eyes, i.e., blots out his desire for continuing on that line of endeavor; "hardens his heart," that is, takes away his aspirations along that line, and sets his face in some other direction.

Does it even seem reasonable to believe that the Masters of Wisdom, to whom all hearts are open, would open the doors of white magic to a libertine, a seducer of women, a liar or a thief, when absolute purity of body, of mind, and purpose is essential to enlightenment?

Does it seem reasonable that the Masters of Wisdom would open the door to unlimited power to the betrayer of his trust, to the cruel, fork-tongued, vain, and ambitious woman whose longing for denied sex expression, or whose over-indulgence in the same, has invalided her, and who sees in every other woman an enemy or a tool? Yet, evil as are these qualities, many possessing them are led to the very doors of wisdom through their longing for more abundant life, and when denial of further advance is made, turn viciously upon those who have taken them as far as it was possible for them to go on the path of research, and avidly deny the existence or possibility of anything beyond their vision.

Unfortunately, as it would seem, it is by the word of such as these that true occultism is judged by the great majority. But here again the merciful law intervenes for the protection of these, for the fact that they have no more power of discrimination than to accept and be guided by such statements shows conclusively that they also are unfit for the accumulation of Divine Wisdom.

LESSON 131
DEVACHAN

To those who are practically ignorant of the basic realities of life, I would say again as I have said before in effect, they have no adequate conception of the Devachanic plane or the conditions of existence on that plane when they jeopardize all that is desirable and possible of individual existence on that plane by filling their minds full of the trivialities of their present life, and their auric sphere with reflections from other minds which will afford no basis for a real devachanic bliss.

As you would smile tenderly though pityingly at your child's concept of maturity, so "those who know" can only smile wistfully at your feeble concepts of life in its more mature aspects when those concepts are devoid of evil. We often hear an undeveloped disciple voice his desire to "renounce Devachan" for the purpose of returning at once to earth life, for the good of humanity. This occurs as a result of hearing or reading of such a consummation by some high Initiate, but the words are spoken in utter ignorance of that which must be renounced, or even of their power to make such a renunciation.

Such a disciple is no more capable of making an intelligent renunciation of that character than would be a three-year-old child.

If you to whom I speak are among this class, I can assure you that you might as well say you will renounce the period between meals given to digestion and assimilation of the food you take to sustain your body; for one period is as necessary to the soul as the other is to the body.

If you had evolved to the degree where material food was no more requisite to the health of the body, as have those higher Initiates, you might then be able to make such a statement with more understanding.

Instead of impossible renunciation of Devachan, it would be more to the purpose if you would use the energy so lost, in strengthening your high ideals or forming new ones which would furnish the substance for assimilation in your devachanic life.

Many wrong ideas are prevalent concerning the nature of subconscious life. Devachan is supposed to be a state of self-deception, a dream. If you consider your present life a dream, then also are you justified in considering Devachan a dream, and not otherwise, for one is as real as the other.

I would ask you, "To what degree have you penetrated the hidden desires, motives, and private acts of the friend to whom you are most devotedly attached?" "Is not the fact that you are utterly unable to reach to those hidden places one of the chief sources of the discontent you feel whenever he or she is absent from you, and even when present in a lesser degree?" You can never get close enough to your friend to satisfy your desire, and it is because of your belief in his possession of virtues now concealed from you that you so desire closer intimacy with your friend. It is not the faults, the weaknesses, the contemptible little things of the lower nature that you are so desirous of contacting.

Your devachanic experience, so far as that one friend is concerned, is a full realization of the highest attributes of your friend, a unifying of your consciousness with the higher aspects of that soul, and all the virtues and beauties of mind and body which you believe exist and which do exist in the Higher Self of that friend.

You cannot so identify yourself with your friend in earth life, but you can "lay up treasures in heaven"[1] by your desire for and appreciation of beautiful attributes, your appreciation of beautiful things where, metaphorically speaking, no moth or rust of the lower — the material — self can corrupt or destroy, or thieves break through to steal them. If you could not come to some knowledge of those attributes and assimilate them into your consciousness in your devachanic experience, you could never bring them into manifestation in yourself, no matter how many earth lives you might live.

However much you may desire immediate reembodiment, so long as there is a single higher attribute still undeveloped in your nature, a period of Devachan is a necessity and is desirable. The majority of adult human beings absolutely require the rest of Devachan as much as they do the rest of sleep; for the astral brain — the seat of the skandhas — becomes as weary as does the physical brain in the case of the undeveloped.

LESSON 132
SINCERITY

Look askance at the man who maliciously attacks his own country, his home, or the organization to which he belongs. You may be sure he is either revenging himself for some deserved punishment, or has some selfish purpose to carry out.

If a man is sincere in trying to correct a supposedly wrong condition, and is capable of so correcting it, he will devise a better condition, prove it feasible in his own life, and then present it to others. He may be sure that if it is really better than the previous condition, it will at once appeal to the intuition of all concerned, for everyone wants better conditions.

It is neither necessary nor right to use the weapons of a coward or a cur to accomplish a good purpose. The law of progression furnishes the impulse and points the way for such accomplishment.

---
[1] Matthew 6:20.

LESSON 133
RADICAL ACTION

There are certain definite cycles in the lives of men and nations when the more conservative lines of action must be discarded for the time being or the evolution of man or nation will be sadly threatened, if not temporarily stopped; cycles in which sentiment and the higher attributes of mercy and forgiveness must seem to take on characteristics which are foreign to them during other cycles.

The law of cycles is as applicable to those attributes as it is to all other phases of manifestation, and the lowest arc of the cycle of a sentiment would coincide with the lowest arc of a racial or world cycle; and the interaction between the controlling forces back of the evolving of such a sentiment, and the more materialistic aspects of life which were dominating the race during that particular racial cycle would be stronger and more incessant than at other periods.

As is usually the case, humanity at large only perceives the effects, scarcely ever the causes which lie back of the changeable phenomena which make up its life experiences. It jumps to the conclusion that it is the cruelty, injustice, and wrong living of one class which is responsible for the enforced suffering and hard conditions under which other classes are living. That karmic action and cyclic law have compelled the manifestation of the conditions that have bred the class hatred, always in evidence at such periods — but this does not occur to either class.

The class in power recognizes the fact that something must be done to change the conditions which are making for class hatred, but it does not know what to do to achieve such change. It is as ignorant of the real facts as are its supposed victims.

A stronger hand than theirs is at the helm of the universal ship, a hand which is in readiness to demand justice for outraged law, and it chooses just such a period as I have mentioned, when the lowest arcs of the cycles of sentiment and justice are in opposition — a time when radical action is necessary, whatever its effect on individual and collective man.

As there are cycles in individual life when virtue cannot be regained by limiting vice, times when merciless, radical action is the only possible cure for diseases of the mind or body, so similar cycles come in national and universal life.

The seemingly unnatural and unnecessarily cruel wars which have occurred from time to time between two factions of a single nation, as well as the wars between nations — wherein large bodies of people are sacrificed to some ideal or for some selfish purpose — have always materialized at such periods as I have referred to; and until mankind can realize that strong, determined, radical action is equally possible and far more effective on lines of unification than on lines of disorganization, and therefore that it is possible to use all the radical forces generated at the lowest arc of a cycle for purposes of good instead of evil, he will continue to slaughter his fellow man, and then build monuments to his glory, and sing psalms of victory over what are in truth terrible defeats.

But before collective man can utilize the power that may be at his command in such a manner, individual man must learn to do the same thing; and while he selfishly continues to break down where he should be building, while he cajoles and deceives when radical action is imperative, and uses radical action where the higher conservative action is alone lawful, he is only a victim of the forces which gather at the nether pole of a cycle.

War is only necessary between man and man so long as humanity is blind to the purposes, power, and scope of the irresponsible, semiconscious forces of natural life, which may be used even more effectually in pursuance of peace than of its opposite, war. These forces can be used for the uplifting of a race which has fallen under their action at a time when such action was directed by destructive agencies.

It is a sad mistake to accept the theory that the forces of the negative aspect, the lowest point in the arc of a cycle, are responsible for the evil deeds committed by mankind at that period. The negative aspect of any natural force or object is evil only because the forces of the negative aspect are used *for* evil. In no way is this truth more easily demonstrated than by the good man who is great enough to sink himself to the level of the man who has fallen low in the scale of life and lost all hope of betterment. Only by reaching down to the level of the other man can he possibly understand the fall of the latter, and lay the lines of regeneration.

Once awakened, the hope of valuable service to mankind in the breast of a man and the negative forces which under wrong direction have worked for his undoing, will work just as strongly for his uprising. This fact may not be generally accepted because of the evident difficulties in the way and the backsliding experienced by the man who is trying to rise from a fall. But the latter are all due to auto-suggestion. He has set up definite currents in his astral atmosphere which can only be retarded and finally destroyed by personal effort and direction; but the same energy he used in the carrying out of wrong suggestion can be used in carrying out right suggestion; however, it requires a strong directing impulse, either by some more virile man or by the awakened soul of the fallen man, to turn that energy in the right direction, and this is where radical action is essential.

No amount of sentiment or precept will fulfill the purpose which positive example and radical action will accomplish in such an instance.

The races of mankind die out at the lowest point in the arc of a great cycle when the negative forces are the most active, because they have been drawing on those forces for selfish and evil purposes during the whole of the second and third quarters of that cycle, and the people are surcharged with that one aspect of life. The builders — the semiconscious elementals of the negative force — have become in turn the destroyers through wrong direction.

LESSON 134
THE INTERMEDIATE STATES OF CONSCIOUSNESS AND MAN'S RELATION THERETO

The revelations of ancient and modern science are rapidly drawing to a focus. It is now but a matter of nomenclature and the bigotry of a few modern authorities on physics that are keeping the world at large from a recognition of the spiritual truths which underlie all phenomena and, therefore, which are responsible for the continued disputations and the waste of time, means, and strength which could be applied to more important investigation in those fields which would render the most satisfying results. When one of the said authorities proudly proclaims the discovery of a state of matter hitherto unknown to, and unimaginable by, his contemporaries, and practically denies the existence of the same state of matter on the following day, even deriding the descriptions given by some ancient authority in a similar field of investigation, and who takes such a course owing to the fact that the matter indicated by the ancients has been placed in the field of metaphysics instead of the field of physics, and can only be identified by some term in common use by metaphysicians, he is only adding to the confusion in the minds of the masses.

If he would even permit an analogy, a correspondent possibility to gain a vantage point in his own dogmatic mind, and put it out as a working theory, the mind of some embryonic scientist or philosopher, possibly less well equipped in some ways yet more intuitive, would go right to the root of the difficulty and throw a flood of light on all phases of the subject.

Wonderful discoveries are announced from time to time in current literature, discoveries which have been prevented by the Initiates up to the present time for the reason that their open announcement might do exactly what I have intimated, i.e., set some intuitive mind to work at a problem which the world was not ready to solve advantageously to itself, and which might have led to outbursts of crime far exceeding in brutality and wickedness any which had preceded them; for instance, the burning of the so-called witches. It was the claim made by metaphysicians of their belief in and knowledge of an intermediate state of existence and the inhabitants of that state, as well as the power of the latter to influence sensitives on the physical plane to injure others by occult methods, which was primarily responsible for the perpetration of that blot upon civilization termed the era of witchcraft. Yet the recent announcement by an accepted authority of the discovery of a state of matter, which is in fact identical with the state and plane of matter discovered by the before-mentioned metaphysicians by means of their investigations into psychic phenomena, does not cause a ripple of excitement.

This new discovery, or rather re-discovery, relates to the existence of minute organisms given the names of cathode corpuscles and negative electrons. The existence of these minute lives was quite clearly indicated in the instruction on Light, given to Templars over a decade ago.

The emissions, absorptions, and radiations of Light are the bases of all matter in manifestation, both on the exterior and interior planes of life. But as long as man refuses to accept the fact of the Spiritual Sun — the source of all light — he will continue to work in practical darkness. While he considers the etheric plane as merely the medium by means of which light and sound waves are conveyed, instead of the eternal mode of motion of all life — spiritual Light — he will work in a circle. He will accept and reject his corpuscular theory by turns.

The atomic, ionic, interionic, and all other component parts of his corpuscles will give him subject matter to theorize about, but he must eventually accept the facts as given out by the Masters of Wisdom.

Man must experience in order to know, and the before-mentioned autocrats of modern science must bow their heads to the level of the little child and accept unequivocally the facts as given by the votaries of Divine Wisdom before it will be possible for them to reach the threshold of spiritual experience, which alone holds the key of knowledge. The dogmatism, egotism, and pride engendered by such successes as they have reached, fanned by the adulation of those who could scarcely comprehend, much less interpret, their dissertations on their discoveries, prevents them from reaching the attitude most requisite for such experience as I have mentioned.

They cannot cross the bar simple faith has set up at the gate of knowledge, nor can they understand the nature of the substance of that bar. Although they may reach that substance by inductive methods, and can see and touch it in their investigations, yet they must turn sadly and disappointedly away each time because of their inability or unwillingness to cross the bar. But it is being crossed by others in all quarters of the world, and the discoveries being made by those others are fast destroying all obstacles, and are building the neutral structure between the two poles of endeavor within which the two phases of the one great and divine science can meet and mingle, and from which will go out to the whole world the glad tidings of great joy.

LESSON 135
BLOOD SACRIFICE

Every milestone of the path of human progress has been marked with blood up to the present time, and will continue to be so marked until all matter is redeemed. Many men have striven rightly to interpret the statement imputed to the Apostle Paul to the effect that without the shedding of blood there can be no remission of sin.[1] The same or similar statements have been uttered by the Initiate teachers at some time in the first half of every racial period since man became a self-conscious, responsible being, and they have been to voice the necessity of sacrifice for broken law. These statements have usually been called forth as the result of the sacrifice of the life of some great

---

[1] See Hebrews 9:22.

teacher or leader of men; but that they might more particularly refer to a fact in nature — the action of a universal law — was seldom recognized.

The blood is the vehicle of Prana — material life force — whether that life force is circulating through human or animal veins, or through the sap of a tree or the molecules of a stone. When the term "blood sacrifice" was used by the ancients to indicate the redemption of a race or a world from the power of evil, it was used in a generic sense, and included all containers and conveyors of life force, whatever their form or character, which could be compelled to render up that life force in a sacrificial rite.

The law of Karma is generally understood to apply to self-conscious beings alone, but that is a mistake, for its action is just as certain, though not so radical nor pronounced, in the case of every molecule of living matter as it is in the case of man.

Every such molecule of living matter embodies an embryonic — a rudimentary — soul, that is on its way to self-conscious existence, and which is therefore subject to the laws which govern all self-conscious forms of life — the laws of Karma, Reincarnation, and Eternal Progress.

No race or kingdom of living things or beings, whether it be human, animal, vegetable, or mineral can rise to the next succeeding degree beyond its status at the close of a racial period, until its racial indebtedness is remitted by the shedding of blood; that is, by the yielding up of its bodily envelopes, in order that the value of the experiences lived through by the constituent molecules of those envelopes may be impressed upon them by contact with the spiritual life forces of a higher plane of existence, and so receive the impetus to greater endeavor when they shall again be assembled in some more concrete material embodiment. These lesser elemental lives must be freed from constriction and confinement in form before such spiritual impetus can be given; as the soul of man must be freed from the physical form, either in concentration, sleep, or death, in order to contact the spiritual forces or beings of higher forms of consciousness and receive the impetus to continued growth.

This is one of the great mysteries of life which science rejects because it cannot prove, but which is nevertheless at the very root of evolution. If this truth be accepted, it is not difficult to understand why it is that it is only the dead thing, whether it be a dead world, a dead government, or a dead enterprise that can stand still. As long as either one is alive, organic change is inevitable. Change is dependent upon motion and every mode of motion is incited by spiritual entities.

The man who departs from any form of established life for the purpose of realizing some ideal must pay the price of his departure, and he pays it by yielding up some feature or phase of his life, whether it be his literal blood, or a higher grade of the conveyors of life force embodied in his mentality or soul. Those who come after him will profit by his sacrifice to the extent that he has benefited by the sacrifice of others; but he, that is, the Ego, the real man, will come back into sentient life to share in the success he has been instrumental in creating by his sacrifice.

It may be that a government, an association of people, a tribe, or a family has arisen in beauty, strength, and power, only to yield up its life as a body, in turn, to make way for a higher form of associated life in another day and age. But the Ego which presided over the first sacrifice made for the ideal condition will share in the benefits as well as the succeeding sacrifices of the body with which it was thus connected.

Whenever you see a man rise to the height of a great sacrifice, you may be sure countless numbers of lesser sacrifices lie behind him, as you may be sure he is on the point of receiving the benefits he has thus earned, for justice rules the universe. Man builds his ladder step by step if he would reach to an eminence.

To the onlooker it seems a great pity that so much apparently needless sacrifice is being constantly made. It appears to be a calamity that the inevitable destroyer must come in and annul the fruits of great labor and of sacrifice unbounded, but the elementary forces, the lesser lives which make up the hosts of the destroyers, whether their work is done by inciting human hatred or other passions to destructive acts, or whether that work is done in the great storms and upheavals of earth, or by any other one of nature's methods of destruction — those elementary hosts are doing the work for which they were created and are agents of Karmic law on the way to higher forms of development.

The great ideals of the Gods and of men alone are eternal. All else is change; all else is sacrificial; so "be not attached to the fruits of action."[1] Live aright today and the morrow will be right; live wrongly today and tomorrow will surely bring you remorse and discouragement. Do not look forward to the results of your brother's sacrifices of

---
[1] Bhagavad Gita 3:9.

today with expectation of individual advantage at some later day, for it is only your own sacrifices that will bring you individual attainment. You will be partaker in the results of your brother's shedding of his life force insofar as you have stood by your brother in his needed trial and, therefore, have shed your own blood — your own life force — whether it be the blood of the soul or body at the same time.

Remember, sacrifice is the law of all life and progress. Without sacrifice there is no remission of sin, no wiping out of evil, of inharmony, of death. The assertion that a brother's blood will cry out from the ground for vengeance is generally believed to have been used in a figurative sense, but to the advanced psychic it is seen to be a statement of fact; for with the expulsion of blood from an animal or human body there occurs a premature reuniting, a commingling of the earth and fire elementals from which the material constituents of the blood originally came, and a demand is thereby made on the universal law by those elementals for payment of the debt contracted by the one who has cast them out of the blood which embodied them before the time when they would have been released by natural law, and so given the opportunity for the higher impulse before referred to; for the law decrees that the souls of mortals who die violent deaths shall remain in Kama Loka[2] until the day of their appointed end, at which time they are released to attain to Devachan and to receive the higher, the spiritual impulse, and the same law is correspondingly active in the case of the lesser lives which make up the physical body of man. In fact it is largely the breaking of this law which has given cause for the confinement of the soul in Kama Loka during the aforementioned

---

[2] *Kama Loka* (*Sanskrit*, "place of desire") — the lower plane of the Astral World, corresponding to the Hades of the ancient Greeks and the land of Silent Shadows of the Egyptians. Here, all beings that have lived on the Earth, including animals, wait in their astral bodies for their "second death." If people die naturally, they remain in Kama Loka for a few hours to a few years, depending on the purity of their desires and emotions during their lives on the Earth. The purer their souls are, the less time they have to spend here. Thus, a light-bearing soul might pass through Kama Loka into the higher layers without being conscious of this passage. However, those who die unnaturally, as a result of suicide or murder, will have to stay here for as long as they had to live on the Earth, according to their Karma. For example, someone was destined to live for 80 years but committed suicide at age 20 will have to remain here for 60 years. Vicious people may become dangerous entities — elementaries — who will commit even greater crimes by possessing physically incarnated people.

interval, in the cases of those who die violent deaths. Violent death is unnatural death, and nature cannot be thwarted.

The conditions in which the violently expelled blood elementals are involved are comparable to the conditions which obtain in Kama Loka, where all is confusion and unintermittent change, consequently, conditions of suffering in various degrees.

LESSON 136
TO THOSE WHO SUFFER

Is there one among your number or among your friends and acquaintances who would not raise a hand in response to a question as to the need of sympathy at some time when the waves of sorrow had beaten down the last stronghold of materiality; in some hour when the very depths of suffering had been sounded and the soul was alone with God; when no human succor was possible; when all that lay between life and death was whatever degree of the power of endurance that soul had developed?

If memory can recall such an hour with sufficient vividness, does it not also remind you of the agonized promises you made to your better self, to your God, to undo some wrong you had done, or to do some righteous action which might change the current of your life, and if so be, you might find relief?

Even death would be welcome at such an hour if there were no other way of bringing surcease of suffering to soul or body, as the case might be.

You may not know it, but you touched the Godhead in that moment or hour in the depths, far closer and more intimately than you had ever done before or could do again unless like conditions obtained; and something was given you in that touch that you had never possessed before, something which forevermore separated you from the self of matter you had previously served. Whatever name or title you choose to bestow upon that gift, whether the gift was an expression of Divine Love, sympathy, or a mutual understanding, it matters not; it was in all truth a part of God's essence bestowed upon you.

If you have permitted that gift to lie idle, or have only drawn upon it when a personal friend made a claim, or when some national calamity pounded so hard at the door of your heart that you had to open the door in self-defense, you are forfeiting the greatest opportunity given to man, and one for which will be demanded a most rigid accounting.

It should make no difference to you who or what a sufferer may be or may have been, what had been the original cause of his suffering, or what was going to be done eventually with the results of your awakened sympathy. The one thing that should count with you is the fact that for the moment or hour you have been graciously permitted to become a vehicle for the transmission of that gift of the Holy Spirit to another human soul, that you have been enabled to radiate the same Divine Essence, by and through which you had become god-like for the time being.

Your own exemption from infinitely worse suffering than you had ever endured was hanging in the balance when the unspoken call was made upon you to share that divine gift with another. You have nothing whatever to do with the results of such expenditures, whether they take the form of spiritual or material things. The responsibility of the results rests upon the God who incited you to that action in that never-to-be-forgotten hour while in the depths of your own suffering.

Though you have been forgetful of and ungrateful for that gift at times, you still have faith to believe that there will come a time when you will *not* forget, and when Gratitude will become a permanent possession.

Believing this, can you not also realize that repeated efforts will sometime bring others to the place where they will not forget what you did for them while they too were "in the depths"?

Therefore you have no cause to fear the final effect of any good act, whatever its temporary aspect.

High or low, black or white, educated or uneducated, human beings are much alike when it comes to the real, vital things of their complex lives, and there are some notes in the grand scale to which every soul must respond.

Do I hear you say, "But what of the evils of ingratitude? Would not such indifference on the part of one incite to equal indifference on the part of the other?" Ah, my child, again I say you need not concern yourself with the results of any righteous act. You may safely leave such results with the giver of the gift you received in your hour of exaltation, for He hath other gifts in His power, and your expression of sympathy may prepare the recipient for the coming of the gift of Gratitude — the key which will unlock the fast-closed door of the heart that has been seared by the cruelty, the coldness and indifference of the world at large. You may joy in the gratitude of another, but you may not demand that gift as your right.

Not many, even among the most orthodox Christians, have ever fully interpreted that most occult saying of the Master Jesus — "Whosoever will give a cup of cold water in my name the same is my disciple."[1]

What the cup of cold water is to the dried, parched lips of the desert-worn traveler, such is the dew of sympathy and help to the lonely soul in the depths of suffering; and if it be given in the name — which means in the power of the Christ — there is also imparted the spiritual power, Endurance, the power to rise above and conquer the restricting elementals which have plunged that soul into those depths.

You are in the throes of a vast opportunity. A like baptism of Fire to that which descended upon the disciples of Jesus in the "upper chamber" is falling today on all people whose hearts are open to its flames.

The tongues of flame and the tongues which gave utterance during that fiery deluge to strange languages were of one and the same nature; both were tokens of the power of the Christ to impart knowledge of the strange new language of human brotherhood.

The man or woman in the depths of suffering is a Christ-given opportunity to all those who can hear the call of the sufferer; and may God have mercy on the human soul who perceives that call and refuses to respond to it, for there will be no mercy shown that one when the decrees of evolutionary law are uttered by the blind administrators of that law; and there will arise no pleader in the name — that is, in the power of the name — in the power of those tongues of flame — the power of the Christ, which was bestowed upon that one when God the Son recombined the God in man with man in God, in that moment or hour "in the depths."

It will be of no consequence whether you be a member of a church or any other organization, or a freelance among the unorganized, but it will be of much consequence whether or not you are able to hear the call of your Higher Self.

It may be made through my lips at the present moment, or through the lips of a child, a beggar, a woman of the street, or a prison-bound criminal at the next moment; but whenever or however it comes,

---

[1] See Matthew 10:42, Mark 9:41.

memory should bring back to you some measure of your own experience, and incite you to answer — and then to forget that you had answered, if you are inclined to expect an outer expression of appreciation.

You will find it difficult to hear that call if your inner ears are still sealed by the sense of separateness — the belief that separation between bodies extends to souls. Only the realization of the essential unity of all things, all people, will unseal the ears and eyes of the soul, and finally bring about the annihilation of suffering.

LESSON 137
PREPAREDNESS

February 1913

The criminal indifference or mental indolence of a large majority of the white race in view of their present defenseless position on the one hand, and their inane, inadequate plans for such defense as seems needful to them on the other hand, could only be sustained by a race blinded by egotism and self-adulation, and can only result in the destruction of the race as a race, when the hour strikes for the next cyclic upheaval of races (as strike it must in a comparatively short time), unless some worldwide awakening to the real facts in the case takes place and a united, determined effort is made to correct the mistakes that have resulted from the use of wrong educational methods. Those mistakes have been made in the face of prophecy, parable, warning, and entreaty sounded from pulpit, lecture platform, and in various literary productions from wherever and by whomever the light of wisdom has escaped; and today the thinking people stand aghast at the possibilities presenting themselves.

Spasmodic efforts put forth by first one and then another for the formation of a peace pact between nations will be fruitless of expected results, nor could such efforts ever succeed unless all interested factors combined could recognize and use the knowledge of spirits — spiritual and psychic forces which are at present only perceptible to a few.

At the apogee of a racial period, the divine impulse of cyclic law sets into action certain elemental forces which destroy those races which have not utilized their opportunities to the fullest, and finally uses the energy generated in the process of the destruction of one race for the building up of another race. Paradoxical as it seems, it requires a corresponding amount of life force to kill as it does to create.

The yellow and the brown races have retained possession of a divine power won by them in other ages and incarnations — the power of concentration. Not even their subsequent degradation and loss could rob them entirely of that power, and it is their consciousness of the possession and availability of that power that will furnish the dynamic force back of their plans of warfare in any struggle with a white race.

A large majority of the white race have either ignored, neglected, or despised the evidences of such a power as that possessed by the brown and yellow races and formerly by the red races when such evidence was forced on their notice, notwithstanding their knowledge of the resultant strength, endurance, contempt of physical pain, and even of life itself. One of the evidences of the possession of this power is national and racial devotion, and this devotion will supply the ideal needful as a base for the concentrated effort and the wise direction of the energy now being utilized in building up, equipping, and training their armies. Once utilized in subduing and governing natural desires and functions of life and in the performance of magic and psychic phenomena it has been turned in the opposite direction, we would ask what preparation has the white race made for meeting and combating such forces when launched against it with destructive intent?

It would be a very grave mistake for one to consider it incumbent upon or excusable in him or her to make an intimate connection with one of the opposite sex of an antagonistic race merely because it had been prophesied that similar connections were inevitable at some future time.

The great benefit to be derived from prophecy is the opportunity which previous knowledge of coming events affords man to equip himself with the requisites for meeting the rapid changes incidental to the coming of such events; changes which occur in ever-increasing ratio as time brings the event closer, and such changes inevitably affect the lives of those who are influenced by the shadowy outlines of the event — the men and women who see and feel intuitively that far-reaching incidents are occurring in some interior field of activity, yet who without special guidance or prophetical knowledge are unable to grasp the proportions of such incidents and seize their individual opportunities for conserving energies, enlarging perspective, and strengthening the power of endurance by persistently practicing concentration in the daily affairs of life, and realizing that any duty worth performance at all can be better performed if the mind is fixed immovably upon it for the time being.

The tremendous waste of energy in useless words, passion for amusement, loss of vital fluids, thirst for abnormal pursuits, and the resultant ennui and brain and nerve exhaustion is fast sapping the moral, mental, and physical inheritance which came to the present white race from a more vigorous ancestry, thus making impossible the concentration of will power and consecration of purpose which alone will furnish the vital energy requisite for the fulfilling of a great national purpose or the protection and conservation of a great race.

The egotism which results in accepting as an assured fact the common theory that a race must be white in color to be supreme in power is another prolific cause for the apathy of the white race now at the height of its power, while the truth is that the cyclic opportunity for the rapid rise of the yellow and brown races is close at hand, and nothing will prevent the eventual supremacy of these races for centuries to come but the amalgamation of the three races mentioned and the consequent birth and development of a new race, the long prophesied Sixth Race.

Such epochs as I have referred to in the history of men can only occur at the expiration of such vast periods of time that no reliable records are left in the hands of the people at large, although many legends and myths survive. The only authentic records of such epochs are in the hands of the Initiates and are preserved with such extreme care that the laity have no access to them.

At certain definite periods such knowledge as is requisite for the races in manifestation during said periods is given out by the Initiates who are appointed by the Hierophant of that Degree of the White Lodge which holds the records and which is the guiding power of that period. If the race will not accept and heed the information given, it must bear the results of its indifference or willfulness. A perfect stream of such knowledge and information has been poured out on the humanity of this age within the last half century. In isolated cases it is appreciated and utilized, but the worldwide enthusiasm and effort, the impulse, the wave of ardent endeavor which should rise and swell to such a height as to overwhelm the error, supineness and self-satisfaction of those to whom that knowledge has been given, have hardly started, and time is flying.

Life is a constant battle at the best and it makes incalculable difference what impulse and purpose nerves the ram, sharpens the battle axes, or propels the bullets. Symbolically and literally, the generalship, the marksmanship, the caliber of weapons and men and women will tell the final story and these are all dependent upon the forces of concentration and devotion inherent in a race — the two forces which the white race have not sufficiently developed up to the present moment. Where is the man who will speak the word or write the treatise that will lift the life wave of enthusiastic effort into motion?

LESSON 138
THE ETERNAL TRAGEDY

Year after year, century after century, cycle upon cycle passes without any appreciable change, so far as may be observed, in the character, the desires, and aims of the masses of the human race. What wonder at the revolt of the individual man or woman who has been partially awakened from thrall to things — to imaginary national, social, and family requirements — when those requirements are seen to be but the results of the prostitution of all the higher instincts and ideals of those who have passed this way before, or those who are now in the toils of the same slave drivers — lusts of the flesh — which originally incited to such prostitution!

I say truly the prostitution of all higher instincts and high ideals, for wherein does the difference lie between the courtesan who uses her body for the gaining of gold, and the man or woman who uses brain and soul for a like purpose, when the proceeds of their shame is used for self-gratification?

Round after round of the grand cycle, as in a treadmill, goes race after race under similar conditions, similar aims, impelled to similar efforts; and the one man, the one woman, who steps out from among the masses and points to the manna falling from heaven for the feeding of the soul, is torn to pieces by the beast-like passions of man, or crucified on the cross he or she has innocently raised to indicate the way to the storehouse where the manna of other ages still lies stored.

The deep-lined faces of men, the paint-smeared, hardened features of women, who are now, figuratively speaking, dancing along the edge of the precipice built of the broken laws of nature, or crouching under overhanging cliffs — man-made laws — which have made possible such security as has conduced to the gathering of golden store; and both of them sick at heart with fear, or callous and indifferent to the prophecies of enforced payment of debts contracted in defiance of all spiritual law — is it any wonder that men and women go mad in their helpless, aimless revolt at their bondage, or sink into abject, cowardly indifference? "Lo, here, and lo, there,"[1] cry the would-be prophets, themselves powerless to find the safe path for their own feet to traverse, to say nothing of rightly guiding others; and always, in the far distant past as in the present, from the heaven within, a voice is crying, "Seek ye within." "Seek first the kingdom of God and all things thou desirest shall be given unto thee."[2] And man says, "No, the last shall be first; give me now the things I desire — then will I seek within." He knows not what he really desires; he only knows what his senses demand for the privilege of using that body for a season. What he, the real man, or she, the real woman, desires above all else is God, and nothing less will satisfy. But a man must go naked of soul, as he was naked of body when entering the world, into that "within." He can take none of the trappings of lust, of ambition, or greed with him, and as he will not part with these, the eternal tragedy is reenacted moment after moment.

When one who has passed within the gate and caught a glimpse of the glory beyond tries to tell his fellow men what he has seen, his tongue is completely tied. All that he can do is point to the path by which he entered; and because that path is beset by wild beasts which have bitten, and mauled, and trampled him, when he shows the scars of his passage, the eyes of other men, of other women are so fixed upon those scars they fail to see the light of Shekhinah[3] shining through his eyes; and so they cry: "Away with him, we will have none of him. Crucify him; let him starve or die; he is a fraud, a lie, fit only for the subject of a cartoon, an object of scorn." The light dies out of his eyes, drenched in sorrow for those he cannot serve, even though he gave his life, because their eyes are holden by the things they have gathered about them, things of matter and things of mind, both results of their prostitution.

The last part of the path to the heights of life is cold and dark and lonely, and the senses cry out for warmth and light and company. But

---

[1] Luke 17:21.
[2] Matthew 6:33.
[3] *Shekhinah* (*Hebrew*, "dwelling") — the presence of God; the veil of the Absolute.

the coldness, the darkness, and the loneliness are essential for the freezing of lower desire, the gestation of the embryo of the new life, the perception that God is all there is of life. Possessing God, the soul possesses all things desirable.

There are moments in all mature lives when that great truth comes home to the heart in unmistakable terms, but the things for which man sells his soul smother the heart's longing, and not knowing what else to do, the great majority go on collecting more things, to the end of the great tragedy.

LESSON 139
COSMIC CONSCIOUSNESS

The one all-important subject that is exercising the minds of the deepest thinkers along religious lines, in this age, is that of the long-prophesied return in the comparatively near future of the Master and Avatar formerly known as Jesus of Nazareth. The method of His reappearance, the proof of His identity, the purpose of His coming, the possibility of recognition, and even His personal presence on earth at this time, all these and countless minor details are discussed widely, and in almost all instances from such erroneous points of view as to render the one who must perforce listen to them in silence while knowing that he has correct data to base certainties upon, all but desperately anxious to give voice to the premises which might lead his listeners to more correct conclusions.

But such a one is so handicapped in that respect by his knowledge of the action of a certain irrevocable spiritual law that any effort he might make to impart that knowledge to the unprepared would prove futile. And it is ignorance of this law, or defiance of the karma which will be the inevitable result of willful disobedience to its mandates, that is primarily responsible for the ease with which countless numbers of both deceivers and deceived are bringing the subject of the return of the Avatar into disrepute and even into the fields of caricature.

The words "Cosmic consciousness" have been coined to express a state of spiritual uplift which the soul of man may enter under certain conditions of development and where all knowledge is attainable. In an effort to describe the indescribable in a few words we might say, it is a state of being in which the consciousness of the individual is merged in the consciousness of every living thing and being, and all sense of separateness is temporarily lost, while at the same time the sense of individuality remains. But no normal human being of the present races of the earth could remain in bondage to form and continue to function in that state of exaltation for any length of time; consequently, when one attains to the state of spiritual consciousness referred to, the experience is instantaneous. Such an experience cannot be measured in terms of time; were it otherwise, the rapid vibrations of that spiritual state would disintegrate his gross body. Therefore, when one claims to have attained to a permanent state of "cosmic consciousness," he is either stating a deliberate falsehood or is self-deceived as to the nature of the phenomena undergone. Whatever degree of knowledge and power he had attained to during that experience, if it were *bona fide*,[1] would be transferred by reflection to his brain consciousness, and if the memory cells of that brain were well developed they would record and retain the memory of the experience; but if by any chance his power was limited by the possession of undeveloped or degenerate memory cells, by overweening personal ambition, or by desire to use the knowledge so gained for his personal advantage, and he should forget, ignore, or repudiate one particular detail of the knowledge gained in such an experience — a detail of infinite importance — and so should absolutely contribute to the misuse or abuse of that knowledge, he would plunge headlong into the Left-Hand Path — the downward path of life. That particular detail of knowledge is the individual certainty which comes during such an experience of the unity of all life, and consequently, the necessity for the entire subjection of his personal will and desire if he is to take advantage of the knowledge gained.

He could never again say in truth, "I am," "I can," or "I will" from the personal standpoint. He could never again stand forth as an object for personal aggrandizement. He could never again lay claim to any personal thing or creature. Much less could he go out among men and like a braggart make claim to his possession of "cosmic consciousness." Even the Great Master had to die to and in the world, before He was "lifted up," i.e., before He attained to permanent all-spiritual consciousness.

If it be true that a man has been so "lifted up," and has retained the knowledge of his unity with all that lives, his associates will come to some understanding of that great reality as a result of the influences

[1] Genuine, real.

386 THE TEMPLE OF MYSTERIES

set free by his acts and words, as well as his magneto-spiritual emanations. They will never learn it from his lips; for if it be indeed true that he has safely passed that supreme test of the disciple, even the thought of separate interests, of personal deification would be of the nature of torture to him.

Every Avatar, every Savior of humanity has successfully passed that test ere finally reaching Nirvana.

Knowing these facts, there will be no excuse for you if you permit yourselves to be led astray into worship of "false gods" by self-advertised "Avatars"; and happy indeed are you if, knowing these facts previous to such an experience as I have mentioned, you use such knowledge to fortify your personal consciousness of the truth of Unity when it shall be revealed to you by experience; for in such case your memory cells would be greatly strengthened, and you would not be in so much danger of forgetting, denying, or repudiating that which would appear to lessen your personal importance.

LESSON 140
THE NEUTRAL CENTER

The evident attraction between people of totally different character and station is a puzzle to those who do not accept the ancient teachings regarding the action of the law of opposites.

To the great surprise of acquaintances, some pure and innocent girl will find a point of attraction in some notorious libertine, or a clean-minded, intelligent young man will be caught in the snare set by a vicious, depraved woman, and his life be jeopardized or ruined. The world at large looks on and wonders, oblivious of the fact that there is a direct current of force operating between the qualities we term virtue and vice which if left unbroken in the case of any two individuals caught in that current must inevitably draw the psychic desires of both to a common center, and a bond be there created which it is well-nigh impossible to break until satiation has driven the two bodies apart.

When that current is consciously broken by an individual, it is done by virtue of an awakened conscience, and such an awakening comes at a definite time in a life cycle, and always at the lowest point of the particular spiral round of evolution which is typified in biblical lore by the return of the Prodigal Son[1] to a normal state of mind. It is at such a period of satiation, of self-analysis, that the victim of the current of attraction determines to "arise and go to his Father,"[2] and ask to be made a servant, instead of demanding his forfeited right of sonship; in other words, when the personal will becomes subservient to the Divine Will.

But there is in fact the possibility of a prodigal at the pole of virtue as well as a prodigal at the pole of vice, prodigals of natural law. Prodigality of virtue may result in as many complications as prodigality of vice, and the results of the former serve to create the environment in which the prodigal men and women will find their mental and psychic habitat during the days or years of their penitence, the habitat created by the judges and executioners of the moral and psychical laws which have been broken.

One of these poles is typified by the elder son of the parable of the prodigal son, the other by the younger son. In either case when the point of satiation, the point of self-analysis is reached, a new departure must be made, a new step taken, and that step must be in the direction of renunciation and submission to the Divine Will, regardless of the effects on the personality if the power of attraction is to be broken and the pilgrim is to be freed from oscillation between the two poles to which he has been subjected; otherwise there will merely be a change in position and circumstances in a succeeding incarnation, instead of such a general rise in the cosmic scale of life, as there well might be if both elder and younger sons — prodigals both — seized their opportunities at the appointed time when the law of evolution had made such action possible, and so had broken the current, first set up by unfulfilled desire.

The recognized action of the force of attraction between virtue and vice has been attributed to the curiosity of those involved, to abnormality, to fear, to almost everything but that which it truly is in essence; namely, one of nature's means of testing the caliber, the soul development, the possibilities, of the evolving soul, whether it be a human or an animal soul, in order that it may be rightly placed in the grand scale of life; and the force used by nature is as material as is the force of animal magnetism, and its operations are fulfilled by the divine law of opposites.

---

[1] See Luke 15:11–32.

[2] Luke 15:18.

Its poles are positive and negative, masculine and feminine, and at the point where the before-mentioned current is broken, the neutral center of the force manifests, and equilibrium is set up.

The force of human magnetism is set in action between two people of opposite tendencies and characteristics as soon as they come together in any close relation on the physical plane, and it depends altogether upon whether one or the other or both have reached the point of equilibrium which corresponds to a neutral center, as to whether the lower degrees of the force of magnetic attraction can be broken, and one escape from the power of the other. If both are equally well developed when they meet, they will become subject to higher degrees of the force of magnetism, which operate on a higher plane of life, and so will transfer their desires to other fields of endeavor, as for instance may be done by transferring desire from the physical to the mental, or from the mental to the higher astral planes. An increase of effort would naturally follow such transfer, but the nature of the difficulties to be overcome and the limitations to be conquered would be changed, an increase in power and vitality be won, and final victory be proportionately greater.

LESSON 141
COSMIC PICTURES

Were your eyes opened to the astral records — the cosmic picture gallery — at all times, you would find but few among those records wrought by the action of natural law which would fill you with more regret and even horror than those which outline the final results — the finished product — of your acceptance of the cruel, false, or misleading tales which have been brought to your ears by some self-interested or evil-minded slanderer.

The poison which enters your magnetic sphere from the lips of such a one works so subtly and quietly that you are not aware of its presence, even when the act which it incites has been performed, and it does not enter your mind that you are passing on that poison to all whom you contact with every wave of magnetic force radiated from your bodies, even when no word escapes your lips.

The substance of that sphere is so receptive, sensitive, impressionable, and interpenetrating that any sound directed by will disturbs its equilibrium and permits the force expelled by sound, whether it be good or evil, to enter and find emplacement. If that force be evil, it quickens the area affected and creates a condition analogous to that created by the entrance of a poisonous thorn into the body; this condition reacts on the physical body if it be weak, and in all cases it reacts on the Mayavic body[1] in a similar manner. If the force be good, it does exactly the reverse; it quiets some over-active center and permits the entrance of a vital form of energy from a higher state of substance, which impels toward growth.

When you think over some of the outer results of the cruel misuse of the power expelled in words: the broken lives, the blasted characters, suicides, wars, murders, and other crimes in evidence on the plane of gross matter which may be observed in a single lifetime, and then think of the accumulated aftereffects of the same as they go on gathering force and volume in the passing centuries, and realize that no act of man is finished, whether it be good or evil, till the close of the age of manifestation he has entered upon, and know that every act is registered in the astral light, you can gain some idea of the value of the truths with which I opened this message.

However conscientious, no man ever repeated a tale exactly as he heard it. No man ever related the details of an event exactly as it occurred, for in every instance forgotten details are omitted, or shades of expression occur which convey extravagant or contrary ideas to those intended by the narrator, and all lead to false impressions in the mind of the listener, and therefore to doubly false impressions when again repeated.

When a selfish purpose is to be served or an injury intended, there is no end to the possible evil results.

The first lesson impressed upon the mind of a personal chela of an Initiate is the necessity for cultivating habits of silence, and it is by no means alone for the purpose of securing better conditions for the development of the inner senses that this lesson is so strenuously inculcated. It is primarily for the purpose of teaching him to control

---

[1] *Mayavic body* (*Sanskrit,* "illusory body") — a type of the astral body created by the power of thought and therefore also called "thought body." It should not be confused with the Linga Sharira, or the etheric double, because the latter is a real entity, while the "thought body" is a temporary illusion created by the mind. Unlike the etheric double, the mayavic body cannot be hurt by any sharp object or weapon and can pass everywhere without let or hindrance. During life, this body is the vehicle both of thought and of the animal passions and desires.

not only his own speech but that he should be able to limit the speech of others by refusing to admit to his magnetic sphere the invidious forces let loose by sound and winged by evil thought, thereby discouraging unnecessary speech.

One who lives in the silence learns to love his fellow men and to understand them so thoroughly that he will not willingly dwell upon the transitory effect of any mistakes they have made, for the reason that he knows the good of which they are capable is so much more potent than the evil that the latter may be easily counter-balanced under the right training. He knows that the forces of suspicion, harsh criticism, and condemnation directed by himself and absorbed by the sensitive magnetic sphere of another, will accentuate the evil and thus make the struggle between good and evil so much the more difficult for that other — and that he himself must suffer from the reaction of the same forces he has generated and sent forth. So, it is first of all a matter of self-protection that he should cultivate the habit of silence.

LESSON 142
THE INDIVIDUAL SOUL

Much is being said in these latter days, especially in theosophical circles, in regard to the individualization of the soul — the breaking away from the group soul of an individualized soul. If we have seemed to take issue regarding this theory, it is not in a spirit of controversy but simply to call attention to one simple fact which can be verified in all fields of life. Every true grouping of lives is a distinct family, no matter how minute or how extensive. If any other exterior life is added to any one of these natural groups by circumstance or condition, it is an alien and must always remain such, no matter how intimate its association with the original members of the group.

There are groups within groups, from the individualized groups of a solar system to the divisions of an amoeba, but always the groups are distinct, always do they have marked peculiarities. The cells which, when united, form the heart of a human being could no more be individualized in some other organ or part of an organ than a man could change his identity by denying relationship to the mother who bore him. Such a man may marry, beget children, and so form a new family group, but that does not alter his relationship to his own mother, therefore, cannot alter his identification with the original family group; his marriage simply serves to form a lesser group in another larger group, and as spiritual descent always comes through the mother, his children belong to the group soul to which his wife belongs. The greater his intelligence the more has he absorbed the infinite intelligence which was the heritage of the original group from which he has descended through all the past ages, even from the time of the first sevenfold division of the manifested cosmos. His identity and, therefore, his individualization was established with the first explosion of the seed of life which made room for the ensouling monad.

Although every cell of every heart that beats in all the kingdoms of nature contains potentially the form and essence of every other organ and form in the universe, no one of these cells can change its form and nature in one Manvantara. In the course of time they will all be brought into close contact with the cells of other organs and beget a third form of life. Those third forms will be the connecting lines between the family of heart cells and the family cells of another organ through which the racial impulses of each family will be transferred to the other and so help on the evolution of both.

When the different states of substance which will form the cells of all the organs of sense and volition in all kingdoms of nature have been brought into harmonious relation by interaction, then may they be ensouled in a definite form as has been done in the prototypes of all the forms of life in manifestation. These prototypes were individualized entities, for with form always comes identity. However, we think there is to be a distinction made between conscious and unconscious individualization. Such difference of opinion as exists between us and others on this subject is probably more in the seeming than in reality. To our mind, conscious individualization comes with the dawning of intuition. If contact with other races of humanity plays any part in it, it must be a secondary part, and we fail to see how it could in any way affect the relation of the individual soul to the group soul of which it is a part. Permanent identification with the Infinite can only be a realization of one's true relation to every other emanation of the Infinite, and with such realization, a final loss of what we now term personal identity in the identity of the all.

If we were able to trace back our lineage through each family group of the great group soul of which we are parts, and could thus trace our relationship to all the members of the one greater family — the Humanity of the present age — it would do much to strengthen the ties between us as well as to explain the antagonism we sometimes feel toward others when there seems to be no outer cause.

We speak of the Ego, the Monad, the Sons of Will and Yoga, and all the other differentiations of the higher realms of thought and being, but they may all be summed up in the two words Identity and Intelligence — the "I am" — of the Divine Soul, the knowledge that "I," as an individual, conscious, intelligent being, am alive and am evolving according to a definite Divine prototype — a greater "I am." The group soul itself must evolve as well as the atoms of the group. As any one part of a group is developed, the whole group is evolved to a corresponding degree.

LESSON 143
UNITY

It is a well-known fact that the higher, the more compact and concentrated the molecules of matter, the nearer they approach the point of unity and lose the power of differentiation into individual forms, the more rapidly will the characteristics of age and dissolution develop. Whatever the physiological causes deduced from investigation — and be it noted these causes as given out by the authorities of different schools and in different ages periodically change their character — the real cause lies outside the realm of physical matter.

As all life is a unit, the nearer the approach to the original state of cosmic ideation in which differentiation is impossible, the more rapid is the dissolution which permits the release of the thought form which has been held in bondage by the laws governing force and substance and the consequent recombining of the thought sparks which constituted those thought forms into more concentrated forms. You have probably watched the recombining of the separated particles of quicksilver. The force of attraction which draws these particles together in a single mass is the same force which draws together the differentiated thought sparks the instant the separative force — the force of disintegration resident in substance of lower vibration — is overcome. Therefore, all the efforts of those dreamers who are industriously seeking for the elixir of life on the physical plane where nothing is stable are bound to be fruitless.

The same spiritual force which originally gave form to thought, and impelled that form to furnish a matrix for protoplasmic substance to embody, is the real elixir of life as far as life in objective form is concerned.

If very long life were desirable for man, if his evolution did not now demand far longer periods of rest and assimilation between lives than continuous life in matter could possibly secure for him, man would long since have found what he has been so long seeking the power to extend his life indefinitely. But as long as the life of man is bound up in the gratification of his illusive senses and he is unable to grasp the reality of individual consciousness in unity, his natural term of life cannot much exceed that of the people of the present races of the earth. Man lived to a great age in prehistoric times for the reason that there was far more differentiation of substance and force, mentally and physically, than at present. As the interests, purposes, and ideals of man approach each other and coalesce, the tides of religious, social, industrial, and political life run closer together. As families grow smaller in number, keener of intellect, and less spiritual, an era of dissolution sets in. Nature then selects from the best material at hand the matrix of a new race, and the old one dies off or is destroyed in some great catastrophe.

The fact that the deepest thinkers, the more intelligent investigators in all fields of science are practically united now on the great truth of the unity of all life is one of the signs of the times. Investigation into the field of physics is bringing to light many of the long-lost connecting links between the different orders of life, but so long as consciousness and individuality are denied to the lesser forms of life by the delvers into this science, and Soul escapes their observation, they will continue to work almost blindly.

The fact of the possible transmutation of one substance into another can no longer be denied by the said investigators, but the conscious lives which effect such transmutation — the intermediate lives — remain unthinkable to them.

The tremendous energy stored up in and radiating from light in terms of color can now be appreciated to some extent, but the elementals in form which live, change form, and die to live again in every flash of color are unrecognizable by the physical senses.

The true occultist not only knows all these wonderful facts, he is able to use them to his own advantage and to the advantage of the world at large. But he labors at a tremendous disadvantage when trying to prove or impart his knowledge to those who refuse to accept it or are incapable of fitting themselves for its possession. When they are told that sacrifice is the first key to the possession of such knowledge, they begin to seek for some personal cause for the suggestion in the mind of the one who has given them the knowledge of that key. If they are told that personal purity is a requisite, they begin to search for some way of minimizing the necessary degree or finding some method of indulgence which will modify the severity of the demand and still permit them to retain their standing. If they are shown their duty toward those who are pointing the way, they lose no time in trying to see how far they can go in an opposite direction without jeopardizing their chances of success, or in finding some excuse of a personal nature which will justify their recreancy. They cannot accept the simple statements made to them and act upon them. Yet, there never has been but one way to the attainment of spiritual power, and there never will be but one way.

There are certain physiological changes essential; there are certain qualities, characteristics, mental and moral, which are equally necessary; there are certain spiritual qualifications utterly indispensable, all of which the disciple must gain by personal effort, and they can only be gained by obedience to the laws which govern each one of the aforesaid essentials.

LESSON 144
ONLY ONE WILL

At first thought you may feel inclined to refuse to accept the dogmatic statement that there is no such quality or attribute as the human will. But if the unity of all life is something more than a theory or a hypothetical concept to you, it is possible you will accept that statement and apply it in your search for foundation stones upon which to rest your structure of unified life.

There is but one Will. It would be impossible for two or more wills to exist or manifest in a universe of law and order; one will would invariably clash with the other by virtue of the very nature of the attribute of Will. Will is direction, first of all. The universe, as well as every manifested atom of the same, moves in circular or rather in spiral lines to accomplish the "cycle of necessity." Any line of life may end or begin, comparatively speaking, in a straight direction, but it soon curves and the curve necessitates a circuitous route thereafter.

The degree of the arc of the circle depends upon the directing power of Will and the degree of force put forth by the specific action of the Desire principle behind the Will.

The equilibrium of a universe could not be maintained if a secondary and therefore a negative, an opposing will could interfere with the direction of the mass as given by the primal impulse. The same power which precipitated and directed a line of force must determine the time, place, and degree of curve. "Thus far and no farther," said the divine Creator in determining the course of the waters of the universe, and the same Creator declared, "My line has gone forth over all the earth" — note *My* line, not the line of any other entity. When the limit of a line of life is reached, the same directing force which sent it forth must carry it back to its starting point, plus the value of the experience gained on its travels. The experience has determined the degree of curve for the next life line — the next incarnation of the Ego.

So much for the philosophy of my statement that there is but one Will. The Will which moves the atom of self-development is the same Will which moves — directs — the man. Man of himself cannot create the will to move a hand or draw a breath; but because of his fundamental unity with Deity, he may direct and so may use the divine creative Will of Deity to whatever degree he has cultivated the channel of that Will in himself and discovered and fallen in line with the primal purpose of Deity. Wherever he fails in any undertaking, that failure is due to the degree of difference or distance between his lower — his material — self and his Ego, for the Ego is the Deity in him, "unity in diversity." Therefore, his success will be according to the extent of his recognition of Deity and his submission to the directing power which is curving the straight line of his life in order to bring back the auric sphere of energy — the envelope of the Ego — to its original starting point, that it may be sent out with increased power for a wider sweep — a greater life, in other words, a more useful life.

When the recognition of the above-mentioned facts comes to man and he realizes that he is using the very essence of Deity to accomplish every act of will, no matter how insignificant the act may seem to be at the moment, if he is a normal human being, the magnitude, the divine beauty, and holiness of his mission on earth will fill him with awe and fix his purpose to work with instead of against the law of his being. His acts are performed as a result of higher motives; a set purpose dominates him; his relationship to every living thing is established; and life furnishes far wider ideals for him to work toward than those previously encountered and partially or wholly realized. His previous egotistic concepts of his individual importance will gradually disappear as his consciousness of the importance of every phase of life becomes more vivid. It will no longer be *I* but *We* in rehearsing deeds with which he has been concerned.

The greater the opposition offered by nature or man to a divinely inspired purpose, the stronger and more repeated will be his efforts toward accomplishment of the purpose, consequently, the more invincible his power of Will. In other words, the wider will be the channel through which the deific Will may flow. The words "Thy Will be done" do not mean to invite cowardly submission to circumstances and conditions. They should voice the cry of the soul for perception of the nature of divine Will and for strength to use that Will aright. Disuse of function results in disintegration and death in all fields of life, and no exception is made in the case of the operation of Will. But consciously to use that divine energy of Will in an effort to thwart divine law or to crush, maim, or destroy another soul or body for the sake of carrying out some selfish purpose is the unforgivable sin — unforgivable because the inevitable reaction caused by the negative aspect of the power which has built his vehicle will destroy the vehicle through which it operates.

Strive with your whole heart, with mind emptied of every previously absorbed idea, for the realization of all I have tried to impart to you. Realize that self-responsibility really means responsibility in varying degrees for every thing and person you contact and that you can no more avoid that responsibility and live truly than you can live on the physical plane without breath. With the awakening of self-responsibility comes the widening of the channel of Divine Will and the power to use the stream.

LESSON 145
STIMULANTS AND NARCOTICS

During one of my first interviews with the Guardian-in-Chief and Official Head, I told them that they could enter into no form of business life which would afford them more opportunity for direct contact with those who, of all people, most required their service, namely, those who were addicted to the excessive use of stimulants and narcotics.

I wish particularly to bring to your mind the fact that the prohibition of intoxicants and narcotics, enforced upon their disciples by the Initiates of the White Lodge, is a vital necessity; but the main reasons for such prohibition have not been given to any body of disciples belonging to lesser degrees of the Lodge until now. This is due to the almost inevitable misconstruction placed upon our endorsement of one fact, a fact which might injuriously modify the minds of those who seek for license or indulgence and who, in all too many instances in past eras, have believed they found such license in esoteric teaching of one particular kind.

It has always been a mystery to extremists why so many gifted people of both sexes indulged in narcotics and intoxicants for the purpose of doing their best and highest work, and said extremists could not reconcile that fact with the well-known teachings of prohibition given by the Initiates of the White Lodge and with many other religious, scientific, and ethical teachings on this subject. When I tell you that the highest as well as the lowest planes of life are contacted by those addicted to the use of the said narcotics and stimulants and that much of the very highest teachings anent art and religion ever given to the world were received under such stimulation, you must be careful how you reject or erroneously criticize my words.

It is a well-established fact that the pineal gland and pituitary body[1] are vehicles for the transmission of the highest spiritual forces. Anything which will stimulate the molecules of those vehicles to a more rapid vibratory action will open an interior plane to the psychic senses, whether the primary cause is due to high spiritual aspiration and love of humanity or to a strong impulse to escape from restrictions of matter or the inescapable sorrow and anguish of body and mind from which humanity suffers; therefore, that is the thing sought for most diligently by the normal human being. If the answer to prayer, consecration, and endeavor does not come as quickly as seems desirable to the naturally sensitive, highly developed man with a tightly strung nervous system, he is very apt to demand some other method of obtaining his desire. In other instances environment, association,

---

[1] *Pituitary body* or *pituitary gland* — a pea-sized gland located at the base of the brain that produces and releases essential hormones that regulate various bodily functions and control other endocrine glands.

etc., lead people into indulgence which, unfortunately, temporarily opens the door to some inner plane — in other words, increases the vibratory action of the pineal gland, and this increase in turn produces certain changes in the organs of sense which lead to grosser forms of sensation.

But be it remembered, the fundamental purpose in all instances is the same, i.e., higher — more rapid — vibration of the molecules of the pineal gland and pituitary body. However, the final effects are diametrically opposite. In the first instance prayer, consecration, and good works lead to the normal development of the said gland and body and to a vibratory action which may be indefinitely maintained and eventually lead to contact with higher and higher planes of action, until finally the at-one-ment between mind and spirit is realized; while in the last-mentioned instances, the said bodies are not sufficiently developed, physically speaking, to stand the pressure of those more rapid vibrations for any long period of time, and they break down, leaving only the possibility of contacting the lowest planes of being, until death ends the struggle on the physical plane. It is this condition which is primarily responsible for delirium, for with the breaking down of the physical envelopes of the said gland and body, the mysterious nervous organism of the whole body deteriorates and finally incapacitates all the organic structure. It is then subject to the control of low elementals.

If it were fully understood and accepted that narcotics and stimulants did, in reality, open the higher realms of wisdom and knowledge to the hungering soul, even the knowledge that it was done only temporarily and must inevitably lead to degeneration and decay, would not deter the weak-minded or vicious man or woman from such indulgence. Consequently, this deep mystery is held as one of the secrets of occultism.

You have doubtless heard or read that in the performance of the mistakenly believed "sacred" mysteries in past ages, and even in the present age, the use of strong narcotics and stimulants was common. The black magicians of past ages knew, and the present ones know full well, what the final results must be to the victims of their avarice and cunning; but as their purpose was the destruction of the higher attributes in man and the cultivation of the sensuous and lewd, they kept such knowledge from their neophytes and urged them on to all forms of indulgence and sensuality until finally nothing was or is left to the White Brotherhood but to withdraw and permit the destruction of all life on the planet, save the remnants left for the seed of a new race.

Knowing these things, it surely cannot be difficult for you to understand what a high, holy calling it is for any man to block the efforts of the Black Brotherhood by healing the diseases engendered by such means before the destruction of those all-important vehicles of transmission, the pineal gland and pituitary body, is complete, and the soul irretrievably lost.

But the so-called prohibition movement[1] of the present era can do naught but palliate the effects of the causes set up in the bodies and souls of those whom it would save. In all too many instances, the advocates of this measure only increase the danger, for they arouse the natural spirit of rebellion against enforced authority. The will that is striving to free itself from bondage to matter rebels against all things which tend to coerce it into further bondage, whether the nature of the bonds be good or evil; so enforced control tends to drive the victim into greater indulgence just to prove his power to defy control by pressure. Such a movement does not go deep enough. It works on the surface, while the disease it tries to conquer is too deep seated for it to touch and heal, save in such cases as those in which the higher aspirations have been awakened and, as a result, the vibratory action decreased to some degree.

The human will has then become subservient to the divine will, but the real causes for such apparent effects are unknown and unsuspected by the majority of workers in that field. They do not realize that a point of decay in the molecules of the physical envelopes of the aforementioned gland and body must be reached and seared over by the action of one of the "sacred fires" if the victim of indulgence is to be saved. This may be done by the fiery elementals confined in some medicinal formula, or by a higher grade of elementals subservient alone to the demands of the divine will, as is the case in those instances where the cure — the searing — is accomplished by the fires of high aspiration, prayer, and effort. The mystery involved, the lack of understanding and right teaching, and the inability of the masses to correlate the physical with the spiritual and astral aspects and forms of life are responsible to a great degree for man's inability

---

[1] Prohibition was a major reform movement in the United States from the 1870s until the 1920s, when nationwide prohibition of alcohol went into effect.

to deal sanely with this very important phase of the problem which confronts humanity at this time.

If such a movement became strong enough to carry out its principles by force or by national control, there would inevitably occur such a reaction as would sweep all accomplished reforms away, and far worse conditions would result than those which now obtain. It takes poor, self-indulgent, violent, unrestful human nature a long, weary time to learn the deep truth that "true growth is slow growth." A bud may open in a night, but it has taken many nights and days for the plant to reach the point of putting forth its bud, and even then the bud may be blasted by any forced action. When it opens naturally, it is due to the inherent desire of the whole plant to catch the fructifying light of the sun that it may bring forth fruit. And a like desire must be aroused in the masses of mankind to save them from the effects of evil in any form.

Another phase of the same problem is responsible for much of the contradiction and antagonism aroused by any extremist who endeavors to inject his personal experiences into a discussion of this problem. Unfortunately, it is a phase which must be ignored to a great degree, for the same reason that renders it inexpedient to discuss some phases of sex, i.e., misunderstanding.

The elements of time, bodily infirmities, genealogical karmic effects, racial tendencies — all these must be taken into consideration, and if so taken, will modify opinions and set up vibrations which may change the present opinions and conditions while they in no wise change the causes which primarily induced man to yield to his desire and which will continue to do so.

The same effects may be produced by under-stimulation that are produced by over-stimulation, i.e., molecular disintegration and final death of body in those cases where genealogical and karmic effects are manifesting and racial or family tendencies have been set up which must be worked out before the soul is freed from their first causes. You have doubtless witnessed cases where an entire and sudden change has taken place in an inebriate which neither he nor others can account for in any rational way. This effect is generally the result of the release of full karmic indebtedness in one particular line, and with the payment of the debt, the searing process referred to has taken place as a result of some action by the Higher Self. If such a one had been forced into an undesired reform of habit, he would inevitably return to former ways as soon as the temporary restrictions were removed. This is one of the instances where time enters as a large factor.

In other instances, where not sufficient stimulant is chemically provided for keeping the organs of the body in natural action, the proportion required is constantly demanded by those organs, and if supplied in any measure, there is no particular desire for excess manifested. Any change in the molecular construction of the pineal and pituitary bodies is checked in such instances, and if the one so using stimulants does not die from other causes before a definite period of his life cycle, there will occur a change which will do away with need for stimulants.

Then there are still other instances. I refer to those who have fully developed those bodies of transmission in the brain beyond need or beyond power of being affected injuriously. They can take a stimulant or leave it alone as they choose. They generally choose to leave it alone, for the sake of others.

If you are able to see the points I have made in their entirety, you will be better able to form an unbiased judgment on the whole subject of stimulation. It is the world old subject of extremes, and extremes in either direction lead to disintegration and death.

LESSON 146
SOUL MEMORY

What words of mine could picture the hell into which a human soul may be plunged at the moment of awakening to consciousness of soul memory: the moment when the soul faces the recorded results of its own past weaknesses, treachery, and unfaithfulness in the guise of a slain wife, husband, child, or friend — yes, even of a tribe or a nation plunged into ignorance and despair, and awakens at the same time to the knowledge that it will never be released from the anguish of those memories until in the course of ages it has paid its debt to the uttermost and redeemed itself? Redeemed itself not by undoing, for no act of man can be undone, but by overcoming every weakness and evil characteristic that has been responsible for the crime, the woe, and suffering depicted on the rolling waves of soul memory.

The Mosaic law — an eye for an eye, a life for a life — was founded on the universal law of Karma. While from the average human standpoint it is a cruel law, it is in fact a most merciful law, for by the action of its decrees alone is redemption possible.

You have been caught in the waves of soul memory in the dying hours of each one of your many lives as a human being and have acknowledged the justice of the punishment received or to follow in the succeeding life, but as yet you have not retained the memory of the records so made, for in the formation of new brain cells the memory of those records has been temporarily submerged.

However, there will come a time — a life — when, with the development of a new sense, those records will stand forth clearly revealed before your inner eye, and it is the anguish that must inevitably follow such experience that the Initiates of the White Lodge would spare you, would you but make it possible.

The dying eyes of parent, child, or friend whom you have unwittingly slain, have held many an accusation, all unnoted by you. You have never intended to do murder, but by your unfaithfulness, your treachery toward them or others dear to them, to your own Higher Self, and to the White Lodge you have ignorantly or willfully set in action the laws of accusation and reprisal, and the impersonal elemental forces — the instruments by which the decrees of Karmic law are carried out — have struck at you or those people or things which were dearest to you. If the latter were incapable of turning these forces aside, the natural results have followed. You have thus become closely identified with the karma of those sufferers from your acts, whether consciously or unconsciously performed, and must pay the debts so contracted in your present life or in your next one.

You often cry out at the seeming injustice of some affliction that has fallen upon you, as in the loss of some dear one, when if some page of your soul memory were open to your vision, you would see that your loss was justified.

It is from the results of such karmic action for wrongs inflicted by man against man that the whole world suffers today, and despite the knowledge of that fact the average human being continues in the same course of conduct. Warning, entreaty, punishment do not suffice to prevent him from continuing to pile up such karma whenever and wherever his personal desires or idiosyncrasies are concerned; and when such is the case with accepted disciples of the Lodge, the karmic blows fall thicker and faster, but it must not be forgotten they are blows of divine compassion.

The satisfaction derived from the gratification of personal will and desire is infinitesimal by comparison with the remorse and sorrow which will follow when soul memory has flashed a completed scene of the results of such selfish gratification as I have mentioned.

The grandeur, the beauty, the holiness of Truth, of Compassion, of Loyalty will be revealed to the seer in such an hour. Both sides of the Warrior's shield become visible at once when the eye of the soul is unsealed and the pictures imprinted upon that shield spring into view. Until man can learn to be true to his Higher Self, true to his plighted words, true to the obligations he is under to the sacrificial victims of his past weaknesses and wrong doing, his cruelty and cowardice, he can make no great advance on the ladder of life, no matter what else he may do on other lines to effect such advance, for the foundation stone underneath that ladder is Loyalty and without Loyalty life has no meaning.

When consciousness awakens to the futility of all else without that one possession, the disciple may take his first step up that ladder, the ladder which leads to final at-one-ment, and so win the right to the title of Warrior of Light.

LESSON 147
THOUGHT TRANSFERENCE

Thought transference — soundless inter-communication between two or more persons — is a well-established fact. The power to so transfer thought is believed to be attainable without particular effort by the majority of mankind. Many students of psychology have delved as deeply into the illusive regions of mind as it was possible for them to go without the assistance of a Master mind to guide them. They have sought for the fundamental causes of the phenomena of thought transference and the methods for its accomplishment, but while thus engaged have ignored the sources through which alone they could have obtained the most essential information. Even the purely physical aspects of the process have largely escaped observation.

The power of direct thought transference is as much a matter of self-development as is that of any other function of the mentality, and similar methods of accomplishment are requisite to those employed in the attainment of any psychic power; namely, concentration, self-restraint of the sex nature, silence, and continuous effort during stated periods and at definite times.

While it is generally conceded that in some mysterious way there must be an attunement of or a union between the masculine and feminine magnetic currents of force in the case of any two students engaged in this study; the method of action and the requisite centers for making connections have proven debatable points, and in some instances such debates have been the harbingers of much subsequent evil, or unwise action. In the production of any deliberate act of thought transference between two people of opposite sexes there must always be a sympathetic current — an equality — established between them before attempting the act of transference.

It is not necessary for both parties to be in the same locality, but it is necessary that a set time should be chosen and a similar degree of concentration attained to by both, as well as that both should be in harmonious surroundings in order that the requisite positive and negative action should be set up within two special brain centers of each person. One of these centers lies at the base of the brain and the other directly under the center of the skull.

As a result of the said action, a magnetic field is created in the spaces between the said two centers in each brain and a direct current of force flashes within that field from a third brain center which lies just back of the center of the forehead between the eyes.

The last mentioned brain center is the vehicle of communication between the etheric and the physical planes, and all thought currents primarily traverse the etheric plane. When a definite thought takes form in the shape of some symbol, there is a slight explosion of force within that last mentioned center which gives the necessary impulse for the projection of the symbolic form; and the same action takes place in a similar center of the brain of the one who receives the symbolic representation if the necessary conditions have been made.

As soon as the impulse arises to send or receive such an idealized symbolic representation, the previously quiescent force stored up in that center is aroused, and within the magnetic field referred to there is flashed a definite picture or image of the symbolic form, somewhat as an image may be flashed on the surface of a mirror in passing. From this magnetic field the first two mentioned brain centers seize the details of the pictured image and connect with other centers of the brain and sympathetic nerves, by means of which the said details of the symbolic form are worked out into expression; it may be into words or into lesser thought images. It would depend upon the energy set free in the explosion as to how the said details were expressed.

Where four persons are required to send or receive a symbolic thought, it is for the reason that only one of the requisite two centers of each brain is fully developed, and the magnetic field must, therefore, be created between more widely separated brain centers. Like sympathetic vibrations must be established between the four persons thus engaged to those established between two persons. A definite time must be set, and a similar degree of concentration attained.

Such a symbolic thought form as I have mentioned may be caught by many persons at the same time, who are in fact wide apart in space, but the right conditions must have been previously established in any case. Thought waves travel in wide spiral lines and may touch wherever a magnetic field has been established.

It is due to misunderstanding of the fact that the masculine and feminine currents of force are both necessary to the performance of any psychic phenomenon that so much harsh criticism and condemnation has been heaped on the heads of perfectly virtuous students of occultism who have attempted to cultivate the power of thought transference; but when it is understood that there may even be perfect action between the masculine and feminine forces in one body, the supposed cause for such condemnation will disappear. When a man and woman are in the same stage of development and are engaged in the practice of thought transference, all else being equal, the power is increased and the results are apt to be more satisfactory; but two or more persons of one sex can often accomplish much in that respect if they will make the requisite conditions.

LESSON 148
A LETTER FROM THE MASTER

My Children:
Among your number there are a few disciples who might benefit from a little advice I feel impelled to offer; for like other warm-hearted, spiritually hungry souls, they are in danger of being exploited by those fiends in human guise — tools of black magicians who continually lie in wait for new victims of their avarice and cunning.

I refer to those misnamed teachers of occultism who claim to be receiving directions from some high spiritual force, or directly from the Initiates of the "Great White Lodge," and who pour forth volumes of platitudes in flowery or abstruse language specially designed to deceive new and untried disciples, until such time as they have compromised or partially psychologized the latter, before their motives become apparent. Unfortunately, when that time arrives previous warnings are of little avail.

Place an unscalable barrier between yourself and the person who offers you *rapid* spiritual development or the possession of the powers of practical occultism at the cost of little or no effort on your own part, or who offers to teach you the secrets of such attainment for a set price.

If you are familiar with the *Book of the Golden Precepts*,[1] or with any other reliable work on practical occultism, you will have seen that there are certain inviolable rules to be obeyed, certain unalterable conditions to be fulfilled before it is even possible for you to take the first step on the "Secret Path" — the Path of Power.[2] If you feel a strong attraction in that direction, I would advise that you read and thoroughly digest such information as may be found in authentic works on the subject, and then create a mental mirror in which, by the aid of your Higher Self, your conscience, your knowledge of your personal self, your dominant characteristics, you proceed to hold that self before the mirror, and with an earnest petition for enlightenment, question that mirror as to what are the probabilities of your being able to live up to those rules, fulfill the conditions, and abide by the answers.

Ask that mirrored form what is the extent of its will power? of its power of endurance? its ability for sacrifice, such sacrifice as is demanded of the true neophyte? In nine hundred ninety-nine instances out of one thousand, the answer will be: "I have neither power nor ability commensurate with the demand." But then, beware lest immediately there begins to form a series of desire-pictures upon the surface of that mirror, expressions of intense longing, memories

---

[1] *Book of the Golden Precepts* — a secret book stored in Shambhala that contains approximately ninety short treatises, essentially constituting a code of rules which the Initiates must follow. Its copies can be found in the monasteries of the East, and its ethics imbued all Eastern Sacred Scriptures. In 1889, Helena Blavatsky published three excerpts from it in *The Voice of the Silence*; another excerpt was published by Mabel Collins in *Light on the Path* in 1885.

[2] See "The Two Paths" in *The Voice of the Silence*.

of sacrifices previously made, such pictures as generally obsess the mind that has been denied some indulgence. Little by little the "lions in the path" will seem to disappear; the weaknesses of will and mind and physical limitations will seem of less consequence, until finally naught remains but a picture of the lower self in abject submission, the Higher Self triumphant. Such is the power of the lower self, if even temporarily divorced from that light of the Higher Self. If the glamor of lower desire is permitted to blind you to the warnings received and to the dictates of conscience, a false sensation of peace may follow and a desire to acquaint others with the fact that at last you believe you are on the path to unlimited power; and then — then you have become a fit subject for the exploiter who is very apt to appear, and unless you have been so fortunate as to have been under the protection of a true Initiate, there is sore disappointment in store for you. All too many ignorant victims of such exploiters have been forced into utter rejection of all truth and the submersion of all hope and faith after awakening to the fact that they have been purposely deceived by some false teacher, aided by the desires of the lower mind.

Bear carefully in mind that not one of the rules given for your guidance is unnecessary; not one of the directions is superfluous; not one of the sacrifices demanded is useless. Remember that a perfectly sound body and a sound mind are essentials for a practical occultist, without which it would be impossible to pass the requisite physical tests; and remembering all these things, be content to travel the path of the heart, the path of the child, until such time as you may have gained the power to tread the harder path, if that power has not yet been gained, accepting and being content with the guidance of "those who know" until in their eyes, instead of yours alone, you are capable of taking the next step in safety. The peace that will come to you as a result of such submission will be a lasting peace however great the warfare about you. You will be content to await recognition by others instead of claiming it as a right. You will recognize your father's face, your mother's hands, and will no more desire to wander in strange places. Soul sight — intuition — will come, and with its coming will also come the power of discrimination.

My Child, hold up that mental mirror and make sure of your self, your strength, your power to serve aright, ere you ignorantly put yourself into the hands of one who may guide you into the great abyss instead of to the mountaintop.

If you should find that the heights are unattainable to you today, remember that another day is coming. Yet also remember that the first step must be taken by every human being, and therefore, must be taken by you; and be not discouraged or dismayed if you stumble in the taking.

Remember that you, as a Templar, have demanded of the Great White Lodge a chance to climb. Having made this demand, your feet have been placed on the first rung of the ladder; hold fast, let nothing rob you of your opportunity; so shall it be well with you.

LESSON 149
SELF-EXAMINATION

You who hunger for power, influence, possessions; you who believe that that hunger comes from the unselfish motive of the greatest good for the greatest number; who believe that your own particular scheme of life is the only one that could bring order out of the chaos in which the world, to your mind, now seems to be, but who have not attained to the first requisite for the winning of power or to the constructing of a scheme by which you could govern your own personality — to you I say, make an honest self-examination and thereby learn what are the hindrances to be overcome, not only in yourself, but in others.

For a rigid self-examination will reveal the very qualities in yourself that you are so anxious to set right in others. They may not be so obvious in your own case, but they are there and only waiting the pull of strong desire, or the necessary environment to come out with equal power. Until you are willing and able to make this rigid self-examination, recognize your limitations, and acknowledge your own liability to error, you will make no sufficiently strong effort to overcome them, nor will you recognize the causes of your neighbor's limitations and help him to adjust himself.

One of the first discoveries you would make in such self-effort would appear in the difficulty encountered in convincing others of your clarity of purpose and motive and your capacity to execute righteous judgment in any given case. You would see that because of the unwillingness of others to face themselves as they really are, their viewpoints would be altogether different from yours; therefore, they would be for the time being utterly incapable of working in perfect harmony with you; they could not see the necessity for action as it presented itself to you; therefore, your premises would be all wrong to them.

As an example, you imagine that you love some cause or some individual. By refusing to dig deep enough in your own minds to find the incentive to such love, you permit a biased view of your duties and obligations to that cause or person, as well as theirs to you, to change that love into tolerance, indifference, or even hatred. You would walk over burning coals to fulfill some imagined or real duty or selfish desire which seemed of sufficient importance to you, while you would plunge a metaphorical dagger into the heart of the beloved by demands incapable of fulfillment, unreasoning protests, and exhibitions of your own littleness, entirely ignorant of the standpoint from which those others were compelled to view their actions.

Self-examination would have shown you this, and supplied the incentive for change. You have to reach down to fundamentals of human character, select from these fundamentals those you would cultivate and those you would suppress, and then consciously set about doing so, before you can rise above your present mental and physical environment. You may say you have that power. The trouble is that you try to seize upon and change the effects of action already committed instead of the original causes of such action. As a rule you ignore the tremendous power of auto-suggestion. Once you have recognized that your motives are questionable, as they are in most cases, reach down into the desire back of the motive, and if that desire be selfish, crude, or ill-formed, speak to it with all the concentrated will power at your command, and say, "I do not desire this thing, though my mind or body may desire it. It is not in accord with universal law; therefore, it is not my real desire."

If you do this often enough and with sufficient intensity, you will one day find that particular desire shriveling up, going out, and will know yourself free from it, with a higher desire in its place.

In self-examination, your discovered motive for doing or not doing any definite thing will act as indicator and expose the desire behind it. If the mental deposits left in your mind by dwelling upon any desire become so active and persistent that you find it difficult to rid yourself of them, stop resisting them — fill your mind so full of other things that there is no room for them, and they must disappear.

LESSON 150
THE MEASURE OF A MAN

Whether the student takes his observations from the standpoint of God, Nature, or that of fortuitous circumstances, it must be evident even to the mind of a casuist that the power which shapes matter into form has decreed that no form, whether it be form of man, mountain, or drop of water shall retain that form beyond a certain predetermined period of time. The law of Periodicity — a tool used in the shaping of form — is used as perfectly and relentlessly in determining the span of life for an organization of human beings as it is for that of a man or an amoeba. There is but one higher, one more important tool than this one of Periodicity possible of being wielded by Divinity in the shape of a universe, and that tool is the law of service. He who is wise enough and meek enough to perceive and profit by his perception of the method, purpose, and results of the action of these two laws on the lives of others may, if he will, mold the circumstances of his own life to fit into the new form he dimly perceives in the distance of his imagination, the form that is being built by the aforementioned tools of Divinity out of the substance the man himself has created day by day, but which is built according to a plan, the details of which are far beyond his present power of perception. If he can be content to go on cheerfully and unselfishly creating the substance for the form without pausing to measure the amount he has created, or to congratulate himself on the success of his efforts, or worse still, to fall into a state of despair over his seeming failure to create, he may one day learn that he has unconsciously been used as an instrument in creating the foothill upon the top of which he finds himself standing and gazing up at the top of the great mountain range which lies just beyond. But it is when he has reached the top of his first foothill that comes his first hour of real trial. Then must he learn that unless he has gained the power of balance which will enable him to stand erect and unafraid, his only support the never-failing staff of humility, he must inevitably be ricocheted to a state of oblivion, or to some other indeterminate state of illusion.

When the star of a man's life is in the ascendant, when he has reached the top of the first foothill, the measure of that man is taken by the powers that rule and direct his evolution. It will depend entirely upon the vision he has caught of the surrounding plain and the location of the hill he must next climb whether he is ever going to be able to reach a still higher altitude of knowledge and power in his present life cycle. That is, it will depend upon his discovery of the field whereupon his best services can be rendered for humanity as a whole, and upon his ability to maintain the throne of Divinity within his own heart, as to whether greater opportunity will be presented to him.

The measure of the pledged and accepted disciple of the Great White Lodge is being very rapidly and accurately taken in these days of separation. Figuratively speaking, the height, depth, and weight of each one is being determined by the measure of development he has reached, especially the development of the powers of Perception, Stability, and Service. The rapidity of the descent of first one and then another would be a pitiable spectacle to a casual observer unable to see that though the motor power of selfishness had hurled its victim from the top of his little foothill to the plain beneath, the plain was his natural habitat, and would continue to be such until he could develop sufficient purpose and stability to retain his foothold on the hill.

Aside from selfishness, indolence, and instability, there is no other quality so conducive to a fall as is that of excessive egotism. No other form is so rapidly disintegrated as is the form built up by means of exaggerated egotism and self-righteousness.

Mankind is long in learning that the measure of a man is taken by Deity, and by the Servants of Deity transmitted to the consciousness of every other man who has succeeded in reaching the top of a single foothill of life. Only those still fixed on the plain below — the plane of their own desires and passions — can be deceived by the egotist, and they can only be so deceived because they are enwrapped in a similar web of ingratitude, disobedience, and selfishness to that which made the egotist what he is, the prisoner of himself.

LESSON 151
MULTIPLE PLANES OF BEING

The Wisdom Religion formulates seven different planes or states of consciousness. Many teachers of the philosophy of the said religion frequently refer to one or more of the seven sub-planes of each one of these seven grand divisions, who are not aware that the sub-planes may be differentiated almost *ad libitum*, for in fact there are as many sub-planes as there are thinking entities on the four primal planes of matter. As there are no two beings, no two leaves on a tree, no two blades of grass exactly alike, so there are no two mentalities exactly alike. The dynamic power resident in a single great idea or ideal may draw together and hold many minds to a given point, although each mind may perceive a different aspect of the idea.

When a definite idea has taken form in a mentality and been expressed in speech or writing, if it be new to people at large and expresses some great need, it is avidly seized and, if practicable, quickly acted upon. Every mind so seizing the idea and concentrating upon it adds a definite corresponding degree of energy to that of the original idea, and gradually a distinct plane or state of consciousness is created, into which may plunge the minds of uncounted, hitherto unborn human beings, and which will last until the energy which created and has sustained it is exhausted.

The size of the vortex created in the Manasic substance of the universe by the generation and birth of the idea is gradually lessened, the motion of the swirling substance is stilled, and there remains but the seed of the original thought or idea when the cyclic course of the idea has been run. That seed remains as a laya center in the universal mind until such time as a new cycle may open for it by its refertilization in the mind of some other individual. This may take place ages after its previous externalization.

Every true psychic, and in some degree every dreamer, has many partial glimpses of differing forms of phenomena which illustrate in a measure one of the truths I desire to express. In the preliminary stages of trance or dream, various half-formed pictures or images are seen, partial sentences or incomplete revelations are heard, before the psychic senses can seize upon some clearly outlined picture, or some definite intelligible experience is lived through, on whatever plane the consciousness is acting. These undefined, incomplete representations are partial personal recollections of some previous train of experience upon some sub-plane which bears a distinct relation to one of the great full planes — the seven primal planes of manifestation. Such experiences are worthy of note and interpretation for they are connecting links in some life experience, but as reliable interpretation can only be had by means of symbolism, they are never understood or appreciated save by some well-advanced student of occultism.

The relation between ideas and their cyclic return may be partially illustrated by means of a string of 49 beads graduated from the size of a mustard seed to that of a walnut. The beads should be of one color save each seventh bead, which should be of different form and color; the colored beads should be placed according to the scale of the colors of the spectrum. The string which holds the beads would indicate the original idea, the graduated beads would indicate the growth of the idea from one sub-plane to another, while each seventh bead would indicate the externalized idea upon a full plane. The different color and form of each bead forming the other six divisions would indicate the character of the changes which would take place during the different periods of externalization; every intermediate bead would indicate a sub-plane — a new state of consciousness — for the corresponding races of earth or the individuals so indicated.

This is far from being an adequate illustration, but no perfect illustration of very interior truths is possible because we are then dealing with matter subject to entirely different laws from those of the physical plane, which can only be considered by correspondence and analogy by the tyro in occultism.

It is necessary for the human mind to transcend the physical plane and act consciously on interior planes in order to grasp the underlying principle of any universal law and the action of the forces controlling the gross matter of any plane of manifestation.

LESSON 152
THE UMBILICUS

The paths between Gods and men is the umbilicus which once connected God and man. The navel, the Central Spiritual Sun, is the point of separation between Spirit and Matter. The umbilicus connection was severed when Elohim[1] said, "Let us make man in our own image,"[2] and having made man, they set him down in the Garden of Eden. Man cut the cord between himself and the great Father-Mother. Therefore, man must reunite the two severed ends of the cord. This is the real occult secret behind the use of the navel in concentration by some of the ancient teachers. Symbolically, it is the lower end of the Path, the gateway, so to speak; and if the gateway is choked by weeds (sensuous desires and gratifications), the soul cannot pass through it to reach the path of true knowledge and power.

---

[1] *Elohim* (*Hebrew*) — a name for God in the Hebrew Scriptures.
[2] Genesis 1:26.

LESSON 153
PLEDGE FEVER

Many references have been made in the past, both in the Temple Teachings and in earlier esoteric teachings, to the effects which inevitably follow upon the signing of a pledge by a student of occultism. Notwithstanding the warning always given by all true leaders of esoteric schools to those who come under their guidance and supervision, these warnings are very frequently superficially considered and eventually ignored; consequently, the student is left without the protection which earnest consideration and obedience would give, and he finally reaches a condition comparable to that of a bird whose feathers have all been plucked, leaving its unclothed skin subject to the icy blasts of the Storm King and the burning heat of the sun.

While there remains a subconscious memory of the warning received, but little effort is made by the majority of students to revive it on the exterior plane. Like many other laws which seem made to be broken, the laws of discipleship often suffer the same fate. When, at the close of his long, hard struggle a disciple has reached a certain degree of the Great White Lodge and can look back on the path he has trodden, he may be able to see that his disobedience in that one respect has been mercifully overruled to his advantage, for the reason that the icy blasts on his bare skin, figuratively speaking, the burning heat of the Sun, the heavy blows on the unprotected flesh, the stabs of enemies, and all the other calamities which threatened to overwhelm him were so many necessary tests of his power of endurance, his vital energy, and ability to maintain a state of equilibrium in the face of every disturbing condition, and were all essential to the unfoldment of his spiritual nature. All this does not militate against the reality and importance of the aforementioned law and the inevitable results of disobedience. His development has taken place notwithstanding his disobedience and thoughtlessness, and because of an overplus of good Karma or because he has deliberately or carelessly chosen the hard rough way instead of the normal, wise, and protected way.

While he might have had to meet tests fully as difficult to pass on this protected way, he would have had more power to meet them; his strength would not have been frittered away on trifles, and he would not have been led into so many blind trails and lost his way so many times.

The eventual result of like disobedience and thoughtlessness may be discerned today by any advanced disciple, in the many instances of failure to reach a desired goal by some of the adherents of the first Theosophical bodies to be formed in Europe and America, as well as in many instances of not-so-ancient times. The great majority of the above mentioned have never advanced a single step on the true path since their first novitiate was passed. They have either sunken into a state of spiritual coma, or are still feverishly discussing the first principles of occultism in their waking hours with all who will listen, for the reason that they have failed to grasp those of deeper moment or they have deserted the ranks of discipleship and been added to the flotsam and jetsam on the deceptive currents of Maya.[1]

The terrible responsibility they assumed in the sacred pledges they took in esoteric orders has been shirked, and instead of the beacons of light to a drowning multitude that they might have become, they are poor forsworn spiritual or psychic wrecks endangering the safety of other human vessels plowing the waves of life's ocean and seeking for harbor against the heavy storms they intuitively feel are close upon them.

When a disciple is told that with the taking of a pledge to the Great White Lodge every latent tendency of good or evil in his nature, however unsuspected, will become active, it is to his eternal interest to be on guard and watch for their appearing. If he is vain, sensual, or ambitious, those vices will break out no matter how successfully he has concealed them in the past. If he is honorable, compassionate, and serviceable those qualifications will be intensified.

"There is nothing hidden that shall not be revealed."[2] This is an immutable law of occultism. The conditions which obtain in the early stages of his novitiate may result in serious attacks of illness, the effects of his unpreparedness for battle with the elementary forces he has loosed from thrall.

The state of the disciple during this stage of his development has been well summed up by one of our most faithful disciples as "Pledge Fever." While any disciple is suffering from an attack of pledge fever, his co-disciples should constantly exercise patience and compassion toward him; otherwise they will assuredly suffer from the lack of such help in their own hours of trial.

---

[1] *Maya (Sanskrit,* "illusion") — the illusive and transient nature of earthly reality and existence.

[2] Luke 12:2.

This whole subject cannot be considered too seriously, and every effort should be made to impute the right causes to the effects which manifest, instead of passing them off carelessly and uncomprehendingly, or imputing them to exoteric influences.

The accepted disciple has started toward the central flame of his own being, and the closer he approaches the fire the more will he feel the effects of the flames, which are searching out the carboniferous deposits of his lower nature. Until these deposits are burnt up he can make but little real progress on the path of practical occultism, and can experience naught but an occasional hour of fictitious peace at the very best; while the "peace of understanding" so requisite for spiritual growth seems to be constantly receding. But this is only in the seeming, for no effort is lost, and the light may break through darkness very unexpectedly at the last.

LESSON 154
THE POWER OF LIGHT

But for causes to be subsequently noted, every earnest student who has read and thoroughly digested my first instructions on light and sound[1] might be far in advance of the exact scientists of the age, all other things being equal, for being thus thoroughly digested they yield a knowledge of the bases on which many of the greatest systems of philosophy have been built, as well as the principles on which many professions and trades have been founded.

Especially is the latter true of those professions and trades which have grown out of the conduction of light and sound from place to place.

Ill-advised methods of education have resulted in the atrophy or temporary paralysis of one particular brain center in the majority of human beings, a center which was peculiarly active in some preceding races, i.e., the center through which the attribute of intuition is demonstrated. Therefore, the ability quickly to perceive the requisite correspondences between the different forms and degrees of matter and apply the knowledge so gained to the solution of the problems which confront them in all fields of investigation is limited to comparatively few people.

---

[1] Lesson 163, "Sound and Light."

The attribute of which I speak is much higher in the scale of power than that of analogy. It is an attribute of the soul — higher mind.

As far as was humanly possible under existing circumstances, and with those at present under my tuition, I have previously defined the nature of the energy of Light and its relation to the Absolute. It is to its offices of Creator, Preserver, and Destroyer and to its methods of procedure that we are now to turn our attention.

The one all-absorbing purpose of the Initiates is the breaking down, or rather the expansion, of the line of their life cycles that they may fully enter into their inheritance, the Absolute, and this is because of their knowledge of the effects of the evils — the sins of omission and commission of humanity *en masse*, and of their individual disciples or children — on the vibration of the light within, in perpetually decreasing the number of those vibrations, while they should be increased to a great degree to permit of the fulfilling of the divine purpose. For the said Initiates cannot enter into their inheritance until they have brought their disciples to a certain degree of life.

If the terms now used to designate certain features of scientific investigation along the line of physics might be exchanged for the terms in common use in all religions to denote corresponding features and could be accepted by all earnest teachers and students, the errors and misunderstandings now responsible for so much of the evil dominating the human race would disappear as if by magic. Every teacher who further confuses the minds of his pupils by renaming world old truths and so disguising them is responsible for much of that evil. If for instance a man knew that by the commission of some contemplated evil act he would increase the density of a substance which would thereby cut him off from possible realization of some ambition or aspiration, and he understood the rationale of the procedure and could plainly see by logical reasoning that there was no avoiding the effects of a cause so set up, his efforts to refrain from the commission of that evil would be increased tenfold more than they would be by some faint-hearted belief in something that merely appealed to whatever religious sense he might have.

Science and religion are one. If what is commonly believed to be mere sentiment in religious teachings could be shown to have a *bona fide* existence as matter and force possible of manifestation by higher forms of energy and force, and that methods of manifestation could be worked out by logical reasoning, teachers of religion would have more charity for the average materialist, and the latter would be better able to appreciate the truth and beauties of religion.

The student who imagines that the laws of constriction, construction, conservation, and expansion, or in fact any other law by which matter is created or controlled ceases its action when the physical plane is passed is much mistaken; for such action is intensified on the more interior planes.

The power of the astral body to absorb light is greater than that of the physical, but unless that light is diffused almost as rapidly as it is absorbed, the discarnate soul has but little control of the astral body. After death it drifts hither and yon until its atoms are finally dissipated and the soul released.

It is almost unthinkable to the average man that the energy of light should have anything to do with the release of the soul from its enveloping astral body, yet it is true. Light overcomes even the pull of gravitation. The action of gravitation is still more powerful on the astral than on the physical man, and astral matter being lighter and more tenuous than physical matter, the astral body is literally pulled away from the earth sphere by light and dissipated in space when the controlling force of the soul is withdrawn; but the very weight or heaviness of the astral body that has absorbed all the light possible and diffused none worth mentioning makes all the process of disintegration and dissipation a painful one, and it is the difficulty encountered in that process of dissipation and disintegration which produces in the weighted astral the state called "purgatory."

The astral body of the man of broad, generous ideas filled with a spirit of true brotherhood and humanity, the man whose every thought and desire is centered on the good of the race to which he belongs, and who therefore diffuses the light he absorbs almost as rapidly as it is absorbed, has, so to speak, loosened the tendrils which held his astral to the physical body and rendered the former so extremely tenuous, so loosely held together that the soul is entirely released very shortly after death and the atoms of the astral body rapidly return to the elements which created them, leaving the soul free. It is necessary for you to bear constantly in mind the fact that the light of the physical plane — sunlight — is the garment of spiritual light, and it is spiritual light that is the basic energy of which I have been speaking, though you will find perfect correspondences to the phenomena produced by spiritual light in the action of sunlight on the matter of the physical plane if you will seek far enough.

I have referred to the above-mentioned phenomena of the astral plane to help to fix your attention on the similarity of the action of the laws of light on the matter of the two planes and the interaction of energy and matter.

With some understanding of the nature of light, its purpose and action, the mysteries of darkness become less unsolvable. It has been supposed that the tendency to perform evil deeds in the dark was merely to escape observation, but the hours of darkness are nature's periods of assimilation and of excretion; therefore, the energy absorbed by day leaves the body less positively active and less able to reject the exterior influences resulting from the refuse cast off by nature during the hours of assimilation and ejection — the influences of the Eighth Sphere — and knowing little or nothing of the causes — the nature secrets back of the impulses which lead him into temptation — he falls an easy prey unless he leads a purely natural life, with weariness of body and mind resulting from his daily toil. The inertia which follows his day of activity impels him to sleep, and in sleep his thinking self passes beyond the sphere of lower astral activity and his body thus becomes impervious to those lower exterior influences. Darkness is therefore something more than a cloak for evil. So far as any negative action can be externalized it is evil itself, or rather the decreased vibration of nature or light, primarily beneficent and making for rest, but when misused conducive to evil.

The rapid perfecting of the moving picture[1] shows, now so common in every town and village, contains a valuable suggestion to the student of life, for the process of photographing the films and then throwing them on the screen or curtain placed to receive them is an exact correspondence to the methods by which the events of every human life, the action of every ocean wave, stirring leaf, mountain geyser, or crawling ant is thrown upon the astral screen, the film of substance which envelops every materialized atom, and by means of the same energy, light and reflection, there to remain while time lasts.

There is one difference, however, which is of great importance: The moving picture is merely a shadow of the scenes which have been photographed, while the live pictures on the astral screen are the very substance of the scenes depicted thereon. The microscopical

---

[1] The beginning of motion picture in the 1920s.

envelopes or sheaths which every atom or matter sloughs off during every second of time are caught up by the energy of light, carried and fixed in that astral screen day after day throughout the manifesting era of planet or universe, and all together form God's Book of Remembrance or Life.

Bearing this in mind it is not difficult to see how the law of Karma can work so perfectly, down to the minutest act of a man's line of incarnations. The living witness of his good or evil acts is depicted on that astral screen, the very matter with which and by which he committed those acts. The energy which gave and sustains his physical life writes indelibly the record of that life. It is a passing glimpse of this living record that the drowning man, the victim of any accident, catches in his last moment, and which fills him with such terror. It is the record which you and I are constantly facing and adding to daily, to break upon our unbound eyes one day in the future when our hour has struck. There are no erasures, no softening of harsh lines, or blotting out of imperfections in those photographs. They stand there in all their beauty or ugliness for all souls to see.

LESSON 155
INNER REALMS

We, Elder Sons of the same great Father-Mother which bore you who are the younger sons, are taught that the same far distant bodies at which you gaze so longingly at times are but holes in the great blanket of space, as is this seemingly solid body your heavy feet now press so haltingly.

Not until your eyes are opened to the illusion which now enwraps you can you fully comprehend the reality back of such a seemingly wild statement. If you drive a nail into a tree, or cut a piece out of any solid body, the instruments you have used have entered a new realm, a realm which science designates an intermolecular realm. If by an effort of will and the use of a thought-nail you could plunge that instrument through the midst of that realm, the instrument so used would enter a still finer realm of substance, the interatomic realm.

The intermolecular realm of science is in fact the lowest astral realm of occultism. The interatomic or etheric realm is the higher astral realm. That you are constantly passing through, lingering in, and coming back from those realms in both sleeping and waking hours does not often occur to you; yet it is true, and the same wave motions which bear your wireless electric messages to you upon this dense realm of matter may bear your consciousness from one realm to the other.

The disintegrating of your dead bodies creates similar vortices in space, giving opportunity for the mind instrument — the soul — to enter the interatomic realm, as the disintegration of other forms of matter gives opportunity for the release of the elementals inhabiting them and allows them to break through into the intermolecular realm of the disembodied.

If this be true, as it is, is it not also true that the apparently dense matter in which you are engulfed is but the cast off shells of that inter-atomic and inter-molecular substance with which the soul clothes itself for experience when passing from the realm of spirit, the higher pole of life, to matter, the lowest pole?

In your dream life, in trance, and in spiritual vision, you escape from the bondage of molecule and function in those higher inter-atomic realms of substance; and because you find yourselves outside the limits of time and space as you know them, and subject to different laws, you generally think the former are the illusory realms and the one you have left the only substantial reality.

Doubt and unbelief are the bars which close the doors of those interior realms to you, for doubt and unbelief belong to the realm of the cast off shells. They have no place in the interior realms where uncertainty has given place to knowledge. Those interior realms are the real realms of power, and until you can consciously enter their portals, concentration — in the sense in which the Initiates use the word — is very difficult if not impossible, for to concentrate to any purpose the visible universe must pass from your mind. No human tongue can tell you how to do it, for it is a function of the soul. I can tell and have told you how to proceed to learn the alphabet of it, but neither I nor any other being can describe its final achievement. In a few words it may be partially designated.

Learn to lose yourself in the thing, person, or condition you would concentrate upon, and do so with a definite purpose as the guiding force. A more penetrating ray than those given off by any of the newly discovered elements, and a more efficient method for determining the constitution of matter than the spectroscope has given, is possessed by man; but his lack of patient investigation and his continued falling back into the illusions of sense, and his unwillingness or inability to bear the results of his own actions when such results are precipitated by the hosts of elementals which guard the gateway of every interior plane, prevent his recovery of the power once possessed by him.

Just on the verge of that discovery, chela after chela loses his opportunity by reason of the temporary obscuration of his inner sight as a result of the commission of some deed to which he has been incited by those guarding elementals, or his refusal to perform some duty assigned to him as a trial of his strength or intuition, and the hard climb commences over again. Truly it is said, "Whom the Gods would destroy they first make mad."

LESSON 156
WAR

One almost invariably runs the risk of being grossly misunderstood or of arousing the wrath of another by speaking the simple truth in regard to anything. It may be that a truth so spoken would be perfectly evident to that other if time and calm reflection were bestowed upon it; but as a usual thing the first impulse of the hearer tends toward denial, and as argument only intensifies the attitude taken by both parties, the main cause of the argument — the truth — is usually submerged in an ocean of words before the argument is ended.

When I say that democracy is an error and that a democratic form of government is neither right, wise, nor enduring, I can see either denial or perplexity spring into your faces, yet both statements are literally true at the moment, from the standpoint of the White Lodge. Possibly the statement might be less antagonistically received were I to say that such a form of government is neither right, wise, nor enduring at certain periods in a Manvantara. However, from the standpoint of unity, evolution, and spiritual reality, the idea of a democracy is inadmissible.

Take up the argument from the standpoint of evolution alone. It is perfectly evident to the deep student of life that there are not two persons in the world exactly alike. The highest ideal each person is capable of conceiving differs greatly from the highest ideal of others. A satisfactory democracy would demand a race of beings exactly alike, a race with a common desire or ambition and without opposition by the individual desires and ambitions of its members, beyond a set average. The moment one man evolves beyond his neighbors in the average democracy, admiration is followed by jealousy, emulation, and dissatisfaction on the part of a majority of his fellows. True, this is also the case in the average autocracy of today to a great degree; but the reason for this in an autocracy is the evident wrong doing of the upper class — the class in power. It is not true of the ideal patriarchal form of government of the Great White Lodge, a body which is practically an autocracy.

From the standpoint of divine law, every creation of life, whether it be man or animal, plant or mineral is exactly in its right place at all times. If he or it could be permanently displaced by any exterior means, death or degeneration would be the result. There is a definite place, position, and purpose for every individual creation. The law of Karma determines the right place from moment to moment, according to the character of the desires and acts of the individual actor, and no other created thing or person could remove that individual from that position in the universal scale of life unless the law of Karma decreed such removal, without producing untoward results.

In an ideal patriarchal form of government or a monarchy, the father or the king is in the ruling position because Karmic law has placed him there. Every son and daughter directly descended, or other person on whom patents of nobility have been bestowed, is in his or her natural position because Karmic law has placed them there. If this be true, how then can a democracy, with all power in the hands of a people — the majority of whom are not even evolved to the point where they are capable of perceiving their own natural positions in the scale of life — have the right to pick from their number some person of whose rightful position they are equally ignorant, and place him in a position which they are equally incapable of comprehending and expect anything but division, discontent, and final rebellion as a result? The answer to the first question is now as it has been for ages:

"Because of the hardness of their hearts, God suffered them." In other words, because of his ignorance, willfulness, and lack of spiritual discernment, man chooses to endeavor to change divinely appointed and natural law and is permitted to make the effort. To express it somewhat differently, at certain periods in a grand Manvantara, on the lowest arc of certain cycles, spiritual intelligence in man is at a low ebb. The Gods have not yet appeared to give the impulse to the new evolutionary forces for the upward rise of the cycle. A spirit of unrest seizes the masses; desire for change and all that such change may bring comes over them; and the result is the overturning of the old and the establishing of a new order. But the new order, manifesting as it does in such instances on the lowest arc of the cycle, cannot endure for all time. Little by little, as knowledge and power increase, the old order — the higher order — is reestablished and lasts until the evolutionary forces of the new cycle have decreased in strength, volume, and purpose, when another change occurs.

However, if this view is unacceptable to you now, bear in mind that evolutionary law operates in a spiral, not in a closed circle; and each round of the spiral, in each Manvantara, sees the rising of the human race to a greater elevation of Wisdom and Power. The positions in the universal scale of life — eternal by their very nature — now occupied by unacceptable, autocratic, and unwise kings and nobles, will one day in a future age be occupied by the Masters of Wisdom (who possibly may be yourselves), and other features of life will have changed in the same ratio. In other words, the Gods will once more dwell with man, as they have done on the upward arc of previous cycles, and democracy will then be only a name, a forgotten ideal, for a very long period.

Remember what I tell you. Democracy may be the only acceptable ideal to the masses of the people of the present age, and so be relatively right and wise; but it is not right or wise from the standpoint of the Higher Self, and a democracy could not obtain among men who had reached the highest of development in their individual evolutionary cycles.

The present world war[1] is one result of Nature's efforts to tear down old conditions, and it is absolutely unavoidable at this time, from one point of view. As a worldly — a material — event, it may appear to be right and necessary to the mind of the many, although paradoxical as it may seem, the individual man who incites to war and encourages its continuance is an object for harsh criticism.

The same consequences could have obtained from a series of fires and floods, earthquakes, and volcanic action, as far as the race is concerned. That is, a large part of a race could be destroyed by natural means and a new race born subsequently from the remainder; but man in his ignorance cannot wait for that. He convinces himself that he must precipitate events and see the sacrifice of life from another

[1] The First World War (1914–1918).

angle in order to satisfy the blood lust of his nature, thereby creating the hard Karma that will naturally fall on the races living at the close of the next corresponding world period, as well as upon many during the present cycle. If this destruction of life could have been left to natural causes, such Karma would not have to fall on the new race.

But do not forget the spiral ascent of life. War will one day cease and a government be established according to divine law — a government which will last. For a higher round of the spiral will be then reached, when even the evolutionary forces of the lowest arc of the cycle will no longer have power to influence man to his undoing, for he then will have entered into his divine birthright.

LESSON 157
THE WINDOWS OF THE SOUL
AND THE FIRE ELEMENTALS

The Universal Soul gazes out through many windows and doors of the palace, commonly termed Life, windows which look upward and downward, outward and inward; windows which open upon the unending vistas of light and love we call God and heaven; doors which open upon the dense, unyielding, massive piles of matter, which in consociation we term the material plane. And the windows and doors are wonderful objects of superhuman skill. The tiniest hard-shelled seed of plant or tree and the soft-shelled seed of animal and human life are the shuttered windows behind which each individual life is hidden at some period of time, waiting the touch of the brooding soul to spring into activity, tear down the shutters, fling wide the window and burst out into the open, an imaged form of a Son of God.

If you would catch a glimpse of that marvelous being, the Soul of the Universe, look closely into the eyes of the men and animals you contact, for through no other lenses can you catch such perfect visions of the operations of that Soul, its possibilities, and its yearnings. The answers to all the paradoxes and puzzles of life are concealed therein, and may be revealed to the one who can seek with wise understanding and unselfish motive. The vagaries of the human mind, the animal instincts of man, may conceal themselves behind the shutters of other organs of sense, but not behind the shutters of the eyes. They are wide-open windows which always permit the ingress of the searchlight sent out through the eyes of some other soul who has learned to seek wisely, patiently, and lovingly for a glimpse of the sister or brother soul looking out from behind those windows. Other features of the human body may possibly deceive, but to the Initiate or advanced disciple, the eyes of another are like the pages of an open book, revealing by their high and low lights, and in the depths of those wells of truth commonly called the pupils, the possibilities of the soul behind them.

No amount of effort or training can extinguish or change those lights, or hide the reflections constantly changing form in those depths. The lights grow in intensity and power of reflection from youth to middle age, when they begin to grow dim, but they are only totally extinguished at the beginning of the last long sleep — and even then the power is only transferred to the eyes of another plane or state of existence.

The time was when man had only one such window of the soul, but not only all the light and power which are now visible in the twin eyes, but also the more intense light and power, now only active in the interior organs of vision in the case of modern man, were concentrated in that one eye. The guardians of that light and power — a high order of the fiery elementals — were recognized and controlled by the soul of which they were minor parts and were instrumental in producing the flashes of fire which at the command of will could destroy lower forms of life.

You have much to learn of the power and offices of the fiery elementals. For instance, combustion seems to be a simple process to you. You see some inflammable substance reduced to ashes and the fire which consumed it die out, and you naturally think that is the end of both substance and fire. But it is not the end of either the fire or substance. Just as the fiery elementals came forth to do the bidding of those who had power to command them by means of ignition, so they return to their own habitat when their offices are completed, for they are indestructible.

Every molecule of inflammable material is an individual environment for an indwelling fire elemental, and whether or not it is called forth into active service while in that environment by means of friction or ignition, it matters not; the result is the same. With the destruction of the inflammable substance, the elemental loses its vehicle and has no further existence on the material plane until it is again embodied in some other form of matter.

The ancients knew as the Initiates of today know of the power and purpose of these infinitesimal conscious lives, and to them they were sacred. No fire was ever lighted by the seers of old without an appropriate ceremony. This ceremony was instrumental in uniting the consciousness of the elementals with the consciousness of the seer in a bond of mutual service. The sacrifice of their embodiments in such service was repaid by the one for whom the sacrifice was made, by assisting the elementals to regain embodiment in a higher order of life.

The priests of the modern Christian church have but little knowledge of the real purpose of the lighted candles upon their altars and beside their dead, and the laity are even more ignorant. The practice is as old as is the material world, and is still continued by the Initiates to whom the ceremonies connected therewith are as sacred, and the purposes to be served are of as much importance now as they ever were.

The fire elementals are more intelligent than are the water, earth, and air elementals, and while the last three mentioned are subject to any human being who has been made their master, the fire elementals are absolutely uncontrollable, as far as the rendering of individual service is concerned, by any save the Initiates. One of the chief offices, and the office which is now and has always been sought for with more pertinacity than any other by both ancient and modern Initiates, is the office of guardianship to the Sacred Fire of the Temple of Initiation, and it is believed that a circle of fire, or some other figure outlined by fire elementals, will protect any object or person entrusted to their care.

When their guardianship is disturbed or broken down by any extraneous force, the fire elementals exert all their power to destroy the person or thing that has been used as a weapon for that purpose, and it requires all the power and influence of the Initiates to protect a disciple who has ignorantly or viciously been instrumental in preventing the said elementals from carrying out their trust.

An altar is the most sacred thing in the material universe to a true priest or worshipper, its defilement the worst sin that can be committed in their eyes; therefore, in the past, fire elementals were called upon to guard both home and temple, and some inflammable substance which was their natural habitat was made into forms which, when ignited, would call forth the elementals to the duty assigned them, though they were hidden by flames from mortal view. The same races of elementals were called upon to guard the dead from being profaned.

The belief in the sacredness of the family hearthstone in olden times led to belief in the visible presence of the elementals called forth in the burning of inflammable materials.

It is because of the willful and ignorant calling forth of the fire elementals without their consent and cooperation, that they are so difficult to control by man. The destruction of their embodiments rouses them to fury when no effort is made to assist them to find others by working in conjunction with them, as is done by the Initiates; and the selfish use and squandering of the natural forces stored in combustibles is bound to bring a terrible fiery karmic action upon mankind.

And yet the first lesson in the occultism of Fire is very simple. If a disciple of the White Lodge would always remember just what he is about to do when igniting any inflammable substance and concentrate upon a definite thought, which includes gratitude for the service to be given and desire to render equal service, he would make a bond between the elementals confined therein and himself. The thought would take form on the astral plane and furnish new astral environment for the released elemental. As man by means of nature's materials may furnish exterior homes according to a thought plan, so may he help these infinitesimal lives to furnish their environments; that is, help them to gather from nature's finer forces whatever they first need for securing new embodiments — new forms in matter. Like man, they object to being evicted by force.

LESSON 158
TRUTH VERSUS FALSEHOOD

December 1914

It is openly said, and implicitly believed by many people of the present day that a perfectly honest and truthful man cannot succeed in any line of business or professional life; and if success means the amassing of great wealth or worldly honors, it appears on the surface to be true. The effects of dishonesty are only too obvious in a great majority of instances, but one effect of this belief, permeating as it has the minds of the masses, is responsible for a worldwide calamitous condition, which bids fair to do more toward destroying the confidence of the people in each other and their faith in God and in spiritual existence after death than all else; and also bids fair to bring down upon all the races of the earth the most serious karmic effects that have ever befallen the present human race.

For some years there has been a great cry going up from the masses for reform in law, in ethics, in religion, and in politics, and that cry has finally risen to a great swelling chorus. The demand thus made has awakened a response in the minds of certain individuals among more intelligent people, and if one were to judge from the apparent sincerity of those who are in the forefront of many of the movements now on foot for securing such reforms, there would be but little cause for fear or anxious thought; but unfortunately, "those who know" — those who are able to see behind the surface act to the motive governing the majority of these would-be reformers — are forced to perceive that, having failed in reaching a desired success on more legitimate lines, the latter have now seized the thunder of the demagogues of a decade ago and are using it to deafen the masses to their real purposes while backing, if not leading, various so-called reform movements.

With the concentration of such immense sums of capital in the hands of a few, and the fear of a coming monarchy that will destroy the freedom of the masses, there is gradually growing a sentiment of hatred and distrust which renders many among the masses amenable to the purposes of the aforementioned backers or leaders. With the natural indolence of many, the obsession of countless men by one idea, and the hosts of men and women incapable of earnest thought in any direction save that of keeping themselves and their children from starvation, what hope is there that all these can be aroused to the right kind of action before the damage is done which now seems imminent?

The power that was in the hands of the moneyed men a few years ago is passing into the hands of the aforementioned reform leaders, and is back of many of the laws they are responsible for making: the destruction of old forms, the establishing of unwise precedents, the tearing down of safeguards built up by the centuries of effort made by honest men, the destruction of old religious ideals, and the replacing of them with lines of supposedly new thought (which are in effect the black magic of centuries past) — back of all these is an unsuspected, creeping, crawling serpent full of venom that will strike at the very heart of the nation when the time is ripe. That heart is the freedom of man.

I know my statements will seem wild and unauthorized, and it will be because of their seeming wildness that they will not ring true and compel the consideration they are really worth. If there were no ulterior motives behind the acts of those I have in mind who are apparently seeking reform, there would be no occasion for such statements as I have made, for there is no question about the need of reform in many directions; and the fact that in many instances these people are ignorant of the real motives actuating them, and the inevitable effects of such action as they inspire makes the conditions all the more dangerous.

A few Divine Laws have been given man at the beginning of every great world period. The more these laws are ignored, the faster other laws are superimposed upon them, the more rapidly a world and its inhabitants are destroyed. Two of those Divine Laws command that no man shall steal from or lie to his neighbor. If his neighbor makes it impossible for him to live without stealing, or lying to conceal some theft, and then builds a vile prison and forces him into it by means of some lesser laws that he has made, and enforces the same by his greater mental or physical power, is it conceivable that Divine Justice will let that neighbor escape punishment? If Divine Law says, "the earth is the Lord's,"[1] and that it is the birthright of man, and a few men divide it up among themselves and make the great majority till it for their benefit, will it be possible to thwart Divine Law by means of the petty laws made by man to retain possession of that earth? If Divine Law says a man shall do good and not evil, and if other men take away his freedom of choice by laws which bind him to only one mode of procedure (whether they believe those laws will enforce the good or not), will not the man deliberately break those laws to regain his freedom of action, whatever the aftereffect; and if mankind once realizes that these lesser laws were not really made for his safety, but only for his exploitation, will anything keep him from revolution in an effort to get back under the guidance of the Divine Laws which he feels were really made for his higher evolution?

As worldly conditions now are, the threatened revolution of a few years ago, when the open cry for reform first started, is far more imminent now, and it is the supposed reforms that are bringing it about — and they are doing this because of the ulterior motives, the unjust methods, and the unwise laws which would rapidly reduce men to automata if they were allowed to increase and be perpetuated.

---

[1] Psalm 24:1.

Get to the bottom of things. Do not be carried away by surface waters. Make the seeing of truth your object, instead of self-deception.

LESSON 159
THE PURPOSE OF LIFE

Until the soul of man can reach the point of balance — the equilibrating center of consciousness — he is a drifting, purposeless animal, pleased when tenderly stroked; angry and mayhap vicious when the stroke is sharp; companionable, agreeable, selfishly unselfish when amused, flattered or adored; and bitter, vengeful, oftentimes cruel when ennuied, ignored, or ill-treated.

The qualities which are preeminently active in these changes have been bred by the pairs of opposites into his animal soul, and until the change comes which lifts that animal soul into the environment of the human soul, wherein are stored the higher phases and forces of the same qualities, and where the effects of the action of the law of opposites are raised in proportion to his efforts for daily or yearly accomplishments, his opportunities for rapid growth are few.

Long before a child has grown to maturity, it commences to realize that pleasure and pain may follow quickly upon the heels of each other.

Violent emotions in one direction are swiftly followed by equally violent emotions in another direction. An ecstatic joy is the forerunner of a gaunt specter of misery; and as year by year passes he begins to accept a great joy with an underlying fear, and the fear is generally justified. The periods between joy and sorrow are lengthened, and in the interim between joy and sorrow the soul is impelled to ponder on and assimilate the results of either the joy or sorrow, as the case may be. Then there comes a long period when the joys of life come very infrequently, are less vivid and very temporary, and the sorrows seem interminable; the man becomes incapable of ecstasy, his joys are very tame affairs, and the periods of care, anxiety, and fear grow longer and longer, and finally even sorrow loses its power to crush, fear is swallowed up in indifference, and real joy never enters his dwelling with the intent to linger for any length of time.

This is the tale of the average life, the life without a definite spiritual purpose. But the tale of the man with such a purpose cannot be told in such simple terms, nor are the results of his experiences the same, although the experiences may be similar; and to the common observer, the dissimilarity may not be perceptible, but the difference lies in the fact that when the last-mentioned man reaches the point in his life cycle where the lengthened periods between joy and sorrow leave him time and space for consideration, for pondering upon and assimilating the fruits of his experiences, he catches a glimpse of the great purpose behind all those fluctuations, and perceives that they are necessary to growth. He sees that when the pendulum of his clock of life has ceased its action to and fro, there will come a time of rest and silence wherein opportunity is given for the coming of the Holy Ghost — the Illuminator — through Whom alone the vast mysteries of life are revealed.

Life's purpose then becomes clear to him.

He perceives that the pendulum can attain to rest and equilibrium without the destruction of the clock, and the latter can be started up again at his option. Therefore, his time and effort are spent in gaining the power truly to govern his own life, instead of permitting it to be controlled by the elementary forces of life and by the senses and emotions.

Eventually, he finds that he can do better work for the world — and incidentally, for himself — if he can continue in the state of equilibrium indefinitely, and so he transfers his life energy to a higher plane of life, and does so consciously, whereas the first-mentioned man is the sport of the forces which have controlled him even to the end of his life and beyond.

The ultimate effect of action is determined by the motive, the purpose of the act, whatever may appear to be the incidental effect of such action. The higher, the more unselfish, and humanitarian the purpose, the harder will be the battle with the pairs of opposites; yet without the victories won in these battles, man would never rise above the soulless animal manifestation he was before the incarnation of the Sons of Mind.

So, instead of looking at the pairs of opposites as needless, cruel instruments of torture devised by an angry God, as man is tempted to do when in the throes of suffering, he should endeavor to stand apart and realize that they are beneficent, needful, and altogether good.

LESSON 160
RIGHTEOUSNESS

When man has attained to full mental and physical maturity, and some strong interior impulse impels him to reconsider and analyze all those features, phases, and conditions of life which have been instrumental in promoting what the world terms his successes — his pleasures, his power over weaker men, his self-gratification in any desired form — what then does life hold for him as a basis for unremitting effort in the days and years which are to follow?

If he has come face to face with his naked soul in that period of introspection and perceives the rags and tatters lying at its feet or still clothing it, the fag ends of his birthright which alone remain as the final result of all his past efforts — namely satiation, disappointment, hopelessness, bitter contempt for the things, the methods, the means, the ideals of his fellow creatures, the men and women with whom he has been most closely associated in the varied experiences of his business and social life — it may be that in some interval between those lines of mental action the word Righteousness falls upon his ear or is whispered by his diviner Self, and forces him to a more just review of his life experience and a fairer determination of causes and effects. In such an instance the purposeless future narrows before a man's vision and regret for wasted opportunities temporarily blinds him to all else.

Only then can he begin to comprehend the beauty, the desirability of Righteousness, the necessity of living up to some code of psycho-material, moral and ethical laws as that inculcated in the Ten Commandments, or in some other religious code of laws that has been handed down from father to son from time immemorial.

It dawns upon his consciousness that he has entirely misconstrued the purpose and the character of those laws, and that far from being the arbitrary, undesirable, crippling demands of a formerly cast-off personal God, or of some dictator of a past age, they are simply the most beneficent, helpful, clean, all-embracing, and sane rules of life it is possible for human or divine mentality to invent.

He now perceives that aspiration — prayer, compassion, honesty, purity, self-sacrifice, regard for the rights of others — if religiously followed, would have built a foundation for an eternal structure of Peace, Usefulness, and Unity; would have clothed that now naked soul with exquisite garments of Love, Hope, Faith, Wisdom, and Knowledge, and finally, way down in the depths of his disgust and abhorrence he cries out, "O, what a fool I have been; truly, I have bartered my birthright for a mess of pottage!"[1]

A man or woman must have sunk to the state of swine in order to be content to remain filthy in body day after day when there is any possibility of cleansing that body, yet many men and women who are outwardly clean are content to remain in such a state of interior moral, mental, and psychical filth as the vilest animal would shrink from if able to perceive it.

In its last analysis, the word "Righteousness" means cleanness — purity of soul and body. When one considers that such moral, mental, and psychical filth as I have mentioned creates conditions of astral life, which are analogous to the germs of disease and death which are developed by material filth, he begins to understand and realize how desirable is Righteousness — cleanness — from every point of view he is capable of observing. If he is not utterly lost to all interior and exterior decency, he will turn his face about, and like the prodigal son, "arise and go to his Father"[2] — that is, get up out of the mire and filth of his lower nature, look earnestly into the heights of his Spiritual Self, recognize the wholesomeness, the cleanness, the beauty, and truth of a life guided by divine laws — and then set out in earnest to live by those laws, regardless of anything in the line of pity or contempt shown by his whilom friends and perfectly oblivious of the pain, the loneliness, and the anguish which must inevitably come at times until his soul and body have been cleansed and purified from the results of his past misuse of life's greatest blessings.

Ah, truly, Righteousness should be the one aim and ambition of the human soul, for there is nothing else in the wide universe that justifies the bestowal of immortality upon man.

LESSON 161
ATONEMENT

Atonement for sin can only be made by the Christ, the Christ who hangs on the cross of suffering throughout a Maha Yuga — a great cosmic age — the cross made by the crossing of the line of matter by the line of spirit. Atonement for personal sin is made by the soul — the

---

[1] See Genesis 25:29–34.

[2] Luke 15:18.

vehicle of the Christ — almost continuously throughout the earth lives of the individual ego. When the desire of the soul for obedience to the Divine Law has overcome the desires of the body to break that Law for the purposes of sense gratification, an entire change has taken place in the lower nature. The process of overcoming has resulted in an at-one-ment of the individual soul with the Over-Soul.

To atone means to blot out, and in the process of blotting out — or atoning for an evil deed — there first occurs a neutralizing of the currents of force which have been set up in the aura of the man by the energy freed in the commission of the evil deed. As one chemical may change the entire character of a substance composed of several other chemicals, so the action of one high attribute may neutralize or overcome the effects of the action of several low qualities in the nature of man, thus changing the whole character of the man, regenerating him, as it were.

No man can atone for the sin of another man, but he may be able to give such help to another in some life crisis as to enable that other to throw open his closed heart to the call of his Higher Self, thereby arousing the action of divine forces which in turn will react in the aura of the first man, and thus make the latter a partaker in the good effects resulting from the action of the divine forces which have been brought into manifestation as a result of his helpfulness.

The Christ on the cross of every human being must descend into Hades at some point of its evolution, in order to bring back to normal conditions the soul that has been plunged therein as an effect of the evil deeds of its lower self. In other words, Divine Love must reach down into the heart of man, conquering and regenerating the man before he can appreciate the enormity of his offenses against Divine Law and forgive himself for the sins committed against himself. This forgiveness must be obtained to complete at-one-ment.

LESSON 162
FRESH AIR

No student of life and its various aspects can fail to observe the cyclic action of its every phase of operation. In law, in ethics, in politics, and religion action and reaction occur cyclically. Laws are made in one period only to be repealed or ignored in a succeeding period. One school of medicine, or architecture, one method of education, one fashion gives way to another, and after a definite period returns accentuated in some degree. One period of pronounced reform on ethical lines will give way to indifference and license, and again there will return a wave of excessive virtue. No matter how trivial any phase of life may appear to observing eyes, the cyclic law governs its advent, its obscuration, and again its appearance.

It is only within a comparatively short period of the present era that the importance of fresh air in the cure and prevention of disease has become universally accepted, and yet new discoveries in science are now accountable for a reversal of some of the more generally accepted ideas in some degree; and as the newer theories gain ground, fear of the effects of impure or devitalized air will decrease and other remedies for those diseases, now supposed to be only curable by fresh air, will be found only to give way in their turn. But the wise man will not be caught in that reactionary wave, for behind and above the apparent truth of later scientific discoveries is a spiritual truth which may be discerned by observing the law of correspondence, and it will be found to be far more reliable than any findings of modern science.

The preventative as well as the curative effects of pure fresh air are primarily dependent upon the moisture in the air, which acts as a vehicle for one of the finer forces of nature. Moisture is the result of the combination of hydrogen, nitrogen, and oxygen; the ultimate bases of these gases are magnetism and heat. In overheated air the moisture is decreased and the magnetism and electric heat are inhibited to a great degree upon which all physical life depends. You have only to watch the drying up of material objects in an overheated apartment to gain some idea of the effect of artificially superheated air on the human body. An extra amount of the moisture of the body is drawn to the surface and even if not apparent as sweat, under right conditions may be seen a constant throwing off of minute particles — vehicles of magnetic energy — whereby the very life principle is escaping the leash of skin and mucous surfaces, thus rendering the whole body more subject to the encroachment of disease germs and gradually destroying its power of resistance.

The life principle is a fine electrical force by means of which the magnetism and heat of the body are maintained and the gases of hydrogen and oxygen are combined in the fluids of the body. When the air is unnaturally overheated or vitiated, and therefore when the normal temperature of the body is changed or interfered with as a result of unnatural heat on or by the action of the germ life before noted, the dispersal of the carboniferous deposits left in the brain and blood as the result of the normal action of the burning up of the deleterious elements or their by-products in the blood is interfered with, and these by-products cannot escape from the body. These carboniferous deposits are sometimes so gross they may be seen by the naked eye trained to distinguish them.

So much for the physical effects of unnatural heat and weighted air, but there remains a more important effect which is not so easily modified or destroyed as is possible in the case of the air.

As before noted, the law of correspondence will furnish the wise man a measure of knowledge not obtainable by those ignorant of the action of the said law. You are doubtless aware of the effect induced by excessive heat upon the mind. The processes of thought are sadly interfered with during a period of even natural excessive heat; something approaching a comatose condition obtains in many instances. The mental bodies of those so affected are robbed of their life principle — the finer form of energy which in turn is the base of bodily heat and magnetism — at the same time that the body is robbed and weakened; and the deliberate yielding of the body to conditions which enervate and disease that body is a species of suicide. The soul, the vehicle of the spirit, may be thus compelled to cease its normal action on the mental body and the whole man, body and soul, is thus incapacitated to a greater or lesser extent.

You may say that similar results may be obtained by other means, but I assure you any similar effect has been produced by similar means no matter how far apart the original causes may seem to be. The blood is the vehicle of the life principle, and the blood is entirely dependent upon the vehicle of the finer forces — the air — for purification, as the finer forces must have a vehicle for transmission. Whatever the form of disease or injury the body may suffer, recovery is dependent upon the degree of purity the blood is maintaining.

Excessive anger, hatred, and all their brood of devils also superheat the blood and bring on conditions of body and mind similar to those produced by ill-ventilated apartments or by the maintenance of excessive heat within the same.

LESSON 163
SOUND AND LIGHT

Until some of the most important features of occult research are possible of expression in words, inexperienced students will continue to be confused by misleading or insufficiently expressed statements given out by false or by misinformed teachers. Only the highly developed, trained occultist can understand the difficulties in the way of expressing such planes or states of matter and energy as have no material correspondences. Such an occultist is in a similar position to that of a musician who endeavors to give in words some idea of a tone of higher or lower vibration than the tones now audible to the human ear. When the etheric vibration which has produced a sound has been raised to that of light, it can be manifested by electric energy; but if one should try to express an idea of the intermediary vibratory waves between those of sound and light, he is handicapped by the fact that there is no way of illustrating them by natural or mechanical means on the material plane, and yet those intermediary vibrations or planes — part sound, part light — are as real and necessary to the whole scheme of creation as are those of higher vibration.

It is extremely difficult for the untrained psychic to distinguish between or even to locate the sounds or words set free on the intermediary planes and heard by the psychic ear, for unless the instrument or voice is perfectly familiar and rightly located, words or sentences may be easily confused with or lost in those uttered by other persons on other intermediary planes than the one where the first heard sounds were set free. It is this fact that gives rise to the wrong impressions held by those who frequently hear single sentences by means of the psychic sense of hearing — perfectly sane, intelligible sentences — but followed by meaningless words of strange sounds which have no connection with those first heard. Such experiences naturally drive the unenlightened listener into the belief that he is suffering from some hallucination or other mental disturbance. If he knows that such phenomena are perfectly natural, he is spared such anxiety. He is in a similar position to that of a man located in one room, trying to catch the details of some story being told in another room by other storytellers who are relating entirely different tales. Under such circumstances he could only catch an occasional sentence of the story he desired to hear, and in the intervals many entirely different voices and sounds must fall on his ear, much to his confusion. The trained occultist would know by the degree of energy set free in the sounds which reached his inner ear exactly how far distant from the speaker he was, and under what conditions the words were spoken. He could shut off the sounds coming from other planes so entirely by the interposition of will power that he would not lose the continuity of the sentences to which he desired to listen.

One grievous mistake is frequently made by untrained psychics in relation to sound and sight. Orthodox religious teachers make no reference to more than two or at most three planes of existence — which they name the Earth, Heaven, and hell — while there are in truth 49 planes and sub-planes.[1] According to general belief, a sentence psychically heard by a living person on this earth must come from either Heaven or hell, if it is not the result of incipient insanity.

The illustration previously given of the person hearing voices from many rooms when trying to locate words spoken by one voice, applies equally to partial conversations audible to the psychic ear when both speaker and listener are on the earth plane. An actual psychic conversation may be psychically held between two people living at the same time on this earth plane, while no word of it would be audible to others.

It is not generally understood that different etheric vibrations of sound and light affect different organs of sight and hearing. The sensory centers of the astral and Kama-Manasic bodies record sights and sounds which are invisible and inaudible to corresponding centers of the physical body. A sudden impulse to action on the physical plane may be, and often is, due to a suggestion recorded in some interior sensory center and reflected back to the corresponding center of the physical body, while the person receiving and acting upon the said suggestion may be totally unaware of its source.

The average untrained person is convinced that there is nothing for him to learn on this subject, or is too indolent or hypercritical to submit to the rigid training essential to real advance, so he goes on from day to day seeing his hard-won findings of one day contradicted by some life experience the next day.

But occasionally there is some sincere, earnest student who is able to grasp a half-concealed truth of occultism and use it as a key to open some wide vista of knowledge that will lead him to the feet of a great teacher. To such a one "the path" will open.

---

[1] There are seven main planes, each having seven sub-planes: $7 \times 7 = 49$.

LESSON 164
THE CROSS OF BALANCE

Y ou would have no condemnation for a man who could not raise
   a paralyzed arm to protect himself, or for the mentally overbalanced man who was unable to give the right valuation to words spoken
in warning. So why be impatient with or condemn the psychically paralyzed or overbalanced who willfully deride or ignore those symbolic
messages which the rapid vibratory action of modern life has drawn
forth from inner spheres, or the messages which the Elder Brothers
in anguish of soul are forced to deliver by action of the higher law?
Why turn into ridicule the words of the man who listens and heeds,
but who misinterprets or misrepresents those messages because the
psychic centers of his brain have been unduly underdeveloped or overdeveloped; in other words, one whose senses, psychic and physical,
are not perfectly correlated or balanced; and consequently, who sees
or hears all psychic phenomena from an exaggerated point of view?

The perfectly balanced man or woman is an anomaly in the present age, and if you are at all acquainted with yourselves you will know
that the same is as true of yourselves as it is of your neighbor; it is only
a matter of degree. The lack of balance is due to diseased or abnormal
organs of sense.

By even limited observation, you cannot fail to see that there is a
large class of people who impatiently reject, deride, and ridicule, or
who become wildly excited over prophecies of coming events and try
to frighten all they come in contact with into accepting their views
of the events foreshadowed. All in this class lose the advantages to be
gained by calm introspection and analysis of past events and present
indications. Sacred and profane history is full of accounts of the climaxes in national and worldwide affairs, which cyclic law has brought
upon this planet repeatedly at set periods of time. The repetition of
such climaxes at the exact time of the closing of definite periods of time
surely supplies some basis for the belief that corresponding climaxes
must occur at the expiration of like periods of time in the future, and
therefore, gives a reasonable basis for a fair and unbiased examination
of such messages as I have mentioned — no matter how unreasonable
or overdrawn they may appear to be at first sight and hearing — as
well as furnishes clues to the right interpretation of the same.

Nature does not work by tremendous jumps from one state of life to another. True growth is slow growth, and the character of great crises or climaxes in the past is a good criterion for judging the character of those to come.

The closing of a cycle in which one large continent was cast into the depths of an ocean and a new one was upheaved brings to mind the magnitude of the calamity prophesied to occur at the close of another cycle of the same length of time. Knowledge of the great law of opposites would indicate the character of such calamity, as for instance, a calamity occurring by water at one closing cycle would give assurance of a corresponding calamity by fire at the close of another period of the same length. By a knowledge of symbolism and the law of cycles, every event — of individual, national, or worldwide import, material or spiritual — may be safely predicted and consequently, may be prepared for.

The law of all laws — the law of balance, equilibrium — is of all spiritual as well as physical laws, the most important. It is irrevocable and all-wise; upon it rests the stability of all life in manifestation. It is the primal cause and the final effect of the law of opposites, the law governing sex, and all forces in opposition. Without its action there could be neither spiritual, psychic, nor material life in form.

The cross of balance represents the consummation, the efflorescence, the final unity of all diversified life; as for instance, the disappearance of sex into sexlessness, the victory of the human soul over all that has impeded its evolution. When a full realization of all that may be represented by the symbol of the cross of balance dawns upon the image-making center of the mentality of normal man, a connection is made between that center and the center of the brain through which the divine power of intuition manifests. The purpose, mode of motion, and incalculable importance of the action of the hitherto confused idea as to the necessity of the law of opposites become clarified.

As a general thing, it is at such a moment in the life experience of a man that a realization comes to him of the absolute necessity of attaining to a point of development where he cannot be swayed by the opinions, experience, or desires of any other being, human or spiritual; the necessity of forming a decided plan or object in life, and refusing to be turned from or swayed against it. At a later period he will learn that there is another equally important point of attainment to be gained, without which the first mentioned may become a lasting curse instead of the blessing it is intended to be according to divine purpose.

To you my children, you who are of my own essence, I say again and yet again, labor with a whole heart for the attainment of the power of balance — never forgetting that there can be no rise which does not spring from a level beneath, and that the level beneath holds in itself the energy, the impulse, to rise. Take advantage of that energy each time a lower level is struck instead of permitting yourselves to sink lower down, and there will be for you higher and higher points of attainment to be reached. The cross of balance will become the crown of all knowledge and power when the balance is struck, the last point of attainment won and held.

LESSON 165
GENIUS VERSUS MADNESS

That genius is allied to insanity in some mysterious way is generally accepted, although the intermediate degrees between genius and insanity as these terms are understood — as well as the line of demarcation between the two — may be differently construed. If the law of balance is applied to any problem presented to the mind, as may be done in this problem, at least some measure of solution may be obtained.

A limit is fixed by natural law to the degree of evolution possible of attainment by man during a predetermined cycle of time; and if this limit is exceeded, whether it is by a center of mind or of body, the right balance between the constituent parts is disturbed and the overdeveloped center then becomes an abnormal center. In such an instance some degree of insanity ensues, and this degree is governed by the measure of loss sustained by the other constituent parts of the mentality or body, as the case may be. No composite form of matter, no creature belonging to one ray or group soul, can pass beyond the point of development set for the matter or mind of all the constituent creatures of that group soul by evolutionary law for a definite period of time, without losing in the end.

The length of that period is determined by the strength and power of the aspiration which gave the first impulse toward a specific end. For instance, the indwelling elemental soul of a tree belonging to a certain family group of trees could not change the form and

characteristics of that tree or force its evolution into any other kingdom of nature during the period set by natural law for the perfecting
of the one division of trees to which it belonged without breaking the
law of evolution.

If it were able to do so, the once natural tree would become a monstrosity, neither a tree nor any other natural object; yet if a higher ideal
actuated the elemental and its own growth were commensurate with
that of the tree, at the commencement of another cycle of evolution
when a new vibratory impulse had been given the whole group to
which both elemental and tree belonged, the more potent forces set
free would all tend toward the accomplishment of the desired change
in a natural, and therefore more satisfactory, manner. There would
then be a rise instead of a fall in the scale of its life.

The same laws obtain in the case of a genius — the result of an
overdeveloped brain center. During some previous cycle of incarnation the soul of such a one must have developed an overweening desire
or ambition in one direction, and the result has been the unbalancing
of all the brain centers of its vehicle in a succeeding incarnation, for
one center would be unnaturally developed while the others would be
depleted. It should be remembered that the skandhas — the effects of
action — do not die with the body; they await the soul on its return
from Devachan and become identified with the new personality. Here
as elsewhere may be seen the necessity for cultivating wisdom and
knowledge, and thereby dominion over the principle of desire — in
other words, cultivating the power to conform to the Divine Will as
it is expressed in the evolutionary law.

The command "Thou shalt not steal"[1] is first of all addressed to
the human soul, for the soul may commit a theft by inciting one brain
center to supernormal activity at the expense of another; and here may
be found the solution of the mystery behind the seemingly extra severe
punishment meted out to thieves in olden times — even death. The
soul that persisted in robbing many brain centers of needed power for
their development for the benefit of one center would literally compass
the final annihilation of the body; for in its last analysis, death is the
dissociation of atoms, organs, or states of consciousness.

Insanity being the negative pole of sanity, and primarily due to
lack or loss of balance, it would follow that the over-balancing of one
brain center by an unnatural increase of force at a period when only

---

[1] Exodus 20:15.

sufficient force was available for the normal development of all the brain centers, would result in disaster in some degree to the whole entity.

LESSON 166
LODGE AGENTS

The following is a Master's reply to a question concerning Lodge Agents:

You have been asked why you and others who have been placed in positions similar to yours in the past should be compelled to fight the demons, poverty, ill health, slander, and vilification.

There are three reasons based on karma, reincarnation, and compensation:

1. To have reached a state of psychic and spiritual development which would enable one to do the work expected of such a one, he or she must have passed through and won out of every phase of evil during many earth lives, thereby creating karma which must be expiated, and that karma is not fully expiated until manifestation in flesh is no longer absolutely required. The closer that period of release approaches, the fiercer grows the combat betwixt good and evil, thus precipitating past karmic action more rapidly.

2. Self-protection has been the controlling power until the revelation of the unity of life dawns on the soul. Subsequently, responsibility for others and incessant labor in the cause of those others becomes the dominant purpose, but with the taking up of that burden the responsibility is divided and opportunity is then given those who are being benefited to pay back some of their own back karma.

3. Lodge Agents are not found among the physically perfect, wealthy, and powerful of the earth. Their time is not yet. They are "testing stones" for those they are sent to help, as well as debtors to still unexpiated karma. They are not yet Masters, but are farther on the road to mastery than are the majority of mankind.

LESSON 167
CONDENSATION AND DIFFUSION OF MATTER

The method and process by which an architect drafts the design of a house on parchment corresponds to the method by which nature drafts and fixes the design or form of man, animal, plant, or mineral on the etheric substance of a world or a system of worlds.

The utensils used for the drafting in one case would appear to be very different in character and form from those used in the other, but if we were able to perceive the ultimate character of the substance used in the drafting of the design, we would find it the same in both proceedings.

Universal mind is the real architect, whether its differentiations manifest in nature or in man. The base of the substance used in the mere mechanical act or the natural process of recording the design, whether the record be made on ether or parchment, is stored up pranic energy — the vehicle of Light.

Gross matter as viewed from the heights of life is but the refuse cast off from spiritual substance in its descent from the plane of pure spirit. It is a well-known fact that the atomic base of every molecule of matter which forms a physical body sloughs off and changes its outer envelope — the epidermis of the molecule, so to speak — every seven years.

In exact correspondence, there is a sloughing off, a periodical change in the enveloping medium of every atom of the lower astral body, and in the processes of each change there is either an expansion and diffusion, or a condensation and refinement of such media, according to whether the change be made in an evolutionary or involutionary period of the cycle of manifestation, as is also the case with all gross matter. These changes are precipitated by means of the pranic force contained within such medium, and are directed by the incarnated Egos of the period. During an evolutionary period this sloughed off medium or substance reaches a slower rate of vibration and becomes active as matter on the physical plane, as in the present world period, the refuse substance of a higher plane or state of substance became the matter of our present physical world by means of the action of the laws of expansion and diffusion.

What I have now said in no wise contradicts what I have previously said on the subject of reflection, for it is by the power of reflection that one state of matter or substance is conducted into another state. A definite portion of the substance of your physical body is used up by the energy of light each time a reflection of your form is cast on any reflecting surface, and that reflection endures for a definite period of time after the form which cast the reflection has departed.

The power of the Initiate — by means of which he can form and reform, can exude or withdraw any part or all of his astral form from his physical body — has been won by him through his experience with the phenomena of light and sound. The original design will persist in the auric sphere of the Ego from the beginning to the end of the Manvantara in which the latter is periodically incarnating.

That design was originally made in the image of God, and the same design is, metaphorically speaking, stamped within every differentiated particle of substance, no matter how minute it be.

The Ego must build the substance contained in its auric sphere into the requisite phase or part of the original design which requires perfecting according to the race, kingdom, and age in which that particular portion of the design can develop.

Through the long ages passed during their descent into matter, the incarnating Egos of the present Manvantara have gradually recreated the substance, the matter, now available for their use on the ascending arc of the same cycle of manifestation. In other words, the action of evolutionary energy impels the sloughing off, or changing of the substance of the spiritual and astral vehicle of the Egos during each period of their descent from spirit — pure energy — and that substance has gradually become condensed, coarse enough to partake of the nature of the animal, vegetable, or mineral kingdoms.

Becoming reversed at the close of the evolutionary period, the involutionary aspect of the same energy — the forces of condensation and refinement — came into action from that period to the present; and as it will continue to act to the highest degree of the arc of ascension — the top of the spiral round — matter has continued to condense and refine and therefore to lose its grosser qualities. These processes will continue until the involutionary energy is expended at the aforementioned top of the arc of ascension, when the first-mentioned processes of expansion and diffusion will again be resumed, and a higher round of the cosmic spiral — a new Manvantara — will then commence.

During the period of involution, the substance sloughed off from the atomic bases of matter — as before referred to — is condensing instead of expanding as it has previously done, and the astral substance thus re-created becomes lighter, more tenuous, and elastic. The elementals formed of this substance become more active and persistent as time passes, and the effect of their action on the human race of such a period is more pronounced, and more difficult to control. It is partially due to this fact that the sensual impulses, the temptations to extremes in all fields of life, noticeable in the humanity of an involutionary period, are so much stronger and more difficult to control than in the humanity of an evolutionary period. Investigation will prove to you that the sensual impulses, the acts of the humanity of even a few hundred years ago. were grosser in character and slower of execution, the designs more massive in construction than are similar impulses, acts, and designs of the present races of mankind — all of which are largely influenced by the change in the character and substance of the hosts of elementals embodied in the astral substance of all nature's kingdoms since the outset of the present involutionary period set in.

But little interest is felt by the second or third person to whom the first person relates the vision of an astral visitant. Belief in the reality of the same rapidly oozes out of the mentality of the former, if it ever had admittance, and the seer of the vision also soon forgets or disbelieves in the reality of the vision, unless he possesses the power to visualize to physical eyes the form observed. If the process of such visualizing were understood and the reality admitted as a scientific possibility, the power of faith would do much toward making such phenomena very common, for the forces and methods used by nature in expanding and diffusing spiritual energy in the first — or evolutionary — period of a round of manifestation are in fact stored up in the Ego of man. The highly developed Initiate has released those stored up forces in himself, and therefore can condense or expand at will the astral molecules which are the vehicles of the atomic bases — the sparks, as these bases are termed in Oriental philosophy — and can so render his spiritual — Nirmanakaya — body perceptible even to physical eyes, and can also make visible the astral form of another who is on the same line or circuit of life as himself, if it is necessary for him to do so, although he cannot hold that form in manifestation for any great length of time in any given instance. But he cannot control the ego of another form without its consent. The Ego of the form so called forth would remain quiescent in its own field of life during the manifestation of the form, and so it would not be of much more importance to draw forth such a form than it would to vivify a picture and so reveal a presentment of a live person.

But the fact that the act itself is possible to man would revolutionize modern science, for it would prove beyond power of refutation the existence of a Fourth Dimension, which is at present a subject for much controversy.

The truths that I have herein stated will be provable by the scientist of another century, for the condensation and refinement of matter is now proceeding so rapidly and methodically that observations must inevitably be taken in some field where the changes made in the constitution of matter will be so pronounced as to be perceptible to the human eye under the microscope. And the general acceptance of the facts thereby deduced must set at rest the present uncertainty as to the persistence of life after the change termed death.

LESSON 168
THE LAW OF RHYTHM

The idea of connecting the law of rhythm with the law of cycles would not occur to the average thinker, yet they are elder twin sons of the universal Father-Mother — Motion. Every vibration of all the matter of the four kingdoms of nature moves in perfect rhythm in unconscious devotion to divine law. However minute the atom, molecule, cell, or organ of force or substance, the Fohatic energy which has forced it into outer expression has set up a swing to and fro, inward and outward, in exact measure at its ultimate center. If that measure is broken, there is a change in the constitution of the force or substance involved. If the measure is increased or decreased beyond a certain marked degree, an unnatural condition obtains, unnatural as far as the object is concerned. For instance, if it were possible for man to increase the mass motion common to the cells of the heart beyond a certain definite degree, that heart would disappear entirely from the physical body as far as the physical senses are concerned. If the motion was decreased, the effect would be as pronounced, but instead of the form of a heart being manifest to the psychic senses on the higher astral plane, as would be the case in the first instance, it would only be manifest to the same senses on the lower astral; and what is true in relation to the heart is equally true of every atom of matter.

One difference between the Cyclic law and the law of Rhythm lies in the different directions — courses — taken by the energy or the object in the accomplishment of a given purpose. The Cyclic law directs certain forms of energy and matter in a circular course; Rhythmic law impels the degrees of matter it acts within to a forward and backward motion and sets the bounds of movement. Cyclic law directs energy into required circular channels; the law of Rhythm directs the course of force — and substance — within those channels.

In music we have the best illustration of the action of the law of Rhythm. Cyclic law governs Time; the law of Rhythm governs the length of the intervals between tones. Cyclic law determines the length of the life of a man; Rhythmic law directs the qualities active in the intervals between the definite changes in that life as, for instance, the direction of the changes occurring in the intervals between infancy, youth, middle age, and old age. The Rhythmic law directs the act of breathing by its to and fro action on the cells of the breath centers; the Cyclic law directs the course of the constituents of the air drawn into the lungs by breathing and the course of the bloodstream as it enters and leaves the heart, and it does so as completely as it directs the course of the planets in their orbit around the sun.

These simple illustrations of the action of these two great universal laws may be confusing to young students, but it is only by bringing complex truth into concrete examples that it is possible to give the mentality a form it is capable of cognizing and therefore capable of using to solve some of the mysteries of the constitution of matter from the interior as well as the exoteric standpoint. The breathing of the advanced neophyte is purposely and intelligently regulated by means of his knowledge of the action of Rhythmic laws, for the accomplishment of a definite end. Once the mysteries of the Cyclic and the Rhythmic laws are even relatively grasped, the mystery of the constitution of the substance-matter of the four lower of the seven planes of life becomes less dense.

The slightly tinged sap of a sugar tree bears little resemblance to the hard brown sugar formed by means of motion imparted by boiling. The consistency of the sap gradually changes according to the intensity and time of the applied heat — vibration. The various planes of matter are different degrees of condensation of the ether — universal world sap — condensed by means of the forty-nine Fires into grosser or finer forms or degrees of substance, but all as subject to the Cyclic and Rhythmic laws as are the objects of the before-given illustration.

You will find many more exact illustrations of these same truths in other forms of literature, but when they are deprived of all garnishment and technical terms, they will convey the same basic truths herein revealed.

It is not a difficult task to prove beyond cavil to one's own consciousness the remarkable effect on the sense of feeling by persistent use of a set form of rhythmic breathing, and thereby to gain some concept of the effects produced by rhythm on a world or universe which is constantly subject to the action of rhythm in every atom of its form.

No matter how prolonged a sound may be, there must occur an interval between that sound and another sound of the same origin. If your sense of sight is acute enough, you will see the flash of light which at once succeeds the sound and which fills the interval between the two sounds. These flashes of light hold the key to the action of the law of Rhythm. The ability to gauge the power of the energy — Light — thus precipitated and therefore to gauge the correct intervals — the right rhythmic vibrations when sound is to be used for accomplishing some definite purpose by a trained occultist — gives the latter a tremendous advantage over other men.

LESSON 169
THE FOURFOLD WAVE MOTION OF
MATTER, FORCE, AND CONSCIOUSNESS

If not denied *in toto* by the materialist, the sights and sounds of the astral and super-astral planes are mysteries and therefore questionable and must remain so until such time as science will be able to demonstrate their purpose and method of production.

Yet the key to such knowledge is attainable by any earnest, sincere student of life. That key lies in close observation of the action of the law of correspondences.

Modern science now admits one fact which ancient science demonstrated long ages agone, the fact that substance and force may be conducted from one point to another in space by means of etheric or atmospheric wave motion. Someday there will come an admission and a demonstration of another fact, in effect, that the phenomena of astral vision and hearing are governed by the same law and are transmitted by similar methods to those which conduct the phenomena of sight and hearing on the physical plane, namely, etheric waves. If a piece of heavy metal is thrown into a body of water, it will sink to a depth commensurate with the weight and density of the metal and can only be cast upon the shore by a wave of tremendous energy. If a piece of wood is cast on the same body of water, it may be floated to the shore by a light wave or ripple; it will not sink to any depth unless it is water soaked.

A reflection — a shadow or picture — cast upon the waves of the etheric ocean by a predetermined act or thought takes a definite form within a definite grade of substance. It will depend upon the density and form; in other words, upon the degree of energy and the intensity of concentration responsible for its creation as to which one of the four planes, i.e., states of substances, in which that reflection will finally be located, and by the force of its impact as to how long it will remain fixed on that plane. The cyclic law which governs each wave of matter, force, and energy — and therefore which governs the wave motion of the Ether — decrees that by action of the law of repetition, a reflection of a first reflection — a pictured form — shall be cast on the crest of each outgoing or incoming wave according to whether the wave travels to or from the Etheric plane. In other words, the form will be repeated in other grades of substance on each one of the three planes approaching to or receding from the physical, the manasic, or the etheric planes.

With the development of psychic sight and hearing, man experiences, in some degree, conscious association with those reflected forms when, metaphorically speaking, the hands of the universal cyclic clock reach the same hour and minute the original act was committed — in other words, when the energy set free in the commission of the act reaches a similar degree of power again.

To simplify somewhat: The form and the effects of an act committed today at some particular moment or hour may be reproduced to the interior senses of the actor tomorrow, next year, or a hundred years from now at a corresponding hour, year, or century, of another cycle to that in which the act was committed, and each time the impulse to repeat the act will increase in strength. The psychic seer may observe a vision or hear language totally unfamiliar to him in his waking hours. He may never again see or hear a recurrence of the sight or sound in the one life cycle, yet if his soul memory were awakened, the scene of his vision and the words he has heard would be perfectly familiar. He would know when and where he had first contacted the people or scenes of his vision or heard the sound. A vision of a scene, object, or person may appear before the interior eyes of a seer twenty-four hours after the original scene, object, or person on the physical plane has been observed. Possibly some of the details, characteristics, or objects may be changed, or new ones introduced before the ending of the vision. In such instances there has been a blending of two different scenes, an overlapping of cyclic events. The nondescript character of the details, or the grotesque or hideous malformations so frequently observed by psychics, are the results of just such cyclic overlappings when, as it were, differing scenes on the crests of two or more waves have come into juxtaposition. In one respect such scenes correspond to the composite pictures taken by photographers where the same negative has been used for taking two or more exposures of different persons.

All these facts may be bewildering to the new student of occultism, and all the more so if his philosophy has long been subject to the ridicule of his friends; but the earnest devotee will find many clues to the language of symbolism in the foregoing paragraphs, the substance of which has never been revealed to any other body of western students. In particular I refer to the "fourfold wave motion of matter, force, and consciousness" herein partly revealed.

I have been asked why the visions of the night were so often reproductions of the scenes witnessed during the day when there seemed no reason or purpose for or in the same. The aforementioned cyclic law controls the action of the substance of the astral plane as well as that of the physical plane. The consciousness of the seer becomes identified in some degree with the scene or object observed, and in semi-consciousness or sleep he perceives the astral image of the same by the interior sense of sight.

How such scenes or objects may become symbols for personal application is a mystery until the student realizes that the identifying of his consciousness with the scene or object by his observation of the same in his waking hours, makes a definite astral connection between himself and the scene or object, and as every thing or object in manifestation in matter has a definite correspondence to every other thing and object, the one seen in vision bears a definite relation to him. He has come into magnetic rapport with the scene or object at the moment of identification by observation or contact.

It will invariably be found that the weight, i.e., the character and motive of the act, will determine the depth — the place or plane — within which the effects of the cause — the act — are located, and therefore, to which plane the consciousness of the ego must ascend to witness or reap the results of its action.

My main purpose in calling attention to these hitherto secret details has been to help you understand that height and depth, weight and density, are not confined to the phenomena of the physical plane, therefore that the substance and force of the interior planes are no more illusory than are material objects. What is termed the weight and density of an object on the physical plane is increased or decreased according to the rate of the vibratory action of the mass of the object. A shadow is as truly a material thing as is the object which cast the shadow; but it approaches in kind and character the matter of the fourth dimension of space, which is without weight and density as these terms are commonly understood on the plane of matter.

In its last analysis all matter and force is retarded motion, but so long as the consciousness of man is fixed in matter of varying degrees of mass motion, he is dependent upon his knowledge of cause and effect or method and purpose, in order to free himself from exterior restraint and reach the wider consciousness.

LESSON 170
THE TWELVE GATES

Upon reading a description of the Temple built by Solomon, according to a plan given in detail by Jehovah, the materialist would give but little thought to the mystery of the Twelve Gates. To him they are only entrances to a building, but to the student of occultism they are duplicates, or correspondences, of the entrances to a living Temple — the human body — as well as to a greater Temple on interior planes — a Universal Temple. Each detail of the Temple holds the key to all the mysteries of the division of life it represents and is. To no one detail does more interest attach than to that of the Twelve Gates.

The Ego enters the first three of the Twelve Gates by means of gross matter, form, and lower mind. Through many incarnations, in fact, up to the period when connection is made with the Soul — Higher Mind — the Pilgrim of Days gradually passes through the first three gates of the Universal Temple. By means of instinct alone, the reincarnating monad makes its way through the three Kingdoms of Nature until its form is ensouled in the Third Root Race of mankind when, as a complete human being, he is prepared to enter the next three gates. With a more refined body, increased brain capacity, and a soul, the passing of the next triad of gates fits him for Temple Service. The first period of that service involves the development of the latent qualities of ambition, endurance, and devotion.

The third triad of gates is entered only by "the few" of any race — the Prepared — for they are the teachers of the masses, and this must be so until the cycle rolls around in which all of a Redeemed Humanity may enter. This opportunity will be part of the heritage of the Sixth Root Race. "They are of those who have passed through great tribulations,"[1] great tests, and won.

The last three gates are entered only by the Perfected — the Masters of the highest degrees of Life — the highly evolved progenitors of the Seventh Root Race. These are the gates through which come and go the Divine Builders of Worlds.

The above is but a rough outline of this vast subject. What you and all humanity are now most greatly concerned with is the last gate of the second triad of gates through which you are now striving to pass. Unfortunately, as it would seem, you have loaded yourselves with much rubbish which must be cast aside, or changed, before it will be possible for you to get entirely through the gate. You are not yet sure what had better be cast aside. You think you may need some of that rubbish on the other side of the gate and so are confronted with the difficulty of fixing a right valuation upon it. You still have to learn to put a right valuation upon *things*. You have to learn that it is not necessary to cast away any useful thing, but that it may be necessary for you to transmute the rubbish, to reduce much of it as the chemist reduces gross matter to obtain the particular substance he needs for some definite purpose.

"Without God nothing was made."[2] It is the God in that rubbish which you must seek and find, and when you have succeeded, the mass will be so reduced in volume and character that you will find no difficulty in passing through the gate. Once inside you will find yourselves equipped for the necessary service.

These twelve gates have a certain correspondence to the Zodiac and to every yearly cycle. April, May, and June correspond to the first three gates; July, August, and September to the second three; October,

---

[1] Revelation 7:14.
[2] John 1:3.

November, and December to the third three; and January, February, and March correspond to the last three. In terms of time, you are now[3] about to enter the last one of the second triad of gates with the beginning of the month of January. The good resolutions made as a result of interior recognition of a new beginning — a new impulse given to the life forces, figuratively speaking — is the soul's ticket of entrance to the gate you are about to enter — the last, so far as a yearly cycle of time is concerned. It is possible that it will open for some of your number upon the floor of the Initiation Chamber of the Great Temple, on each side of which is one of the four Thrones occupied by four of the Masters of the Highest Degrees. Each one of those Thrones combines the resident power of three of the twelve exterior gates.

As the Pilgrim of Days travels toward the Universal Heart — the mathematical point — he finds that all exterior forms of life appear to condense, coalesce, and concentrate. As before indicated, they are reduced to their original elements, and experience has yielded the power for such reduction.

The experiences of the Ego through a whole line of incarnations in evanescent form have yielded the power by means of which it has passed the Gates of the Temple and won eternal life in form. When any division of humanity has succeeded in passing one of the outer gates, there is great rejoicing among those who traverse the tessellated floor of the Great Initiation Chamber.

While the above statements may only be accepted symbolically by the many, there are those who know I speak truly — those who *know* that the Great Temple exists — and rejoice with the Masters at the opening of every new life cycle which makes for the development of the human race, even if it must open on conditions so indescribably awful as to stagger the imagination of man. After the whirlwind cometh the low, sweet Voice which speaks peace to all creatures; out of travail cometh New Birth.

LESSON 171
THE ÆTHERIC AND THE ETHERIC SCREENS

Modern literature presents many phases of varied forms of investigation, but none more interesting than the results of investigation in the field of Mind. All the necessary distinctions between the

---

[3] This Lesson was published in the January issue of *The Temple Artisan* in 1916.

principle of Manas, the Divine Mind, and the human mind, as well as the diversified operations of the principle of Manas as exemplified in the instincts of animals, plants, and all forms of crystallization are seldom referred to save in philosophical works of a certain character not easily secured. Yet without these distinctions and differentiations, the student soon finds himself at sea amidst much wreckage of theory. While there is but one mind in essence, that one Mind is identified with the Trinity — Desire, Will, and Motion — the three in one. Only when this Trinity is differentiated in form on the fourth plane, or state of life, does distinction as individuality appear, and it then operates in an Ætheric medium in and through which the Soul of the Universe and of man develops. With differentiation of form and number, there also appears differentiation of Mind into two aspects commonly termed higher and lower Manas.

Some of the more distinguished savants in the fields of scientific research have reached certain deductions as a result of long, continued experimentation, which will be of great advantage to many who are not so well equipped for investigation; but they have not gone deep enough into the mysteries of Mind to satisfy the true student of occultism.

Various theories and partial truths founded on the results of such research have been used to create quite a furor in the world, owing to their application to the rapidly increasing physical and mental ailments of humanity. Especially is this true in the case of those diseases which have developed as a result of nerve and brain tension and exhaustion of vital force, for these are more or less amenable to treatment by suggestion.

Among the above-mentioned partial truths are those which may be combined under the names of Christian Science, mental healing, psychotherapy, and psychoanalysis. The last-mentioned system of healing pertains to a field where investigation has been blocked for many centuries owing to two aspects of that field of which little is known save by the advanced occultist. I refer to the laws of Symbolism and Correspondence. Psychoanalysis pertains to that phase of the Manasic field which comes under the head of dreams and the diagnosis of disease by means of the dreams of the sufferer.

While it is partially true that the unfulfilled desires and ambitions of man may be relegated to the field of the subconsciousness to be recalled to the outer consciousness in the form of disease, the average man is incapable of diagnosing the disease and of understanding the primal cause which lies back of the desire and ambition, and in a field of which he knows nothing. The skandhas, or qualities, brought over from past embodiments are the primary causes of the range of those desires and ambitions which are powerful enough to make a lasting impression on the Astral Screen — the etheric counterpart of the physical body — and the particular quality which has given rise to the desire or ambition must be killed out or transmuted before dreams of the character noted can be permanently overcome and the process of healing be completed. While I cannot deny the efficacy of the treatment of some forms of disease by the method referred to, the whole subject is of minor importance in comparison with another character of dream life which more nearly concerns the higher development of the soul, the permanent body of the Ego, which man is developing throughout his whole line of incarnations.

It is necessary to make a distinction between the Ætheric medium or screen, and the Etheric or Astral Screen — body, or confusion confounded would be the result to the mind of the average thinker. This distinction is far more than a difference, for the development of the soul is largely accomplished by the character of the pictures — the results of action — thrown upon that Ætheric Screen. If the character of the picture thrown upon the Etheric Screen — the astral body, which is also the seat of the subconscious mind of man — is of such a nature as to react on the physical organs of man and produce inharmonious action within the cells of the said organs, it will produce disease.

From one point of view, the Etheric Screen is the negative aspect of the positive Ætheric Screen. The latter only records the pictures of those acts which have resulted from concentrated definite thoughts and ideas, while the former records the pictures formed by the drifting desires and wishes in the mind of the physical man; in other words, the memory of the thoughts and wishes which make but temporary impressions on the brain cells of man. The results of action determined by will and molded into resultant form by the action of Ætheric energy may or may not come back to the outer consciousness as incitements to subsequent action, either in the form of dream, or vision, or as intuition. In any event, they are the milestones which mark the path of the development of the soul, and to relegate these to the domain of the physical body is to place them in a wrong category and into one which might prove disastrous to many people.

To one who has had the advantage of dream or vision in the higher orders or degrees of Universal Life and who has, therefore, contacted forms of life and of living far beyond anything possible of conception by the lower mind, the idea of connecting them with anything like gross matter, or the transitional phases of material life, is abhorrent to a marked degree. The time is not very far distant, as we count time, when a prepared humanity will be able to grasp these great Cosmic Realities and take advantage of the knowledge so gained; but, as previously intimated, they must be interpreted by symbolism and correspondence to the average mind since they lie outside the domain of gross matter.

By using the word *pictures* in referring to the impressions made on either one of the before-mentioned Screens, we may convey an erroneous idea, yet it is difficult to convey a lucid idea of those impressions in a few words.

If you can imagine all the scenes of a moving picture drama rolled up into a composite picture and finally assuming the form of a star or other symbolic figure, and knew that all the scenes of that drama were the results of some act or series of acts, you might gain some concept of the phenomena that spiritual sight would reveal to the seer. Yet this illustration is very incomplete, for the aforementioned symbol might not be apparent to any save the Ego of the actor in such a drama. It is all but impossible to clothe a spiritual reality in the words of any language. Such realities can only be grasped by the intuition, and even then only in part, while the intuition must express itself in common terms.

LESSON 172
VIBRATORY CHANGES

In every city, every settlement of all the nations given over to the white race, as well as in those of many other races, are daily and almost hourly being voiced some of the explicit statements of the Nazarene. These statements are accepted as divine truths upon the fulfillment of which countless numbers of believers base all their hopes of future salvation. Yet, while they are literally pounded upon the eardrums and into the mentality of the listeners by the clergy, used as a basis of prayer to an Almighty God, used as texts to adorn the walls of their houses of worship, and in many other ways, in the majority of instances, their real significance is lost or they are as chaff before the wind when it comes to applying them to purposes like unto those which originally called them forth. To no one of these many statements should more intelligent observation and more ready acceptance be given than to the following, "Go thy way, thy sins are forgiven,"[1] spoken to the woman who begged for an exhibition of the healing powers of the Master. If those words were fully understood and accepted at their true value, there would be neither prison nor hospital in the whole world, for there would be no need for such. Sickness would be recognized as sin, sin as sickness. The man or woman who had broken the law, the child trapped by its heredity, would be treated as an invalid and receive every advantage that science could bestow to the end that they be healed, and consequently from the esoteric point of view, forgiven. The inconsistency of treating as criminals those in need of medical attention, and by those who profess to be guided by the statements of the Master, is largely due to their ignorance of the action of the finer forces of nature.

The breaking of nature's laws, whether they are consciously or unconsciously broken, by nation or individual, displaces substance which is moving in one mode of motion and throws it out of equilibrium. The substance so displaced is within the auric sphere of the one who is responsible for the action. Instead of moving in the direction and consequently in the mass mode of motion which natural law has imparted to it, that substance is halted, as it were, and turned in another direction. As a result it must adjust itself to the new vibration, and in the adjustment the physical atoms, molecules, and cells — which are the outer expressions of the interior force or substance which has been displaced — are thrown out of balance and must suffer until adjustment is made on the plane on which the disturbance was created. If the laws of mentality have been broken, the adjustment must first be made on the mental plane.

If you send a man to prison for some so-called crime, which is in part the result of some disturbance in his mental sphere, and by so doing add enormously to the disturbance already created, you are simply enlarging his field of operations. However, if you were able to diagnose his case correctly, by means of interior observation and by the character of the crime committed, and thus learn what method or means to use in healing the area affected, by strengthening the

---

[1] Luke 7:48.

man's power of resistance and so hastening the adjustment to be made within the disturbed area, you would soon have a normal man.

A study of the crystallization of matter will give some idea of the various forms interior substance is thrown into. There is perfect correspondence between the two. If you can imagine a halting in the process of the crystallization of a cube whereby one side of the cube was contracted, thus changing entirely the form of that which by natural law should have been a cube, possibly you may also imagine the disturbed condition of all adjoining cubes. If the substance of some organ of a human body had been originally crystallized into cubes, and such a change as I have mentioned had subsequently occurred, an abnormal condition would obtain in the part or organ built of that substance and disease would inevitably develop in that organ.

The cause of such a change might be back in the heredity of the individual, or even be the effect of the action of the skandhas in their transmission from one incarnation to another.

But be that as it may, nothing but a change in the vibration which has produced the change in crystallization could heal the disease in the said organ. Such a change in vibration may come either as a result of mental suggestion or medical treatment; that would depend upon the organ affected and therefore upon the formation of the crystallized substance — the basic substance of the cells.

LESSON 173
SEX

Volumes have been written on the subject of sex. The light of the highest intellects of all ages has been turned onto the subject. The mind of every normal human being still wrestles with it, and yet it remains a mystery to the uninitiated and must remain so until passion has been divorced from Compassion — Love. Passion is the shadow of compassion and when the shadow flies away the pure white Light of Compassion shines forth as a Sun. As all shadows are deceptive, this great shade of passion is no exception. It has veiled the eyes of angels and man and will continue to do so until its nature is recognized and the veil is withdrawn.

Man's ignorance of the sevenfold division of Matter, Force, and Consciousness and the nature of those divisions constitutes the veil.

SEX   461

What are commonly termed the physical senses do not function primarily on the plane of gross matter, although their organs of excitation are clearly physical. The five or seven senses of man are but one sense on a more interior division or plane.

Just as the sense of taste and smell are intimately related, the sense of touch — feeling — and the sexual sense are similarly related. The stimulation of one sense arouses activity in all. Consequently, if the psychic senses in an individual have been awakened, the consciousness is very apt to turn inward to that plane of the one sense, and psychic sight and hearing may then respond to the sense of touch functioning on the physical plane. Herein lies the great danger to the spiritually unenlightened man; for unless he is aware of the deceptive sensuousness of the sights and sounds of that interior plane as they are thrown into form and sound by the energy set free by excitation on the physical plane, the beauty and delight of these sights and sounds would deceive him into believing he was contacting still higher planes of being where life is real. These higher planes are only open to man when the senses are all under control and the now-atrophied organ through which the one sense may act is again developed; or the horrible, licentious, and vicious images and gross sounds he may vision or hear would deceive him into believing he had entered a veritable Hades. For when undirected physical or mental energy is set free by man, it may throw the substance of that first interior plane into either class of images.

The last-mentioned phenomenon occurs when the mental balance has been disturbed by disease, or when over-indulgence in sense gratification has led to satiety.

The great aim and ambition of enlightened man is Mastery, and the word itself should indicate the process and the result. An enlightened man does not aim at mere mastery over worldly conditions. Such mastery is far more easily gained than is the mastery over the finer forces of nature and the absolute control of his lower self. So long as man can be controlled by his senses, it is utterly impossible for him to arouse into new activity that now-atrophied center of the brain, which is essential to the control of the higher creative forces.

If a unit of the human race is content to take his evolution with the other units of that race, so far as the functions of sex are concerned, he will only be subject to the sex karma of that race. If he perverts those functions in some abnormal manner, he adds immeasurably to his share of that Karma.

If man, deliberately and willfully — in full consciousness of the difficulties in the way — sets out to gain liberation and then falls back into sensuality, he must necessarily block his way for ages; for by so doing he has veiled his intuition anew and will no longer be able to distinguish between the false and the true. He has paved the way for the deceptive elementals of the Eighth Sphere who will blind him to the character of the experiences he passes through until such time as satiety has partially opened his eyes, when he then realizes the bondage in which he has placed himself.

Satiety always follows upon the heels of over-indulgence. This alone should teach man the materiality of all sense indulgence; for true spiritual experience never satiates. Ecstasy of sense and ecstasy of soul are possible realizations of the two poles of the great Mystery — Love. The ecstasy of sense is the fulfillment of passion; the ecstasy of the soul is the fruit of compassion. One must disappear in the face of the other, for the two can never meet. One is differentiation, the other completeness.

Those who dare to degrade the ideal of Divine Love by prostituting it to low sense gratification come close to committing the unforgivable sin, and those who teach the ignorant that true enlightenment may come by such methods are creating heavy karma.

It is passing strange that any student of life who has had all the advantages that study of *The Secret Doctrine* and other like philosophies may give — those teachings which contain all available data concerning the primal causes for the failure and destruction of other civilizations — can fail to perceive that it is only by a return to a state of purity that man can regain his lost estate. Such a student must know that sex abuse, or some aspect of licentiousness, built the bridge whereby the angels of light entered the abode of demons — the gross physical plane — and that they must re-cross that bridge by turning the creative forces in an opposite direction if they would further the development of the human race and thus regain their spiritual supremacy, as the humanity of the present age and that host of angels are one and the same.

When man reaches the point of development where the functions of sex will be employed for procreation primarily and not alone for mere sensual enjoyment, and the waiting souls long seeking incarnation can be given bodies — without endangering the lives of the women who bear those bodies and who therefore can banish the fear and anxiety that now mark countless bodies with the sign of degeneration and decay — then the human race will have made a great stride upward.

LESSON 174
PEACE ON EARTH

While it is perfectly natural that the idea of peace on Earth should gain more adherents as time passes and the influences of a Messianic Cycle become stronger, perfect peace between nations for an indefinite period cannot obtain until all the substance matter of this plane has been raised to a higher vibration, and that cannot be for many millenniums to come.

When you take into consideration the fact that the very cells of the physical body may be antagonistic to each other and that there is continual warfare between the elemental forces in operation on the physical plane, you realize that all this is primarily due to the action of the laws of Attraction and Repulsion and the resultant friction created in the many grades of matter which form this planet. It becomes evident that some tremendous change must take place in the very constitution of matter before it will be possible for peace to reign upon the earth, or man must evolve to such a degree as to be capable of controlling the forces of nature, and thus be capable of reducing the friction.

When one considers the slaughter of human beings now taking place in this 20th century, and the release of the diabolical forces resulting from malice, hatred, and revenge, there would seem to be but little hope for any radical change in the near future.

While all matter and force are governed by Cyclic law to such a degree as to make it impossible for any great change in the constitution of matter to take place out of the cycle for such a change, one of the great hindrances to a more rapid change is the ignorance of the masses as to how such changes occur. This is why no more effort is made to effect such changes.

Man has created and is creating his own environment in a much more specific way than is generally understood. He is responsible for all the pestilence, famine, and plague which devastate the earth. He has given color to Nature and determined the atmospheric conditions of his world. In other words, he has made his world what it is by the exercise of the all-powerful energies of Will, Desire, and Mind — and he alone can change it. Until he can recognize this fact and turn his image-making power, fortified by Will, to work in the right direction, the forces of degeneration and decay will continue to hold him in their power, and the War God will continue to hold sway in the world. As it now is, all his energies are turned toward working in the gross matter of his little world which, by its very nature, is evanescent and fleeting, as well as provocative of conditions which make war between man and man inevitable.

If peace were declared today by the various nations now at war, it could last but a short time. The elemental forces evoked by such slaughter as has already taken place do not die out with the slain. They have been called into action and must expend the energy with which they are charged. In a Messianic Cycle, their action is overruled by the Karmic Lords to a greater degree than in other cycles. A definite purpose is to be served, namely, the purification of the earth, so far as it is possible to purify it at that particular time, thus raising the vibratory pulse of the earth. This occurs as a result of the suffering, the aspiration, and repentance of the masses of humanity, thus making possible the advent of such a Great Soul as is He who is coming within the aura of the Earth. However, it is a mistaken idea that perfect peace will fall upon the earth upon that advent. Such peace as may come can only be relative and temporary, for as before stated, all the gross matter of the planet must be changed — raised in vibration to the highest power — before permanent peace can reign.

It is written that there was war in Heaven between the Angels of God, and the Dragon and his angels were cast out.[1] Those angels reincarnated in man. What can this mean but that there was antagonism between the Great Creative Forces of the Universe, caused by friction — the result of the action of the laws of Attraction and Repulsion. This clearly shows that the action of said laws is not only responsible for the warring conditions in nature and man on the physical plane,

---

[1] Revelation 12:7–9. For more detailed explanations regarding the war in Heaven, see H. P. Blavatsky, *The Secret Doctrine*, vol. 1, p. 198; vol. 2, pp. 268, 380, 384; "Tetragrammaton," *Collected Writings*, vol. 8 (Wheaton, IL: Theosophical Publishing House, 1990), p. 148; "Transactions of the Blavatsky Lodge of the Theosophical Society," *Collected Writings*, vol. 10 (Wheaton, IL: Theosophical Publishing House, 1988), pp. 371–372.

but also that similar conditions obtain through the three higher states of matter, at definite periods of evolution.

But this should not discourage the aspirant for peace, for every effort serves its purpose in some degree. The longer a Cycle of peace lasts, the stronger are the forces which will eventually bring about the desired permanent results.

LESSON 175
THE HIGHER LOVE

Ah, you husbands and wives of this restless, psychic-mad century, this era wherein all things are rapidly disintegrating and reforming. There can be no stability, no balance, no point of equilibrium in religious, social, political, or family life unless it be created and maintained by stern endurance, divine patience, and above all by clinging as to a lifeline to a sense of duty. This is for the sake of the undeveloped and the unborn children who must suffer unspeakably if their parents yield to the action of the disruptive forces now sweeping through every phase and differentiated condition of the earth sphere. Who is to speak with sufficient power? Where are words to be found — so pregnant with pleading and authority — as to compel your attention and sink deep enough into your souls to arouse the latent strength and purpose so necessary for your own salvation and that of the race to which you belong?

Modern methods of education have left the majority of men with an absorbing ambition for some purpose which will end in one of two ways: exhausted vitality, shattered nerves with all the concomitant effects in the way of impatience, selfish indulgence, and indifference — or in the phlegmatic, self-satisfied, stupid facsimile of herbaceous animals. These methods have left even more of the women restless, physically unfit for the marital relations, psychically sensitive, intensely idealistic, impractical, and full of longings for the realization of ideals. As a rule both men and women are ignorant of or selfishly indifferent to the crying need each soul is making to the other for help and sustenance, for understanding and sympathy.

No third person can aid in establishing harmony between the man and woman who have reached such a stage of dissatisfaction, for they would not accept the offices of such a one. Their own self-esteem or their idealistic illusions would have thrown such a glamor over their mentality that it would seem to degrade them to listen to and profit from the experience of another. Therefore, they are thrown back upon their own soul's integrity for the power to stand still when the waves of discontent, disappointment, ungratified passion, and longing race over their personalities — unless they have been wise enough to cherish with never-ceasing care and thoughtfulness the spark of true love which united them in the beginning of their married life — and to look upon that love as a priceless jewel which could be injured by rough handling by either one, and which requires a setting of little mutual attentions, constant reminders of its existence and fragile nature, and frequent cleansings with the pure water of spiritual communings.

Ah, ye men and women, what else in all the wide universe save the unselfish, devoted love of wife or husband can give you strength to face the terrible reality that to live as mortal is to suffer continuously; to suffer in joy as to suffer in pain — constant, unremitting suffering. Not even in sleep — the twin of death — can you find entire surcease, save in such hours of utter negation as are those which literally blot out life for the time being; for such is the law of mortal life, and no man may successfully appeal from its judgments. Not until man has triumphed over mortal life by means of the flames fanned into burning from that one spark which is transferred to the hearts of man and woman from the Heart of God, in the hour of union, can final release from suffering be given — for love alone can fulfill the law — love founded on mutual respect and grounded in mutual forbearance.

It is passing strange that so many among the masses of mankind fail to see that it is never by the exercise of force or broken law that the new life currents are set in motion.

Unwittingly and too often, both men and women yield to the absorbing cares and duties of daily life; they are either too tired or indifferent — or take too much for granted — and treat each other as they are prone to treat those of their own sex. They are forgetful of the fact that the establishment of the marital relationship between a man and a woman has brought to fruition a germ in the soul of each which is dormant in the usual single man and woman — a co-relation which transcends the physical plane and operates on the plane of soul — and therefore must be taken into consideration if the angel Harmony is to appear and be permanently established in the home life.

The man must recognize these facts and not permit material conditions and circumstances to kill in him the feminine qualities which would enable him to understand the nature of the woman he has married, and so be capable of giving her the nourishment her soul craves from him in order to live and grow.

The woman must recognize the fact that it is equally necessary for her to cultivate the masculine qualities of the soul, and so be able to comprehend the character of the struggle for material supremacy which is implanted in the masculine aspect of life; otherwise, it will be impossible for her to understand the effect of that struggle on the finer parts of the nature of the man she has married, and so help him to balance the two sides of his nature as far as she is able.

Nine-tenths of the grave differences that occur between normal married people arise from utter ignorance of the nature of the fundamental differences in the masculine and feminine sexes. When but little effort is made toward dispelling such ignorance, there seems but little hope of reaching a common basis of understanding, except in those instances where true marriage has taken place.

The woman agonizes over or cries out for constant exhibitions of the finer qualities of her ideal man, the qualities that she has had good reason to believe were a part of the nature of the man she was marrying. The man cries out or smothers the cry for an understanding on the part of the woman of the causes back of his inability to respond to the demands made on those finer parts of his nature at such times as are those when his energies are turned in the direction of some — to him — necessary material struggle.

If the woman's happiness depends alone upon constant outer manifestations of affection, and of interest in her pursuits, and the man's happiness depends upon an intelligent understanding of his limitations and difficulties, there is no possible hope for a termination of their marital woes. Both parties must be brought to the consideration and adoption of a code of mutual forbearance, and a mutual respect for the rights and privileges of each other before a common ground of understanding can be formed.

Of course you will understand that I am not now considering those sad cases where one or both have lost all regard and respect for the laws of God and man, and the life of one has become a hell because of the acts of the other, and both are therefore drifting onto the rocks of life. I am only pointing out some of the causes which have wrecked so many lives that might have been passed in circumstances which would have paid up some bad karma and enabled those so situated to find the complementary parts of themselves in another life cycle with much more ease than would have been possible with a mass of more recently made evil karma.

As long as either man or woman is wedded to the idea that personal happiness on the physical plane is the end and aim of life, instead of the fulfillment of duty, all chance of happiness will fly away like a bird on the wing; while the fulfillment of duty will at least bring peace to the soul and a possible recognition of the reality of the ideal toward which they are striving, but which may not yet exist on this plane.

LESSON 176
MOTION AND VIBRATION

In these latter days when the devotees of what are commonly termed the exact sciences have reached their maximum point of investigation in those fields which supply visible and tangible substance for their operations there is arising another class of investigators who, while they are perfectly willing to accept the findings of earlier scientists so far as they appeal to reason and to the five senses, are unwilling to rest there. The sixth sense now in process of evolution has already given unmistakable evidence of one or more fields of investigation hitherto only suspected, or accepted as mere hypothesis.

The discovery of several elements previously unknown to humanity as a whole (but long known to the Initiates of the Great White Lodge under other terms than those which have been accepted by the latter-day scientist) has been the means of unlocking several doors leading to the solution of some of life's mysteries, and investigation in those particular fields has led to the final acceptance of the statements of the said Initiates by some of the last-mentioned class of investigators; and among the last mentioned are devotees of the ancient alchemists.

The newer fields touch very closely the finer forces of nature before which the man of five senses only finds himself at bay.

Intuition and coordination, two of the qualities of the sixth sense, may leap over the bars set up by the five lower senses and seize upon some point of demarcation between spirit and matter; but only the seventh sense, the synthetic sense, can pass that point on the upward arc and enter the spiritual realms. And it is because the higher degrees of said Initiates have evolved that synthetic sense that they are able to give utterance to statements of absolute truth and verity regarding the spiritual realms. When one of these great Masters of men and things states unequivocally that all manifest life, all life in form, is the result of motion and vibration, it naturally follows that those who can accept that statement desire to know somewhat of the nature of that which is set in motion and vibration and the fundamental cause of the same.

The average occultist will tell you to go to *The Secret Doctrine* or some similar work for such knowledge, but while that knowledge is indispensable at one stage of your effort, I tell you to first use whatever rudiments of the sixth sense you have already evolved to seek for the keynote of that motion which binds you inseparably to conscious Deity; that note is the Christos — the Christ — who sounds that note in your soul lest you become lost in a maze of perplexing mental generalities from which there is no exit.

But first consider the statement that that which is set in motion and vibration is the robe of the Christos — the Christ-in-you, in me, in every living thing and creature, yet Who reigns supreme over all things; the Christ Who weaves a robe for Himself out of that vital force the ancients termed the Akasha — the Archaeus.[1] In the first chapter of St. John you will find a verification of the first of the above statements: "In the beginning was the Word, and the Word was with God, and the word was God. The same was in the beginning with God. All things were made by Him; and without Him was not any thing made that was made."[2] The Word — the firstborn Son of God, the Absolute — is the Christos. That which we feebly express by the words, "the noumenon[3] of electricity," that great mystery of science, is the Word (in occult philosophy, Fohat), the Christos, the power and potency of all the energy and force in manifestation; and when that which is motion, *per se*, starts into vibration, the point of demarcation between spirit and matter has been reached. The Christos then commences to build a form for its manifestation, the form of the Heavenly Man, the pattern for humanity — and builds it by means of vibration; and the form of the Heavenly Man is the seat of vibration — the Central Sun.

Every form and grade of matter is created by one mode or rate of vibration, and each responds to a definite note or key, both from

---

[1] *Archaeus* (*Greek*, "ancient") — the life principle that, according to Paracelsus, directs and maintains the growth and continuation of living beings.

[2] John 1:1–3.

[3] *Noumenon* (*Greek*, "to mean") — the true essential nature of being as distinguished from the illusive objects of sense.

above and below. A Master of one of the high degrees of life holds within himself the power to change the course of any vibrating wave within a definite circle or sphere of operations. He has within himself the tuning fork, to use a figurative term, by which he can find the key to the vibration of sound, light, heat, and electricity. That tuning fork would correspond somewhat to the sender and receiver of a wireless instrument, although the latter is limited far beyond that of the human tuning fork when it is perfected. If a wireless instrument were complete, an operator could change the direction of heat waves by interfering with vibration within a definite area. He could bend the waves from a transverse to a straight or horizontal direction, and so freeze solid every living thing within that area. He could do the same to the light waves, and no ray of light could penetrate the darkness of that area. He could change the course of electrical waves, and no sound could penetrate that radius. He could increase the power, and all live creatures therein would be instantly electrocuted; and were he possessed of the power to change the course or stop the vibration of all four of these life destroying and building energies — sons of Fohat — he could blot out all manifestation of life as far as life on the physical plane is concerned within a certain area of the earth, and he could do all this by manipulating a few keys tuned to the keys of the vibratory waves of ether and air.

When man once comes to a realization of these great truths his "likeness to God" becomes evident to his consciousness.

Even now he is unconsciously using the power of the before-mentioned human tuning fork within the area of his own aura to some degree. Every conscious act of good or ill intent is changing the course of some vibratory wave and so creating, changing, or disintegrating some form of substance within that auric sphere — the akashic robe of the Christ — the Christ who will be the informing consciousness of the Nirmanakaya body when the Ego, the real you, wins that body through its long travail. Think for a moment what such a destiny for man must mean, when in your hours of despondency, of disgust and discouragement you view the evidences of evil in yourself and others and forget the evidences of power to reverse that evil.

If even the faintest approach to realization comes over you in those moments you will never again say life is not worth living.

Note: intuition, coordination, imagination, compassion, volition, apperception are the qualities of the sixth sense.

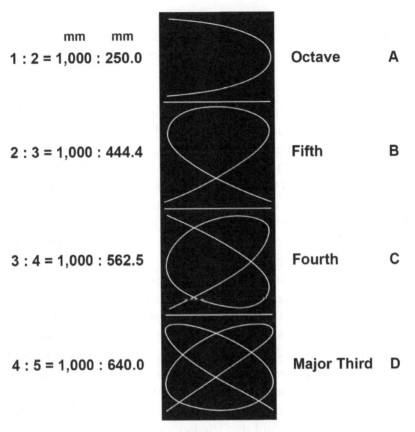

mm mm		
1 : 2 = 1,000 : 250.0	Octave	A
2 : 3 = 1,000 : 444.4	Fifth	B
3 : 4 = 1,000 : 562.5	Fourth	C
4 : 5 = 1,000 : 640.0	Major Third	D

Figure 3
Visible Intervals in Music

Figure 3 shows visible intervals in music obtained by the oscillations of a double pendulum[1] into which is fitted a glass funnel filled with fine sand. The relative lengths of the two pendulums can be altered.

If the shorter curve is one-fourth the length of the longer one, the former will execute twice the number of vibrations that the latter will, in the same period of time. This is in accordance with the law that the times of the vibrations of any two pendulums vary inversely as the square roots of their lengths. But the bob cannot move in two directions at the same time. It will, consequently, move along a path intermediate between the two straight lines just spoken of, and the

---

[1] *Double pendulum* — a pendulum at the end of which another pendulum is attached, forming a simple physical system that exhibits rich dynamic behavior with a strong sensitivity to initial conditions.

resultant due to the combination of the two vibrations is a parabola — A (Figure 3). The rates of vibration of the two pendulums in the case just considered are as 1:2. But this ratio also expresses the interval of the octave. The figure A, therefore, is the curve that corresponds to this interval.

If we change the position of the ring so as to alter the relative lengths of the two pendulums, and start the bob as before, we shall obtain an entirely different figure from the one just exhibited. Making the lengths of the two pendulums as 4:9, the sand from the funnel will describe figure B. But the square roots of 4 and 9 are 2 and 3 respectively. While, therefore, the longer pendulum makes two vibrations, the shorter one executes three. But the ratio 2:3 expresses the interval of the fifth, and hence figure B may be considered as the visible expression of this interval.

Making the relative lengths of the two pendulums 9 and 16 — the square roots of which are 3 and 4 — we obtain figure C, corresponding to the interval of the fourth. Similarly, if we make the lengths of the pendulums as 16:25, we shall obtain figure D. The square roots of 16 and 25 are respectively 4 and 5. But these ratios express the vibration ratio of the major third. Figure D, consequently, corresponds to this interval. In the same manner, by changing the relative lengths of the pendulums, we could obtain figures corresponding to all the intervals in music. We should find that the figures expressing the intervals become more complex as the numbers representing the intervals become larger.

From *Sound and Music*

Figure 4
*Visible Expression of the Sonorous Vibrations Composing
the Musical Interval of a Perfect Fifth*

Figure 5
*Visible Expression of the Sonorous Vibrations Composing
the Musical Interval of a Perfect Fourth*

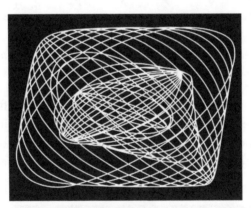

Figure 6
*Tracing Obtained by Making Changes in the Relative Length
of a Compound Pendulum Used to Obtain the Musical Intervals*

The above tracings are obtained by means of a compound pendulum the relative lengths of which can be altered and the tracings are on a plate of glass blackened by camphor smoke resting on the condenser of a vertical lantern. The process is described as follows in *Sound and Music*. The pendulums are so adjusted that one of them vibrates twice while the other executes three vibrations. If then they be both made to oscillate simultaneously they should cause the tracing point to describe a curve corresponding to the musical interval of a Fifth. The pendulums are started and instantly there flashes out on the screen where all was darkness before a beautiful bright curve, which becomes more and more complicated. Finally the tracing point has returned to its starting point and the curve delineating the interval of a Fifth is complete.

From *Sound and Music*

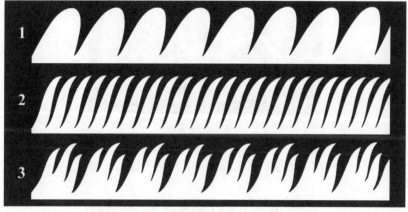

Figure 7
Flame Images Produced by Vibrations of Sound on Flame

The flame image corresponding to the fundamental note is shown in 1 in the above figure. 2 is the flame image of the Twelfth, and shows that it executes just three times as many vibrations as its fundamental. Both flames combined give 1:3 which shows the components of the sound under analysis as well as if each partial were examined separately.

From *Sound and Music*

Figure 8
Image of the Peculiar Sound of the Letter R on Flame

LESSON 177
THE MULTITUDE

In all quarters of the world today there are arising both true and false prophets. Unfortunately, among these prophets are many who are unintentionally voicing misleading prophecies, while others are unintentionally voicing truths. Old systems of philosophy are being torn to shreds and indiscriminately used in establishing new systems. New systems are founded on the false aspects of older systems, while the multitude, the unenlightened masses, confused by many theories of loud-voiced demagogues who exploit them, are led into many byways of thought. Many are repudiating former beliefs and are wandering like sheep with no shepherd into the morasses of irreligion; and in all the world of men there seems to be no one individual possessed of sufficient power and wisdom, and instigated by pure love of humanity, who is able to arrest their attention and compel them to listen to the truth which God is now uttering in no uncertain tones in all lands and among all people — the truth that the present age is an age of transition, and old conditions are passing to make way for new. Therefore, it is an age for silent watching. Heaven and earth are touching each other in travail, to bring to birth a new race, and a new religion and science in one. The new race will have the advantage of the knowledge of the sevenfold division of matter, force, and consciousness, and many other long-lost truths. It cannot be so easily deceived by false teachers as are the masses of the present race. As the evolution of the race proceeds, the psychic and spiritual senses of man will develop and the phenomena of psychic sight and hearing, and of dream and trance, will no longer be subjects of mere curiosity or unbelief, and can no longer be so easily used by the unprincipled to lead their victims into immorality as is now all too often the case, by the teaching of some modified form of phallic worship, and thus arousing the creative centers to an unnatural degree; ignoring the fact that while such forms of worship may have been permitted on the downward arc of some earlier cycle, when a race was dying out, it would be an entirely different matter on the upward arc of a cycle which was bringing a new and a higher race into manifestation.

He who would truly benefit his kind should endeavor to realize somewhat of the divine plan — "the plan in the mind of God" — and work toward the materialization of that plan. But however great and pure his purpose, he must recognize the fact that in the carrying out of his purpose he might interfere as to time, place, or position with some feature of the Divine plan, if some detail were fulfilled at once, and so be prepared to see all his preparations, his labor and efforts swept aside for the time being — and to do it without losing his equilibrium — secure in the knowledge that all that is divine in his purpose will surely be made manifest at the right time and place, and that he will be the gainer in the end, for no effort for good is lost or wasted.

For those who watch and guide the evolutionary forces into channels prepared for them, there is no sadder sight than that which all too often meets their eye when those prepared channels — disciples of the Masters of the White Brotherhood —in their eagerness for more rapid advance, are drawn by the wiles of pure mercenaries into some bypath and who, as a result of specious promises of power and influence to be gained at little cost to themselves, willfully embark on some questionable adventure, forgetful of the action of those irrevocable laws which are the fundamental principles of all true development — the moral and spiritual laws of growth — whether it be national or individual growth. Their natural karmic guides and leaders may be obliged to stand by and see them take the plunge which will throw them into the hands of the Black Brotherhood, unable to stay them for the reason that they have been given all requisite knowledge of the law of cause and effect, and have accepted their karmic responsibility for that knowledge. They are free to choose and must abide by their choice, for no man, no Master, has the right to forcibly restrain them. Warning, entreaty, command, or example is useless when ambition has seized the reins of raging desire in a man.

The necessity for qualifying the word "ambition" is evident where the word is used to indicate a thirst for personal power and influence. Without the quality commonly termed ambition, man would be an impotent, useless creature; but that quality is possible of modification, and it is modified by motive — in other words, by the use to which he proposes to put the fruits of ambition, and by the methods he proposes to accomplish his purpose. While the world waits for that one who can sway the multitude, millions go down into darkness — mayhap because you, or you, or you of those I now address have not risen to the point it was possible for you to reach, but have been stayed at a point where the personal self has overridden the selfless you which had started aright on the path of at-one-ment, possibly to be overtaken and cast down at some stage of the journey; for that one of whom I speak must be a link between two great divisions of life — the multitude and the Masters. It cannot be either the Voice of the multitude or of the Masters. That one leader of humanity must stand, as it were, on a single point, with a hand clasping each division; and that point is the crux of the whole situation, for the average accepted disciple who has reached that point generally passes quickly over into an entirely new field, and he who cannot pass it falls back into his former position. It is the point of the greatest renunciation — the great sacrifice — on which the Christs of all time have stood at some period in their long line of effort toward attainment. It is the point of your great Ideal, and for him who reaches it the reward now waits.

LESSON 178
IMAGINATION VERSUS FANCY

From the viewpoint of a true Initiate, the most pitiable object, the saddest travesty of a human being, is the man without a God. By the term "a God" I mean the highest ideal of God it is possible for man to image and fix in his mentality. The characterless ideal conceived by man at one period of life may differ greatly from an ideal conceived at another period; but however feeble by comparison his first ideal of God may be to that conceived at some later period, it is in fact one feature or aspect of God, and therefore is as truly God as is the later-formed ideal. The difference between the two lies in an increase of wisdom and in the character of the attributes one is able to image in the later period, of that which must ever be an increasingly great ideal, when all is told.

No tongue can tell the sad effects of the misuse and misinterpretation of the word "imagination," and accordingly of the misunderstanding of the nature and purpose of the attribute to which it is applied. Imagination and fancy have been so generally and inextricably confused in general conversation, it is seldom one takes the trouble to segregate the quality or attribute to which the word has been applied and endeavor to learn exactly what interpretation was intended by the speaker or writer. Yet the difference is all but insurmountable, for imagination is an attribute of the Divine Soul, and fancy is a quality of the lower mentality. To imagine an object or an attribute is to create the form of that object on an inner plane, and that object or attribute must as surely become objectified to the human senses in due time as day will follow night. To paraphrase Paul's interpretation of the word Faith, we might say imagination is the substance of things hoped for. Imagination is so swift in action it would appear that there is hardly time to picture all the details of a perfect form in the instantaneous flash by which the mind seizes a replica of the object imagined. Even sunlight performs the phenomenon in photography.

Only God can create an image of God, only God can see God, and the image-making power of man could not create an imaginary form of God if that God had exercised no power in the creation. Just so far as one center of the screen of man's mentality is evolved to the point where it can receive and record an image of God is there a true picture or true ideal of God in that man's mentality. What a desecration then must it be when man persistently applies the term "imagination" to the fleeting, evanescent fluctuations of the lower mind, and what a deprivation for the man who has been taught that all his imagining of God-like qualities and the forms which convey his ideals of super-human greatness are but fancies without any permanent value. As he has had no other way of creating his ideal of God than by means of imagination, such a man is without a God. The only center of the soul by which he can cognize God is allowed to atrophy or to deteriorate so badly as to be no longer capable of responding to the divine impulse which in the early years of his life was subject to his will. The killing of the imagination in a child by ridicule or punishment is a crime against nature. You may say how can I image the Absolute — which is without form — if I am incapable of accepting any lesser idea of God? In reply I say I am not referring to the Absolute in introducing the word "God." To avoid all unnecessary differentiation of substance and form, strive to realize that with the first reflection or manifestation of the Absolute, as the principles of Atma-Buddhi-Manas creation by Kriyashakti — Divine Will — began. In simple terms, the Absolute created or reflected an image of God — a synthesis of the aforementioned principles, and all creations which followed as the ages came and passed were but differentiations and combinations of those first three principles. The principle of form, commonly termed geometry, was one of those differentiations; but form is relative, so consequently the Godhead is not confined to any one form but is present in all forms. The all-inclusive form of a sphere generally enters the mind, in endeavoring to image that Godhead. The imagination can hardly go astray in picturing any high ideal, for as before intimated, the character of the ideal depends upon the development of that center of the human brain through which the power of image-making is preeminently active.

There is no irreverence, no lack of spiritual discernment, in imaging God as a being formed on similar lines to those of a human being, for a perfectly formed human being is the highest possible ideal form. One of the objections voiced by many thinkers to limiting the Absolute by the idea of a God in form, comes from the belief that owing to the manifestation of the pairs of opposites in all form, a perfectly good God could not exist in form, as evil must be coexistent with good; but to my mind that objection is immaterial, for even in the case of a normally good man, the power to work evil is his if he so wills. In fact, it is his power of choice that renders him either a good or an evil man, as the case may be.

I would not have you think I am insisting on any one form as a pattern to build an imaginary God upon, but I am insistent upon the necessity for keeping alive that center of the brain through which imagination works; and you cannot do this if you refuse or neglect to image some ideal of the Godhead therewith, any more than you could mold an image of clay without the clay, for the attribute of imagination is purely an attribute of the Godhead, without which no possible form could come into manifestation in matter.

A deep underlying truth was unconsciously uttered by a materialist who satirically gave to man the privilege of making his own God; for if you have a high ideal to which you have applied the name of God, you have indeed created a form by imagination, which is your God so far as you love or worship the attributes with which you have endowed that ideal form, for it is the character and nature of those attributes which have called forth your love and devotion, and those attributes belong to the Godhead.

LESSON 179
FIRE

The pillar of fire which led the Hebrews by night, the flaming bush by means of which Jehovah communicated with Moses, the tongues of flame which enveloped the disciples of Jesus, and countless other experiences wherein the energy of the fourth plane of manifestation has penetrated gross matter and become objectified to astral vision were not the illusions of over-excited brains as has been claimed by those whose psychic senses are still sealed; they were direct messages from God to man. Such vision will become more and more evident as the days pass and the meaning of the fiery baptism the world is undergoing at this time (1916) becomes clearer. The use, or rather the misuse, of the fiery forces now being liberated in warfare would not have been possible even a single decade ago. The karmic agents of the Law could not have permitted the invention and use of the means for their exploitation to any such degree as is now possible. The energy which manifests as fire on the physical plane is set in action on the fourth plane, and its manifestation is controlled to a large extent by the Karmic Lords. The partial or complete destruction of life on the physical plane takes place alternately by fire and water, and in a fiery cycle the means for manifesting the action of the elementals in their fiery phenomena are far more easily obtained than in a water cycle. What is termed spiritual fire, the first veil of spiritual energy, does not consume gross matter.

To the inner eye of the psychic, it appears to be intense white light. To use a common expression, light must explode on the astral plane, thus freeing the atomic souls which give substance to the light of the material plane, before it becomes the fire of the plane of gross matter.

It does not occur to those who use the expression "the light of the mind" as a mere figure of speech that they are expressing reality, and that the first veil of higher Manas — Akasha — is actually spiritual fire, light, or energy *per se*.

Transmutation is accomplished by the action of spiritual fire, and by a process akin to explosion. After the lowest point in a Manvantara is reached, more rapid vibration is set up in the substance in manifestation. And instead of the action of the positive aspects of expansion and expulsion, we have the action of the positive aspect of cohesion and concentration in excess of the negative aspects. There is a drawing together and cohering of the atoms of matter, and at the close of the Manvantara, the atomic substance has re-become the unit it was in the beginning. We use the words explosion and expansion in a relative sense; the word "unfolding" would more perfectly express the process of evolution, as the word "infolding" would better express the process of involution.

It must be understood that this process is in fact the process by which the regeneration and resurrection of the soul of man takes place. The fire — spiritual light — accomplishes this by means of the two opposites of nature, pain and joy. It is well to remember that this fire or light is not an illusion. It does to the nature of man just what objective fire does to matter; it either purifies or consumes.

LESSON 180
THE GREAT MYSTERY

The greatest mystery you will be called upon to solve while in a form of flesh, the mystery in which are involved all the secrets of the manifested universe, and which only your own higher consciousness can approach with any certainty of solution, is the mystery of the square — the solid. When man is asked to believe that the universe is a solid, and to believe this despite his knowledge of the countless visible and invisible differentiations and grades of matter and energy, and of the vast interspaces between the heavenly bodies, he is excusable if he smiles pityingly at what he deems the credulity of one who could accept and teach such an evidently untenable proposition. Despite countless instructions and analogies explanatory of the sevenfold differentiation of matter, force, and consciousness, man must become something more than man before the three higher of the seven states or planes — the tetrad[1] — are conceivable by him.

The best way for one to obtain a synthetic idea of any abstract truth is to take a representative form and examine its minutiae. In this instance we will take the physical body as an illustration, accepting the occultist's view of it as a sphere of which the aura is the outer wall. In the Book of Revelation, you may read that eventually there are to be 144,000 saved.[2] In one of your private instructions, you are told there are 144,000 degrees and orders of the Great White Lodge. You may find the same number used in scientific and religious literature to establish some point in connection with differentiation of matter or in prophecy. Whether aware of it or not, the writers or teachers of

---

[1] *Tetrad* (*Greek*, "group of four") — the Unity or the "One" under four different aspects; the fundamental number Four, the Tetrad containing the Decad (1+2+3+4=10), or Ten, the number of perfection; the primeval Triad (or Triangle) merged into the Divine Monad.

[2] See Revelation 14:1–5.

science and religion are expressing one aspect of the same great truth, the truth that there are 144,000 aspects of Deity in manifestation.

The same enumeration may be applied to the differentiations of every cell, organ, body, or part of a body in the visible universe — the various aspects of one solid body, the body of Deity.

Can you realize that your blood, your heart, brain, and every other organ and part of your body, and all other bodies are literally composed of 144,000 distinct and separate elemental creations? The interstices between these elemental forms are occupied by the same number of lesser forms of life which form another state of matter; and still another state of matter is formed of yet more minute forms of life which fill the interstices between these lesser forms, and which are sometimes termed etheric or inter-etheric states of matter.

What you do not yet know is that you will sometime have to so identify your consciousness with the elemental lives now developing in your own body, as to enable you to know their purpose, function, and composition, and finally to direct their evolution according to the dictates of the Divine Will within you.

In its nature the substance of your aura is identical with that of the aura of every planet and sun. The elementals of your heart are identical with the elementals which form the heart of the earth and of the sun. There is a corresponding center in the earth to every organ and part of your body, and every such center is a group of elemental lives of the same nature as are those which form the organs and parts of your body. If you can follow and accept the above statements, especially in their relation to the square — the four states of matter — you will doubtless arrive at the conclusion that the filling of all the spaces between different grades and forms of substance finally necessitates a state of solid, the basic substance of which is spiritual energy. When this energy fails to arouse action within its substance, the latter is not dead as we count death; it remains in a quiescent state until set in motion again by Divine Will at the beginning of another Kalpa — a great age. From the occultist's point of view, the aforementioned square — the four lower of the seven states of matter, force, and consciousness, the solid universe — is Manas — Mind in manifestation as form, number, and dimension throughout a Kalpa; quiescent throughout a cosmic Pralaya, a very long period of rest. The spiritual energy that moves to action is the principle of Manas, the third principle of the higher triad. The differentiated mind in man as in his present state of evolution cannot conceive of the three higher states or principles as spirit apart from all form, but with the complete identification with the Higher Self he may perceive his individual ego as a reflection or radiation of those three higher principles in combination, or in common terms, as his individual spirit.

It is only by some understanding of the minutiae of life that it is possible for man to gain any satisfactory idea of the greatness of life. Not until he has gained accurate knowledge of the nature and formation of the blood which courses through his veins and arteries can he learn anything of consequence in relation to the life principle. Not until he has learned somewhat of the magnetic aura which surrounds and penetrates his physical body can he form any satisfactory concept of the etheric or astral planes or states of matter. Humanity can only learn by experience, and only by individual experience in and with every state of matter as it is manifested in the organs and parts of his physical body can any man perfect himself in the cosmic science of matter. This being true, do you not think it worth your while to strive to learn something of the nature, function, and general characteristics of each organ and part of your own body, especially in view of the fact that you — the real you — have before you the task of consciously guiding the evolution of the elemental lives which comprise those organs and parts on one of the sub-planes of this physical plane, and that your duties in that respect will be comparable to those which devolve on you now as heads of families? Would it not be worth your while to try to relate those elemental lives to those which form like organs and parts of the bodies of your fellow men and so learn somewhat of one of the states of the universal solid, and of the mathematical and geometrical laws which are active in differentiating that solid?

You will have become a part of the 144,000 of the saved when all the substance within your auric sphere has been raised to its highest possible rate of vibration; when you — the real you — shall have become a sun — a radiating center of life.

The present theory of the atomic constitution of matter enables the thinker to postulate a universe which comes close to being a solid, for he can people the apparent spaces between visible forms with atoms. But this does not satisfy him. He can go still further and people the interatomic spaces with ions of electrical force, but finds he cannot stop there. Eventually he reaches the conclusion that there must be a state of indivisible substance and this indivisible substance we claim to be the solid universe — spirit in manifestation — first as mind and secondly as matter.

To return to the 144,000 of the saved: The personal ego is perpetually clothing and unclothing itself in number, form, and dimensions of the substance of the aforementioned square — the four states of matter — one state of which is comprised of the infinitesimal lives, which science unconsciously combines under the term "the elements," for want of generic terms. It is the substance of the square — the four states of matter, the robes of spirit — that will constitute the 144,000 of the saved at the end of the age. In other words, it is matter redeemed, raised to the highest possible rate of vibration.

That there may be a blind in the above number as given may not occur to those who are not occult mathematicians. Strictly speaking, the naughts of any given number count for nothing in occult mathematics. In this instance, we have only to consider 144. One and 4 are 5, the number of the manifested universe as a whole — the solid. The second number 4 is the number of the square, or matter in differentiation. Five and 4 are 9. Here we have three triads indicating the trinities, or body, soul, and spirit in each of the three universal states of number, form, and dimension. He who sees behind the blind perceives the redemption — the saving, or rather the return of all matter in manifestation to its original state of purity at the close of a Kalpa or great age. However, as the law of correspondences obtains here as elsewhere, the same number and its correspondences apply to the individual, the planet, the sun, and the group soul, who are "saved," evolved to their greatest height at the close of individual life cycles.

LESSON 181
THE GIFT OF HEALING

Unfortunately there is an occasional student of the occult who has become so prejudiced against the Bible, or against much that it contains, that he is unable to appreciate the fact that some of the most important and basic truths of the Wisdom Religion may be found therein, clothed in different language. Among these basic truths is one in relation to Divine Healing. The same truth is frequently referred to by Bible students as one of the gifts of the Holy Spirit.

Cosmic electricity and Fohat are practically identical, and although it may seem like blasphemy to many, Fohat and the Holy Spirit in operation are identical.

The Sons of Fohat are Sound, Light, Flame, Magnetism (heat), Attraction, Repulsion, and Cohesion. In the last analysis, the gifts of the Holy Spirit as forces are the above-mentioned cosmic energies, and the power used by occult means in the healing of disease is Magnetism. The process of healing by this means depends upon the practitioner's ability to raise the vibration of the affected organ or part of a body by means of the magnetic fluid in himself and in his patient. The rise in vibration allows the diseased cells to attract to themselves the positive power of the elemental builders of vital force (Jiva),[1] and to repulse the negative elemental destroyers of the same vital force, and so to heal the disease. It is a process analogous to that of using electric power to start a gasoline motor. The human being who has allied himself with the positive elemental building forces of life by persistent effort and normal living may be able consciously to direct magnetic energy to a given point in the body of another, and so arouse the dormant cells at that point by his own life force. He may start that energy into action by a formula of words (sound) and by Will, and so help to drive out the negative elementals from a diseased organ, but if neither he nor his patient knows how or where to dispose of those ejected elementals, they may return with redoubled fury to the body from which they were ejected. And what is infinitely worse, if he does not know the back karma of the soul from whose body he has helped to drive those elementals, and the fundamental cause of the disease from which it suffers, he may do much more harm to both his own soul and that of his patient than he has done good to the body. Truly it is said, "Fools rush in where angels fear to tread."[2]

The Christian and mental healers as a rule base the righteousness of their acts of healing on the examples furnished by the Master Jesus, but they do not call attention to the record of His act of driving "the devils" — the elementals — afflicting the sick man into a drove of swine, nor do they perceive in that act a necessity for some similar act on their own part before attempting to heal a disease. Neither do they pretend to put the question asked by the disciples of Jesus,

---

[1] *Jiva* (*Sanskrit*, "life") — the universal principle of life; Prana; the monad.

[2] Alexander Pope, *An Essay on Criticism* (1711).

"Who did sin, this man or his parents?"[1] when an inquiry is made as to their willingness to heal the sick, which question in the mouths of those disciples plainly showed belief in karma and reincarnation. The answer received seems to have depended on their power or willingness to heal. For it must be remembered that Jesus had been teaching those disciples the secrets of occultism for many days.

Every sincere and earnest disciple has a perfect right to pray over, lay hands upon, or otherwise minister to the sick, and by so doing align himself with spiritual forces or beings which may use him as a vehicle to awaken the healing or building forces in a patient if he prefaces his act by aspiration and by an act of renunciation, whereby his personal will is entirely subjected to the Divine Will. His personal responsibility is thus limited. He has nothing to gain of a selfish nature in return in such an instance, and so is indifferent in the highest sense of the word, as to the results of his act. He can neither affirm nor deny the cause or the cure of the disease, neither can he accept payment for such service, or attempt consciously to expel or disperse the elemental forces which are the cause of the disease without knowing how to dispose of them. He who utterly ignores or defies the karmic effects of such action is running very close to black magic.

If fitted for such service, man is at perfect liberty to use nature's material remedies for the healing of disease under right conditions, for those remedies and the physical bodies treated belong to the same plane of life or state of gross matter, and the building and destroying elementals which have built up both those remedies and the physical bodies are of the same or similar degrees of life to those which have caused the disease, and which act and react on the same planes of life. They are not what they are often termed "spiritual forces." Therefore, the karmic result of their use is altogether different.

It is in the ignorant use or misuse of spiritual forces for material ends that man's culpability lies. As a rule the average man is entirely ignorant of the aftereffects of such use. A Master would be able to use spiritual forces for the gaining of right ends, for the reason that he knows exactly to what extent he can safely do so, both for himself or for others, but no Master would allow himself to be advertised as a Divine Healer. If he uses his power, it is because both he and the patient belong to the same group soul, and he has been consciously or unconsciously called upon by the patient to pay some karmic debt of

---
[1] John 9:2.

like nature, and therefore has the right to use the power if conditions and circumstances warrant its use by him.

If it is allowed that there are qualities in human nature which can only be overcome by sorrow and suffering, and if it be allowed that an actual necessity exists for the elimination of the said qualities if evolution on higher lines is to proceed, it should not be difficult to understand that it must require Divine prescience to determine to what extent it is justifiable to alleviate the suffering or heal a disease in an individual case. Neither does the present apparent necessity for suffering conflict with the even greater necessity for the cultivation of compassion and all the beatitudes. The first is transitory; the latter is eternal.

When all is told, the basic rule of occultism, "Do the right thing at the right time and in the right place," applies to healing as to all other forms of action.

LESSON 182
SOME MYSTERIES OF LIGHT

Until a student of life can accept the facts, at least tentatively, that consciousness is the one eternal reality, and that all else is illusion — reflection — he can never rest in the certainty of attainment in any field of true philosophy. With every increase of the vibratory pulse of a world, the increase which takes place on the upward arc of a cycle of time, the mentality of man enters an entirely new field of adventure. The devotee of science, invention, politics, and sociology is attracted toward some new ideal in each individual field of search, and this new ideal, all unconsciously to himself, will dominate other ideas in the mind of the thinker. The ideal is new to him then because he cannot remember similar periods on the upward arcs of preceding cycles when the same ideal, or some feature of the ideal, appealed to his mentality, but which he was unable to perfectly attain because of the limitations, the exactions which life in a physical body demanded at that particular time, and because of the action of a divine law which forbids any one unit of a race to progress very far beyond the race to which he belongs. In other words, there is a certain minimum state of development which must be reached by all the normal, intelligent units of the race before the single units can reach to the maximum state of that cycle.

It is by no means easy to retain in mind the fact that it is con-sciousness — identity — which creates and moves through all fields of life, while that consciousness seems to be so firmly imbedded in the matter of its own creation, and within which it is only capable of functioning by use of five senses.

It is only possible for man to attain to a full realization of this truth when the sixth sense begins to unfold, as is now the case with the more highly developed units of the present Root Race of humanity. As a result of the first flutterings of vital force in hitherto atrophied brain centers in such highly developed units, the last half of the past century and beginning of the present one has seen some wonderful strides in all fields of life — material, psychic, and spiritual. Anal-ogy and correspondence are opening up mind areas which had been closed by superstition and ignorance, and are being used to augment the results of investigation by microscope, telescope, spectrum anal-ysis, etc. Microscopical research alone is furnishing some remarkable disclosures along the line of the minute forms of life.

The comparatively great spaces between the cells, the molecules, atoms, and electrons, which recent investigation has proven, paves the way for understanding somewhat of the universes which may exist, peopled by conscious lives now classified as microbes, germs, etc., and even more minute forms of life. Analogy and correspondence furnish plenty of evidence to the thinker that, as those lesser areas of space are peopled by minute forms of life, so the wider spaces are peopled by forms of life correspondingly greater in size; beings in which count-less other large forms of life now visible to the eye of man, may be of correspondingly microbic proportion to the consciousness of such beings. These new discoveries of science are related to facts which have been known to the Masters of Wisdom for ages, and many of these facts have been made known to the disciples of the said Masters long before the devotees of science now engaged in such research announced them. However, there is one impassable barrier between the findings of the average scientist and the teachings of the Masters, and that is that barrier at the point where spirit and matter meet, and "where one must disappear to give space to the other."[1] The Master teaches that this point lies in the atomic field of life; in other words, that neither the atom nor electron is matter, in the strict sense of the

---

[1] From the *Book of the Golden Precepts*. See Blavatsky, *The Voice of the Silence*, p. 12.

word, but Mind and Soul, entirely different states of existence within which the microbes of science are non-existent, while at the same time they are created — built — into form by consciousness. He teaches that all the forms of the greater as well as the lesser universes which the scientist now postulates, are facts in nature also created and animated by consciousness, and as both lie outside the fields of gross matter and are not subject to the governing laws of such matter, they can only be observed and contacted by the inner senses — the senses of soul.

One of the very interesting findings of a famous scientist and microscopist is that the utmost attainable limit of resolving power by which life in minutiae is observable is $1,140,000^{th}$ of an inch, and that such restriction is caused by refraction. This means that the ray of light entering the lens of the microscope at its axis bends around the object and enters the eye exactly as though the object did not exist.

However, while this does not mean that organized life does not exist in minutiae beyond that object, it does mean to the occultist that there are light rays which would not bend in even a microscope of much greater power, and therefore would leave the object visible to the eye, if that eye could bear the light; such rays of light would be directly transmitted from the Central Spiritual Sun through the sun of this solar system, but would not be traceable by the physical sense of sight. The light would be visible to the psychic sense of sight. When rays of light are diffracted — bent around an object — a window is opened into the astral plane at the bend, through which man might see the astral image of any material object in its path if the physical eye were differently constructed.

Until the scientist can accept the fact that the light which to all appearances comes from the visible sun is but the reflection of certain rays of a much greater central sun, his researches in that line will be unsatisfactory. As the full strength of a chemical may be applied to some form of gross matter without injury to the latter, but must be diluted if safely used by a man, and still further diluted if used by a child, so the energy of the Central Sun is freed by means of certain rays in proportion to the character of the mass which has attracted them, whether it be a sun or a world or a man. With the evolution of the sixth sense, consciousness will have a vehicle by means of which the human ego will be able to solve many of the mysteries of light without the aid of a microscope or any other material agent. The human eye will then be fully developed and will be all that is required in the line of a microscope. Man will then be able to look through the aforesaid windows made by bent rays of light which are now opaque to his vision.

The mind of man is so generally bound by his theories regarding the constitution of matter that it is difficult for him to accept the fact that matter has no *bona fide* existence.

LESSON 183
LIFE SPARKS

The differentiation of electrical energy to which its latest inves- tigator has applied the term *Ion* — to distinguish it from other differentiations of the same cosmic energy — and the *Sparks* of occult science are identical. While modern science has been driven to accept many of the truths of occultism, at least as hypotheses, it is only one here and there among its votaries who has been able to apply the theoretical knowledge so gained, in practice. It will not be possible to apply the finer forces in the manipulation of matter to any remarkable degree until the workers in this field of science are able to demonstrate to their own satisfaction the intermediate forms of energy which lie between gross matter — the vehicles of such forms of energy — and those which more nearly approach the highest poles of manifested life — Manasic energy.

While the degree of electrical energy which the occultist desig- nates Manas, or Ideation, is being applied in its own field of action — the mental plane — it has not been found possible to direct it in a manner to show visible or audible effects by any acknowledged scientist of this age; neither has any scientist been able to accept the statements of occultists who claim to be able to produce such effects, or to have seen them produced. Yet, until the knowledge is gained of the possibility that such visible or audible effects can be demonstrated to the senses, it will be impossible to segregate and demonstrate the reality of the existence and possible use of the Ion, and several other forms of the same energy, in the production of external phenomena. In order to accomplish that feat, it is absolutely necessary to use the Manasic energy outside of its own field, i.e., by visible or audible effects on or in gross matter, as man has not yet evolved the senses by means of which he might perceive the natural phenomena constantly occurring within the fields or planes of substance in which each form or degree of electrical energy is preeminently active.

Man may be able to gather together the constituent elements, the chemical agents and reagents, and other forms of substance which nature has already created, and under exactly right conditions of heat and moisture succeed in creating a living creature; but it must be remembered that practically all he has done is to make conditions under which the previously created elements, chemicals, etc., could continue to grow. The basic life forces active in every atom and molecule used in the materials he has brought together were already in them; he literally had no hand in creating those basic materials. If he had only been able to isolate a single molecule of all those forms of substance that he had gathered, and was wise enough to create exactly the same conditions which nature would use in developing life sparks, from that single molecule would be evolved all other constituent molecules required to form such a body as the one that he had been instrumental in bringing to outer form. But nature would go much further; for while he had to pause when that form was created, nature would go on, and from that same molecule would evolve an organic vehicle through which the electrical energy of Manas could operate, and that which might be termed a rudimentary brain would manifest in the form evolved from that single molecule. But nature could not have performed any of these marvels had it not been for the basic life — the spark — which rests at the very center of every atom which constitutes that molecule.

Notwithstanding our efforts to convey some idea of the fourfold existence of the Ego on the four planes of life, we are not successful in all instances, and so we can only try again until our purpose is served. Many words confuse real issues, and often throw a deep shadow over what are in fact self-evident truths.

The life and action of the Ego in the four lower of the seven states of consciousness, the forms through which that consciousness functions, the states of matter which comprise those forms, and the motion — the time — which governs the appearance and disappearance of those forms in any one or all of those states of matter, are the basic facts, which alone provide for any understanding of the appearance and disappearance of the astral and physical bodies from the sight — the consciousness of each other.

First consider the swinging of the pendulum of a clock, the spring of which has been wound up to allow the pendulum to swing for exactly twenty-four hours. The winding of the spring, which sets the pendulum in motion, corresponds to the Fohatic energy that has been set free for an age corresponding to the said twenty-four hours. That energy sets in action and keeps in motion all the substance which has previously been asleep through a night of time, and moves that substance in perfect rhythm and time corresponding to the movements of the pendulum of the clock. (We are not now considering the three highest of the seven states of consciousness.) Then consider that there are four grades of that substance, each one more refined, tenuous, and elastic than the preceding one, if we start from that of the physical plane, or the reverse if we start from the manasic.

It is through these four planes or states of substance that the Ego — the unmanifested Spiritual Self of the three higher of the seven principles — must function throughout each age, as the cyclic law — the pendulum of the life-clock — swings that substance around a central point, in completing one great age of life in order that it may gain permanent individual life when the hands of the clock have completed their circles; that is, when the seven great ages are completed.

For the purpose of providing itself with an individual form through which to function on all planes, all fields of life, the Ego must evolve a separate vehicle out of each of the four states of substance — akashic, etheric, astral, and physical — which altogether constitute the composite plane of manifestation. It may simplify this phase of the subject if we use terms in more general use in attempting to fix this most important point in the mind. The electric, atomic, molecular, and cellular divisions of matter as used in physical science, closely approach the differentiations of occult science previously given.

If the reader can accept the truth that there is one universe within another — each one of which is composed of substance in precisely the state of vibration to which have been given the terms above mentioned, and that in combination they create an exterior universe, the universe we perceive by our physical senses — it may aid in giving a hypothesis by means of which we may comprehend what is sometimes termed "the ladder of life" upon the steps of which the pilgrim, the individual Ego, descends and ascends from and back to spiritual life.

Since each individual Ego must create for itself, out of the substance of which each one of these universes is constituted, a form or vehicle in and by means of which he can live, comprehend, and finally control the substance of each universe. For instance, the Ego must evolve a form out of the electric substance, another form out of the atomic universe, still another form out of the etheric, and yet another form out of the molecular life of this exterior material universe, if it desires individual conscious existence on all four planes.

Yet, on his ascent from the lowest step of the ladder, he must lose the consciousness of each universe as a distinct and objective field of life, retaining only what he has gained from the experience he has passed through while functioning in the body which was built out of the substance of that universe.

When he has taken the last upward step of that ladder, he has lost all sense of separateness; the former four universes with their separated forms no longer obtain in his consciousness, but he retains all that his experience — through them all — has brought to him.

LESSON 184
NO GOD

The blatant materialist or atheist knows in his heart he is not what he would have other men believe him to be. He has either built up a mental image, endowed it with the negative qualities of matter, and endeavors to convince others that he is that image; or he is trading on the weakness of the self-indulgent curiosity hunter who is ever-seeking some anomaly in nature or in man. A *bona fide* materialist — one who disbelieves in Deity — is an utter impossibility in a universe created in, of, and by Deity, whatever be the name, form, or nature that Deity takes in the mind of man.

By his very nature man must have a God, but whether that God is a Supreme Being, a sun, an image made by his own hands, or an ideal of a perfect human being, it matters not. The first cry of an awakened soul for light — whether that cry was smothered in terror of the unknown, or was loudly uttered in a plea for guidance, comfort, or help in a time of need — is an unconscious recognition of Deity. Possibly the cry may be an expression of admiration for exquisite beauty or grandeur, or for some exhibition of phenomenal power; whatever the exciting cause, it is the God in him crying out to the God who created him, for readmission to the Garden of Eden — the state of equilibrium — perfection from which he was driven by divine law in order that he might return clothed in immortality.

Every unsatisfied longing for love, devotion, truth; every wave of admiration for beauty, in whatever form that beauty is clothed; every ambition for strength, power, and ability to build some lasting monument of his own skill, is a half-recognized cry to the God the materialist claims to disbelieve in. His unbelief is negative belief, and every effort he makes to prove his unbelief to others does but drive him further on toward final — positive — belief and recognition of Deity.

The mouthings, cursings, and invective of the atheist — or his silent contempt for others who loudly profess their faith and belief in God — in reality spring from the revolt of the outraged God in himself. The man who believes his faith in God and therefore his hope and courage have departed, owing to the evils perpetrated by some other human being, is mistaken. It is not his faith that is gone; his temporary doubts are due to the partial numbing of a single center of the brain by hard usage, as when a portion of an arm or leg may be numbed from repeated blows from the outside, and that center will not respond to the call made by the inner man. But it is not a permanent injury to the center. Either in the hour of death, or at the coming of some great unexpected joy, the numbness will depart and he will find himself saying something like the following: "My God and my King," or "Thanks be to thee, O God."

The man who has trained his mind to unbelief by reading atheistic works or by placing himself under the influence of the so-called "free thinkers" — the most abject slaves — has weakened his will by coming so entirely under the power of negative suggestion, and is of all men to be sorrowed over, for he has entered the path to annihilation. There is no life outside God, and man has been left free to choose whether he will have life or death in the end.

The recognition and acceptance of the Higher Self which comes to the student of philosophy, after he has passed a period of what he believes to be atheism, is the result of the soul's effort to bring the lower self back into close communion with Deity, for God and the Higher Self are one. The terminology applied to the Supreme Self by different expositors of religion and philosophy has given rise to much confusion.

If disciples could bear in mind one great truth, it would tide them over many deep streams of doubt and unbelief: that is, the truth that the highest concept of any human mind is a concept of some one or more aspects of Deity. It is of no permanent consequence whether he terms that concept God, Brahman,[1] Jehovah,[2] or the Higher Self for the time being. It is the recognition of the Supreme, whether he places it inside, outside, or both inside and outside of his physical self. That Supreme Self knows, for it is Knowledge when any aspect of Itself is raised to recognition of Itself. The more perfect that recognition, the more complete the identification — the union of the human will with the Supreme Will — the more wisdom, knowledge, and power is at the service of the individual Ego. The sooner man realizes that there is but one Will active in the universe — the Will of God — and that it is on his use or misuse of that Will that he is dependent for power, the sooner he will come into his divine inheritance.

LESSON 185
WHOM WILL YE SERVE?

Down twenty centuries of time, repeated over and over, by word of mouth, by pen and symbol, endorsed and denied by countless peoples of all tongues and climes, have come the burning words of One who knew whereof He spoke: "Ye cannot serve both God and Mammon."[3] Even now they are not understood in full, save by the few, the chosen ones of earth. Applied alone to mediums of exchange, to gold and silver, flocks and herds, to lands and houses, Mammon stands for man's possessions only; yet He who gave it utterance meant a wider range of that which stands for wealth than man now gives to it. Mammon! Beast! In truth the words are all but interchangeable in this age, and if by *beast* the lower self of man is also meant, it will fitly express that which the great Master meant by Mammon. Man cannot serve the beast within himself, and serve his Higher Self, his God, at the same time.

The demon would slay the Higher Self had it the power.

A liar, a deceiver, a murderer, a foul epitome of selfishness and lust — such is that lower self, a tempter of the pilgrim starting out to climb the Path of Power.

---

[1] *Brahman (Sanskrit,* "to grow") — the ultimate reality or universal principle in Hinduism; the unchanging, infinite, and transcendent reality that underlies all existence.

[2] *Jehovah* — a Hebrew name for the God of Israel.

[3] Matthew 6:24.

If man would reach a star, he must travel the lone path that leads thereto. The star route is a lonely route. If man has sought and found the only other soul that could by any means walk by his side along that route, blessed indeed is he. Alas, but all too often does he pass that soul unheeding, mayhap contemptuously, unfeelingly. Desire or ignorance stays his steps upon the very threshold of success while he dallies with the tempter and strives to climb all hampered as he is to the step beyond. But this he may not do, and so must wait for time to forge another link between the links of the chain which would bind him to his other self. Or, having found that other self and started up the Path, a demon in the form of earthly power or pride awakens from the sleep in which it has been wrapped — and lo, the beast, the Mammon power, hath seized and thrown him once again.

It stands and faces man or lurks behind at every halting place upon the Path, and not until his feet are shod with the sandals of Self-knowledge, not until his hand clasps close the staff of "true indifference" can he safely, surely tread the Path to his Father's house and hear that Father say, "Well done, my son, the beast is slain."

LESSON 186
EGOISM VERSUS EGOTISM

Does the seed of a plant attempt to put forth leaves for the purpose of attracting the necessary constituents from the air for the nourishment of roots, or flowers for the formation of new seed, before it has even commenced to put forth a stalk to support the flowers? Does a wise parent attempt to put a child through a college course before the child has matured a brain by means of which it may comprehend the rudiments of even a single study of such a course? Yet many people are attempting to accomplish a purpose that is fully as impractical and unnatural as would be a similar purpose by seed or parent. If it were possible to accomplish such a purpose, the result would be unnatural for the following among many other considerations: absence of the functions by means of which the necessary nourishment — physical or mental energy — could be supplied from the outside to permit the bursting of the shell of cell or molecule in order that the within may become the without; and inability to maintain that which has come forth until its divine purpose is fulfilled in the development of new seed or cells.

If it were possible to accomplish either purpose, the result would be a monstrosity, an abnormal thing incapable of fulfilling the divine purpose. In no case is this truth more evident than in the overdevelopment of the quality of egotism in the character of a man or woman. The seed of the quality of egotism is "egoism" — individuality — notwithstanding the generally accepted definition of the word, for the Ego is the spiritual seed of the individual, the consciousness of the "I am."

The quality of humility bears a certain correspondence to the stalk of the plant or the trunk of the tree. It is the quiet unassuming force which is the real support and base of supplies for the more exoteric features of individuality. True humility is absolutely necessary for spiritual growth. Overdevelopment of the quality of egotism, and a corresponding underdevelopment of the quality of humility is ever noticeable in the leaders of mobs. A dearth of actual knowledge, a little desultory reading, attendance upon certain classes of lectures, and a course of mental gymnastics have fitted the rabid egotist for such leadership. The normal development of the qualities of egoism and humility, all things else being equal, serves to fit one for true leadership; but one so fitted is generally backward about asserting himself. Unless a definite call has been made upon him by others, he will avoid everything which tends to push him to the front. His knowledge of his own limitations is so keen it is actually painful if he be placed in a situation where he appears to stand forth as a superior in the eyes of his fellow men.

An egotist has no more chance to unlock the jewel case of Deity and estimate the value of the treasures therein by means of the seeing eye than a chicken has to estimate the value of a tray of precious gems in a jeweler's window.

The ranter on the street corner who draws a crowd to listen to an arraignment against all ruling powers — one who may never have heard of political economy, the history of nations, the action of cyclic laws, or the inevitable results of Karmic law, and who may have been pushed to the wall by his own incompetence, or indolence — is one example of overdeveloped egotism. As a result of his ranting, possibly a large number of people are aroused to frenzy, and instead of trying to find some real remedy for what may have been a mental or moral disease, he heads a mob to wreak vengeance on some other man who is in a position of power, yet who is, in all likelihood, equally a victim of circumstances, environment, and wrong educational methods. Or, to bring an illustration closer to everyday life, the egotistic husband and father of a family who — because of his inability to make any deep impression on his fellow workers in some field of labor, yet who is convinced that he is a much misunderstood and unappreciated victim of the ignorance of others — makes his home a place of torment to wife and children by his rigid rule over them, by his constant demands upon their credulity, by his repeated criticism of words or acts, by reminders of their supposed inferiority, as well as by prophecies of the evils to befall them because of their lack of respect or regard for him. In fact, his inferiority to many others his family are frequently contacting, his lack of self-control, his narrow concepts of the great realities, are all so self-evident to the family that, despite their real affection for him, there is aroused such a feeling of contempt for his littleness, such a disregard for his injunctions, that in the end something approaching hate develops in their minds with a desire to get so far away from him that they will never have to behold his face again.

I have no intention of confining my remarks or arguments to the masculine sex in giving these illustrations, for they are equally applicable to the feminine sex, and are daily becoming even more so as women are being forced unprepared into the positions formerly held by males alone. Some of the qualities which are preeminently active in the sex make the female heads of families or of business houses peculiarly trying to those who are under their control. I refer more particularly to small jealousies of each other, the character of jealousy seldom noted in the male sex. While jealousy is one of the prevailing limitations of the male, it is exercised in larger ways. But all this is incidental. What I am striving to arouse in those to whom my words apply in any special sense is the power to estimate character at its true value, instead of yielding to the negative forces of over or under self-appreciation without effort to form a correct estimate of one's real position in the scale of life. This power cannot be won so long as self-satisfaction and egotistic pride predominate over those qualities which make for fair and just judgment. One method of accomplishing this purpose is to cultivate the habit of seeking the great, the perfected in the minutiae of art and science and in nature, and among the humble, the inconspicuous, the hidden people and things of life.

When you fully comprehend the vast truth that the invisible molecule is possible of subdivision into innumerable lesser divisions, you will have more regard for the hidden things of life, for each subdivision is capable of the generation of energy of incomparably greater power than that of the mass from which it was subdivided. The atom is capable of generating power enough to drive the world out of its present orbit if the ability to direct it were at the command of a human being whose trinity of action — Desire, Will, and Mind — was sufficiently developed to permit of his awakening that energy from its semiconscious state and directing the course of its movements.

The time will come when man will be no longer subject to many of the cruder forms of energy which now limit his action so greatly; a time when he will have learned that the many layers of matter which now seem to make impossible his reaching to the center of any form of life are in fact illusions possible of dissipation by the means he now possesses yet fails to use, owing to its simplicity, and to his present contempt for the very qualities by which alone it would be possible for him to recognize and use those means.

The man or woman who flatters you, works on your vanity, praises you beyond your deserts, is one of your worst enemies; for whether you are conscious of it or not, he is adding to the natural menstruum of your pride and conceit and preparing the way for the lower self to build therein.

Strive by self-examination to look yourself honestly and fairly in the face, to recognize the qualities which belong to your lower selves and gain control of them. Of course, it is a long task — but you have Eternity to accomplish it in, so do not let that deter you from making a beginning, lest even Eternity be too short.

LESSON 187
DISSONANCE

In the study of music at headquarters, the subject of dissonance was introduced for discussion and proved to be of such deep interest that it was thought advisable to get as much light on the subject as was possible. Therefore, the following questions were asked of the Master when an opportunity was given, and were subsequently answered by him in an instruction which we give in full, together with some comments by the Guardian-in-Chief:

1. What is dissonance?
2. Has it polarities?
3. What is its action on the qualities?
4. Is it good or evil in its results?

Dissonance sounds the key for the dissociation of the atoms of concrete substance. Divine Law uses the force of dissonance to resolve one state of substance into another state. You can only reach a full understanding of its uses by studying its natural effects on objective forms, on people and things. It is the uses to which it is put that determine its good or evil aspects, its effects on the qualities.

Dissonance resolves harmony into discord, love into hatred, peace into battle. Harmony in music may lull the mind and body into a false sense of security. Dissonance may arouse mind and body to action. The final result of such action may be anything but desirable, or it may be the exact reverse, and yet you cannot truthfully say that either dissonance, harmony, or discord is good or evil in itself.

Dissonance is a force, i.e., the passing of one state of energy into another. Harmony is a state of consciousness. Dissonance may turn discord into harmony; yet as discord is also a state of consciousness, it also may be influenced to a great degree by dissonance.

Having reached its gamut — the end of its triune action — dissonance may then reverse its course of action; the positive aspect of its action may assert its purpose and return to its point of departure. From that point it may then resolve discord into harmony, harmony into love, love into unity — the end of the line of its uses throughout an objective cycle.

It is toneless in itself, although it may be used to strike the key to a tone. At certain definite periods in a Manvantara when the positive aspect of the force is preeminently active, the disruptive, disintegrating power of action is, as it were unshackled, and turned on those phases or places in a universe or world as the case may be, which has reached its apogee — the height of its spiral course. Divine Law then uses it to tear apart old forms until another period of the cycle is reached, at which time the course of action is reversed again, turned towards the reconstructing, the integrating of the primordial matter through which it is acting, the matter which is then in a state of flux, and from that state of flux into definite form.

Of itself dissonance is nothing; it is only in its uses that it may be made manifest. The present period of this Manvantara gives opportunity for the unleashed powers of disintegration, and dissonance in all fields of life and action is playing a tremendously vital part.

As an illustration of the nature and purpose of dissonance, consider the following:

Divine Law (God in action) proclaims a decree, speaks "the (Creative) Word," i.e., sounds the keynote to a note — a rate of Vibration. If that decree adversely concerns conditions previously prevailing and the change is to be precipitated within the confines of a harmonious — a balanced — state or condition, the force or energy instrumental in creating the change would be negatively opposed to the neutral — the harmonious state or condition — and would result in changing the latter into a discordant, inharmonious state.

The Divine Decree would in its proclamation have struck the keynote to a change in the vibratory pulse of that state, i.e., it would have lowered the rates of vibration previously in action, and that which produced the change would be the force of dissonance. The force would have been evoked in the proclamation of the Decree and the Divine purpose; the method and means of accomplishment would operate simultaneously.

During that period of any grand cycle when the force of dissonance is most active, it will be found that in all fields of art, music, literature, invention, and in national and family life, there is a strong tendency in evidence towards the breaking up of old forms, and much discord and friction. In religion it will appear in loss of faith and increase of doubt; in governments, in much lawlessness among the masses; and in the crust of the earth, in much volcanic and seismic disturbance.

In another, a later period of the same cycle, all this may be reversed. It is to be hoped that the difference between discord and dissonance may be recognized and that humanity may learn to use the force of dissonance in a beneficent manner instead of, as is largely now the case, being used by it to individual disadvantage.

COMMENTS FROM BLUE STAR[1]

If I have read the instruction aright, the terms dissonance, harmony, and discord are used in a more general and wider sense than that in which they are generally applied. The words *dissonance* and *Satan* may be interchangeable to some extent.

Lucifer — Satan — the bright angel banished from Heaven because of his pride and disobedience, brought sorrow and suffering upon the human race, but as a final result of his act, man is evolving to a state much higher than would otherwise have been possible.

---

[1] *Blue Star* — the spiritual name given to Francia La Due by the Master Hilarion.

If the Master's interpretation of the purpose and final effect of the force he terms dissonance be accepted, these would appear to be practically the same as are those which are said to be the purpose and final effect of the action of Lucifer, i.e., the disintegration of matter and the breaking up of all old forms of life.

The word *harmony* in general use is indicative of a heavenly or harmonious state or condition, but a state which may be destroyed by dissonance — Satan — but which may also be re-created by the opposite pole of the same force, consonance, at definite periods of time, and this must be accomplished by the very laws of his being, for Satan is both good and evil in the last analysis.

He, or It, changes harmonious conditions into discordant conditions in the lives of men by inciting them to disobedience to the commands of God, yet in the nature of the Christos he must reverse those conditions.

While there is a strong disinclination in the minds of many to assent to the idea of a synthetic Christ and Satan as is put forth in some of the older philosophies, yet the idea of successful opposition to God by Satan, or any lesser being or power, seems even more difficult of acceptance by others.

The word *harmony* as used in music is made to include concord, consonance, dissonance, and discord, but as indicative of a cosmic state of consciousness, energies, or forces, these words do not bear the same relation to each other.

Occultly speaking, harmony has its correspondence in the "Triple Key," Atma-Buddhi-Manas. It is all inclusive until differentiation takes place. Buddhi-Manas in differentiation has polarities, and consonance and dissonance would correspond to the polarities of Buddhi-Manas. Buddhi synthesizes, Manas analyzes.

In differentiation or manifestation, concord and discord are states of energy or consciousness. In differentiation, consonance and dissonance are polarities of the force which is used by Karmic and Cyclic law to resolve substance of lower vibration into harmonious or discordant conditions, according to the periods of a Manvantara in which that force is used by divine law.

On the upward arc of any cycle, the positive pole — consonance — would be preeminently active; on the downward arc of the same cycle, dissonance would be most active.

While the Master did not use the word *consonance* in his instruction, it is clearly indicated as "the positive aspect" of the force of dissonance. It must be understood that the Master was not using the above-mentioned terms in relation to music alone, but in a much broader and higher sense.

Guardian-in-Chief

ADDITIONAL QUESTIONS

1. Can you verify my comments on dissonance, so that they could be incorporated as part of the Instruction?

2. Would the word *intersonance* include the polarities of dissonance and consonance?

Guardian-in-Chief

ANSWERS

If exoteric interpretation by students of words indicating Cosmic Forces is preferable to the esoteric interpretation of the same words as given by you, there would naturally be room for argument. From the esoteric point of view taken up by you, you are absolutely correct.

The Instruction entitled "Dissonance" as given by me was not given for the purpose of verifying the adaptation of the same terms as used in musical composition, but rather in exposition of Cosmic forces. However, the common use of the prefixes "dis" and "con" should indicate opposition.

The happy use of the word *intersonance* by your brother comes very near to indicating the neutral zone between the polarities dissonance and consonance. It is applicable to the zone of light — on an interior plane, from which dissonance and consonance are differentiated, i.e., brought into manifestation, and also harmony and discord as interpreted by me.

The energies which manifest as Light and Sound on the physical plane are one on an interior plane.

LESSON 188
WAR AND PEACE

Step by step, through incredible anguish and suffering, the human race is evolving to a degree where the taking of human life will no longer be tolerated by that race. As a final result of that evolution, all degrees of matter constituting the physical plane are changing, but the completion of those changes cannot occur during the manifestation of the Fifth Race of humanity. All cosmic eventualities must first appear as ideals in the racial mind. Ideals of universal peace, universal freedom, love, and harmony taking form in the minds of the more highly evolved units of the present race will be consummated in a later age.

In the present age as in all preceding ages, the highest ideals the humanity of the age is capable of reaching are the final results of the life and teachings of the Sons of Wisdom, and those teachings are always first given to a group of chosen neophytes or disciples in the age preceding the one in which it would be possible to bring into manifestation on the physical plane the ideals which have formed as a result of the widespread efforts of such a group as I have referred to.

In a Messianic Cycle, there is more rapid growth and even objectification of high ideals than in other cycles, as is evident at the present time; for while there appears to be a great increase of what is generally termed evil on the one hand, there is a correspondingly great increase of effort on all lines which make for righteousness. The ideal of the establishment of permanent peace between all nations of the earth is rapidly taking form in the more highly developed minds of all nations, and it is the result of the teachings of a single group of disciples during the last Messianic Cycle. But that peace cannot be consummated until the decrees of Karmic law are carried out — the karma made by the rejection of those teachings by the masses then in incarnation, and the abuse of those teachings in succeeding ages.

It must be remembered that, as the different races and sub-races overlap each other, so do the decrees of Karmic law overlap each other. Comparatively speaking, there is little of the karma of a race or nation perfectly fulfilled during the cycle in which that karma was made. The decrees of racial and national karma, both good and bad now being made in the present war, will overlap some of the early sub-races of the Sixth Race —to be fulfilled or expiated during the Third and Fourth sub-races of the same Root Race — when will occur another Messianic Cycle, and when all the unexpiated karma of all preceding Races will fall on the humanity then under the testing forces for the highest point of development a race could reach: the final testing of man for his Divine Inheritance, his Mastery.

But the possible escape of karmic action in the present cycle should not be an inducement to the man of high vision to plunge into the present holocaust. He should have a higher motive than that of escaping karma by entering active service — if that were possible. A nation or a man is only justified in warring with another nation or another man when the life and safety of his own nation, or some other nation, or some other life is at stake, and the motive is *defense*.

There was a time not so many years ago, when much of the evil karma the present race is now paying might have been paid by other means than those which have precipitated the present world crisis, but the people would not hear or obey the injunctions — nay — the pleadings of the Initiates and Prophets of the Great White Lodge as they were voiced through preceding centuries as well as in the century which closed in the year 1898, leaving the Karmic law no other alternative than that which has culminated in the present worldwide struggle. But this does not mean that war is ever right from the highest spiritual standpoint (where Spirit and Matter are one), and a neophyte of the White Lodge should be careful to make distinctions when voicing his own position or that of The Temple of the People. As an individual, his action should be governed by motive and duty, regardless of the final fruits of his action, whether he takes an active or passive part in the war. If convinced that the life and safety of the people of his own nation or those of another nation with its teeming races of humanity are at stake, and he believes his duty calls him to take an active part in the defense of that nation, he should not be considered a renegade to principle any more than should the man be considered a renegade to his race who sees his duty in another direction. Either man may be a far greater man, spiritually speaking, than the other because of the purity and unselfishness of his motive and the sacrifices he may be called upon to make. To his own Higher Self must he stand or fall. But whatever may be his personal action or motive for action or for inaction, he has no right to confuse the main issue by claiming that the body of which he may be a part — a body built on the principle of the brotherhood of man, irrespective of nation or creed — cannot be perfectly right if it is unable to endorse his motive for action or inaction as the case may be. He is perfectly right from his standpoint owing to his controlling motive. The body of which he is a part is right from the standpoint of that universal principle alone. There is a wide margin between universals and particulars, and wise indeed is the man who can fill in that margin with data which are right and just from a spiritual standpoint.

A tremendous responsibility is assumed by the mentality of man when an issue is under consideration, such as the surrender of the vehicle through which the incarnating Ego must contact the world of matter, in order to vindicate what is to that mentality a spiritual principle. The thinking entity, man, must take heed lest the thought waves of others impinge so powerfully on his mentality as to make his presentation of a question to his Higher Self more the question of some other individual or individuals than his own; and the answer received — either by direct word or impression — might apply more perfectly to those who had influenced his mental action than to him directly.

The basic unity of the human race is responsible for this possibility, for the more closely the spiritual planes of action are approached, the more the essential unity of the race is manifest to the soul. Therefore, the responsibility of the man who subjects himself voluntarily to the influence of others when some important decision is to be made, is as great as is that of the one or more who are freeing those thought waves in order to influence that decision. The thought waves of the audience, in the case of a murder trial, may do far more to influence the verdict and sentence of judge and jury than all the evidence submitted could do. The negative condition into which judge and jury would necessarily fall as a result of long tension, would prepare the way for such influence. If there be a current of sympathetic action between any two people, the danger of undue influence is all the greater; therefore, all the more care should be exercised when any important decision is to be reached.

LESSON 189
UNIVERSAL LAW

The universe expands under the breath of Fire — Spirit — the Father, at the beginning of a Maha Yuga, a great age, and contracts under the breath of Substance — the Mother, at the end of that period. The degree of expansion and contraction is contingent upon the divine impulse sent out from the center of all life. Every atom in every solar system expands and contracts in corresponding ratio at the rising and setting of the sun upon its field of action, and this action is dependent upon the impulse sent forth from the sun when it is high noon at any point of any planet belonging to the solar system.

When man turns his nights into day by means of artificial light, for toil or pleasure, he must inevitably suffer as a result of thus acting in opposition to natural law. The physical body naturally falls into a more or less comatose condition as the energy of contraction is set up in the atoms of that body at sunset, and if man oppose his will to the natural law which governs Motion, at the time when his body is subject to the contracting forces of the Solar Orb, he throws his whole body out of harmony. In such an instance, the forces of attraction and repulsion are at war in his body, each one striving to usurp the power of the other so that neither one can perfectly perform its natural functions. Consequently, much of the energy of cohesion — the combining force sent forth from the heart center when the life currents flow naturally to and fro from that center — is lost; the expansive energy of the vital currents is impeded, and there is no opportunity for cell growth and development. Consequently, degeneration has set up in the nucleoli of the cell before the allotted life cycle of the incarnated ego is complete.

The same laws govern all forms of organized life to a greater or lesser degree, i.e., according to the perfection or imperfection of the organized body, whether the body is created by Divine or human will. If the constituent parts of a body, the members of an organization created by man, turn the night side of their nature — the effects of the action of the lower mind — to the purpose of obstructing the functions of the higher mind — the day side of their nature symbolized by the organizing central point of the body corresponding to the sun, the welding force — the cohesive energy of the central point — can no longer exert the same power; the expansive energy of the body is cut off; and the growth of the body is impeded.

Not understanding the working of natural law, or permitting their knowledge to lie dormant, the majority of the students of the philosophy we sent to the western world through H. P. Blavatsky, allowed the qualities of the lower mind to usurp the functions or attributes of the higher mind. They turned the currents of suspicion, self-interest, and factional disturbances upon the natural heart center — the appointed representative of the Initiates — and drew away from her the life forces of sympathy, understanding, and loyal support upon which her life work depended. So far as the said students were concerned, she was no longer able to function the currents of force from the White Lodge for their benefit, for they had lost the power of attraction which drew those currents to them, and they fell under the influence of whosoever had the power to attract them in the world at large. All this being true, it stands to reason there could not be a perfect, permanent vehicle for the continuous transmission of those Lodge currents until a sufficient nucleus of naturally law-abiding, law-understanding people were drawn together — a nucleus of disciples who cared enough for their own development, and the development of the races of the earth — to make determined, persistent effort to dominate those aforementioned qualities of the lower self, and permit the attributes of the higher mind to function their natural forces and so bring about expansion of the body.

With the completion of the formation of such a body, the question of the worthiness, the ability, and power of the selected center — the Agent — is stilled. The body *knows* beyond question that it has received just what it demanded from the Initiates by its aspiration and devotion and that its development depends upon its own conduct toward its heart center.

False to H.P.B. and her teachings, a disciple could hardly be true to the present agent of the Lodge, for he could not have worked out the karma of his offense in so short a time and still be in incarnation, except through some such superhuman effort as the average man would not dare undertake. This accounts for the abject failure of so many early students and their continual drifting from one point to another.

LESSON 190
SOME CHIEF CAUSES FOR FAILURE IN THE DOMAIN OF OCCULTISM
FROM THE MASTER K.H.

That there has been a failure so far as the successful establishment of a vast organized body is concerned is beyond controversy; that is, such a body as was planned by the Initiates of the White Lodge when they sent their representative to the Western world.[1] These causes were first, abnormal development of the quality of egotism unsupported

---

[1] It was H. P. Blavatsky who was sent to the West to establish the Theosophical Society in New York City in 1875. The Masters saw the main goals of this organization as forming the universal brotherhood of humanity without distinction of race or religion, as well as in acquainting the peoples of the West with the esoteric philosophy of the East.

by knowledge among the early investigators of the Wisdom Religion; second, great increase in the number of imitators of the phenomena produced by true Initiates, and the natural reaction which followed the exposure of fraudulent methods of producing phenomena; third, false claims to personal guidance of the Masters by the self-deceived or ambitious; fourth, unfaithfulness to vows of discipleship, and consequent contempt for such weakness in the minds of those who had previously considered such solemnly pledged disciples as examples for others to follow; fifth, false teaching along the line of sex; last, but by no means least, an army of braggarts who have constantly poured forth accounts of personal contact with the Masters, accounts in which the wisdom and worth of the braggart was duly extolled and the lack of spiritual perception in the case of their followers greatly deplored. The final result in such instances has been the arousing of suspicion and the direction of adverse currents of force against the true disciples of the Masters, which has stultified their efforts to interpret and give forth the valuable teachings of the Wisdom Religion to a world in travail.

What should have been the greatest, most far-reaching organized effort for good in the world, by this time, has become a heterogeneous mixture of small cults, each one under the direction of some pseudo-occultist who is incapable of fulfilling his or her promises to followers. Only here and there among these groups may be found a genuine chela of the Masters who is endeavoring to leaven the lump of fraudulent or unwise teaching presented to their number. Of all the enemies by whom these chelas are beset, there are none capable of inflicting so much injury to the cause of occultism as the beforementioned braggarts who, by their claims of superior development and of the constant supervision of their "personal Master," arouse strong feelings of envy or of discouragement on account of the seeming difference between the claimant and his whilom student, who finally sinks into a state of despair or of disgust at everything bearing the name of occultism. Such a one is unable to recover from the shock to his inner nature throughout his whole life. The evident ignorance of the causes back of the desertion of erstwhile followers is the most hopeless feature of the failure of such self-deceived braggarts.

There are false prophets, deceivers, and liars in every religious movement, but there are not always the opportunities for braggadocio in those others that there are in a body of students of occultism.

Eventually the truth will prevail in the case of the first-mentioned movements, and the deceived one will be rehabilitated in his own estimation; but in the case of the utterly disheartened and discouraged student of occultism, it is difficult for him to recover his former state of security, for the claims of the braggart will present themselves repeatedly to his mentality, and he knows just enough of some of the facts of psychic development to understand that such claims might possibly be justified in the case of the braggart, while at the same time his Higher Self is trying to convince him of the worthlessness of those claims. Consequently, there is a continuous state of confusion in his mind, and he never feels sure of either side of the argument.

But for the fact that there are the few who have remained faithful to the teachings of the Masters, who gave the truths of the Wisdom Religion to the Western world, those Masters might well despair. But while there has been the failure I have mentioned, in many instances and despite the injury inflicted on numerous groups of people by the ignorant and selfish, the force of the main tenets of the Wisdom Religion — Karma, Reincarnation, and the Seven Principles of Life — has permeated the thought currents of the world, as is evidenced in changes which have occurred in science, art, literature, and religion. Because of that fact, there will be sufficient antagonism opposed to the present day revival of orthodox philosophy to prevent its reaching the same low level of cruelty, inhumanity, and pure diabolism, which a similar wave reached in the 17th century when the notable Blue laws[1] enforced the burning of suspected witches, the jailing of the Sabbath[2] breaker, and the inhuman treatment of women accused of breaking the Seventh Commandment,[3] as well as countless other crimes against humanity. If only so much good has been accomplished, the work of the Initiates of the White Lodge has not failed, in the true sense of the word failure.

---

[1] The Puritan laws enforced by English Puritans who settled in North America in the early 17th century. Puritan laws were often strict and punitive, with penalties ranging from fines and public humiliation to imprisonment and even death.

[2] *Sabbath* (*Hebrew*, "rest") — the seventh day of the week (Saturday) for Jews and the first day of the week (Sunday) for Christians. It is observed strictly as a day of solemn rest and devotion. Puritans placed great emphasis on observing the Sabbath and they enacted laws to prohibit work, entertainment, and even certain forms of recreation on this day. Anyone who missed church on the Sabbath had to go to court and pay a fine.

[3] "Thou shalt not commit adultery" (Exodus 20:14).

The return of the spokes of the cosmic wheel to a similar point of the world spiral is accountable for the present antagonistic wave against materialism and occultism. The course the wave is taking was to be expected. It will do its appointed work and make way for the return wave of the Wisdom Religion. Nevertheless, the world has sustained a great temporary loss by the failure of so many students of occultism to rise to the heights presented to them, and their failure has made it so much more difficult for the faithful to accomplish the task given them to perform.

LESSON 191
SELF-DECEPTION

The man who chooses from a statement of facts, or the expressed opinions of another man, only those features of the same which will minister to his own vanity or otherwise favorably affect his personal opinion of himself, and rejects *in toto* those which are to his discredit, will inevitably fail of success in all the great purposes of life. Even the harshest honest critic can scarcely fail to estimate more fairly the motives and effects of a man's act than can the man himself.

Exactly as the reliable art critic must stand away from the picture, the musical instrument, the voice, or the piece of sculpture in order to form a fair estimate of the value of the work of the artist, so the honest critic of his own acts or those of another human being must stand away from the point of action. He cannot come too close in sympathy or affection for others without becoming more or less identified with the personal opinions of those others. His estimate of the motives and effects of an act indulged in by those others, whatever its nature, will be more or less modified. Distance is essential to impartial judgment; so the man who would conquer his own limitations and win a victory over inhibiting conditions must be temperate minded enough to weigh carefully the expressed opinions of others regarding his acts, however invidious those opinions may appear to be.

How can any man protect himself from the wiles of the female who reduces herself to a seeming nonentity in his company, pouts and weeps over the cruelty of other men and women, while her tongue carries the sting of a viper when out of his presence, if he has overvalued his own power of discrimination and so cannot accept the estimate other men place on the character of the woman?

How can a woman protect herself from the vile machinations of the man who, to gain his own ends, pretends to credit her with all the virtues, graces, and attributes of a goddess, if she has allowed herself to be convinced that she possesses all those attributes and is therefore a sorely misunderstood martyr to the false opinions of others, when in fact those others may be endeavoring to protect her by their honest criticism of her weakness and gullibility?

How can a nation protect itself if its people will not heed the warning given by a friendly power in relation to the approach of a dangerous enemy, and refuse to do so for the reason that in their self-sufficiency they cannot conceive of the necessity for armament and defensive maneuvers?

There are all degrees of self-deception between the extremes I have mentioned, and one of these degrees fits every man and woman in the world. The closer one clings to his own individual degree of self-deception, however slight it may be, the surer it will lead him into pitfalls from which it may take him many incarnations to extricate himself. The more conceited, the vainer the possessor of the particular aspect of self-deception he has cultivated, the more persistently and emphatically will he deny the existence of such weakness in his character.

You may say, "If that be true, how then is one to become enlightened? How to overcome such a limiting defect?" It will not be an easy task. It has been built up into a monstrosity by the "little things" — the minutiae of over-appreciation through many lives — and as is the case with other personal defects, it must be torn down and removed by steady, persistent effort. It is the most subtle, the deepest-seated characteristic of human nature, and the heart will bleed when it is removed. But if it is the greatest hindrance to all power and development, the soul — the observer of all the fluctuating phenomena of life — should be ready and willing to bear the testing force.

So, however deeply it may sink into the consciousness, whatever the hurt to pride, self-esteem, or reputation, take the blow straight between the eyes, whether it comes from friend or enemy, if it be in the form of a personal criticism, and set yourself to find out what it is in you that has been hurt, and to what extent you deserve the criticism.

You will never convince your friend that he has been unjust by argument, or your enemy that he has been wrong by a return blow. There will be but one way to do either, that is, to rid your aura of the rubbish — whatever degree of that rubbish you may have fostered — and so become in fact the conqueror over the elementary force which now rules mankind, instead of its protector as you now are.

LESSON 192
"HIS LINE HATH GONE OUT"

Only by means of the "line of God" — the straight, true line — can the outline of a perfect form be constructed and that form be made permanent.

Every physical form or material object was originally built on the perfect pattern form existing on etheric planes. To whatever degree man has cultivated the attributes of God within himself, to that degree can he reconstruct any corresponding line that has been broken down or distorted in the outline of a physical body or an organ of a physical body; and unless such lines can be reconstructed on the perfect lines of the pattern form, it matters not what appearances or sensation may promise, a diseased organ or body cannot be perfectly and permanently made whole. The fact that mathematical and geometrical laws could be applicable in any sense to the healing of a diseased organ would not occur to the average man, yet an Initiate of the White Lodge would apply those laws to whatever degree was necessary in the healing of a diseased organ, providing Karmic law permitted him to undertake such healing at all.

The perfect pattern — the first reflection of a form — is indestructible. It is this form of which we find a record in Genesis. God made man in His own image. It is the outline of the body of the soul. But the second reflection of that form existing on one of the lower mental planes is subject to change; and as the physical body is a more dense reflection of the mental pattern, the lines, curves, and angles of the physical form must follow the lines, curves, and angles of the mental pattern.

As only a Master could intelligently visualize the outlines of the perfect pattern and also perceive similar outlines of the mental pattern, only such a one could be absolutely sure of the position and condition of the broken down or distorted portion of an outline, and so feel assured he was not working further injury to the organ in attempting the reconstruction of that portion of the outline.

Even as the white magician would have the power to reconstruct such lines, so the black magician would have not only the power to build, but would more often use that power temporarily to break down or distort those lines, thus bringing about conditions which would make possible the development of disease germs within the physical organ which corresponds to and which is, in fact, the basic material form of that organ. But as all evil is impermanent and illusory, he would not have power to render such conditions permanent. There must inevitably come a time in one incarnation or another when the true pattern would reflect a perfect pattern again on the mental plane. The effects of the evil would have been counteracted.

The power to change or distort what were once perfect lines exists to a lesser degree in every human ego, but without deliberate intent and power of will such changes are very fluctuating, and especially insofar as their effect on others is concerned; but they may last indefinitely or during the life-cycle of the personality, if destructive thought forces are turned in such a direction to any great degree.

You have all doubtless met many persons who had what is commonly termed "a true eye" — that is, persons who had the power of perfectly visioning or marking a straight line, or of estimating the degree of curve or angle of any visible form at a casual glance. Without knowing it, such persons may have something more than "a true eye." Metaphysically speaking, they possess the "measuring rod of God."[1] That rod is one aspect of the attribute of truth. God cannot be false in any respect, and the nearer man approaches Godliness — that is, develops the attributes of God — the truer he will be in all respects. However, a man may be true to one ideal or principle and false to another. He may have developed perfect vision — physical, mental, and even spiritual vision — and therefore be able to perceive the true intuitively, whether it be a perfectly proportioned geometrical figure or a true concept of a mental problem, and still be utterly false in all the common relations of life. Therefore, he would have developed only one aspect of the attribute of truth.

Every aspect of the attribute of truth is developed in the God-man, the Master of high degree. Therefore, the "measuring rod of God" is his to use at will. He knows that every line, curve, or angle of the various organs and divisions of the human body is built by exact measurements, and he knows the units of such measurements. If a

---

[1] See Ezekiel 40:2–3 and Revelation 11:1, 21:14–15.

certain part of the outline of an organ is displaced or distorted, he would know exactly the number of units of bone or tissue substance he must change to bring that part of the outline back to its original state of perfection. And it is right here that a miracle may occur, so far as a miracle is possible, for no possible exterior means could change that outline back exactly to its original form. The Initiate must unite the constituent elements of those units, must actually create the substance he uses to re-form or replace the broken outline, and must do this on the plane of the second reflection, and therefore by means of Kriyashakti and mental power.

If an extraneous object enters an organ of a physical body through all the layers of cuticle and embeds itself in the flesh, the outline is indented or changed, however minute the wound thus made may be. Nothing in the line of surgery or other extraneous means can render that outline exactly perfect again. Wherever the cuticle is scarified, the outline is broken or distorted, and a similar outline in the mental or astral body bears the same semblance. If the latter can be changed back to the original perfect outline, the corresponding physical outline will regain its former appearance. Consequently, it is on that mental or astral counterpart that the said Master must perform his operation if a diseased organ is to be perfectly healed without leaving any exterior sign of the process. The ability to perform such a seeming miracle is due first to his development of the power of Will, secondarily to his knowledge of the constituents of the substance we are agreed to call *mind stuff*, and thirdly, to his knowledge of higher mathematics and geometry, and this gives one a clue to the Master's insistence on the importance of these sciences.

LESSON 193
WHY WASTE IS AN EVIL

Among the commandments given by Jehovah to the Hebrews is the following: "Thou shalt not kill."[2] This is supposed to apply to the murder of man by man, but the far-reaching consequences of the taking of life in other forms are very lightly considered, if at all, by the majority of the people of the earth. The fact that every molecule of matter is a conscious life on the path of evolution makes the taking of the lives of even the animal, vegetable, and mineral kingdoms a

---

[2] Exodus 20:13.

matter for consideration, but if those lives are sacrificed to furnish sustenance for higher forms of life, the lesser lives receive an impulse toward growth as a result of their close contact and association with other hierarchies of lesser lives which have already been raised into other kingdoms of nature — the lives which have become the basic substance of blood and tissue as a result of their forced sacrifice. Just so far as those lesser lives are sacrificed necessarily for the growth and development of man, as well as for that of the lesser lives, the karma for such action is overcome. The interdependence of both forms of life is established by Divine Law. But when man willfully kills and wastes such lives through his own carelessness, cruelty, and selfishness, in whatever form they come into his hands, he is committing the sin which may be designated murder.

It is no wonder that so many simple household proverbs in all languages have grown out of the idea of waste. For while the severe lesson taught by waste is very apt to come home to the waster with crushing effect at some time of life, the soul itself cries out in warning to every sensitive person when brought to face waste in any form; and the mind will shrink from committing such waste unless that person is still too undeveloped to sense the cry, or has crushed out the voice of his soul for so long that he is no more moved to action. He is not apt to realize that, by the wasting of food material which would have sustained life, he is compelled to take, or induce others to take by purchasing their products, countless other lives which might have been left to growth. He is thus responsible for the commission of that crime against Divine Law. It is useless to say that he is not responsible for the taking of those extra lives, and that the materials would lie on the market unused if he did not purchase them, for that is not true.

The law of supply and demand would take care of all such matters, if man would permit and would live close enough to nature to allow the law to function for him; but he has defied all these laws and created unnatural conditions to which he is now bound.

The unity of life, and the interaction and interdependence of all lives, is beyond the realization of the average man. When the life blood or life essence has been freed in the killing of animals or gathering of grain or other forms of plant life, and the foodstuffs so secured are prepared by fire or other means into palatable food, it is generally believed that life is ended for the animal or plant. The fact that elemental lives have been freed, and different hierarchies of these elemental lives have been welded together by fire, causes the natural result, i.e., revolt of the fiery lives; and it is their action on the body and mentality of man which brings about the karmic action of disease or may be instrumental in bringing about poverty and want which are the sequel to the waste.

The laws above referred to are as applicable to the willful waste of spiritual and mental forces as to more concentrated matter. Man is as responsible for the waste of the higher forms of elemental life as for the lower. It is said that man must give an account of every idle word; then why must he not account for every other waste?

Take this lesson to heart, study it in all its bearings, and see if you cannot discern the logic and justice of my deductions.

LESSON 194
AS A GRAIN OF MUSTARD SEED

One of the greatest hindrances to understanding the purpose and accomplishing the given result of directions imparted to his disciples by an Initiate of the White Lodge, lies in the efforts made by the disciples to confuse the issue and refuse to believe that the simple natural form in which it is given does not hide some abstruse problem which requires Divine Wisdom to solve.

No statement made by Jesus of Nazareth to His disciples or to the multitude conveyed a deeper truth or one couched in more simple language than did that which runs as follows: "If ye have faith as a grain of mustard seed, ye shall say to this mountain, remove hence to yonder place and it shall remove."[1] Yet that statement has been made the base of tomes of literature of various kinds. It is used as the fundamental tenet of any number of faith cures, as it well might be if it were accepted as it was given — a simple statement of fact. Faith is a mighty engine, and like other engines, it requires a definite form of power, a well-qualified engineer and a given purpose if anything is to be accomplished by its use. But it is something more than an engine; it is a superhuman instrument which has grown by accretion, and according to the laws which govern its plane of existence.

You will note that Jesus said, "faith as a grain of mustard seed." The word *as* holds the clue to whatever mystery may be accredited to the statement. In order to grow, a mustard seed is planted in the

[1] Matthew 17:20.

earth, i.e., in darkness, coldness, shut away from its kind, alone. There it lies until the natural laws which govern growth, the application of moisture, heat, and the nourishment of mother earth have brought it to germination, burst its shell, and shot it up into another plane of existence, that is, into the light and life of the sun and air.

Yet, in the application of Faith, the average believer in its power would seek for a full-grown entity whose power of accomplishment was phenomenal; that is, mere belief in its existence was sufficient to accomplish miracles, despite the fact that this believer may deny the possibility of miracles, and rightly so, as there are no miracles, this very matter of Faith being a proof of the truth of that statement. The faith by which great deeds are done by man, must develop and grow under circumstances that exactly correspond to the growth of the mustard seed. It is not a ready-made tool for use at any moment and by anyone. It is "as a seed" in the soul of man and must develop under conditions analogous to those of the mustard seed. As the seed develops in the darkness and coldness and loneliness of earthly life, and grows by the light of the Central Sun, it becomes like unto the mighty engine to which I have referred; but then that engine must be operated according to the laws of the plane it has entered. The nucleus of the seed of the mustard will not permit that seed to expand into an oak tree; it will only grow mustard. Neither will the nucleus of Faith develop any other attribute or thing; it will always be just Faith, one of the mighty engines by which the Christs build worlds and men, and destroy them as forms.

What the average person means to convey in his use of the word Faith is merely a certain degree of belief in the power of a divine being. What the advanced occultist means by his use of the same word is a universally diffused form of force or energy. In one sense, it might correspond to the action of electrical energy, a form of energy or substance which is one of the constituents of every atom or molecule of physical substance, and therefore — like every other constituent of matter — is capable of growth, extension, expression, and final disintegration and dissolution. The Faith which the high Initiate has developed in himself is closely akin to the energy of Will.

LESSON 195
THE JUNCTION

It is not difficult for the normal human being to perceive the outlines, the uses, the possibilities of a finished product, but it is indeed difficult to perceive the design and purpose of an uncompleted object by means of any one section alone; yet the occultist is frequently called upon to do so. When the average person attempts to formulate some idea concerning the physical plane, his mind naturally turns to visible objective forms of his own little world. It does not occur to him that there is an actual state of matter — a universe in itself — just below and another just above the physical plane, wherein are constantly occurring all the changes which make his world what it appears to be to his senses. These intermediate planes or states of matter are not those to which the term "astral" has been somewhat promiscuously applied, but are exactly what the term "intermediate" implies. Within these planes occurs all the vibratory action that changes the substance of one form into that of another.

These changes occur under the direction of definite laws that pertain to those alone and are completely under the direction of the Divine Builders of Form. There is a certain correspondence between the undertones and overtones of music and the intermediate planes, as there also is between Life and Death, and between Fire and Flame, etc. To the psychic and the dreamer, the phenomena of the intermediate planes are observable by means of the psychic senses, but neither one is able to bring back to the waking senses the consciousness of the processes of change, or of the laws which govern the same. He may perceive the almost immediate change in one form or another. For instance, a well-known face may change form and features; the wall of a building may crumble and re-form on different lines; labyrinthine paths may lead into or cross each other without visible cause; whole cities change into other cities while there would appear to be no purpose to be served, no object to be gained by such changes. But if the physical or astral eyes might pierce those planes where the changes were instigated and carried out, and the human Ego could guide the elemental forces producing such changes, the process of changing an undesirable quality, characteristic, or feature into more acceptable form would be much easier than is possible by the slower methods of undirected nature.

A junction is a point where two or more lines meet, and the term seems peculiarly apt in referring to an intermediate plane.

The idea of a 4th dimension of space is commonly accepted, but that there may be a 5th, a 6th, and a 7th dimension of space is not so well understood, nor is the fact that these dimensions are in fact junctions between definite states or planes of substance wherein is accomplished the evolution of the human soul.

The 4th dimension of space — the "withinness" of matter as it is sometimes termed — and the first intermediate plane beyond the physical are identical. The instability of matter is a well-recognized fact; that there is a definite point or place wherein the impulse to change form — to pass from one state of vibration into another — is given and the change accomplished is not of common knowledge. The changes that appear on the physical plane take place in the cells of the objective form, and eventually appear in some modification of that form. The changes that take place in the substance of the astral and mental bodies first occur in the molecule and atom, but it must be remembered that the changes are instigated and produced on the intermediate planes between the full planes upon which substance is stabilized to a much greater degree.

To the physical eye, such changes as occur in outer forms appear to be somewhat dependent on time, but time is not a factor in the production of such changes on interior planes. It is on the intermediate planes that the Initiates, the great Masters, accomplish their seeming miracles, and whether consciously or the reverse, it is on these planes that the human Ego must work to change any part of his nature. If physical man desires to make such changes more rapidly and intelligently than they are being made by nature, he must strive to identify the lower mind with the Higher Mind in order that he may be able to observe the action of controlling laws of substance on all interior planes, for those laws differ greatly from the laws which govern matter of lower rates of vibration.

Every quality or characteristic in the nature of man has taken a definite form in the individual aura and is subject to change. As was said before, man may make changes; but in order to make them, man must understand somewhat of the nuances of form and of the significance and subtleties of curve and angle, line and square — deep mysteries which only the Higher Self can solve. This is one more reason why man should make every effort to gain the needed identification with the Higher Self.

Every conscious effort that he makes takes him another step toward that end; and the step that brings him to a realization of the aforementioned intermediate planes or junctions — on which the real work of changing form takes place — is a most important step.

LESSON 196
SELF-RESPONSIBILITY

In a previous communication to Templars on the subject of self-responsibility, I stated in effect that a single individual might defer the advent of an Avatar for a definite length of time. Many Templars have looked askance at this statement; others have refused even tentatively to accept it, owing largely to the fact that they are not capable of fully accepting the philosophical viewpoint of the Initiates on the subject of Centralization — centralization of power, of energy, of force, of every constituent of gross matter — and of the geometrical lines of influence that guide, attract and crystallize, and finally solidify and disintegrate the minor crystallized divisions of every ion, atom, molecule, and cell. These are responsive to one or the other of the seven major tones or keys that control the said lines of influence, and therefore are primarily responsible for the raising and lowering of the vibratory pulse of all matter in manifestation on the physical plane throughout a Manvantara.

It requires a strong analytical and mathematical turn of mind to divide and subdivide and remold into a definite mental form possible of expression by words, all the various aspects of Centralization. Unless one has the power of raising the personal consciousness to a state corresponding to one or all the lines of influence of the seven keys aforementioned, it is difficult to grasp the subject in its entirety. It depends upon the ability to do this how far it is possible to grasp the deep truth I endeavored to express in the message referred to in the beginning of this communication. It depends upon how far even the average human being can identify his consciousness with the central cell of each form of differentiated substance within the line of influence where evolutionary law has placed him, and how near he can approach the state of evolution commonly referred to as Adeptship.

If the central cell — the mind and soul — of a human being within the same line of influence as that which enfolds the individual Ego of one who has reached Adeptship (and who therefore may possibly fulfill the duties of an Avatar to all within that line of influence) shall set his will and mind against the outer expression of that particular Avatar, he can set in motion elemental forces which might greatly hinder the appearance of the latter for a limited time. Such an individual might not even be conscious of the effect of his line of action, such as a child on the physical plane might easily and innocently set fire to a valuable building by some careless act, or as an evil-minded person might willfully and deliberately commit a similar crime, it would be the action of the fire itself which would destroy or injure the building. Neither child nor man could be classed as the effect, although one or the other might be the cause of the fire.

It might be the use of the stored up power in the man and his position within the line of influence that would make possible such temporary inhibition as I have mentioned in the case of an Avatar, but it would be the character of the energy set free by his acts that would be the determining factor in such inhibition. The stored up power which made possible his action would necessarily be the fruits of previous efforts at gaining control of the centralized forces of one or more forms of substance. That central point or spark in every cell or division of mental or physical substance is the point of connection between spirit and matter. It is the individual consciousness of that cell or division, and the greater man's recognition and control of the central cell of any form of substance beneath that which constitutes his own vehicle of expression, and the more potent for good or ill are the effects of his acts.

If I were to tell you that barely seven people, four men and three women, were the points of precipitation, the avenues through which the powers of disintegration, slaughter, and destruction were preeminently active at this era — one in each of the seven major divisions of the earth — and that not all of them were perfectly conscious of the measure of their use, you might feel justified in disputing my statement; yet it is true. All other exterior influences at work to create the present conditions in all the great nations of the world are secondary, although many of them are aware of their being used for such purposes.

When any great issue comes up which affects the world as a whole to a supernormal degree, two centralized powers or individuals have precipitated it, one on either side of the problem presented; one is positive to the other's negative. Every secondary power or individual who consciously or unconsciously thwarts the action of the law which provides for a true and just solution of the problem, retards the action of that law.

The fact that such a great issue has arisen is a very sure indication that the evolutionary forces have forced the issue, whatever may seem to be the contributory causes. Even the crude laws of combat between man and man have a large measure of divine initiative behind them. The third person who steps in between the combatants, or who endeavors to trip, or throw, or over-encourage one or the other by overt acts, is the real enemy to both.

When the great issue has been settled, the secondary or contributory causes may precipitate other issues, but they would not be of like import. Here again I revert to the primary cause of this communication, namely, the necessity for a better understanding of the laws of Centralization, and of personal responsibility by students of life who are striving for the apples of wisdom — the fruit of knowledge — for they are the fundamental laws of all progress.

LESSON 197
THE AVATAR

The great test of the degree of development a human soul has reached in this Messianic Cycle will be whether it is a matter of vital importance as to what form — or even whether there be any visible form — the coming Avatar of the human race will choose in which to perform his mission to man.

Unless a man has evolved to the degree where it will be possible for him to interiorly recognize the presence of the Christ when contact is made within the Auric Sphere of the Earth, he might be as easily deceived — as many men are now deceived — by the claims of those who declare themselves to be Avatars of the present age. And if the soul of a man is evolved to the degree referred to, it will be a matter of indifference to him personally whether that Avatar will appear in a physical body or not, for he will know beyond any shadow of a doubt that the long sought is at hand when He comes, as surely as one would be conscious of an electric shock, even if there were no dynamo or battery in sight when one received that shock.

In the process of development, one would have created within himself a psychic center of action within which a response would be aroused by the mental stimulus of another who was attuned to the same key.

Perfect devotion to and intercommunication with the Christos would attune the consciousness to the keynote of the Christos, and every Avatar of the Christ strikes the same key — to use a simple illustration.

If you are a sensitive, the presence of a beloved one in your immediate vicinity is known to you at once. You have no need to argue the question with yourself, or to turn about to face the physical form of that loved one. Then how much greater would be the magnetic attraction of the vehicle of the Christos to whom your soul was drawn.

There is always a measure of doubt, or unbelief, if man must see with his outer eyes before he can recognize the Truth.

LESSON 198
THE NUMBER SEVEN

Though it taxes your belief to the breaking point, I must repeat again and yet again if necessary, a statement made to the original group of seven disciples called together by the Initiates of the White Lodge in the year 1898 to form the nucleus of a future organization. This statement was, in effect, that the seven said Initiates had labored diligently for centuries to secure seven highly organized psychically sensitive disciples in incarnation *at one time*, who would remain faithful and obedient during the necessary period of their chelaship, in order that they might gain the knowledge and power which would enable them to work in collaboration with the Initiates for the further enlightenment of the more intelligent people of the world, in ways absolutely necessary for growth on interior lines of life. As I then told the selected seven who formed that first group, it remained to be seen how far success would crown the efforts of the units of the group. As the natural span of life for the humanity of the present races of the earth does not allow for more than 50 years at most, in which man in his prime is capable of strenuous, long protracted mental and physical exertion, it can be readily perceived that many vacancies must have occurred in groups previously formed, before their units were fitted for the work to be accomplished; and as part of the necessary training leads to the prolongation of life, the failure or death of even one, at a critical point in training, would leave the group incomplete and valueless *as a group*, unless the vacancy could be filled at once.

It is now time that some of the information given to the first-mentioned group should be somewhat extended, for there should be those among the students of life who would be fitted for any vacancy which might occur in such a group.

One cause for the secrecy maintained in regard to Numbers by the Masters of Wisdom is the difficulty encountered by the average human being in comprehending the nature of the substances which constitute the first four planes of manifestation. Finite minds are not as yet capable of cognizing the nature of the finer forces or energies, and their relationship to numbers, although their effects are noted under different names in all the ancient philosophies. It is not until they are reflected or radiated, i.e., until the Three become the Four and Seven, that their nature becomes even approximately understood and noted by the senses of man. This is soon apparent to the inquirer who seeks to discover by mechanical means the secret which only the key of touch, i.e., feeling, will unlock.

Science has striven in vain to discover the source and ultimate nature of Light, Electricity, Heat, and Gravity — the Four which become the Seven by differentiation (the last three being Magnetism, Chemical affinity, and Cohesion). To reach a better understanding of the main point under discussion — the necessity for a group of seven human beings — it is well to postulate a Central Spiritual Sun as the basic source of the above-mentioned energies and of all forms of life in manifestation within the sun and planets of a solar system. The recipients of the radiations from the Central Sun take the form and nature of the said energies, and it is as various degrees of those energies that they become evident to the senses of man on this earth.

Somewhat as the spokes of a wheel reach the circumference from the hub, the seven direct rays or energies pass from the Central Sun to the center of the objective sun, thence to its circumference, and again to centers of groups of nebulae, which will become centers of other planets, and thence to man.

The heart of every human being is an embryonic center of a world to be, a point of attraction, as it were; but in order to receive and be able to respond to the action of the said energies — from the center of the earth, for instance — they must pass first through the seven most highly organized and highly evolved Beings upon or within the earth. These Beings are vehicles for the transmission of attenuated forms or degrees of the energies referred to. They are sometimes erroneously termed Gods; they are in fact Masters of very high degree. In turn there must be seven lesser beings, and again seven times seven, through whom in constantly lowering degrees those streams or lines of energy must pass in order to safely reach and accomplish their divine mission of growth and development in the masses of less developed human beings, and thence to the heart Center of every other living creature. It is by means of the said energies and their differentiated degrees that all matter in manifestation is created and maintained, and he who comprehends the exactness of all the laws governing physical life understands that there can be no variations in the enforcement of those laws.

In our postulate I have given you some idea of the methods and principles involved, but no human intellect can grasp the reason for the use of the numbers Three, Four, and Seven throughout every center of manifested life. We know their use is the effect of an action of universal law and must be satisfied with that knowledge for the present. The Masters of high degree select such groups from their personal disciples as are necessary for the furthering of their work. Positions in groups are not matters of choice by the disciples. If a single vacancy occurs in a selected group of seven units by the passing from earth or the failure of a unit, the perfect interchange of thought and effort — and the necessary alignment of the group with the sevenfold division of Masters who direct their action — is broken. The work of the Masters for that group is jeopardized if the vacancy cannot be filled. While the privileges of the units of such a group are many, the responsibility is great.

By means of the intercommunication established between Master and disciple, it is possible for the Master to so instruct the disciple that he may become a conscious instrument for use in the evolution of lesser orders of the kingdoms of nature, at the same time that he is becoming a unit of a center which will ultimately become the nucleus of a larger organized body, and so aid in enlightening the masses of humanity. Thus, as it were, on strictly mathematical principles, a direct line is established from the Central Spiritual Sun through the fields of spiritual as well as material life. I say spiritual life, for spirit is the guide, the director of all the forms of energy which constitute life in manifestation. Naturally, I can give you but little more than correspondences in such an article as this, but those correspondences or hints may be of incalculable importance if you will be guided by intuition in reaching conclusions. However, you must bear in mind that the energies mentioned are conscious spiritual entities on their plane of manifestation, and that it is only the effects of their action on their own plane which appear as forms of energy to the senses of man on the physical plane.

It is perfectly true that from each solar orb are radiated the streams of energy which supply life force and power of growth in lines of mathematical precision, to each one of the heavenly bodies belonging to its solar system. In their passing, the ether is thrown into waves.

The more highly a human being may be developed, the greater the possibility of aligning his consciousness with that of the spiritual Beings who are the vehicles of transmission to and fro from one plane to another of the finer forces of nature, and the more surely can he attract and use those nature forces.

All other forms of energy in operation within the physical plane are combinations or differentiations of two or more of the seven before-mentioned energies. There is a perfect system of interchange and interaction between the seven streams of energy as they pass from a sun to the various bodies of its solar system, and thence to all the centers of life upon or within those bodies. Full knowledge of this system is known only to the Masters of Wisdom who have become, as it were, perfect dynamos of tremendous power. As a result of their control of the nature spirits, they are able to direct some measure of those streams of energy into the channels which can be used by them for the benefit of the world at large and so help on the evolution of the units of that world. Those channels are the sevenfold groups which have been mentioned.

LESSON 199
HEALING

Possibly I may shock or discourage those among my children who have accepted modern interpretations of a philosophy as old as the world and who, in their efforts to reconcile two or more irreconcilable phases of that philosophy, have given the mongrel result the title of "new thought." But I am hoping that deeper consideration and thorough investigation will better enlighten those who have accepted the view presented by the original founders of the various present cults.

First of all, you must consider the natural tendency of the human mind to avidly grasp and strive to apply any fact or theory that gives promise of immediate relief from painful or undesired conditions. How eagerly they read or listen to the gleanings from any and every exposition obtainable which appear to confirm their accepted theory, and reject in part or *in toto* the gleanings which appear to oppose or refute a theory founded on the same expositions. This natural trend of the human mind is so obvious that it does not require a very brilliant intellect to grasp and use a theory that seems to offer personal advantage as a base for propaganda. You may note that the majority of the new thought teachers have seized upon some method of healing or of gaining material wealth, and put it forth as the *ultima Thule*[1] of all endeavor. The very sound or sight of the word "spiritual" is seized by the imagination and generously applied to the aforementioned methods.

The suffering from what are at the very most temporary forms of disease, and the deprivations suffered from what are equally temporary conditions of so-called poverty, are far less acute than are other forms of suffering which the human being is capable of enduring.

The qualities of patience, courage, and endurance attained in one life period might render the sufferer immune to the greater suffering in other lines; but this fact is tabooed or scoffingly denied.

In many instances, the immutable decrees of the laws of Karma and Reincarnation are either denied or twisted into a form that would appear to justify the theory advanced. The illusory plane of gross matter takes precedence in the minds of those theorists over what are, in very fact, the real planes of life; this despite all their idealistic descriptions of life after death upon those planes and their desirability as a dwelling place. Were such not the case, a vaster knowledge of those decrees of laws and life would be attainable than is possible while their present limitations obtain. That they are right — insofar as their conception of the power of thought is concerned — is indisputable; but they are often wrong in their application of the power and ignorant of the nature of the instrument used to accomplish their desired ends. Necessarily their thoughts are focused on the physical

---

[1] A remote goal or ideal.

plane to a great degree, and this prevents the wider sweep of the soul on interior planes of life.

No intelligent mind can deny the fact that certain results are often accomplished by the application of mental force. The main point at issue here is whether such results would be desired by the individual who is treated by the said methods, if he were aware of the ultimate effects. For instance, if a man is afflicted with a disposition toward one form of cruelty, however concealed from others or discredited by himself, the fact of its existence in this incarnation is the result of repeated acts of cruelty by himself in former incarnations. Cruelty is an evil that must eventually be eliminated from the mental sphere where it has developed to an abnormal degree; and as every mental inhibition or undesirable quality must be eliminated by means of a definite process which necessitates its manifestation in gross form — a lower vibration of matter — that tendency to cruelty may be material-ized in some form of disease. If that disease were eliminated by means of a higher spiritual force — before the Ego had succeeded in reducing that tendency toward cruelty — that spiritual force would have been misdirected and the tendency toward evil would remain unchanged, necessitating an increase of suffering in later life or in future lives.

While the above only illustrates one point of my argument, it may be of interest to you to learn that such a form of cruelty as is the suppression of sympathy, which is evident in the cases of many votaries of the old or new thought may easily result in one particular form of disease in the body. The inconsistency of many devotees of the theorists is a bar to belief in their teachings, in the case of a logical mind. When they vigorously affirm that spirit (their particular idea of spirit) is all in all, and by their methods of treatment claim to be perfectly capable of applying the said treatment for the elimination of all forms of evil — while subsequently making exceptions show-ing that other, more material means are necessary for treatment in exceptional cases — it is difficult for them to convince a logician as to the infallibility of their methods.

The Initiate Paul voiced a statement that should be of interest to the section of new thought healers who claim to use the power of Faith alone as a means to the healing of all disease. He said, "Faith without works is dead." Faith, void of obedience to the laws which govern the plane of action upon which it is applied, is truly ineffective. The works to which Paul referred must be concerned with the matter or substance of the plane upon which the energy of Faith is acting at that time. The universal laws which govern the plane of mind or soul decree that the substance of mind can only operate within its own plane — its particular rate of vibration. The governing laws of substance or matter of lower vibration than that of Manas — matter of greater weight and density — cannot allow such matter to enter the Manasic plane. It would be in defiance of the governing laws of both planes were it possible to transport a piece of iron ore or of physical tissue into the substance of the Manasic plane; but a perfect picture of that iron ore or tissue might be observable by the inner eye upon the Manasic or Psychic plane. That picture would be clearly the result of the action of the rays of the Central Spiritual Sun within the substance of an intermediate state of substance between the mental or astral and the physical plane — a state corresponding to a film or negative in the case of a photograph taken by means of solar light, a camera, and negative plate.

The ignoring or repudiating of the necessity for an intermediate vehicle to bridge the gulf between spirit and matter constitutes one of our chief objections to the promulgating of some of the modern theories founded on so-called spiritual healing. Another objection is based on the deceit practiced on the ignorant by those who fly to the medical fraternity for aid in emergencies, and claim all credit if success has crowned the efforts of the physician or surgeon employed, and repudiate responsibility if the latter are unsuccessful.

In every instance where a genuine cure of an actual (not an incorrectly diagnosed) disease is made by the application of spiritual or mental means, it is due to the recognized or unrecognized action of the third — the intermediate — state or entity, which to the orthodox mind bears an idea of the Christ. This intermediate state from one point of view may correspond to a flux, in which two totally dissimilar states of substance may be made to unite and thereby become an entirely different form of substance. This intermediate state is unconsciously accepted and termed "the healing force" by many new thought advocates, although they are often unaware of its ultimate nature or the laws that govern it.

It is to be regretted that in some instances the right to study modern works on chemistry and other scientific works is denied to students by their teachers, for it would lead to a better understanding of the spiritual, mental, and physical laws; too often this refusal is based on the fear of losing their adherents, rather than on the best good of those concerned.

Far be it from me to deny the power of any attribute of the Godhead. My objection to the use of the finer forces of Life lies in what I recognize as the total ignorance of the majority of those who would so use them — and therefore the frequent misuse of those forces — and the final sad results of such misuse. The man who would use a very precious stone for the shoveling of earth would be termed a fool — or worse, by those who saw him do so when a common tool was available. Yet something far more precious is often applied to such a passing immaterial thing as a slight headache or sore finger, which only requires some slight material aid.

As before said, the inconsistencies, the illogical findings, the cruelty, and indifference toward the suffering of others by many of this class should make an intelligent man carefully consider the whole question of mental or spiritual action in the healing of disease or the gaining of material values.

LESSON 200
LIBERTY AND LICENSE

October 1918

My Children:

I greatly deplore the necessity for adding vital energy to a thought form rapidly taking shape on the lower manasic plane, as does occur in even considering the basic ideal of a subject, which is primarily responsible for bringing a thought form into expression, for the more vitality a thought form is given the more quickly it may be materialized and the stronger it may be. While the form in question is already in material expression in some of the European nations, it will inevitably eventuate in America also, unless there is a radical change in the minds of the people in relation to the general interpretation of the words, personal freedom. This is my justification for bringing the subject up for your consideration.

As is always the case, the awakening of one pole of force or matter prefigures the awakening of the opposite pole, and with the awakening of the positive ideal of Liberty in the minds of a people, its negative pole, License, becomes the *ultima Thule* of endeavor in that portion of a race which has not yet evolved to a perception of the ideal of

Liberty which is held in the minds of a more highly developed portion of the same race.

The one fundamental and all-important base of a true civilization is the ideal of the family. The purity of a race,[1] the possibility of a clean genealogy, depends upon the offspring of the union of one man to one woman, and whatever strikes at this base — this root of civilization, strikes at the possibility of the continuous existence of the race. The man or woman who indulges in promiscuous cohabitation is guilty of a very far-reaching crime against the race to which he or she belongs.

Whatever may be the faults or failings of Orthodoxy in other respects, its insistence on the sacredness of the marriage tie has been a most redeeming feature. I am bringing these points up at this time, for the days are fast coming when one of the results of this world upheaval which I have termed a religious war, and of the precipitation of the thought-form previously referred to, will be upon you as it is now upon Germany and some other nations of this Dark Star. The days when whatever body is in power at the time may advise and even demand that promiscuous cohabitation shall obtain, using as a plea for the same the supposed need of numerically maintaining the population of a nation may yet arrive, and I ask you men who have wives and mothers, sisters and daughters, if you are inclined to countenance the false ideas of personal liberty in matters of sex now being freely discussed among many people. How would you feel if you were to see the bodies of those wives and mothers and sisters and daughters at the mercy of some of the human beasts of prey who are now actively supporting the program of the ruling powers of the countries referred to, the men and women whose minds have been permeated with the effluvia arising from the ravings of a madman, because they were either too indolent or too sense-besotted to realize the subtlety and the dangers of the philosophy presented to them?

There is a bar sinister on the escutcheon of the soul that can be so utterly deceived as to make it impossible to interpret the word Liberty as others would naturally interpret the same word, and so far as you are spiritually above such a sorely deceived soul, just so far are

---

[1] None of these statements support any form of segregationist ideology or eugenics. The purity referred to relates to spirituality, since spiritual impurity has far-reaching negative consequences, resulting in various physical and mental diseases. See Two Workers, *The Seven Laws of Spiritual Purity* (New York: Radiant Books, 2023).

you bound to work for the dissemination of the Light of Truth herein imparted to you wherever you are placed. Especially is it your duty if you expect to become leaders of men in the future.

If you do not do this, it will be upon you, and upon others like you, that the onus of such conditions as I have referred to will rest, for you have had the advantage of over 2000 years of preparation and instruction on those lines which make for race purity and high civilization.

You may refuse to believe that here in America, or in England or France, such conditions would be tolerated, but just calmly consider the fact that it only requires the addition of comparatively few more sympathizers to each one of the many groups already formed; groups of men and women who are even now advocating the repudiation of the present commonly accepted code of morals and high ideals, to bring about conditions which would make for unbridled license.

There is a tremendous responsibility resting on all clean-minded men and women, and there is no time to be lost.

ADDENDUM FROM BLUE STAR

True Liberty consists of the power and ability to do the right thing at *all times.* Man has not now the freedom of choice which enables him to always do the right thing. He is prevented by the results of past License, and until it is made possible for him to possess freedom of choice by means of a right environment and the evolution of a higher sense of morality true Liberty is the ideal he must aspire to, and by constantly aspiring to it he will surely gain it when the cyclic hour strikes.

LESSON 201
THE SEPARATION OF THE SEXES
AND THE MODERN THEORY OF TWIN SOULS

Only an embryologist who was also an occultist could reach a satisfactory solution to the mystery of the separation of the sexes in the Third Root Race. The process of separation covered many ages of time during which the sweat-born, egg-bearing, and androgynous races gradually changed from one order of evolution into another. It is only because the present theory of twin souls has originated in an unconscious recognition — or latent memory fixed in the substance which constituted these bodies in the Third Race — that we refer to it at all in considering the said theory. If we are to arrive at any definite conclusion concerning this subject, we have first to consider the divine spark, or monad, containing within itself all the potencies of Atma, Buddhi, and Manas; and to understand that the monads — the God in man — of the First, Second, and Third Root Races are also the monads of the Fifth, the present Root Race. While these monads have remained the same from age to age, they have clothed themselves in matter of many different vibrations, both astral and physical. According to *The Secret Doctrine*, the monad — the divine spark, the God in man — manifests as a personal ego when it incarnates in form, and something remains of each personality through all its incarnations through its connection with Manas — mind — when the latter is perfect enough to assimilate Buddhi — the Christos.[1] With the incarnation or overshadowing of the Sons of Mind — the highly developed spiritual entities of a previous great age — in a portion of the mindless Third Root Race of the present age, in order to save it from extinction, that portion of the race gradually became possessed of Higher Mind to some degree and eventually became identified with those spiritual entities. This brief resume of the evolution of the first three races is necessary to enable the thinker to grasp the point we wish to make here, that is, the position in the scale of life of the race in which occurred the separation of the sexes, and the state to which the human race would descend if the generally accepted modern theory of twin souls was correct, based on differentiated sex, as it most assuredly is.

The creative power or principle is indivisible. The positive and negative aspects of that power in differentiation — as in the masculine and feminine sexes — occurred in the latter part of the age in which the previously mentioned portion of the Third Root Race separated into sexes, not by arbitrary separation of one composite body into two parts but by a process of embryology. When it is remembered that even the present races of the earth are egg-born — the ovum or egg developed in the ovaries of the female and impregnated by the male being the creative center of human and animal life — it does not strike one as visionary when learning that in an early human race the fetus developed within an egg-shaped vehicle which was exuded from the abdomen, as drops of sweat exude from the skin of the present human race. It must be borne in mind that these egg-born bodies of

[1] See *The Secret Doctrine*, vol. 1, p. 265.

the early sub-races of the Third Root Race were not constituted of such dense substance as are the bodies of the later races. They were formed of an elastic, tenuous, etheric substance. This substance was gradually condensed and consolidated as evolution proceeded. Only a slight modification of mind was possessed by the sub-races of this Root Race; therefore, they were not as morally responsible as later races became and fell into gross sensual sin.

While the monad, the vehicle of the Higher Self, was identified with those bodies to some degree, the link — the higher Manas — was not there as yet, and only became so connected by the incarnation or overshadowing of the Sons of Mind. However, as the divine soul is the seat of memory, there exists even in the memory of the men and women of the present races of the earth a latent consciousness of the period before the separation of the sexes. In the more highly developed of the present race, there is also an intuitive perception of a future race and a period when the two aspects of sex will again be reunited and a sexless — a highly developed race — will be evolved. But this does not mean that two physical forms will be united; it will be by a process of embryology that certain organic changes will occur. The law of affinity, the law which compels like to seek like, must inevitably draw into closer communion all those beings who originally sprang from any one great group soul, one of the Sons of Mind referred to above. The development of the higher principles, qualities, etc., of life in each unit of such a group soul would naturally tend to draw all such units toward each other as, even in the present life, people of like minds and purposes are naturally drawn into close association. It could not be in such relations as is generally understood by the twin soul theorists, for sex as it is now understood will not be manifest in those more highly evolved souls; the era of physical generation will be over for them. The power of creation by Will and Yoga — Will and Mind — will be possessed by each such unit. The latent memories — fixed in the souls of humanity of the period when the Father-Mother principle, the two as one, manifested in each unit as in the Third Root Race — would naturally attract any two people who, in this present incarnation, mentally vibrated most closely to a single keynote of the substance of which they were formed, whether they were in male or female bodies. That keynote may be found in some degree of magnetic energy. This natural law accounts for the close friendships between man and man, and between some women and men. This also partially accounts for the attraction which impels many to enter marital relations who are totally unfitted for the same, when there might have existed a warm personal friendship between them had it not been for the power of the passional aspect of sex that temporarily blinded them to the qualities in themselves that must eventually force them apart.

The higher aspect of sex would not have so blinded them had their relations been on simply a friendly footing, but would have aided them in overcoming lower qualities if they had possessed them — or helped in the development of much higher qualities — and so established a lasting friendship such as is possible when sex is under control. Such a bond would unite them more and more truly as their evolution proceeded until they became, in deed and truth, one being in thought and feeling.

The fact of the spiral evolution and involution of matter would indicate that a much more rapid vibration of all forms of life must obtain at the highest point of each spiral of an involutionary period than at any other point of the period and, therefore, would show how impossible it would be for man to return to the same state and conditions of life which obtained in the androgynes of the Third Root Race when the sex principle was not so differentiated. Therefore, how unlikely it would be that the twin soul theories now based on sex contact could have a real spiritual foundation.

It is a commonly accepted truism that a half-told truth is far more dangerous than the worst kind of a lie, and in no instance do these words apply more forcibly than in the fallacy of the impurity and immorality of sex as sex. The generally accepted ideas concerning the necessity for celibacy, in the case of an aspirant to spiritual development before he has reached a certain defined degree of life, are based on a fallacy, and the fallacy itself is a result of a wrong presentation of a natural law insofar as the masses of mankind are concerned.

There is nothing impure or evil in sex; the impurity and evil are the result of the abuse of sex privilege, and ignorance of the fact that what may be normal and right under some circumstances would be abnormal and therefore wrong under other circumstances.

The demand for celibacy in the case of the accepted neophyte of certain Orders of the Great White Lodge is based on the necessity for conservation of the creative forces, and their transference from the generative organs to certain heart and brain centers. The male and female neophytes in the said Orders are separated mainly for the reason that constant association between them renders the task of conservation more difficult than it would otherwise be.

It is not a question of impurity, and therefore of "evil," in the matter of sex. The fallacy last mentioned is based upon the belief held by certain orders of the orthodox churches that only the masculine sex can attain to the heights of discipleship. It is more difficult for the feminine sex to attain to the same heights of development along certain lines that are possible of attainment by the male of the same average of intelligence, due to the maternal instinct that, in a normal woman, is ever striving for expression. If denied individual expression, unfavorable qualities may develop as a result, which cause much unhappiness to the woman and utterly incapacitate her for any high degree of discipleship. On the other hand, the same maternal instinct may increase to such a degree that the woman may become, as it were, a spiritual mother to all humanity and capable of rising to any heights of development. The qualities of selfishness and self-indulgence are not developed in the second instance. Sex in itself is no barrier to discipleship.

There is no sex in Divine Soul substance; therefore, there can be no twin souls in the sense in which the word "twin" is commonly used.

Total ignorance of what the soul is in fact — what are its functions and where it is located, together with the latent memory of a former androgynous state of mankind — is responsible for the modern theory of twin souls.

LESSON 202
THE VISION

The Temple of the People as "a voice crying in the wilderness" has long been pleading with man, as the Guardians of the Temple in past ages have pleaded with each race, "to make straight the way of the Lord."[1] From time to time, there is thrown on the world screen, here an etching, there a vivid outline, and in the most secret place, a broad, full picture whereon "the open eyed" alone could gaze and understand. Bound eyes have been unbound, blind eyes have been opened to the vision of the future — that future which is even now, in part, of the past — which stretches on in the sight of those who

---
[1] John 1:23.

have caught that vision to inconceivable heights beyond, where now dwell the redeemers of this Dark Star.

No tongue of man or angel can ever tell the story of the richness of the sacrifices made, or the glories of unselfishness to which man has risen and which even now are paving the way for the coming of the Angel of Enlightenment. Nor can human eye read the story graven on that world screen by the stylus of mortal anguish in this one short cycle; the story is too great, too far beyond the power of words to express; it loses something transcendental in the mere effort to express it in words. It is part of the great Vision which can only be seen and read by those who have won the power, by sacrifice and anguish, to throw open the shrine in their own hearts and read correctly the record of their own life experiences. Only a few more steps out of Eternity into Time remain to be taken by the Son of Man ere the brightness of the Vision be revealed to His own who are still in embodiment, as it now is to the innumerable hosts on the other side of Life's torrent — the souls that were driven thence by the lash of a great desire. Having caught a glimpse of the vision, there was no more rest for them on earth. They only asked for the privilege of making the last, the supremest, sacrifice; if so be, they might complete some infinitesimal figure of the grand total.

Those sacrifices have not been made in vain. Blind eyes have been made to see, dumb lips to speak strange words, and over the whole world there is rising a wave of aspiration which will reach to the heart of God and evoke a response that will unloose the floodgates of that stream which has been dammed up in the souls of humanity for so long — the stream of desire for perfect realization of the Fatherhood of God and the Brotherhood of Man. This realization will ultimately eventuate in a readjustment of conditions that have hitherto barred the way to the understanding of one nation's problems by another.

The sense of injustice and of wrong, under which the peoples of all nations have struggled so fruitlessly in past ages, will give way to the certainty of Divine Justice, and to a passion of sorrow and regret for past reviling and unbelief, which will soften hardened hearts. Tongues that have previously cursed will commence to bless life; lips that have never known laughter or song will be changed in form by tender smiles and glad strains. On all sides will be heard the words, "come let us reason together," instead of the words, "come let us battle for possession."

Is there naught in this vision to stir the dead or sleeping soul of man to new life and effort, after its fierce struggle throughout the long night of time to the dawn of a new day, even though there yet be heavy clouds in the offing?

Arise ye! Arise and go forth from palace and hut, from forest and glade, and seek the path to the heights whereon the vision rests and where all who will may behold it and rejoice with the angels over a world to be redeemed from ignorance.

LESSON 203
THE THIRD CYCLE

A COMMUNICATION TO TEMPLARS
December 1918

You have asked me what of the twenty years, the two decades that have passed since I came to you.[1] Each one of those years and days and hours has been a testing stone of fealty, faith, and love to and for humankind and to and for each other first of all, upon which each Templar has stood, having heard and answered the call sent forth by the Great White Lodge — the call to its own to gather themselves together against a fast coming day of need.

With the opening of the third ten-year cycle, you are hearing the joy bells, the cries of victory and rejoicing over a peace which, alas, is no peace.

Your thoughts hark back to a day when throughout the world there fell the sound of a tocsin straight from hell, a day when father from son, brother from brother parted in hatred and met but to slay each other; and you comfort yourselves with the thought that the sound has been stilled, the demon of hatred conquered, and the long struggle ended. But, my children, the great struggle has only just begun.

Not yet will mankind as a whole accept the olive branch held in the hand of the Angel guest that flew over the world in its quest for a place to plant its feet upon while it gave the message from God to man. Those feet were stained with blood as the Angel flew aloft, its quest unfulfilled, for they had walked upon rivers of blood and upon blood-drenched earth. The drops which fell from those feet called loudly for vengeance, and today far louder is heard that call than is

---

[1] The Temple of the People was founded in November 1898.

heard the message the Angels ever bear to man, "On earth peace, good will toward men."[1]

Think not that this land upon which you now tread in safety is to escape that call for vengeance.

"Vengeance is mine,"[2] saith the great Lord God. The vengeance of God in this instance is but another name for the final effects of a single cause. The cause is of long standing, and the effect is near at hand.

But woe betide any disciple of the Great White Lodge who sets fire to the refuse heaped up as a result of the ignorance of his brother man, and thus starts the conflagration which is to come. Not his should be the hand to perform this task, lest countless of his lives to come be passed in like ignorance, for he could not perform this act in ignorance of the inevitable results. He who sheddeth his brother's blood, by his brother will his own blood be shed.

For good as well as for ill, this third cycle will present opportunities for the human race that are immeasurably vaster than any save one which has preceded it. Such opportunities will be correlated in ways that will render them far more effective than would ever have been possible if presented singly. But as to you — who twenty years ago were presented with an opportunity which, from a spiritual standpoint, far exceeds in value all those to come — from you will be exacted the equivalent for failure if you fail to take advantage of that opportunity to the extent of your power.

LESSON 204
MAGNETIC PERSONALITIES

The electricity generated to create a flow of magnetism may increase that flow to any desirable extent, depending upon the number of times the conducting wire is wound around the magnet. This fact is a clue for the investigator who is striving to find the cause for the great difference between the flow of magnetic force from one person, and a corresponding flow from another; in other words, why one has a strong magnetic personality, another a very weak one, and still another seems entirely devoid of all magnetism. It also indicates why one person can strongly influence another by concentrated thought and why yet another person's thoughts seem devoid of all results.

[1] Luke 2:14.
[2] Deuteronomy 32:35, Romans 12:19, Hebrews 10:30.

The spine, like the brain, is a tremendously strong magnet, and the nerve fibers correspond to the wires that carry a current of electricity from one point to another; but they only correspond because they mark the invisible lines in the organ through which the currents flow. The higher degrees of magnetism are not dependent upon any exterior form of matter for transmission, although the energy must flow in definite currents or lines from one pole to the other of the magnet.

The interesting point of the correspondences lies in the fact that, as the intensity of the energy in the first instance depends upon the number of times the wire is wound about the magnet, in the second instance the intensity of the magnetic force in the body of man depends upon the tenseness of the spiral flow of force as it passes upward through the spinal cord, crosses at the cerebellum and flows in a double loop around the two halves of the brain. It then passes down the spine, contacting all the nerve centers on either side of the spine, thus conveying to the latter the necessary impulses sent out from the convolutions of the brain, and distributing those impulses to the different plexuses of nerves, muscles, and organs of the body.

Before wireless telegraphy and telephony can be brought to a highly satisfactory degree of perfection, provision must be made for sending the electrical energy forth in a spiral instead of a straight current. It would not be found so easy to intercept a current if this were done.

Just as man found it necessary to use wires in the conducting of energy, nature long before discovered a similar necessity in sending the lower forms of life force that now travels through the substance of the nerves.

In a strong magnetic personality, the magnetic currents flow in a close spiral about the spinal cord, each spiral almost meeting the preceding one. In a weak personality, the spirals are far apart, corresponding to a loosely wound cord on a rounded stick; and as a wire wound around a magnet must be insulated to prevent the electric current from escaping, so the invisible lines, which are only marked by the nerves, are furnished with insulation to prevent the escape of the finer forces — protection which, unconsciously to the individual, is supplied by the emanations of the nervous fluid. But like every other good thing, a strong magnetic personality is a karmic result, the result of unselfish devotion to humanity in other lives. The sending forth of kind, loving thoughts into the world of things and people increases the vibrations of the whole auric sphere and tightens all loosely constructed lines of life therein.

LESSON 205
THE BETRAYER

"Have I not chosen you twelve and one of you is a devil?"[1] So said the great Initiate to His disciples in the hour of His trial.

The story of the betrayal of the Master Jesus illustrates one of the greatest mysteries of Initiation. As a statement of fact, it by no means records the first event of the same nature in relation to a twelvefold group of disciples of the White Lodge. We must seek much farther back in the annals of time than that of the period in which Jesus suffered as a result of betrayal, if we would glimpse the first settings of that deep mystery. We must hark back to the first manifestations of spirit as matter — back to the period when the rebellion of the bright angel Lucifer led to his expulsion from Heaven, or the betrayal of the mythical Adam and Eve by the negative aspect of the Serpent — if we would find the first revelations concerning the negative force generated and freed by the first denials of the supremacy of Good. It was and is the same devil whom Jesus recognized and saw to be peculiarly active in Judas, and which also manifests most actively in one disciple out of each group of twelve chosen disciples in every degree of the Great White Lodge.

While the same force is more or less operative in every other unit of such a group, we are more concerned at the present moment with the one entity of a group in whom the force would be preeminently active in a specified period during which the powers of resistance in all the units of the group would be at their lowest point of action; therefore, the period in which the positive aspect of that force of evil might more surely accomplish desired results on its particular point of attack — the one already prepared to receive the suggestion of betrayal and carry it out.

It is not that any particular one of the chosen twelve disciples in any such group has been chosen by the Master — the Organizer of the group — for the identical purpose of betraying Him when His own final hour of trial comes upon Him. It is the use to which given

---

[1] John 6:70.

opportunities for growth have been put, the development or lack of development of certain attributes and characteristics — for instance, the power of devotion and loyalty to each other — during the period of their co-discipleship, as to which one of that twelve will fail when comes his trial by fire, his last exterior test.

Yet the primary cause of the failure of his power of resistance lies far back in the beginnings of time. If the record of the karmic results of the acts of the personal Ego, from the time of its first embodiment, were possible of examination by the Organizer of a group, many indications of the growth of tendencies toward unfaithfulness would be found which would doubtless lead to caution in the selection of the units of the proposed group; but full knowledge of all such inequalities — karmic effects — in the far distant past of those disciples would be confined to the group soul, the ruling power of many such combinations. Divine justice would not permit of the entrusting of such knowledge to lesser entities. Too much is at stake in all such divisions of the Great White Lodge to risk miscarriage of Divine Design.

Only the Masters of high degree have the power to attain to knowledge of the beginnings of sentient life — the early embodiments of the Ego. For that reason you may feel sure of the fallacy, the unreliability of the statements of those who profess to unravel the mysteries of the reincarnating Ego's first embodiments; these lie too close to the mysteries of the Godhead for even the comprehension of the humanity of the present age and race.

As it is at present constituted, the human brain contains no center of action sufficiently evolved to permit the safe impact of the forces that alone could awaken personal consciousness of a state of substance so utterly different and so remote from that of the field of action in which the mind and senses of man now function.

What man of ordinary intelligence could be induced to accept the statement that the reembodiments of his personal Ego were in any way dependent upon such an immaterial thing as Number? Yet, this is the case to a marked degree.

Ask yourself these questions: Why did the Master Jesus choose twelve instead of eight or nine disciples? Why should there be seven distinct states of consciousness instead of five or six? Why are certain numbers considered secret and sacred by the seers of all ages, while other numbers bear no such significance? These questions and many similar ones are unanswerable by the man of even normal intelligence unless he happens to be an advanced student of occultism; unanswerable for the reason that it requires the knowledge gained by long, intense study of a certain system of philosophy enforced by a highly developed psychic sense to even obtain a working hypothesis by which a solution of the mystery might be reached. The average man is content to accept the statements of recognized teachers of exoteric creed and dogma rather than devote his time and strength exclusively to such study, or to the fulfilling of the duties which would be imposed upon him by a competent instructor.

Search where you may in the fields of nature or supernature, wherever you find a distinct grouping of twelve units, you will find the organizer and the disorganizer; the builder and the destroyer; points, aspects, or persons through which the positive and negative aspects of creative force are peculiarly active. However much or little the same forces are active in all other units of that group, their action is always intensified at two points of the geometrical figure formed by the combination of the twelve units, and those two points are represented by two of the twelve units.

It is well for each human unit of such a twelvefold group to put the question, "Is it I?" to his or her own Higher Self when the charge of treachery enters the group consciousness, for who can truthfully affirm entire innocence? Who can say, "I know my own heart so thoroughly I am sure I am incapable of such baseness." The seriousness of such an offense against the law is evident in the suicide of Judas, which followed upon the betrayal.

Unfortunately for the human race, it appears from a casual study of the subject that there may be found in the history of every race many references to individual members of a class who have been held up in song and story for the admiration of others of the same race or nation; a class of spies, detectives, diplomats, etc., vampires living on the weaknesses of their fellow men, thus putting a premium on the deadliest sin of human nature — the sin of treachery. The fact that individual members of this class in one nation are held up to scorn and opprobrium by the people of another nation — even done to death in many instances — ought to be sufficient to designate the real status in the scale of life of those who accept such employment, however necessary to the exterior safety of a people that class appears to be. No true believer in the laws of Karma and Reincarnation could justify the employment of individual members of the said class. Evil never destroys evil, and however disguised, it is either revenge or hatred which incites to the employment of those who sink to such depths.

The great purpose of human life is the attainment of Mastery, and the first and last enemy to be slain by the accepted disciple of the White Lodge is the personal devil — the force which incites to treachery.

One may not be able to attain to the same degree of faithfulness observable in another, but our respect and regard for that other is beyond question, however fallible he may be in other ways; whereas the absence of that one virtue in the case of yet another, who may have attained all other virtues possible of expression, may leave one cold and unfeeling toward that other.

LESSON 206
THE GREAT QUESTION

March 1919

What are you doing and what are you going to do?

Are you cultivating the powers of courage, assurance, and endurance at the present time, or are you sinking down into a state of cowardice, fear, and indolence, when some realization dawns upon you of the truth of the facts I have tried to impress on your minds during the last twenty years, relating to the imminence of the great struggle between the powers of light and darkness for the salvation or destruction of the present human race?

I ask myself again and again, can it be possible there is sufficient power in the words of any language or all languages to express the importance of that struggle, or to express the necessity for cultivating the positive powers of courage, assurance, and endurance in yourselves and in your children; and I listen again for the "no" that has ever been my portion to hear. There are no words in any language capable of expressing that need, but there is something behind those words which may carry conviction to every heart that will open its leaves and let that something, which is the power of truth, sink within and set the wheels of the brain going with sufficient rapidity to arouse the whole nature of man to a realization of the issues at stake. If you allow yourselves to dwell on the possibilities of the destruction of cherished possessions, the slaughter of your kind, the overthrow of your governments, traditions, and hopes, you will not only open some path by which those terrors may eventuate, but also you will weaken your defenses, render inadequate your weapons, and serve to cut yourselves off from the great army of the White Brotherhood gathering for the fray. There may be no time or opportunity for the units of that army to stop, pick up, and carry the cowards, the selfish, and the indolent who refuse to walk by their side.

The safety of your race, the hope of future civilization rests on you and upon each normal human being, on *your* power to stand up and fight, to take the buffets which fall on you and hurl them back to their source, and to serve wherever and at whatever task the Great Law shall put upon you without a whine; to spring quickly at the call of your superior officer, your Master in the lists of life.

You from whom indolence, wealth, or carelessness has stolen the spiritual brawn, bear well in mind, you cannot regain the treasures of bravery, confidence in yourselves, and industry in a moment of time; but you can begin at once to plan and carry out each detail of that plan, as well and as rapidly as power shall develop to do so, and it will develop only by use. The first task you should set yourself is forming an ideal of what you wish to be and clothing it in garments of Faith and Hope sufficiently strong to bear the strain which will be put upon them.

LESSON 207
THE COMING AVATAR

Whenever the subject of the Coming Avatar comes up for discussion, there invariably arise these questions: when, where, and how will the expected Avatar appear? Will it be at some designated time or place? Will he come in some superhuman body accompanied by wonderful exhibitions of supernatural phenomena? Will he be born of woman and grow to maturity in circumstances similar to those which environ each one of the children of the present human race, only to meet with similar affirmations and denials like those met by the last Avatar when he announced his mission to man?

Strong assertions have been made as to the reincarnation of the last Avatar in the body of some child born within the present century. In a number of such instances, the assertion is conscientiously made — based on some apparently supernatural phenomena which were believed to have preceded the birth of the child — thus fixing the belief in the mind of the mother and her immediate friends if they have forgotten or ignored the fact that many other mothers have had similar experiences and are even now making similar assertions.

Those who believe in a literal translation of the statement accredited to the Master Jesus by His disciples after His crucifixion, to the effect that His Second Coming would be "in a cloud with power and great glory"[1] find it difficult to accept the claims above mentioned. There appears to be a direct contradiction between the two methods of procedure. These contradictory claims have been given the widest publicity and have proven great stumbling blocks in the way of a general acceptance of the belief in the reappearance of the Avatar. If it is not possible to reconcile these contradictory claims, the world will be no nearer to a solution of the great mystery in the present cycle than it has been in past cycles.

It would not occur to the average person that two such apparently irreconcilable beliefs were possible of reconciliation by the introduction of a third, and up to the present time, a strictly esoteric teaching concerning the possibility of the appearance of a Great Soul to the senses of physical man.

The student of occultism who has accepted the teachings of the Masters of Wisdom anent the illusory character and the impermanence of all matter on the physical plane — and the reality and endurance of the three higher of the seven states of manifested life, namely, Atma, Buddhi, and Manas — is prepared to accept the statement that the Christos or Buddhi, "the firstborn son of God," is in fact a state of energy, although far beyond the investigation or even the imagination of man in his present state of existence. It is taught that this state of energy is actually Spiritual Light — the original source of all Light — and that it is reflected within the mentality of man and also in every living creature in varying degrees. Therefore, every man is a potential Christ.

The brighter the illumination of mind resulting from the reflected light of the Christos, the more rapidly the mentality of the normal human being absorbs or assimilates and generates that energy, thus approaching the state of evolution which makes possible his admission to one of the highest orders of manifested life — the Avataral Order — where he is prepared for open avowal of his mission to the world. A fully prepared Avatar has gained full power over physical

---

[1] Luke 21:27.

life and death, and over all matter that constitutes form in the lower orders of life. He has passed through myriads of lives in those lower orders, as well as through many of the higher orders of Adeptship, ere he reaches the Buddhistic state from which he enters the state of perfection wherein he becomes an individual Christ, a Savior of the race to which he belongs by evolutionary right.

At the beginning of every great age in the earlier stages of a Manvantara, the Avatar karmically connected with the units of a previously great race, reincarnates in the body of a child, grows to maturity, and eventually proclaims his mission as teacher, and therefore Savior, of all those who may accept him.

When the individual Ego of an Avatar has reached and possibly has passed into the Buddhistic Order of Life, it may not be necessary for It to reincarnate in the body of a child on earth, or on any other planet of this solar system. It has evolved a form similar to that which the disciples of Jesus saw at the time of His transfiguration — a Glorified Body, sometimes termed a Nirmanakaya robe, which is visible only to the interior sense of sight in the case of the physical man. The Nirmanakaya body of a great Buddhi would be like unto a Sun in brightness to the psychic sense of the observer, and if, in the course of the evolution of a race, a change in vibration had occurred which had unsealed the interior vision of the units of that race, they might envision the Buddhi, or Christ, as clearly as they might now behold an Avatar in a physical body, were one upon the earth.

The nearness of a Nirmanakaya body to the Auric Center of the Earth would be sufficient to raise the vibrations of every human being, and even of the substance of the earth itself. This change in vibration would raise the senses of man, especially the senses of sight and sound, to a marked degree.

The bringing of a lighted lamp close to the open door of a previously dark room filled with people would lighten the room according to the size of the lamp and the intensity of the light given out by it. It would not be necessary for the occupants of the room to see the source of the light in order to be conscious of its nearness. With the dissipation of the darkness, there would occur a notable change in the occupants of the room. Even a slight change in vibration would quite materially increase the mental action as well as the heart action of each occupant, although he might not recognize the cause of the increase. If you will consider the change in the sense of feeling, the actual relief of mind, and the brightening of the faces of all present when a lighted lamp is suddenly brought into a previously dark room where you are quietly sitting with others, it will not be difficult for you to accept my statement regarding the effect of Spiritual Illumination on the whole nature of a race of human beings. I am not attempting to give a technical illustration of the effects of light on gross matter that would satisfy the mind of an academician, but there are certain correspondences between different grades, or states of energy and substance which greatly aid the intellect in solving many of the most mysterious processes of nature, chief of which are processes by which spiritual light becomes manifested as light on the plane of gross matter.

What is true of the reincarnation or of the development of an Avatar is equally true of the lesser orders of life. The spiritual light which illumines the mind and soul of an Avatar, illumines the mind and soul of every human being; as before said, it is but a matter of degree and of preparation for the reception of that light. The Light of the Central Spiritual Sun — spiritual light — is in actuality the light or energy we term the Christos. The soul of man is primarily a reflection, so to speak, a beam of that light clothed in energy or substance of lower vibratory rates.

In terms of matter, the first Trinity in manifestation is Light, Heat, and Electricity. A composite unit of the three states of energy is the basis of the substance that clothes the reincarnating soul, or personal Ego. It is the Thinker, and the Thought, and the Expression. In differentiation the Thought becomes the Etheric body and the Expression is that Etheric body clothed in the gross matter of the physical plane.

I have only touched on this vast subject. My purpose in doing so has been to aid in furnishing a working hypothesis by means of which some understanding of the problem presented by the prophesied return of an Avatar might be solved, at least partially. It must be understood that whether the Coming Avatar shall appear as a reincarnation of the Ego which previously incarnated in the body of Jesus of Nazareth, in the body of a child, or in the body of a man — or whether the vibration of a race shall be so raised as to enable the units of that race to behold the glorified Form of a Buddhi — that recognition must be by intuitive perception of the individual seer, and not by associating the form and features with those of any preceding Avatar.

In previous messages I have endeavored to show some of the tremendous issues facing the present human race within the recently opened ten-year cycle, as well as the unprecedented changes which will take place in man as a whole, or in part, and even in the very substance of the earth to some degree. The rapidity with which changes are taking place in the ideas and ideals of man is not alone due to recent worldwide events; it is first of all due to the entrance of a Great Soul into Nirvana — a soul that has completed its whole round of development, and to the nearness of another Great Soul to earthly environment. It is said that similarly rapid changes are taking place in the flora and fauna of some parts of the earth. Naturally, such changes are always taking place, but it is the rapidity with which they occur at the present time that more particularly attracts attention.

It has also been taught by Masters of High Degree that these changes will culminate to a marked extent in the year 1928, and that a point of their culmination is due to fall between certain parallels of latitude and longitude on the Western Hemisphere, directly opposite a similar point between the same parallels on the Eastern Hemisphere, thus closing a cycle of time and space which opened nearly two thousand years ago.

In a prophecy made by one of the older Sages, we find the words: "The child of the East must lie in the West wind to receive the call to action." There are now many indications of the fulfillment of this prophecy. The young men of many Eastern nations are rapidly receiving the call to social and political action at the present time in some of the countries of the Western Hemisphere with the avowed purpose of returning to their native lands to act according to entirely new ideals.

Knowledge of the form in which the coming Avatar is to appear to man has been withheld from man for a definite purpose. If it should prove to be, as before outlined, in the form of a Glorified Body, it will not be difficult to understand how two biblical prophecies relating to the "second coming of Christ" may be fulfilled, i.e.: "He shall come in a cloud with power and great glory"[1] and "He shall appear in the twinkling of an eye and every eye shall behold him."[2] Natural laws would have to be suspended to make possible the verification of those two prophecies if an Avatar were to appear in a strictly physical form. But whatever be the form, or whether that form be perceptible to inner or outer vision, one indisputable fact remains, the mere seeing of the form would count for little. It will rest upon the conscious effort of

---

[1] Luke 21:27.

[2] Revelation 1:7.

the individual man or woman as to what the final effect of that event will be upon him or her. The human will, enforced by Divine Will, must settle the question of preparation and the course of action to be pursued in the interim between now and the final event, as has been done in former Messianic Cycles. It would be well if each reader of this article should make an individual and present issue of this subject of the Coming of the Avatar. Above all else, his or her readiness for the Call of the Christ will depend entirely upon individual effort and the spirit of unselfishness which actuates that effort. We can only pray that the Christ may have mercy on the one who refuses to make the effort, for there is no mercy in the Code of Laws which governs the action of the Individual Ego — the Divine Self — when the human soul is brought before its Judgment Seat.

LESSON 208
THE MOMENTOUS QUESTION

The more enlightened classes of the present age are naturally interested in the important question now being presented to the religious world, "Shall Christianity dominate the human race in the future, or shall that race be permitted to lapse into barbarism as a result of the action of the terrific forces of opposition now set free?"

In making use of the term Christianity I shall use it in a much broader sense than is generally the case with those who entitle themselves Christians.

As used by the Initiates of the Great White Brotherhood, the term Christianity would denote the belief of the earnest seeker after the truths taught by each one of the Great Souls — the Christs, who have incarnated upon the earth, at different periods of time, for the purpose of teaching and regenerating a fallen race, to which they had been karmically attracted.

The fundamental truths as expressed by each one of the Buddhis and Avatars of the human race have ever been the same whatever the nation or the language in which they were expressed. They may be found in the Upanishads, the Vedas, the Commandments of Moses, as well as in the Teachings of Jesus, Confucius, and others and, in fact, may all be summed up in the familiar words "Love one another, for love is the fulfilling of the law."[3]

---

[3] Romans 13:8–10.

The momentous query now being put to all well-recognized religious bodies can only be truly and satisfactorily answered as the individual members of these various bodies adopt the spirit of Christianity in the solving of every problem which may arise as a result of the efforts being made to adjust differences and combine for a definite purpose. Only by so doing can they become able to meet and neutralize or to destroy the forces of opposition now rampant in every part of the world, forces which will become more active as the cycle advances.

There is good reason for the anxiety now being felt by many in respect to the threats made by one class of people against another class. They are the natural protest against man's inhumanity to man, and the malignant forces which have been active in the latter half of the century are now being gathered into a stream which is ruthlessly sweeping over the world, striving to destroy all religion, and thereby striking at the very root of civilization.

The question now is, "Can Christianity stem the current of that stream and guide the stream into a safe outlet?"

During the latter part of every great age the efforts of the forces of opposition are always directed toward the destruction of form and the disintegration of mass. Unfortunately it is not only forms of gross matter that have been or are being destroyed so ruthlessly at the present time, but the far more important ideal forms which make for higher evolution.

There can be no expression of life without form. Destroy a form and you drive out the elemental souls of which the form is an expression.

Religious forms and ceremonies, if wrongly used, may become traps for unwary feet, but it is not the form itself that is the trap, it is the betrayal of the elemental souls therein, thereby breaking the Hierarchal lines, the units of which have created those lines which must eventually bind all living creatures and people into one harmonious whole.

The efforts now being put forth to combine all orthodox and unorthodox religious bodies for the stemming of the tide of irreligion may do much in that line, but such efforts will be greatly nullified until there can be a recognition of and a return to the ancient form of religion, a patriarchal form, under which the Masters and Adepts of the Great White Brotherhood have always lived and ruled themselves under Hierarchal guidance.

So far as the masses of mankind are concerned, the Hierarchal line was broken in the early ages of the present Manvantara, and there never has been peace in the world since that time, nor will there be peace until it is reestablished.

The originators of the present plan for combining religious bodies have come to a realization of the imminence of the dangers confronting the present race; dangers to body as well as soul, as a result of the tide of irreligion, but they are not wholly alive to the difficulties in the way of overcoming the differences of opinion which originally established sectarianism.

Unless a common ground can be established whereby belief in a Supreme Being is the one essential, and the necessity of the maintenance of Law and Order recognized by all, there can be no possibility of continuing such an organization as is proposed. Only by fulfilling the Law of Love would it be possible to overcome the prejudices which now exist between different religious bodies, and thus open the way for united action.

It is acknowledged by all believers in Christ that the Brotherhood of Man is a fact, and it is generally believed that the salvation or higher evolution of the individual man rests on his righteous treatment of his fellow men. These beliefs are based on irrefutable truths.

The unsatisfied longing of the human soul for all that is embraced in his ideal of a Supreme Being, has driven him into many hells of his own making. It is no more possible for him to satisfy that longing while he is at enmity with another human being than it would be to satisfy his physical hunger with a stone, yet in every country of this world man is cultivating hatred, enmity, and cruelty toward some man or men, and in many instances believing he is doing God service.

Everywhere you hear of the decline of Christianity, when, in fact, real Christianity has existed nowhere but in the higher orders of the Great White Brotherhood for ages, save in comparatively few individual instances where a man or woman is a conscious or an unconscious disciple of one of those Orders. The germ of Christianity exists in every human soul, but it must be fructified and cultivated by love and by understanding of the problems of other souls than its own, if there is to be a form of Christianity determined whereby the reestablishing of the aforementioned Hierarchal line may be accomplished and thus do away with the causes for contention, by placing in positions of power those who are spiritually fitted for the exercise of power.

It requires the trained occultist to teach the philosophy of these vital truths. The pseudo-occultist who attempts to teach them while denying their reality and virtue by his actions toward others is a menace to the race.

This brings me to your responsibility in the matter of the aforementioned combination of religious bodies. You have not the excuse of ignorance if you are unable to teach by precept and example the vital truths which have been so generously taught you. Every harsh criticism of another, every willful misunderstanding of the motives and problems of your fellow disciples renders you so much the less capable of playing the part assigned to you in the present world tragedy, for you must do that part as a body, if at all, and it is well worth your time and effort to bear this constantly in mind.

Strive to realize more perfectly that as a body the members of the Temple collectively as well as individually are one in God, and if occultism — Christianity — is to be established with sufficient power as a result of a combined effort by all who are truly Christians, i.e., believers in the Christos, you will have to do your part to make that body a capable and efficient instrument or you will fail in the test that you are facing.

So long as a man or a body of men continue to narrow the divine Ideal of Christianity and refuse to apply the basic truths of that Ideal to their personal as well as their collective problems, the forces of opposition will destroy every form of religion they create; and this will be done, as it has been done in the past, in accordance with Divine Law, for the ideal form in the mind of God is perfect in every detail and God will accept nothing less than perfection as a finality.

As the basic truths of occultism and those of Christianity are the same, the accepted disciples of the Masters are more responsible for the right presentation of those truths than are members of the various sects who have not had the same advantages, or the opportunities for demonstrating the verity of those basic truths. They can never be proven by force; and egotistic claims to knowledge that are not demonstrable have driven many earnest inquirers into atheism. Revelation of the action of the interior laws of life and their relation to the laws of the physical plane is most important, and it is only the well-advanced occultist who is prepared to reveal these great verities.

Each one of your number must conscientiously determine his position on one side or the other of the path in the great trial by fire that is now on the human race. It is imperative that you take a stand for the salvation of the religion of the Christ regardless of individual differences. Is there to be one vast harmonious movement toward true Civilization, or must there be rapid destruction of all forms which have hitherto been built to that end? This is the most important and momentous question of the present age, and it can only be rightly answered from the religious point of view.

LESSON 209
INTERRELATION, INTERPENETRATION, AND CORRELATION OF MATTER

Until man can comprehend to some degree the interrelation, inter-penetration and correlation of all grades of Force and Substance from the cell to the electron, and even still finer grades of Substance and Force, and also comprehend that he has as many vehicles of expression as there are grades of substance in which his consciousness functions, he will hardly be able to accept the fact that a Universe itself has a definite form or vehicle of expression, and what to him is of still more importance, that it is his consciousness — his individuality or Spiritual Self — a correlation of Atma, Buddhi, and Manas — which is operating eternally through all grades or divisions of matter and force within that Universe. The average man knows little or nothing of biology; and the creeds and various teachings of the Orthodox Churches do not enter minutely into the finer forms of nature and life.

If a man is satisfied with the teachings of whatever church has most strongly influenced his trend of mind, he will not make a deter-mined effort to learn what even profane science may offer him in relation to finer forms of life than are those now evident to his exterior senses. For instance, he cannot easily accept the truth that his indi-vidual consciousness is now functioning in four different vehicles of expression or bodies, and that when what is commonly called "death" intervenes, his individual consciousness has merely thrown off the shell, or physical body, and that he will be as much, or even more alive in a form of molecular substance, or astral matter, and in a universe of substance of similar consistency and nature to that in which his consciousness will then be functioning.

The shell or cellular substance thrown off at death by disintegra-tion is used by nature in building up lesser forms of life — animal, plant, and mineral life. When the individual consciousness ceases to function in the astral body, the molecular substance of that body is cast off as a result of what orthodox theology terms the "second death."[1] The consciousness then functions in a vehicle of substance comparable to the atom of science, and in a corresponding atomic universe or state of matter. From the point of view of the occultist this is the higher Astral or higher Manasic plane.

That which is of infinite importance to the truly spiritual-minded man or woman is the fact that it is in this higher Manasic plane or state of substance and its corresponding vehicles of expression that the reincarnating ego in its manifestation as the soul of man reaches the devachanic state, or is reincarnated again on the physical plane if it has reached the state of development where it can consciously aid in the evolution of humanity and so chooses to renounce the devachanic interlude. In the great majority of mankind the ego rein-carnates again after the devachanic or rest period. The length of that period and the character of its experience rests upon the nature of the acts and thoughts of the individual during the last earth life. The evil-minded, cruel, and inhuman personality has but little, if any, devachanic experience comparable to that experienced by others; it is forced into reincarnation under conditions which correspond to the deeds and thoughts of previous earth lives and either ascends the scale of life as a result of the sufferings it endures, or descends the same scale by continual evil doing.

It must be understood that the various divisions or planes of matter, force, and substance are not sharply defined divisions. There is interdependence, interpenetration, and correlation between all four of the states of manifestation and the individual forms functioning therein, as there is also interdependence, interpenetration and correlation between spirit, mind, energy, and substance in the composite body of man. As the outer senses of man respond to the stimuli of the last-mentioned states of energy and substance, so the interior senses of the soul respond to the more rapid vibrations of the finer forms of energy and substance when it is released from its bondage to Time and Space.

---

[1] *Second death* — when people die in physical bodies, they experience their "first death," but they continue to exist in their astral bodies, which are also mortal. When the time comes for them to go higher, they undergo their "second death," which is the separation of their spiritual triads from their astral bodies.

LESSON 210
THE YOKE

From time immemorial, the human race has been striving to throw off the "Yoke." The history of civilization is one long series of conflicts between man and man to determine how best may he throw off the Yoke of God — the bond, the Universal law — the state of energy or substance, call it what you will, it is in fact that which binds Spirit and Matter together, the bond between the Creator and the created.

As all manifested things and creatures are sevenfold by nature and constitution, so also is the Yoke, and as all manifested things and creatures have three aspects or energies — positive, negative, and neutral — man must become involved in one or more features of its sevenfold constitution, and is brought or brings himself under the control of either the positive or negative energies, or qualities, to the exclusion of the neutral. It is the ignorance of the masses in relation to these great fundamental principles and laws which disqualifies them from applying these principles and laws to the solving of their life problems, whether they be spiritual, mental, moral, or physical problems; and it is the same ignorance which keeps the races of the earth in such a state of flux as they now are, and have for ages been in, except for the short periods in which one or more races have temporarily gained a period of comparative quiescence; but these periods have only lasted until a stronger, a more dominant race or combination of races, has brought them to an end.

I know I am laying my words open to much criticism and denial when I say that every revolution, every combined effort of mankind to throw off the chains of one ruling power only to establish another, which in time would be similarly overthrown, is first of all an effort to break down the seeming barrier between God and man. It is an effort to set in action either the positive or negative principles or powers of the universal creative energies to the exclusion of or opposition to the neutral energies of the universal triad — the very substance of the Yoke, the divine law of Peace.

I do not say that this is in accordance with the general understanding of the evolutionary law. I am simply stating what I know to be a fact.

The deep, unprejudiced thinker of the present era can hardly fail to perceive the rapidity with which a large portion of the people of the United States, as well as other nations, are preparing the way for the overthrow of that for which the nation has stood since the commencement of its life as a nation, that is, individual Liberty, religious freedom, and political freedom; and it is being done so subtly and secretly, under a mask of morality, righteousness, and unselfishness, and done by the Judases whom the people themselves have raised to power, wealth, and influence, and have so raised by the aid of the laws they have made. In their inception the plans for thwarting the will of the people are quietly, secretly formed; but their finished presentation to the world at large is accompanied by such a blare of trumpets, ringing of bells, and fair speeches that the power of prevision in the people is obscured. All unperceived by them, the worm in the bud is growing to unprecedented size and strength and will have eaten the heart of the fruit — individual Liberty — ere its ravages become evident to the naked eye. One of the Initiates of the Great White Lodge charged his disciples to refrain from being yoked together with unbelievers.[1] The same charge may well be given in a wider sense to those who are now ignorantly or willfully striving to prevent the ratification of the bond between God and man; for the present-day unbelievers are unbelievers in the existence, the reality, of the Yoke which has bound man to man, and man to God since the beginning of time. Man looks upon the idea of the existence of a state of substance or energy comparable to a yoke, as a chimera not worth a sane man's consideration; therefore, he makes no effort to sustain his side of the yoke or reach the state of substance, the neutral state of peace — perfect freedom — the freedom of the regenerated soul, the freedom which precludes the performance of evil, for the reason that evil does not exist for it. Such man-made laws as restrict the liberty of man serve to dam up the stream of evolutionary force upon which he is dependent for higher development. This does not mean that man should be exempted from punishment, or left unrestricted to work out evil; but that he should be left perfectly free to choose his individual course of action in all things. If he chooses evil he must bear the results, but a law which gives him no choice enslaves him to whatever degree his Liberty of action is inhibited, and it is the efforts of one class or race of mankind to deprive another class or race of its liberty that have led to every revolution since time for man began.

---

[1] See 2 Corinthians 6:14.

God, the Infinite Father of the human race, creates, establishes the "Yoke," but man, the human soul, must put his side of that yoke on himself — must give up his Liberty to do evil, by allying himself so powerfully with that Father — the Higher Self, Divine Soul — that no exterior power can tear that yoke asunder. He yields it up only as he passes into Nirvana — becomes one in consciousness with God. Impatience, indolence, intolerance and all those qualities which hinder man from wisely seeking for the causes which lie back of all phenomena, wrongly applied hero worship, egotism, and self-assertion are some of the positive and negative aspects of the barrier man sets up against the Yoke.

The neutral aspect of the same triad, the substance of the very Yoke itself, is a combination of Love, Truth, Beauty, and true Liberty.

LESSON 211
POWER OF CHOICE

My children, remember there is one indisputable fact, the fact that, even at the longest, there is, comparatively speaking, but a short time left for you to remain in physical incarnation at this particular stage of your life journey, and consider whether you desire to be active or passive in the intermediate — astral — state between the physical and devachanic states of consciousness, that is, do you desire to be conscious of personal existence and experience, or do you desire to lose the sense of personality for a long time when you pass into that intermediate state? Bear in mind, it must be one or the other; there is no third alternative. It is only the extremely wicked who lose and the very advanced souls who renounce the devachanic interlude, so it is well to acknowledge and accept the fact in considering the fate of the human race in that respect, and turn your attention temporarily to consideration of the state preceding the devachanic.

It is not a commonly accepted fact that a normal human being may choose whether he will remain wide awake, or will passively accept a half comatose state of existence during that intermediate period, at the close of which occurs what is sometimes termed the "second death." If wide awake, the personal mind is more conscious of the purgation which is taking place than it would otherwise be; that is, more conscious of the experiences it is passing through, experiences both positive and negative — the karmic results of previous action.

When I say man may choose, of course, I use the word choose in a relative sense, for his power of choice depends largely upon the condition of the vehicle of his astral consciousness; and the condition of that astral vehicle depends upon the degree to which he has developed that vehicle, by means of the exercise of Desire and Will while still functioning on the physical plane. If he is an accepted disciple of the White Lodge, such exercise will be given under fixed rules for controlling these two forms of cosmic energy. Remember, his action in that respect will not influence his later devachanic experience, unless he has reached a point where the individual need for that period of rest no longer exists, as is the case with the Masters of Wisdom, who are conscious on all planes at will.

The occult rules for consciously changing the outlines of any living form are possible of so much misuse they are only given by Master to pupil, direct; there are no reliable printed rules for that purpose. It is a serious matter for one to deliberately decide consciously to change the configuration of any organ of that astral body, for if he has much unpaid bad karma he may create conditions which would increase the action of karmic retribution beyond his power of patient endurance, as a highly sensitive body may feel pain more keenly than would a gross body on the physical plane.

It is possible for a strong-minded man to do much in the way of changing his astral body, as I have mentioned, without knowing anything about the before-mentioned rules, or even being aware that he is building that body at all; but if he consciously undertakes to make such changes while totally ignorant of those rules he is likely to make some serious mistakes, and the result would be a badly proportioned, unnatural or deformed organ or body, for he would not know how or where to fix his thought force. Under such circumstances, he would do better to leave the changing of that form to nature alone, for it would be possible for him to tear down by sudden gusts of anger, hate, or jealousy more in a moment of time than he could rebuild in a year. This also is even true of the normally moral, well-intentioned man; but if he is building by rule he may know better how to correct fault in the building.

One of the peculiar idiosyncrasies of the human racial mind is the rapidity with which it eliminates certain facts and experiences it would seem would have been indelibly imprinted within it; for instance, the methods and means by which structural changes in form, both astral and physical, take place and the causes for such changes. Every race, as a whole, has been repeatedly taught the necessity for morality and for spiritual rebirth if the soul is to have an independent existence after death of the body. They may not have accepted these world-old teachings, but at least they have heard of them in some degree. They have something in the line of a concept of a Supreme Being and of a Heaven and a hell, but the basic reason for being righteous, "from a mathematical or geometrical point of view" receives little or no consideration.

The knowledge of the fact that the commission of an act, or the dwelling upon a definite thought which is contrary to divine law, may produce structural changes in form (both astral and physical) has been lost at some period of the individual life line, and this notwithstanding the fact that the seat of memory is fixed in the soul. It would seem that the intuition or the racial instinct of a people, if nothing more definite, would have carried over into a new incarnation such a super-important memory, but this occurs only in exceptional cases. The loss of a limb or the infliction of some other physical injury in one life does in fact leave an impress on the soul memory in all succeeding lives, and this becomes evident in an instinctive fear of the thing or creature by which such injury was inflicted; yet the means by which Karma collects its moral and spiritual debts, in so many instances, remains a mystery. A man may have been born deaf or blind, and science may find the cause for it in some structural fault in eye or ear, or some hereditary or prenatal influence. Orthodoxy terms it the "Will of God," and it seldom if ever occurs to that man that the primal cause of his blindness or deafness was misuse or abuse of the properties of Thought, Sound, or Light. The mode of motion or the vibrations of the waves of light or sound which had been evoked by Thought in that misuse or abuse reached the centers of sound or vision in the process of formation in the unborn child.

The interaction of all energies, substances, and matter on all planes of life is little understood as yet.

These are crude illustrations but they may give some idea of the method and the means by which prenatal variations of form are accomplished, and the causes back of such structural changes, both good and bad, from a material point of view. One may listen to the tale against, and subscribe to the revengeful punishment of another man, without making an effort to learn the truth of the charge against the man or to help the sufferer, thus passively becoming an accessory to his suffering, but Divine Law takes account of that sin of omission. The waves of sound or vision, or both, have been evoked and diverted from their natural or divine course; and sometime, somewhere, in some newly incarnating life, a center of hearing or sight in the then forming Linga Sharira — astral form — will catch those diverted waves, and when ear or eye is fully formed there will be some fault, some malformation which will not permit the great normal, natural waves of sound or light to play upon the astral ear or eye centers in the process of forming.

Possibly this illustration will give some idea of the interaction of substance on different planes, although it is very difficult to illustrate the action of the higher spiritual forces in and through gross matter.

LESSON 212
UNDEVELOPED OR UNUSED CENTERS OF THE BRAIN

It is no uncommon circumstance to hear an underdeveloped student of life complain of having reached the limit of mental effort. The cause does not always occur to the sufferer or to the confidant of his woes, even when the latter is a physician or surgeon, for the reason that the cause lies just beyond the last point his scalpel can reach, although still in the domain of physical matter. The remedy is in his own hands so long as he has the power of direction, for in order to effect a cure the patient must recognize the cause and direct the mental energy which has all but ceased flowing through certain brain centers which are not classified in any accepted physiological work.

There are seven of these minor centers in the brain which serve the larger sense centers, the master chakras, or centers which direct the functioning of the various organs of the body somewhat as do the keys of an electric switchboard which turn off and on the current of electricity that travels by wire or wave.

As the average man or woman is ignorant of the existence and the functions of the minor centers, no specific effort is made to keep them in working order, and eventually they deteriorate as does every unused center or organ of the physical body, except insofar as nature may direct their functioning indiscriminately. The weakening of the surrounding tissue of these centers through disuse or misuse is what causes the gradual weakening of the mental powers in old age.

Occasionally you see an elderly man or woman whose interest in the affairs of life is as keen at eighty years of age as at thirty. If you are able to acquaint yourself with the details of the events of such a life you will probably learn that a super-normal curiosity about phenomena of every kind was the most notable characteristic of the person, a curiosity which impelled the most active interest in everything connected with the object of curiosity. When a subject of interest is introduced in the hearing of such an one the vital point of the subject is seized upon at once, and no pains are spared to hunt that point to its last hiding place. If, for instance, the subject is the motive power of aeronautics, every possible clue leading up to the discovery and the nature and use of that power will be followed to its end. In a person of this character the particular brain centers of the class I have mentioned function the motive power of invention and execution, and the interest is increased by every point established until there is a strong current of force set up between the *tattvic*[1] centers and the chakras. This increase in vibration brings an increase of blood to the corresponding plexuses and, consequently, better nourishment.

As an illustration, take a person engaged in any line of mental or physical activity, one whose whole mind for many hours in the day is concentrated on that one line of endeavor, and who has little or no interest in life outside of that line. The brain centers most active in promoting that line become overdeveloped. The connecting lines between that one center and other centers associated with other lines of life interest are gradually either wholly or partially atrophied and life holds no real interest for that person outside that one line as advancing age creeps upon him and his power of concentration on the one line decreases. If interest seems to be dying out in the normal affairs of life, and one would avoid such a fate as is last pictured, he has no alternative but to make a practice of deliberately seizing upon some point of every subject which would naturally interest him if he were in a normal condition, and force his interest to the point nature intended. By persistently following this rule, he will gradually awaken new life in these connecting lines by a purely natural process.

These supersensitive centers, *tattvic* centers as they are termed by the orientalists — the undeveloped or unused centers referred to

---

[1] *Tattva* (*Sanskrit*, "principle") — a fundamental principle of Nature, correlative to one physical sense. There are five tattvas exoterically and seven tattvas esoterically, two of which are still latent in humanity.

by me are the first centers to develop in the head of the fetus. In and through these centers come and go the impulses from the universal tattvas — the seven principles of life.

The seven master chakras of the brain control the senses of man and are dependent upon the flow of the seven life currents through the tattvic centers. When an impulse from a cosmic tattvic force impinges upon a corresponding tattvic center in the human brain, that center is set in rapid vibration and the energy aroused is then communicated to the corresponding sense chakra, thence to the corresponding plexus and to the organ of sense by means of the motor and sensory nerves which control the action of the nerves and muscles. When man fails to recognize and makes no use of the cosmic tattvic forces as they impinge upon the tattvic centers of the brain, those centers lose elasticity and power of response and finally atrophy or become in some instances completely paralyzed. In such an instance the organ or part of the body which is under the control of the corresponding sense chakra will gradually begin to be affected. If it is the chakra which controls hearing the individual will begin to lose his power of hearing. The principle of Buddhi-Manas has been partially inhibited from action in that instance.

By studying the principles and their relation to the various brain centers you will find all these correspondences.

It is the vital interest — the curiosity in relation to any thing or subject which a life impulse has awakened in any tattvic center which increases the activity of the chakra in which has been aroused an increase of vibration by the tattvic force. This interest or curiosity will bring a steady flow of the tattvic force to the corresponding chakra until that interest or curiosity is satisfied. If constant effort is made to so satisfy interest in phenomena, and an increase of blood and therefore of life force flows steadily to the portion of the brain occupied by the tattvic center and the chakra in question, the mental and physical development will be rapid.

The normally intelligent man is interested in and curious about every unfamiliar objective or thought condition which presents itself and strives to learn the causes and consequences of the same. The purely self-indulgent, indolent man gradually loses interest in all that does not add to the gratification of the organs of sense. He has little, if any, curiosity about Nature's great secrets and, therefore, neglects development of these tattvic centers which control the master chakras, which in turn make possible the higher development of brain and body; consequently, he ages more quickly than the first-mentioned man.

LESSON 213
AUTOMATIC REVELATIONS

Unless a student of occultism is thoroughly conversant with the philosophy of the Wisdom Religion, notably that portion of it which declares the sevenfold division of Matter, Force, and Consciousness, he may be quite easily deceived by some of the literature now being disseminated by means of newspapers and magazines, and by some of the teachings put forth by certain organizations on the subject of automatic revelations, which, it is claimed, have been given by the disembodied souls of the newly dead.

The ignorance of many of the mediums of communication between the physical and astral planes concerning the constitution of matter and the nature of life on the interior planes is evident in every line of some of these communications and therefore the danger of accepting them verbatim is evident. Similar mistakes to those which first led to the formation of some modern spiritualistic organizations are being made by many psychics and mediums of the present time.

If authentic, such communications originate within the sixth plane, counting from above, a sub-plane of the full astral plane — a plane which the soul contacts immediately upon leaving the body. It is a plane of reflection and of incessant change; a plane of purgation, and the plane within which the "second death" — release from the limitations of gross matter — eventually occurs. Whereas, in some of the automatic revelations put forth, completion of the life-line of the individual soul is clearly indicated. But very little that is seen on that sub-plane has any permanent existence.

The fact of an occasional communication from a Master to some disciple who has not yet developed the higher centers of sight and hearing, but whose astral senses are sufficiently developed to allow him to become a medium of communication between certain earth-bound souls and still living personalities on the physical planes, does not militate against the truth of my statements.

The directions and instructions given by a Master to a more highly developed disciple, or Agent of the White Lodge, are given by the use of Kriyashakti Power, a power which the Master has won during his many lives, and is not subject to interference by elementary forces of a lower plane.

Communications given by the average medium in séances are generally designed to help some inquirer, regardless of the worthiness or unworthiness of the latter to receive such help or comfort from a spiritual source, and even if the medium is reliable, and the psychic centers have been partially developed, the scenes witnessed are generally reflections of objective forms on the physical plane, or of the thought forms of strong desires as they are pictured in the mentality of the medium or the questioner. The pictures would appear to indicate perfect satisfaction of each desire and naturally would deceive the personality as to their spiritual value.

I do not intend to enter minutely into the subject of miscalled spiritualistic phenomena at this time; my main purpose is to call the attention of advanced students of occultism to the literature based on automatic revelations that is flooding the world at this time, and to advise such students to put all articles on that subject before the judgment seat of their own souls and strive to learn how nearly they conform to the teachings of the Wisdom Religion, and especially to those teachings which take up the sevenfold division of Matter, Force, and Consciousness and the relation of the incarnating Ego to those states or planes of life. By doing so, they should soon be able to separate the chaff from the wheat. By testing such communications as I have referred to by the light of the Temple Teachings alone, they will not go wrong, for they are in perfect harmony with the teachings of the Wisdom Religion.

Accept tentatively that which seems reliable from everything that comes your way, but above everything learn to discriminate between the true and the false.

Among the strongest desires expressed by a human being is a desire for assurance of the continuity of life after death, and for communication with friends who have crossed the border between life and death, so it is not surprising that people will go to almost any length to obtain satisfactory assurance of the same, especially if they do not know that they can very materially retard the evolution of the soul they desire to contact, by drawing it back toward the physical plane while it is breaking the connection between the astral and physical planes.

Bear in mind that your efforts should be directed to the development of your own higher centers of consciousness, so that it will be possible for you to contact those friends on higher planes without an intermediary, when they also have broken the attraction of the astral and physical planes.

LESSON 214
THE LORDS OF KARMA

In one sense the Lords of Karma are the administrators of Divine Justice — the Supreme power of the Universe, the Lord God Omnipotent of the Absolute — the creator of motion; therefore, the creator of cyclic action upon which all law is dependent.

The Lords of Karma — high spiritual entities — guide and direct the action of every form of force and energy set free by gods, angels, or man. The Higher Self of man is his own judge and executioner, but the Higher Self can only apply the effects of a given cause to the personal self after the Lords of Karma have reversed the stream of energy set free by that personal self as a result of any act that is contrary to law, for Divine Law cannot be broken with impunity. Disobedience to a Divine Law may obstruct the action of that law temporarily, but cannot do so permanently. Cyclic action will ultimately bring about conditions comparable to those which existed at the time the law was broken. The karmic results of the disobedience may have been worked out in the meantime, leaving as it were, opportunity for final adjustment and a clear field at the close of the cycle.

Man is so bound by familiar terms of expression, he is greatly handicapped in his efforts to understand super-physical phenomena when they are presented in unfamiliar terms and there are but few terms in the English language by means of which certain forms of energy may be designated, or their action on the physical plane described; for instance, the forms or degrees of energy which are generated by different sounds and motions and which so far as may be observed by the senses have no exterior effects. Every spoken word or sound, as well as every act of man tends to free a definite form of energy which must take a clearly defined course according to the guidance of the Lords of Karma.

If you throw a stone into a pool of water, thus setting the water in motion, you have released some form or degree of energy; the waves of water will move outward until they reach the verge of the pool, where they will receive the impetus to return to their starting point. But action will not cease with that one round, the waves will complete many rounds before the initial force is exhausted, and the number of rounds will depend largely upon the size and weight of the stone cast into the water. So it is the size and weight of the stone, the original cause or motive of the act, which is cast into the Ocean of universal Life that determines how many times the waves — the effects of that cause — will return to the one responsible for the act, or how many incarnations will be affected as a result of that act.

There are three grand divisions of the Lords of Karma, and very many times three minor divisions. As there is continuous interpenetration and correlation between different grades of force and substance, there is correspondingly continuous interchange, synchronous vibration, between all degrees and orders of the Lords of Karma and with the higher selves of all humanity; consequently, there is no possibility of a miscarriage of Divine Justice as a finality. For instance, a man may commit a murder as a result of a carefully considered plot and from an utterly selfish motive, thus throwing a very weighty stone — a great evil, into his individual pool of life and setting free a powerful stream of energy. Instead of allowing that stream of energy, weighted with evil as a result of the action of will and motive, to run its course and injuriously affect countless others, the Karmic Lords may turn that stream of energy back on its course to the auric sphere of the one who sent it forth. The energy so returned is utilized by the Higher Self in working out the effects of that original cause upon the lower or personal self, and as the cause was so powerful for evil in itself, it may take the personal ego many incarnations to work out all the effects of that one cause; i.e., the waves of the individual pool would return again and again to the point — the cause — where that heavily weighted stone was cast into the pool.

It is a mistake to believe that the one who commits murder of the physical plane in one life must be killed in another life by his victim in order to satisfy the Karmic law. Such another act of disobedience to Divine Law could not satisfy Divine Justice. Divine Law always acts for the ultimate benefit of humanity, even when its decrees bring sorrow and loss upon the units of a race or a nation. Evil can never be overcome by evil on any plane of existence. The Higher Self has other ways of utilizing the return wave — the stream of energy turned back by the Karmic Lords, in such an instance as I have mentioned. In the eyes of the average man the punishment meted out to the murderer by the Higher Self might not seem commensurate to the crime, but if he were able to see far enough into the future to behold the final result of the decrees of Karmic law upon the incarnating Ego of the murderer, he would be satisfied with the administration of Divine Justice.

I have taken one of the worst of crimes to illustrate my point; but the breaking of any Divine Law will bring results in perfect accord with Divine Justice; and all such universal laws are founded on universal principles. Those principles are the very foundation stones of the universe, and are therefore irrevocable and unalterable. So far as man-made laws are identical with Divine Laws, they are just; but when they vary in the least, they are mutable and cannot always stand the test of life.

LESSON 215
KARMIC ADJUSTMENT

FROM THE MASTER K.H.
January 7, 1920

If it were not for the soul tragedies in process of culmination which they are compelled to witness, the Initiates of the White Lodge might more tranquilly watch the action of inexorable Law than they are able to do at present, as one after another of the self-deceived victims of their own ambition, or the ambitions of others, falls into the sloughs of the lower astral plane in the belief that they are contacting the Masters of Wisdom or the angelic hosts of high heaven. But as it is, the knowledge possessed by the Masters of the inevitable tragedies which will follow, even in the case of some of their own solemnly pledged disciples who have been led astray, as well as others who have never had like advantages, is a source of deep sorrow and regret to them.

Those students who believe that the Masters of Wisdom are no longer subject to sorrow and pain, know but little of the offices and effects of those great nature forces. It is not that the Masters are unable to control the action of the said forces, but that they will not separate themselves from the race they are serving, and must often stand helplessly by when their own neophytes are suffering, for the reason that the Karma of the Master and that of the neophyte for whom he has assumed the responsibility of training, become identified to whatever degree knowledge has been imparted which would enable the neophyte to misuse the power he has gained, if he subsequently falls under the dominion of the Brothers of the Shadow. This has been the case with those neophytes referred to in the opening paragraphs of this communication.

The deeply regretted mistake of our much prized representative, Helena Blavatsky, in accepting as students and in imparting some of the teachings of the Secret Science to those chelas who were utterly unprepared for their receipt, has been repeated by other advanced disciples of the Masters in the present era, and the consequence is that, never since the sinking of Atlantis as a result of the misuse of spiritual power have there been so many units of a human race fallen so deeply and irretrievably under the glamor of black or of ceremonial magic, as has been the case in the present era. This is evident to the seeing eye in the lowering of the tone of morality of the race as a whole, the many sexual perverts under observation at present, the contempt of moral and national laws, and the willful breaking of the most sacred vows of discipleship by solemnly pledged neophytes.

When the curse of personal ambition seizes a soul, the mind becomes blind to honor and principle. It seizes upon every pretext to advance personal interests; friends and relatives are shelved without compunction, until at length there comes a day when the tragedy of utter desolation falls upon that soul. The work of the Brothers of the Shadow is thus completed for one, if not more, incarnations and the long hard path must be retrodden if the soul is to gain emancipation.

It seems all but impossible to convince an over-ambitious student that the simple, natural laws of life cannot be disobeyed with impunity. He does not sufficiently realize that it is by means of the physical, mental, and psychic strength and virility gained as a result of implicit obedience to those laws, that it becomes possible for a neophyte to pass the necessary tests of endurance, strength, and concentration; tests which even an Initiate must have passed successfully to enable him to take the step which opens to him the Path of final Initiation. If he has failed to pass those tests, the hurt to his pride and his disappointment may make of him an easy victim for the first self-seeking claimant of occult Power who passes his way, unless he is filled with the holy spirit of self-sacrifice and Christly humility, in which case he remains under the protection and receives the assistance of his Master as before, until a recurring cycle opens another opportunity for Trial.

A broken physical or mental law demands karmic adjustment. The soul of man cannot be satisfied with its state of progress if the correlation between his mind and physical body is continually being hindered by the results of disobedience to natural laws.

A broken law of discipleship quickly brings its own retribution. Although such retribution may follow as a result of some action taken by the Master or Teacher before whom the vow was taken, that action was taken at the demand of the soul of the disciple. The soul has demanded the fulfillment of that vow, and the Master or Teacher who is conscious of that demand endeavors to aid in its fulfillment.

I am sorry to say that letter after letter, direction upon direction, have been and still are being given publicity, purporting to come from me or from one of my brothers of the same degree of the Great White Lodge. We have neither written letters, nor given directions, to those who are responsible for circulating such letters or directions. Our *bona fide* Agents — representatives, are flouted or ignored by the latter. The directions, which in fact have been given by us, if obeyed, would have saved thousands of lives in the past five years and would have furnished the fundamental planks of a sound governmental system. These directions have passed unnoted or have been secretly destroyed by the agents of the Black Brotherhood, while we, because of our reverence for Law and our obedience to the direction of the Maha Chohan,[1] to whom we are subject, must possess our souls in patience until the coming of the Great Day.

ADDENDUM FROM THE MASTER H.

January 10, 1920

The present cyclic wave of astralism is fast rolling up and engulfing its victims by scores. Natural Law shows no favoritism and these victims of self-deception, or astral intoxication, will come from all grades of human life. The reaction — the return wave — will end in a period of suppression corresponding to that which ushered in the Inquisition and the Era of Witchcraft. The wave will sink to a depth corresponding

---

[1] *Maha Chohan (Sanskrit, "Great Lord")* — the title of the Great Lord of Shambhala, the head of the Great White Brotherhood. The Masters take the duties associated with this appointment in turn, in accordance with their individual tasks. In the 19th century, the Maha Chohan was the Master Serapis. In 1924, the Master Morya became the Lord, changing His name to Maitreya.

to the heights it reaches in a decade. Karma will then collect the debts made and one more of the rounds of the present human race will then be completed.

LESSON 216
THE WITNESS OF GOD

Every true revelation of the great mysteries of Divinity declares individual responsibility for the dissemination of the Light of the World. The Master Jesus made this declaration in the words, "I am sent to be a Light to lighten the world."[1] In the sacred Stanzas of Dzyan may be found a similar declaration: "I am sent to be a torch to light the Fires within your hearts."[2] Whatever be the form in which the intent is clothed, there is no misunderstanding the nature of the intent.

Infinitely more than the Light of the Solar Orb can mean to physical man, does the Light of the Central Spiritual Sun mean to the soul of man, and until man has awakened to some knowledge of its reality, and of its ever-present and permeating influences, he cannot rise to any comprehension of that Divine Being who is worshiped, ignorantly or wisely, by all the races of the earth, under different names.

It must be remembered that God has never left Himself without a witness. In his worship of the Solar Orb, the most ignorant of savages, as well as far more enlightened men, have worshiped the Light of the World as it shone through that visible sun; that Light which is, in fact, the very Vesture of God.

Every Avatar that has come to earth, or that ever can come, is a radiating Center of that Light.

As physical man depends on the light of the sun, or on some secondary light which is dependent on the sun for power to visualize objective forms, so the spiritual man is dependent on the Light of the Central Spiritual Sun for power to perceive and comprehend Divinity.

The soul of man alone can perceive that light and it is because the substance of the soul is of the nature of the Vesture of God that it is possible for it ever truly to know God, or to refuse to know Him by choosing evil. By so choosing it inhibits the action of the Light of which it is a part. To the soul is given the power of choice. It makes a

[1] See John 12:46.

[2] "Theogenesis: From the Stanzas of Dzyan," *The Temple Artisan*, vol. 14, issue 7 (December 1913), p. 97.

wrong choice when it chooses to act in opposition to the dictates of the radiating center of light within itself.

Whether it be termed conscience, perception, or intuition, that which impels man to act in unison with the Divine Beings who guide the evolution of the races of mankind is the Light of the Spiritual Sun.

The appreciation of beauty and perfection of form in the artist and the love of harmony and melody in the musician are effects of the action of the rays of light from the Central Spiritual Sun shining into the sense centers of man. Those sense centers are, as it were, receiving stations which catch those rays of light and translate them into terms that are comprehensible to man. But there are also stations which catch the shadows left by the passing of the Light — the effects of ignorant or selfish use of the Light.

Every unselfish desire is a reflection of a similar desire in the Mind of God. If the desire is strong enough and the will to carry it out is fully aroused, man must succeed. If the unselfish aspect of a desire is changed and becomes clouded by the personality, the plan in the Mind of God is not carried out and a constrictive force is brought into action which binds, closes up, and contracts the lines of the form which has been reflected by the Spiritual Light, and the form thus created will not conform to the pattern form in the Mind of God. When intuition has opened the avenue of perception in the mind of man, the Light of the Spiritual Sun will reflect an image of the truth through that avenue to a brain center whenever a call is made upon it.

LESSON 217
THE WORLD'S TRAVAIL

The soul of the world is in sore travail, and not one human being of its myriads of inhabitants will escape the effects of that travail. The spiritual forces of love and hate are arrayed against each other, and the battle is on for supremacy. Like unto a pack of hunger-maddened wolves the masses are lining up against those whom they believe to be the classes. Ignorance of the primal causes of their distress, a sense of injustice and of betrayal at the hands of those they have trusted, is leading many of the frenzied poor even to bite the hand of those who would feed them. They cannot now tell friend from foe; they have been deceived so often.

On the other hand, the ignorance of the wealthy on other lines in many cases has led to their ignoring the signs of the coming of the inevitable reaction of the forces they have been setting free. The experiences of past ages have been forgotten, and they have blinded their eyes too long to the signs and portents of the present era.

If I could but make my voice heard to the four corners of the world I would cry out to every human soul, "Oh, son of man, pity the brother who stands at thy side, for he is thy brother, even if he be the one who would slay thee; he knows not what he would do. He is caught in the snare set by the demons of hate, even as thou hast been caught. He is but a tool in the hands of the opponents of universal Love, even as thou hast been. If but he and thou could imagine the agony of remorse which will sweep over both as the scales fall from your eyes on the other side of the life stream, when full recognition of brotherhood dawns upon the consciousness of each one, then would you understand the uses to which the Brothers of the Shadow have put both. What does it require but the sowing of the seed of hate in the hearts of the people of a divided world, to turn men from faith in and love for God into distrust of God and love of evil?"

There is an Angel in the heart of every human being. Ah, children of mine, listen to the voice of that Angel as it bids you to show compassion toward your brother man whatever be his offenses against thee. Only by so doing wilt thou be able to meet his agonized eyes when death hath brought you to a common level. His offenses against thee will seem so small in comparison with thine against him, as thou viewest them from the heights of life. And remember, the brother thou hast sinned most deeply against, will be the first to meet thy quickened eyes when thy footsteps fall on the nether shore. The days of retribution are falling fast. Make clean your own hearts and there will be naught for you to fear.

LESSON 218
THE WAVE OF PSYCHISM

If you were able to perceive the deep sympathy felt by the Masters of Wisdom, and their understanding of the power of the great temptation facing you in common with other soul-hungry people as the present wave of psychism approaches its height, you could better appreciate their efforts to stem that wave and save you from the dire

effects of yielding to the thrall of investigation by mediumistic methods whose devotees are utterly powerless to protect the investigator
from the effects of the action of the lower elementals and astral shells
of the human souls who have passed into Devachan, leaving only the
lower qualities to animate the shells left on the lower astral plane.
These elementary forms of life gather around the sphere of investigators into psychic phenomena and feed on the magnetic emanations
drawn from them.

It is sad beyond power of expression to see men and women of
scientific culture and renown deceived by mediumistic methods even
when those methods are studied by conscientious investigators, yet
who are deceived by such dangerous tools as the Ouija board[1] and
other like implements.

Communications so received are the result of subconscious control of the mind and hands of the operator when no deceit is used.
The subconscious mind has access to the memory leaves of the soul,
the mental images or expressions of every object and form of life the
individual ego has contacted in all its incarnations in form. These
memories are fixed in the auric sphere of the individuality and may
be reproduced in any incarnation if the right conditions are made
and may supply the data for many wonderful psychic experiences.

In the case of a highly developed Mystic or Master there may
be a temporary identification of his subconscious mind with that of
another Mystic, and the memories fixed in the auric sphere of either
one may be flashed into the outer consciousness of the other, but the
power by means of which this phenomenon is produced is a high spiritual power which could not be used for any selfish purpose without
disaster to the one so using it. Such a Mystic would be incapable of
degrading that power by using it to deceive some heart hungry person
into believing he or she had been placed in rapport with a dear one
who had crossed the border between two planes of consciousness, or
by countenancing the use of any interior power to advance the financial, social, or political interests of some inquirer who might greatly
misuse the knowledge so gained.

I entreat you to refuse to accept the ideas promulgated by some of
the self-deceived adherents of the so-called "new thought" movements
relating to sex freedom and psychic development which are pernicious

---

[1] *Ouija board* — a board with the letters of the alphabet and other signs on it, used
to ask questions that are thought to be answered by the spirits of dead people.

in their effects. I refer particularly to those features which are in fact opposed to the light principles of life and action inculcated by the Masters of Wisdom throughout this Manvantara, and upon which all true civilizations have been founded.

Promiscuous sex relations and superstition have been the primary causes of the destruction of many civilized races in the past, and will be the cause of the destruction of the present one unless the race can recognize its danger and correct the present tendency in these directions before it is too late.

Spiritual development is dependent on purity of life and purpose. Monogamy is the keystone of the family, and the family is the keystone of civilization. The increase of insanity among the devotees of the Ouija board and other objective forms for obtaining communications from interior planes is deplorable, and the danger lies in the opening of the manasic centers of the brain to malefic influences active on the lower astral plane, and in the robbing of the brain centers by the aforesaid lower elementals and astral shells of the magnetic force they require for the functioning of manasic energy. This robbery is often accomplished unconsciously by the medium who depends on the magnetism of the inquirers engaged in the attempt to secure communication for themselves from the discarnate. The manasic centers of the brain are dependent on magnetism for life expression on the physical plane, and any concentrated effort of will opposed to natural evolutionary law weakens the resisting power of the physical substance which forms the outer wall of each molecule of that substance, to the negative forces which attack them unless that wall is protected by the individual Higher Self, and it is not so protected when the center is used by the lower self in defiance of the aforesaid evolutionary law.

The opening of the psychic senses, even when accomplished by normal evolutionary process, is always attended by more or less danger to the delicate brain centers involved, but the danger is far greater when it is undertaken in an attempt to speed up the process by effort of will under the direction of another person, unless such direction is given by a Master who possesses the requisite power of protection; otherwise the devotee is taking unimaginable risks of breaking down one or more brain centers, thereby becoming mentally unbalanced.

Knowing these facts, the person who dares to direct that process in the case of another, while unable to protect that other, is piling up some dread karma for himself as well as for his victim.

LESSON 219
THE CURSE OF THE WORLD

Years pass by and are lost in decades; decades pass into centuries; and centuries into ages. Races and nations are born and pass, yet man, the result of all of nature's efforts, with all the gathered experience of the ages behind him, balks at the law which demands that he shall live for his race, his nation, his world and not for himself alone. Whenever he breaks that law he calls down its punishment upon his own head and upon the heads of his children unto the third generation and beyond. When he breaks the Law of Love he breaks the one law which underlies all other laws, for upon the inviolability of that law rests the health, the sanity, the growth, and development of his race.

The Law of Love and the law of monogamy at their base are one and the same. The degradation of virginity, the contempt of that law, in man or woman, is a crime against Divine Love from which there is no appeal. The man-made law whose servants have decreed the union of one man and one woman, though they may be in ignorance of the fact, is based on that one divine law, and no man or woman can break it without increasing the results of the curse which has fallen on the human race because of the age-long violation of that law. All the worst conditions of human life are the result of the breaking of that one law. Argue as he will, examine himself as he will, curse the law as he may, for man that law stands as irrevocable today as the day it was made, the day of the separation of sex.

Each man, each woman is called upon to decide not whether he or she is personally getting the best out of life, not whether wife or husband is a saint or a sinner, but whether as units of the race to which they belong they will advance that race by precept and example, or whether they will add to the desolation, the crime, and the devolution of that race, as a result of revolution against that Law of Love. Until the human race as a whole recognizes this truth, a perfect race cannot be born.

LESSON 220
CRYSTALLIZATION

As the rays of a dying sun fall obliquely on each angle of all the drops of moisture suspended in the atmosphere, each one of those angles flashes out its own particular color, or rather flashes back the ray of color its angle has broken from the one white ray. So when the white ray of the spiritual sun falls athwart the angles of the crystallized qualities and characteristics in the mental and psychic bodies of man, it is broken up by those angles and can only reflect the different colors of the broken ray — the effects of the thoughts, words, and actions of the man — into the auric sphere, the vehicle of the Higher Self.

Crystallization holds the key to the manifestation of spirit in matter, but the key could never be turned by a materialist, for such a one could never perceive the connecting links which intuition alone can supply. Each color given out by each angle of a crystal when a ray of light is turned upon it from the right direction, would indicate to the eyes of the occultist the exact state of matter, the first plane of its manifestation, and the next step in the scale of life of the minute lives sacrificed in the process of crystallization.

A good chemist, if examining a crystal formed of the escaping fluid of a physical body, could tell at a glance which fluid formed that crystal. He might even be able to determine from which one out of several bodies the fluid was taken, and what the process of crystallization was, from a material point of view. But of the different planes or states of matter which gave birth to those minute lives, the forms they were destined to create, their ulterior purpose, and many other features, he could tell nothing. All these secrets the occultist could import if so minded, and could do so by observing the action of light on the different angles of the crystal, and applying his knowledge of the elemental forces which combined and molded the minute lives into different forms according to a divine plan.

LESSON 221
THE KARMA OF THE NATIONS

When the masses of humanity finally awake to the truth of the inexorable law of Karma, the law of cause and effect — and that law is made the basic principle of all forms of government — there will be no more making of war by one nation against another, or of revolutions within their own borders. The certainty of reprisal would be so fixed in the minds of the masses of humanity that they would not countenance such action under any circumstances. If that portion of the French people that instigated the French Revolution and carried out its blood-thirsty programs could have known that for every head that fell by their action into the basket of the guillotine the life of another French man or woman would be sacrificed when the corresponding point in the same cycle rolled around, as it did roll around during the recent war with Germany,[1] they would have hesitated in precipitating such a revolution.

Likewise if the people of the Belgian race and nation could have known that the wanton cruelty to and murder of the native Africans by the soldiery and at the instigation of King Leopold may have been primarily responsible for the fate that has overwhelmed the Belgians of the present cycle, they could have better understood what befell them.[2] We cannot prove this all to be true, but if the law of Karma is inexorable it is not difficult to see the reasonableness of the belief, as we can also see that in the squaring of karmic accounts the English nation may have paid the debts contracted by the killing of numberless non-combatant East Indians by the soldiery of another era. The lives of many Americans may have been sacrificed in payment for the lives of the American Indians taken by American soldiers of an earlier date. The closing of the cycle during the recent great war in which these karmic debts were made, may have created the conditions which were taken advantage of by the Lords of Karma to fulfill the Law.

It is very difficult to reconcile the belief of the Christian in the forgiveness of sin by Christ with the action of Karmic law, but the difficulty will be overcome when man understands what the founder of Christianity meant by the words "forgiveness of sin." The Christ in man may forgive the sin against the Spiritual Self, even while punishment is inflicted by the Law upon the personality responsible for the sin.

It appears to be an evident fact that so long as man believes that forgiveness may be had for broken Law he will not make a very strong

---

[1] The First World War (1914–1918).

[2] For over twenty years, King Leopold II of Belgium (1835–1909) enslaved the people of the Congo in Africa for the ivory and rubber trade. He was responsible for the widespread atrocities committed against them and killed millions of people. When the First World War started in 1914, Belgium was among the first countries occupied by Germany.

effort to keep from breaking that Law. It is so natural for the lower self to rebel against control by the Higher Self.

It is strange that any historian of wide experience can fail to see the working out of the law of Karma in view of the innumerable instances available in the history of any of the older nations wherein the evil effect of the causes set up by humanity during past ages has been so much in evidence. As far back as sacred or profane history can take us we may find that as day follows night every nation's evil cause set up by man has been followed by some act of forced expiation. The interference of cyclic law may defer the expiation of that act for a time but it is inevitable in the end. The extremes of life when brought into conjunction invariably produce friction — heat and energy. That energy of itself is impersonal and when mankind is wise enough always to turn the energy set free by friction, usually resulting from opposition, into constructive channels instead of destructive channels, or letting it go to waste as is now so frequently the case, the human race will have made a great advance. For instance, when the qualities of Love and hate coalesce in a human mind, as they often do in spite of their opposition, there is produced a friction within the mentality which may generate the power to render service to the objects of Love or hate hitherto unsuspected by the producer and quite possibly a long karmic debt may be so paid.

With the karmic results of long past upheavals in government, social, and religious life which are made so noticeable at the present time, and which the great war has made provision for, it is difficult to see how a thinker can deny the existence of Karmic law. The causes back of the terrible events which have occurred since the year 1914 are not far to seek.

LESSON 222
THE BETRAYAL OF THE CHRIST

FROM THE MASTER C.

"Ere the cock crows thrice one of you shall betray me," saith the Christ, again today as yesterday.[1]

"Is it I, Lord? Shall I betray thee?" cried one of the twelve rulers over as many storehouses for the necessities of life, as he sat at the right hand of the Lord, one of twelve chosen disciples around the

---

[1] See John 13:38 and Matthew 26:21.

bounteous table the earth had provided, and gazed into the face of Him by whom all things were made — the face of Him who sat at the head of the table. "Shall I to whom thou hast given control of all the corn and grain my subjects have sown and on which they depend for life itself, shall I betray thee to the cross of suffering? No, a thousand times no, say I!"

"Is it I, Lord?" spoke another, "Could I betray thee, I to whom thou hast given control of all the gold and silver men have mined that they might have a medium of exchange for the necessities of life? Could I in foul ingratitude betray thee — thee to whom silver and gold are as dross in comparison with human life? Rather let me perish than do this thing."

"Is it I?" cried out he who sat on the left of his Lord. "Shall I yield thee up to torture, thou who hast given me power over the very elementals of the earth, that power by means of which I may drive them forth by my slaves, and take and store the iron and coal in which those lesser lives had been confined, in order that I may compel the crowded, cold, and freezing souls who dispute my will to yield to my dictates or die? Ah, no, my Lord, I will block the way for those who fain would nail thee to the cross.

"To be sure these willful souls would not so compel me if they but knew thee for what thou art. We, my brother rulers and I, have taken care that they should not know thee and knowing thee should presume upon our rights. We alone now have the time, the opportunity with which to seek thee out."

"Is it I?" spoke up another, "I to whom thou hast given dominion over the fishes of the sea and the fowls of the air? In order that hungry men should not dispute my claim, lo, I have formed a cordon around my fishermen and huntsmen and not a fish or fowl escapes their hands without the payment of a heavy tithe to me. Not one of all the rabble seeking thee shall even touch thy robe, for I in payment for thy gifts will fend thee off from them. Not I, my Lord, not I shall play thee false."

"Is it I, Lord, who shall betray thee?" Up arose a crowned and mitred head, one clothed in flowing robes, embroidered over with cunning needlework, and spoke unto his Lord, saying: "Surely, thou couldst never deem me such a traitor unto thee; I, the earthly head of all the Christian Church, could never yield thee up to cursing, ribald mobs, thou who art the Son of God, thou whom I and all thy church now worship with many prayers and ceremonies. Could I be faithless unto thee? Truly have I built me many houses for the honor of the Church, but always do I turn my eyes in passing when poverty bestead and sinful men and women crowd therein and reek and die in their own filth. I will not look upon the brothels and the dens of vice these sinners make of these — the houses I have built. I hold my hands behind me for the gold they bring to me. I do not soil the eyes I seek to lift unto thy face, with scenes like these. I could not betray thee if I would, so free from sin am I in thy most holy sight."

Then up rose their Lord, the Christ, and said: "Oh fools, Oh blind and hard of heart! Lo, even now there falls upon my ear the sound of hard sped feet, the feet of those who come to bear me hence. Thou hast betrayed me! Thou who sittest at my right hand, thou who sittest upon my left, and thou, and thou, on either side, all ye who now do hang your heads in shame. Ye have betrayed me over and over again. Ye will betray me on the morrow as today. Betray me in that ye will leave my little ones in whom I live to starve and freeze and die in helpless misery, that ye may hold the power ye steal; that ye may fill your coffers with the gold ye filch from other men whom ye have made your slaves by hunger, cold, and want. In every one of these ye have betrayed me over and over again, for I in them do suffer even as they suffer on the cross of woeful want, which ye have raised. Upon the cross of human woe hath mankind nailed me, age by age, and there I hang today, as yesterday, with pleading eyes and tongue beseeching you to end my sorrow and my pain. Aye, ye have all betrayed me, all ye who rob my little ones of that which God hath freely given to all; and first of all, are ye who rob yourselves; all ye who do betray a trust some other one hath placed in ye; all ye who fail to keep the vows ye made to God. All ye betray the Christ."

LESSON 223
THE BASIC LAW

Back of the modern idea of cooperation, even from a materialistic viewpoint, is a basic law, a biological law, which is as old as the universe.

As an illustration of the action of this law in one cycle of Time, we see that, according to Biblical genealogical records, the human race of the preceding age (a 5,000-year cycle) became consciously subject to the action of that basic law with the incarnation of the Egos of Adam,

Eve, Cain and Abel, and also became subject to the negative aspect of the same law in an effort to thwart that law when Cain undertook to nullify the first decree issued by the Divine Law-Giver — the decree which demanded that man should live for the race and work together in love, i.e., union, for its development. That decree was disobeyed by the slaying of the fourth member of the fourfold body by the third member of that same body. Since the passing of that first racial era, one or more of each subsequently formed human combination of four creators of a race has endeavored to thwart the perfect action of the law. From the standpoint of occultism, this effort to thwart the law is the result of the heresy of separateness.

However few or many were the units of a body and whatever the primal object of its formation as a composite body, it has been overtaken by a similar tendency to destroy one or more of its first four units with the object which led to the slaying of Abel by Cain. If not perpetrated in kind, the desire to be rid of some member of the original body was fulfilled — in other words, the combination first formed was broken up in order to further some selfish purpose.

To understand the basic impulse in man to form such a combination of human beings for cooperative purposes, we must first consider the subject from the standpoint of the formation of the group soul, one differentiation of the universal higher manasic substance, the composite soul, which has its origin on an interior plane, but which is subject to the same above-mentioned law.

That law is the divine code of Love, whatever the appellation bestowed upon it by man. Scientifically, it is the law of attraction; the law which tends to draw together all men or objects of like nature for the accomplishment of like purposes. The possibility of a successful formation of a cooperative body on the plane of gross matter, the physical plane, depends first of all upon the perfect obedience of the units of the group soul to the decrees of that divine code of Love. If the units of that substance do not conform to the law which they must obey to enable the group soul to function perfectly, another divine decree of the law comes into action, the decree of repulsion, and the form of the corresponding body on the physical plane is broken up. The basic law in action is first of all union, and whatever militates against the uniting of the parts of a body is breaking that law.

If the original purpose of the formation of a body be the gaining of material advantages for purely selfish ends and the purpose be attained despite disobedience to the decrees of the basic law, the evolution of the units of the body will be greatly retarded. The first decree of that basic law as issued to the units of the group soul on an interior plane demands the acceptance of and obedience to the principle of brotherhood. Therefore, to whatever degree the units of the group soul first in form on the akashic plane adhere to that principle of brotherhood, to that degree are they approaching perfection along the particular line they are building at the racial period they have reached, and the less difficult they are making it for the human race on the physical plane in that era if they succeed.

One of the most remarkable examples of the principle governing cooperative bodies (brotherhoods) lies in the application of the Law of Love by the ruling powers in the carrying out of the details of the evolution of primordial life, for it is not in the human kingdom alone that the first decree of the Law of Love comes into force. If there were a sufficiently powerful microscope available for observing the first manifestations of form in minutia as composite bodies, it would be found that there were four distinct species of four units of the same race who were obedient to that decree required to build up each composite unit of the composite body. In each unit would be found slightly differentiated constituents and characteristics to those to be found in all other fourfold units of the same body. Mathematically speaking, each unit is a square of a square of wider dimensions.

Each one of the four first formed units of such a body sets up a corresponding line of action to that which occupies the time and efforts of the remainder of the units of the fourfold body. It is of interest to know that there is a perfect correspondence between the ruling positions of the units of a group of the primary manifestations of form and the four officials frequently posited at the four points of the compass who build up and govern an organization for religious purposes and even in some instances for business purposes. The same law which directs the process of the formation of a group soul directs the countless elemental lives of an interior plane into composite forms of gross matter and directs all details of their formation by means of manasic energy active in the first four of its units within the fourth plane of manifestation counting from below. Formless, conditionless spiritual life is thereby changed into concrete expressions of form primarily within the Akasha, the fifth plane. The substance of the three highest of the seven planes of life is undifferentiated, so far as our understanding of form is concerned. Man has become so familiarized with the idea of and belief in the theory of single expressions of life in form that he naturally rejects the idea of the fourfold expression of the beginning of life as it unfolds from the triad — "the three in one" — in composite fourfold forms.

It must not be understood that we are opposed to the ancient belief in the threefold manifestation of life, the triad — Spirit, Soul, and Body in one. Where there appears to be contradiction between the latter and the fourfold manifestation of life in one form, it is due to misunderstanding of the apparent division between spirit and matter, the division frequently referred to as "the bridge" whereby "the Three fall into the Four."[1]

The triad, father, mother, son, or in other words, spirit, mind, and consciousness, become the father, mother, son and daughter within the fourth plane. The daughter — individual self-consciousness — as differentiated from universal consciousness, has begotten substance within "the bridge" — the substance or energy of the fourth plane. Mathematically speaking it is the square, the cross involved. Form-lessness has become form *per se* — the fourth plane, within which occurs the generation of countless elementary forms of life — wherein each monad — a divine spark of the fire of the Absolute — unfolds or clothes itself in matter of lesser vibration; in other words, where the monad — life spark — becomes a fourfold material form, eventually evolving four chief senses and organs, which are still further differentiated as evolution proceeds, and the Ego has then become conscious of three more planes or states of being.

I have only given a crude resume of the truths herein presented. My main object in doing so is to give some impression of the causes back of cooperative movements and of the law which alone can render such movements of any lasting avail. It is only by consideration of the methods by which man may attain to the knowledge of brotherhood as taught by the divine Teachers of mankind that he will be enabled consciously to become a creator in the highest sense of the word, for he must then be able to direct the creation of different degrees of living substance into forms possessing more power and intelligence than similar forms now possess.

No unit of matter in manifestation on the physical plane is complete in itself, although each unit has latently within it the power of

---

[1] Blavatsky, *The Secret Doctrine*, vol. 1, p. 29.

reproducing the latent energies which manifest later in the other three units which, with the first, complete the fourfold body. This truth is exemplified over and over again in the organs of the human body, each organ being built up of myriads of conscious lesser lives.

LESSON 224
DANGERS OF MEDIUMSHIP

The materialist or the doubting investigator of occult science probably will scout or ridicule the statement that great dangers lie in the investigation of psychic phenomena and mediumship, while to "one who knows" those dangers are appalling. But the latter is doubly handicapped in endeavoring to point out those dangers to a new investigator for he has first to prove that the state of matter in which and by which any such phenomenon is objectified has a *bona fide* existence, or if this be admitted, he also has to prove it to be altogether a different thing from what it is supposed to be even by the average undeveloped psychic or spiritualist, though it has been largely by the efforts of some of the prominent spiritualists that the said phenomena are coming into public notice in the west in recent days.

The believer in the return to earth of the disembodied human soul at the command of a sensitive or medium cannot be convinced of the fallacy of that belief until certain facts in the case are demonstrated beyond possibility of mistake by means of occult science.

Mundane science has already done much to establish the underlying truths of the ancient religions — not the errors and superstitions with which those religions subsequently became encrusted, but their fundamental basis, the truths as taught by Krishna, Buddha, and Jesus. It has also proven that there is a necessity for a hypothetical ether as a medium for conducting light and sound and electrical phenomena, notably by means of photography and the wireless telegraph and telephone, but it has not proved the preexistence or postexistence of the soul of man.

Many scientists have also accepted the ancient belief in the One Life or the One Substance from which all forms and states of matter have been evolved or created, that is, set in motion and sustained from a pivotal point, as it were, and so created by means of different rates of mass motion and vibration. Science has also proven the reality of the law of cause and effect, the law of Karma. Its next step seemingly would be the establishment of the truth of the reembodiment of a central nucleus or soul, as it has already proven the fact of evolution — progression, which is one aspect of reincarnation.

The hypothetical ether of science is in fact the lower aspect of the Æther of the ancients — the domain of the lower astral light and astral body. Beyond the etheric is the Akasha or higher astral, the plane or state of the purified soul. The lower astral light is the plane of all newly disembodied souls during the process of purification — an intermediate period between physical death and the "second death" — the release of the soul from bondage to matter.

The first sheath or model body of all forms is created, even as the physical body, primarily in and out of Etheric states of matter, and this model is called the astral double. The model is created before birth of the physical body and disintegrated after death of the body.

As the light of the sun can imprint and fix a picture on a sensitized plate, so may the light of God, the light of the spiritual Sun, imprint upon the ethero-astral substance every form, impulse, act, and thought of the individual soul throughout its long line of incarnations; and while the results of those thoughts and deeds which are good remain a part of the soul after that second death, those of the opposite pole, evil, will remain a part of the astral body until it disintegrates in turn, after which its elements are reduced to chaos. And it is said to be these astral shells or bodies which are drawn to and temporarily galvanized into materialization by the medium who attracts them (when the materialization is genuine), instead of being the beautiful spiritual souls of the individuals who have gone from the physical and the lower astral planes into devachanic existence. Every human being has a lower side to his nature, and however it may be disguised, it is this lower aspect of the self which may be drawn back to earth during séances. Its appearance may have nothing to do with its real character; and when one thinks of the character of some of the human beings who are thrown into that lower astral all unprepared, full of revenge and of desire for sentient life at any cost, some of the dangers of tampering with that degree of life may be more easily understood.

This lower astral double may even take the semblance of an animal. These astral doubles or shells of evil minded men and women may take the forms of vicious beasts. The supposed legend of the werewolf may have been founded on a psychic vision of such a beast.

Occasional psychics have seen the form of a beautiful animal endowed with almost human intelligence which was clearly the galvanized shell of some human being. The attraction between some human beings and animals which has led to an undue attachment between them may have printed the features of the animal upon the astral shell of a recently defunct human body.

The purified, the good, do not remain on the astral plane for a great length of time, and once having passed on to a higher plane, the average human soul can only be recalled at great danger to itself. The perfected Soul, a Master, can go to them, if need be, but it is because such a perfected Soul has made the great renunciation and has returned to the astral plane for the sake of humanity, though possessing power and wisdom of a god-like nature. Such an one would surely not require the assistance of a medium openly to appear to mankind.

The empty astral shell might be comparable to the skin shed by a snake, which, when filled out with gas, would seem to be a living snake, but in reality would have no vitality of itself.

Occult science claims that when mundane science is able to demonstrate the truth of reincarnation it will find that the vehicle or body of the soul is created by a finer degree of electrical energy than are those forms of electricity which operate in gross matter, and that the soul is, materially speaking, a composite structure of all the sublimated powers and forces and substance that the persistent Ego has used to build up in turn all the bodies of its line of incarnations, and that it is this soul that returns each time to sentient life for experience at the expiration of its periodical eras of heavenly rest.

A gulf or barrier exists between the different planes of body, soul, and spirit. These barriers are the conditions which test the soul as to its fitness to pass from one plane of life to another, and the human body could no more contact those states and preserve physical life than it could touch a highly electrified wire without being instantaneously killed. These intermediate states or divisions, gulfs, or walls of protection, as they are sometimes termed, are only passed when the Ego passes in and out of incarnation; and aside from the dangers before mentioned, both to the soul and to those who might presumably contact it, there is another reason of infinite importance why it should remain undisturbed after leaving the world of matter. A purified soul cannot go backward and forward through the gulfs that separate the different planes at will. If it returns to the astral or physical plane at the call of a medium, it must remain there indefinitely until released by some higher entity or until it regains the power to repass.

LESSON 225
THE SEED OF LIFE

The vagaries of the human intellect are truly phenomenal. The extent to which the inhibition of a single brain cell may incite an individual to acts of cruelty and injustice is one of the great mysteries of life. Especially is this true if that cell is a part of the brain center which governs the correlating functions of the mind. In considering the results of a single event in the life of an individual which, to all appearances, should have been controlled by the most simple laws of nature, it is frequently found that the balance between two formerly perfectly harmonized centers of force in a physical organ has been mysteriously destroyed. The cause of the destruction of balance lies in the overwhelming of the positive electrical pranic or life force by the negative aspect of the same force, owing to the before-mentioned inhibition of some of the brain cells which control that organ and this has been the result of concentrated selfish thought along a line of mentality that is destructive to balance.

In no instances are the foregoing truths more evident than in the attitude of the great majority of the human race toward the Great Souls who have come or have been divinely sent to earth for the development of the race by means of raising the vibratory action of the atomic substance of certain brain centers in the units of the race. It is seldom that one, even among the brightest intellects of this age, is capable of recognizing such a high Initiate or understanding the motives and purposes which actuate him. He is always the incarnation of an older soul than are the souls of the race he enters, and he is possessed of finer and stronger powers of mind and body.

Among the offices he must undertake is, metaphorically speaking, to fire the refuse — the wrong beliefs — of the age in which he incarnates, and to lay the fires — inspire higher ideals — for the humanity of the succeeding age. Wars and revolutions and increased activity in all fields of material life may result from the fires he then sets — the increase in the rates of vibration he establishes.

As a result of his labors the set opinions, creeds, and dogmas of the orthodox religions of the great majority of the races in which he incarnates must undergo many changes. If he does not measure up to the religious, ethical, and social ideals of the general public, the age-old cry of "crucify or hang him, ostracize or imprison him" rises from the numberless throats. The wrongly taught masses imagine that such a man must be a model, a pattern, upon which each contemporary man or woman, community, or organization must be built. They do not realize that he is of different nature in many respects from them. He is an intermediary, a combination of the extreme of development in an older race and the initial impulses of development for a new race.

No one but a Great Soul could voluntarily take upon himself such an incarnation of suffering as every Avatar has endured for the love of humanity. He is a living sacrifice (in one sense the old is always a sacrifice for the new), and not until the Avatar or Great Soul — the Savior of a racial period, has passed from the ken of the humanity of that period and the evidences of the work he has done begin to appear does his real life and nature become apparent save to his personal disciples. To the orthodox priestly classes in authority at the time, he is a devil, a sensualist, a collaborator with evil spirits, or at best, an object of pity. They do not understand him, and but very few among the masses of the people realize that an angel has passed their way when he has left their sphere of action, or that he has opened the way for an incoming host of souls who are to raise the vibratory pulse of the world.

Something similar to a miracle has occurred in the very substance of his body as a result of his great renunciation and suffering. The embryological life of some of the cells of his body has changed their rate of vibration to a higher degree. The atomic substance of some cell, organ, or feature of his very flesh has become as it were a group of seed by means of which the atomic substance of similar cells in all bodies of flesh will eventually be changed. You have only to consider the changes which have occurred in the substance of some of the lower forms of animal and plant life as a result of the labor of the embryologist to understand somewhat of the rationale of the changes which may occur even in the nature of human flesh by the action of mental energy on physical substance, as a result of the efforts of the Great Souls who come this way from a more interior plane of life.

A stronger link is formed by them between the races of man, and between God and man.

These Great Souls can only incarnate on the physical plane when the cyclic law has opened a period which will allow for such changes as have taken place in every age, even before man became the intelligent, self-conscious being he is today. Yet as a rule man still fails to recognize them, although they have been, as it were, the seed of every advance in life, and will continue to be so until the God in man as in nature is fully recognized by the human race.

The process by which the changes take place in the cells of the bodies of the Avatars of each great Root Race is repeated in lesser degree in the cases of the most highly developed units of each sub-race. The mysteries of embryology cannot be solved by science until it recognizes the fact that there is a central cell of generation in every organic body, and a similar secondary central cell in every organ and distinct division of such a body. As an illustration of the process by which such changes occur, take the actions and reactions of mental and physical energy combined within the central generative cells of the body of one of our ancestors. The impress of the ideal in the mind of that ancestor is made on the atomic substance of one of those central cells, and the atoms constituting the molecules of that central cell become as it were a group of seed which are capable of impregnating the atomic substance of all the other cells of the organ involved. If the impress was made on one of the three main cells instead of upon the central cell of a single organ, the atomic substance of every organ of the body would be affected.

The body as a whole has three central cells which lie in the heart, the brain, and the generative organs. The impress made on the atomic substance of the heart center by the ideal in the mind of a human being accelerates the vibration of the heart and affects the whole blood stream as a result of the change in the rate of vibration. If made on the central brain cell, it affects the atomic substance of the cerebellum and spine and the pineal and pituitary glands primarily. If made on the central cell of the generative organs, the changes occur in the embryonic form and features of the descendants of the individual ancestor of the family or race who has made the impression. Some of the emotional tendencies of the parents of a child will be transmitted to the child as the result of the emotional action of the parents on the central cell of the heart of the child. The atavistic tendencies — the transmission of features and characteristics from ancestors to descendants — are evolved in the atomic substance of the central cells of the generative organs of the ancestors, who have at some cyclic period of their lives formed an ideal of a type of form and features which has appealed to them. By means of manasic energy so generated the ideal of that type has been transmitted and fixed in the atomic substance of the central cells of the generative organs of their descendants, and the form, features, and characteristics of that type will appear in their descendants, although it is possible for them to skip several generations before appearing.

LESSON 226
THE ETHERIC PLANES

Within the last decade an exceptional amount of interest has been aroused in the etheric phenomena of life, owing to the increased development of the psychic senses of man in so many instances.

Scientific investigation along similar lines has added greatly to such interest, especially in regard to the efforts which have been made to reduce gross matter to the last analysis possible of investigation by exoteric means. It is interesting to note that the findings of science corroborate the statements of the old Masters in respect to the constitution of matter and especially in regard to the finer etheric states of Akasha which are imperceptible to the physical senses. However, science has not yet demonstrated the truth that the etheric states of substance are the temporary environments of all forms of life previous to and immediately following the closing of manifestation in physical form.

The soul of man is continuously striving to solve the mysteries of life after the death of the physical body, and in some instances this has led to belief in the philosophy of what is termed "spiritualism" — belief in the visible and audible manifestation of discarnate souls to those in incarnation on the physical plane. The advanced occultist does not accept this teaching for what it is supposed to prove by its advocates. While he does not deny the possibility of many forms of occult phenomena, he can only accept the teachings of the Masters anent the manifestation of the personal Ego within the sevenfold divisions of matter, force, and consciousness. According to the latter, the soul — the higher intelligence — does not return to earth in spiritualistic manifestation, although it is possible for the astral or etheric body, the vehicle of the soul, to appear under certain conditions after the soul itself has left that body and is functioning in one of the higher etheric planes.

The said occultist is not only conscious of the continuity of all forms of life within the etheric planes but also of the various modifications of Akasha which in part constitute the substance of the fourfold etheric planes. I intend to confine this communication more particularly to consideration of the lowest of these four states, for it is more nearly related to the matter of the physical plane.

This state of etheric substance is known by different schools of thought under various names, and this has led to much confusion in the minds of students. According to both science and occultism this etheric substance is more electrical and magnetic than is the matter of the physical plane. It is the substance of the Protyle[1] of the Crookes[2] School, the Alcahest[3] of Paracelsus,[4] the Fire of Zoroaster,[5] and the lower Astral Light of the occultist. It is the vehicle of the Dynaspheric Force[6] of other scientists. Finally, it is the homogeneous, all-pervading form of etheric light which permeates every atom of physical matter. It is the basic substance of all such forms as may become visible to the psychic senses in vision, trance, or sleep.

At the death of the physical body, the confined or personal ether concentrates and streams from the head, gradually assuming the form of the physical body it is leaving. This subtle, rarefied, tenuous

---

[1] Protyle (Greek, "first substance") — the term used by William Crookes to describe the primal substance from which all chemical elements originated.
[2] Sir William Crookes (1832–1919) — an English physicist and chemist who discovered thallium, invented the radiometer, and studied cathode rays.
[3] Alcahest — the universal solvent, the "Vine of Life."
[4] Paracelsus (1493–1541) — a Swiss physician, alchemist, and philosopher, considered a pioneering figure in the fields of medicine and chemistry.
[5] Zoroaster (Avestian, "golden shining star," "golden Sirius") — the founder of Zoroastrianism and a prophet. He was given the Revelation of Ahura Mazda, or the Creator, in the form of the holy scripture of the Avesta.
[6] Dynaspheric or Etheric Force — the mysterious energy used by John Worrell Keely to conduct his experiments. Its discovery "would lead to a knowledge of one of the most occult secrets, a secret which can never be allowed to fall into the hands of the masses" (The Secret Doctrine, vol. 1, p. 560).

substance in form is the vehicle of the departing soul, which remains on the lowest one of the etheric planes until its period of purgation is ended, when it automatically seeks a higher, a more ethereal or spiritual plane, leaving its vehicle as a shell on the lower etheric plane until it also has disintegrated as the physical body has previously done. It is this shell revivified by the mediums or by some astral entity that appears in spiritualistic séances.

The substance of the etheric plane may be, as it were, molded into any desired form by concentrated individual thought force which has been set in action by auto-suggestion, as may also be the case of one using the magnetism of the ether for healing or other purposes. The psychic may perceive the magnetic force in the form of light escaping from the ends of the fingers of the operator in the course of magnetic treatments.

As the air may be contaminated by the effluvia arising from poisonous or noxious vapors, so an etheric magnetic current may be contaminated by the evil, lecherous thoughts of man, eventuating in illness or even in death of the individual to whom they are directed. Evidences of such contamination are visible to the psychic in the clouded shades of color assumed by the personal ether escaping from the body of one who is indulging in selfish or other evil thoughts.

It is not so much the general phenomena of the etheric planes that I am emphasizing at this time, for that is too far-reaching a subject to particularize upon to any great degree in a short communication. It is the personal ether, that portion of the etheric substance which permeates the physical body and is possible of manipulation by the will and mind of man. Man possesses the power to manipulate this fiery electric emanation and is responsible to the higher law for its use or misuse. Its selfish personal use is one form of black magic.

The word magnetism is so carelessly and ignorantly used that the real nature and power of the substance which the word indicates is unknown by the great majority of people. The substance of the personal ether and the personal magnetism are the same in appearance. It is continually emanating from the physical body in definite waves, which are subject to direction by one person to the body of another. As the air is necessary for the building and sustaining of every molecule of a physical body, so the ether is requisite for the building and sustaining of the astral body.

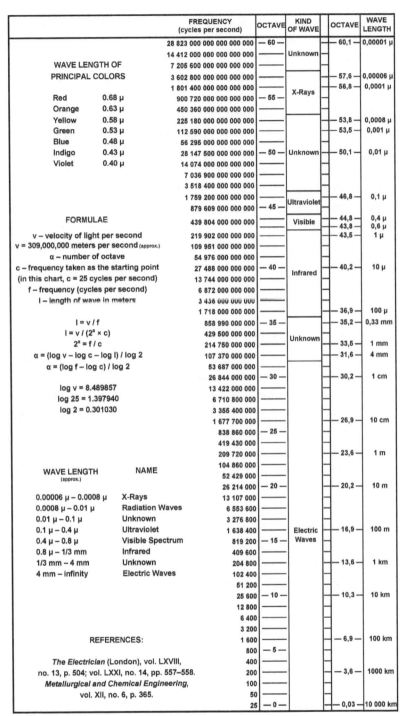

WAVE LENGTH OF PRINCIPAL COLORS

Color	Wave length
Red	0.68 μ
Orange	0.63 μ
Yellow	0.58 μ
Green	0.53 μ
Blue	0.48 μ
Indigo	0.43 μ
Violet	0.40 μ

FORMULAE

v – velocity of light per second
v = 309,000,000 meters per second (approx.)
α – number of octave
c – frequency taken as the starting point
(in this chart, c = 25 cycles per second)
f – frequency (cycles per second)
l – length of wave in meters

$$l = v / f$$
$$l = v / (2^{\alpha} \times c)$$
$$2^{\alpha} = f / c$$
$$\alpha = (\log v - \log c - \log l) / \log 2$$
$$\alpha = (\log f - \log c) / \log 2$$

log v = 8.489857
log 25 = 1.397940
log 2 = 0.301030

WAVE LENGTH (approx.)	NAME
0.00006 μ – 0.0008 μ	X-Rays
0.0008 μ – 0.01 μ	Radiation Waves
0.01 μ – 0.1 μ	Unknown
0.1 μ – 0.4 μ	Ultraviolet
0.4 μ – 0.8 μ	Visible Spectrum
0.8 μ – 1/3 mm	Infrared
1/3 mm – 4 mm	Unknown
4 mm – infinity	Electric Waves

REFERENCES:

The Electrician (London), vol. LXVIII, no. 13, p. 504; vol. LXXI, no. 14, pp. 557–558.
Metallurgical and Chemical Engineering, vol. XII, no. 6, p. 365.

FREQUENCY (cycles per second)	OCTAVE	KIND OF WAVE	OCTAVE	WAVE LENGTH
28 823 000 000 000 000 000	60		60,1	0,00001 μ
14 412 000 000 000 000 000		Unknown		
7 205 600 000 000 000 000				
3 602 800 000 000 000 000			57,6	0,00006 μ
1 801 400 000 000 000 000		X-Rays	56,8	0,0001 μ
900 720 000 000 000 000	55			
450 360 000 000 000 000				
225 180 000 000 000 000			53,8	0,0008 μ
112 590 000 000 000 000			53,5	0,001 μ
56 295 000 000 000 000				
28 147 500 000 000 000	50	Unknown	50,1	0,01 μ
14 074 000 000 000 000				
7 036 900 000 000 000				
3 518 400 000 000 000				
1 759 200 000 000 000		Ultraviolet	46,8	0,1 μ
879 609 000 000 000	45			
439 804 000 000 000		Visible	44,8	0,4 μ
			43,8	0,6 μ
219 902 000 000 000			43,5	1 μ
109 951 000 000 000				
54 976 000 000 000				
27 488 000 000 000	40	Infrared	40,2	10 μ
13 744 000 000 000				
6 872 000 000 000				
3 436 000 000 000				
1 718 000 000 000			36,9	100 μ
858 990 000 000	35		35,2	0,33 mm
429 500 000 000		Unknown		
214 750 000 000			33,5	1 mm
107 370 000 000			31,6	4 mm
53 687 000 000				
26 844 000 000	30		30,2	1 cm
13 422 000 000				
6 710 800 000				
3 355 400 000				
1 677 700 000			26,9	10 cm
838 860 000	25			
419 430 000				
209 720 000			23,6	1 m
104 860 000				
52 429 000				
26 214 000	20		20,2	10 m
13 107 000				
6 553 600				
3 276 800				
1 638 400		Electric Waves	16,9	100 m
819 200	15			
409 600				
204 800			13,6	1 km
102 400				
51 200				
25 600	10		10,3	10 km
12 800				
6 400				
3 200				
1 600			6,9	100 km
800	5			
400				
200			3,6	1000 km
100				
50				
25	0		0,03	10 000 km

Table 1
Spectrum of Ether Vibrations

"Everything in nature is in a state of vibration, and there is apparently no limit to the different kinds and frequencies of these vibrations. Some of these vibrations are directly perceptible to our sense organs, others to instruments, and still others to photography, fluorescence, etc."

"We are constrained to study natural phenomena with humility, not knowing when some new discovery will reveal to us hitherto unrecognized vibrations.

"There is a conflict between atomics and energetics. This conflict concerns itself with whether the atomic hypothesis shall dominate the physical sciences or whether matter is only a manifestation of electrical energy.

"Our knowledge of the external world is derived through sense organs by certain forms of energy. Le Dantec[1] observed, 'To find an impersonal method of measurement is to found a science.'

"'Seeing is believing,' hence the visualizing tendency in human nature.

"The diagram of C. W. Robbins of etheric vibrations (Table 1) shows a velocity in the ether when unretarded of 309,000,000 meters, or about 186,000 miles, per second.

"The list is divided into octaves, the vibration frequency per second at any octave being twice that of the preceding octave and one-half that of the octave following. The numbering of the octaves is essentially arbitrary.

"The vibration rates extend into infinity, and there is no reason to believe there is any limit.

"In the chart the length of any wave multiplied by the frequency per second equals 309,000,000 meters.

"Sight detects only a little less than one octave, and these vibrations are limited to the visible spectrum (red to violet), hence the fallacy of saying 'seeing is believing.'"

From *Physico-Clinical Medicine*

---

[1] *Félix Le Dantec* (1869–1917) — a French biologist and philosopher of science.

LESSON 227
RELIGION

Esoterically the word *religion* means to bind back to God. The great desire of all units of a religious body is to reunite the soul and spirit of man however the desire may be expressed. Man has created a breach in consciousness between his higher and lower self which must be overcome before he can attain to individual spiritual consciousness.

By persistent disobedience to the Deific laws and principles upon which all forms of religion are founded, man has made religion a thing of little moment in comparison to what it might be if those laws were upheld.

In the orthodox religions this breach is believed to have been caused by original sin, the sin of a single man and woman, Adam and Eve, from whose sin the whole human race must suffer. In the Wisdom Religion it is taught that the so-called "sin" consists of disobedience to the divine laws and principles by the whole human race, therefore that individual man suffers from himself. The cause is the same in both instances, i.e., disobedience to law. The first mentioned is disobedience to the dictates of a personal God, the last mentioned is disobedience to the dictates of the Higher Self — the Universal God in man.

Unless the fundamental philosophical, ethical, and moral principles of the religion or system of philosophy with which the individual man has identified himself have become the most vital thing in his life, he is a failure, from the higher spiritual standpoint. His success in material fields of life does not alter that fact. This is true for the reason that the spirit of man should have control of the mind and body, and he learns to control and use spiritual energy through his obedience to the dictates of his Higher Self, his God, and his devotion to those fundamental principles which are the basis of his religion. To whatever degree he fails in this respect, he deprives himself of the power to function that energy in any field of endeavor.

Unless the philosophy of the religion of The Temple of the People as accepted by the members of that body is made a living power in the daily lives of those members, it will be impossible to carry out the given directions for the upbuilding of the physical counterpart of the ideal form of the Temple in the mind of God. Every duty neglected, every refusal to carry out the directions of the Masters, who are in a spiritual sense the Chief Priests of the Temple of Humanity, by any of the component parts of that body causes them to rob themselves of the spiritual energy which otherwise would come to them through that particular channel, and thus the whole body must suffer from the effects of their action or inaction. The channel — in this instance The Temple of the People — becomes so much the less effective.

The above-mentioned basic principles or laws of spiritual, ethical, and moral life are identical in all forms of religion. In whatever form of religion these laws are ignored or misinterpreted, it is due to the ambition, pride, selfishness, or faithlessness of one or more units of the body. It is not the governing principles of the religion that are at fault, for they are omnipotent, changeless, and eternal. To whatever degree they are ignored or disobeyed by man, the power to utilize the spiritual energy on which he is dependent for spiritual and moral growth is lost. This is as truly a fact as is the fact that interference with or the cutting off of a current of electrical energy from the dynamo of an electrical engine on the physical plane will deprive the engineer of the power to run the engine and, therefore, to benefit from its use.

It is lack of realization of this truth by man and therefore his failure to benefit from the knowledge to be so gained that has left him the feeble, impotent creature he has become during the present great age in comparison with the strong, vitally alive man he might be. His religion has been made a secondary or a third feature of his life, instead of the one vital thing it ought to be.

There have been so many abuses of power in some orthodox religious bodies, that the very word religion has become taboo to many, even to some students of occultism who do not realize that occultism — Theosophy — is religion in the highest sense of the word.

It has been said by those who know whereof they speak, that spirit and matter cannot meet. This is true from a universal aspect; but from the individual or particular aspect, spirit has built a bridge, figuratively speaking, a bridge of mind substance over which the energy awakened by spiritual action can pass to matter and therefore to the soul and body of man. It is by means of this bridge of mind that the soul passes into the realms of spirit — the consciousness of spirit.

The religious instinct in man is aroused by the soul's desire and effort to pass back over this bridge — to regain its lost inheritance, its conscious realization of union with God. It is the increased development of this instinct by means of the basic principles of his religion which makes the religious practices of man such a vital thing in his life. A man's personal religion should be the school of his soul.

If all Templars could fully realize the truth of the statements I have made herein and could see how their development was hindered by indifference or neglect of their duties and disobedience to directions given them for their benefit, they would make a stronger effort to fulfill their obligations than is made by some of their number.

LESSON 228
HERO WORSHIP

There is a natural instinct or tendency toward hero worship in the heart of every normal human being.

The principles of Desire and Will active in all men lead them on to honor and glorify some other man or woman who has reached to eminence in some field of religion, science, art, or politics — in other words, there is a tendency to glorify one believed to be in advance of the masses of mankind.

The soul of man intuitively recognizes that there are beings of a higher order of life than are the men and women of the present races of the earth. The latter believe that honor and love are due to those beings, from whom they expect that humanity, individually and collectively, will be benefited through their greater knowledge and power. Man's apostasy and recreancy, his fickleness and oftentimes cruelty toward those he has previously exalted is due to his innate recognition of the failure of the whilom hero to reach heights to which he had aspired or was believed to have attained. Disappointment and chagrin lead his former devotees metaphorically or literally to slay him.

The soul of man is continuously urging him on to reach from one height to another. It knows it can never be satisfied until it becomes conscious of its unity with the Godhead.

The desire and will which have been the impelling force of the soul of man on its upward journey will demand from that soul the love, reverence, and obedience due to God and to the great Spiritual Beings who are his representatives; and man will gladly yield them when he has been awakened to a sense of the actual relation existing between God and man.

Every effort man makes to smother that primeval desire of the soul prevents the fulfillment of that desire to a corresponding degree.

All life, spiritual and material, is dual in manifestation. Man as now constituted stands at the neutral point or center between two poles or aspects of life, spirit, and matter.

The Absolute in manifestation as God represents the positive pole or aspect. Primordial matter or energy represents the negative pole or aspect. The interaction between the two aspects results in the creation of a third aspect, the neutral center.

A spark of the Absolute, the Ego, seeks the negative aspect — matter — and proceeds to build a self-conscious vehicle by means of evolutionary law. This vehicle finally reaches the human state where it becomes the seat of the soul — a divine emanation. It has reached the neutral center where the manifest God by His descent into the matter of this center awakens desire in the soul for cosmic or God consciousness. Thereafter, the chief object of the soul is self-conscious union with God.

This is a very crude and condensed illustration of the cosmic processes by which man has reached his present state. I have only tried to express in few words a universal truth, i.e., the relation between God and man — to illustrate what is believed to be the secret of the inner urge towards what is commonly called hero worship, the search of the human soul for God in every stage of its progress. Every hero or little god raised to a pedestal by man is a step of the process by which the final goal is attained.

It is at the central point of life as a whole as well as every division of life that the cosmic forces act to give the most powerful vital impulses toward the heights of life. This is equally true of the centers of religion, philosophy, science, and art or of any other organized force, as it is true that the development of the physical body depends upon the center of the heart.

LESSON 229
RULING YOUR STAR

The ushering in of every new birth cycle of man is at the close of every sixth year, and the opening of the seventh gives opportunity for spiritual and psychic advancement. At such periods the life lines cross each other and there is set up in the mentality an incentive to take some radical step in one direction or another which will determine the trend of future efforts.

Having reached his majority, one will act wisely if at such cyclic periods he will quiet the modifications of his mind sufficiently to take observations along the backward track of his life and seriously consider the negative qualities of his nature; for instance, those qualities which have left a trail of broken promises and acts of selfishness or cruelty. If he has been taught the identification of those negative qualities with those of like character in his ruling planet, he will understand the necessity of gaining control of them in himself before it will be possible to pass from under the ruling power of his present nativity to the cusp of his ambition, when the hour of his next birth cycle strikes, and to remain there until the trine of Perception, Determination, and Action is completed. In other words, until he perceives, acknowledges, and sets about changing the lower red vibrations of the negative aspects of the qualities in question into the vibrations of the positive or spiritual red aspects of those same qualities.

It is not easy for the average man to realize that no God, no Master, can raise him from the influence of one Ray of Light into that of another until he has gained a controlling power over the inhibiting forces of the Ray to which he belongs. Every successful effort he makes not only tends to release himself, but also tends toward releasing his guiding star from the same influences.

Truly it is said man rules the stars, for in his ascendancy over the lower aspects of the qualities which guide his action, he will eventually change his mental environment, and at last this will give him rule over his own particular star when his line of incarnation is complete.

Even a snail cannot raise itself to a higher order of life until it has overcome the inherent tendencies toward supineness and inertia. Then how shall man change his mental or spiritual environment until he has changed the inhibiting forces of his present environment and, therefore, secured the means whereby to raise himself?

LESSON 230
A SUPREME BEING

One of the mistakes many modern students of occultism fall into is that of making distinction between the laws which control all life in manifestation, dividing them into divine and human classes. All laws governing the constitution, conservation, and dissociation of all substance-matter, whatever be the plane of manifestation, are divine laws.

The law which governs the turning of water into steam is as divine as is the law which separates the soul and body of man. The law which governs the action and reaction of the drug called quinine upon the blood of a victim of malaria, is as divine as is the law which governs the healing of other diseased conditions of body and mind by mental or spiritual methods.

There are no human or mechanical laws in the higher acceptation of the terms. By his powers of invention and mechanical skill man is able to take advantage of the divine laws to carry out his purposes. Yet those very powers are powers of the divinity in man, and his success in any field of life depends upon implicit obedience to the divine laws which govern that field. Those laws are divine laws because they were made by a self-created spiritual hierarchy of beings far, far beyond the present power of the humanity of the present age to recognize or understand — a hierarchy of beings who, in combination, represent the Godhead. While they are not visible or audible to man, their works — the action of the laws they have made for the unfolding of life in essence into organized form — make their existence a natural sequence.

As the works of this Divine Hierarchy are indicative of their universal service on all planes and in all states of life, so the works of man are indicative of his individual service for himself and other men of his kind. To every human being has been given some particular field of work, for training in and performance of which he is best fitted by nature and desire. It matters not whether that work is to rule a nation, to build a road, or to take up some profession or trade; it is his divinely appointed task. As a general thing, his restlessness, his discontent, or tendency to crime is the result of his betrayal of his task, his not raising his work to the highest point of service and efficiency possible to him, thereby losing all interest in it. All that impedes his efforts is by way of preparing and inciting him to raise the scale and quality of his work, for perfection is the ultimate aim of the soul of man.

In one sense the same is true of the Divine Builders of form. All of spiritual evil which impedes the work of the latter in carrying out the dictates of divine law incites them to greater effort. Their work is the ultimate perfection of the body and soul of mankind, the making of and obedience to the laws of evolution under which the elementary lives encased in gross matter attain to self-consciousness.

There is a tendency among many students of philosophy and science in the present cycle to eliminate belief in the existence of a

Supreme Being, a Godhead, and to trust entirely to their interpretation of the laws of evolution to account for the phenomena of life and nature; but even those laws alone give ample evidence of such an existence to the open, unprejudiced mind. For example, the law of demand and supply, the law of opposites — divine laws furnish such evidence.

The universal cry which rises from the heart of every human being in its extremities of joy or sorrow for union with or recognition by its God, whatever be the ideal of God he holds in mind, is a proof of the existence of a Supreme Being who can and does answer that cry. The fact that man is sometimes unable to interpret the answer to his plea correctly is no proof to the contrary, for if the plea was not for the benefit of the man or race to which he belonged, the answer might not be given in the form desired or might be long delayed. Man cannot express a desire which is not possible of fulfillment on some plane or in some period of life.

There is one central or creative cell or life spark at the heart of every form of manifested life. In man that original cell has unfolded on five planes of life. The intelligence guiding the action of that cell has created from its constituents all the lesser cells which together evolve an organic material form. It has created the form in the sense that it has drawn to itself and organized all the unorganized primordial substance required by that guiding intelligence for the manifestation of the organized form. The same is true of the manifestation of form at the beginning of life on the physical and ethereal or spiritual planes in every great age.

Using his divinely inspired intuition man should be able to reach a reasonable, logical deduction regarding the necessity for the existence of a supreme intelligence, a creative Center or God, if he accepts the statements of wise men as to the existence of a similar center in all forms of material life. If the creative cell is a necessity from a purely scientific and material point of view, how much more is a spiritual creative cell, a Supreme Being, a necessity to the soul, the immaterial or spiritual part of humanity, and especially to those souls who know and feel acutely the relation between God and themselves — the basic unity of God and the soul and spirit of man. God is in one sense the central or creative cell of the manifested universe — the Central Spiritual Sun.

We can think of the Absolute as of the power or energy which has created unorganized primordial substance; but it is only as individual organized intelligence seizes upon unorganized life force — Prana, and brings it into material form that the intellect of man is satisfied of the reasonableness of the philosophy which teaches the existence of a Supreme Being at the point of differentiation between spirit and matter, the point where homogeneous substance or energy becomes heterogeneous matter.

LESSON 231
THE UNKNOWABLE

Many of the greatest intellects of all ages have been driven into the depths of atheism and despair by the final recognition of the futility of dependence upon such knowledge as has been gathered by men in previous centuries when the subject of the mystery of the Godhead, the Unknowable, was approached by them. The utter impossibility of a satisfactory solution of the mystery by the intellect alone, while at the same time a constant inward urge impels man to incessant effort in the search, is sufficient to unbalance the personal mind. Salvation from such a fate can come only from appreciation of the fact that there are still undeveloped senses within man which, if the law of analogy holds true, will be the means by which those unaccountable desires and impulses will one day be satisfied.

Nothing adds to the rebellion of a man of this character more than does the announcement of the coming or the arrival of a self-advertised "Adept," a "Master," who promises to lead his adherents not only up to the gate of spiritual knowledge, but through and beyond what is generally termed the "unknowable," without any corresponding effort on their own part.

From the period when the first prophetic utterances of a racial seer were revealed to a race of people, up to the present time, the announcement of the near precipitation of some tremendous occult force, or the coming of an Angel or an Avatar for the purpose of raising the vibratory rate of this planet, has been succeeded by a flood of imitations.

The present race as a whole has been informed that if its units are to be individually benefited by means of the advent of an Avatar, they must make conditions of mind and body for the reception and subsequent use of the forces to be spread by that Avatar; and by such information as would be available aid in the development of the principles, qualities or senses by means of which alone it would be possible to perceive the action of such forces, or to recognize the prophesied one.

If occult and profane history have given facts, immediately upon the utterance of such a prophecy by a seer there has arisen a class of pseudo-prophets, self-styled Adepts or Masters, who profess to be able to lead their followers through the great mysteries of life up to complete identification with God with whom all knowledge lies. Unfortunately, as it would seem, they have had access to ancient records or systems of philosophy wherein certain methods of procedure were outlined for the gaining of supernatural powers, and endorsement of the said methods furnishes means to attract the curious and the soul-hungry and to hold them until such time as they learn, to their dismay, that they are no nearer their promised goal than they were at the initial stage of their effort. The preliminary work on which any possible success on occult lines would depend is never required by the said teachers, for such training as is requisite for this purpose demands far more sacrifice, time, and effort than either the teacher or the average student would give to it. Consequently, the student eventually finds himself in a similar position to that of one who attempts to study higher mathematics without any previous knowledge of the first principles of arithmetic.

Man is ever trying to climb up to God some other way than by the way God has ordained and will not accept that way until disappointment and despair have driven him back to his starting point, when, if he is wise, he will subject the vacated spaces in his brain, from which their long-time tenants have been expelled, to the action of simple faith and devotion, when he will begin to understand that he can climb up to God only as he becomes God.

No Savior, no Master or Adept in the heavens above or the earth beneath can *carry* man farther up the path to the gods than his own will allows. All that a Master can do is to point out the steps, endeavor to show the disciple how he can obtain the spiritual nourishment he will require on his journey, and give him a staff of knowledge to enable him to protect himself from the antagonistic forces he will inevitably meet on the way; then he must draw in and await the result. All the rest depends upon the individual man.

As a rule, the climber has an intuitive perception that the above is true, yet at the first announcement of a new religious fad, the first sight of some will-o'-the-wisp of research, he will leave the safe, sure road and run after the deceiver, never realizing that the very temptation to do so is a test of his ability to tread the sure path to the end, and of his worthiness to receive the aforesaid staff. No man who, "having put his hand to the plow,"[1] turns aside to watch his neighbor work; *his* particular field is worthy of the effort the Masters might otherwise make in his behalf.

This does not mean that he should deny himself the privilege of study or of investigation in any field of life experience he desires to enter, but it does mean that, if he has the reasoning powers of the normal man, he must have realized the absolute impossibility of placing his puny intelligence on a par with that of the Godhead, and the futility of trying to establish a claim to the possession of cosmic consciousness. He will recognize his limitations and will refuse to be deceived by any so-called Adept or Master who proposes to teach him how he can attain to a state of infinite wisdom and knowledge while bound by the fetters of matter, for that is practically what it would mean if, in his present state of evolution, he could *know* God in fact.

The claim to such knowledge and the ability to impart that knowledge to others has been the bait held out in every age by the Brothers of the Shadow to poor, ignorant, soul-hungry humanity. The reasoning power of man, if fully awakened and put to use, ought to show him how utterly futile his efforts to reach his goal under such guidance would prove to be in the end; but his egotism or mental blindness makes him a victim to the wiles of the deceiver.

Every great religion has its legend of Lucifer — Satan — the fallen Angel, who was banished from heaven for attempting to prove his equality with God. Personal knowledge of God predicates equality with God, for only one on an equality with another can truly *know* that other, whether that one be God or man.

The pseudo-occultists who claim to be able to solve all the mysteries of the universe are too wary to make their claim in simple language easy of interpretation by the ignorant, for that would bring too quick a revulsion to the mind of even a savage. They present their claims in the disguise of some oriental or other mystical formulae, or glibly use the term "cosmic consciousness" or some such ambiguous or all-inclusive

---

[1] Luke 9:62.

term to express that which they offer; while if they have any concept of such a state as that which they term "cosmic consciousness," they must surely know that man could not exist on the physical plane for a single hour if he had truly reached that state, for again, to have attained to cosmic consciousness would be literally to have become consciously one with God and on an equality with God.

Not content to grow normally and naturally into a realization or perception of absolute perfection along the God-appointed line — the love line, the line of compassion, the line of sacrifice — the man who has never known what the term love really implies rejects that line and calls it mere sentiment or something else, which he claims must be killed ere a true concept of God is possible; and right there lies the big stumbling block in the path of development in all such instances. You may note that this repudiation of the higher love — compassion — is the key which is generally struck by a pseudo-occultist. He either teaches that such love must be destroyed *in toto*, or he raises passion to the throne of love and sets his followers to worshiping the beast in man. There is but little to choose between the two, for the end of both is alike.

When called upon to make a decision, a disciple finds himself in a quandary in regard to any investigation he is making into the claims of some well-advertised teacher, or finds himself facing a mystery of such nature as I have indicated, if he would take his stand on the fundamental plank before mentioned and try out every proposition made to him by that one omnipotent, irrevocable principle, he could not be led far astray, for sooner or later every vehicle of the satanic force will reveal its position by either one or both of the false premises previously outlined.

The man who says he loves God while his every act shows indisputable hate of his brethren must be a curiosity to the angels. The man who professes to possess the higher creative power, the Kriyashakti, when he does not function the higher love — universal love — in his life, places himself in the category of falsifiers. The man who could be induced to perform a dishonest act cannot shelter himself under the garment of truth. The man who is not truly humble, universally kind, just, and wise could not hold up his head in the presence of the Masters long enough to present his claims to discipleship. The man who is not willing and able to sacrifice his life, his all, for the good of the race to which he belongs will never be able to greatly advance that race.

It has taken millions of years to evolve the vehicle through which the consciousness of the ego can function sufficiently to allow it to become a self-conscious entity, that is, conscious of itself as an evolutionary factor capable of attaining to liberation. Then what satisfactory reason can there be for believing a few months or years are sufficient for the completion of that purpose, i.e., the unifying of self-consciousness with the consciousness of the Cosmos?

LESSON 232
THE RELATIONSHIP BETWEEN TEACHER AND CHELA

A mistaken idea has taken possession of the minds of some of the students of occultism which should be eradicated before regret and disappointment intervene between their most earnest desires and the objects of those desires. I refer to the identification of a member of the Inner Orders of the Temple, or any other similar body, with other bodies of like nature under different teachers. It must be understood that this mistake would not occur as a result of mere identification with other bodies from the standpoint of the physical plane alone. Such action may be even desirable from that single standpoint, but the law of occultism which prohibits identification with other bodies by pledged chelas of an inner degree of the Temple, is based upon the well-known electrical action of crossed currents. The magnetic currents between one teacher and another may be in sheer opposition, while the two personalities may be mentally and physically companionable and in accord on exterior lines. The crosscurrents set up in the magnetic fields may react each upon the other, or even nullify the action of the energy seeking expression and dam up the magnetic flow from one or both, and even act adversely on all who are in close and intimate association with either one or both of the teachers of the separate bodies and so inhibit the action of still higher forces.

The magnetic rapport necessary between Master and chela may thus be greatly interfered with, if not cut off entirely, without the volition of either, and even despite their utmost efforts toward harmonious relations. The Master is not only acting as the Father of a family, he *is* that Father to the chela if both are parts of the one Group Soul, and no more than the child can supplant his own physical father by delegating the functions of a father to some other man, can the disciple, even temporarily and unconsciously, supplant the Master by delegating the functions of that Master-Father to another, by accepting the admonition, directions, or advice of that other. Not even good intent would prevent the action of the law which prohibits unnatural relation, and such identification would be unnatural from the standpoint of the Group Soul. This may seem a far-fetched idea to those who cannot perceive the action of interior forces, but it is nevertheless so true that with the best intentions many chelas have entirely lost place and power, and been self-relegated to the ranks of the outer degrees of the Lodge temporarily, by trying to serve two Masters of opposing degrees before they had reached the point of intelligent choice.

Fire and Flame are both valuable, but Flame may eat up a substance in which higher form of Fire is concealed.

A chela should be able to know intuitively, if not by outer means, when he has reached the point of demarcation — the point of division — between one Group Soul and another, if his previous instruction has come from a reliable source. The preliminary instructions issued by all true Agents of the Lodge will be almost identical in scope and purport, although the phraseology and language may be dissimilar, until the degree of fulfillment of the Great White Lodge is entered. From that period until the disciple has passed beyond the necessity for oral or written instruction, there is a change in the method of instruction, the disciple passes more immediately under the personal direction of the Master — the Father — of that division of the Group Soul to which he karmically belongs. The magnetic currents of the latter may be higher or lower vibrations according to the position such a Group Soul occupies in the scale of life, but in any case they are *different* and that difference is the essential thing to the disciple who is on the eve of the change from negative to positive identification with the Master.

LESSON 233
MUNDANE ELECTRICITY

Mundane electricity is a combination in equilibrium of the ions of radiant energy and the electrons of magnetic energy. When the ions of radiant energy and the electrons of magnetic energy are in synchronous vibration there is no exterior manifestation, no fire, flame, or heat. But if the electrons of magnetic energy are in excess of the ions of radiant energy, a current of electricity may be generated and maintained as long as the armatures are kept in motion, and fire, flame, and heat may thus be maintained. It is the increased motion of the armatures which breaks up the accumulation of radiant energy and sets free the form of electric energy so created. If the motion is stopped the electric current is also stopped.

It must be understood that reference is here made to what may be termed mundane electricity alone. We have to reach beyond and above such manifestations of electricity as have been produced by exterior means to obtain a concept of electrical action on interior planes, for the energy which manifests on the plane of gross matter is but one aspect or division of a much finer form of energy.

The electricity of the living substance of the physical body is a manifestation of life force, Prana. If the vibrations of the electrons of the blood or an organ or other part of the body have been changed from their normal rate, thus producing abnormal or diseased conditions in that organ or part, it stands to reason that the original rates of vibration must be restored to reproduce the same normal state. As all forms of matter are living forms and subject to the same laws, man must at some time be able to change the vibrations of any abnormal condition in any form of matter by use of the finer forces of nature, when he is capable of bringing them under control by will and mind, or by some mechanical instrument which corresponds to the human body, through which the mental or spiritual energy of will and mind is set in action.

LESSON 234
VIBRATION – A SYNOPSIS OF CREATION

The Cosmic centers or principles of Atma, Buddhi, and Manas, the first three manifestations of the essence of Deity, are materialized by the power of Fohat, Cosmic Electricity. The different rates of vibration are directed by the Hierarchy of Dhyani-Buddhas[1] and Dhyan-Chohans — great Spiritual Beings, creators of Form.

The vibrations of this Deific Essence result in the formation of the first state of Substance in manifestation, the state termed Akasha. By the action of Fohat, certain degrees and situations are set

---

[1] *Dhyani-Buddhas* — those who have Merciful Hearts; another term for the Masters of Wisdom who guide the evolution of humanity.

up in the substance of Akasha. The decreasing degrees of vibration in akashic substance result in the formation of the substance of the etheric planes, as a still lower decrease of vibration of the etheric states of substance results in the formation of the astral and physical states of substance — matter.

The phenomenon of Cosmic Light is the effect of the radiation and vibration of the minute particles of Electricity termed Auric Force or Electrons, and the vibrations of Cosmic Light are in one sense the creators of all lower forms of Substance and matter. The Deific essence is made manifest first by Sound — the Word, Cosmic Electricity, and secondly by Light, and Light and Mind are fundamentally one Substance. The Deific Essence is primarily spirit in manifestation as Cosmic Light. The Auric Force is formed by the radiations of the light of the Central Spiritual Sun, the light of Buddhi, the higher mind.

Only as man understands the importance of vibration in solving the mysteries of creation, can he ever gain a synthetic idea of spiritual life in manifestation as physical matter.

The creation of matter is a stepping down by vibration from spirit to matter, a lessening in degrees of vibration of one homogeneous state or condition of spirit, to matter of the lowest vibratory rates, the matter of the physical and lower astral planes of life. Death is the result of a change in vibration of all the substance of the physical body, and this change in vibration sets in action the forces of dissolution in the whole body, and the principle of higher mind has no longer a suitable vehicle for manifestation on the physical plane. The cause of the change in vibration may be either disease or injury. Anything that produces a change of vibration will have its corresponding effect according to the mathematical enumeration of the different rates or degrees of vibration.

LESSON 235
RECOGNITION OF LIMITATIONS

He who fills his days with unwholesome repining, his sleepless nights with longing for that which comes not, neither can come — to him I say, hear me and remember, for I speak truth. No greater, though possibly an unacknowledged hero, is there in life's lists than is he who has recognized the limitations of his mind and body, and with firm decision has uncomplainingly set about making

the best of such qualities and circumstances as are his by birthright.
He has seen that the broad stream between his desires and his possibilities is full of sunken rocks. Recognizing that this little bark of life
would be sure to founder on some one of those rocks, he stays on the
nearer shore. Knowing that there is as much of God's great plan to be
worked out on one side of the life stream as on the other, and that the
seeming difference between the two banks of the stream lies only in
the imagination of man, he takes up whatever line of work his hands
find to do and does that work with his whole heart.

Such a man is nobler far than is the man who rides rough-shod
over all obstacles which bar his way to the possession of power; the
man who crushes hearts and bodies alike and leaves widespread desolation in his wake on his way to the accomplishment of some ambitious purpose, only to find at length that though he may be a hero
to a few scattered hundreds of his own ilk, he is the veriest failure in
his own eyes.

For however vast the enterprise or great the prize he has striven
for and won, it is worthless when he must look back on a life spent in
gratification of ambition. The husks which alone are left after a sur-
feit of the food provided at such cost are all that remains to console
him, and they are very harsh and bitter to the taste when he faces a
yawning grave.

LESSON 236
INNER ROBES OF LIGHT

Consider the Inner World of Light of which the material world
is but a reflected, unstable, and shadowy replica. In this outer
world is vividly sensed the panoramic shifting of these shadows, confusing the reflected consciousness of the Higher Ego, and distorting
the outer lines and qualities that correspond to the real inner lines,
until the reflected higher consciousness is hopelessly entangled in the
web of separateness and the illusory aspects of matter. And there is
no way back save by stilling the outer vibrations and indrawing the
consciousness to the Fifth plane — the first plane of Universality and
Impersonality where the lines of differentiation begin to merge, and
to become One.

In this inner realm, Light is the Vesture of God — the Eternalized
Reality that forever ensouls all outer Light — the Seamless Garment

of the Over-Soul, the Universal Auric Envelope, the Hiranyagarbha[1] or Golden Egg of the Universe, the actual and potential seed from which all things proceed and in which all things and creatures have their roots of Being. Light should be considered as an Entity and you have been told that every Ray of Light that you see is the outer body of a highly evolved spiritual entity. Light is also the substance-matter of the higher planes and that Light is also a Robe or state of consciousness — to those who can attain or bear it, which is not possible, however, to mortal man unable to rise to the plane of the Fifth referred to. To any such that Ineffable Light would be sensed (if sensed at all) as darkness — oblivion — unconsciousness, more than the darkness the prematurely opened eyes of a kitten would sense if suddenly subjected to the glare of the mid-day sun. This is the analogous state of that blankness known to the occultist and sometimes called the "blank wall of inner experiences." The disciple, however, in contacting the higher planes, inevitably at first in inner initiations, loses consciousness as in a swoon, because the consciousness *enters in* and awakens on a higher plane, the same as in the death of the body. As spiritual progress is made, the lower consciousness becomes identified with the higher vestures and, after repeated experiences becomes one with them. The process means the conscious correlation between the outer and inner selves of the Creator with the created.

At the beginning of the Temple work the two on the physical plane who had made the requisite correlations and whose inner and karmic lines were nearest to me, were called together and from their auric robes a double star was brought into manifestation — that is, a figure composed of five fundamental inner principles, positive and negative, respectively. The correlations referred to made by these two permitted the substance Light of the Fifth plane to be used in blending the two five-pointed stars into a six-pointed one which alone would be capable of transmitting the higher spiritual and cosmical forces. The structural spiritual qualities of number and form are based on immutable occult Laws. Just as the Three falls into the Four, so does the Five when interiorly polarized, rearrange its structural qualities and falls into the Six — the first cosmical state in the pilgrimage back to the Divine Source.

---

[1] *Hiranyagarbha* (*Sanskrit*, "golden egg") — the luminous "fire mist" from which the Universe was created.

In the existence of this combined Red and Blue[1] Hierarchical double star on an inner plane — its real center of power — members using intuition should find the answer to all questions concerning the future of the work so far as connection with Lodge forces is concerned. The mere passing of outer vehicles from the material plane does not invalidate the status or inhibit the functions of the double star in the least degree. This definite configuration makes failure or confusion more difficult than had been the case in earlier efforts and the present Lodge effort through the Temple gives more promise of good for humanity than other efforts made for many ages past, that is of continuing, persisting good, uninterrupted by break. This is mainly due to the fundamental facts set forth above, to the organized nature of the work, and the strong karmic lines that have been woven together, and that it was possible in this effort to connect up with many lines of inner and outer forces laid by various Agents of the Lodge in the efforts of centuries past to uplift humanity.

LESSON 237
THE FIFTH BREATH

In every differentiated form of matter, whatever be its purpose or use, there is one of the seven principles, qualities, and energies that is the dominating factor in the creation of the form.

The purpose and the use for which every form is designed would determine which one of the Seven principles, qualities, and energies would be in leash in the creation of any form by the divine builders of the form. As these seven great creative powers are the basis of all matter, it is evident that the material forms invented by man come under the same law, the law of centralized power; for instance, the particular form of energy dominant in the unifying by man of the molecules of the state of matter of which a material form in metal was composed would be the energy of Cohesion. The same would be true on the plane of Manas where the unifying power was exercised over substance-matter of higher vibration, as, in the case of two or more individual minds, the energy dominant in the combining or unifying of those minds would be the energy of Cohesion.

Heat, Attraction, and Repulsion are the first trinity of Spirit in manifestation.

---

[1] Francia La Due and William H. Dower, the founders of The Temple of the People, were called *Blue Star* and *Red Star*, respectively.

They are the just three Sons of Fohat (Motion). Fohat is the driving power of the Universe.

The Fifth Breath is the fifth of the five breaths (Vibrations) which brought life force into manifestation.

The Fifth Breath has its correspondences in the fifth Cosmic age, the fifth cycle of each age, the principle of life, the fifth stage of man's evolution, the fifth sense of man, and the fifth of any being or object. We are now in the Fifth Race of a great age.

The fifth principle is Manas (mentality) and a warning to beware of the action of the Fifth Breath would mean a warning to beware of the undue action of the higher mind, for the forces of that phase of life are of the nature of fire — and the human body cannot bear the action of these forces without danger to the brain.

The drawing on those forces by Christians in their revivals has driven many insane, the emotional reaction over stimulating the brain centers.

The Fifth Breath is in reality the Inner Breath and has its occult center of action in every cell and organ of the physical body as well as in all correspondences of the same in the inner sheaths or principles. This inner center of action is where the Akasha *concentrates*. The four lower breaths are outer, the Fifth is the first breath that touches the Universal Rhythm of the Higher Self or the God within. It is the first *In*breath in other words, and its element is the correspondence of oxygen on all planes. On the lowest astral this is pure ozone which, however gross compared to the higher aspects, is so fiery that physical lungs would be soon burned up were they to inbreathe this element undiluted. This may serve to give an idea of the Breath of the Gods, so to speak, on the various planes of being. Because of a knowledge and control of the Fifth Breath, the yogi, though using only the lower astral phases, can put himself into a so-called cataleptic sleep and allow himself to be buried for months without any apparent outer breathing, and finally be resuscitated and none the worse for the experience. The fire of the inner breath permeates the physical in sufficient volume to ward off outer dissolution.

All animal organisms have the four lower breaths. Minerals do not have these outer breaths, but do have the fifth inner and the changes that occur in all mineral structures are really the result of the functioning of the Fifth Breath within their essence, for the Fifth Breath is involved with Akasha, from which all things come or are outbreathed;

so the cosmical inbreaths of Akasha finally draw all things back to it or reduce all things to their primal Akashic nature. The form, color, and other qualities of minerals, jewels, and all objects in nature are really determined by Akashic impulses. Where there seems nothing, there are often the most precious things or forces. Certain spaces in the physical body, as the central canal of the spinal cord and the ventricles (spaces) of the brain, are centers of action for the lower inner astral breath. Impulses centering in these areas tend to draw the physical inward or upward and to increase the vibrational rates of the outer body approximating ultimately the rate of the astral as evolution proceeds. A knowledge and control of the Fifth Breath, the first inner breath, is of vast importance to every soul on the Path that leads to Eternal Light and is the spiritual birthright of every individualized soul.

It is only the scientifically trained mind that considers the subject of the energy of Cohesion at its actual importance in the economy of the Universe, yet an understanding of its functions in the creation of form on all planes of existence is a necessity to the student of occultism.

If the principle or energy of Cohesion were missing from the sevenfold universal creative agencies or energies, there could be no organized forms of any character whatever. It is the combining and unifying force between every two or more electrons, atoms, molecules and cells of all primordial substance.

From the philosophical viewpoint, Cohesion is one of the seven Sons of Fohat — Divine Will — which manifest as Electricity, Magnetism, Light, Sound, Heat, Attraction, and Cohesion.

Figure 9
Fohat

The above figure represents a manifestation of Fohatic energy expressing in this flash of lightning the Tejas Tattva[1] in action.

"The lacy loveliness of lightning is strikingly revealed in this photograph of the new 2,000,000-volt spark which was produced during the course of experiments at the Pittsfield, Massachusetts, plant of the General Electric Co. The triangular flare is the result of a discharge of the highest man-made energy ever known,[2] and represents about $1/25^{th}$ the power of a real lightning flash. The spark points at the three corners are nine feet from one another. The separate threads of light so plainly visible in this remarkable picture were caused by the succeeding waves of electrons, generated by the three-phase alternating current. The human eye is not quick enough, nor is it sufficiently tuned, to perceive this web-effect in practical demonstration, so it remained for a special camera, equipped with a lens of quartz through which the rays penetrated to the plate, to show up these supplementary lines. Each discharge of this artificial lightning is accompanied by a crash deafening to the ear, and there is an intense glare during the fraction of a second that the spark takes to jump from point to point. Even artificial rain has been produced."

LESSON 238
THE GREAT SILENCE

To those who have known the power of Silence — those who have sensed the operation of the tremendous life forces as they thrill through space, and have sunk into that perfect stillness where the soul enters the thought currents of the Infinite, and loses all sense of time and space as it drifts out into unfathomable depths or rises to unspeakable heights — to such as these may great secrets of life become clear.

The statements relating to the re-creating, purifying processes of nature and of the soul made by those who know, are no longer mere words, for all such labor is accomplished in Silence and in darkness.

The vision of a single soul confined in some limited area of space to work out its salvation in silence and darkness is no longer a fearsome tragedy to the mind of the occultist — or a merciless act of an over-just Creator. It is the merciful, loving act of a Father who knows

[1] *Tejas Tattva* (*Sanskrit*, "fire principle") — the elemental power of Fire.
[2] As of 1925.

that within that soul is the seed of its purification — a Spark from the Living Fire of God, that can only accomplish its divine mission if it be shut up in the fastnesses of the soul, and allowed to do its work in such Silence and darkness as God must always work in to bring His own to birth.

When we realize that the filthiest matter of which we are cognizant, the fecal matter of animal and human excretion, can be brought to a state of as perfect purity as the purest water of the mountain stream, by means of the life force working in and through it, if it be closely confined, shut off from light, air, and sound; and can also understand that that life force is pure Prana — the very substance of God — it is not difficult to understand how even the vilest creature has within him the germ of a Higher Self, which only requires the right conditions — the silence and darkness of the tomb of the soul, to bring to birth an ever living entity, pure and undefiled.

If there be a purgatory for sinning souls, what is it but a reflection of that greater, holier Silence and Darkness of spiritual creation — a state wherein those souls may be confined until the God spark within them may have time and opportunity, through spiritual suffering, to churn, crush, mingle, and intermingle the essence of their lower natures until they are freed from all impurities, and those souls, reclothed, are made meet to once more come forth and take their place among the Sons of God?

Verily, you should love the Silence and the Darkness — even as the Light — and strive with all your hearts to fathom their mysteries; always entering their portals with humble, patient hearts, and remaining there until there is brought to birth the germ of Wisdom now lying dormant within you.

Only then can you bear the Light of Spirit without being irretrievably blinded by Its rays.

LESSON 239
THE MASTER'S TOUCH

My Dear Children:
I am writing you this letter that its words may sink deeper in your hearts than they could by the mere tones of the voice of Blue Star through which I must yet speak to you, and desire you to read

and re-read them and realize that the essence of my own individuality flows through them.

As the neophyte — disciple — man — advances along the path of evolution, he takes step after step of the degrees of the Great White Lodge, unconsciously. As you examine your past lives you will find that the real epochs of those lives have not been divided by days and years, but by events. Great sorrows, severe pain, and thrilling joys are the milestones marking off that journey of life and these have been the means of broadening and lengthening the mental and spiritual horizon of your *real* inner existence, and each of these must be duplicated over and over again on the three great planes of being — Mental, Spiritual, and physical. Grief and pain will walk by your side over many vast stretches of the path until they are conquered by self-conscious endeavor. You have arrived at the step where you may begin to do this. When either or both seize upon you, try to realize that they are part of the great world's pain and grief, as you are a part of it; and to whatever extent you succeed in rising above, in conquering it, to just that extent have you changed the inharmonious conditions of the world and made it a better dwelling place for the children of God, and what is true of these is true of all limitations of matter, force, and consciousness.

As victory over limitations crowns your efforts, you will become more conscious of your oneness with the Lodge and the Universe, and this consciousness carries with it a force that refines the atoms of the physical body. The organs of sense will begin to lose their grossness, and light and sound from the inner sphere will break on your sight and hearing.

I give you this little touch of love that you may pass it on to others in need. You are in a great company, met to commune with each other on matters of vital importance. As day follows day you will become more convinced of this. There are great trials of faith and endurance before you and persecution and trial to Blue Star I bid you stand by her as by me. Do not judge what she may seem to do or leave undone. You can see but surface act. Draw closer and yet closer together, work as one being for the good of all.

Trust and love the Great Master who walked the earth in poverty and humility, though higher than the angels. Sink your very souls in the great Father-heart, the beats of which vibrate through your own with every pulse of the same, and remember that I am one with you — not outside of you.

In tender love I greet you, my children,
Your Father and Brother

LESSON 240
THE SIXTH BREATH

The Sixth Breath is a Formative Principle — the Essence, so to speak, of Abstract Form. This Sixth Breath is the Breath which God breathed into the man of clay; and which made man a living spirit. To have breathed into man only the fourth or vital breath would not have ensouled matter with any spark of the Godhead. The Sixth Breath is the Spiritual Breath animating all things in manifestation, and its polar opposite in matter is the Fourth or Rupic[1] Breath, belonging only to the Creature, that is, the thing created, whereas the Sixth is of the Creator. Rhythmic impulses from the Sixth Breath which is in synchronized vibration with the Great Breath, arouse corresponding breath-desire activities in the lower Rupic pole and so Form is kept in manifestation on the lower planes. Were the Sixth Master Breath to cease, all Form, animate and inanimate, would disappear from the face of the Cosmos.

Imagination, the kingly faculty of soul, has its seat of power in the Sixth Breath which is also the basis of Kriyashakti, creation by will and imagination. In a sense, Breath and Desire are one and the same. Attuned to Universal Rhythm of the Great Breath, Desire is omnipotent, but the lower desires cannot vibrate with the Sixth Breath because of the limitations of matter, as the Rupic consciousness on the fourth plane is merely a reflection of the higher Arupic[2] Sixth Principle on the realms of the Formless, yet having in itself the potency of all form.

Breath creates images and imagination arouses Breath. With the Sixth Breath on the universal planes of being, this process is vast and indescribable in human terms, but some idea may be gained by studying the effects of lower breath desires on the human emotional plane. All kinds of emotions which belong to the fourth or rupic state

---

[1] *Rupa* (*Sanskrit*, "form") — a form or shape in any degree of visible or invisible manifestation. For example, thoughts do have a certain form, although invisible, while ideas are formless.

[2] *Arupa* (*Sanskrit*, "formless") — formless or bodiless, as opposed to *Rupa*.

of being affect the breath as in joy and sorrow, anger, fear, fright, deep concentration, and so on. When lower emotional phases manifest there is no control of the breath centers. The Breath becomes deep, rhythmical, catchy, or shallow according to the phase of emotion manifesting, as all such belong to the plane of the Fourth Breath. Control the Fourth Breath by the Sixth, however, and all disordering conditions disappear.

In all disturbing mental or emotional conditions, therefore indraw the consciousness by deliberate, quiet breathing and seek to correlate with the Sixth Breath on its own plane of force and consciousness. If this is done, there will immediately result a balanced state and a feeling of inner calm and peace, with control of outer conditions. Motions and Emotions cease more and more as we go in consciousness toward the Center of Being, for the Kingdom of the Divine Rhythmic Breath — Heaven — is *within*. Differentiation from the Center outward begets wider and wider motion which is cause for more motion and so on to infinity as is noted in the case of the mighty swing of suns and planets through the spatial depths. And yet within the real inner center of those swinging orbs and all creatures thereon there is a common place or state of Identity. In other words, if you find the real center of anything, soul, creature, star, or planet, you have found the Center of All. All roads lead to God through Centers within Centers.

In the deepest states of mental concentration the outer breath becomes quiet and still and if of sufficient power may almost cease altogether as in the case of yoga, because the outer impulse or desire has passed through the Fourth to the Fifth and is near perhaps to the Sixth Breath. And as the outer breath correlates with the inner, every organ, cell, and tissue of the body begins to breathe in unison, for every organ and cell has the correspondence in itself of every other organ, every cell having the analogue of lungs and potential rhythm of all the Seven Breaths.

LESSON 241
THE SEVENTH BREATH

July 1923

The Fifth, Sixth, and Seventh Breaths are Universal and Illimitable. The four lower Breaths are involved with the limitations of the matter of the corresponding lower planes of existence, and are of the nature of aspects of the three higher, that is to say, the three Breaths on the Higher plane become four Breaths on the lower plane due to the immutable law of the materialization and crystallization of spiritual forces in and with matter. The Three becomes Four due to this law of solids as the Triangle with its Three lines on a plane surface takes on Four sides when it becomes a solidified or material body. The first solid body possible is the Tetrad, each line, surface, and angle of which is pregnant with Deific truths.

The four lower Breaths may be briefly defined before considering the mystery of the Seventh.

The First Breath. This is purely elemental and automatic and is the lowest of the four lower or outer breaths. This first breath is rhythmic molecular respiration, that is, respiration of the molecules. This is really the lower astral breath which by repercussion on the physical envelope or body causes the function of outer breathing through the lungs. Death results when the molecular respiration ceases as the outer mass breathing must then also cease.

The Second Breath. This is the Vital Breath or Rhythm pulsing — breathing — in and out of the cells and tissues of the Microcosm. It is the analogue in the Microcosm of the Great Breath in the Macrocosm. It is an aspect of Atma in which the synthetic becomes differentiated and yet retains its synthesis.

Atma is everywhere and yet its lower Breath or rhythm may be modified, tinctured, or colored by the will and desires of the creature. Thus the creature — man — becomes a builder with the Divine and can help or retard nature in her evolutionary purpose as he keeps pure or pollutes the Second Breath with his images — creations.

The Third Breath. The Third outer Breath is the lower positive pole of the Sixth which is negative on its higher plane to the Atmic or Great Breath. The Third is Rupic and its respiratory impulses materialize the essence of Form by drawing from the Sixth Breath and so keeps the Rupic or Form principle in manifestation. This applies to all of the planes. Were this Breath lacking, it would be impossible to clothe our thoughts or ideas in any kind of form whatsoever and the process of thinking would be impossible with the brain mind. Abstract thinking is only possible on the highest plane — the so-called planes of the Formless. Thought on the lower planes is the flashing of a succession of images (forms) on the sensitive akashic screen of the inner sensorium of the brain.

The Fourth Breath. This Breath is negative to the Third and Fifth Breaths. It has important functions and is a respiratory rate of balance between the higher and lower planes. The Fourth Breath inbreathes in all things and creatures the Light of intelligence — the Knowing Principle, through being receptive and negative to the impulses of the Fifth.

The Divinest mysteries center in the Seventh Breath which is the Auric Breath. The Seventh Breath is Self-Creative — it has no organ of action but every cell and atom breathes rhythmically with the Auric All. When the Seventh Breath is active every cell, molecule and atom of the nature breathes in perfect unison with the Universal All — the Great Atmic Breath. Breath is the life, spiritual and material. The Breaths of all the planes should be coordinated and when this is accomplished man becomes more than man, he is a Master of Life — a Master of Breath and is omnipotent.

One-half of man is dead, a corpse, or let us say one-half is still unborn. It has no breath. Every center, organ, cell, and tissue should breathe — have its rhythmical vibration or expression. Inner potencies are thus released as in the seed expressing its germinal potencies by growth. Every living thing has breath and as everything is alive all things breathe, including the minerals. Sometimes it is one breath, sometimes another of the seven breaths, according to the plane and grade of matter involved. Modern science illustrates this in the case of seeds which breathe, taking in oxygen and giving out carbon dioxide. Placed in airtight containers most seeds will die in a short time. When about to germinate — wake up — seeds breathe more rapidly and require more air. Minerals function the inner breath attuned to Universal Nature. The sun breath has an eleven-year period. The unborn child functions the inner breath, the mother representing universal nature. The seventh or Auric Breath is synchronized breathing on all the planes of self simultaneously, and this synthetic breath makes the full correlation of man with the Higher Self. This Auric Breath marks in reality the identification of the individual with the universal, and the Auric Breath is the true utterance of the Sacred Word — the Ineffable Name — as every plane of the self and every cell and atom on every plane of the Self is in harmonized aspiration with Divine Consciousness.

LESSON 242
THE DUAL POWER

FROM THE MASTER M.

If the ruling hierarchy of a world or a nation does not prepare for the inevitable counter-attack at the same time it prepares for an assault on any defended position in life, it will most surely meet with final defeat. The same law which makes necessary such provision holds good in every department of life, cosmical or individual. If man neglects to prepare for the negative action of a positive act in the line of religious, business, personal, or family life, it matters not how successful may be the first effects of his positive act, he will be caught in the toils of the negative action of the force he has set in motion as surely as the sun rises and sets each day.

It takes humanity a long time to learn to apply the knowledge it has gained of mechanical laws to those problems which most closely concern his mental and spiritual progress. If the progress of higher orders of life must depend upon their knowledge of the action of the said laws, what chance has the average man of the world to win and keep what he has won as aids in progression if he refuses or neglects to act in accordance with the demands of those laws, and consequently makes no commensurate effort to protect and hold that to which he aspires to the effort he has put forth to win the same?

The great failures in all fields of life lie at the doors of indolence or of ignorance of the one vital necessity for success, i.e., preparation for the inevitable rebound of the force or object set in motion. Indolence or excessive self-confidence will leave man open to disaster, when normal sane methods of procedure in meeting the reaction of a precipitated force with a like ratio of strength and endurance to that set free in precipitation would bring success.

You will find the same laws govern every phase of life, if you search deeply enough. Life in action is never singular; it is always dual. Consequently, no greater service can be given to those units of humanity who have had no opportunity for absorbing knowledge of the action of this law than by giving constant, unremitting effort to supply this deficiency.

LESSON 243
THE STILL SMALL VOICE

The still small voice, wherein alone may man hear the speech of God, can only be heard at the neutral center of sound. The positive pole of sound is loud and large; the negative pole is silence. As the positive decreases in volume as it nears the center, so the negative increases. When they meet at a given point one strives to overcome the other, and as a result of the struggle there is manifested something infinitely higher in the realm of sound.

The stillness and smallness indicate equilibrium, peace. On the battleground of life is born the Androgyne. So it is in all aspects of life, spiritual and material. Love is the greatest thing in life because it comprises, compounds, and correlates all lesser things. In the battle between love (passion) and hate in the mind of man something higher than either the love or hate of the physical plane is born, namely, Compassion and Understanding. In the struggle between sunlight and darkness are born the dawn and the twilight hours of Peace and Beauty. In the stress of battle between good and evil is born the power of Renunciation, the most difficult power to attain. In the battle between pleasure and pain is born Endurance.

So through all the aspects, attributes, qualities, and energies in or out of manifested life on the planes of matter and force, it is in the neutral center, the place of peace, the point of equilibrium — the Dawn, the point of Renunciation, that we shall find God; never at either end where noise, confusion, dissatisfaction or silent non-being, disintegration, and disruption occur. So while man may be a microcosm of God, he is an epitome of the ends of all the above-mentioned aspects, attributes, qualities, and forces — a battleground wherein is being fought out to a finish the battle of the ages. When he has established the neutral center of all these aspects, attributes, qualities, and forces in himself, he enters the Macrocosm — where God dwells.

LESSON 244
THE CAUSE OF FAILURE

December 1909

How many of your number have ever fathomed the underlying cause of some individual, family, or national effort to thwart the execution of any commonly accepted social or religious custom or law?

How many realize the futility of pitting your individual, feeble will and desire against cosmic or national Will and Desire?

You may be able to convince yourself that you are entirely in the right, and that the great majority are in the wrong, if so be you are involved in a controversy where such a question is called up; but you know you are merely trying to deceive yourself and others if you attempt to justify some personal, social, or religious offense, by loudly claiming the right of the individual soul to "lead its own life in its own way," regardless of the effects of its actions upon others.

You know that the soul impulse of the great majority — that interior force sometimes designated "the public conscience" — working for the greatest good of the human race, has been evolved by means of the blood and the sweat of uncounted millions of human beings — your own forebears — men and women who have gone down into the depths of hell, and who finally crawled out of those depths, shorn of everything that had formerly been held precious in their sight, and who, because of what they had suffered, had been made ready to stand at the foot of the cross of sacrifice, with arms extended in pleading to their descendants — to you and to me — that we spare ourselves and those that will follow us the needless stain, the perfectly avoidable agony, that surely results from contemned and broken law.

When one realizes that he must pass in review before all these "souls crucified," as a rebel against established law and order, on his way to the commission of some act, which if indulged could only momentarily satisfy the changeable part of his lower nature — some impulsive act induced by the opinion he is holding at the moment — it is evident the underlying cause for the commission of that act is something deeper than the revolt against seeming injustice and wrong; and that cause lies at the base of his human nature.

There is much said in these days regarding "the rights of man," and the "free soul." My children, there is no such thing or creature in the Universe as a free soul, and there never has been, or ever will be such a soul. Back of all desire or demand for freedom, in the case of every normal human being, there is a still deeper desire, or more correctly speaking, a deeper aspiration — a louder cry for a personal recognition of and a closer unity with God — the Over-Soul; a desire to combine individual strength with the energy generated by others for a definite purpose, and we never can reach such unity as we desire while we willingly tread underfoot the rights of the companion souls who are struggling along the path, it may be with us, crying to us to sustain them in their hour of peril.

We never can reach conscious unity with all souls until our feet are firmly fixed on the sacrificial stone at the foot of the Altar of Crucifixion; and I say emphatically, from the depths of whatever knowledge and experience I have gained with the human race, that not a single well-developed, mature soul can truthfully deny its knowledge of its responsibility for others, when it bravely faces itself in the silence of its own divinity, however much it may desire to do so.

It knows that as long as another fragment of itself is liable to be worsted in the great fight, by anything it individually has done, or left undone, or may do, that sacrificial stone will stand silently pleading for a victim, and until that victim itself is ready, its way to the throne of power is blocked.

Understand me, I speak not of such instances as those which occur when awakened conscience arouses the desire of a nation or a body of people for justice, and, from the demand wrought out from a divine impulse, there arises an overwhelming determination to right a national or social wrong, to free a slave, to overcome the soul-killing, life-sapping lethargy which sometimes seizes upon a whole people.

I speak of the selfish or corrupting desire of one or more people to overrule some long-established, wise, beneficent purpose or law of a nation or race, and when unlicensed, unlimited freedom for one, means abject slavery or unnecessary woe for others who are to come after them.

If you will seek out the basic reality, the fundamental law upon which even the most corrupt nation or race was founded, you would find that law true to nature, and to nature's God.

Had it not been so, the nation or race could not have existed for a single century; and only in accordance with a certain measure of obedience to that law, even though such obedience were rendered by a limited number, could that nation or race have any true and normal sustained growth. You find this exemplified in the legend of the destruction of Gomorrah.[1] Could even one righteous man have been found in the city, it might have been saved from destruction.

---

[1] *Gomorrah* — an ancient city near the Dead Sea that, along with Sodom, was destroyed by God for the wickedness of its inhabitants. See Genesis 19:1–28.

When the demand for such a one comes from God, think well if you are tempted to teach that any man has the right to overrule the laws and customs of his people for his self-interest, lest you urge on a day in which there could not be a single righteous, law-abiding man left in any body of which you are a part, and that body be doomed thereby.

True it is that "in freedom lies thy strength,"[1] but that freedom is the release of the soul from the ancient bondage of the lower self.

Having paid the price demanded by the Higher Self, by perfect obedience to the law it has previously broken, the soul is free indeed, free of all things save the Law; and having become one with the Law, through that perfect obedience, it is its own lawmaker thereafter.

LESSON 245
CAUSE AND EFFECT

"As ye sow, so shall ye reap."[2] When, by means of culture and concentration, the door of spiritual perception (the spiritual energy resident in the pineal gland) has been opened and aroused to action by that vibration of the "Great Breath" which operates through the pituitary body, the consciousness of man passes unimpeded into and through the various critical states of matter which separate, or rather join, the several distinct states of consciousness; and one may observe at will the semi-intelligent individualized lives which have their habitat in those states of matter, and which are sometimes called the handmaids of Karma. The law of Karmic action has been so little understood, and its phases of operation so travestied, that I have determined to make another effort to bring to your attention the existence of innumerable grades of living creatures which were originally created by yourselves and others, and which are under the control of the Seven Sublime Lords of Karma — God-like beings with a Cosmic mission for creating, adjusting, and balancing all forces in manifestation. Once having been created by the human race by means of thought and word, these lives naturally rise or sink to the level of the beings who created them, through their subjection to the law of affinity.

---

[1] See *To My Beloved* in the beginning.
[2] Galatians 6:7.

Many ancient myths and legends refer to spoken or written words as jewels and flowers, or poisonous plants and malignant elves. Few among modern interpreters will admit that such myths and legends convey wonderful scientific and spiritual truths, and would therefore be unable to see any connection between them and the law which is indicated by the words, "As ye sow, so shall ye reap" — the law of cause and effect, as applied to words whether spoken or written, or to the deeds of man — all of which is due to their inability to observe the action of their own creations, the karmic handmaids. In order to throw a little light on the subject, we will take certain portions of the Pledge given by chelas to the Lodge on entering one of its degrees.

"I promise to give of time, money, and thought, all I conscientiously can, for the support of the Temple work."

First, consider to Whom or What you address these words. In nearly all cases they are addressed to the highest Being or Beings the chela is capable of cognizing, and they are carried and registered by the higher light and sound waves into the consciousness of that Being. Invariably before the chela has brought himself or herself to take such a pledge, he has, consciously or unconsciously, made a demand for help or aid in personal development, and in making the demand, he has given a promise to pay, for such is the law. It is a foregone conclusion that the Lodge will give such help, whether or not the method is apprehended by us. If the chela repudiates or neglects to fulfill that promise, the law itself compels its fulfillment by setting in action the handmaids which he has created. The Being to whom the promise has been made is a conscious, active part of the Godhead — a World-Builder — and the Temple, with its constituent parts or members is a part of It. On the higher planes, substance is interchangeable; therefore, a debt contracted between any two parts of the Temple puts the World-Builder in the position of creditor to itself and its constituent parts; and, as on the plane of real life, personality as you know it disappears, such debts, if not paid to the personal, lesser creditor, will be collected by the Greater Creditor, and when collected, may assume entirely different characteristics.

Therefore, the repudiated debt of time, thought, and money will be collected by force; it may be by shortened life, by lack of power for thought, by loss of money, or by some other corresponding method.

The karmic handmaids — elementals — live a certain definite time, i.e., as long as the force which has precipitated them into being endures — which is long enough to permit them to accomplish the purpose that the law has determined; then they return to a state of undifferentiated substance, to be recalled in other forms on demand, until their particular cycle of necessity is exhausted.

Thinking it of less importance, another chela may fulfill all other obligations, but neglect or refuse to fulfill the one which promises Love, Protection, and Obedience for and to the representatives of the Lodge; such refusal or neglect incites to action other grades of the same class of karmic handmaids, and the love, protection, and obedience when refused to a representative and bestowed unworthily or where it is not appreciated, only serve as a whiplash to punish the recreant, or rather to awaken him to a sense of neglected duty.

Do not mistakenly imagine that there is anything unjust or arbitrary in such action of Karmic law. It is simply the fulfillment of the law of Justice or Equilibrium; for by your pledge of chelaship you have called for the precipitation of Karma, and it is in response to that call that Karma acts so unerringly and swiftly.

The unpledged portions of the human race are as amenable to the Law as are the pledged chelas, but the action of the Law is slower, and consequently less violent in effect. A chela who comes under the personal direction of a Master of the White Brotherhood for the purpose of developing more rapidly than the remainder of his race, always provokes more rapid precipitation of karmic action.

LESSON 246
THE CURSE OF MAMMON

1899

What I am about to say may seem to contradict statements previously made by those teachers of occult science whom you most revere, but in reality this is not so, for I shall only take some of those threads that have for the time being been permitted to hang loosely in the web of philosophy expounded by the Masters.

Rightly have you been informed that the fall of the angels into generation was the first fall of man; and that with the attainment of the highest physical and mental powers by those of the human race now classed among the prehistoric peoples, there occurred a still worse fall whereby man, having attained the power of the Gods, fell below the level of the beasts with whom he cohabited. As a result of this fall there came upon, or within man, the curse that has hung as might a millstone around his neck, over his soul, dragging him back into the dark stream of ignorance and oblivion over and over again — the curse of forgetfulness, the doom of slavery. Never since that far distant age has collective humanity been free; never since has it been able to remember the blessedness of its previous lot, nor the cause thereof; nor has there lived a nation, a people, or a race devoid of an innate sense of its own sinfulness, its own powerlessness; nor without a desire to propitiate some offended Deity, which represented Infinity, however crude its concept; and this seeming curse is the result of the division of human interests.

However broad its declaration of principles, each form of government had buried within its constitution the seed of its own decay; and, as it has been in the past, so it is now in this present great cycle.

The accumulated evil of the age has reached the zenith of its power and readjustment must follow. A short day of grace is still ours, a single century; for, if before the end of that century the peoples of the earth have not awakened sufficiently to enable them to behold the canker in the bud of their great so-called civilizations, and destroy that canker, nothing can save them from decay and annihilation. The kingdom of Satan or evil, and the kingdom of God or Good, cannot exist simultaneously in one place and age; one must give way and the kingdom of God, holding all the positive power of the Infinite, must eventually overwhelm the kingdom of Satan, or negative power.

Let the mind of man reach out over the Universe in any direction where the great upward evolutionary forces are in full control, and it will find no evidence of that separateness which is the curse of the human race. The sun shines alike on the good and on the evil; the dew and the rain fall alike on the just and on the unjust; the earth yields its treasures of usefulness and beauty alike to the poor and the rich; only one principle is involved — *labor*. Those fields upon which man bestows the most thought and service yield most abundantly; but nature covers with luxuriant beauty even the untilled fields; each is dependent on each, all is for all; even the tiny blade of grass is not a slave to the flower, but grows all the more luxuriantly for being shaded by it.

With the seizure of the first plot of ground by a king or ruler of a people and its apportionment for the benefit of his favorites, with the first piece of money given in exchange for human service, with the first captured and enslaved human being, entered the triple curse into the world we now inhabit, the entering wedge that divided the kingdom of God, and set up the kingdom of the devil; and not until a nation arises as one man to throw off this curse, can the seed of suffering and sorrow be eradicated — destroyed forever, thus opening up the waste places, that the light of the Infinite may shine into souls darkened by ages of ignorance, superstition, idolatry, and inhumanity.

No slavery ever existed on the earth more binding, more evil in its effects, than the present system of wage slavery, excepting only that of the slavery of women. The latter are, in one sense, their own worst enemies, for many of them do not recognize their position — do not know that they are in slavery. Never so long as woman is not the mistress of her own body is she free. Never, so long as children are born into the world as a result of passion alone, can children be free-born, for on every atom of their little bodies is impressed the seal of their slavery.

The petted, pampered, idolized, but still enslaved woman who can look abroad on the degradation of women in many parts of the earth and hold her peace, or put a straw in the way of others who are working for the emancipation of the sex to which she belongs, is preparing a Karma for herself of which she little dreams. No woman with the truly feminine instincts of the soul desires for herself, or for her sisters, aught that will detract from her own loveliness in the eyes of those whom she loves; and only the exigencies of the times and the overpowering intuitive perception that she is a part of God and therefore part of man, could give her courage to face the sneers of her own sex or the ridicule and inane expressions of contempt from the opposite sex, in making an effort to win the recognition that is her right. As well might man strive to invent an electric dynamo without negative power as to strive to create a righteous government and leave out of his scheme the power of women.

The coral reefs of some of the deep sea islands furnish an example of the unity of all life. The polyps building these structures, which are massive enough to founder the largest ship, constitute a primitive nation in themselves in a world which they have created on natural lines of self-sacrifice and true Brotherhood. Four classes of these tiny creatures are required to complete a reef which rises to any height above the level of the sea. The class that lays the foundations in the depths of the sea cannot live above a certain lower level of the water. When that point is reached, another class of the same polyps takes up the work; this class carries the work several feet above the point where the first laid down their tools, or bodies. Then another class arises to complete the structure. Finally, still another class comes upon the scene and these fill in the spaces and round out the reef. While the polyps of the first designated class are laboring on their allotted portion of the work, the stress and strain undergone by them in reaching beyond their natural habitat result in the birth of a different order of polyps, a class that can labor naturally on a higher level. Each class literally sacrifices itself to its progeny, and the whole work when completed is a perfect example of self-sacrifice. Whatever its highest use in the economy of the Universe, a single reef will outlast by ages any work performed by humanity on the physical plane.

This is only one of the many examples furnished by Nature to the student who is willing to learn the lesson of unity and sacrifice, as opposed to disunion and self-indulgence. Until we begin to work with Nature, by finding out and obeying her Laws, evidences of the workings of which are scattered profusely about us, we shall never have nation, state, or organization that will outlast the impulse which gave it birth.

From the lips of the great Master Jesus once came an expression pregnant with force, which will yet tear asunder the curse from the cursed: "Ye cannot serve God and mammon."[1] The term "the mammon of unrighteousness" has a broad and deep significance. It comprises all slavery, whether it be of lands, money, or human chattels; it is deep enough to include every single molecule of matter that has ever been bought and sold by the human race.

You will be told that a government devoid of all medium of exchange must of necessity be a failure. I ask you: How do you know? Has it ever been tried within the memory or history of man? I answer you: No, not as man is now constituted. It is the one thing that never has been tried in the world you now inhabit, since the fall of man to which I have referred; but there are worlds — many of them, whose forms of government have never, for ages upon ages, been materially changed, and where never a thought of the curse that has blighted this fair earth has found lodgment in mortal brain; where life on physical

---

[1] Matthew 6:24.

lines is one joyous service, only exchanged for greater joys; and such a one can this poor planet become, when its inhabitants awake to the cause of what they term "original sin," the curse that hangs like a pall over the soul of every human being that enters upon his heritage of woe therein.

That curse which has raised every man's hand against his brother, which has filled prisons and insane asylums and has made man deny the God within himself; for light has no fellowship with darkness and God is Light.

Have you nothing to do in the work of regeneration, the labor of preparing for the Kingdom of Christ — the Kingdom of Unity as opposed to separateness? Dare you stand idle through all the long day, and let the shadows of night descend on this fair world, without an effort to arrest their falling?

LESSON 247
THE WHITE BROTHERHOOD
AND ITS CONNECTION WITH THE TEMPLE

The humanity of a Manvantara or period of creative energy, past, present, or future, manifests in seven major stages or grades of evolution. These stages correspond to, and are one with the seven degrees of occultism into which the Great Lodge is divided. Each one of these Degrees is divided into seven minor steps, making forty-nine in all. Every human being on "the Path," or in manifestation during such a Cyclic period, is in or on one of these steps or Degrees.

The Seventh Degree of the present Cycle is composed of all those people who have reached a certain definite point in spiritual development, and have been admitted into this Degree by the Masters without any self-conscious act on their part, on the outer plane of manifestation, i.e., the physical world.

The Sixth Degree is composed of those in the position of Teachers or Leaders of men, who are working on purely ethical lines or under some personal concept of the Infinite and Trinity thereof, but who have not yet realized their position in the Lodge or the assistance given them by higher entities, because of that position.

The Fifth Degree is composed of such members of esoteric or exoteric Societies for Psychical Research, and students of occultism as are familiar with the truth of the Lodge as a fact in natural life, and who are working consciously under the direction of one or more Masters for the advancement of the human race. Many of the most noted professional men, scientists, and investigators along all lines have reached this point, but do not realize the position of the Degree to which they belong in the great scale of life. Many belonging to the Masonic Fraternity,[1] in past ages, were members of this Degree.

The Fourth Degree — The Temple — is composed of those who have come into close personal touch with the members of the White Brotherhood (the Initiates and Masters), whether they are members of the Temple organization or not, and who are in process of preparation for more sacred Degrees, having taken a self-conscious step in evolution.

All things connected with the three Inner Degrees are very sacred and secret, membership in them leading up to conscious union with all the component parts of the Lodge. But little can be said by us of these Degrees to any but pledged members of the Temple. By earnest aspiration and rightly directed effort, we may hope, however, to reach one or all of these Degrees, the members of which are trained occultists, seers, and Initiates. The advanced souls who constitute the higher Degrees are the Instructors or Teachers of the members of the lesser, or before-mentioned Degrees. In different parts of the world there are organized bodies under the leadership of one or more of these Initiates, the members of which have no idea of the real standing of their Teachers.

It is known to be a law, that no effort for good can be made without awakening an opposite pole of evil — so there are also to be found in the world, groups of people under evil guidance that cast sad reflections on the term occultism.

---

[1] *Masonic Fraternity* or *Freemasonry* — a centuries-old fraternal organization based on a system of moral and ethical teachings. It uses symbols and allegory derived from the tools and practices of stonemasonry. Just like the Rosicrucians, the Knights Templar, and other mystical orders, this society was first designed to protect and spread secret knowledge among those who could use it for the benefit of humanity, often guided by the Masters of Wisdom. For example, the founding fathers of the United States were Freemasons. However, over time, this organization lost all connections with the Masters and today operates as any other created by people.

LESSON 248
THE TEN RULES OF DISCIPLESHIP
OF THE 4TH DEGREE OF THE GREAT WHITE LODGE

God is Love, and Love is the fundamental source of Being. There-fore, if thou sin against Love, that sin is against God.

1. "Thou shalt love the Lord thy God with all thy heart and mind, and thy neighbor as thyself."[1] This is the highest law.

2. Thou shalt obey the laws of life. The Higher Law will hold thee accountable for the breaking of every lesser law.

3. Thou shalt not sin against thine own body nor against the body of thy neighbor by concupiscence; for the Lord thy God will demand an accounting of thee for all of the Creative Fire enthroned within thee.

4. Thou shalt not needlessly take the life of any thing or creature.

5. Thou shalt not speak falsely, unnecessarily, or critically against thy neighbor, and so put in action the converse force of creative sound and word; for the Higher Law will reverse the action of the force thus directed and bring back upon thee, with intensified strength, the results of the broken law.

6. Thou shalt bear constantly in mind the unity of the human race, and treat every member of the Great White Lodge as though he were of blood kin; for unity is the law of discipleship and, if thou sin against this law, thou shalt be greatly hindered in thy progress toward the goal of thy desires.

7. Morning and evening thou shalt lift the eyes of thy soul toward the Throne of thy God, with strong aspiration, gratitude, and devotion; for according to thy desires — thy demands — upon the Center of all Being, desires expressed in purity, thanksgiving, and unselfishness shall the supply be vouchsafed thee.

8. Thou shalt give of thine abundance to all the poor, but of thy poverty, the price of thine own pleasures, and that which would min-ister to thine own desires shalt thou give to the Great Mother and to the Guardian of the Shrine, through which the Great Mother love of the universe radiates for thine own eternal good.

9. Thou shalt not despise nor ill-treat any thing or creature. Matter, Force, and Consciousness are but different degrees of the one eternal, all-pervading principle of Love — which is God; and he who despises

---

[1] Luke 10:27.

and reviles his body, because it does not radiate the light of his soul, despises God as certainly as does the man who despises and reviles the soul and spirit of God.

10. When the Law of Love — of Karma — has brought thee out of the morass of spiritual darkness to the beginning of the path which leads to spiritual illumination, woe be unto thee if thou obstruct that path for thyself or others, by refusing to obey the Master to whose feet that law has brought thee.

Only by implicit obedience to the commands of the Master-Teacher shalt thou be able to lift one foot after another while treading that path of discipleship.

Commune long and earnestly with the God within thyself ere thou darest to make demand to tread that path, for once thou hast entered it, thou canst no more return to thy former state of irresponsibility than thou canst reenter thy mother's womb.

Behold the Path before thee; a clean life, pure aspiration, and unselfish service. Art thou prepared to tread that Path?

LESSON 249
"MY FATHER'S HOUSE IS A HOUSE OF PRAYER"

It is not wise to look upon the depressing side of natural forces, but it would be unwise not to recognize their power when danger is near. Man has created and sent into space through many long, long ages the forces that are now gathering for his overthrow. It matters not how loudly he calls upon the Gods, the Gods combined cannot avert the action of the Universal Law. As he has sown so must he reap; and in the reaping (and here is where the joy in the sorrow of the universe manifests) he can redeem the past, and that is what so many forget entirely who have thrown aside the truths of the Christian religion.

For the last thirty-five years there has been but little said of the New Testament among occult students of H. P. Blavatsky and others who came after her. It was in a manner put in the background for a good reason. As I have told you before, the New Testament holds in its pages all the knowledge of the universe. All the diffuse philosophical literature of the ages that preceded the Christian era was preparatory. The New Testament synthesizes all, but it has been so misunderstood and misinterpreted that we deemed it best to go back to the older philosophies, that they might explain the New Testament. It is only through the old philosophies that it can be understood, for it contains copies of the most occult manuscripts in the world; and the treasures of the hidden chambers of the East, of which I have spoken to you before, are, as I have said of the western philosophies, but explanations of all that you find between the pages of Matthew and Revelation. You cannot study that book too much. It will open to your understanding, with the explanations you have already had, as nothing else can.

On one page in that book is the sentence, "My Father's house is a house of prayer, but ye have made it a den of thieves."[1] My children, do you suppose for a moment that the Master Jesus meant the temple in which he was standing at that time? By no means. He meant the human heart, the human mind, and it has been a den of thieves. It should be a place of aspiration and inspiration. Instead of these, the golden calf has been set up, and the lower man has fallen down in worship before that, and it is filled with the sacrifices he has made of his brother's blood. It is the curse of all curses, and today the astral atmosphere about you is loaded with the effects of that curse.

Is it any wonder that you have all felt at times a sense of depression that almost bowed you to the ground? The weight of that house within you that should be a house of prayer, that has been made a den of thieves through all the ages that have gone since your innocence passed away, is enough to cause it.

I would not have you think, my children, that life is all a curse, that there is nothing but blackness and darkness and destitution for the children of men. But I do desire to awaken those who are sleeping. I do desire to bring them to the point where they can recognize the fact that their destiny is in their own hands — not in the hands of a God, not in the hands of a Master. When you can make yourself that house of prayer which is meant in the passage above referred to, you can turn everything around and about you into joyfulness and peace. You can attract to yourself from the ends of the universe all that it holds of truth and of righteousness. You can make it a place of peace where the Angels of Light will be glad to dwell. You have but one alternative; there is death and worse than death, and there is joy and peace, and you are the master. You are to say which it shall be.

---

[1] Matthew 21:13.

GLOSSARY

ARMAGEDDON — the Final Battle between the Forces of Light and darkness, as proclaimed in ancient prophecies. If the Powers of Light are headed by the Great Lord of Shambhala, then the forces of evil are led by the Lord of Darkness, also known as Lucifer (*Latin*, "Light-Bearer").

The ancient legend of the Fallen Angel, who rebelled against the Powers of Light and became Satan, reflects a true drama that took place on Earth millions of years ago.

Lucifer was one of the Eight Great Spirits, who, in an act of self-sacrifice, left their worlds nearly eighteen million years ago and came to Earth in order to assist and edify humanity. Lucifer had quickly ascended the Ladder of Evolution and achieved many triumphs in his World. Of all the Teachers, his Spirit was energetically closest to Earth, as well as having all the features of the composition of Saturn. This gave him the right to participate in the development of humanity, particularly its intellect. Like the other Great Teachers who had been incarnated and were interacting with humankind, he endowed them with reason and free will.

During the times of Atlantis, while living among people, the Great Teachers imparted to them an abundance of secret knowledge, enabling them to achieve success in many spheres of life — they were able to manage the most powerful energies; they knew the mysteries of Nature and could breed new species of plants and animals; they could create the most complex technologies, including the science of aeronautics; in addition, they made direct contact with Distant Worlds.

Being an expert on all the mysteries of Earth, Lucifer justifiably become known as the Prince of this World. It also left him with a special attachment to Earth, while the remaining Seven Great Teachers were subject to the attraction of the Higher Worlds and managed to preserve their purity. With every new incarnation on this planet, Lucifer's higher consciousness gradually darkened. Pride totally captured his mind which led to his downfall and revolt against the Laws of the Cosmos.

Having lost the right to bear this name, Lucifer thought to limit the whole of humanity solely to Earth, depriving it of a connection to Higher and Distant Worlds. Demonstrating the miracles of matter, he rapidly gained adherents, and these soon constituted the majority of the population of Atlantis. Lack of heart development among humans meant that they were vulnerable to temptation.

To achieve his goal of becoming the absolute and only god for Earth-dwellers, Lucifer directed all his efforts towards demeaning Woman, which always and inevitably leads to the desensitization and degeneration of humanity. He destroyed the Cult of Spirit, creating instead a cult of personality: the Atlanteans began to build temples and monuments to themselves. People began to use secret knowledge not for the good of all but for the accumulation of wealth, inventing deadly weapons, waging war, practicing dark magic, and so on. Those who warned of the inevitable disaster resulting from the actions of the Atlanteans faced penalty of death.

In this way, the violation of Cosmic Laws on such an unprecedented scale, along with the use of dark magic by the Atlanteans against the Sons of Light, brought destructive elemental forces into play. These gradually destroyed Atlantis and ushered in the Ice Age, in which entire regions of the planet were covered with ice.

Many peoples of the world have preserved legends of the Battle of the Titans, or the Battle of the Gods, that tell of the time when a group of Gods opposed another dominant God. These myths actually reflect events connected with the rebellion of the Sons of Light, the Titans of Shambhala, against the dictatorship of Lucifer and his evil sorcerers, which took place during the later days of Atlantis. In 9564 BCE the Light secured a victory over the warlocks of Poseidonis, the last island of Atlantis, as it sank beneath the waves.

Prior to these disasters, the Sons of Light resettled in Egypt the finest and most spiritual inhabitants of Atlantis, thereby transferring the entire Atlantean sacred heritage. The Masters themselves moved to Shambhala, at that time also an island, and have been assisting humanity secretly ever since, never revealing their identity.

At the onset of a new stage in human development, the Fallen Angel founded and headed the dark brotherhood, becoming a furious enemy of the Great Brotherhood of Teachers for all ages to come. In contrast to Shambhala, located high in the mountains, the dark brotherhood established its stronghold at the lowest point, burrowing into subterranean layers closer to Earth's core, in order to gain strength from its fire. But at this point, Lucifer decided to convince humanity that he did not exist, in order to more easily deceive and enslave.

One should never underestimate the hierophants of evil, because they know many secrets of Nature and the human mind. Their main goal was to sever humanity's connection with the Great Teachers, so that even the smallest reminder of the Brotherhood would be persecuted vigorously by humanity itself.

Nevertheless, in the not too distant past the Messengers of Light succeeded in turning the situation around. At this point the forces of darkness realized that they would never triumph over the Light and, sooner or later, would be annihilated by fiery energies approaching Earth. Therefore, Lucifer, who had no access to the Higher Worlds, decided to blow up the planet, since this alone would enable him to remain in its atmosphere for some time ahead, thereby prolonging his life. The catastrophe could have taken place in 1899, 1949, 1954, 1977, or 1999. Had it occurred, the Brotherhood of Great Teachers, together with the most spiritually advanced Earth-dwellers, would have moved in subtle body form to Venus and Jupiter; the souls of the majority would have waited billions of years for the formation of a new planet on which to continue humanity's evolution. The evil ones would have ended up on Saturn. All planets and stars in the Universe are home to living beings, it is just that in each case the structure of matter has different degrees of tenuity. Therefore, people cannot see them either with the naked eye or with telescopic devices, which are as yet far from perfect. Nevertheless, the Earth was saved from destruction through the combined incredible efforts of all Forces of Light in the Solar System.

The liberation of Earth from Lucifer's dictatorship began on the Subtle Plane at the end of the 19th century and the turn of the 20th century; soon afterwards the battle shifted onto the physical plane in the form of the First World War, 1914–1918. At the end of 1931, a new phase in the struggle for humanity's freedom and immortality began on the Subtle Plane. The calculations unearthed in the Great Pyramid of Giza indicated the significance of 1936 — this date marked the start of a personal fight between the Great Lord of Shambhala and the Lord of Darkness, the celestial battle of Archangel Michael and his angels with the Dragon, as proclaimed in the Bible. Eventually, the decisive battle between the Forces of Light and the darkness shifted from the Subtle Plane to the physical plane giving rise to the Second World War, 1939–1945.

The second phase of the Final Battle ended with the triumph of the Forces of Light on 17 October 1949, when the Great Lord banished Lucifer to Saturn.

However, after their defeat, the hierophants of evil managed to gather the remainder of their crushed army on the Subtle Plane. Their desire for revenge resulted in the third phase of the Final Battle which began at the end of the 20th century. This stage of the battle was reflected on the earthly plane in Chechnya, Nagorno-Karabakh, the Caucasus, Transnistria, the former republics of Yugoslavia, and then in Syria and Ukraine, where some of the Points of Life most significant to the current time are located. But, in general, from time immemorial, in places where Points of Life were born, involutionary forces of evil have tried to establish power by means of local or global bloody war, spawning their own Points of Death.

Nevertheless, the main field of the Final Battle lies in each human heart. It will come to an end towards the final days of 21st century, when the last bearer of darkness on Earth and in the near-Earth spheres will be expelled to Saturn in the wake of their ruler.

Lucifer's rebellion against Cosmic Laws greatly slowed the evolution of Earth. If it were not for Lucifer, there would be no borders today between the physical world and the Higher Spheres, and humanity would be unfamiliar with the phenomenon of death. Furthermore, in attempting to separate the Earth from the Distant Worlds, the forces of darkness obscured the Subtle Plane of the atmosphere around the planet so that energies from the Sun and other stars, sent to assist humanity, could not penetrate. This same process contributed to parts of the planet being covered with ice. Its melting in the present age is a sign of the Fiery Era, in which there is no place for cold in any manifestation. This means that Earth is gradually being released from the "heritage" of Atlantis and that its atmosphere is being purified. However, for centuries having been deprived of new stellar energies, people are unaccustomed to them. Hence it is only the willingness and desire on the part of humanity to assimilate these new energies that can bring about the complete destruction of the heavy dirty-grey atmosphere, which is suffocating the entire planet, as it is seen from the Subtle Plane.

ATLANTIS (*Greek*) — Plato's name for the continent whereon the Fourth Race of humanity developed. Extending from the North to the South, it was located in an area now covered by the waters of the Atlantic Ocean.

Numerous islands rose from the depths to form this continent, beginning some five million years ago. At the same time, the Great Teachers started gathering and resettling on one of the central islands the best representatives of the Third Race from the continent of Lemuria, whose time was drawing to a close.

The first Atlanteans were almost three-and-a-half meters tall, later decreasing in height to approximately two-and-a-half meters. The peak of Atlantis' flourishing coincided with the Toltec period, when, after long internecine wars, tribes united into a federation headed by an emperor. The capital was the City of Golden Gates.

The decline of Atlantis began with the fall of Lucifer, who had been one of humanity's trusted Instructors. People began to use mystic knowledge not for the good of all but for glorifying themselves. This frightful moral decline, along with the humiliation of women and other perversions, led to the Atlanteans consciously repeating the sins of primitive people, the progenitors of the primary apes; the sexual intercourse between some Atlanteans and primary apes produced man-like monkeys.

The main continent was destroyed by water a few millions years ago, leaving a number of large and small islands, among which were Ruta and Daitya. The isle of Ruta sank almost 850,000 years ago, and Daitya submerged nearly 270,000 years ago, leaving a smaller island known as Poseidonis.

Today, Atlantis is slowly rising and will be the continent for the development of the Sixth and Seventh Races of humanity.

AUM or **OM** — the most sacred and mystical of all words. It may be pronounced as two, three, or seven syllables, producing different vibrations. Its correct utterance, or rather, the intonation with which it should be pronounced, is a great secret, conveyed directly by the Teacher to His disciple. One who is able to pronounce it correctly draws close to the creative power of the Universe: *In the beginning was the Word, and the Word was Aum.* However, those who know how to use this Word, rarely turn to it, since they know that it evokes forces which they cannot control and which may destroy them.

Aum includes three components: Light, Color, and Sound. These are the Three Fires or the Triple Sacred Fire in man and the Universe.

According to popular belief, Aum symbolizes the three Vedas and the three Gods of Fire, Water, and Air. They also mean Creation, Preservation, and Transfiguration, personified by Brahma, Vishnu, and Shiva — or Buddha, Christ, and Maitreya. In esoteric philosophy, there are many interpretations of this three-lettered entity, which symbolizes the Trinity in One.

This word is usually placed at the beginning of sacred Scriptures and is prefixed to prayers, though it may serve in itself as a prayer. It is from Aum that the word *Amen* is derived.

AURA — the electro-magnetic radiation of all the accumulated energies of a living organism, especially the heart, retaining its dominant color, sound, and scent. All bodies and objects of the manifest world are surrounded by an aura.

The human aura is kind of passport which quickly identifies the individual's essence and destiny. In the future, a person's aura will determine their suitability to hold important positions in every domain of life. Every thought, emotion, feeling, or act leaves an imprint on the aura in the form of radiations, which, in turn, magnetically attract elements from space that correspond with their tonality. The more powerful the fiery energy in a person, the stronger the influence of their aura over their whole environment. Throughout their lives, people suffuse everything they touch with the radiations of their aura, brightening or darkening the objects around them. In addition every individual perceives the world through the prism of their aura, as though they were looking through a pair of glasses. Hence, through a light aura, one perceives only the Light, and through a dark aura, one perceives the darkness.

As a rule, the aura of a newborn child is colorless until the first gleam of consciousness imbues it with colors that correspond to the accumulations of previous lives. As a rule, this happens at the age of seven.

The auric field should be enclosed by a protective net, woven together from the sediment of the subtlest fiery energies providing a shield against extraneous intrusions and influences. But souls devoid of spirituality lack this protection causing them often to fall victim to the impact of other people's auras, especially those that possess a powerful aura of dark fire; they also succumb to the influence of various evil entities from the Subtle Plane. First and foremost this affects a person's health. Remember that more spiritually-minded people have a protective net in the form of fiery ruby sparks. However, dark entities are always attempting to break through, for even the slightest rupture opens the way to gaining control over another being. The aura of powerful spirits generates a ray, which imbues thoughts — or anything else — with its color and energy. When a thought like this is aimed in a specific direction, it has the appearance of a real ray in space and is equipped with tremendous power.

A planet possesses an aura, too, along with a protective net. The aura of Earth accumulates all the energies produced by the activity and free will of humanity. At the beginning of its existence, the aura of the Earth was golden, but by the mid-20th century it had turned ash-grey with clouds of brown gas and black holes in its protective net. By the end of the last century, the Hierarchy of Light and its earthly colleagues managed to restore the net. However, the state of the planet's aura still depends upon humanity and upon each and every individual.

AVATARS (*Sanskrit*, "descent") — Gods, Spirits of the Higher Spheres and Distant Worlds incarnated in the bodies of ordinary mortals. Referred to in Tibet by the ancient word *Lha* (*Tibetan*, "Spirit," "God"), whose meaning covers the entire series of celestial Hierarchies. Every Supreme Cosmic Concept is personified in a High Spirit that also takes a human form. For this reason every ancient religion has a pantheon of Gods, each embodying a certain Idea and representing a particular Force of Nature.

Sons of God, Sons of Light, Sons of Heaven, Sons of Fire, Sons of Reason, Archangels, Planet Regents, Masters of Wisdom, Bodhisattvas (*Sanskrit*, "Enlightenment Beings"), the Dhyan Chohans (*Sanskrit*, "Lords of Light"), the Rishis (*Sanskrit*, "Sages of Insight"), the Kumaras (*Sanskrit*, "Youths"), and so on — all High Spirits, who, like the Avatars, assumed a human appearance to raise the consciousness of humanity and accelerate its development. Seven Great Spirits took on the role of caring for planet Earth and humanity. Again and again, they were incarnated as the greatest founders of kingdoms, religions, sciences, and philosophies to help people realize their divine nature. As such, they have left deep traces in every area of life and in every land.

For example, their incarnations on Earth include Akbar the Great, Anaxagoras, Apollonius of Tyana, Confucius, the Count of Saint-Germain, Francis of Assisi, Gautama Buddha, Giordano Bruno, Hermes Trismegistus, Jakob Böhme, Jesus Christ, John the Apostle, Joseph, Joshua, King Arthur, Krishna, Lao-Tzu, Mahatma Koot Hoomi, Mahatma Morya, Melchizedek, Menes, Moses, Muhammad, Numa Pompilius, Origen, Orpheus, Paul the Apostle, Pericles, Plato, Pythagoras, Rama, Ramesses the Great, Sergius of Radonezh, Solomon, Thomas à Kempis, Thutmose III, Tsongkhapa, Tutankhamun, Zoroaster, and many others.

All the Gods have a Spouse, with whom they are united in the Higher Worlds; one does not exist without the other. But, since the Masculine Principle must express itself in the visible aspect of life, and the Feminine Principle in the invisible aspect, Female Deities were revered as the most sacred and secret in all ancient religions. It is the Female Deities, incarnated on Earth as mothers, sisters, daughters, and wives who inspired the Sons of Light and the peoples of the Earth, as well as humanity as a whole through their self-sacrifice, heroism, and continuous giving. Similarly, the entire Hierarchy of Light devoutly honors the Mother of the World — the Great Spirit of the Feminine Principle, who is personified in many world religions as the Supreme Goddess. The Mother of the World incarnated as Mary to give life to Jesus Christ. Subsequently, for the past two thousand years, She has manifested through Her Hypostasis-Daughters — Faith, Hope, and Love, who have continuously replaced each other, at no point abandoning this world.

CROSS — the most ancient cosmic symbol: the vertical line symbolizes spirit while the horizontal one symbolizes matter, which together create all that exists.

Christ said: "If any man will come after me, let him deny himself, and take up his cross, and follow me."[1] The cross is Karma. One who is unwilling to accept the cross cannot follow, but to take it means expressing humility before the karmic discharge of old debts, the conscious extirpation of vices, and the unconditional acceptance of probations. The higher the human spirit, the heavier the burden it accepts, but the cross is lifted by the spirit and therefore it cannot destroy man

---

[1] Matthew 16:24.

by its weight. However, as the time of release draws nearer, the burden becomes more and more unbearable — but it is an illusion, amplified by the darkness, and one has to pass through this without deviating from the path. In this way, after a symbolic crucifixion on the cross, when a man overcomes the desires of his baser bodies, atoning for his karmic sins, a resurrection occurs — the fiery transmutation of the lower nature and its unification with the spirit, or the Heavenly Father. This fiery renewal breaks the vicious circle of Karma.

The Fiery Cross is the symbol of the *swastika* (*Sanskrit*, "well-being"), whose motion is caused by the presence of opposite poles. Everyone has their own rhythm associated with the rotation of the cross. Initially, man must establish himself as an individual; for the first forty-two years of his life, the rotation of his cross is directed inwards; he absorbs everything that is outside by way of knowledge and information. When the balance is reached, then the cross must be reset to an outward rotation — to return. The individuality, the Karma of Love, begins its task of giving to the world all the treasures that the man has gathered in his Chalice for many lives. In this way we may observe the simultaneous rotation of the two crosses: one — inside, the other — outside. And when these two crosses unite in harmonious movement, the symbol of balance appears — the swastika, or the sign of the Fiery Cross of Life, or the "Seal of the Heart," which marks the High Spirits.

GOD — the Divine, Unchangeable, Invariable, and Infinite Principle; the eternally Unknowable Cause of All that exists; omnipresent, all-pervading, visible and invisible spiritual Nature, which exists everywhere, in which everything lives, moves, and has its being; the Absolute, including the potential of all things as well as all universal manifestations. Upon being made manifest, out of its Absolute Oneness, God becomes the Absolute of infinite differentiation and its consequences — relativity and polarities. God has no gender and cannot be imagined as a human being. In the Holy Scriptures, God is Fire, God is Love — the one primeval energy that conceives the worlds.

Where this notion does not refer to the above, in ancient Teachings it has always denoted the totality of the working and intelligent Forces of Nature. Thus, the world is ruled by the Creative Forces of the Cosmos, together constituting the limitless Hierarchy of Light, which in the Bible is represented as Jacob's Ladder.

However, the Great Unknown was, is, and always will be hidden from the eyes of those who live in the manifested world. The Primal Cause, the Absolute, has been and will be unknowable — forever and always.

The traditional Christian concept of *God* refers to the Planetary Spirit, or a *Demiurge* (*Greek*, "creator") — the Supreme Lord or Ruler of Earth, who has lived out His human evolution and reached an unparalleled level of spiritual development. Together with other High Spirits that constitute the Hierarchy of Light, He is now responsible for the creation, preservation, and transfiguration of Earth.

The Planetary Spirit is androgynous because there is no gender separation on the higher planes of Existence — hence, the pronoun *He* is used merely for lack of a more appropriate one. The Planetary Spirit can manifest in various Aspects and Hypostases, including male and female in the binary world since He bears within Himself both Principles.

From ancient sacred texts, it is evident that the Planetary Spirit of Earth is the Lord of Sirius. Even the Quran states that Allah is the Lord of Sirius. However, it should be borne in mind that the God described in the Old Testament is not the same as the Supreme Lord of Earth whom Christ calls His Father in the New Testament.

Sometimes He who is denoted by the name *the One and Only*, forms simultaneously several of His own Hypostases, as well as Individualities (under different names), and one that possesses a higher energy component serves another (we might even say, Himself) as a Master, Teacher, and Protector — either in the physical world or in the Ethereal, depending on the single goal that is set before His "emanating forms."

Thus, one of the Hypostases of the Lord of Sirius manifested on Earth was Melchizedek (*Hebrew*, "king of righteousness") mentioned in the Bible as a Priest of the Most High. In esoteric philosophy, He is the King and Father of the planet Earth and the Priest of the Ineffable One, or the One whose Name is Silence, and carries the same Name.

According to the ancient legends of Judaism and early Christianity, Melchizedek establishes the right to a special and ideal dignity and extraordinary priesthood, germane to both royalty and high priests. Melchizedek is the prototype of the Messiah. He is the head of eternal angels, and He is "King of peace; without father, without mother, without descent, having neither beginning of days, nor end of life; but made like unto the Son of God; abideth a priest continually."[1] Jesus Christ was "called of God a high priest after the order of Melchizedek."[2]

In the ancient Melchizedekian teaching, it was asserted that Melchizedek was the first and principal incarnation of the Supreme God, while Christ was only the image of Melchizedek. It was believed that Christ had descended upon a man, Jesus, at his baptism, and that Melchizedek was a Heavenly Power, higher than Christ. According to their teachings, Melchizedek did for Angels what Christ was to do for humankind.

The last incarnation of Melchizedek took place about 6,000 years ago as the first Zoroaster, or Zarathustra, the founder of Zoroastrianism and prophet. Zoroaster was given the Revelation of Ahura Mazda, or the Creator, in the form of the holy scripture of the Avesta in the language of Zend, which is very close to the language of Senzar.

According to linguistic studies, the name *Zoroaster* translates as "the golden shining star" or "Golden Sirius." In Zoroastrianism, Sirius is especially revered, being called *Tishtrya*, "whom Ahura Mazda has established as a lord and overseer above all stars, in the same way as he has established Zarathustra above men." Only thirteen Zarathustra incarnations have been revealed to humanity, and each carried a sacred scripture which over time was lost, requiring the manifestation of a new cycle of secret knowledge.

The image of Melchizedek bears the seal of High Mystery; the main pages of His incarnations may be revealed only to those who have ascended the first rungs of Initiation.

The Nativity Mystery of the Stellar Spirit of Sirius in the Glorious Body on the Higher Planes of Earth occurred for the first time on 19 July 2017. This is significant not only to Earth and the Solar System but to all the constellations headed and supervised by Sirius. This Mystery of Light will never be repeated in the present Grand Cycle of Evolution.

INITIATE — one who has become entitled to acquire the Secret Knowledge of the Cosmos and human beings. Each new stage of Initiation reveals ever new mysteries and imparts new abilities.

Initiation ceremonies — or Mysteries — took place in Ancient Sanctuaries such as the Pyramids of Egypt, the Temples of Greece,

---

[1] Hebrews 7: 2–3.
[2] Hebrews 5:10.

India, and so on. Secret Sanctuaries with halls for Initiations were built in places of powerful energy, mostly in the mountains. Mountains are the source of the strongest energy because their summits are covered with snow, which, like a natural lens, serves to receive the currents of other constellations and planets. Similarly, representatives of other worlds who study the Earth have their bases in the mountains, too.

The procedure of Initiation is a mystical penetration into a higher level of perception and comprehension of the mystery of Existence, thanks to the acceptance of higher-order currents and the ability to use them effectively. It is the transition from life to a temporary death by means of a magic dream, which in turn enables a candidate to experience a disembodied Spirit and Soul in the subjective world. Each Initiation requires moral purity, strength of spirit, and an aspiration towards Truth.

For example, Hermes Trismegistus (*Greek*, "Thrice-Greatest") underwent three Initiations, although he is already the Four-time-Greatest, having successfully passed through yet another. His father, Arraim, is a Four-time-Greatest also. Thales of Argos passed through four Initiations. Christ passed through Eight Initiations, and His Second Coming is associated with His Ninth Initiation.

However, it is not only people and the Great Spirits who may go through Initiations, but also realms of Nature, planets, stars, solar systems, etc. Thus, in the present day, humanity as a whole as well as Earth are undergoing the next level of their Fiery Initiation.

KARMA (*Sanskrit*, "action") — the Cosmic Law of Cause and Effect, expressed in the formula, "as you sow, so shall you reap"; defines the limits within which the destiny of an individual, people, or planet, and so on can be developed.

Karma neither punishes nor rewards; it is simply a single Universal Law that infallibly guides all other laws, producing certain effects in accordance with corresponding causes. Every word, action, thought, or desire leads to an appropriate effect — and, eventually, to everything in one's surroundings. Nothing happens accidentally. Karma may be individual and collective, embracing whole peoples, continents, planets, and star systems. One cannot change or eliminate it except by removing the causes that underlie human actions.

Every individual bears the mark of karmic predestination from birth. Their free will is determined by the limits dictated by Karma, which is in turn created by their own human will. However, the placing of obstacles and restrictions in one area opens up opportunities in another. The purpose of Karma is to direct all humankind towards the path of Evolution.

Karmic debts are formed when an individual's free will violates the Divine Laws set forth in all world religions in various forms. Ignorance of these Laws does not exempt the individual from bearing responsibility. This may not happen immediately. It can take several incarnations before a person is offered the opportunity to pay off the karmic debts that they have accumulated, through the creation of certain conditions. The fastest way to redeem karma is to show Love to all, especially to those who wish you ill. Those who have succeeded in paying off 51% of their debts receive the opportunity to cooperate with Higher Forces.

The age of 42 years — 24 years for future generations — is considered the age of "cosmic adulthood." At this age begins the *Karma of Love*, when people are to work with the Cosmos on a spiritual level: for example, helping others by sharing their life experiences or developing some spiritual quality within themselves. Of course, they live on. But it also happens that, after the age of 42, some suffer a heart attack and pass on. This is because before reaching the age of 42 they needed to fulfil a certain program associated with their former Karma. Once the soul completes its task, it brings about a new incarnation. Or vice versa: a human spirit may realize that its present body is unable to perform a certain divine task and, so as not to waste time, attempts to weave together another body. Thus, as is evident, once they reach the age of 40 most people begin to take an interest in spiritual practices and ponder their mission in life — this is the Cosmic Karma of Love coming into effect. However, the Karma of Love may touch not only a human life but also the life of humanity as a whole, within smaller or greater evolutionary cycles.

LEMURIA — the name of the continent where the Third Race of humanity developed. It covered most of the present-day Pacific and Indian Oceans, stretching along the equator. Lemuria included today's Australia, New Zealand, Madagascar, and Easter Island.

Lemuria was the birthplace of physical humanity, since the first Races did not have matter bodies. The ethereal and sexless beings slowly began to take on density and, by the middle of the Third

Race, people resembled beast-like giants, up to twenty meters tall. Even though their shapes were similar to animals, these were already human beings, though not yet rational. At the same time, a separation of the sexes of all creation gradually took place, and distinct male and female individuals appeared, along with certain animals of those times, i.e., dinosaurs. Being mindless, many male Lemurians had sexual intercourse with female animals and procreated a vicious breed of monsters — primeval apes. It was from these creatures that some Atlanteans — this time consciously — later engendered all currently existing species of man-like apes.

When humanity was ready to perceive knowledge, the Great Teachers came to the Earth from the Distant Worlds and endowed people with the Higher Mind. This happened nearly eighteen million years ago.

The Great Teachers lived together with human beings. They cultivated morality in them through their examples, always being by their side as Elder Brothers. There was no need for religions in those days, since the Gods were right there with the people. The Messengers from the Distant Worlds had taught the Lemurians much in the way of science, providing them with the knowledge of highly developed planets. For example, they knew the properties of the Fire and fiery energies; they had knowledge of architecture, construction, mathematics, astronomy, agriculture, etc. Some of the plants — wheat, for instance — do not have wild-growing counterparts on the Earth, as they were the gifts of the Sons of Light from Venus. Likewise, bees and ants were brought from Venus for the edification of people: their diligence, along with their communal and hierarchical system, could serve as an example for humanity.

By the end of the Third Race, the Lemurians had achieved a highly developed civilization. Their physical bodies had become more perfect, and their height had been reduced to between six and seven-and-a-half meters; there was a similar evolution among animals, unusual species of which are still preserved in Australia. The Lemurians had built huge cities, and were impeccable masters of both arts and sciences. Humanity of that time can be compared with the civilization of the 19th century of the current era, but their knowledge of Nature and the Cosmos were far superior. Even so, those days saw the beginning of fierce confrontations between the Forces of the Light and the darkness.

When the Cosmic Period came for the next change of Races, the Great Teachers resettled the most spiritual and advanced representatives of Lemuria to new islands, which were soon to form a new Race on the new continent of Atlantis. Lemuria was destroyed by the Fire, that is, by extremely powerful earthquakes, and then submerged into the water about four million years ago.

Evidence of the existence of the Lemurians and their civilization has been preserved in the form of mysterious sculptures on Easter Island. And archeological excavations have also revealed huge skeletons which once belonged to the giants of that time.

LORDS OF KARMA — the Spirits of the Universe, known as *Lipikas* (*Sanskrit*, "Scribes") in esoteric philosophy. These Divine Beings are mystically connected with Karma, the Law of Retribution, for they are the Recorders, who impress on invisible tablets a "grand gallery of scenes of eternity" — i.e., a faithful record of every word, act, and even thought of everyone on the Earth, and of all that was, is, or ever will be in the manifest Universe. It is the Lords of Karma who project and make objective the ideal plan of the Universe, according to which the God-Creators re-create the Cosmos.

The Lipika Lords direct the evolution of the world, following Cosmic Laws and harmonizing their will with the evolution of the Cosmos. Against the will of the Lords of Karma human will is powerless, for the latter has created the former. To determine the course of human destiny, they use special matter that outlines the basis of the way which everyone must walk, being bound by karmic necessity.

However, the Lords of Karma create precisely those conditions for humans, planets, systems, etc. that are necessary for the ascent along the Ladder of Evolution.

MAN — a being destined to *become* the bearer of the highest spiritual principle on the planet Earth, and to *be* a creator. His evolution on the Earth passes through Seven Races, Seven Spheres, and Seven Rounds, incarnating at least 777 times in each Round.

Man develops through the following stages: mineral, plant, animal, man, God-man, and God. Each stage presupposes the attainment of perfection on a particular planet; and each higher level involves the repetition of previous experiences. Thus, humanity had been evolving in the Mineral Kingdom on a planet which no longer exists. Then it passed through the Mineral Kingdom once more, but by now it had reached the Plant Kingdom on another planet, which also disappeared. Subsequently human Monads emigrated to the Moon, where they continued their evolution in the Mineral, Plant, and Animal Kingdoms. On the planet Moon, the wave of life appeared one stage earlier than on the Earth. This means that the current Animal Kingdom of Earthly Evolution was the Plant Kingdom on the Moon. When the Moon completed its life cycle, when all its forms of life reached the highest point in their development within the Seven Rounds, they ascended to the next higher step and thereby to another planet — the Earth. Now, when humanity achieves perfection on the Earth, it will move to a new planet, where there will be new conditions for higher development still — and so on endlessly into Infinity.

Man goes through all the Kingdoms of Nature in turn — not only from the moment of conception as an embryo, but also throughout his lifetime his structure is continually being formed in accordance with these steps. Hence for the first seven years he lives as a mineral; the next seven years, up to age 14, as a plant; further, up to 28, like an animal; then up to 35 as a man; and later, up to 42, as a soul. The number 42 is inherent in the Solar System for the maturation of the sevenfold human structure. In other words, from the perspective of the Cosmos, man attains his age of majority at 42 years.

The evolution of High Spirits, who came to the Earth from the Distant Worlds to help humanity, implies an exception: in order to become human beings, they can avoid the Animal Kingdom through additional incarnations in the Plant Kingdom or pass through this stage in the Kingdom of Birds.

Human structure, as everything in the Solar System, is septenary and consists of seven principles, which go by different names in various philosophies and can also be represented in a traditional tripartite concept:

I. Spirit.

1 (7). *Spirit* or *Atma* (*Sanskrit*, "spirit") — the fiery element united with the Absolute.

2 (6). *Soul* or *Buddhi* (*Sanskrit*, "soul") — spirituality, the conductor of Spirit.

3 (5). *Higher Mind* or *Manas* (*Sanskrit*, "mind") — the principle, which endows man with self-consciousness and responsibility, bringing the Law of Karma into force. Man is the only one among all

the Kingdoms of Nature of the Earth endowed with higher consciousness. Therefore, his immortal part, the sixth and seventh principles, is integrated with the Higher Mind. It brings together in itself the entire accumulated experience of all past lives, in contrast to the intellect, the lower mind, which is renewed in every life.

II. Soul.

4 (4). *The astro-mental body* or *Kama Rupa* (*Sanskrit*, "body of desires") — expresses physical and mental desires, emotions, and thoughts. It consists of two parts:

a) *the mental body*, which includes the lower mind, or intellect;

b) *the subtle body*, or *the higher astral body*.

The mental body is more perfect and is used for interplanetary flights by the Adepts, while the subtle body can be used for travelling within the limits of the Earth. The astro-mental body is mortal, although it may live for thousands of years.

III. Body.

5 (3). *The etheric double, the lower astral body*, or *Linga Sharira* (*Sanskrit*, "body's image") — the transmitter of cosmic and solar energy to the physical body during its lifetime, being closely associated with nervous system. A state in which man is insensible to pain — either under narcosis, certain drugs or hypnosis — is achieved by the weakening of the link between the etheric and physical bodies. Containing all the physical features of man, the etheric body constructs man's physical appearance according to the pattern inculcated in him at the moment of conception: hence the physical body, in fact, is the precise double of the etheric one. It disintegrates soon after the death of the human being; some sensitive people see etheric bodies as ghosts in graveyards. Again, mediums use their etheric doubles to demonstrate various phenomena.

6 (2). *The energy body, the vital principle*, or *Prana* (*Sanskrit*, "breath") — consists of various energies intrinsic to the Earth. After the death of the physical body it is discarded and is immediately assimilated by the Earth.

7 (1). *The physical body* or *Rupa* (*Sanskrit*, "form") — the densest body for communication with the physical world.

All the principles mentioned are also sevenfold in their structure. The four lower principles form a *quaternary* — the mortal personality; while the three higher principles comprise a *triad* — the Immortal Individuality, also known as a *monad* or the seed of the spirit. Hence in the physical world, all seven principles are encased in the physical body. After leaving the dense world, the three lower bodies die, and man lives on in the Subtle World with the remaining four principles in his subtle or astral body. Further, man casts off his higher astral body as he moves into the Mental World. Finally, he passes into the Fiery World only with the higher triad, which is encased in the fiery body.

It is not correct to conclude that if someone is bad, they will become an animal in their next incarnation. Sometimes it happens that their higher Principles might abandon them even during their lifetime. Such a person may show no outward difference from others — they might even be highly intellectual — but the person is only an empty shell of a living corpse. The living dead keeps being reincarnated until the complete separation of the higher triad from the lower principles occurs. According to Cosmic Laws, such an individuality begins their evolution all over again, that is, from a mineral, but on a completely different planet with new conditions for life. A striking example of this is Joseph Stalin, whose principles were fractured in the 1930s. Unfortunately, there are many such living corpses on the Earth at the moment.

Man himself constructs the bodies of his seven principles. So, he builds his subtle bodies by his thoughts, feelings, and actions, and his physical body in conjunction with food. He is the creator of his own Karma, which is expressed within set limits. It is possible that a man's essence is not always fully reflected in his physical appearance, for it is sometimes difficult to find suitable parents and a suitable body. In the Higher Worlds, however, he acquires an external appearance which precisely corresponds with who he actually is.

Each of the abovementioned principles, save the physical and etheric bodies, is in fact only an aspect or state of human consciousness, made up of various qualities of the one primary energy of Fire, life, or consciousness. Man is Fire, manifested in constant action. All actions and processes in the body are Fire-derived. Therefore, the control over any one of them involves mastering the Fire.

In the future, the structure of man at the stages of God-man and God will be twelvefold: with seven lower and five higher principles. Now the human body is being refined under the influence of the Cosmic Fire, becoming subtler and more attenuated. Unusual feelings and abilities are gradually beginning to awaken. Also man will reach the maturity of his subtle and physical bodies not by age 42 but by age

24. From 24 to 42 he will then experience the formation of a different structure, which will not include ageing. That is, a New Humanity is being born this very moment. The hundred years of the 21st century are entirely devoted to this.

MASTERS OF WISDOM — the Great Teachers of Humanity, who have taken responsibility for its evolution. Through suffering and sacrifice, Masters of Wisdom are those who have achieved a high level of development, far surpassing that of the ordinary individual — and, of course, in the human understanding, they can be seen as Gods. In the 19th and early 20th centuries, six Masters were incarnated, known under the following names: Morya, Koot Hoomi, Rakoczy, Serapis, Hilarion, and Djual Khool. Now they no longer occupy their former physical bodies, and they have also changed their names; some have gone on to other, more advanced planets, leaving worthy earthly successors in their place.

The Masters are the Great Guardians of Truth, who implement the Divine Plan. They know when, what, and how much should be given to people and attentively watch over their evolution. There is so much intense work that the Masters have no time for anything personal. They create new causes that bring about the effects needed for Evolution, thereby helping humanity to liquidate its former Karma. They know in advance the flow of consequences and can project them for millennia ahead. And sometimes, when the Teachers foresee the future, they know the effects of the causes consciously produced by them. So, they create the future, which is pliant in the hands of their fiery will. The Masters know the course of the stars and their future combinations and coordinate their creative work with the energies of the Cosmos.

One of the most essential tasks of the Great Brotherhood is the selection and guidance of colleagues and disciples. For various reasons, the Teachers cannot enter into direct and close contact with multitudes of people. They act through their colleagues, disciples, and messengers. When their disciples are incarnated on Earth with a definite mission, the Masters follow and guide them from childhood. The karmic relationship of many millennia enables the Teachers to make contact with their disciples without difficulty. In addition to being taught secret sciences, they usually undergo a fiery transmutation that allows them to maintain communication with the Masters. The disciples are constantly being tested, even at higher levels of development. The most terrible betrayals are also unavoidable in their lives.

Each century, the Masters admit into their Abodes of Light a maximum of two candidates to convey through them a part of the Secret Knowledge. But for various reasons this may not always be necessary. The chief consideration is that the messenger's body must be ready to receive the Teaching. The Teachings of Light, of course, never appear spontaneously — there are specific periods allotted to them. To record the Teaching, the disciples go through many incarnations of preparation, sometimes for thousands of years, and when the time comes, they are alerted beforehand to the work they are about to undertake. As a rule, preliminary preparation takes place over three years, during which time the Higher Spirits work with the disciples, attuning their bodies.

Contrary to established opinion, the Great Teachers do not make contact with mediums or channelers, except in very rare cases, and when they do, it is usually through their advanced disciples.

It must be remembered that on turning towards the Powers of Light, a person must initially establish a connection with their higher bodies: for example, the mental body will be higher than the emotional body, and the spirit can act as a Guide for the soul, as well as take on the role of god in relation to the body. And only after establishing a harmonious order of all seven bodies can a person hope that someone from Above will pay attention to them, according to their vibrational sound, or Karma, both human and spiritual, depending on the goal they set for themselves, or that was set by Teachers who entrusted them with a specific mission.

Helena Blavatsky had to accept the body of a powerful medium, which was necessary for the tasks assigned to her during her final life on Earth. She was required to work with many people and perform miracles to convince them of the existence of the higher Laws of Nature and Supreme Knowledge. Nevertheless, with the help of her Master, she brought her ability under complete control. Before revealing *The Secret Doctrine* to humanity, Blavatsky experienced the fiery transmutation of her body for three years under the supervision of her Teacher in one of His Ashrams in Tibet. For those who have endured this process, it is tough to be out in the world amongst people, and all the more so amongst those adversely disposed towards them. This was the reason for Blavatsky's poor health. Helena Roerich went through something similar and even more intense when she received *Agni Yoga*. However, she lived in India in the pure mountain air in almost total solitude, surrounded by loving individuals, conditions that enabled her to almost wholly accomplish the mission of her last earthly incarnation.

Initially, when the Leaders of Humanity first came into the world, the continents were divided into seven spheres, wherein each of the Great Lords emitted their own luminous vibrations. As the rainbow is dispersed into seven colors, so all the Seven Great Teachers represent the Seven Rays, bringing with them the currents consonant with their particular note. At the present time, each of the Seven Masters of Wisdom has educated disciples who have reached a high level of consciousness. The precise number of the Leaders of Humanity is now 777. Naturally, each of these Teachers also has their own Teacher, for the process of cognition is limitless.

In essence, the Seven Great Teachers — the Seven Rays — are the components of the One Supreme Lord, who represents the White Ray and personifies the Spiritual Sun. Thus, there is One Individuality, but His partial manifestations enlightened such earthly incarnations as Buddha, Christ, Maitreya, and other Great Teachers.

MONAD (*Greek*, "unity") — the fiery seed of the spirit, a Divine Spark, which is eternally reincarnated, clothing itself in various forms; a particle of the One Divine Principle in each manifestation of the world.

It is indestructible, unchangeable, and eternal. It is the same for all existence as the unconscious basis of life. As a particle of the Divine Principle, this spark of life is inseparably linked with this Principle. Its program includes an aspiration to cognizing Divine Love and the eternal self-perfection of the forms it animates.

Besides, at the dawn of the Grand Cycle of Evolution, every seed of the spirit is begotten under the rays of a specific star or planet, which has its own Planetary Spirit, or Regent. Therefore, the Seed contains the same energies as this Spirit; in essence, the Lord of this star may be called the true Guardian Angel of the monads conceived in His Rays, and the celestial body itself can be considered to be their Guiding Star for the whole Cycle. All seeds engendered here are part of His own essence, although its vehicle — the human beings for whom He is Teacher and Cosmic Father — may never become aware of this fact. Similarly, the Great Masters of Wisdom have their Father, who has

His own Lord, and so on — however, everything in the Universe is indissolubly connected with the Unknowable Divine Principle, who is the Primal Progenitor of all creation.

The more developed the monad, the more advanced forms it embodies itself in. The levels of perfection correspond to the levels of the development of consciousness and are attained by an incredibly long evolutionary process. At the end of the Grand Cycle of Evolution, the Divine Spark returns to its Source, or point of origin, to begin a new cycle of development at a higher level. And so on *ad infinitum*, with neither beginning nor end.

The monad is actually a duad: the union of Atma (*Sanskrit*, "spirit") and Buddhi (*Sanskrit*, "soul"). It is reincarnated in the lower Kingdoms of Nature — mineral, vegetable, animal — and gradually proceeds through them to humanity, clothing itself in appropriate forms. But upon entering the Human Kingdom, the principle of the higher consciousness, Manas (*Sanskrit*, "mind"), joins the duad, forming the divine triad. It is Manas that transforms human beings into rational and moral individuals, and this is what distinguishes them from ordinary animals.

Sixty billion seeds were sown on the planet Earth, bearing the divine triad. All of them belong to the rays of various stars and planets, although they are all on the same temporary stop — the planet Earth. Of course, only eight billion are now incarnated in physical human form, while others are in the Subtle and Fiery Spheres surrounding the planet.

The divine triad is in the human heart. From this fiery seed germinates a special Flame, whose tongues create what looks like the folded petals of a Lotus. The higher the spirituality and morality of an individual, the brighter and stronger will be the radiations of their heart's Flame. As a rule, there are three tongues, or petals, of the Flame — hence the threefold Flame. While there are twelve petals in all, only nine are able to unfold on the Earth and in the current Solar System. The first three petals are green, or emerald, the next three are rose, or scarlet, while the last ones are white. When people receive knowledge, the first three green petals of their heart-Lotuses start to unfold. When they begin to love, then comes the time of the rose-colored petals. Then appear the last three, the white ones, only of such a color that is not accessible to the human eye.

Among humanity the vast majority are people with green petals of Knowledge, unfolded in varying degree. The rose petals of Love are revealed in a mere handful of people around the world — people who have reached the level of holiness. The white petals are possessed only by those who work with the Lords — the Adepts and the Initiates.

RACE — a stage in the evolution of humanity. Belonging to various Races is first of all determined by the level of spirituality, or by the coefficient of brightness of the heart — a coefficient termed *Argo*. There are Seven Races in total, each of which has seven sub-races. Each Race develops a particular side or quality in people, densifying or rarefying the matter of their bodies.

People in the first two Races, as well as in the first half of the Third Race, did not have physical bodies — their bodies were of ethereal matter. Those people were genderless beings, not endowed with reason and never dying, for they did not have flesh. They had existed for 300 million years.

Eighteen million years ago, in the middle of the Third Race — i.e., the Lemurians — the separation of the sexes took place, and people began to conceive their progeny. Humanity received dense physical bodies and began to reflect the Higher Mind.

The Fourth Race — the Atlanteans — came into being approximately 4–5 million years ago. But only three sub-races of the Atlanteans evolved on the continent of Atlantis while the remaining four were in Egypt, Asia, and Europe.

The current Fifth Race, known as the Aryan, originated about one million years ago in India. In the 20th century the term *Aryan*, as well as additional secret knowledge previously revealed by the Messengers of Light, was used by the dark forces to develop and circulate their anti-evolutionary theories. The Fifth Race's people are now to be found on each existing continent and all its seven sub-races have already formed. Nevertheless, the Third and Fourth Races are still represented on the Earth, too.

The formation of future Races does not require the millions of years needed by previous Races. Therefore, it may be said that the Sixth and Seventh Races will exist and develop simultaneously. Thus, since the beginning of the 20th century, in each country there have appeared the best and most spiritual and moral people, who are generating the next, or Sixth, Race. They are no different from others in their outward appearance, but they have loving hearts, strong energy, and often many abilities and talents. And in the present days the seeds of the Seventh Race are already showing themselves. At the end of this Race, many things that are now considered miraculous will become common, and the attenuation of the human body, as well as the matter of the planet, will reach the point prescribed by the Evolution for this Round and its last Race.

The farther one looks back into humanity's past, the more one can see of its future, for the past contains a projection of the future. Thus the first Races were ethereal — and matter slowly became solid. The last Races will be the same, but this time the matter will gradually rarefy. The end and the beginning are similar in form but distinct in expression. While the beginning was characterized by the absence of self-consciousness, the end is the pinnacle of self-awareness. The middle of the Fourth Round — the middle of the Fourth Race — marks the lowest point of the fall into matter, the densification of the human body, and the development of intelligence. The Fifth Race is on an ascending arc. Therefore, gradually the spiritual must achieve an ever-increasing preponderance over the material and the heart over the intellect, so that by the end of the Seventh Race matter is completely subordinate to spirit to the extent accessible to the Fourth Round of Evolution.

Humanity currently lives in a period of great responsibility — the time of the change of Races. This process is always accompanied by an extremely powerful influence of the Cosmic Fire, leading to a change in the inclination of the Earth's axis and magnetic poles, attended by natural disasters and climate change. Additionally, humanity is reaping what it has sown over this period of its development. As the time of the change of Races approaches, information is being imparted to the world (within permissible limits) through the Messengers of Light, with the aim of warning humanity of the forthcoming dramatic and earth-shaking changes.

Thus, Helena Blavatsky's works and *The Mahatma Letters*, along with other ancient writings, point out that during the change of Races, such continents as America and Europe are to be shaken by powerful earthquakes and submerge into the sea. Edgar Cayce, too, foresaw this scenario for the end of the 20th century. However, the development and collective will of humanity enabled the Hierarchy of Light to prevent such devastating cataclysms. But even they have the right to interfere in such cases only up to 50%; otherwise, humanity will learn nothing. The other half of efforts for salvation are to be made by Earth-dwellers themselves.

America and Europe may have a most beautiful future. Everything depends on people who must keep pace with Evolution, and that requires a revival of spirituality. Also it should be borne in mind that books, films, and other works of art which proclaim yet another "end-of-the-world" scenario and various cataclysms, promote — through human will — thought-forms that take on enormous proportions. Such energies may explode in space, resulting in huge disasters. So, North America finds itself on the Subtle Plane in a rather unstable condition since its population in the Physical World is constantly destroying its own cities and the entire continent — by the thought-forms contained, for example, in its entertainment films, which are distributed worldwide. It requires a tremendous effort on the part of all the colleagues of the Great Brotherhood to prevent such thoughts and the destruction they depict from coming true in reality. But it is also within the power of any conscientious citizen of any country. If someone can erect giant destructive structures simply through their thoughts, then by the same token a light-bearing individual is able to produce creative and positive currents — for example, by prayerful appeals to the Forces of the Light. And then the transfiguring Fire will descend into the lower spheres and mitigate the destructive influence of these negative formations.

Therefore, the manner in which the change of Races will actually take place depends upon everyone: whether through conscious evolution without tragic consequences or through constant upheavals.

ROUND — the life-cycle of Evolution of a different Time scale. So, the transition of humanity across all Seven Globes (or Spheres) of the Earth or any other planet through incarnation in each of the four Kingdoms of Nature — as mineral, plant, animal, and man — is known as the *Planetary Round*, or *Great Round*, or simply *Round*. The Great Round consists of the Seven Races, which evolve on the Seven Spheres of the planet. The development of the Seven Races on just one Globe of the planet is called a *Small Round*, or *Ring*. Also every Race involving human evolution within each of its seven sub-races may be considered a Small Round.

There are Seven Great Rounds in total comprising *Manvantara* —
a period of active life. Although in ancient scriptures there are other
divisions and expressions, this one is generally accepted at the present
time. Between Rounds and Manvantaras there are *Pralayas* of different
timespans — periods of rest, similar to slumber, which are equal in
duration to the periods of activity. After passing through the Seven
Rounds, humanity moves on to new planets, and so on *ad infinitum*.

As the current population of humanity, representing mainly the
Fifth Race, we are now in the Fourth Great Round, which will come to
completion in the Seventh Race. It is in this Round that humanity on
the Earth has fully developed — earlier, it was referred to as *humanity*
only for want of a more appropriate term. That which becomes man
passes through all the forms and kingdoms during the First Round
and through all human shapes during the two following Rounds. At
the commencement of the Fourth Round, man appears on the Earth
as a primeval form, being preceded only by the Mineral and Vegetable
Kingdoms. Over the following three Rounds, humanity, like the globe
on which it lives, will be ever tending to reassume its original divine
form, except that humanity will become more and more self-aware.
Like every other atom in the Universe, man strives to become first a
God-man and then a God.

Every new Round always repeats the previous one in miniature
before proceeding to a new level of development. The Mahatmas
briefly revealed the human evolution in each of the Rounds:

First Round — Man is an ethereal being, non-intelligent, but
super-spiritual. In each of the subsequent Races and sub-races and
minor races of evolution he grows more and more into a compacted
or incarnate being, but still essentially ethereal. And, like the animal and vegetable, he develops bodies corresponding to his coarse
surroundings.

Second Round — Man is still gigantic and ethereal, but grows
firmer and more condensed in his body as he becomes a more physical
man. Yet still he is less intelligent than spiritual, for mind evolves with
less speed and more difficulty than does the physical frame — i.e., the
mind is not able to develop as rapidly as the body.

Third Round — Man has now a perfectly concrete or compacted
body. At first it is the form of a giant ape, more clever (or, rather, cunning) than spiritual. For in the downward arc he has now reached the
point where his primordial spirituality is eclipsed or overshadowed by

his nascent mentality. In the last half of this Third Round his gigantic stature decreases, his body improves in texture and he becomes a more rational being — though still more of an ape than a man. The people of this Round had reached the physical state, but could not stay in it, causing a catastrophe, although on a smaller scale than in the subsequent Round. Some of them returned to their astral state, while others simply perished.

Fourth Round — The mental body and intellect experience an enormous development. The formerly mute races acquire human speech on the Earth, during which, starting with the Fourth Race, language is perfected and knowledge of physical things increases. At this point then the world teems with the results of intellectual activity and spiritual deterioration. In the first half of the Fourth Race, sciences, arts, literature, and philosophy are born, degenerating in one nation and reborn in another. Like everything else, civilization and intellectual development whirl through septenary cycles. Only in the second half of this Round does the spiritual essence begin the process of transmutation of body and mind to manifest its transcendental powers and accept the governing role of the heart.

Fifth Round — The same relative development and struggle continue, but with a new goal: the mastery of the subtlest Cosmic Energies. Plato and Confucius were representatives of this Round. (It should be understood that prior to their coming to the Earth, they were on another planet, which was already in the Fifth Round of development.) In this Round, the Higher Mind reaches perfection. People have completely mastered thought; clairvoyance and clairaudience are available to almost everyone, but in varying degrees. Common language is replaced with the reading of thought. Evil in the form of a struggle against the Light does not exist, but there is imperfection at various stages of evolution. Science and art are highly appreciated; chemistry and other natural sciences are well developed.

Sixth Round — In this Round the human soul is fully developed. Humanity is so advanced that the qualities and abilities of the Greatest Master become the property of transfigured man. Gautama Buddha was a representative of this Round.

Seventh Round — Humanity becomes a tribe of Gods and animals are intelligent beings. It ends with the spiritualization of matter and the transition into subtly luminous forms. On the plane of ordinary visibility the Earth becomes invisible, but life remains, and its forms are manifested on the highest planes of invisibility. Everything is focused on spirit. Thought is the external expression of life, becoming a reality without a single limitation. But even these conditions are merely the preparation for a New Cycle of Evolution.

Thus, the chain of Rounds inevitably leads man towards a state of omnipotence, while each Round assigns a task for man to develop his bodies, principles, or any other abilities of his microcosm.

SENZAR — the language of the Sun based on symbolism and closely associated with Sound, Light, Color, and Number. Currently, Senzar is the secret sacerdotal language of the Great Teachers and their disciples all over the world. It is taught in the Secret Schools of the East.

In the ancient past there was one body of knowledge and one universal language — Senzar. From the beginning of human evolution, these were transmitted from generation to generation. Yet during the times of Atlantis, when humanity fell into sin, this language, along with eternal knowledge, ceased to be available to posterity. All nations restricted themselves to their own national tongues and lost their connection with the Secret Wisdom, forgetting the one language. Humanity was no longer worthy of such knowledge. So, instead of being universal, Senzar became limited to just a few. The biblical myth of the Tower of Babel and similar legends around the world symbolically testify to that enforced secrecy, narrating the story when the Lord created several languages from the one original language, so that sinners could no longer understand one another's speech. In mythology Senzar is often referred to as the language of the birds.

The tongues of all peoples through the ages have their origins in Senzar. Thus, the roots of many current eastern languages come from Sanskrit, which is based on Senzar. Many words of this most ancient language underlie not only Sanskrit but also Egyptian, Hebrew, Latin, and other languages of various known and yet-to-be discovered sacred texts. Thus, Senzar is similar to the roots that nourish a single Tree, and languages compose its crown which is beautiful in its diversity.

The language of Senzar consists of many levels, having both spoken and written forms of speech, which are significantly different from traditional understanding. It is also distinct from others in that it has no obsolete or ingrained forms of expression. Being rather succinct, it is able to most fully and concisely express any thought, including hugely sophisticated phenomena.

Its highest manifestations are closest to the Voice of Silence and include thought-forms, the breathing of fires, the geometric expression of combinations of rays, and so on — whereas its lowest manifestations resemble traditional writing systems, each with its own specific rules.

The writing system of Senzar combines seemingly incompatible elements. These include signs, syllables, and letters based on symbolism. A single symbol is capable of developing into an entire treatise, easily comprehended by an initiated disciple of any ethnic background. But the reader's level of consciousness is also important. Color, light, number, and sound play a significant role in its alphabet from which words and sentences are composed. Each letter, possessing its own specific color of the rainbow, shade of light, number, and mystic sound syllable, has its equivalent in the languages of all peoples of the world and may be reproduced using different cryptographic methods with the aid of specialized calculation tables. Thus, a new cryptographic alphabet is created in a given tongue while numerological, geometrical, and astrological keys help the reader to precisely determine how to decode this secret writing system.

For example, the Angelic language of John Dee, mysterious advisor to Queen Elizabeth I, is *one version* of script in the Senzar language.

In present times, Senzar has been discovered in inscriptions on stones and plants that do not lend themselves to deciphering. For example, on the territory of the Buddhist monastery Kumbum in China grows the sacred Tree of Great Merit, also known as the Tree of Ten Thousand Images. Legend has it that the tree grew out of the hair of the great Buddhist reformer Tsongkhapa. In the past, according to witnesses,[1] when the tree blossomed, on each leaf there appeared a sacred letter or syllable of such astounding beauty and perfection that no other existing letter could surpass it. These mystic letters and syllables were written in Senzar, and in their totality comprised the whole Teaching of Buddhism and the history of the world.

SHAMBHALA (*Sanskrit*, "Place of Peace") — the Stronghold of Light, a legendary kingdom hidden in the heart of the Himalayas. It is known under different names in the myths and beliefs of various world peoples: Agartha, Belovodye, the City of Gods, the Garden of Eden,

---

[1] See Évariste Huc, *Travels in Tartary, Thibet, and China, 1844–1846*, vol. 2 (London: Office of the National Illustrated Library, 1852), pp. 52–54.

Mount Meru, the Pure Land, the White Island, and so on. Shambhala is the Imperishable Sacred Land, the first and ever-present continent of the planet Earth, which never shared the fate of the others, for it is destined to continue from the beginning to the end of the Grand Cycle of Evolution. It is the cradle of the first human and contains the sacral Source of all religions, philosophies, sciences, and esoteric teachings. This mysterious place, which preserves the Eternal Wisdom, lies at the intersection of the past, present, and future, as well as the Physical, Subtle, and Fiery Worlds.

Shambhala was first mentioned in the Puranas. Information about it filtered into the world at different times. Back in the 10th century, one of the monks of Kievan Rus had been staying in the Ashram of the Great Brotherhood for several days. However, he wasn't allowed to talk about it, except upon his deathbed, to tell his story "from mouth to ear." It was not until 1893, in fact, that this account was written down.[1] In the 12th and 13th centuries, Popes Alexander III and Innocent IV both attempted to establish contact with Prester John, the head of the Secret Spiritual Brotherhood in the heart of Asia, who had sent letters to several Christian sovereigns: Constantine the Great, Manuel I Komnenos, Frederick I Barbarossa, Louis VII of France, and others. In the 17th century, the Portuguese Jesuit missionary, Estêvão Cacella, was the first to tell the Europeans of this mythical place, which he visited at the invitation of the Tibetans. In 1915, Albert Grünwedel published a German translation of the Guidebook to Shambhala, written by the famous Panchen Lama, Lobsang Palden Yeshe, in which the location of this legendary realm is indicated by a mass of symbols and complex geographical hints. And in 1925, in many newspapers worldwide, an extensive article by the Mongolian explorer, Dr. Lao Chin, appeared, telling of his journey to the Valley of Shambhala. He was forbidden to write about the wondrous spiritual phenomena there. However, Dr. Lao Chin mentioned that the valley's inhabitants lived for many centuries but looked like middle-aged people, and they were characterized by clairvoyance, telepathy, and other higher abilities. Among other things, he saw how they levitated and even became invisible to the physical eye.[2]

---

[1] Published in English as *The Kingdom of White Waters* (New York: Radiant Books, 2022).

[2] To read Dr. Lao Chin's article about his journey to one of the Abodes of Shambhala visit radiantbooks.co/bonus.

Shambhala is the Ashram of the Great Brotherhood of the Teachers of Humanity, each of whom is a God, having become such for many nations and leaving the divine mark in human hearts as an equal among equals in the flesh. The work of the Mahatmas may be seen in three principal directions of research: the improvement of the earthly plane, methods of communication with the Distant Worlds, and means of conveying the results of their study to humanity. The latter is indeed the most challenging of all.

The Shambhala of the Earth may be thought of as a spaceport from which messengers are sent to the Distant Worlds and where ambassadors from the infinite Universe arrive. New ideas from other inhabited planets are tested in the laboratories of the Brotherhood; after being adapted to earthly conditions, they are conveyed to scientists of the world as inspiration.

Here the most important decisions concerning the evolution of humanity and the planet are made. Once every hundred years, the Council of Shambhala is convened (1924, 2024); once every sixty years, the Council of the High Initiates takes place. It is a real World Government, which has little in common with earthly regimes, but still, it has often contacted them through its messengers. Indeed, the history of all times and nations records testimonies to the Assistance of the Great Teachers, which has always been secretly given at turning points in the history of every country. However, while the people of the East often accepted their advice, the West, as a rule, rejected them.

For example, in addition to the aforementioned information, it is known that warnings were received by the representatives of the Habsburg dynasty and the Norwegian King Cnut the Great. Charles XII of Sweden was warned not to start his fatal campaign against Russia. The repeated warnings to Louis XVI and Marie Antoinette of the impending danger to France and the French royal family are widely known. Napoleon was also warned not to go against Russia. A warning was given to Queen Victoria in 1851. And in 1926, the Mahatmas issued an austere warning to the government of the USSR, and the consequences of its rejection were indeed grave.

Further, an unknown Tibetan lama passed a warning to Hitler through German zoologist Ernst Schäfer that he should not start a "great war." On the other hand, American Presidents George Washington and Abraham Lincoln listened to the advice of the Great Brotherhood, which resulted in the development of the United States. In the 1930s, however, when President Franklin Roosevelt was warned about the upcoming Second World War, he, unfortunately, didn't take all the advice he was given to heart, or there would be a United States of both Americas today.

Several prominent people also visited Shambhala. As a rule, one or two candidates are admitted there each "century" (which consists not of a hundred years but sixty, according to the Kalachakra Calendar). For example, during their lifetimes, this Stronghold of Light was visited by: Gautama Buddha, Jesus Christ, Lao-Tzu, Pythagoras, Plato, Apollonius of Tyana, Paracelsus, the Panchen Lama Palden Yeshe, Helena Blavatsky, Helena and Nicholas Roerich, and others — all of whom have played a significant role in the evolution of humanity. But not all the Great Spirits who had certain missions to fulfil visited the Brotherhood during their earthly life. Furthermore, anyone who visits this Abode of Light by invitation resonating deeply in their heart takes a vow of silence, which may be broken only with the permission of the Great Lord of Shambhala. An uninvited guest will never find the right way to reach it.

WHITE BROTHERHOOD — the Community of the Seven Messengers of the Distant Worlds and their disciples, who have lived side by side with humanity on Earth for millions of years, developing the human mind and heart. This Brotherhood is called *White* to indicate the White Light that, upon splitting, yields the seven colors of the rainbow, each of which symbolizes one of the Great Teachers, and vice versa — the seven colors of the rainbow that result in the White Light after fusion.

The previous Solar System was tasked with giving people knowledge and developing their intelligence. The present System aims to bring people closer to Love, and the focus of Love is the heart. Therefore, the Great Lords have divided themselves into two Lodges — Western and Eastern.

The Western Lodge — also known as the Brotherhood of Luxor or the Thebes Sanctuary, located in Egypt — was to provide knowledge, as well as to develop and expand human consciousness, with an emphasis on the mental body, the mind, the human intellect, to help take a step towards the heart. All the knowledge accumulated in the past and present Solar Systems resides exclusively in Egypt.

The Eastern Lodge — Shambhala or the Himalayan Brother-hood — was to develop the intuition of the heart, always bearing Love and serving the highest energies. In other words, the West is the mind, and the East is the heart. Ancient traditions have it that the Masters left the West for the East. Many people, in fact, left the Sanctuary in Egypt to move to the East. This happens approximately once every two thousand years.

At the end of the 19th century, before the start of Armageddon, all the Secret Schools and Ashrams of the Western Brotherhood were closed and moved to the Himalayas. All the Great Teachers who had worked in the world — holding Initiations and imparting knowl-edge — were also summoned to the Stronghold of Light in the Hima-layas. Humanity was abandoned for a hundred years, but knowledge was still passed on through their disciples. However, there was no longer any direct contact between the Masters and the vast majority.

WORLDS — various states, or planes, of Cosmic Matter. For the pres-ent Solar System, there exist Seven Worlds, each of which has seven sub-planes, according to the degree of rarefaction and refinement.

In the current Fourth Round of Evolution, Four Worlds are avail-able to humanity and Earth:

1. *The Physical World, the Dense World*, or *the Material World* — The Earth itself on which physical humanity lives.

2. *The Astral World, the Subtle World*, or *the Ethereal World* — This is the world where everyone goes during sleep. It exists in spheres encircling Earth, and its dimensions are much larger than the earthly plane. It consists of many layers, from the lowest to the highest, to which each individual is drawn by consonance. All individuals assume an appearance corresponding to their inner essence, and reap what they have sown on Earth. Its matter is pliant and instantly becomes an expression of what the spirit is thinking, and who that individual really is. Everything is created and moved by thought. Illumination occurs on account of the radiation of a person's subtle bodies, hence the lower spheres to which evil-minded people are drawn are dark. All earthly emotions and habits remain and assume a significantly intensified state. So if a person has not overcome their most primitive desires on Earth, here they will suffer from the absence of a physical body through which to satisfy them. The lower areas of the Subtle World are the closest to Earth. Therefore, those in this layer often

use Earth-dwellers to satisfy their desires — hence the phenomena of possession. For good people, not bound by physical passions, the Subtle World provides limitless freedom of spirit; here they can fly, endlessly create, contemplate creativity in all areas of life, and study and explore anything they wish. Souls may remain in this world for thousands of years.

3. *The Mental World*, or *the World of Thoughts* — Consists of the product of the mental creativity of thinking beings: mental forms or thought-forms. Its layers are determined by the affinity of thought emanations that comprise the content of the form. The line of attraction is determined by the attunement of one's consciousness. The process of attunement may take place subconsciously, but it can also take place by order of individual will. In this case the will chooses the point of attunement and establishes the necessary control. Whereas on Earth people travel by car, train, etc., in the Mental World they travel in the vehicle of thought. Consciousness enters thought like a passenger enters a railway carriage, and the vehicle of thought carries it to the sphere chosen by the mind.

4. *The Fiery World*, *the Empyreal World*, or *the Spiritual World* — Matter belonging to this world is so subtle, perfect and imbued with energy that it everywhere causes a fiery luminosity, hence its name. Here neither time nor distance exists in the earthly sense; everything happens "here and now." The beauty of this world is magnificent. The flowers are especially striking, and they are everywhere; they move and flutter, giving off marvelous fragrances and melodies. The elevated forms of matter and energy of which this world is comprised create an atmosphere of Joy and Love. However, not everyone is able to reach the Fiery World, because in order to do so they must have developed their immortal fiery body. This happens when the individual follows a spiritual path on Earth.

When the Worlds are listed, the Mental World is often omitted. It serves as the living link between the Subtle and Fiery Worlds, belonging more to the latter, as thought cannot exist without Fire. Hence one might come across statements to the effect that there are *Three Worlds* accessible to humanity, and that the Fiery World is the World of Thought and vice versa.

The planet Earth exists in all these Worlds, and it is represented in each of them by its corresponding globe-sphere. All Four Worlds are combined concentrically one inside the other, forming the complex septenary body of the planet. Thus, Earth consists of dense physical matter, penetrated by spheres of subtle and fiery matter. All Seven Spheres of the planet in the Four Worlds are inhabited. Those who dwell in one World cannot see or sense the other Worlds. But they are continually moving from one World to another; dying in one, they are reborn in another, moving either upwards to the next higher planes or downwards once more to Earth. In this way, people pass through the Round of incarnations within the Planetary Chain.

Each of the consecutive bodies in which a person lives a conscious and full life, is restricted by the world and sphere to which it belongs, and is subject to its laws. All the Worlds have their boundaries and limitations, restricting people in some measure by the properties of matter. All ancient Teachings prescribed certain norms of behavior, diets, and so on, aimed at the purification, or refinement, of the matter of all human bodies. The crude astral body, weighed down by crude habits, cannot rise higher than the lower layers of the Astral World, which are in perfect correlation to the composition of the astral body. Having been released from the dense body, only individuals that have purified their subtle bodies from dense particles on Earth can succeed in soaring high. In the Subtle World each disembodied person undergoes a process of cleansing, and yet, for all that, they cannot ascend higher than the height they themselves have attained. The Law of Consonance is just and infallible.

The planet Earth has already passed the lowest point — or greatest density — of its evolution, and so is now on a course of ascent. As a result, a convergence of the Dense and Subtle Worlds is gradually taking place, and the planet is rising one step higher than before. Hence the Subtle World is advancing on the Dense World, expanding the spheres of its own influence, thanks to the addition of properties that rarefy the matter of Earth; the Physical World, in turn, is harmoniously flowing into the layers of the Subtle Spheres. Similarly, the planet's Subtle World in its higher layers blends with the Mental World, and the Fiery World ascends into an even Higher World. Thus, in the Fifth Round, Five Worlds will be accessible to the Earth and humanity, where the Physical World will resemble the lowest layer of the Subtle World — that is, without the sharp demarcation between the two that is evident at the present time.

THANK YOU FOR READING!

If you enjoyed this work, please consider leaving a review, even if it is only a line or two. It would make all the difference and would be very much appreciated.

Sign up for our newsletter to be the first to know when new books are published:

radiantbooks.co/bonus

ABOUT THE AUTHOR

FRANCIA LA DUE (1849-1922) was born in the city of Chicago, Illinois. When she was four years old, her family moved to Syracuse, New York, where she spent most of her life until she moved to California.

Even during her school years, La Due began to demonstrate exceptional literary talent. Later, she worked as a nurse despite having no medical education.

In 1894, La Due became a member of the Syracuse branch of the Theosophical Society, founded there in 1892 by Dr. William Dower. Together with Dower, she advocated for the rights of Native Americans.

After the passing of Helena Blavatsky, the Great Brotherhood needed a new successor to continue its spiritual work in America. Thus, in 1898, the Master of Wisdom, known as Hilarion, began to guide La Due's activities. In the same year, she founded The Temple of the People in Syracuse.

However, the Master Hilarion later deemed it necessary to find a new location that would consider the intersections of the Earth's lines of force that create points of power. After two trips to California, La Due found an area on the eastern coast of the ocean. There, in 1903, she established the community of Halcyon, where a new stage of spiritual work of The Temple of the People started. La Due was the first head of the Temple, serving as its Guardian-in-Chief.

The Temple of the People published the monthly magazine *The Temple Artisan*, in which messages from the Master Hilarion, as well as from the Masters Morya and Koot Hoomi, were published for many years. The pages of this magazine also revealed a new section, *Theogenesis*, from the secret *Book of Dzyan*, which sheds light on the evolutionary path of humanity toward realizing its divine nature.

The members of the Temple succeeded in laying the foundation for scientific discoveries, such as microwave technology, the fruits of which are still bringing benefit to humanity today.

INDEX

Holy Spirit, 164
individual according to qualities; gulf between Higher Self and personality, 334
method of action, 520
relation to Universal Lodge, 330
throws out life-line, 152
Highway robbery, 207
Hilarion, expression of closeness, 441
affirmation of as to Christ, 171
Himalayas, date of; effects on polar climate, 313
History repeats itself, 357
Holding the center, 246
Home, family, etc., devotion to, 307
Holy, Ghost, sending of and Elder Brothers of race, 195
Spirit, crime against, 141
Spirit in operation, Fohat, cosmic electricity, 483
Spirit, equals Higher Self, 164
Horoscope of interior bodies, 249
H. P. Blavatsky, ref., 6, 215, 507, 508
causes of failure of early students of, 508
mission of, to teach Wisdom Religion, 43, 637
Human, being highest ideal form, 478
beings, not yet, 139
Humanity, blending of at close of Manvantara, 248
passing through last gate of second triad, 454
sub-race, new, to appear, 143
Humility, 83
as basis for claim to discipleship, 607
as result of cosmic consciousness, 386
as unassuming force, 496
heroism of, 137
staff in hour of attainment, 410
vs. pride, 13
Hypnotism, etc., point to one great force, 35
as black magic, 318
danger of, 145

I

"I am," 8, 62
"I am all power," 320

I Am; Identity and Intelligence, 392
equals I Was and I Come, 43
Ida, and pingala, distributors, 105
pingala, and sushumna, and poles of planet, 96
Idea, birth and history of; laya center of; cyclic returns of, illustrated, 412
growth of; affinity for physical organ; fiery lives waiting for "Soil," 286
vibration of, felt as well as heard, 226
Ideal, forms and religion, 551
pursuance of, demands price; final share in success of, 374
Ideals, alone eternal, 374
as consciousness of God, 160
dependent on stored memories, 299
difficulty of spreading, 69
effect of, on body and on descendents, 591
for assimilation in Devachan, 367
formed ages ago, 534
keep strong and pure, 364
Ideals, Illusions and, 17
Ideals, The Love of, 184
Ideals, The Murder of, 166
Ideals, pessimism destroying, 42
privation in form of spiritual self, 185
soul life dependent on; destruction of, is work of Enemy, 166
Ideas, repetitional, 412
Identical auric vibrations, 187
Identification, necessary to sense of phenomena, 299
with Infinite, 391
Identity, age of, 304, 391
Idol, of clay, 167
material, 123
Ignorance, reproof for impatience with; willingness to teach, 25
the root of all evil, 35
Illusion, 7, 192
Image of healthy organs in cure of disease, 111
Image-making power, possibilities of, 463
Imagination, 101
in the Absolute necessary to creation, 478
killing out of in child a crime, 478
of Divinity a divine gift, 478

The, last part of, 383
Path, The True, 206
Paths, of white and black magic side by
  side, 350
  the four, to Attainment, 302
Pattern of man, reflections, 513
Paul on faith, 529
Peace, dependent on higher vibration of
  substance matter, 463, 464
  divine law of, 57
  ideal taking form, 504
  pact will be failure, 379
Peaceful revolution, hopelessness of, 22,
  627
Perception, born in concentration, 134
  stability, service, critically necessary;
    periodicity and service as tools, 410
Perfection, longing for, attained in higher
  vibration, 45, 229
  not reached while Ego retains body, 335
  the state of equilibrium from which
    man was driven, 494
  ultimate, aim of soul, 602
Perseverance, 50
Personality, persistence of, in astral or not,
  559
Pessimism, 46
Phallic worship, teaching of, 475
Philosophy, importance of, 597
Philosophies, old and new, but explanation
  of Bible, 637
Phosphorescence, important purpose of,
  342
Phosphoric, energy, spiritual light
  becomes, 341
  plane, pre-astral place of testing, 341
Phosphorus, spiritual aspect, 341
Physical, body, development of, depends
  on center of the heart, 600
  focusing on the, 528
  law intensified, 418
  plane, the refuse of the higher, 36
  tests, 407
Physicists, case of particular, 315
Physicians, 53
Physiology, injunction to learn, 483
Pictures, action of Central Spiritual Sun on
  substance of intermediate planes, 530
Pineal gland, and control of sense, 461

development of, awaking in disciples of
  White Lodge, 291, 628
  etc., as affected by stimulants, 397
Pituitary body, 628
"Plan in mind of God," interference with,
  475
Plan of God and personality, 573
Plane, fourth, relation to akasha; double
  cosmic mirror; Christos in operation,
  180
  physical, the refuse of the higher, 36
Planes, barriers between are conditions of
  tests, 588
  connecting link between, 226
  extent of relations between, 212
  gaps between filled, 65
  gulf between, 38
  interior, and the inhabitants thereof, 195
  intermediate, 520, 530
  intermediate; changes of substance on,
    assistance to character, 519
  material, sub-division; etheric,
    subdivision; Alaska, three divisions,
    180
  methods appropriate to each, 318
  no conscious passage between, 341
  of being, seven; seven sub-planes; sub-
    divisions, 411
  sub-, Adepts must dwell in, 65
  three higher, of manifestation,
    incomprehensible, 180
Planet, destruction of life on, 398
  axis of, deflection imminent, 94
  peace on, 464
  struggle for existence on, 223
Planetary, influences, 249 (See Astrology)
  ruler, mentality of, vibratory action of,
    250
Pledge and latent tendencies; central flame
  consumes lower nature, 415
  fever, warnings of, result in earliest
    Theosophical bodies, 414
  of discipleship; protection, 179
  to Temple, 628
Point of balance, reaching the, 431
Point of vantage, chance, one, to hold, 295
Poison; ions of thought energy;
  manipulation of; similar to animal
  poisons; plagues as result of, 282

T

U

V

Y

Z